Communications in Computer and Information Science   **947**

Commenced Publication in 2007
Founding and Former Series Editors:
Phoebe Chen, Alfredo Cuzzocrea, Xiaoyong Du, Orhun Kara, Ting Liu,
Dominik Ślęzak, and Xiaokang Yang

Andrei Chugunov · Yuri Misnikov
Evgeny Roshchin · Dmitrii Trutnev (Eds.)

Electronic Governance and Open Society: Challenges in Eurasia

5th International Conference, EGOSE 2018
St. Petersburg, Russia, November 14–16, 2018
Revised Selected Papers

 Springer

Editors
Andrei Chugunov (ID)
eGovernance Center
ITMO University
St. Petersburg, Russia

Yuri Misnikov (ID)
Institute of Communications Studies
University of Leeds
Leeds, UK

Evgeny Roshchin (ID)
North-West Institute of Management
Russian Presidential Academy of National
Economy and Public Administration
St. Petersburg, Russia

Dmitrii Trutnev (ID)
eGovernance Center
ITMO University
St. Petersburg, Russia

ISSN 1865-0929   ISSN 1865-0937 (electronic)
Communications in Computer and Information Science
ISBN 978-3-030-13282-8   ISBN 978-3-030-13283-5 (eBook)
https://doi.org/10.1007/978-3-030-13283-5

Library of Congress Control Number: 2019931945

This Springer imprint is published by the registered company Springer Nature Switzerland AG
The registered company address is: Gewerbestrasse 11, 6330 Cham, Switzerland

Preface

The 5th EGOSE conference was held during November 14–16, 2018, in St. Petersburg, Russia. Like the previous conferences, it was organized by the ITMO University's Centre for e-Government Technologies. This year it was done in cooperation with the North-West Institute of Management, a branch of the Russian Academy of National Economy and Public Administration (RANEPA).

The conference's call for papers asked for research papers to be submitted under the following thematic tracks:

- eGovernance and Eurasian Integration
- Open Government Prospects
- Information Society and eGovernance
- Open Government Data
- Citizen Centered E-Government
- Building Smart City
- Convergence in E-Governance Services
- Smart City and Quality of Life
- eGovernance and Policy Modeling
- Participatory Governance
- Comparative trends in Digital Government
- Disruptive E-Governance
- Social Media: Tools for Analysis, Participation, and Impact
- Big Data, Computer Analytics, and Governance
- Cases and Perspectives of the Government Transformations

As many as 98 papers were submitted to EasyChair for a double-blind peer review, with around three-quarters coming from Russia. The Program Committee selected 36 for publication. Maria Wimmer of the University of Koblenz-Landau (Germany), and Marijn Janssen of Delft University of Technology (The Netherlands) delivered the keynote speeches.

The papers accepted for publication were presented in nine academic sessions:

- Research Session 1 – Smart City Infrastructure, Policy
- Research Session 2 – Digital Privacy, Rights, Security
- Research Session 3 – Data Science, Machine Learning, Algorithms, Computational Linguistics
- Research Session 4 – Digital Public Administration, Economy, Policy
- Research Session 5 – Digital Services, Values, Inclusion
- Research Session 6 – Digital Democracy, Participation, Security, Communities, Social Media, Activism
- Research Session 7 – Social Media Discourse Analysis
- Research Session 8 – Digital Data, Policy Modeling
- Research Session 9 – Digital Government, Administration, Communication

A specific feature of this conference was a visible rise in papers devoted to machine learning and other issues relating to the use of artificial intelligence models and algorithms for textual analysis, often in combination with computational linguistics. This resulted in having a special session (session 3) to report on such research.

November 2018

Andrei Chugunov
Yuri Misnikov
Evgeny Roshchin
Dmitrii Trutnev

Organization

Steering Committee

Maria A. Wimmer   University of Koblenz-Landau, Germany
Marijn Janssen   Delft University of Technology, the Netherlands
Dmitrii Trutnev   e-Governanace Center, ITMO University, Russia

Program Committee

Artur Afonso Sousa   Polytechnic Institute of Viseu, Portugal
Olusegun Agbabiaka   Softrust Technologies Limited, Nigeria
Martynov Aleksei   Lobachevsky State University of Nizhny Novgorod
                               (UNN), Russia
Luis Amaral   University of Minho, Portugal
Dennis Anderson   St. Francis College, USA
Francisco Andrade   University of Minho, Portugal
Farah Arab   Université Paris 8, France
Arry Akhmad Arman   STEI - Bandung Institute of Technology, Indonesia
Sören Auer   TIB Leibniz Information Center Science
                               and Technology and University of Hannover,
                               Germany
Mohammed Awad   American University of Ras Al Khaimah, UAE
Johnstone Baguma   Toro Development Network (ToroDev), Uganda
Maxim Bakaev   Novosibirsk State Technical University, Russia
Alexander Balthasar   Bundeskanzleramt, Austria
Luis Barbosa   University of Minho, Portugal
Vladimír Benko   Slovak Academy of Sciences, Ľ. Štúr Institute
                               of Linguistics, Slovak Republic
Anna Bilyatdinova   ITMO University, Russia
Svetlana Bodrunova   St. Petersburg State University, Russia
Radomir Bolgov   St. Petersburg State University, Russia
Nikolay Borisov   St. Petersburg State University, Russia
Francesco Buccafurri   UNIRC, Italy
Luis M. Camarinha-Matos   NOVA University of Lisbon, Portugal
Sumandro Chattapadhyay   The Centre for Internet and Society, India
Sunil Choenni   Research and Documentation Centre (WODC),
                               Ministry of Justice, the Netherlands
Andrei Chugunov   ITMO University, E-Government Center, Russia
Cesar A. Collazos   Universidad del Cauca, Colombia
Amihalachioae Cornelia   e-Government Center, Moldova
Vytautas Čyras   Vilnius University, Lithuania
Shefali S. Dash   National Informatics Centre, India

Saravanan Devadoss	Addis Ababa University, Ethiopia
Subrata Kumar Dey	Independent University, Bangladesh
Elsa Estevez	Universidad Nacional del Sur, Argentina
Omololu Fagbule	Megastride Global, Nigeria
Behnam Faghih	Technical and Vocational University, College of Bushehr, Iran
Isabel Ferreira	Escola Superior de Gestão, Instituto Politécnico do Cávado e do Ave, Portugal
Olga Filatova	St. Petersburg State University, Russia
Simon Fong	University of Macau, SAR China
Enrico Francesconi	ITTIG-CNR, Italy
Galindo	University of Zaragoza, Spain
Despina Garyfallidou	University of Patras, Greece
Carlos Gershenson	UNAM, Mexico
J. Paul Gibson	Mines Telecom, France
Christoph Glauser	ArgYou AG, Switzerland
Tatjana Gornostaja	Tilde, Latvia
Elissaveta Gourova	St. Kliment Ohridski University of Sofia, Bulgaria
Dimitris Gouscos	University of Athens, Greece
Ronald Greenberg	Brown & Weinraub, PLLC, USA
Stefanos Gritzalis	University of the Aegean, Greece
Ahsan Habib	Shahjalal University of Science and Technology, Bangladesh
Karim Hamza	Institute for European Studies, Vrije Universiteit Brussel, Egypt
Martijn Hartog	The Hague University of Applied Sciences, The Netherlands
Naiyi Hsiao	National Chengchi University, Taiwan
Wan-Ling Huang	Tamkang University, Taiwan
Tongyi Huang	National Chengchi University, Taiwan
Vigneswara Ilavarasan	Indian Institute of Technology Delhi, India
Diana Ishmatova	APEC e-Government Center, Tokyo, Japan
Marijn Janssen	Delft University of Technology, The Netherlands
Yury Kabanov	National Research University Higher School of Economics, Russia
Christos Kalloniatis	University of the Aegean, Greece
George Kampis	Eotvos University, Hungary
Vitalina Karachay	ITMO University, Russia
Sanjeev Katara	National Informatics Centre, Govt. of India, India
Nikolay Kazantsev	Alliance Manchester Business School, The University of Manchester, UK
Maria Khokhlova	St. Petersburg State University, Russia
Bozidar Klicek	University of Zagreb, Croatia
Andreas Koch	University of Salzburg, Austria
Sergei Koltcov	National Research University Higher School of Economics, Russia

Liliya Komalova	Moscow State Linguistic University, Russia
Evgeny Kotelnikov	Vyatka State University, Russia
Akmaral Alikhanovna Kuatbayeva	Shokan Ualikhanov Kokshetau State University, Kazakhstan
Mohammad Lagzian	Ferdowsi University of Mashhad, Iran
David Lamas	Tallinn University, Estonia
Christine Leitner	Centre for Economics and Public Administration, Austria
Lessa Lemma	Addis Ababa University, Ethiopia
Sandro Leuchter	Hochschule Mannheim University of Applied Sciences, Germany
Yuri Lipuntsov	Lomonosov Moscow State University, Russia
Natalia Loukachevitch	Research Computing Center of Moscow State University, Russia
Euripidis Loukis	University of the Aegean, Greece
Olga Lyashevskaya	National Research University Higher School of Economics, Russia
José Machado	University of Minho, Portugal
Latéfa Mahdaoui	USTHB, Algeria
Ignacio Marcovecchio	United Nations University Institute on Computing and Society, Macao SAR, China
Ricardo Matheus	Delft University of Technology, The Netherlands
Nor Laila Md Noor	Universiti Teknologi MARA, Malaysia
Giovanni Merlino	University of Messina, Italy
Bundin Mikhail	Lobachevsky State University of Nizhniy Novgorod, Russia
Inna Miroshnichenko	Kuban State University, Russia
Yuri Misnikov	Institute of Communications Studies, University of Leeds, UK
Harekrishna Misra	Institute of Rural Management Anand, India
Olga Mitrofanova	St. Petersburg State University, Russia
Robert Mueller-Toeroek	University of Public Administration and Finance Ludwigsburg, Germany
Ricky Munyaradzi Mukonza	Tshwane University of Technology, South Africa
Kawa Nazemi	University of Applied Sciences Darmstadt, Germany
Alexandra Nenko	National Research University Higher School of Economics, Russia
Galina Nikiporets-Takigawa	University of Cambridge, UK
Paulo Novais	University of Minho, Portugal
João Luís Oliveira Martins	United Nations University, Portugal
Prabir Panda	Independent Researcher, India
Ilias Pappas	Norwegian University of Science and Technology, Norway
Theresa Pardo	Center for Technology in Government, University at Albany, SUNY, USA

Catalin Vrabie	NSPSPA, Romania
Vasiliki Vrana	Technological Education Institute of Central Macedonia, Greece
Wilfred Warioba	Commission for Human Rights and Good Governance, Tanzania
Maria Wimmer	Universität Koblenz-Landau, Germany
Vladimir Yakimets	Institute for Information Transmission Problems of RAS, Russia
Kostas Zafiropoulos	University of Macedonia, Greece
Nikolina Zajdela Hrustek	University of Zagreb, Croatia
Sherali Zeadally	University of Kentucky, USA
Hans-Dieter Zimmermann	FHS St. Gallen University of Applied Sciences, Switzerland

Contents

Digital Public Administration, Economy, Policy

Digital Services, Values, Inclusion

**Digital Democracy, Participation, Security, Communities,
Social Media, Activism**

Social Media Discourse Analysis

Smart City Infrastructure, Policy

Agent Based Modeling of Smart Grids in Smart Cities

Bauyrzhan Omarov[1], Aigerim Altayeva[2], Alma Turganbayeva[1],
Glyussya Abdulkarimova[3], Farida Gusmanova[1], Alua Sarbasova[1],
Batyrkhan Omarov[2(✉)], Yergali Dauletbek[2], Aizhan Altayeva[2],
and Nurzhan Omarov[4]

[1] Al-Farabi Kazakh National University, Almaty, Kazakhstan
[2] International Information Technologies University, Almaty, Kazakhstan
batyahan@gmail.com
[3] Abai Kazakh National Pedagogical University, Almaty, Kazakhstan
[4] Kazakh University of Railways and Communications, Almaty, Kazakhstan

Abstract. The goal of the study is to explore Smart Grids with a system of multi-agents and aspects related to the Internet. Smart cities are created at a high level of information and communication technologies (ICT) structures capable of transmitting energy, information flows multidirectional and linking another sector that includes mobility, energy, social and economic. Smart cities concern the connection of subsystems, the exchange and evaluation of data, as well as ensuring the quality of life and meeting the needs of citizens. We have different models of transport systems, energy optimization, street lighting systems, building management systems, urban transport optimization, but these models are currently being considered separately. In this article, we present an overview of the concept of an intelligent city and discuss why multi-agent systems are the right tool for modeling intelligent cities. This article represents simulation results with a Smart Grid as a case study of Smart City.

Keywords: Smart grid · Smart City · Multi-agents · Agent based modeling

1 Introduction

The development of Smart City is now directly related to the concept of energy and energy potential. Energy to a greater or lesser extent has always been the locomotive of urban development, but it is quite obvious that, with the advent of the Smart City concept, its role is constantly increasing. Mankind has faced a serious challenge. The population of the earth is growing steadily, while the specific consumption of energy per capita is increasing, all the more so because the reserves of the main energy source (organic fuel) are steadily falling. From the fact whether alternative sources of energy will be found, and also on how effectively society will use energy, the prospects for sustainable development of modern civilization depend. In this regard, energy efficiency and energy saving is one of the priority areas of Smart City.

In recent years in the West in the electric power industry the concept of Smart Grid (smart/intelligent networks) is developing very actively. First of all, it covers

A. Chugunov et al. (Eds.): EGOSE 2018, CCIS 947, pp. 3–13, 2019.
https://doi.org/10.1007/978-3-030-13283-5_1

transmission and distribution, but it has something to do with generation. The term Smart Grid became known from the middle of the 2000s and immediately became so popular that it overgrew many different properties and meanings. Now it is very capacious, not without a hint of marketing brilliance, a term that is also interpreted differently in different parts of the world. It is rather a kind of vision of what the future of the electric power industry should become, its new innovative model, which in many respects differs from the modern one both by the principles of functioning and by the technological basis.

"Smart grids" refer to "breakthrough" technologies and innovations. Like classic breakthrough technologies and innovations [1, 2], they are able not only to significantly change the technical and technological basis of the industry, but also the markets, the composition and roles of the subjects, the fundamentals of the economy of the electric power industry. Their potential influence on the markets of energy carriers, auto-billet building, information and communication technologies (ICT) and electrical engineering is also significant, mainly due to new opportunities for the development of renewable energy sources (RES) and electric vehicles, the formation of complex intellectual infrastructures based on advanced software and hardware solutions. In addition, the long-term functionality of smart networks in the field of reliability and quality of electricity is fundamentally important for the development of a high-tech industry and a sector of high technology services.

The value of technology is confirmed by the scale (40–70 billion US dollars in 2012–2014) and rapid growth (average annual growth rates for the next decade - up to 20%) of smart grid markets [3, 4]. According to the estimates of the International Energy Agency, during 2014–2035, the volume of investment in intellectual solutions can range from 340 billion to about 1.17 trillion US dollars (in 2012 prices, the scenario "New Energy") [5].

2 Background

2.1 Smart Grid

The concept of "Smart grid" or "intellectual network" does not have a clear definition. It can be defined as a concept for the modernization of energy systems by integrating electrical and information technology. However, to determine the concept of "intelligent network" it is better to use the capabilities and performance of the network instead of certain technologies. Typically, an intelligent network means an increase in the degree of auto-matting and a gradual upgrade of the electrical networks of many owners for the transmission and distribution of electricity with traditional distributed and especially renewable generation units and batteries connected to the point of consumption. The same customer can be both a producer and an energy consumer. This requires a two-way flow of energy both at the junction point and in other parts of the supply grid.

In the developing DOE8 (U.S. Department of Energy) [6] concept of Smart Grid, the diversity of requirements is reduced to a group of so-called key goals (key goals) of the new electric power industry, formulated as:

availability - providing consumers with electricity without restrictions, depending on when and where they need it, and depending on its quality paid by the consumer;
reliability - the ability to withstand physical and informational negative impacts without total disconnections or high costs for restoration work, the fastest recovery (self-recovery) of operability;
economy - optimization of tariffs for electric energy for consumers and reduction of system-wide costs;
efficiency - maximizing the effectiveness of the use of all types of resources, technologies and equipment in the production, transmission, distribution and consumption of electricity;
organic nature of interaction with the environment - maximum possible reduction of negative environmental impacts;
safety - prevention of situations in the electric power industry that are dangerous for people and the environment.

In the European Union, among the key values are [7]:

flexibility in terms of response to changes in consumer needs and emerging problems with electricity supply;
availability of electricity for consumers, in particular renewable energy sources and high-efficiency local generation with zero or low emissions;
reliability of electricity supply and quality of electricity while providing immunity to hazards and uncertainties;
economy through the introduction of innovation, effective management, rational combination of competition and regulation [8].

2.2 Microgrid

The wide interest in renewable energy sources presents new challenges. Placing generating capacities (solar, wind, based on heat exchange or combining electricity and heating) in close proximity to the consumer requires a completely new approach to managing the electricity grid. One of the new approaches is the MicroGrid concept. Microgrid, in a simplified form, is considered as a physically distributed structure, which is characterized by the following features:

- the fulfillment of the main task
- life support or production process;
- Power Supplies
- Distributed (decentralized) production of electric energy, including renewable energy sources [9];
- territorial limitation-the concentration of all electrical devices in a user-defined area;
- human presence
- a user or an expert (a microgrid manager) who can make adjustments to the management functions of individual subsystems or the entire facility [10].

The desire to create the most comfortable conditions for a person has led to a high degree of saturation of microgrid electrotechnical, electronic and other technical devices and systems, control and regulation of operating parameters is carried out by specialized control systems. The microgrid control system is an information and intelligence system that integrates information coming from a variety of heterogeneous microgrid components, such as: alternative power supplies, loads, sensors and characterized by different types of physical data. Such a system is created to control energy resources taking into account the user's wishes.

3 Proposed Architecture

The architecture of our control system of the energy and network systems of the building is illustrated in Fig. 1. In our study, we consider the Smart and Micro Grid system for building energy management based on multiagent technologies. The system consists of three types of agents. The first control system is a grid system that is responsible for connecting to the Utility Grid and Microgrid, which is controlled by the Switch State Agent, Fig. 1. Next level of the building energy management system (BEMS) is the Multiagent system. There are different types of agents that are used to manage the entire system. Another part of the system is the Management system, that is responsible for the management of HVAC, grid control and electrical lighting.

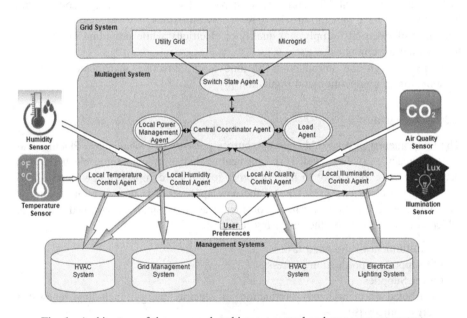

Fig. 1. Architecture of the proposed multi-agent control and management system.

In our study, we consider two types of energy sources: a utility grid and a microgrid. The utility grid takes energy from the main grid of the city. Microenvironments are supplied with renewable energy sources. The second part of the system is a multiagent system. Since each agent assumes a high level of intelligence for making a local solution, the system requires a new architecture of the agent model. The multi-agent system takes data from sensors and passengers as input data and decides on the introduction of control over the drives. Control systems are the systems that must be controlled and supplied with comfort and energy.

The sensors are distributed throughout the building to monitor its operation. Three types of data, including environmental, user settings and energy data, can be obtained from the sensor network. Environmental data refers to the environmental parameters of the building, such as indoor and outdoor temperatures, light levels, CO2 concentration or even the detection of intrusion or fire alarm signals. The filling data usually includes the number of passengers and the presence or absence of passengers. The energy data is mainly focused on the status of energy supply, such as the state of the utility network, the price of electricity and the availability of renewable resources. These measured data will be used by various local agents to determine their behavior.

To realize an effective, user-oriented control over the building system, another important element for the multi-agent system is the passenger behavior model. Personal agents in the multi-agent system are designed to study and predict the preferences of residents through their behavior. Studying of preferences of inhabitants is carried out by observation of their behavior and definition of the person who has carried out these actions. By providing the identity of a particular user to a personal agent and respecting his behavior, the personal agent will be able to find out the preferences of this particular user, rather than all the residents of the building.

The central coordinator-agent is the coordination of all agents and the built-in optimizer to maximize the composite comfort index, which can be determined in several ways based on the specific needs of the clients. In this study, we define the terms "general comfort index", "comfort index", "comfort level" and their ratio from the point of view of the mathematical model.

Based on this information, the central agent manages the regional agents to distribute the available capacity in the area of the building in which comfort is provided. Regional agents turn control over local agents. Consider the assessment of comfort in buildings and zones based on the index of comfort (CI) [11] and general comfort (OC) [12]. These figures can range from 0 to 1 and record information about temperature, light and CO2 concentrations in the building zones. The comfort index CI characterizes the internal environment of certain sections of the building and is determined by the method of combining comfort information using the average level of ordered aggregates. Mathematically, comfort index can be written as:

$$CI = OWA(\delta_T, \delta_H, \delta_L, \delta_A) = \sum_{j=1}^{n} \omega_j b_j \qquad (1)$$

where OWA is an ordered weighted average,
$\delta_T, \delta_H, \delta_L, \delta_A$ are the parameters that construct comfort level for inhabitants. In our case comfort parameters are temperature, humidity, lighting, and air quality into the indoor environment;
ω_j is corresponding comfort index; $\omega_j \in [0, 1]$

Formula 2 computes comfort level of the people depending of four comfort parameters.

$$Comfort\ Level = \delta_T\left(1 - \left(\frac{e_T}{T_{set}}\right)^2\right) + \delta_H\left(1 - \left(\frac{e_H}{H_{set}}\right)^2\right) + \delta_L\left(1 - \left(\frac{e_L}{L_{set}}\right)^2\right) + \delta_A\left(1 - \left(\frac{e_A}{A_{set}}\right)^2\right) \quad (2)$$

Here, $T_{set}, H_{set}, L_{set}, A_{set}$ – temperature set, humidity set, luminance set and air quality set, respectively.

e_T, e_H, e_L, e_A – Temperature error, humidity error, luminance error, and air quality measuring error, respectively.

$\delta_T, \delta_H, \delta_L, \delta_A$ – Parameters that construct comfort level for inhabitants.

4 Experiment Results

In this case study, we will consider the utility grid mode. Carrying out experiments with the mode used and measuring the required power, we can further predict the ability of the micro network to supply the building with energy.

In the simulation, the comfort ranges of residents for various management tasks are set in the illumination range from 750 to 880 (lux), air quality ranges from 400 to 8,800 parts per million, and temperature and humidity ranges are based on international European standards and ISO recommendations/FDIS 7730 [13] (Fig. 2). These comfort

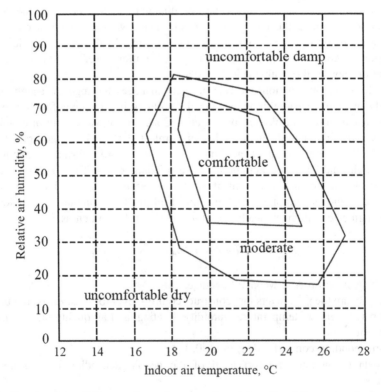

Fig. 2. Comfort data of the premises, given based on international European standards and recommendations ISO 7730 [13].

ranges serve as limiting constraints in the stochastic multipurpose genetic optimization algorithm to optimize the optimal setting of the given points at each time step. The set points for each comfort parameter are set in Tset = 22 oC, RH = 50%, Lset = 800 lux and AQset = 800 ppm, and the same weight factor for each comfort parameter is set to one fourth (1/4).

Figure 4 demonstrates comparisons of conventional system and our proposed system for comfort temperature into the room. As illustrated in the figure, temperature changes of the proposed system belong between 21 and 25.5 °C, while temperature of the conventional system went out of the comfort area with the indexes between 26 °C and 29 °C, most of the explored time (Fig. 3).

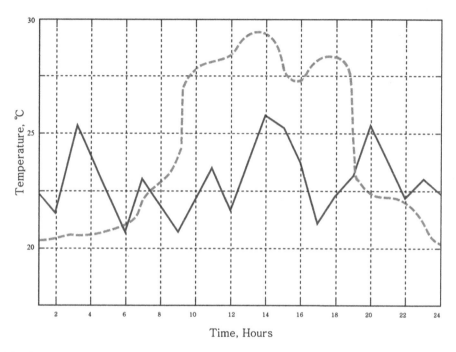

Fig. 3. Temperature set points comparison (Blue line: temperature changes using our approach; Green line: casual temperature changes;) (Color figure online)

Figure 4 demonstrates the humidity changes by applying two different systems as a conventional and the proposed system. There, we can observe that, the proposed system humidity changes between 30% and 40%, when a conventional system shows a very dry microclimate.

Results of the experiment with indoor illumination level were given in Fig. 5. The proposed system gives much more comfort illumination level comparing the conventional lighting level. Also, the figure shows, that it easier to control illumination level than the other comfort parameters.

Figure 6 illustrates air quality level of indoor environment when using the two different systems. In our study, we consider CO_2 level as an indicator of air quality.

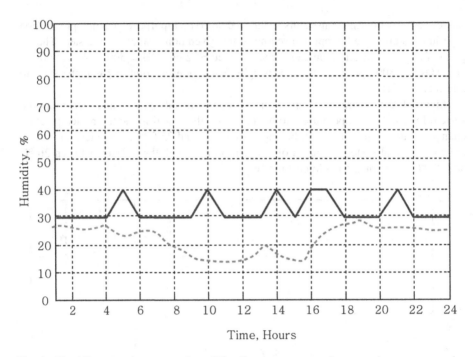

Fig. 4. Humidity set points comparison (Blue line: temperature changes using our approach; Green line: casual temperature changes;) (Color figure online)

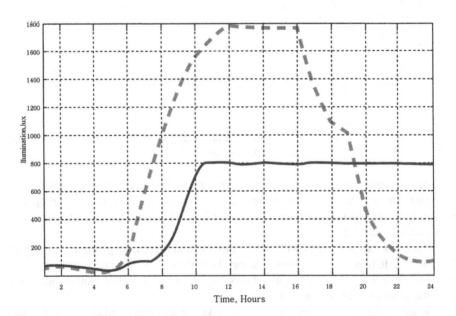

Fig. 5. Illumination set points comparison (Blue line: illumination using our approach; Green line: casual illumination;) (Color figure online)

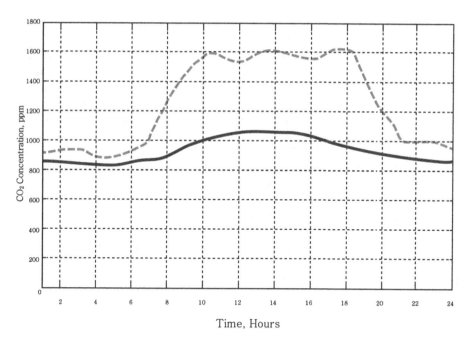

Fig. 6. Carbon dioxide set points comparison (Blue line: carbon dioxide level using our approach; Green line: carbon dioxide level using conventional system;) (Color figure online)

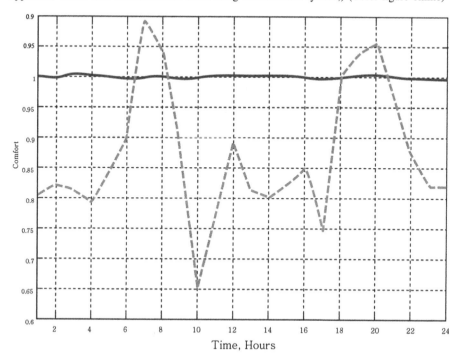

Fig. 7. User comfort level set points comparison (Blue line: user comfort level using our approach; Green line: user comfort level using conventional system;) (Color figure online)

When using our system we kept the indoor air quality index in acceptable level, while the conventional system shows worse result. It can be explained that, by increasing the people in the room, CO_2 level will increase and it needs control every time and immediately react for changing the air quality level. In the conventional systems does not control the CO_2 level, and, in most cases, people are not able to estimate air quality level into the room. For this reason, CO_2 level should be controlled by the system.

Figure 7 shows the comfort level into the room considering all the parameters. The results demonstrate that the proposed system comfort level is over 1 that means, comfort for the people. Conventional system comfort level changes between 0.65 and 1, while most of the experienced time less than 0.9.

Figure 8 demonstrates power expenditure comparison of the two systems. There, we can observe that, the proposed system shows less power consumption comparing the conventional system excluding 8.00 to 10.00, even that time, the proposed system does not spend more energy that the conventional system. Spending more energy between 8.00 to 10.00 can be explained with the proof that, the given time is start of working day, and all the heating, ventilation and air conditioning systems starts to preparing ensure the comfort microclimate. After, they continue working in normal mode.

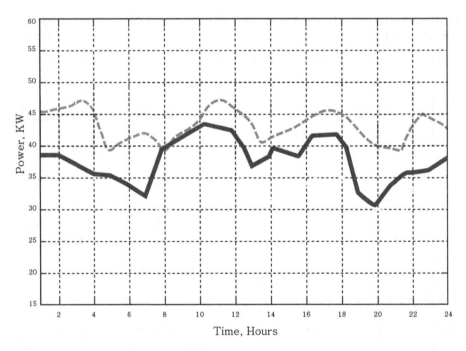

Fig. 8. Power expenditure comparison of two systems (Blue line: power consumption using our approach; Green line: conventional system power consumption) (Color figure online)

5   Conclusion

This study developed an intelligent multi-agent energy management and management system with heuristic optimization, and it was shown that it is capable of achieving management objectives by coordinating several agents and an optimizer. The proposed structure of the multiagent based smart grid system can optimize basic tools to achieve energy efficiency, providing thermal comfort in the room. In the future, we intend to improve the proposed model by applying algorithms of machine learning and using the training agent to make decisions based on controlled learning.

References

1. Christensen, C.: Innovator's Dilemma, p. 255. Harvard Business Review Press, Boston (2016)
2. Christensen, C., Rejnor, M.: The Innovator's Solution: Creating and Sustaining Successful Growth, p. 320. Harvard Business Review Press, Boston (2003)
3. Global Smart Grid Market to Reach US$118.1 Billion by 2019 Due to Transmission Upgrades. T&D World Magazine, 14 May 2015. http://tdworld.com/smart-grid/global-smart-grid-market-reach-us1181-billion-2019-due-transmission-upgrades. Accessed 11 Nov 2016
4. Northeast Group, LLC: Global Electricity Transmission and Distribution Infrastructure Dataset (2016–2026), 3 p. August 2016. http://www.northeast-group.com/reports/Brochure-Global%20Electricity%20T&D%20Dataset%202016-2026%20-%20Northeast%20Group.pdf
5. OECD/IEA: World Energy Investment Outlook, Paris, Special Report, 188 p. (2014). https://www.iea.org/publications/freepublications/publication/WEIO2014.pdf
6. Grids 2030: A National Vision for Electricity's Second 100 years. Office of Electric Transmission and Distribution of USA Department of Energy (2003)
7. European Commission Directorate-General for Research Information and Communication Unit European Communities: «European Technology Platform Smart Grids, Vision and Strategy for Europe's Electricity Networks of the future», European Communities (2006)
8. European Technology Platform SmartGrids. Strategic Deployment Document for Europe's Electricity Networks of the Future, April 2010
9. Shawkat, A. (ed.): Smart Grids: Opportunities, Developments, and Trends. Springer, London (2013). https://doi.org/10.1007/978-1-4471-5210-1. 23 p.
10. Xenias, D., et al.: Scenarios for the development of smart grids in the UK: literature review. Working Paper. REF UKERC/WP/ ES/2014/001. UK Energy Research Centre (UKERC), London, 184 p. (2014). http://www.ukerc.ac.uk/support/tiki-download_file.php?fileId=3510. Accessed 11 Nov 2016
11. Omarov, B., Altayeva, A., Suleimenov, Z., Cho. Y.I., Omarov B.: Design of fuzzy logic based controller for energy efficient operation in smart buildings. In: 2017 First IEEE International Conference on Robotic Computing, pp. 346–351, April 2017. https://doi.org/10.1109/IRC.2017.26
12. Omarov, B., Altayeva, A., Cho, Y.I.: Smart building climate control considering indoor and outdoor parameters. In: Saeed, K., Homenda, W., Chaki, R. (eds.) CISIM 2017. LNCS, vol. 10244, pp. 412–422. Springer, Cham (2017). https://doi.org/10.1007/978-3-319-59105-6_35
13. ISO/FDIS 7730:2005, International Standard, Ergonomics of the thermal environment—analytical determination and interpretation of thermal comfort using calculation of the PMV and PPD indices and local thermal comfort criteria (2005)

Smart City Implementation and Aspects: The Case of St. Petersburg

Sergey I. Drozhzhin[1,2](✉) [iD], Artem V. Shiyan[1] [iD],
and Sergey A. Mityagin[1]

[1] ITMO University, Kronverkskiy pr. 49, Saint-Petersburg 197101, Russia
{sergey.drojjin,avshiyan,mityagin}@corp.ifmo.ru
[2] ETU "LETI", Professora Popova st. 5, Saint-Petersburg 197376, Russia

Abstract. Cities in the world face the problem of combining competitiveness and sustainable development at the same time. Urban space forms a much more subtle matter in terms of the simultaneous scale and point of processes spectrum. Certainly, the city is the primary source of generation fundamental anthropogenic factors within the framework of human activity (ecology, transport, society and security). However, on the other hand, in the current realities, it also becomes a structural tools mechanism for creating qualitatively new drivers of development (for example, intelligent infrastructure networks for urban mobility or closed-loop water supply).

The city as a dynamic system has a certain set of patterns. The basic ones regulate the system development, complexity of mechanisms and diversification of modules designed. The critical ones regulate system stability and the preservation of existing stable state. Providing modularity of urban management architecture will allow scaling the interaction chain within the socio-technical system (i.e. the city), which make it possible to minimize the risk of destructive strategic decisions.

Smart city as a platform provides transparency of the urban space processes and forms a two-level management (citizen-government). An effect indicator of high technology implementation is not so much a formal achievement of indicators values, but as the parameter of the complex infrastructure regime of a certain urban area in a given chronological period.

When we have such projects of this level, the citizens themselves act as the center of aggregation of new meanings, values, and needs. On the basis of their everyday life situations, a framework of knowledge is designed for further strategic urban space planning.

The authors of this article propose to revise the traditional understanding of the concept of "smart city" and consider the case of development of St. Petersburg as a "smart city", based on the value-oriented approach.

Keywords: Smart city · Value-oriented approach · Urban studies · Human-oriented approach

© Springer Nature Switzerland AG 2019
A. Chugunov et al. (Eds.): EGOSE 2018, CCIS 947, pp. 14–25, 2019.
https://doi.org/10.1007/978-3-030-13283-5_2

1 Introduction

Today, cities, within the trends of global economic development, are considered a kind of network nodes of world resources. They aggregate human, financial, scientific and technological, historical, cultural, commodity and civilizational (i.e., quality of life standards) flows. In addition, the modern city, as a complex infrastructure object, is an extremely complex system. And dynamically changing trends and threats are constantly expanding the list of critical parameters of this social engineering system.

The life-cycle of the city behind the paradigm of historical processes was transformed from a purely utilitarian direction of development (city-plant) into a mechanism of self-generation of new points of activity (city-functions) and meanings (city-people). In addition to the already formed framework of infrastructure, the urban area needs to be reorganized from the point of view of the impact of life situations of citizens [9]. Such fundamental decisions are pushed by numerous factors of resilience in the era of rethinking of everyday processes.

On the one hand, there is an increase in the population density of large cities due to over-urbanization and the chaotic use of adjacent areas, which leads to the risk of loss of the basics of strategic planning. But the redevelopment of former industrial areas leads to the revitalization of urban infrastructure. Engineering, transport and information infrastructures of the modern city are the arteries for the delivery of quality services. On the other hand, the role of every citizen, regardless of his or her activities, in ensuring the global competitiveness of cities is increased [5].

Because of continuous configuration changes, as the urban fabric covers various aspects of human scale, a priori there is an impact on a lot of other parameters, which in turn affect the socio-economic situation and, perhaps, even more worsen the situation than it was before. Thus, the smart city as a platform is aimed at monitoring and detailing the ongoing urban processes, regardless of the scale of the tasks.

2 Mechanisms of Smart City Design in the Context of Technological and Infrastructure Framework

«Smart city» suggests a rational strategy of advanced integration of innovative technologies with the urban infrastructure in order to improve the life quality [2]. All this is aimed at algorithmization of management of an effective service-oriented model of urban processes. The absolute organizational and economic condition for the design of this kind of ecosystem is the actual format of the technological and infrastructure base. The background of the emergence of a smart city as a kind of new formation of the territory is associated with the efficiency of resource use for a strictly limited cycle of services. Therefore, smart urban space provides the opportunity to use distributed entry points to the infrastructure guided by standardized regulations of interaction.

During the popularization of the strategy of smart cities around the world, there is a different trend of approaches to the formation of smart infrastructure for a qualitative leap in the integrated development of the territory [3]. Based on the existing types of urban space, the following basic features can be identified in the formation of smart cities:

- Historically formed urban infrastructure (megacities New York, Moscow, London, Barcelona, Tokyo and St. Petersburg)
- Development of territories "from scratch" through the introduction of smart infrastructure (Songdo, Masdar, etc. new projects)
- Cities with underdeveloped infrastructure (for example, single-industry towns and small towns, for further preservation and development they need such a complex project-driver).

Most modern technological solutions are aimed at the installation of a single platform with a strictly built vertical modular architecture. This kind of boxed solutions are in demand in such standard projects as Masdar or Songdo. Of course the effect of ready-made and tested solutions in some cases justified. However, in the long term, a city without developing a platform for its specific management, territorial development strategy and infrastructure risk losing its competitiveness and digital independence in just five or ten years. Therefore, each city strives to choose a certain initiative and a key role of urban space for citizens in the future [16]:

- Moscow - unified information space;
- New York - city sustainable and resilient;
- Barcelona - technological sovereignty, increasing opportunities for citizens in the digital environment;
- Vienna - city of equal opportunities for all groups of citizens;
- Singapore - human-oriented approach and smart use of technology.

Due to the more transparent optimization processes in the urban infrastructure framework and the availability of flexibility in building tasks on life cycles, the most modern case is the approach to the phased implementation of a smart city. The specificity of the problems is due to the so-called "technological symptoms of scale", when the decisive feature of the quality of information is the creation of distributed information systems for each public service, and not the modularity of the architectural approach on the fundamental layers of a single platform.

As of 2017, St. Petersburg occupies a leading position among other Russian regions in regional information, development of the information society and the level of ICT penetration into urban process [14].

The city information infrastructure of St. Petersburg has a sufficiently developed, with great potential, but a complex structure, with an ever-growing volume of heterogeneous and fragmented data, services, systems, functions, which does not fully meet the modern requirements and needs of citizens, business and the city economy as a whole [15].

In this regard, the task was to restructure the existing complex of systems to create an intelligent network of interaction within the integration of various services. A smart city should transform the everyday life situations faced by different categories of citizens into personalized requests and a standard of urban service mobility [10].

For St. Petersburg, the priority goal is the fundamental deployment of technological and infrastructure base around the values of citizens, for a more flexible response to the current needs in the given conditions [11].

3   Methodological Support in the Development of the Concept Smart St. Petersburg

«Smart city» is considered as a system of urban resources management, designed for a new format of interdepartmental cooperation and the formation of a competitive economic space [16]. Due to the universal reasonable use of advanced intelligent information technologies, it is planned to gradually improve the quality of life of citizens starting from the first annual cycle of Smart City events.

Within the logic of integration processes, a structural and functional smart city model is proposed. Such a platform is an interconnected set of functional elements of the digital economy infrastructure of the city, consisting of four layers. The General scheme is shown in Fig. 1.

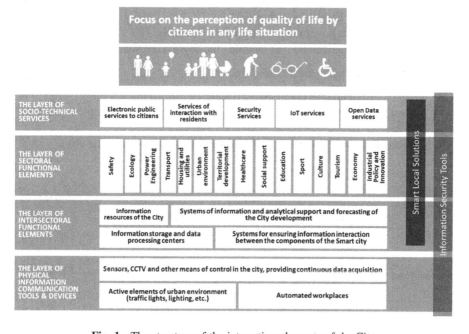

Fig. 1. The structure of the interacting elements of the City

Each functional element characterizes a group of functions of the city in relation to residents, businesses or authorities [4]. The development of elements of the basic layers (physical means of information interaction and inter-sectoral functional elements) is a necessary condition for the creation of the framework of the highest-level infrastructures. This kind of distribution of the smart city architecture into layers allows to prevent the emergence of unnecessary intermediaries of interaction and to streamline the phased implementation of modules to preserve the principles of the ecosystem [13].

1. Layer of physical information communication tools and devices:

   - hardware and software systems accompanying distributed urban processes;
   - seamless integration of digital technologies into the urban environment;
   - monitoring of automation objects.

2. Layer of intersectoral functional elements:

   - ensuring smooth interaction at the applied level of all subjects of urban information space;
   - aggregation of different data sources into a single urban repository;
   - organization of the required level of infrastructure performance for guaranteed access to urban data.

3. Layer of sectoral functional elements:

   - transparent coordination of urban development within the framework of the activities of the Executive authorities;
   - optimization of e-government information resources;
   - component implementation of modules for day-to-day management tasks.

4. Layer of socio-technical functional elements:

   - mobility of public and municipal services;
   - formation of conditions for the expansion of services in the digital profile of citizens;
   - infrastructure entry points to the unified information space of the city.

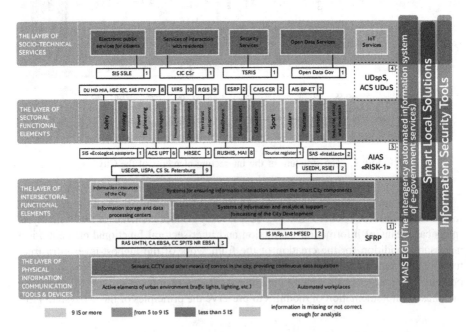

Fig. 2. Current situational scheme about IT infrastructure status of St. Petersburg

Table 1. Terminology explanation of urban information systems in St. Petersburg

№	Abbreviation	Full meaning
1	SIS	State information system
2	SAS	State automated system
3	CS	Classifier system
4	ACS	Automated control system
5	AIS	Automated information system
6	CAIS	Complex automated information system
7	IS	Information system
8	RAS	Resource accounting system
9	HSC	Hardware and software complex
10	IAS	Informational and analytical system
11	CA	Certification authority
12	CC	Control center
13	AIAS	Automated information and analytical system
14	TSRIS	Territorial and sector-based regional information system
15	RSIEI	Regional system of interdepartmental electronic interaction
16	UDspS	Unified dispatch service
17	FTV CFP	Fixing traffic violations and control fines payment
18	MAI	Management of ambulance infrastructure St. Petersburg
19	ESRP	Electronic social register of St. Petersburg population
20	ClC CSr	Call centre of citizens service
21	IASp	Information and analytical support
22	SFRP	System of the formation and projects registration

Figure 2 shows a comparison with a model of smart city architecture by overlaying the current set of resources with a planned information platform. Table 1 provides brief reference for technical names of urban systems.

4 Formation of an Integration Platform for Effective Implementation of Smart Driver-Projects

The implementation of the Smart St. Petersburg is made in the logic of the project approach, in which each project occupies a certain place in the overall structure according to its functional purpose [16]. Thus, the «smart city» is structurally a set of interacting projects, jointly ensuring the achievement of their own local goals and common goals of «Smart St. Petersburg». The concept implementation in St. Petersburg assumes the use of the existing potential of the city due to the active and initiative participation of business and citizens as participants of the city development process [12].

The process of implementing projects within the «Smart St. Petersburg» involves an annual cycle of activities. The project platform is described in Fig. 3.

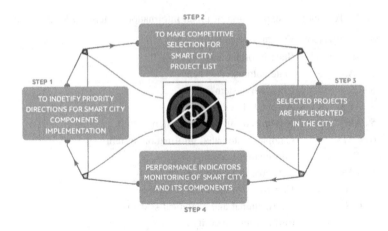

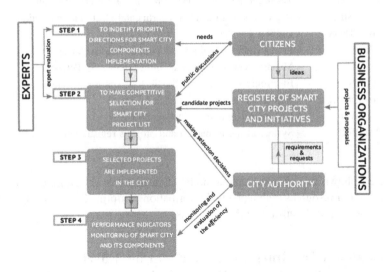

Fig. 3. Annual cycle of selection and ranking of projects

The purpose of the first stage is to determine the priority directions for the development of the city. The directions are determined by following factors: expected effect in terms of improving people's quality of life; advance development of the city; necessary elements of infrastructure [6]. At the first stage, the most popular areas of development should be identified, according to current problems and the needs of the population, as well as the formation of an infrastructure for the introduction of "smart" solutions. There must be a balance between these areas.

At the second stage, projects are selected based on methodology and regulations.

At the third stage, the projects of "Smart St. Petersburg" are being implemented. The implementation of projects is carried out in compliance with the standards adopted in the industry of the implemented project, while respecting the principles and objectives of Smart St. Petersburg. Control over the implementation process is carried out by the relevant state authority of St. Petersburg [8].

At the last stage of the cycle, the dynamics of the target indicators of "Smart St. Petersburg" and the performance indicators of the implemented projects are analyzed. Based on the monitoring results of the target indicators of Smart St. Petersburg, the results of the first and second steps can be slightly adjusted, and the cycle can be continued from the third stage. In the case of a significant deviation in the values of indicators or inability to achieve the target values - the cycle of activities is repeated from the first stage.

5 The Strategy of Human-Oriented Design to Improve Citizens Life Quality

There are three options for identifying priority areas and areas for introducing smart city technologies.

The first option assumes an orientation toward successful global and Russian practices of building "smart cities". Focusing on specific solutions and positioning the city in subject ratings are the advantages of this option. Possible immature of the city to implement a set of technologies due to lack of infrastructure (or serious problems in it) is disadvantage of this option. Current problems of the city can also be a difficult obstacle to the introduction of technology.

The second option involves focusing on current urban problems and their consistent solution. This allows to achieve the desired effect of improving quality and standard of living. Advantages of this approach are the initial social orientation and ensuring the maximum social effect at each iteration. The disadvantage of the approach is that strategic goals and intensive development of the city are not achieved.

The third option involves the identification of areas for the city development, based on its personal characteristics and capabilities and orientation to them. Advantages of the approach are: certain determination of development and the possibility of achieving significant results by focusing efforts. The obvious disadvantage is the lack of consideration of current problems in the city.

As part of the preparation of the "Smart St. Petersburg" concept, a combination of the second and third approaches was considered as a basis [1].

First of all, it is necessary to understand the position regarding the smart city of those stakeholders that are in St. Petersburg. The first component is a survey of active residents of the city, the second is a survey of employees of the authorities in St. Petersburg. It is important to determine how the concept of "smart city" is perceived now and how ready the two groups are to actively use smart city technologies today. The detailed survey and extended statistics are presented in Fig. 4.

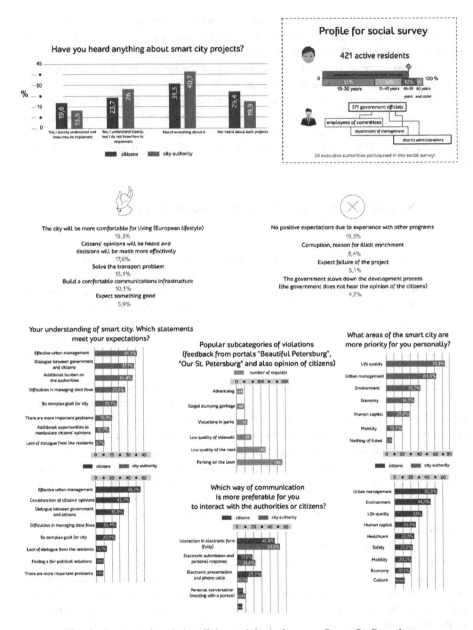

Fig. 4. Stages and statistics of the sociological survey Smart St. Petersburg

In general, according to the results of the research, it can be noted that the representations of St. Petersburg authorities on the priority areas of the city's development focused on the management of the city and the prospects for its development. Citizens focus mainly on current problems.

For this reason, when composing the final priority ranking of the directions for introducing the «smart city», both components are considered. Figure 5 shows the final rating of directions in the abstract format according to the structural and functional model of «Smart Petersburg».

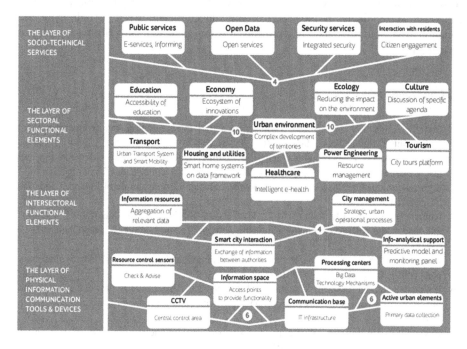

Fig. 5. Priority directions and areas for introducing smart city technologies in St. Petersburg based on needs and proposals of citizens and city authorities.

The conducted sociological survey has demonstrated a kind of snapshot of the development ideas about smart city in the specific context of the space transformation needs. This kind of dynamic tracking of the «urban pulse» will help to avoid misinterpretation of the basic values of citizens and the principles of technological progress [7].

Many cities are trying to gain a rating score by implementing various "smart projects" chaotically without feedback and overloading the fundamental infrastructure. Thus, the agenda of complex development of the territory is formed subjectively and without a full-scale discussion. The trend of over-urbanization obliges the government to use predictive modeling to understand the needs of citizens in a balanced and long-term Smart City strategy.

6   Conclusions

This article considers the vision and main features of smart city in St. Petersburg: structural and functional model of the "smart city"; main steps of selection and ranking of projects for their implementation in the urban environment; results of sociological survey. Results of the survey confirmed necessity of considering opinion of citizens and other stakeholders in processes of city development. Even though there are common expectations of smart city projects, it is important to make priorities to achieve certain effect.

References

1. Minelli, A., Ruffini, R.: Citizen feedback as a tool for continuous improvement in local bodies. Int. J. Public Sect. Manag. **31**(1), 46–64 (2018)
2. Fernandez-Anez, V., Fernández-Güell, J.M., Giffinger, R.: Smart city implementation and discourses: an integrated conceptual model. The case of Vienna. Cities **78**, 4–16 (2018)
3. Sikora-Fernandez, D.: Smarter cities in post-socialist country: example of Poland. Cities **78**, 52–59 (2018)
4. Kumar, H., Singh, M.K., Gupta, M.P., Madaan, J.: Moving towards smart cities: solutions that lead to the smart city transformation framework. Technol. Forecast. Soc. Chang., 1–16 (2018)
5. Kummitha, R.K.R., Crutzen, N.: How do we understand smart cities? An evolutionary perspective. Cities **67**, 43–52 (2017)
6. Borsekova, K., Koróny, S., Vaňová, A., Vitálišová, K.: Functionality between the size and indicators of smart cities: a research challenge with policy implications. Cities **78**, 17–26 (2018)
7. Bakıcı, T., Almirall, E., Wareham, J.: A smart city initiative: the case of Barcelona. J. Knowl. Econ. **4**(2), 135–148 (2013)
8. Mora, L., Deakin, M., Reid, A.: Strategic principles for smart city development: a multiple case study analysis of European best practices. Technol. Forecast. Soc. Chang., 1–28 (2018)
9. Alawadhi, S., et al.: Building understanding of smart city initiatives. In: Scholl, H.J., Janssen, M., Wimmer, M.A., Moe, C.E., Flak, L.S. (eds.) EGOV 2012. LNCS, vol. 7443, pp. 40–53. Springer, Heidelberg (2012). https://doi.org/10.1007/978-3-642-33489-4_4
10. Fernandez-Anez, V.: Stakeholders approach to smart cities: a survey on smart city definitions. In: Alba, E., Chicano, F., Luque, G. (eds.) Smart-CT 2016. LNCS, vol. 9704, pp. 157–167. Springer, Cham (2016). https://doi.org/10.1007/978-3-319-39595-1_16
11. Haarstad, H.: Who is driving the 'smart city' agenda? Assessing smartness as a governance strategy for cities in Europe. In: Jones, A., Ström, P., Hermelin, B., Rusten, G. (eds.) Services and the Green Economy, pp. 199–218. Palgrave Macmillan UK, London (2016)
12. Monzon, A.: Smart cities concept and challenges: bases for the assessment of smart city projects. In: International Conference Smart Cities And Green ICT Systems 2015, pp. 1–11. IEEE (2015)
13. Braude-Zolotarev, M., Grebnev, G., Yermakov, R., Rubanov, G., Serbina, E.: Interoperability of information systems. Compendium INFO-FOSS. RU, Moscow, pp. 100–108 (2008)

14. Level of IT development in Russian subjects. http://minsvyaz.ru/uploaded/files/vopros-2-prezentatsiya.pdf. Accessed 21 Mar 2018
15. Disposal of Government of St. Petersburg № 21-rp, 14 April 2017. http://base.garant.ru/43424628/. Accessed 13 Mar 2018
16. Concept of Smart St. Petersburg. http://petersburgsmartcity.ru. Accessed 30 Apr 2017

Risk Factors in Smart City Development in Russia: A Survey

Lyudmila Vidiasova[1]([✉]), Felippe Cronemberger[2],
and Evgenii Vidiasov[1]

[1] ITMO University, Saint Petersburg, Russia
bershadskaya.lyudmila@gmail.com, vidyasov@lawexp.com
[2] University at Albany, Albany 12205, USA
fcronemberger@alumni.albany.edu

Abstract. Public managers and academics continue to express interest in smart cities. In contrast with flagrant enthusiasm with regards to technology applications towards achieving such goal, threats to local governments continue to grow across the globe, while risks and concerns remain underexplored in research. By examining a survey where experts rate factors and risks in smart city development, this paper sheds light to an array of vulnerabilities that may be overlooked by public managers and executives and may compromise their smart cities goals. Expanding on literature, findings suggest the most critical smart city development factors are technological (infrastructure development, open data services, availability of information resources), organizational (clear KPIs, coordination procedures, strategic planning, creating business environment, transparency in decision-making) and social ones (preferences in getting e-services, human capital growth). Markedly, experts understood the most serious risks involve technological and social adaption. The results achieved could be of interest for counting risk factors in the emerging smart cities.

Keywords: Risk · Smart cities · Development · Technology

1 Introduction

Smart cities are a topic that keeps growing in importance. Although different scientific perspectives and approaches exist [1], most researchers see the undeniable advantages of active IT adoption and smart cities creation [2]. Taking into account the variety of interpretations used in the studies [3], it can be concluded that smart cities consider as multidimensional and complex sociotechnical systems [4].

In recent years, nevertheless, some attention has been paid to the "dark side" of information technologies in the context of smart cities. While researchers started observing concerns on future development of IT and how it may affect society [5], a special attention is also paid to the emerging risk factors in the context of smart city development. This paper addresses such gap through a survey with experts who have been in touch with what Russian cities' that only recently started to explore the idea of smartness at the local government level. The practical importance of this research is in

A. Chugunov et al. (Eds.): EGOSE 2018, CCIS 947, pp. 26–37, 2019.
https://doi.org/10.1007/978-3-030-13283-5_3

forecasting the most critical risks and inform actions that are needed to prevent or mitigate them.

The paper consists of six sections. First, the literature review is focused on an overview of factors, risks and threats faced by smart cities as they develop. In the sequence, the methodology section describes the approach and data sources used in the survey. The results section gives an estimated list of development factors and risks considered important by respondents in smart city development initiatives in Russia. Finally, "Discussion" and "Conclusion" sections respectively open some prospects for research limitations and the unexpected results, and offer suggestions for practical uses of research results.

2   Literature Review

As many frameworks have demonstrated, smart cities are complex interorganizational environments, composed of multiple different systems (see [6] and [7]). In such capacity, challenges involving those systems can be understood through socio-technical lenses, which includes studying them as technological, organizational, and social issues affecting local governments.

In the literature such terms could be found regarding smart cities unexpected side: risks, challenges, barriers. In the literature review the authors refer to all similar formulations found in scientific works.

Smart cities development faces challenges, and associated risks have been mapped in literature. Research has found that those risks relate to the extent to which those cities are capable, as organizations, to respond to issues they are expected to address. Such ability has in governance one of its pillars [8], have also been identified as compromising the ability one city has to respond to emergencies [9]. According to Angelidou [10], those challenges may also include existing practices such as poor physical planning, or economic factors, such as the ability to attract investment and new businesses.

Smart cities' risks and challenges should also consider the complexity of issues being faced by local governments. Those challenges may involve socio-economic vulnerabilities [11], and may encompass unemployment, poverty, and high crime rates [12], urban planning issues such as traffic congestion [13] and exposure to emergencies [14]. All those issues are contextual and environmental in nature, and, while common to many cities in the world, tend are likely manifest in particular ways in each different locality [15]. For example, Borsekova et al. [16] observed a correlation between smart city progress and its' size: more innovative spirit has been detected in medium-sized cities.

Some unpredicted social impacts have been noticed in San Diego where the economic growth of territory raised the level of poverty [17]. Risk of social and economic polarization could increase inequality in work, space organization and other activities [18]. The inequality issues are also raised in work of Vanolo [19] with a special attention to reinforcing long-standing social order. To avoid some negative consequences, a paper on the Italian experience with local governments suggests smart city projects' orientation on the most vulnerable population groups (the elderly, children, poor families, immigrants, multi-child families) [20, 21]. Overall, those sociodemographic issues suggest that smartness at the local level involves not only intraorganizational capabilities, but also an ability to understand problems that are external to local government.

Furthermore, it is important to highlight that data and technology are central components of smart cities and may play a critical role in its development in results measurement [22]. Despite being considered an enabler of the smart cities vision, nonetheless, the use of information and communication technologies can expose vulnerabilities of a city. Because smart cities benefit from information sharing and integration across technologies [12], those risks usually fall within the realm of cybersecurity [23, 24] and information safety [9]. Within the same scope of concerns, a variety of technological treats were presented by Baig et al. [25], including information leaks, unauthorized access, data interception threats, multiple ICT attacks, malicious code execution. Privacy risks, some skewed incentives in IT application [the benefits and risks] and even loss of life [26] are also among the list of possible smart city risks. Baig et al. [25] would also refer to such phenomenon as the "cascading effect", an issue that spreads risk towards important spheres such as healthcare and social service. In this context, the same way a smart city may benefit from information sharing and use, information users' reluctance to provide information to be used for smart cities' purposes is another issue that may be problematic [27].

Finally, the ability to solve those problems involve a multi-stakeholder perspective on issues faced by smart cities [28]. That ability encompasses the development of "urban systems models" that bring together "citizens, entrepreneurs, civic organizations, and governments" and foster collaborative understanding around how a City functions or should [29]. This approach involves considering citizens as a central enabler of smartness [30] and has increasingly discussing collaborative governance [31] and co-creation [32] as the modus operating for public value creation in local governments. According to [33], "inadequate citizens' upskilling, training and education, loss of humanity through over use of technology, lack of vision, poor governance and unsustainable policies" are a few of the challenges that that may compromise smart cities' goals and make local governments socially and politically vulnerable. Such a participatory view of smart cities suggests that a deterministic view of smartness, one that considers approaches exclusively engineered in the City Hall.

In summary, smart cities development is likely to face risks and challenges that are internal and external to local government scope of action. Internal risks could be associated to organizational capabilities, such as human capital and proper use of data and technology. External risks relate to environmental circumstances that can be social, political and economic in nature, or jointly reflect the intersect of each one of those realms.

The literature review also revealed that many risks are technology-related, and that consequences associated to the use of those technologies are often discussed hypothetically. At the same time, the review found the importance of some categories that do not relate to the "smart" aspect but still can be influenced in the process of smart city development. Given the scarcity of empirical research on such a broad topic, this paper may expand knowledge on the what is known about smart city development risks thus far.

3 Research Methodology

3.1 Smart City Development in Saint Petersburg

Smart city development started in Saint Petersburg in 2017. That occurred in accordance with the principles of strategy, economic and social development of St. Petersburg for the period, and may last until 2030. In April 2017, the city governor gave a start to the urban innovation program "Smart St. Petersburg" indicating the following principles:

- Context accounting- understanding the current city situation about by using urban data, including big data.
- Interaction and coordination based on ICT of all participants of city processes, including G2C, B2B, B2C, G2C, IoT.
- Realization of short-, medium- and long-term planning on the basis of mathematical models and artificial intelligence.
- Motivation and trust - incentives for intersectoral communication and an open transparent format for interaction between authorities, citizens and businesses.
- Reasonable control - achievement of the goals on the basis of monitoring KPIs.
- Economy and balance - reasonable management of urban resources and saving money through ICT.

For the coordination of the development of a smart city plan, a special projects office was created (https://www.petersburgsmartcity.ru/). The office is located inside ITMO University. The concept of St. Petersburg development with the help of "smart city" technologies states that smart city construction is conducted in order to overcome the current challenges: urban population growth, territories' need of renovation, complexity of city management processes, limited resources, technological and socio-economic stress factors of the urban environment (environmental pollution, information overload, violation of natural biological rhythms, lack of healthy physical activity, stressful factors).

In the research the following working definition was used: smart city is a "city resource management system designed to improve the quality of citizens' life, the quality of urban management and the formation of a competitive space for economic activities due to the widespread rational use of advanced intelligent information technologies" [34]. According to the Smart city concept, the smart city technologies count a set of methods, processes, tools, services that are used in the city to improve the quality of life of city residents (ensuring the security of the urban environment, providing services to the population or business, the implementation of public administration functions) with hardware and organizational and technical means for more efficiently solving social problems -economic development of the city. From the review of the Smart City concept the importance of technological components should be noticed. Technological tools consider as special conditions for life quality increase. However, the social processes taking place in the city life should not be ignored.

Smart city building in St. Petersburg is made in the logic of the project approach. The process of introducing smart city technologies involves an annual cycle of activities, including the identification of priority areas, conducting projects contest, implementation of selected projects, monitoring the smart city performance indicators. During the monitoring, the results of public discussions should be taken into account, as well as collection of citizens' opinions. This process has just begun, and at the time of writing the article, 53 projects have been submitted for contest.

Assessment of indicators' achievement is assessed on a scale where the highest results are: (1) needs of all population groups are met in the city; (2) residents have clear and positive expectations of living in the city; (3) prospects for living are of a positive nature and are understood by the majority of the population.

The Conception may have changes not more than once a year, that's why some critical research on possible development and risk factors could make a ground for better adjusting of smart city course.

3.2   Research Method

The research was conducted using a socio-technical approach describing interconnections between innovative progress, social institutions, their forms and processes [35]. According to established approach, smart city development is accompanied with development factors' influence and chances of risks.

The literature review revealed a variety of risks and challenges appeared in the smart city. Taking into consideration the Saint Petersburg conditions the research attention was focused on revealing the parameters and factors of a smart city success and the possible risks. The research question was as follows: what are the risk factors that influence smart city development in Saint Petersburg? Also, it was important to figure out if social and organizational factors matter as well as technological that are mentioned in the city conception quite wide.

For revealing the level of development and risk factors importance the expert survey was conducted. For the expert survey a Delphi method was used. An expert panel was formed, including experts in the field of e-governance, digital technologies and communications, among the staff of government authorities, the scientific and business community. The expert panel was formed as a result of cooperation with the project office "Smart St. Petersburg", which functions at ITMO University.

The survey included the following steps:

1. Expert group formation- this process started in Autumn 2017 when the Saint Petersburg governor has formed a project office and the responsible authorities selected their experts to participate in all activities as well as active IT- companies and expert organizations.
2. Consideration of the problem – the expert group had monthly meetings with presentations on smart city topics of different nature: scientific background, the world best cases, comparative research results, citizens' opinions etc. The expert group discussed the emerging topics and worked together for the development of the city program "Smart Saint Petersburg".
3. Collecting experts' opinions via questionnaire. The questionnaire was distributed at a meeting of the working group.
4. Consideration of results. The research team collected the answers and provided analysis of experts estimated.

5. The research team decided the importance of factors according to the experts' proposals and assessments.
6. The expert group was notified of the survey results to use them as the prioritization criteria of smart city projects in Saint Petersburg.

3.3 Data Collection

In the survey two main categories were used: smart city development and smart city risk factors. The development factors counted those categories that in experts' opinion influence positively on the smart city development. The risk factors involved those possible adverse consequences and circumstances that may be caused by smart city development. Both types of factors were grouped in three directions: technological, organizational and social. Then averages scores for each development and risk factor were calculated, and final ranking of factors' importance was built.

The survey was conducted in April 2018. Twenty-six experts took part in the study: 76% - men, 24% - women. The age structure of the expert group was as follows: 20–29 years - 8%, 30–39 years- 36%, 40–49 years - 24%, 50–59 years - 20%, 60 years and over-12%. 44% of the experts are working in the field of informatization, information society, e-government and smart cities for more than 10 years, another 12% - from 5 to 10 years, 8% - from 3 to 5 years, and 36% less than 3 years.

Among the survey participants, 32% were representatives of government bodies and subordinate organizations, 28% from private companies, 4% from non-profit organizations, and 36% from scientific and expert community. The absolute majority of experts are top managers (39%) and middle level- managers (30%), another 4% are managers of the lowest level and 26% are ordinary specialists. The research team believes that working in connection with practitioners (presented by the project office "Smart St. Petersburg") helped a lot to receive realistic estimates for development and risks factors.

In the survey a special questionnaire was developed addressing the following parameters:

- understanding of a smart city concept (open-type question),
- acceptability of various scenarios for the development of smart cities for Russia (closed question with an opportunity to draw their own scenarios),
- assessment of smart city development factors (5-point Likert scale),
- assessment of smart city risk factors (5-point Likert scale).

4 Results

According to most experts, a smart city is a city space in which a comfortable and safe environment is created based on the use of computer technology. When such environment is created, it is important to minimize the human factor in managing urban processes, to ensure a high quality of life through the optimization of urban processes. Some experts also expressed an idea of a "smart city" as an ecosystem of interaction and management of the urban environment as well as the need to increase the involvement of the population in urban development processes.

As the most acceptable scenario for smart cities development in Russia, experts identified the modernization of existing urban systems (10 experts). In addition, 9 experts announced the need for prioritization of specific industries and starting the smart city implementation from them. Another 3 experts expressed the opinion that the construction should go from the bottom up, that means on citizens' initiative.

For the ranking of development and risk factors, a 5-point scale was used. According to experts' marks, organizational factors were ranked as the highest important with an average 4 points. If we consider the whole spread of factors, then the most significant in experts' opinion are technological (infrastructure development, open data services, availability of information resources), organizational (clear KPIs, coordination procedures, strategic planning, creating business environment, transparency in decision-making) and social (preferences in getting e-services, human capital growth) (see Table 1).

Understanding of the organizational factors importance lead the experts to proposal of criteria for smart city development assessment, such as: the level of citizens' satisfaction, improving the quality of life, raising social capital, reducing complaints about the state of the urban environment, matching services to user expectations, the utility of "smart services" in terms of consumers, information accessibility/reduction of information asymmetry, economic efficiency, high level of security, raising of citizens' awareness, publishers in the open data formats of all data on urban systems, the availability of competition between the social and technical means of interaction between citizens and the authorities, the transparency of interaction between citizens and authorities, the growth of investments in the urban environment, the reduction of fuel consumption resources, the reduction in the number of accidents (crimes, accidents, traffic jams, road accidents, environmental pollution) and negative social phenomena such as unemployment, etc., the effectiveness of IT solutions (optimization of labor, financial, time resources), increase in GRP, volume investment in GRP, availability of public services and social security, the possibility of electronic discussion of decisions with the legal significance of feedback from residents, positive emotions of citizens from interacting with the city, the implementation of feedback within different spheres from end users.

At the same time, the distribution of the importance degree of risks looks different (Table 2). The experts have appropriately estimated average values for the risks associated with technology and their social adaptation. According to experts, with the development of smart cities, unexpected and sometimes risky consequences should be pierced in these areas rather than in the management environment.

The most critical expectations are linked with cybersecurity treats (also highlighted in the literature review), fear of not be in time with technological progress with the old architecture and growing the mistrust to new technologies and their abilities to citizens' real involvement in decision-making.

Table 1. Experts' estimates on smart city development factors

Technological (3.98)	Organizational (4.04)	Social (3.78)
Development of technological infrastructure (4.5) Open data/services (4.4) Availability of city information resources (4.4) Presence of agreed single reference books and classifiers (4.1) Development of mobile technologies (4.0) Wide use of technologies for informational modeling of industrial and civil objects (BIM) (3.9) Availability of standards for information systems implementation (3.9) High level of Internet use by residents (3.8) Broad development of VR technologies (2.9)	Clear KPIs for projects' implementation (4.7) Coordination of services (4.3) Development of programs and strategies for city development (4.3) Creating conditions for a comfortable business environment (4.3) Transparency in decision-making (4.3) Forecast and planning of urban systems development (4.3) Development of industry programs and strategies (4.1) Existence of proper regulatory framework for new technologies use (4.1) Creating conditions for the development of urban communities (4.0) Use of smart technologies in government (4.0) Increase digital literacy of government officials (3.8) Growth and use and processing of data in government (3.8) Monitoring of processes in real time (3.8) Use of smart technologies in subordinate institutions (3.7) Prioritizing the spheres of development and technologies (3.7) Increase of digital literacy of employees of subordinated institutions (3.5)	Getting public services mainly in electronic form (4.2) High level of human capital (4.0) Use of electronic resources for the interaction of citizens with each other (3.7) Use of electronic resources to participate in the decision-making process (3.7) Emergence of initiative smart projects from citizens (3.7) Citizens' ICT skills (3.6) Presence of an active urban community, leaders-activists (3.6)

Table 2. Experts' estimates on smart city risk factors

Technological (3.15)	Organizational (2.97)	Social (3.1)
Cybersecurity, vulnerability of information systems (4.0)	Inflexibility of power, resistance to the citizens' inclusion in political decision-making (3.5)	Development of cyberterrorism and hacking (3.7)
Obsolete architecture for new technologies (3.3)	Absence of necessary competencies of authorities in a smart city (3.5)	Mistrust of society to new technologies (3.2)
The impossibility of forming a single information base (3.3)	Enhancement of patchwork informatization (3.1)	Disappearance of many professions, and as a result, the growth of unemployment (3.1)
Complicating the processes of maintaining a smart city (3.0)	Inability to harmonize the interests of all stakeholders (3.0)	Preservation of preferences for non-electronic technologies use (3.0)
Threat of data loss when they are open (3.0)	Complication of city management processes (3.0)	Increase in entry migration to comfortable for life smart cities (3.0)
Incompatibility between smart systems and less developed areas (3.0)	Erosion of power, the possibility of social conflict (2.5)	Inequality between citizens due to different competences in ICT (2.7)
Uncontrolled development of artificial intelligence (2.5)	Complexity of managing migration flows (2.2)	Strengthening the digital divide between Smart and other Cities (2.6)

5 Discussion

The research revealed a wide spectrum of technological, organizational and social factors' influence on smart city development. The experts ranked highly the importance of technological components, these parameters were also reflected in government programs and strategies.

Risks of social adaptation received almost the same average point as technological ones. The experts believe that building a smart city without orientation on citizens' is impossible. Citizens will live in smart cities, without them, their trust and loyalty to modern technologies it's impossible to imagine an effective smart environment.

The intensity of development and risk factors should be stressed in this regard. For instance, average ranks for risks are lower than the development factors had. The experts expressed not so much fear in the link with risks, but a kind of concern that might happen but not necessarily appears in recent years.

Saint Petersburg develops a smart city within already existed environment providing new technological solutions for solving critical urban issues. This case of a smart city differs a lot from those established as new cities (Songdo, Singapore etc.). That means smart city development within existed social ties as well as significant historical background. The research results stressed the necessity to focus on citizens-centric projects and their values. In the Concept of St. Petersburg development with the help of smart city technologies, the results obtained are reflected in the formation of a socio-technical functional elements layer, including e-services provision, interactive C2G communication, participation in city management, open data and IoT services.

A smart city is planned to be implemented through a mechanism of competitive selection of projects. Criteria for their evaluation include achieving the goal of a high quality of life, assessing the needs of residents, expectations in the short, medium and long term, values and behavioral attitudes to living in the city. According to research results, a special attention should be paid to criteria that measure progress in risks' overcoming.

6 Conclusion

The study results suggest a complex vision on smart city development. Literature on smart cities, risks, emergency management and threats seem to be marching separately. Addressing development and risk factors showed the picture in complex and draw the perspectives of positive and negative nature. Risks should be understood individually, but in the context of smart cities they should be examined holistically and as far as its impact in the city.

Significant efforts should be addressed to building proper organizational environment: the most critical factors received more than 4 expert points count transparency indicators, development of comfortable business environment, proper regulations and urban communities' development.

It's important to encourage those smart city projects that have a special component on social adaptation such as promoting new services, increasing IT-competences, involving citizens into decision-making, collecting initiative ideas for city development.

Technological side of smart city development should count the modern infrastructure requirements. Each project submitted to the contest should be tested for compliance with the requirements of cybersecurity, the harmonization of the classifiers and categories used, as well as the standards of information systems.

The main research limitation is connected with a pre-defined list of factors that was used in the questionnaire (based on literature review). The respondents were able to identify factors that are important from the list. That offers little latitude for them to elaborate on issues that are interdisciplinary and do not fall exactly within one of the two categories. That could be further explored through qualitative methods such as semi-structured interviews centered around results obtained from the survey. Future research should also focus on smart city adaptation measurement, achieved goals assessment and providing criteria for development and risks detection.

Also, the Saint Petersburg is a good case for studying the factors in the emerging smart city. To disseminate the findings globally, it is necessary to carry out comparative studies focusing on different smart city types: newly created/developed on the basis of existing cities, successful cases/failure experience, as well as situated at different global regions.

Acknowledgements. The study was performed with financial support by the grant from the Russian Science Foundation (project №17-78-10079): "Research on adaptation models of the Smart City Concept in the conditions of modern Russian Society".

References

1. Neirotti, P., De Marco, A., Cagliano, A.C., Mangano, G., Scorrano, F.: Current trends in Smart City initiatives: Some stylized facts. Cities **38**, 25–36 (2014). https://doi.org/10.1016/j.cities.2013.12.010
2. Hashem, I.A.T., et al.: The role of big data in smart city. Int. J. Inf. Manag. **36**(5), 748–758 (2016). https://doi.org/10.1016/j.ijinfomgt.2016.05.002
3. Vidiasova, L., Kachurina, P., Cronemberger, F.: Smart cities prospects from the results of the world practice expert benchmarking. Procedia Comput. Sci. **119**, 269–277 (2017). https://doi.org/10.1016/j.procs.2017.11.185
4. Nam, T., Pardo, T.A.: Conceptualizing smart city with dimensions of technology, people, and institutions. In: Proceedings of the 12th Annual International Digital Government Research Conference, vol. 282 (2011). https://doi.org/10.1145/2037556.2037602
5. Gil-Garcia, J.R., Pardo, T.A., Nam, T.: What makes a city smart? Identifying core components and proposing an integrative and comprehensive conceptualization. Inf. Polity **20**(1), 61–87 (2015). https://doi.org/10.3233/IP-150354
6. Chourabi, H., et al.: Understanding smart cities: an integrative framework. In: Proceedings of the 45th Hawaii International Conference on System Science (HICSS), pp. 2289–2297 (2012). https://doi.org/10.1109/HICSS.2012.615
7. Gil-Garcia, J.R., Zhang, J., Puron-Cid, G.: Conceptualizing smartness in government: an integrative and multi-dimensional view. Gov. Inf. Q. **33**(3), 524–534 (2016). https://doi.org/10.1016/j.giq.2016.03.002
8. Castelnovo, W., Misuraca, G., Savoldelli, A.: Citizen's engagement and value co-production in smart and sustainable cities. In: International Conference on Public Policy, pp. 1–16. Milan (2015)
9. Wu, Y., Zhang, W., Shen, J., Mo, Z., Peng, Y.: Smart city with Chinese characteristics against the background of big data: idea, action and risk. J. Clean. Prod. **173**, 60–66 (2018). https://doi.org/10.1016/j.jclepro.2017.01.047
10. Angelidou, M.: Smart city planning and development shortcomings. Tema. J. Land Use Mob. Environ. **10**(1), 77–94 (2017). https://doi.org/10.6092/1970-9870/4032
11. Gasco-Hernandez, M.: Building a smart city: lessons from barcelona. Commun. ACM **61**(4), 50–55 (2018). https://doi.org/10.1145/3117800
12. Musa, S.: Smart cities-a road map for development. IEEE Potentials **37**(2), 19–23 (2018). https://doi.org/10.1109/MPOT.2016.2566099
13. Batty, M., et al.: Smart cities of the future. Eur. Phys. J. Special Top. **214**(1), 481–518 (2012). https://doi.org/10.1140/epjst/e2012-01703-3
14. Mustapha, K., Mcheick, H., Mellouli, S.: Smart cities and resilience plans: a multi-agent based simulation for extreme event rescuing. In: Gil-Garcia, J.R., Pardo, T.A., Nam, T. (eds.) Smarter as the New Urban Agenda. PAIT, vol. 11, pp. 149–170. Springer, Cham (2016). https://doi.org/10.1007/978-3-319-17620-8_8
15. Nguyen, M.T., Boundy, E.: Big data and smart (Equitable) cities. In: Thakuriah, P., Tilahun, N., Zellner, M. (eds.) Seeing Cities Through Big Data. SG, pp. 517–542. Springer, Cham (2017). https://doi.org/10.1007/978-3-319-40902-3_28
16. Borsekova, K., Korony, S., Vanova, A., Vitalisova, K.: Functionality between the size and indicators of smart cities: a research challenge with policy implications. Cities (2018, In press). https://doi.org/10.1016/j.cities.2018.03.010
17. Hollands, R.G.: Will the real smart city please stand up? Intelligent, progressive or entrepreneurial? City **12**(3), 303–320 (2008). https://doi.org/10.1080/13604810802479126

18. Chatterton, P., Hollands, R.: Urban nightscape: Youth cultures, pleasure spaces and corporate power. Routledge, London (2003)
19. Vanolo, A.: Is there anybody out there? The place and role in tomorrow's smart cities. Future **82**, 26–36 (2016). https://doi.org/10.1016/j.futures.2016.05.010
20. Beretta, I.: The social effects of eco-innovations in Italian Smart Cities. Cities **72**, 115–121 (2018). https://doi.org/10.1016/j.cities.2017.07.010
21. The benefits and risks of policymakers' use of Smart City technology. Mercatus Center. Research Summary (2016). https://www.mercatus.org/system/files/mercatus-hamilton-smart-city-tools-sum-v2_1.pdf
22. Albino, V., Berardi, U., Dangelico, R.M.: Smart cities: definitions, dimensions, performance, and initiatives. J. Urban Technol. **22**(1), 3–21 (2015). https://doi.org/10.1080/10630732.2014.942092
23. Braun, T., Fung, B.C.M., Iqbal, F., Shah, B.: Security and privacy challenges in smart cities. Sustain. Cities Soc. **39**, 499–507 (2018). https://doi.org/10.1016/j.scs.2018.02.039
24. Kumar, H., Singh, M.K., Gupta, M.P., Madaan, J.: Bowing towards smart cities: Solutions that lead to the Smart City Transformation Framework. Technological forecasting and social change (2018) In press. https://doi.org/10.1016/j.techfore.2018.04.024
25. Baig, Z.A., et al.: Future challenges for smart cities cyber-security and digital forensics. Digit. Invest. **22**, 3–13 (2017). https://doi.org/10.1016/j.diin.2017.06.015
26. Dallaway, E.: Smart City risk factors could lead to loss of life (2016). https://www.infosecurity-magazine.com/news/isc2congress-cmca-smart-city-risk/
27. Mustafa, S.Z., Kar, A.K.: Evaluating multi-dimensional risk for digital services in smart Cities. In: Kar, A.K., et al. (eds.) I3E 2017. LNCS, vol. 10595, pp. 23–32. Springer, Cham (2017). https://doi.org/10.1007/978-3-319-68557-1_3
28. Schaffers, H., Komninos, N., Pallot, M., Trousse, B., Nilsson, M., Oliveira, A.: smart cities and the future internet: towards cooperation frameworks for open innovation. In: Domingue, J., et al. (eds.) FIA 2011. LNCS, vol. 6656, pp. 431–446. Springer, Heidelberg (2011). https://doi.org/10.1007/978-3-642-20898-0_31
29. Harrison, C., Donnelly, I.A.: A theory of smart Cities. In: Proceedings of the 55th Annual Meeting of the ISSS - 2011, Hull, UK, vol. 55 (1). ACM (2011)
30. Waal, M., Dignum, M.: The citizen in the smart city. How the smart city could transform citizenship. It-Inf. Technol. **59**(6), 263–273 (2017). https://doi.org/10.1515/itit-2017-0012
31. Bolívar, M.P.R.: Governance models and outcomes to foster public value creation in smart cities. In: Proceedings of the 18th Annual International Conference on Digital Government Research, pp. 521–530. ACM (2017)
32. Bryson, J., Sancino, A., Benington, J., Sørensen, E.: Towards a multi-actor theory of public value co-creation. Public Manag. Rev. **19**(5), 1–15 (2017). https://doi.org/10.1080/14719037.2016.1192164
33. Brolchain, N.O., Ojo, A., Porwol, L., Minton, D., Barry, C.: Examining the feasibility of a Smart Region approach in the North West Atlantic and Borders Region of Ireland. In: Proceedings of the ICEGOV 2018 (2018, in press)
34. Concept of St. Petersburg development with the help of "smart city" technologies (2017). (In Russian), https://docs.wixstatic.com/ugd/548461_be60daeea6ca4768944e3af8344ba8b5.pdf
35. Orlikowski, W.J.: Using technology and constituting structures: a practice lens for studying technology in organizations. Organ. Sci. **11**(4), 404–428 (2000). https://doi.org/10.1007/978-1-84628-901-9_10

A Multi-criteria GIS Based Methodology for Smart Cities Site Selection

Nada A. Fashal[1], Ghada A. El Khayat[1(✉)], Boshra B. Salem[2], and Saleh M. El Kaffas[3]

[1] Faculty of Commerce, Alexandria University, Alexandria, Egypt
ghadaek@gmail.com
[2] Faculty of Science, Alexandria University, Alexandria, Egypt
[3] Faculty of Computers and Information, Arab Academy for Science and Technology and Maritime Transport, Alexandria, Egypt

Abstract. Building a Smart City (SC) is a practically irreversible decision that needs large investments. The success of a smart city in realizing its objectives of economic prosperity largely depends on its ability to reach its full potential; which in turn depends on its location. This research contributes a site selection method for SCs that satisfies the decision maker's criteria. Through the analysis of relevant literature, the main criteria to be considered when locating a SC were identified. Interviews with subject matter experts enabled retaining the most relevant criteria to the Egyptian reality. Layers corresponding to these criteria were built in a Geographic Information System (GIS). The Intersect process was then applied to perform site selection and identify the region respecting the decision maker's criteria. The developed GIS-Based Multi-Criteria Evaluation (MCE) methodology was tested on a study area that spans Alexandria, El Beheira and Matrouh governorates in Egypt. The prototype developed is a very beneficial instrument that enables facts based decision making as opposed to the current subjective practices used in selecting a SC location.

Keywords: Geographic Information Systems (GIS) · Smart Cities (SC) · Knowledge Precincts (KP) · Site selection · Multi-Criteria Evaluation (MCE) · Decision support · Location analysis

1 Introduction

A Smart City (SC) can be defined as a territory with high capacity for learning and innovation, which is built in the creativity of its population, its institutions of knowledge creation, and its digital infrastructure for communication and knowledge management [1]. SCs are the result of knowledge-intensive and creative strategies aiming at enhancing the socio-economic, ecological, logistic and competitive performance of cities. A Smart City is based on a promising mix of human capital, infrastructural capital, social capital and entrepreneurial capital [2]. It operates over four main dimensions: the intelligent city, the digital city, the open city and the live city [3]. A Smart City is an area where a mass of technological activities has structural benefits for individuals and companies located in there [4–6].

© Springer Nature Switzerland AG 2019
A. Chugunov et al. (Eds.): EGOSE 2018, CCIS 947, pp. 38–51, 2019.
https://doi.org/10.1007/978-3-030-13283-5_4

A Knowledge Precinct (KP) is a smaller form of a Smart City. Its contemporary practice moves from work focused knowledge precincts e.g., science and technology parks, innovation parks to multi-activity focused Knowledge Community Precincts where people, work, live, play, and cyber within their boundaries, as in Crossroads Copenhagen, Helsinki Digital Village or Singapore One-North [7, 8]. During the last few decades, the knowledge economy has been the essential boost of the global and local economic development [9]. The concept of Knowledge City (KC) has evolved from concepts such as 'knowledge clusters' [10, 11], 'ideopolis' [12], 'technopolis' [13, 14], 'science city' [15], 'learning city' [16], 'intelligent city' [17], 'sustainable city' [18] and finally 'smart city' [19]. The meaning of SC involves several definitions depending on the meanings of the word "smart": intelligent city, knowledge city, ubiquitous city [20], sustainable city, digital city [20, 21], etc. Many definitions of Smart City exist, but no one has been universally agreed upon [22].

To achieve their planned social and economic impact, the SCs, or KPs have to be well-located and planned in a way that integrates services of different kinds and from different sectors and to do this researchers need to use Geographic Information Systems (GIS) which form, more and more, a backbone for the location analysis problems. Geographic Information Systems can be defined as computer systems designed for capturing, storing, checking, integrating, manipulating, analyzing, and displaying all forms of geographically referenced information since it derives information from digital maps. [22–25]. The term "location" is defined as locating a business, facility or a group of facilities of a specific size and type in an area [23]. Building SCs is being considered by many countries in the recent years as an important arm of development. Egypt's ICT strategy (2012–2017), adopted four main goals, which are: (supporting democratic transformation, fostering digital citizenship, supporting sustainable social development and finally fostering knowledge-based national economy. For the last goal to be achieved, the strategy set several steps, among them was working to increase the number of SCs/KPs to reach 20 areas all over the Egyptian society. Egypt has already developed a number of SCs/KPs. Evaluation of existing SCs/KPs is also important as [24] argues that most of the KPs within the Arab region have failed to achieve their goals. Location analysis tools are needed to locate new SCs. These are modeling, formulation, and solution tools for a class of problems of siting facilities in some given space within a pre-established set (site selection) or without (site search) to identify the most suitable location for the decision maker [25–27].

This research aims to develop a selection method that satisfies the decision maker's criteria when selecting a location for SC. This is done through investigating a set of criteria for site selection of Smart Cities, developing a GIS-Based multi-criteria evaluation methodology for the site selection and testing the proposed methodology on a case study. The rest of this paper is organized as follows. Section 2 presents the main related concepts and reviews recent studies related to GIS, Smart Cities and site selection. Section 3 introduces the proposed GIS-based Methodology for Smart City site selection. It also handles the proposed approach and prototype development. Section 4 presents the results of the study and the discussion is given in Sect. 5. Finally, the conclusion and future work are included in Sect. 6.

2   Background and Literature Review

In this section, a review of the related literature is provided. The section is organized as follows: Sect. 2.1 presents GIS and its components, GIS data models are defined in Sect. 2.2. In Sect. 2.3 the role of GIS in Location Analysis is discussed. In Sect. 2.4 the Multi-criteria Decision Making (MCDM) is demonstrated; then in Sect. 2.5 MCDM and its relation to GIS is further explained. The elements guiding the location of SCs are discussed in Sect. 2.6.

2.1   GIS and Its Components

GIS is taking over and extending the role of spatial data storage which was previously played by maps. Once spatial data is represented in digital form it becomes very much easier to perform analyses and to make changes to them. Operations can be applied without reference to any graphic map [28]. The GIS has four main components: hardware, software, data, and liveware (People) [29]. Data processing systems use hardware and software components to process, store and transfer data [30].

2.2   GIS Data Models

The GIS' graphical interface is linked to a relational database, which presents data as a series of layers. So, according to the stored data model in the geodatabase, one can distinguish vector and raster approaches [31]. Most GISs have the capability of converting raster to vector and vector to raster. Spatial data types are used to represent geometric data. These include point, line, and polygon [32] as shown in Fig. 1.

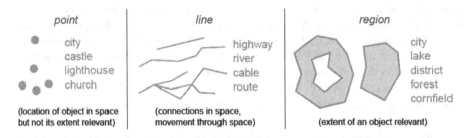

Fig. 1. Fundamental abstractions for modeling single, self-contained objects [32]

Vector Data Model

In this model, entities in the real world are divided into clearly defined features represented by point, line, or polygon geometry. The simplest vector features are points that are represented by an x (easting) and y (northing) values and possibly z (for elevation). Lines are one dimensional and defined by x, y coordinates. A polygon is a two-dimensional representation defined by a series of points and line segments connecting the points with the start and ending points being the same x, y location [33].

Raster Data Model

This model defines the space into an array of cells, each having a value that represents some aspects of the real world (e.g. elevation, land use) [34].

2.3 GIS Role in Location Analysis

The GIS have been used in urban planning throughout the past decades. The applications of GIS vary according to the different stages, levels, sectors, and functions of urban planning [35]. Recent advances in the integration of GIS with planning models, visualization, and the Internet will make GIS more useful to urban planning. An advantage of geographical spatial data is that it can be analyzed and worked with easily. GIS and Remote Sensing, the two variants of digital spatial data, work side by side in urban planning. Spatial decision problems require the evaluation of a large number of alternatives based on many criteria; hence they are multi-criteria in nature [36].

GIS has an extraordinary role in the development and implementation of the concept of SCs; as the intelligence of a city should be measured by its ability to produce favorable conditions to get urban operators (citizens, organizations, private companies, etc.) actively involved into socio-spatial innovation dynamics [3]. Citizen involvement can be realized through group decision making procedures that can be followed using artificial intelligence technologies [37]. The GIS tools used in KPs location problems are presented in [38]. GIS tools are used in conjunction with other systems and methods such as decision support systems (DSS) and methods for MCDM to solve location problems [39]. In MCDM, the different factors considered for making the decision can possibly interfere, which can influence the decision results [40]. This can be taken into account in cognitive modeling methods.

2.4 Multi-Criteria Decision Making (MCDM)

Multi-criteria decision making (MCDM) can be defined as "the process of making decisions while having multiple, usually conflicting, criteria" [41]. MCDM is suitable for addressing complex problems featuring high uncertainty, conflicting objectives, different forms of data and information, multi interests and perspectives [42].

MCDM can be grouped into two main sections: multiple attribute decision making (MADM) and multiple objective decision making (MODM). MADM is used when the decision maker has to choose only one alternative from a set of discrete actions, but MODM is a continuous decision problem. MADM is often referred to as multi-criteria analysis (MCA) or multi-criteria evaluation (MCE) [31]. These terms MCDM, MCDA, MADM, and MADA are used interchangeably. In this work, we adopt MCA to identify suitable locations for building a SC.

2.5 MCDM and GIS

A literature review was conducted regarding the GIS-based multi-criteria decision analysis (GIS-MCDA) approaches from 1990 to 2004. There are five generic steps of the GIS-based MCDA process regardless of the variations between the GIS-MCDA frameworks: (1) The goal(s) an individual (or group of individuals) seeks to achieve and the corresponding evaluation criteria for the alternative courses of action; (2) the decision-maker or a group of decision-makers involved in the decision-making process along with their preferences; (3) the set of decision alternatives (4) the set of states of nature; and (5) the set of consequences associated with each alternative-criterion pair [43]. GIS provide a powerful platform for performing logical and mathematical analyses that use the weights of each map layer. However it does not have the capability of objectively assigning the weights to each map layer [44].

Different contributions used GIS in conjunction with MCDM. These include applications in forestry [45], landfill site selection [46], locating optimal sites to the hillside development [47], wind turbine farm site selection [48], river catchment management [49] and site selection of aquifer recharge with reclaimed water [50]. In order to consider weights, MCDA and overlay analysis using GIS were used for siting landfill [51]. MCDA process that combines GIS analysis with the Fuzzy Analytical Hierarchy Process (FAHP) was used to determine the optimal location for a new hospital in Tehran. GIS was used to calculate and classify governing criteria, while FAHP was used to evaluate the decision factors and their impacts on alternative sites [52]. GIS-MCDA continued to be an interesting area of research throughout the last decade and contribution tackled a diverse set of problems from different sectors [53].

2.6   Elements Guiding Smart Cities Site Selection

There are five intangible key elements and principles that judge the nature and potential for building KPs in towns. The five elements are: (MIXED-USE ENVIRONMENT: helps living and working purposes, CENTRALITY: provides accesses to different infrastructure, services, and amenities, BRANDING: forms new niche markets and marks the name of the emerging knowledge city with a landmark development such as Barcelona city, LEARNING AND PLAYING: suggests the existence of Urban playfield, R&D facilities, places of interaction, and technological innovation and creativity hubs, CONNECTIVITY: happens through tacit knowledge, face-to-face interaction, places of interaction, and social networking between the citizens [54]. These five elements are reflected in the criteria identified in the following section and used in the study. A more comprehensive review on SCs location analysis is found in [55].

3   Proposed GIS-Based Methodology for Smart Cities Site Selection

The current study applies to the Alexandria Region; which includes: Alexandria Governorate, El Beheira Governorate, and Matrouh Governorate in Egypt, as shown in Fig. 2. Data relevant to this region was obtained from bodies holding statistics such as Ministry of Housing, Utilities and Urban Communities, General Organization for Urban Planning, Strategic Plan for Alexandria Region Project; and from experts in the field. Table 1 provides the criteria used in this study and their respective values for smart cities at the local, regional, and international levels. The land cover criterion was also considered in this study but is excluded from the comparison table as it was found suitable for all the studied cities. In order to undergo MCE, interviews were conducted with subject matter experts in Egypt including officials and scholars who work in SC projects and representatives of the Ministry of Communications and Information Technology to identify the relevant criteria presented below.

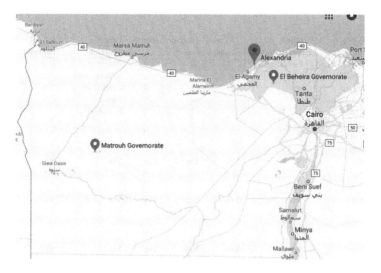

Fig. 2. Study area

Preparing Criterion Maps
The first step in the study is to prepare the criterion maps. The thresholds upon which the criteria will be treated were estimated according to secondary sources and expert opinion. The criteria considered are *Land Cover;* which is the classification of land according to what activities take place on it or how humans occupy it, *Soil Type;* which refers to the different sizes of mineral particles in a particular sample, *Elevation;* which is the height of a geographic location above or below a fixed reference point, *Proximity to High Ways*, **Proximity to Residential Areas** and *Proximity to Universities and Proximity to Airports*. Table 2 shows the used criteria and the threshold of every criterion. The open street map basemap was added to the GIS project. The geodatabase contains seven layers corresponding to these different criteria that were then added to the project as shown below from Figs. 3, 4, 5, 6, 7 and 8.

Table 1. Comparison between local, regional, and international SCs

Criteria	Egypt		Regional			International		
	Smart Village Giza	Borg El Arab's Technological Zone	Smart Dubai	Abu Dhabi (Masdar)	Riyadh	Japan (Yokohama) (YSCP)	Europe (London)	USA (New York)
Elevation https://www.latlong.net/	28 m	18 m	0 m	7 m	638 m	13 m	15 m	7 m
Soil type	Highly calcareous, gypseous and saline **Parent material**: Argillaceous sandstone of the continental terminal	**Other quaternary formations**	Torripsamments	Torripsamments	Jurassic	**Parent material:** Weathered volcanic ash material of Tertiary formation	**Parent material:** peat	Aquic +UDIC soil
Proximity to high ways	**Yes**	**No**	**Yes**	**Yes**	**Yes**	**Yes**	**Yes**	**Yes**
Proximity to residential areas	**Yes**	**Yes**	**Yes**	**Yes**	**Yes**	**Yes**	**Yes**	**Yes**
Proximity to universities	**Yes**	**Yes**	**Yes**	**Yes**	**Yes**	**Yes**	**Yes**	**Yes**
Proximity to airports	**Yes**	**Yes**	**Yes**	**Yes**	**Yes**	**Yes**	**Yes**	**Yes**

Table 2. Threshold of criteria

Criterion	Threshold
Land cover	Bare rock - Bare soil stony
Soil type	Bare soil stony - Bare rock with thin sand layer
Elevation	From 0–100
Proximity to high ways	Buffer 5 km
Proximity to residential areas	Buffer 30 km
Proximity to universities	Buffer 30 km
Proximity to airports	Buffer 30 km

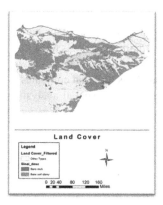

Fig. 3. Land cover

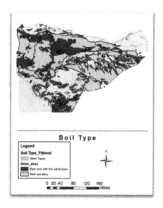

Fig. 4. Soil type

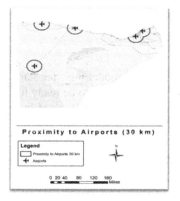

Fig. 5. Proximity to airports

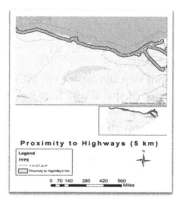

Fig. 6. Proximity to highways

Fig. 7. Proximity to residential areas

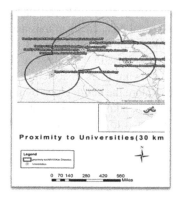

Fig. 8. Proximity to universities

Data Processing
The second step is the data processing procedure for generating criterion maps based on the following GIS functions. ***Buffer*** which is one of the proximity analysis tools that can create influence zones for points, lines and polygons. The influence zone is shown in Fig. 9 [56]. The second function ***Intersect*** is an overlay analysis tool that computes a geometric intersection of the Input Features and will be used for the spatial analysis.

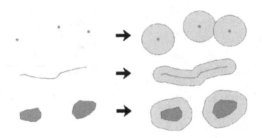

Fig. 9. The influence zone [56]

Spatial Analysis
This third step consists of the MCE and the overlay. The MCE model includes standardization of spatial data from its original format into a general format to be ready for analysis [57]. Various spatial input layers can be combined when MCE is used in a GIS-based environment to facilitate decision making [58]. The overlay was realized applying the ***Intersect*** function over the four proximity layers after filtering the three other layers according to the chosen threshold. The complete process of intersect is shown in Fig. 10.

Software
ArcMap10.5, used in this work, is the main component of Esri's ArcGIS suite of geospatial processing programs. It allows the user to explore data within a data set, symbolize features, and create maps. ArcMap is a kind of Desktop GIS. It performs several powerful tasks such as creating and editing maps, analyzing the maps and their relevant spatial data, create graphs and reports, etc. Google Earth which is a free online geographical tool that allows users to navigate the globe and create customized maps [59] was also used. It displays a 3D representation of the Earth based on satellite imagery allowing users to see cities and landscapes from various angles and allowing them to explore the entire globe by inputting coordinates, or names of the locations. In order to do so, a kml file was created in Google Earth Pro desktop application and then it was imported to a shapefile in ArcMap environment.

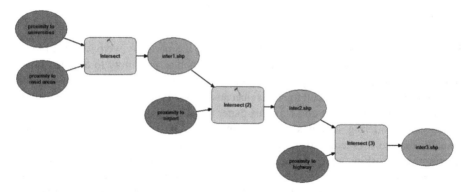

Fig. 10. The complete process of intersect

4 Results

The area defined by the outer red polygon in Fig. 11 satisfies the seven criteria considered in this research and provides a wide area where decision makers can locate new SCs.

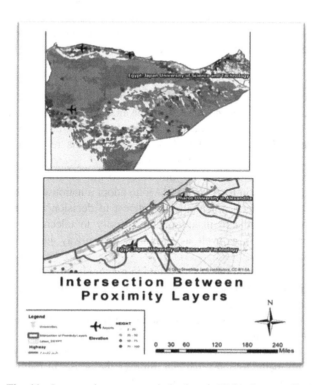

Fig. 11. Intersect between proximity layers (Color figure online)

5 Discussion

In this paper, the selection criteria used for locating a Smart City were identified to be land cover, soil type, elevation, proximity to universities, proximity to airports, proximity to residential areas, and proximity to highways. SC site selection is considered a crucial decision as it is difficult to reverse because of the high cost of relocation and the potential waste of time and effort. In this paper the site selection of the smart city was addressed considering strengths and capabilities that GIS offers such as the ability to visually analyze sites and to display data and information on a map which helps better interpret relationships within a specified area. Since Decision Making is a subjective case, criteria are chosen by concerned experts. Thus, it is impossible to arrive to the same results using data obtained from different experts. Another way for getting criteria is using an aggregate measure representing the opinion of a group of experts obtained through applying techniques such as Delphi technique.

6 Conclusion and Future Work

This paper contributed a GIS-based MCE methodology to meet the requirements of SC site selection. The spatial model considers a number of criteria of interest to the decision maker. First criterion maps were prepared; data processing and GIS spatial analysis involving MCE were undergone and the overlapping area is the area to be proposed to the decision maker. The development of the proposed system was carried out using ArcGIS 10.5 with Spatial Analyst extension as well as Google Earth Pro. The proposed system was tested to determine the potential sites for SCs in the identified study area in Egypt.

A big region was identified where it is suitable to build a SC. Interestingly, an area such as the Abis region in Alexandria seems to be an excellent candidate location for a SC. However, it never attracted the decision makers' attention. It is also recommended to do further detailed studies on the identified area in this research to assess the feasibility of establishing a SC on one of its sites.

The proposed methodology can be introduced to the Central Agency for Public Mobilization and Statistics in Egypt (CAPMAS) to adopt it nationwide and to add more data relevant to other criteria potentially of interest to decision makers. These may include proximity to healthcare institutions, proximity to telecommunication hubs, electrical distribution hubs as well as proximity to railway junctions as well as developed railway stations.

Future work includes building and developing a dynamic prototype where the user can input the criteria of interest to the ArcMap project. The interface can also have buttons for different analysis and conversion tools embedded in ArcMap.

Another future avenue of research is testing the proposed methodology in a real environment, on an existing smart city to evaluate whether the location chosen by the decision makers was appropriate or not. The proposed methodology may be integrated with weight setting methodologies that can improve the output to the decision maker. These include the Analytical Hierarchy Process AHP. Finally, the described approach was used for the location of SCs which is the focus of this paper. However the methodology is generic enough to be applied to the selection of industrial and residential areas, among others. The relevant criteria of interest to the concerned decision maker would then be used.

Acknowledgement. The authors would like to thank Mr. Ahmed El-Sobky (ITIDA and Chairman of Silicon Waha), Dr. Mohamed Meheina (Bibliotheca Alexandrina), Dr Walaa Sheta (Dean of the Institute of Informatics) and Eng. Mohamed Hanafy (ITI) who acted as subject matter experts in this research.

References

1. Komninos, N.: Intelligent cities: variable geometries of spatial intelligence. Intell. Build. Int. **3**(3), 172–188 (2011)
2. Kourtit, K., Nijkamp, P.: Smart cities in the innovation age. Innov. Eur. J. Soc. Sci. Res. **25** (2), 93–95 (2012)
3. Roche, S.: Geographic Information Science I: why does a smart city need to be spatially enabled? Prog. Hum. Geogr. **38**(5), 703–711 (2014)
4. Chan, K., Lau, T.: Assessing technology incubator programs in the science park: the good, the bad and the ugly. Technovation **25**(10), 1215–1228 (2005)
5. Westhead, P., Batstone, S., Martin, F.: Technology-based firms located on science parks: the applicability of Bullock's 'soft-hard' model. Enterp. Innov. Manag. Stud. **1**(2), 107–139 (2000)
6. Yigitcanlar, T.A., Martinez-Fernandez, M.C.: Making space and place for knowledge production: knowledge precinct developments in Australia (2007)
7. Yigitcanlar, T.A.: Knowledge-based urban development. In: Mehdi, K.-P. (ed.) Encyclopedia of Information Science and Technology, 3rd edn, pp. 7475–7485. IGI Global, Hershey (2015)
8. Yigitcanlar, T., Velibeyoglu, K., Martinez-Fernandez, C.: Rising knowledge cities: the role of urban knowledge precincts. J. Knowl. Manag. **12**(5), 8–20 (2008)
9. Yigitcanlar, T.: Evolving definition of knowledge cities. Int. J. Knowl.-Based Dev. **8**(1), 1–4 (2017)
10. Huggins, R.: The evolution of knowledge clusters: progress and policy. Econ. Dev. Q. **22**(4), 277–289 (2008)
11. Luis Arboníes, A., Moso, M.: Basque Country: the knowledge cluster. J. Knowl. Manag. **6** (4), 347–355 (2002)
12. Garcia, B.C.: Developing futures: a knowledge-based capital for Manchester. J. Knowl. Manag. **8**(5), 47–60 (2004)
13. Scott, A.J.: Technopolis: high-technology industry and regional development in Southern California (1993)
14. Smilor, R.W., Gibson, D.V., Kozmetsky, G.: Creating the technopolis: high-technology development in Austin, Texas. J. Bus. Ventur. **4**(1), 49–67 (1989)
15. Anttiroiko, A.-V.: Science cities: their characteristics and future challenges. Int. J. Technol. Manage. **28**(3–6), 395–418 (2004)
16. Larsen, K.: Learning cities: the new recipe in regional development. Organisation for Economic Cooperation and Development. The OECD Observer, no. 217/218, p. 73 (1999)
17. Komninos, N.: Intelligent Cities: Innovation, Knowledge Systems, and Digital Spaces. Taylor & Francis, London (2002)

18. Camagni, R., Capello, R., Nijkamp, P.: Towards sustainable city policy: an economy-environment technology nexus. Ecol. Econ. **24**(1), 103–118 (1998)
19. Yigitcanlar, T.: Technology and the City: Systems, Applications and Implications. Routledge, New York (2016)
20. Anthopoulos, L., Fitsilis, P.: From digital to ubiquitous cities: defining a common architecture for urban development, pp. 301–306. IEEE (2010)
21. Couclelis, H.: The construction of the digital city. Environ. Plan. **31**(1), 5–19 (2004)
22. Cocchia, A.: Smart and digital city: a systematic literature review. In: Dameri, R.P., Rosenthal-Sabroux, C. (eds.) Smart City. PI, pp. 13–43. Springer, Cham (2014). https://doi.org/10.1007/978-3-319-06160-3_2
23. Szymańska, A.I., Płaziak, M.: Enterprise and classical factors of its location on the market. Procedia-Soc. Behav. Sci. **120**, 13–22 (2014)
24. Alraouf, A.A.: Knowledge cities: examining the discourse smart villages, internet cities or creativity engines. Plan. Malaysia J. **4**(1), 31–48 (2006)
25. Revelle, C.S., Eiselt, H.A., Daskin, M.S.: A bibliography for some fundamental problem categories in discrete location science. Eur. J. Oper. Res. **184**(3), 817–848 (2008)
26. Vito, A., Giuseppe, D., Guido, S.: A decision based support system based on GIS technology. In: Nilmini, W., Eliezer, G. (eds.) Encyclopedia of Healthcare Information Systems, pp. 383–390. IGI Global, Hershey (2008)
27. Captivo, M.E., Clímaco, J., Fernandes, S.: A bicriteria DSS dedicated to location problems. In: Encyclopedia of Decision Making and Decision Support Technologies, vol. 1, pp. 53–60 (2008)
28. Jones, C.B.: Geographical Information Systems and Computer Cartography. Routledge, London (2014)
29. Chakraborty, D., Sahoo, R.: Fundamentals of Geographic Information System. Viva Books, New Delhi (2007)
30. Huisman, O., De By, R.: Principles of Geographic Information Systems. ITC Educational Textbook Series, vol. 1, p. 17 (2009)
31. Belka, K.: Multicriteria analysis and GIS application in the selection of sustainable motorway corridor. Institutionen för datavetenskap (2005)
32. Schneider, M.: Spatial data types: conceptual foundation for the design and implementation of spatial database systems and GIS (1999)
33. Sugumaran, R., Degroote, J.: Spatial Decision Support Systems: Principles and Practices. CRC Press, Boca Raton (2010)
34. Information Resources Management Association: Geographic Information Systems: Concepts, Methodologies, Tools, and Applications: Concepts, Methodologies, Tools, and Applications. Information Science Reference (2012)
35. Yeh, A.G.-O.: Urban planning and GIS. Geogr. Inf. Syst. **2**(877–888), 1 (1999)
36. Chakhar, S., Mousseau, V.: Spatial multicriteria decision making. In: Encyclopedia of Geographic Information Science, pp. 747–753 (2008)
37. Raikov, A.N.: Strategic planning of science city socioeconomic development. In: Alexandrov, D.A., Boukhanovsky, A.V., Chugunov, A.V., Kabanov, Y., Koltsova, O. (eds.) DTGS 2017. CCIS, vol. 745, pp. 295–306. Springer, Cham (2017). https://doi.org/10.1007/978-3-319-69784-0_25
38. Fashal, N.A., El Khayat, G.A.: A survey on knowledge precincts location problems and their GIS tools. In: Proceedings of ICT in Our Lives, Alexandria, Egypt, 19–21 December 2015, pp. 59–64 (2015)
39. Rikalovic, A., Cosic, I., Lazarevic, D.: GIS based multi-criteria analysis for industrial site selection. Procedia Eng. **69**, 1054–1063 (2014)

40. Raikov, A.N., Avdeeva, Z., Ermakov, A.: Big data refining on the base of cognitive modeling. IFAC-PapersOnLine **49**(32), 147–152 (2016)

41. Xu, L., Yang, J.-B.: Introduction to multi-criteria decision making and the evidential reasoning approach. Manchester School of Management Manchester (2001)

42. San Cristobal, J.R.: Multi Criteria Analysis in the Renewable Energy Industry. Green Energy and Technology. Springer, Heidelberg (2012). https://doi.org/10.1007/978-1-4471-2346-0

43. Malczewski, J.: GIS-based multicriteria decision analysis: a survey of the literature. Int. J. Geogr. Inf. Sci. **20**(7), 703–726 (2006)

44. Nyeko, M.: GIS and multi-criteria decision analysis for land use resource planning. J. Geogr. Inf. Syst. **4**(04), 341–348 (2012)

45. Phua, M.-H., Minowa, M.: A GIS-based multi-criteria decision making approach to forest conservation planning at a landscape scale: a case study in the Kinabalu Area, Sabah, Malaysia. Landscape Urban Plan. **71**(2–4), 207–222 (2005)

46. Chang, N.-B., Parvathinathan, G., Breeden, J.B.: Combining GIS with fuzzy multicriteria decision-making for landfill siting in a fast-growing urban region. J. Environ. Manage. **87**(1), 139–153 (2008)

47. Chandio, I.A., Matori, A.N.B.: Land suitability analysis using geographic information systems (GIS) for hillside development: a case study of Penang Island (2011)

48. Van Haaren, R., Fthenakis, V.: GIS-based wind farm site selection using Spatial Multi-Criteria Analysis (SMCA): evaluating the case for New York State. Renew. Sustain. Energy Rev. **15**(7), 3332–3340 (2011)

49. Chen, H., Wood, M., Linstead, C., Maltby, E.: Uncertainty analysis in a GIS-based multi-criteria analysis tool for river catchment management. Environ. Model Softw. **26**(4), 395–405 (2011)

50. Pedrero, F., Albuquerque, A., do Monte, H.M., Cavaleiro, V., Alarcón, J.J.: Application of GIS-based multi-criteria analysis for site selection of aquifer recharge with reclaimed water. Resour. Conserv. Recycl. **56**(1), 105–116 (2011)

51. Sumathi, V., Natesan, U., Sarkar, C.: GIS-based approach for optimized siting of municipal solid waste landfill. Waste Manag. **28**(11), 2146–2160 (2008)

52. Vahidnia, M.H., Alesheikh, A.A., Alimohammadi, A.: Hospital site selection using fuzzy AHP and its derivatives. J. Environ. Manage. **90**(10), 3048–3056 (2009)

53. Yalcin, M., Gul, F.K.: A GIS-based multi criteria decision analysis approach for exploring geothermal resources: Akarcay basin (Afyonkarahisar). Geothermics **67**, 18–28 (2017)

54. Bajracharya, B., Too, L., Imukuka, J.K., Hearn, G.N.: Developing knowledge precincts in regional towns: opportunities and challenges (2009)

55. El Khayat, G.A., Fashal, N.A.: Inter and intra cities smartness: a survey on location problems and GIS tools. In: Sami, F., Khaoula, M. (eds.) Handbook of Research on Geographic Information Systems Applications and Advancements, pp. 296–320. IGI Global, Hershey (2017)

56. Pucha-Cofrep, F., Fries, A., Cánovas-García, F., Oñate-Valdivieso, F., González-Jaramillo, V., Pucha Cofrep, D.: Fundamentals of GIS (2018)

57. Hansen, H.S.: GIS-based multi-criteria analysis of wind farm development, pp. 75–78. Citeseer (2005)

58. Jankowski, P.: Integrating geographical information systems and multiple criteria decision-making methods. Int. J. Geogr. Inf. Syst. **9**(3), 251–273 (1995)

59. Ellen, Y., Nicholas, S.: A learner-centered approach to technology integration: online geographical tools in the ESL classroom. In: Jared, K., Grace, O. (eds.) Handbook of Research on Learner-Centered Pedagogy in Teacher Education and Professional Development, pp. 1–22. IGI Global, Hershey (2017)

Development of Decision Support Systems for Smart Cities

Fedor Georgievich Maitakov⑩, Alexander Alekseevich Merkulov⑩,
Evgeny Vladimirovich Petrenko⁽⊠⁾⑩,
and Abdurashid Yarullaevich Yafasov⑩

Kaliningrad State Technical University, Kaliningrad, Russian Federation
maitakov@mail.ru, vsmcenose@mail.ru,
petrenkoe@hotmail.com, yafasov@list.ru

Abstract. Modern decision support systems (DSS) for a rapidly developing sector of smart cities significantly reduce decision-making time and improve their quality. However, a huge amount of time, material and intellectual resources, spent on the development of such systems, in conditions of transition to a digital economy, makes it necessary to unify the elements and methods of synthesis of the working environment. The aim of the work is to develop a technology for the synthesis of a unified virtual work environment for heterogeneous territorially distributed teams (HTDT) that arise in the ecosystems of smart cities. The authors offer a model of a unified virtual working environment and a method for its synthesis, which allows to significantly reduce the costs of developing and implementing DSS in a specific subject area and management level. The technology of synthesis of the virtual working environment for HTDT was tested in the creation of a line of software complexes that implements various components of the smart city management system: "Tourism Industry", "Electronic Budget", network interactive NBICS.Net laboratory, open interactive 3D laboratory. Using this technology has significantly reduced the amount spent on the development and deployment of resources.

Keywords: Smart city · Technology of working environment synthesis · Unification of elements and methods of working environment synthesis · Configuration · Widget · Plugin

1 Introduction

Computer decision support systems are actively used in a number of countries in public administration. Being initially developed to solve national defense tasks (National Defense Operations Center of the Russian Federation) and to monitor in emergency situations (National Emergency Management Center of the Ministry of Emergency of the Russian Federation) for top managers, today, DSS is distributed horizontally - to other branches of government (energy, economy, healthcare, education, etc.), and vertically - from the upper levels of power to the lower ones.

In order to ensure sustainable social and economic development of cities and to improve the quality of life of their population, the "smart city" initiative is actively

© Springer Nature Switzerland AG 2019
A. Chugunov et al. (Eds.): EGOSE 2018, CCIS 947, pp. 52–63, 2019.
https://doi.org/10.1007/978-3-030-13283-5_5

promoted. Within the framework of this initiative, electric, thermal and transport net-works are being reconstructed, production facilities are being modernized, and social and economic infrastructure (residential, cultural, entertainment and commercial complexes) is being constructed. The introduction of the latest developments in the field of information technology increases the degree of automation and intellectual-ization of the branches of municipal government.

The use of smart technologies has high economic feasibility. For example, the introduction of an energy efficiency management system in Barcelona can save about 9.5 billion euros per year. In Vienna, more than 15% of energy resources come from renewable sources, including the use of the largest power plant in Europe working with bio-mass.

To implement effective management of all smart city sub-systems, the DSS is needed, which is capable of monitoring, analyzing, modeling and forecasting the sit-uation in the control facility.

Development and creation of DSS is a complex high-tech and cost intensive task that is solved individually for each specific application [1], and the smart city system covers at once many different subject areas: energy, health, housing, education, etc. It is necessary to take into account the subject (profile) and official heterogeneity and ter-ritorial distribution of the DSS user community. The heterogeneity of the team is determined on the one hand by different field-specific knowledge of each of the par-ticipants in the team (economist, accountant, engineer, etc.), and, on the other, by their different positions in the job hierarchy of the organization (director, department head, specialist, etc.). It should also be noted that during the normal work of the DSS, modernization of its various subsystems may occur, which imposes additional requirements on the flexibility of the system.

The authors have proposed a unified model of a flexibly configurable DSS, applicable in different subject areas, and a technology for the synthesis of virtual working environments for HTDT that reduce the time, intellectual and financial costs of creating and implementing DSS, as well as their subsequent integration and synchronization.

2 Approaches to the Creation of Virtual Working Environments for HTDT

In the context of the problem being solved, HTDT is considered as unification of people jointly implementing a certain programme aimed at achieving a given goal, and acting on the basis of certain procedures and rules [1, 2]. Different models of the organization, its management structure, and ways of expert interaction among them-selves, development time of the system, number and competence of the design team predetermine the choice of a particular approach to the creation of DSS. As a rule, the list of different types of working environments is determined at the early stages of DSS development and is rigidly fixed in technical specifications. However, specific char-acter of management activity, constantly changing conditions of the internal and external environment of the organization [3] and uncertainty [4] in which decisions have to be made dictate the need for maximum flexibility of the working environment of the expert and the decision-maker (DM). Another necessary requirement in the development of DSS is their network integration with a view to creating distributed intelligent control systems for large areas in different spheres [5].

There are many models of software development in general and DSS for such vertically and horizontally integrated systems in particular - sequential [6], iterative [7], spiral [8], flexible [9], etc. All these models involve several steps of development:

- requirements analysis;
- design;
- programming;
- testing;
- system integration;
- implementation;
- support.

As a result of the development of the DSS software using any of the approaches, a rigid system is created that implements a limited set of functions. The approach proposed by the authors of this article, allows you to create a flexible system with dynamically expanding functionality. At the same time, the VSMCenose platform is used, the ideology of which is based on the use of categorical framework: description of the subject area model and description of the expert's working environment model. Both frameworks consist of limited sets of abstract concepts.

The categorical framework for the description of the subject area model allows storing and processing heterogeneous data in repositories with a single unified structure. A unified structure and a limited set of abstract concepts (category, essence, relation) allow you to implement the tools of logic layers and user interface to solve a whole class of tasks rather than a specific task. For example, a task is being solved not just to plot a chart of "income/expenses" of an organization, but to plot a chart for the entity (organization) by categories (Income/Expenditure), i.e. for any combinations of entities and categories. Thus, instruments operate only with abstract concepts and do not depend on the subject area.

The categorical framework for the description of the working environment model provides a possibility of individual flexible adjustment of the expert's workplace using visual programming technology. Combining any quantity of different tools in the working environment allows you to get new functionality, as well as to move beyond a "monolithic", hard-programmed user interface to solve expert tasks.

Joint use of the categorical frameworks for the description of the subject area model and the working environment model in the VSMCenose platform provides opportunities for flexible system configuration without participation of the programmer. This allows any participant of the HTDT to determine the structure of the content stored in the database and adjust its workplace, as well as to reduce costs during the design, programming, testing, system integration, implementation and maintenance of the product.

3 The Model of the Unified Virtual Working Environment for HTDT

Pospelov, Tarasov and colleagues [1, 2] note the problem of constructing objective control criteria in complex systems. The management criteria become subjective and depend on the DM. Complex tasks being solved in the organization, are reduced to simpler ones and are distributed among the members of the heterogeneous collective. Each member of the team decides its range of tasks in accordance with its work profile and position held, i.e. fulfills its role in the team. The role stipulates the management criteria, as well as the functional capabilities, i.e. determines the list of tools and outlines the amount of access to information that is used to solve the tasks. A role model is the basis for organizing joint work of the heterogeneous team in the DSS.

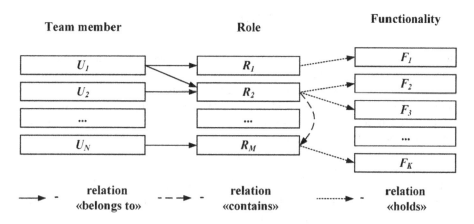

Fig. 1. Roles and functionality in a team.

Figure 1 shows the diagram of the role model of the team members work, where: $U = \{U_1, \ldots, U_N\}$ – the set of all members of the team, $R = \{R_1, \ldots, R_M\}$ – the set of all roles in the team, $F = \{F_1, \ldots, F_K\}$ – the set of all functional capabilities. An employee can have several roles in the team (for example, a member U_1 of the team belongs to roles R_1 and R_2 in Fig. 1). The role can include other roles (for example, the role R_2 includes the role R_M in Fig. 1). The role determines functionality of a member of the team (for example, a member U_1 of the team has functional capabilities F_1 through the role R_1, F_2 и F_3, and through the role R_2 и F_K and through the role R_M in Fig. 1).

The literature notes the usefulness of visual metaphors in the design of user interfaces for computer systems [10]. To facilitate perception of technological processes taking place in HTDT, DSS is constructed as a visual metaphor of a situation room (Fig. 2).

A situation room is a room equipped with hardware and software and intended for prompt decision-making and monitoring of objects of different nature and situations. Each workplace of a specialist in a situation room is represented in the form of an

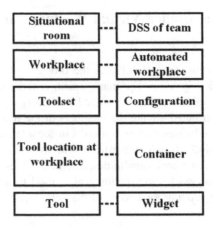

Fig. 2. Visual situation room metaphor.

automated workstation (AWS) in the DSS. AWS is designed to solve a range of tasks for specific groups of users and consists of a set of configurations. Each configuration is a set of visual representations of tools - widgets, arranged in a certain way and configured to solve a specific task. Widgets are grouped in configurations by means of containers. Each container occupies a specific area of the configuration screen and contains the tabs with the widgets.

An example of the organization of the user interface of the virtual working environment of HTDT is shown in Fig. 3.

The screen is divided into the area of communication, navigation and alerts (ACNA) and the current task area (CTA). The ACNA is constantly present in the user interface when solving any particular task. Widgets $I = \{I_1, \ldots, I_K\}$ that provide communication functions and report new events (new tasks, exceeding permissible sensor values, emergency situations, etc.), as well as tools for navigating between configurations are located in it. The CTA reflects the current configuration designed to provide a specific functionality, $K_i = \{C_{i1}, \ldots, C_{iM}\}$, where $C_{ij} = \{W_{ij1}, \ldots, W_{ijP}\}$ j is the j-th container of the i-th configuration, which includes a set of widgets, where W_{ijk} – k-th widget of the j-th container of the i-th configuration.

Widgets placed in the same configuration have a common working field and can interact with each other by exchanging typed signals. Thus, if widgets are tools that implement artificial intelligence methods (artificial neural network, fuzzy system, genetic algorithm, etc.), then their interaction is coarse-grained hybridization [11].

When solving a task, the expert may need to quickly contact another member of the team or he can receive an alert about an event. When an alert is received, the expert can stop execution of the current task and focus on a new event or ignore it. A similar scheme of the work of heterogeneous team members can be observed in the situation room, but the DSS, designed in this way, gives important advantages to the team members - territorial distribution and transparency of technological processes.

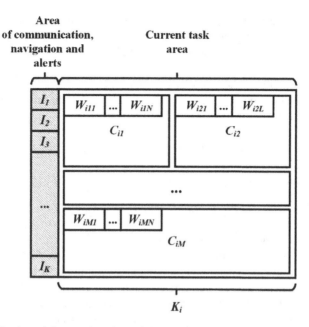

Fig. 3. Organization of the user interface of the virtual desktop environment of the HTDT.

The role model of work organization of heterogeneous team participants, applied to the visual metaphor of the user interface, provides a clear delineation of the functional capabilities of each team member (Fig. 4).

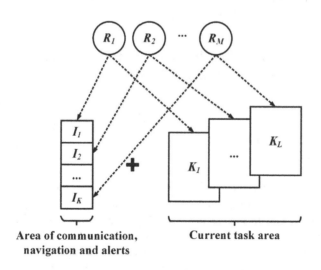

Fig. 4. Application of the role model to the virtual desktop environment HTDT.

Users with a role R_1 have the rights to access the widget I_1 in the communication, navigation and alerts area and to the configuration K_1 in the solution area for current tasks; users that have a role R_M can access the widget I_K and the configuration K_L (see Fig. 4).

Thus, functionality of the role consists of widgets in the area of communication, navigation and alerts and a set of configurations displayed in the area of solving current tasks:

$$R_i = \{F_{i1}, \ldots, F_{iN}\},$$

where: R_i – a range of functionality of i-th role

$$F_{ij} = \{I_{i1}, \ldots, I_{iN}, K_{i1}, \ldots, K_{iL}\},$$

where: F_{ij} – j-th functionality of i-th role.

Each expert receives notifications only about the events that he or she must monitor, and only necessary tools for solving tasks within his or her role in the team. Redundancy of functionality, which can adversely affect the speed of task solution and making managerial decisions, is excluded. On the other hand, the problem of increasing the number of functions performed by an expert in a team is solved by expanding his or her list of roles.

Thus, the model of the unified virtual working environment (MUVWE) is formulated, constructed with the use of key concepts: role, configuration, container, widget, signal. The proposed model allows to quickly synthesize individual flexibly configurable virtual working environments, and using the visual metaphor of the situation room when organizing the user interface facilitates perception of technological processes by HTDT participants.

4 Implementation of the Model of the Unified Virtual Working Environment of HTDT

The virtual working environment model is implemented in three-tier architecture: a data layer, a logic layer, a user interface layer. The data layer provides storage, processing and selection of data. The logic layer performs calculations and is a buffer layer between the data layer and the user interface layer. The user interface layer provides an interactive user interaction with the system and provides information in a convenient form. The tools are executed in the form of plugins - independently compiled dynamically connected programme modules. Each plugin is designed to expand functionality of the system and can provide solutions to both a whole class of tasks, and specific highly specialized ones. It is a functional unit of the system, independent of other plugins. The plugin consists of components that function in each of the three layers. These components interact with each other and with the components of the kernel directly, and with the components of other plugins in the user interface layer by means of the event manager (see Fig. 5).

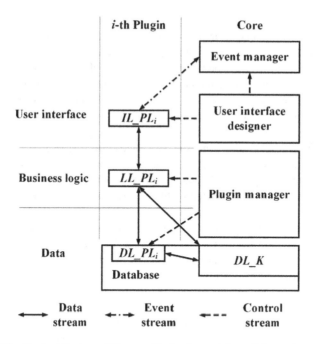

Fig. 5. Architecture of the specific implementation of the system.

Figure 5 shows an overview diagram of interaction of the system kernel with the i-th plugin:

$$PL_i = \{DL\_PL_i, LL\_PL_i, IL\_PL_i\},$$

where DL_PL_i – data layer component, LL_PL_i – logic layer component, IL_PL_i – user interface layer component (view).

DL_K – kernel component in the data layer.

This component implements the universal *Categories of Entities and Relationships* (MCER) data model [12], on the basis of which the framework for the description of the subject area model is built. The basic categories of this model are: subject, object, territory, action and ground. If the necessary functionality for storing, processing and selecting the plugin data cannot be provided by the kernel component in the data layer DL_K, the plugin can expand the MCER by implementing its own data layer component DL_PL_i.

The plugin component in the logic layer LL_PL_i interacts with the plugin component in the data layer DL_PL_i and the kernel component in the data layer DL_K, as well as with the component of the user interface layer IL_PL_i.

The kernel of the system in the layers of data and logic contains the "plugin manager" component, which provides connection of the components of these layers of the i-th plugin when it is installed into the system, as well as disconnection of the specified components when removing it from the system, i.e. it controls its life cycle.

In the user interface layer, the kernel is represented by a user interface designer (UID) and an event manager that provide flexible customization of the working environment. UID allows you to arrange widgets into configurations using containers and to configure event routing between widgets using the event manager. Each container occupies a certain area of the configuration screen and contains tabs with widgets. The event manager regulates the transfer of events between widgets during the user experience in the system. There are two modes of the system: editing and functioning. When you turn on the editing mode, it becomes possible to arrange containers and widgets into configurations using the "drag-and-drop" technology. After the layout is complete, the widgets must be linked together to ensure that they interact with the help of the event manager. Each widget contains a list of incoming and outgoing events. Outgoing events are generated by the widget, and incoming events are received from other widgets in the configuration. Configuring events between widgets allows you to achieve the necessary configuration behavior. After the configuration is completed, the configuration settings are saved. From the configurations made, the AWS roles of the users of the system are collected. To provide capabilities of a new AWS, users are assigned a corresponding role. The system is put to the normal operation mode. The described sequence of steps implements a method of synthesis of a specific user working environment.

Let's consider an example of creation of a workplace of the chief engineer of the amber extraction plant. The list of tasks solved by the chief engineer is broad. One of them is monitoring and controlling execution of the amber extraction plan. To solve this task, a configuration in Fig. 6 is created in the chief engineer's AWS. The configuration consists of three containers, including the following widgets: widget-histogram, widget-circle chart, widget-information about the user.

The widget-histogram displays information about the planned and actual production volumes in the current planning period, as well as the deviation of the actual volume from the planned volume in absolute (in tons) and relative (in percent) terms. When you select a histogram element (plan, fact, deviation), the widget-circle chart is loaded with the information about the structure of this element on the extraction site. By performing a visual analysis of the production structure, the chief engineer identifies a problem area and, after selecting it in a circle chart, receives detailed information about it: full name of the site manager, his contact details, number of incidents per shift, etc. When choosing the method of communication with the site manager, the system will allow communicating with him or her with the help of the widget-communicator, located in the ACNA. Thus, a configuration has been created that solves one of the tasks of the chief engineer of the plant. It should be noted that the widgets used to create the configuration are independent and communicate purposefully with each other by means of the event manager. The logic of this interaction is the result of the installation of the system by the administrator or the chief engineer himself, rather than the result of the programmer's work.

Operating with abstract categories makes it possible to use widgets in creating different configurations of other specialists of the plant in order to solve their tasks. The internal logic of each widget can be arbitrarily complex and intelligent.

The proposed mechanism for visual programming of the interface allows you to remove some of the problems associated with the need to solve new tasks in DSS, by

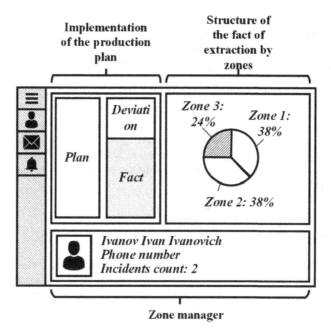

Fig. 6. Example of the chief engineer's workplace of the amber extracting plant.

customizing new configurations from the existing tools. Using plugin architecture allows you to dynamically update and expand the functionality of the already implemented system without interrupting its operation.

5   Conclusion

A unified model of a flexibly configurable DSS for a heterogeneous geographically distributed team is proposed, implemented in practice using two frameworks: description of the subject area model and description of the working environment model. The categorical framework for description of the subject area model based on the MCER provides a unified structure for storing and processing heterogeneous data using a finite number of abstract concepts. This makes it possible to significantly facilitate the subsequent integration and synchronization between DSSs built using this technology. The categorical framework for description of the working environment model based on MUVWE, implemented using visual programming technology, eliminates the need for a rigid fixation of the monolithic user interface for each group of the DSS users and allows for flexible configuration of the working environment from already existing tools to obtain new functionality.

MUVWE for HTDT has been tested when creating a software products line:

- *Tourism Industry* information and analytical complex [13];
- NBICS.NET network interactive laboratory [14];

- *Cogno* Cognitive Center [15];
- *TOT-CREATOR* cloud educational service [16];
- open interactive 3D laboratory [17];
- *Municipality* universal virtual situational center [18].

The results of the implementation of the DSS developed with the use of MUVWE in a new subject area demonstrated a reduction in the resource cost up to 5 times. The main resources in the re-implementation of DSS were spent on organizational issues and on the development of special features missing in the system for a new subject area. The proposed technology stack in combination with the use of plugin architecture can significantly reduce time, intellectual and financial costs for creation and implementation of DSS.

References

1. Pospelov, D.A.: Situational Management. Theory and Practice. Nauka, Moscow (1986)
2. Tarasov, V.B.: From Multi-agent Systems to Intellectual Organizations: Philosophy, Psychology, Computer Science. Editorial URSS, Moscow (2002). 352 p.
3. Merkulov, A.A.: Situation Center VSM Cenose. Publishing house of Technocenosis, Kaliningrad (2014). 312 p.
4. Demidova, L.A., Kirakovsky, V.V., Pyl'kin, A.N.: Decision-making under uncertainty. Hot line – Telecom (2012). 288 p.
5. Kostrikova, N.A., Merkulov, A.A., Ya, Y.A.: Technology of synthesis of distributed intelligent control systems as an instrument of sustainable development of territories and complex objects. Mar. Intellect. Technol. T.1., **3**(37), 135–141 (2017)
6. Royce, W.W.: Managing the development of large software systems. In: Proceedings of IEEE WESCON, 26 August 1970
7. McConnell, S.: The influence of iterative approaches to preconditions. Code Complete. Russian Edition, Peter (2005). 896 p.
8. Selby, R.W.: Software Engineering: Barry W. Boehm's Lifetime Contributions to Software Development, Management, and Research. Wiley, Hoboken (2007). 834 p.
9. Kon, M.: Succeeding with Agile: Software Development Using Scrum. Addison-Wesley Signature Series. Williams (2011). 576 c.
10. Averbukh, V.L., Bakhterev, M.O., Baydalin, A.Y.: Searching and analysis of interface and visualization metaphors. In: Human Computer Interaction: New Developments, pp. 49–84 (2008)
11. Kolesnikov, A.V.: Hybrid Intelligent Systems: Theory and Technology of Development. In: Yashin, A.M. (ed.) Publishing House SPbSTU, St. Petersburg (2001). 711 p.
12. Dmitrovsky, V.A., Maytakov, F.G., Merkulov, A.A.: Data model Entity and Relationship Categories. Immanuel Kant Baltic Federal University, Kaliningrad (2014)
13. Merkulov, A.A., Maitakov, F.G., Petrenko, E.V., et al.: Informational and Analytical Complex Tourism Industry. Rospatent St., 2016614097 (2016)
14. Merkulov, A.A., Maitakov, F.G., Petrenko, E.V., et al.: Network Interactive Laboratory NBICS.NET. Rospatent St., 2016616206 (2016)
15. Merkulov, A.A., Maitakov, F.G., Petrenko, E.V., et al.: Cognitive Center Cogno. Rospatent St., 2016615910 (2016)

16. Petrenko, E.V., Maitakov, F.G., Merkulov, A.A., et al.: Cloud educational service TOT-CREATOR. Rospatent St., 2016617107 (2016)
17. Merkulov, A.A., Bondarenko, R.V., Ginter Ya, A., et al.: Open interactive 3D laboratory. Rospatent St., 2016617572 (2016)
18. Ya, Y.A. Merkulov, A.A., Petrenko, E.V., et al.: Universal virtual situational center Municipality. Rospatent St., 2013661281 (2013)

Digital Privacy, Rights, Security

Risks and Societal Implications
of Identity Theft

Tarmo Kalvet[1]([⊠]), Marek Tiits[2], and Pille Ubakivi-Hadachi[3]

[1] Tallinn University of Technology, Akadeemia tee 3, 12618 Tallinn, Estonia
tarmo.kalvet@ttu.ee
[2] Institute of Baltic Studies, Lai 30, 51005 Tartu, Estonia
[3] Tallinn University, Narva maantee 25, 10120 Tallinn, Estonia

Abstract. Transactions that involved identity theft are becoming increasingly popular in today's society. Identity theft causes not only a violation of privacy for the victim, but also raises the possibility of increased stress for the victim and potential financial and/or legal consequences. Due to this, it is important to understand the nature and extent of the problem in detail so that novel identity management systems may be developed and eventually accepted. The focus of current exploratory research is to understand the spread and consequences of identity theft and fraud in Europe. A census representative on-line survey was carried out in Austria, France, Germany, Italy, Spain, the United Kingdom, and, for comparative purposes, in the United States of America. The research found that 25–30% of the adult population in the surveys countries experienced some form of misuse or attempted misuse of their personal information within the past three years. Extrapolating from the initial results, it is expected that around 100 million European citizens have dealt or experienced misuse of their personal information within the last 3 years and close to 40 million EU citizens had, because of the misuse of their personal information, incurred significant personal consequences ranging from debt collection to legal problems. Government issued electronic identity cards for on-line transactions are needed for electronic authentication and signatures, and their use in the private and public sector should become more widespread. Mobile ID can also service as a convenient and secure alternative to more traditional electronic identity cards.

Keywords: Identity theft · Identity documents · European Union

1 Introduction

Obtaining someone else's personal information or identity document (ID), such as identity card or passport, is where identity fraud begins and it is becoming increasingly popular [1, 2]. With a stolen identity, the fraudster can effectively become someone else, access the victim's financial or other accounts, access communications, set up new contracts, or present false information to the authorities. The above is not only a violation of privacy, but may bring about substantial financial and/or legal consequences to the victim.

© Springer Nature Switzerland AG 2019
A. Chugunov et al. (Eds.): EGOSE 2018, CCIS 947, pp. 67–81, 2019.
https://doi.org/10.1007/978-3-030-13283-5_6

Understanding the nature and extent of the problem in detail is needed for the development of novel identity management systems and, ultimately, their technological acceptance. For example, knowing where the major societal risks are, allows one to design a system that takes the concerns properly account.

Only limited comparative studies on identity theft and its financial and societal consequences exists in Europe. The results of the various earlier (national) studies are not comparable either, as the definition of identity theft and the exact wording of survey questions varies from one study to another. Furthermore, most of the earlier work overlooks on-line transactions and identity theft that involves various Internet accounts. This is why the current research set to create a unique framework and obtain new data that allows us to analyze the ID use patterns, ID theft, and the views of the general public on the novel forms of establishment and checking identity. The focus of the current exploratory research is to understand the spread and the consequences of identity fraud in Europe.

In Sect. 2 the theoretical analytical framework is created on the basis of literature review. Section 3 introduces the research method and data collection and Sect. 4 the experience of identity theft in Europe, its discovery, and financial and personal consequences. In Sect. 5 the findings are discussed and implications for the government issued electronic identity management approaches discussed.

2   Literature Review

The United States Department of Justice and the Bureau of Justice Statistics have commissioned and co-operated on regular studies on identity theft, e.g. [3–7], and the various private consultancy firms, e.g. [8, 9], have studied identity theft issues in the recent years as well. The availability of public data on identity theft is much more limited in Europe. European Central Bank, e.g. [10, 11], analyses the card fraud, and European Commission addresses identity theft as part of regular studies on cyber security in Europe, e.g. [12, 13].

A Eurobarometer survey on cyber security from 2017 is the most recent and comprehensive source that covers the whole EU. Large share of respondents expressed concerns about identity theft (69% of the respondents) and bank card and online banking fraud (66%). As compared to the previous survey from 2013, the number of respondents being concerned about identity theft has risen by 17% points. Some 38% of the respondents have received an email or phone call fraudulently asking for access to their computer, logins or personal details. [13] However, the study does not cover the consequences of identity theft.

In our earlier work, e.g. [14, 15], we have discussed predominantly theoretical literature that discuss personal and societal risks deriving from identity theft, such as loss of privacy. We conclude, however, from our analysis of literature that the majority of earlier research on societal aspects of identity management systems has focused primarily on theoretical discussion of identity, autonomy, and societal values such as privacy. Crucial technological details of specific implementations of electronic identity documents and related systems have been addressed very rarely, if at all. An even more complex variety of public perceptions emerges as one starts discussing the specific choices in technology design, such as the various ways of storing or using biometric data. Yet, it is only at this level that technology developers can actually start discussing potential public concerns, and potential ways of alleviating these in the course if the technology development.

Research is growing on the economic impacts of cybercrimes, e.g. [16, 17]. However, these studies mostly fail to inform about the costs and benefits for all actors involved in cybercrimes and further research is needed to fill in the gaps [18].

While financial losses are clearly related with identity theft, more recent research is drawing attention to victims' experience emotional (e.g., depression) and physical (e.g., poor health) symptoms [19, 20].

Finally, research has been also increasing on reporting of identity thefts to the police. Studies have been done on associations between victim characteristics and crime reporting behavior for traditional crimes versus cybercrimes, several concluding that cybercrimes are among the least reported types of crime, worth investigating it further [21, 22].

3 Research Method and Data Collection

Building on the literature and earlier studies summarized above, a survey on the common use patterns of identity documents, identity theft and acceptability of novel identity management solutions was carried out over the period of 20 May – 5 June 2015 in the following countries: Austria (AT), France (FR), Germany (DE), Italy (IT), Spain (ES), United Kingdom (UK) and the United States of America (US). These countries represent a selection of countries in the core of the European Union (EU), and, in addition, the United States for comparison.

The above mentioned countries represent different cultural contexts. The establishment of identity and identity management are also handled differently in different countries covered by this study. Some governments, such as ES or DE, are relatively more advanced in issuing electronic identity cards; some, such as FR, issue only non-electronic identity cards while there are also governments like UK or US that do not issue any identity cards at all.

For the data collection purposes, a survey questionnaire with 57 questions was developed. The survey questionnaire was designed in such a way that a substantial part of it was shown only to the respondents who have personally experienced identity theft within the last 36 months. Accordingly, a major share of the respondents did not fill a full version, but a shorter version of the questionnaire. The survey was carried out as an online survey using SurveyGizmo (www.surveygizmo.com) web survey service. Cint survey panels (www.cint.com) were used to target and recruit individuals between the ages of 16 and 65 from respondent database. The collected responses are generally representative of the gender and age distribution of the population of respective countries.

More than 500 complete responses were collected from each of the seven countries covered by this survey. The responses that showed obvious signs of the lack of responder's attention or had been filled in unrealistically speedy manner (in less than

240 s) were removed from the survey data set. As the result, 3,278 fully completed responses were retained for analysis.

According to Eurostat, approximately 5–15% of the 16–74 years old population (Eurostat 2014) does not use the Internet and are thus automatically excluded from online surveys. We are aware of this inherent weakness of the survey data set and acknowledge in the subsequent analysis that online surveys exclude a minority who has no sufficient knowledge or skills for using Internet. However, such people are generally of older age [23] many of whom we would expect would be unable to respond to the technology specific questions that deal with electronic identity cards or biometrics. Thus, we expect that the share of persons how are uninformed or undecided about various technology specific questions or scenarios for using eIDs (electronic identity documents) would have been greater if we would have been able to cover also persons not using Internet.

Statistical tools utilized in this study include cross tabulations, analysis of variance, chi-square tests, simple and multiple linear regression, as well as simple and multiple logistic regression models. Thus, data distribution, relationships between variables or sets of variables, as well as possible strengths and directions of these relationships are explored. Both effect sizes and the significance of results were accounted for. Every variable was carefully explored, cases were checked and necessary outliers were excluded from the subsequent analysis. Statistical tests are carried out with the IBM SPSS Statistics software package. In order to do so, a comprehensive dataset was created and cleaned in SPSS.

4 Identity Theft in the EU

4.1 Experience of Identity Theft in Europe

Approximately 25–30% of the respondents have experienced misuse or attempted misuse of personal information in the selected EU member states, and 35% of the respondents in the United States within the last 3 years. Around 10% of the European respondents have experienced multiple incidents of different types (Fig. 1).

Misuse or attempted misuse of existing Internet accounts, especially private e-mail accounts and social network accounts, emerges from the current survey as greatest area of concern. Existing credit cards or financial accounts are also a major target for the thieves, while all other types of existing or new accounts play, in comparison to the above, only a minor role on the identity theft landscape (Fig. 2).

New e-mail or social media accounts, financial accounts and telephone contracts dominate the scene as far new accounts or contracts that have been established under false identity are concerned (Fig. 3).

Public confidence in banking and credit card services remains, despite frequent misuses, fairly high. Furthermore, personal experience with falling a victim of the misuse of a bank account does not influence the consumer confidence in the above services in any statistically significant way. The persons, who have experienced the misuse of their credit card(s) are, however, less confident in security of credit cards as such.

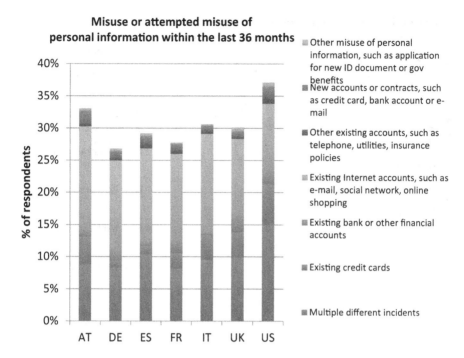

Fig. 1. Identity theft and attempted identity theft within the last 36 months. Source: Authors.

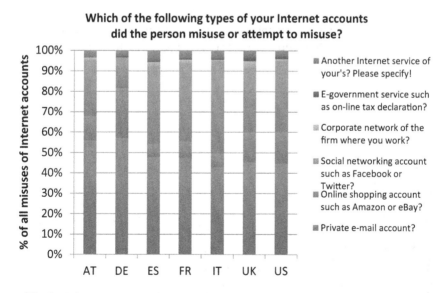

Fig. 2. Misuse or attempted misuse of existing Internet accounts. Source: Authors.

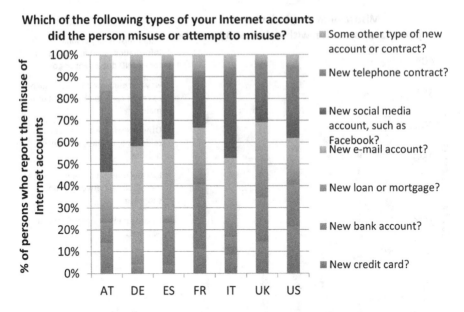

Fig. 3. Misuse or attempted misuse of new accounts and contracts. Source: Authors.

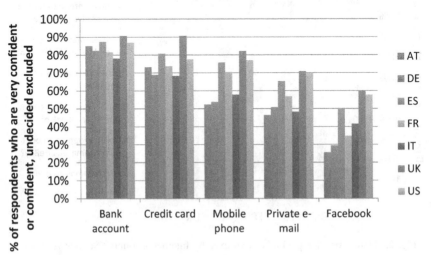

Fig. 4. Confidence in private sector services. Source: Authors.

We notice also that the public confidence in Internet services, such as private e-mail or social networks is fairly low Europe (Fig. 4). Further statistical analysis reveals also that the persons who have experienced the misuse of their existing internet accounts are less confident in security of their personal e-mail and social network accounts. They put also less trust on the security of their bank accounts and credit cards.

4.2   Discovery of Identity Theft

The misuse of personal information was discovered very rapidly in majority of cases. It took less than a day in half of the cases, and less than a week in in 2/3 of the cases. Misuse of the existing financial and Internet accounts is detected the quickest. Relatively rarer types of misuse, such as utility or insurance fraud, take usually longer to discover. The victims of the misuse of the government issued identity documents are likely to learn about identity theft only with huge delay, if at all. Such fraud may take

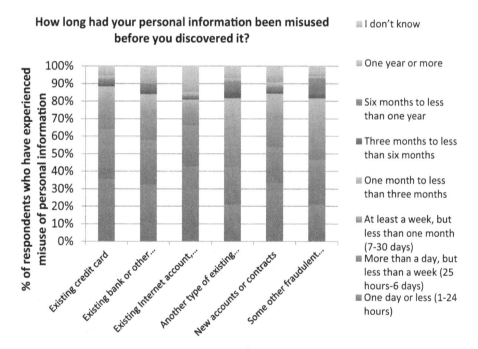

Fig. 5. Duration of misuse of personal information.   Source: Authors.

especially long time to detect, if identity documents are issued or used for opening new accounts or contracts in geographically far away locations (Fig. 5).

Victims detect themselves fraudulent or otherwise strange activities on their accounts on 20–25% of the cases. Fraud detection systems of the banks and credit card companies, and Internet service providers play an even more important role in discovering misuses (Fig. 6).

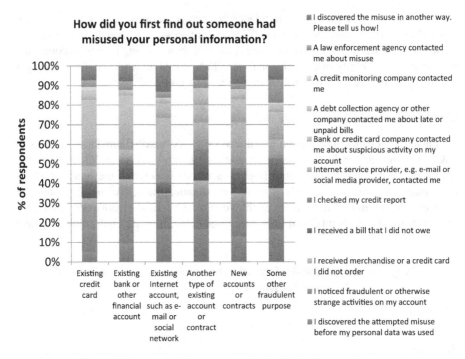

Fig. 6. Means of the discovery of identity theft. Source: Authors.

Almost half of the respondents, who have fallen victim of identity theft, believe that they know how their identity document or personal information was accessed or taken. Computers and credit cards are primarily seen as the source of leakages, which is not surprising given the prominent role of identity theft that involves internet accounts or financial accounts. Lost or stolen passports or identity cards play, however, only a relatively minor role on the identity theft landscape (Fig. 7).

95% of victims claim that they start to use better passwords, and change their passwords or PIN (personal identification number) codes more frequently after the incident. They change their banking details or credit cards, and check financial statements more carefully. They are also more careful about sharing personal information, and using social media. We find, however, a lot of room for improvement in the introduction of better security software, which would warn about fraudulent web sites or e-mails, to the computers and mobile telephones (Fig. 8).

4.3 Financial Consequences of Identity Theft

Across countries, the thief was able to obtain financial benefits, in the form of money, goods or services or anything else from the misuse of personal information in 15–20% of the cases. Additionally, respondents are not sure in 10–20% of the cases, if the thief was able to obtain financial benefits.

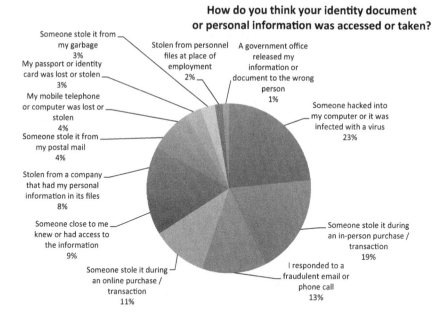

Fig. 7. How was the personal information taken? Note: This figure reflects on respondents, who think that they know how their personal information was taken. Source: Authors.

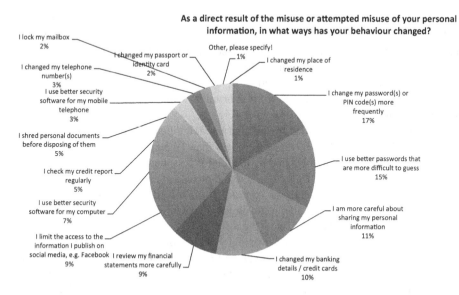

Fig. 8. Change of the behaviour of the victims of identity theft. Note: This figure reflects on respondents, who changed their behaviour. Source: Authors.

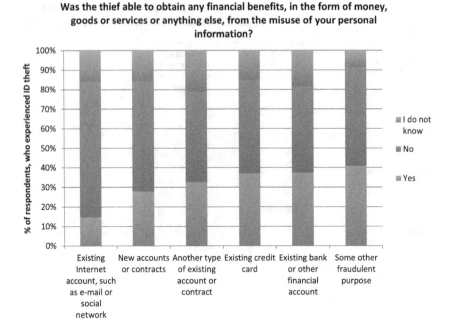

Fig. 9. Share of the cases, where the thief was able to obtain financial benefits. Source: Authors.

Further analysis reveals that the misuse of existing Internet accounts is the least likely to bring immediate financial losses. However, the thief has been able to obtain financial benefits in 1/3 of the cases of bank account and credit card fraud. Other fraud, such as applying for a new passport or identity card, getting medical care, a job, or government benefits; renting an apartment or house; giving your information to the police when they were charged with a crime or traffic violation, etc. is also very likely to lead to the financial benefits to the thief (Fig. 9).

The financial benefits obtained by the thief vary significantly across different cases, as the value obtained by thieves varies from less than 10 euros to tens of thousands of euros per case. Median value obtained by the thief is less than 500 euros. The financial consequences are greater for the cases, where the misuse of existing financial accounts, or establishment of new accounts or contracts is involved, and in other fraudulent purposes, such as the fraud involving government issued identity documents, medical insurance or government benefits, etc. (Fig. 10).

Roughly half of the victims lost eventually their money, as their financial losses were not reimbursed, e.g. by bank or credit card company. Furthermore, the misuse of personal information brought about additional costs, such as legal or other expert fees, or miscellaneous expenses to 15% of the victims. Such additional costs, which were from less than ten euros to thousands of euros, were around 200 euros on average.

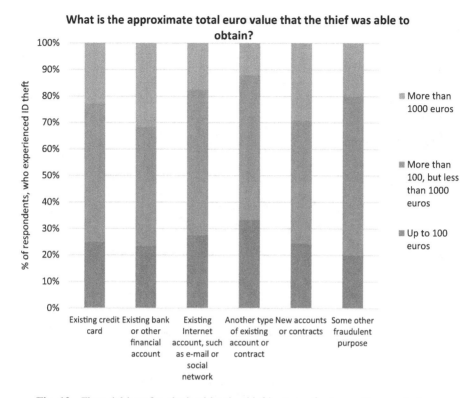

Fig. 10. Financial benefits obtained by the thief by type of misuse. Source: Authors.

4.4   Personal Consequences of Identity Theft

Falling a victim of the misuse of personal information is rather likely to lead to a call from debt collectors, problems with family members or friends, denial of a service, or legal problems. Also, there appears to a substantial share of serious cases, where the victim was turned down for a job or lost a job, or became subject of an arrest or criminal proceedings. Altogether, close to 40% of the victims had at least one of the consequences shown on Fig. 11.

15–20% of the victims of the misuse of personal information indicate that the incident was severely distressing for them, and 25–30% of the victims indicate that the incident was moderately distressing (Fig. 12).

It emerges also that the longer it took to clear up the financial consequences of the misuse of personal information, the more distressful the incident was. Also, the longer it has taken to discover and resolve the incident, the less likely it is that the victim has been successful in fully resolving the case.

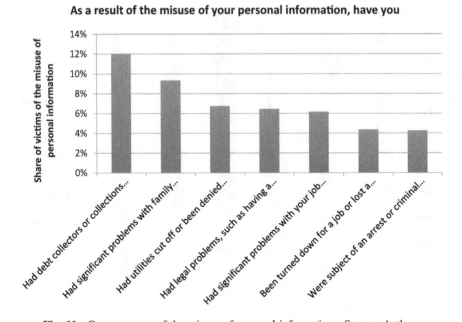

Fig. 11. Consequences of the misuse of personal information. Source: Authors.

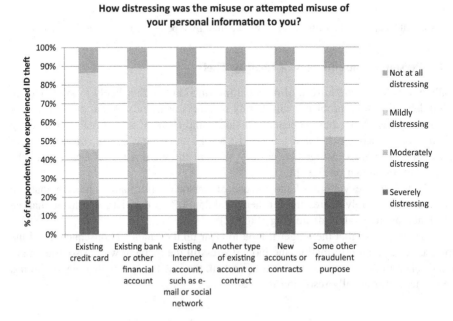

Fig. 12. Distressfulness of the experienced misuse of personal information. Source: Authors.

5 Discussion and Conclusions

The current exploratory research has found that roughly 25–30% of the population of Austria, France, Germany, Italy, Spain, United Kingdom have experienced some form of attempted misuse or misuse of personal information within the last three years. Only 10% of these cases were detected before personal information was actually taken. Identity theft data is likely to vary across countries and we do not have data on all 28 member states. We assume, nonetheless, that, broadly speaking, around 100 million citizens were forced to protect their identity during the last 3 years in the European Union. Almost half of them had to do so more than once, as they experienced multiple different incidents during the last 3 years. Furthermore, close to 40 million EU citizens had, as a result of the misuse of their personal information, significant personal consequences, such as debt collectors contacting them, or significant problems with their family or friends; they were denied a new service, or had to face legal problems, etc.

The total value of the money, goods or services obtained by criminals was roughly 12–16 billion euros in the European Union, and around 7–9 billion euros in the USA in 2015. This is, however, only 'consumer side'. Various intuitional actors, e.g. financial institutions or health insurance, are likely to have incurred, due to misuse of personal information, additional financial losses that are unknown to the individuals and, therefore, not reflected in the current study. For instance, in the United States of America, Internal Revenue Service (IRS) has estimated that it paid 3.9 billion euros in fraudulent identity theft refunds in filing season 2013, while preventing fraudulent refunds in the amount of 18.2 billion euros (based on what they could detect) [24]. It is, given the above, very much possible that the above rough estimate of the financial cost of identity theft in Europe reflects only on the tip of the iceberg, and the real problem is even bigger than a sociological study like this one is able to grasp.

Our earlier research has shown that the public has little trust in security of Internet services [14]. Widespread misuse of Internet accounts, bank accounts and credit cards does not foster trust on these services. Further statistical analysis reveals, nonetheless, that the personal experience with the attempted misuse or misuse of personal information does not lead to decline of confidence in government issued identity documents. Confidence in electronic identity cards and passports remains very high [25]. This is likely to be because of the fact that the misuse of government issued identity documents remains, in citizens' view, negligible as compared to other forms of identity fraud.

Government issued electronic identity cards for on-line transactions, are, thus, an obvious choice for bolstering the security of Internet services and broadening the use of electronic authentication and signatures both in the public and private applications. Furthermore, the experience of front-runner countries in widespread acceptance of electronic identity documents, such as Estonia, shows that mobile ID can serve as a convenient and secure alternative to more traditional electronic identity cards. In fact, majority of the users of mobile ID turn seldom back to their electronic identity card when on-line authentication in Internet or electronic signature is required in Estonia.

Furthermore, the persons, who have experienced misuse of personal information are more likely to prefer identity documents that are more difficult to misuse, e.g., when lost or stolen. Victims of the misuse of personal information are also more likely to accept modern forms of on-line authentication, such as electronic identity cards or mobile ID in combination with PIN codes or fingerprints, or even biometrics (for a study on live enrolment in issuance of identity documents, see [26].

Acknowledgements. This work was supported by the European Commission through the project "Harmonized framework allowing a sustainable and robust identity for European Citizens" (EKSISTENZ, grant 607049) funded from FP7 and a grant "Public sector innovation: The case of modern identity management technologies" (PUT773) from Estonian Science Foundation.

References

1. Piquero, N.L., Cohen, M.A., Piquero, A.R.: How much is the public willing to pay to be protected from identity theft? Justice Q. **28**, 437–459 (2011)
2. Reyns, B.W.: Identity-related crimes. In: Reichel, R., Randa, R. (eds.) Transnational Crime and Global Security, pp. 161–179. Praeger Security International (2018)
3. Langton, L., Planty, M.: Victims of identity theft, 2008. The U.S. Department of Justice (2010). https://www.bjs.gov/content/pub/pdf/vit08.pdf
4. Harrell, E., Langton, L.: Victims of identity theft 2012. The U.S. Department of Justice, Washington (2013). https://www.bjs.gov/content/pub/pdf/vit12.pdf
5. Federal Trade Commission. Consumer Sentinel Network Data Book for January-December 2013. Federal Trade Commission (2014)
6. Harrell, E.: Victims of identity theft. Bureau of Justice Statistics (2015). https://www.bjs.gov/content/pub/pdf/vit14.pdf
7. Oudekerk, B.A., et al.: Building a National Data Collection on Victim Service Providers: A Pilot Test. Bureau of Justice Statistics (2018). https://www.ncjrs.gov/pdffiles1/bjs/grants/251524.pdf
8. Javelin Strategy and Research. Identity Fraud Report: Card Data Breaches and Inadequate Consumer Password Habits Fuel Disturbing Fraud Trends (2014). https://www.javelinstrategy.com/coverage-area/2014-identity-fraud-report-card-data-breaches-and-inadequate-consumer-password-habits
9. Javelin Strategy and Research. Identity Fraud: Fraud Enters a New Era of Complexity (2018). https://www.javelinstrategy.com/coverage-area/2018-identity-fraud-fraud-enters-new-era-complexity
10. European Central Bank. Third Report on Card Fraud. European Central Bank, Frankfurt (2014)
11. European Central Bank. Fourth Report on Card Fraud. European Central Bank, Frankfurt (2015)
12. TNS Opinion & Social. Cyber security, Special Eurobarometer 390 (2012). http://ec.europa.eu/commfrontoffice/publicopinion/archives/ebs/ebs_390_en.pdf
13. TNS Opinion & Social. Europeans' attitudes towards cyber security, Special Eurobarometer 464a (2017). http://ec.europa.eu/commfrontoffice/publicopinion/index.cfm/ResultDoc/download/DocumentKy/79734
14. Tiits, M., Ubakivi-Hadachi, P.: Common use patterns of identity documents, EKSISTENZ D9.1. Institute of Baltic Studies, Tartu (2015)

15. Kalvet, T., Tiits, M., Laas-Mikko, K.: Public acceptance of advanced identity documents. In: Ojo, A., Kankanhalli, A., Soares, D. (eds.) Proceedings of the 11th International Conference on Theory and Practice of Electronic Governance. ACM, New York (2018)

16. Moore, T., Clayton, R., Anderson, R.: The economics of online crime. J. Econ. Perspect. **23**, 3–20 (2009)

17. McAfee. Net Losses: Estimating the Global Cost of Cybercrime (Economic Impact of Cybercrime II). McAfee Center for Strategic and International Studies (2014)

18. Holt, T.J., Smirnova, O., Chua, Y.T.: Exploring and estimating the revenues and profits of participants in stolen data markets. Deviant Behav. **37**(4), 353–367 (2016)

19. Shapland, J., Hall, M.: What do we know about the effects of crime on victims? Int. Rev. Victimology **14**, 175–217 (2007)

20. Golladay, K., Holtfreter, K.: The consequences of identity theft victimization: an examination of emotional and physical health outcomes. Vict. Offenders **12**(5), 741–760 (2016)

21. Cross, C., Richards, K., Smith, R.G.: The reporting experiences and support needs of victims of online fraud. Trends & Issues in Crime and Criminal Justice, Report no. 518, Canberra, Augustus (2016)

22. van de Weijer, S.G.A., Leukfeldt, R., Bernasco, W.: Determinants of reporting cybercrime: a comparison between identity theft, consumer fraud, and hacking. Eur. J. Criminol. (2018, forthcoming)

23. Brandtzæg, P.B., Heim, J., Karahasanovic, A.: Understanding the new digital divide – a typology of Internet users in Europe. Int. J. Hum. Comput. Stud. **69**(3), 123–138 (2011)

24. U.S. Government Accountability Office. Identity theft: Additional Actions Could Help IRS Combat The Large, Evolving Threat of Refund Fraud, Report to Congressional Requesters, GAO-14-633 (2014). https://www.gao.gov/assets/670/665368.pdf

25. Tiits, M., Kalvet, T., Laas-Mikko, K.: Social acceptance of ePassports. In: Brömme, A., Busch, C. (eds.) Proceedings of the 13th International Conference of the Biometric Special Interest Group. IEEE, Piscataway (2014)

26. Kalvet, T., Karlzén, H., Hunstad, A., Tiits, M.: Live enrolment for identity documents in Europe. In: Parycek, P., et al. (eds.) EGOV 2018. LNCS, vol. 11020, pp. 29–39. Springer, Cham (2018). https://doi.org/10.1007/978-3-319-98690-6_3

Personal Data and Privacy Barriers to E-Government Adoption, Implementation and Development in Sub-Saharan Africa

Ebenezer Agbozo[1]([⊠]) [iD], Daniel Alhassan[2] [iD],
and Kamen Spassov[3] [iD]

[1] Ural Federal University, Yekaterinburg, Russian Federation
eagbozo@urfu.ru
[2] Missouri University of Science and Technology, Rolla, MO, USA
daanmq@mst.edu
[3] University of Sofia "St. Kliment Ohridski", Sofia, Bulgaria
kspasov@fmi.uni-sofia.bg

Abstract. Personal data and privacy confidentiality play a highly important role in ensuring user trust in any given Information Communication Technology (ICT) system. In the last decade Electronic Government (e-Government) initiatives have transformed the public sector of many nations and most importantly improved upon the quality of public service delivery to citizens. The issue of privacy and security impedes the progress of any e-government system and potentially causes citizens to lose trust in public e-services. Sub-Saharan Africa (SSA) as a continent has been on the verge of gradual e-government development; though many factors are attributed to its average underperformance according to the 2016 United Nations' (UN) e-Government Survey. Based on a review of relevant literature, a binomial (exact) test was performed to determine the general perception of personal data and whether Sub-Saharan Africans are ready to give it to their governments. Drawing on analysis results, the study offers policy implementation recommendations for the sub-region so as to realize a citizen-centric e-government.

Keywords: e-Government · Security and privacy · Personal data ·
Sub Saharan Africa · General Data Protection Regulation (GDPR)

1 Introduction

1.1 Electronic Government and E-Services

The past decade has experienced an unprecedented upsurge of electronic government (e-government) development across all countries. The implementation of electronic services (e-services) in the public sector for quality public service delivery to citizens, increased government accountability to citizens, ensuring greater public access to information, improve government and public sector efficiency – thus obtaining a more cost-effective government [1, 2]. E-government has played a huge role in policy making [3] transforming the public sector of countries by influencing the business process and encouraging quality service delivery.

© Springer Nature Switzerland AG 2019
A. Chugunov et al. (Eds.): EGOSE 2018, CCIS 947, pp. 82–91, 2019.
https://doi.org/10.1007/978-3-030-13283-5_7

Weerakkody et al. [4] in their comprehensive literary study summarized the benefits of e-government as: reduced production cost, better services, avoidance of personal interaction, convenience, personalization, reducing corruption, efficiency, effectiveness, transparency, greater democratic participation, 24/7 accessibility, flexibility, time saving, and many other benefits. Lofstedt [5] highlighted an important point that e-government is "not only about services or technology; it is about reinventing the way in which governments interact with citizens, governmental agencies, businesses, employees, and other stakeholders". These reasons amidst others are why governments adopt e-government systems.

Presently, researchers and some governments are delving into the paradigm of Government 3.0. According to Jun and Chung [6] it is primarily driven by ICT (the semantic web) and data evolution. These services are intelligent and personalized thereby making information sharing and interoperability transparent at all levels of government. With the gradual transition towards this e-government model which solely depends on data, it gives a clear picture of the relevance of data to e-government.

1.2   The Value of Personal Data in e-Government

Data is essential to every information system - e-government inclusive - and as a result of its value, e-government frameworks and deployments take security into high consideration. The value of data in information systems raise concerns for privacy, transparency, and as such users are cautious as to who and where they supply data to [7].

Personal information and data are the foundation for e-government systems since they give identity to users. In most e-government deployments, citizens' personal information is stored with the national registry so as to obtain an identification card (id-card) with a unique identifier. From research by Igari [8] it has been proven that personal information storage, has effectively contributed to cost reductions by increasing operational efficiency as well as systematizing operations in Denmark since they rolled out their National Personal ID System also known as Central Persons Registration (CPR) Number. These unique identifiers are what give citizens access to perform online public service transactions [9] such as tax payments, fine payments, accessing pension benefits, etc. Without the necessary personal information of citizens, e-government systems cannot function to their maximum potential, hence limiting the attainment of Government 3.0 and the citizen-centric e-government frameworks.

1.3   Privacy and Security in e-Government

Developed economies with the interests of their citizens at heart put effort in ensuring personal data is stored and used securely in order to gain citizen trust. In countries such as the USA, Germany, and China, various forms of Fair Information Practice principles (FIPs) such as Collection limitation principle; Use limitation principle; Purpose specification principle; Openness principle; Individual participation principle; Data quality principle; Security safeguards principle; Accountability principle, are in existence [10]. These policies safeguard the personal data of citizens in countries with well established e-government implementations. In spite of safety measures put in place in both developed and developing economies, there is the fear of having one's personal information hacked into and according to Ambali [11] this form of paranoia gripped public taxpayers in Malaysia a decade ago – this reduced the adoption rate of such e-services.

In their study, Weerakkody et al. [4] indicated security and privacy as risks related to e-government adoption and implementation in spite of e-government's enormous benefits. According to Rehman et al. [12] an e-government system is reliable when it enhances citizens' trust. This is because the primary concern of citizens is how their personal information will be treated, who will use that information, where it will be stored and for what purpose it will be used.

The next section delves into the methodology used in gathering and analyzing data as well as drawing conclusions on results obtained.

2   Method

2.1   Data Collection Method

The study makes use of an online survey with respondents between the ages of 17 and 74 from the following SSA countries: Angola, Botswana, Cameroon, Congo, Gabon, Gambia, Ghana, Guinea, Kenya, Liberia, Madagascar, Namibia, Nigeria, North Sudan, Rwanda, Senegal, South Africa, Swaziland, and Tanzania. The Sub-Saharan African region[1] was selected because in spite of the abject poverty still existing, the region is currently undergoing a dynamic revolution in the area of information communication and technology (ICT) and e-government is gaining grounds gradually [13].

The online survey, comprising of ten questions in total, was conducted using Survey Planet between December 2017 to May 2018. A hyperlink to the online survey was sent out to the target population (group), thus a convenient sampling method was employed.

Despite its numerous advantages as outlined by Evans and Mathur [14], the use of an online survey technique played a role in the small sample size – which is in line with the disadvantages of using an online survey. On the contrary the online survey enabled the distribution of survey material easier to participants who were not in proximity to the authors.

2.2   Data, Survey Items and Analysis

The sample size, due to the difficulty in gathering data from all SSA countries, was not large (i.e. n = 180); yet according to Faber and Fonseca [15], a large sample size is not always ideal for research or statistical analysis because statistical tests were developed to handle samples and not populations and with the increase in computational power today it is possible to utilize a substantial sample size in rejecting a null hypothesis. Despite the limitations of incorporating smaller sample sizes in research, they are

---

[1] About Sub-Saharan Africa,
   Available at: http://www.africa.undp.org/content/rba/en/home/regioninfo.html.

encouraged in confirmatory studies [16] of which this study is not an exception. Thus, this study stands by the usage of the sample size of 180. Thus, this study stands by the usage of the sample size of n = 180.

For the purpose of age categorization[2], we employed the following age groupings:

- Children (00–14 years); Youth (15–24 years); Adults (25–64 years); Seniors (65 years and over).

Another age categorization that was used in classifying the ages of respondents into their respective generations is[3,4]:

- Centennials (<=17 years); Millennials (18–34 years); Generation X (35–50 years); Baby Boomers (51–69 years); Traditionalists (70 and over).

Occupations were categorized according to the International Labor Organization standards – International Labor Organization, International Standard Classification of Occupations (ISCO)[5].

A binomial test [17], also known as the exact test [18], was performed to test the hypothesis of a Sub Saharan African citizen's unwillingness to give their information to their governments using the R programming language [19]. Next, a logistic model was fit to the data to investigate associations among variables. Particularly, it was of interest to know if the odds were higher for females to provide their personal information compared to males. The SAS software was used to perform this test.

The next section discusses results of the analysis from the survey data.

3   Findings

3.1   Descriptive Statistics

Upon performing basic statistical analysis, the results below were derived and tabulated accordingly. Table 1 illustrates the descriptive demographic characteristics gathered from our survey data for all 180 respondents. The larger group of respondents were adults, with 64.44% being males and 86.67% having a higher education qualification. Also, majority of the respondents reside in the Western African sub-region (see Table 1).

---

[2] Statistics Canada, "Age Categories, Life Cycle Groupings", Available at: https://www.statcan.gc.ca/eng/concepts/definitions/age2.

[3] The Centre for Generational Kinetics (CGK), "Generational Breakdown: Info About All of the Generations", Available at: http://genhq.com/faq–info–about–generations/.

[4] World Economic Forum, "How different age groups identify with their generational labels", Available at: https://www.weforum.org/agenda/2015/09/how–different–age–groups–identify–with–their–generational–labels/.

[5] International Labor Organization, International Standard Classification of Occupations (ISCO), Available at: http://www.ilo.org/public/english/bureau/stat/isco/index.htm.

Table 1. Demographic data of survey.

Demographic object	Item	Count	Percent (%)
Gender	Female	64	35.56
	Male	116	64.44
Age group	Adult	106	58.89
	Youth	74	41.11
Generation	Boomer	2	1.11
	Centennial	4	2.22
	Generation X	7	3.89
	Millennial	167	92.78
Educational level	Higher Education	156	86.67
	Secondary Education	24	13.33
Job group	Manager	7	3.89
	None	13	7.22
	Operator	1	0.55
	Professional	131	72.78
	Service Worker	7	3.89
	Technician	21	11.67
Sub-region	Central Africa	4	2.22
	Eastern Africa	13	7.22
	Southern Africa	15	8.34
	Western Africa	148	82.22

3.2   Results from Logistic Regression Model

In this subsection, analysis is restricted to the variables: Gender, Age Group and Education level as the descriptive statistics show that we have somewhat enough data in each level of category to obtain reasonable results. Though other variables may be important in the model, they are heavily associated with each other. The overall model fit to the data is good (p-value = 0.0064) as shown in Table 2.

Table 2. Testing global null hypothesis: BETA = 0

Test	Chi-Square	DF	Pr > ChiSq
Likelihood ratio	12.2998	3	0.0064
Score	11.4660	3	0.0095
Wald	10.7131	3	0.0134

Table 3 represents the parameter estimates and p-values of tests associated with each parameter. Table 4 shows the Odds Ratio estimates of Gender, Age and Education.

Table 3. Analysis of maximum likelihood estimates

Parameter		DF	Estimate	Standard error	Wald Chi-Square	Pr > ChiSq
Intercept		1	1.2008	0.2813	18.2269	<.0001
sex	Female	1	0.5916	0.2000	8.7454	0.0031
age_category	Adult	1	−0.1394	0.1797	0.6017	0.4379
edu	Higher Education	1	−0.1430	0.2630	0.2959	0.5865

Table 4. Odds ratio estimates

Effect		Point estimate	95% Wald confidence limits	
sex	Female vs Male	3.265	1.490	7.151
age_category	Adult vs Youth	0.757	0.374	1.531
edu	Higher Education vs Secondary Education	0.751	0.268	2.106

Amongst the variables considered to explain why one would give their information to the government, our survey reveals that gender is the only significant explanatory variable (p-value = 0.0031). See Table 2.

The odds are higher for females not to give their information compared to males. The odds of females not giving their personal information to the government is about 3.3 times that of males.

3.3 Binomial Test Results

For the purpose of this study and the survey conducted, the null hypothesis is expressed as;

H_0: *At most half of Sub-Saharan Africans are not willing to give their personal information to their governments (1)*

Conversely, the alternate hypothesis is expressed as

H_A: *More than half of Sub-Saharan Africans are not willing to give their personal information to their governments (2)*

Upon conducting the binomial test on the overall survey data, the results obtained are evident in Table 5.

Based on the binomial test results in Table 5, the null hypothesis is rejected. That is, the data provides enough evidence to suggest that more than half of Sub-Saharan Africans are not willing to give their personal information to their governments. In that regard, this study contributes to the extant literature on e-government and the Sub-Saharan African region.

Table 5. Binomial (Exact) test results.

Binomial Test

data: 125 and 180

number of successes = **125**, number of trials = **180**, **p–value =
9.594e–08**

**alternative hypothesis: true probability of success is greater
than 0.5**

95 percent confidence interval: 0.6330513   1.0000000

sample estimates:

probability of success   **0.6944444**

4   Discussion

Results from the analysis reveal a gap in Sub-Saharan African governments' actions to
assure citizens that their personal data is secure in the hands of the government. This
can be associated with the lack in trust [20]. Thus, it can be concluded that a large
percentage of Sub Saharan Africans do not trust their governments with their personal
information. The results of government distrust with personal data can be linked to a
track record of corrupt and inefficient institutions and the undermining of mutual trust
by government officials [21].

The study also, observed a larger percentage of the respondents were of the millennial generation which are the most technology savvy. This generational group is
educated, transacts online and fraternizes via social media yet are not willing to give
government their personal data[6]. This reveals the fact that, millennial generation trusts
private firms with their personal data, much more than governments, regardless of what
those private firms will use their data for.

Though the dataset does not represent the mass majority of Sub-Saharan Africans,
this study confirmed the existing issues raised by Schuppan [22] and Lallmahomed
et al. [23] that citizens' trust in government is pertinent to the success of any e-
government deployment. Lallmahomed et al. [23] concluded that, as trust is increased
(taking citizens' privacy into consideration), citizens' resistance to e-government
adoption decreases. Thus, with regards to implications to practice, governments in the
sub-region must sensitize the general public and raise awareness on security inclusions
into their e-government systems. In curbing the fear of handing over personal data to

---

[6] Schwarz H.: Millennials are a little confused when it comes to privacy, Washington Post, 2015.
Available at: https://www.washingtonpost.com/news/the-fix/wp/2015/05/13/millenials-dont-trust-
government-to-respect-their-privacy-but-they-do-trust-businesses-what.

government for e-services, Sub-Saharan African governments should employ the General Data Protection Regulation (GDPR). The European Union's GDPR policy which came into full force from the 25th of May 2018, driven by a philosophical approach to data protection is made up of six general data protection principles (fairness and lawfulness; purpose limitation; data minimization; accuracy; storage limitation; and integrity and confidentiality) [24]. It is based on the concept of privacy as a fundamental human right (as enshrined in the Charter of EU Rights). The GDPR places personal data in the hands of users and all companies and governments in the EU are to comply with the regulations or face the repercussions (see [24]). A GDPR compliant e-government framework holds citizen personal information (i.e. identity) in high esteem thus truly attaining a citizen-centric e-government.

In like manner, the authors recommend the adoption of the concept of privacy evidence as developed by Sackmann et al. [7], to pave the way for transparency in future e-government deployments.

4.1   Limitation

The major limitation to this study, though catered for by the choice of statistical test, was the fact that the sample size for this study was not large. In addition to this, a large proportion of respondents are from the western countries of Sub-Saharan Africa.

In spite of this, our study gives a general perception which cuts across the whole region and adds to the literature on trust, transparency, privacy and security with respect to e-government adoption in Sub-Saharan Africa.

5   Conclusion

This study's findings reveal important possible recommendations for e-government practice with respect to citizen data security and privacy in the Sub Saharan Africa region. The study discussed the value of personal data to e-government and the fact that security, confidentiality and privacy of citizens' data is important to the success of any e-government deployment. As such a survey was performed in the Sub-Saharan African region to assess whether citizens were willing to give government access to their personal data.

The study confirms that a majority of sub-Saharan citizens are not willing to give their governments access to their personal data/information. It was also observed that millennial Sub-Saharan Africans, which made up the majority of survey respondents, were not willing to provide government with their personal data.

The issue of privacy, confidentiality and trust is still evidently in dire need of discussion in the sub-region and must be brought to the forefront of policy making so as to expedite the development and implementation of quality e-government services. There is the desire for e-government initiatives in SSA countries due to its relevance in transforming the public sector [25] yet privacy concerns are rather high [26]. Evidently, these assertions expressed by researchers are in line with findings in this study.

As highlighted by Anderson et al. [27], e-government is essential in creating a symbiotic relationship between governments and citizens, thereby effectively using

ICTs to facilitate that relationship. Moreover, it promotes transparencies so that the citizens can place greater trust in the activities of their governments. As such there must be a reciprocity in the provision of citizens' personal data by governments providing a secure assuredness of personal data which will build trust and reduce citizen paranoia with respect to personal data. With citizens as the major stakeholders in e-government initiatives, policy makers must also consider adopting the model by Alzahrani et al. [28] which addresses the antecedents of trust in e-government.

In addition, we advise that governments of Sub-Saharan Africa should create awareness by educating citizens on data protection practices and the reason why government needs their personal data – to ensure the success of e-government deployments. The study recommends the privacy evidence concept and the EU's GDPR policy which promises to protect the confidentiality of EU citizens and is a recommendable for Sub-Saharan African policy makers in the inclusion of designing and implementing e-government services.

Future research could delve into obtaining an in-depth overview of privacy regulations and steps governments have taken towards ensuring citizen data safety in each Sub-Saharan African country.

In conclusion, the adoption and survival of e-government implementations are dependent on citizens' perception, trust, security and the integrity of government. As such governments in the Sub-Saharan African region must make the necessary efforts so as to realize the goals for which their e-government and e-services deployments were implemented.

Acknowledgement. This work was supported by the Department of System Analysis and Decision Making, Graduate School of Economics and Management, Ural Federal University.

References

1. West, D.M.: E-government and the transformation of service delivery and citizen attitudes. Public Adm. Rev. **64**(1), 15–27 (2004)
2. Carter, L., Bélanger, F.: The utilization of e-government services: citizen trust, innovation and acceptance factors. Inf. Syst. J. **15**(1), 5–25 (2005)
3. Brooks, L., Henriksen, H., Janssen, M., Papazafeiropoulou, A., Trutnev, D.: Public sector information systems (PSIS): how ICT can bring innovation into the policymaking process
4. Weerakkody, V., Irani, Z., Lee, H., Osman, I., Hindi, N.: E-government implementation: a bird's eye view of issues relating to costs, opportunities, benefits and risks. Inf. Syst. Front. **17**(4), 889–915 (2015)
5. Lofstedt, U.: E-government-assesment of current research and some proposals for future directions. Int. J. Public Inf. Syst. **1**(1), 39–52 (2012)
6. Jun, C.N., Chung, C.J.: Big data analysis of local government 3.0: focusing on Gyeongsangbuk-do in Korea. Technol. Forecast. Soc. Change **110**, 3–12 (2016)
7. Sackmann, S., Strüker, J., Accorsi, R.: Personalization in privacy-aware highly dynamic systems. Commun. ACM **49**(9), 32–38 (2006)
8. Igari, N.: How to successfully promote ICT usage: a comparative analysis of Denmark and Japan. Telematics Inform. **31**(1), 115–125 (2014)

9. Whitley, E.A., Gal, U., Kjaergaard, A.: Who do you think you are? A review of the complex interplay between information systems, identification and identity. Eur. J. Inf. Syst. **23**, 17–35 (2014)
10. Wu, Y.: Protecting personal data in e-government: a cross-country study. Gov. Inf. Q. **31**(1), 150–159 (2014)
11. Ambali, A.R.: E-Government policy: ground issues in e-filing system. Eur. J. Soc. Sci. **11** (2), 249–266 (2009)
12. Rehman, M., Esichaikul, V., Kamal, M.: Factors influencing e–government adoption in Pakistan. Transform. Gov. People Process. Policy **6**(3), 258–282 (2012)
13. Nkohkwo, Q.N.A., Islam, M.S.: Challenges to the successful implementation of e-Government initiatives in Sub-Saharan Africa: a literature review. Electron. J. e-Gov. **11**(1), 253–267 (2013)
14. Evans, J.R., Mathur, A.: The value of online surveys. Internet Res. **15**(2), 195–219 (2005)
15. Faber, J., Fonseca, L.M.: How sample size influences research outcomes. Dent. Press. J. Orthod. **19**(4), 27–29 (2014)
16. Hackshaw, A.: Small studies: strengths and limitations. Eur. Respir. J. **32**(5), 1141–1143 (2008)
17. Zar, J.H.: Biostatistical Analysis, 4th edn. Prentice Hill, Upper Saddle River (1999)
18. McDonald, J.H.: Handbook of Biological Statistics, vol. 2, pp. 173–181. Sparky House Publishing, Baltimore (2009)
19. R Core Team: R: A language and environment for statistical computing. R Foundation for Statistical Computing, Vienna, Austria (2015)
20. Verkijika, S.F., De Wet, L.: A usability assessment of e-government websites in Sub-Saharan Africa. Int. J. Inf. Manage. **39**, 20–29 (2018)
21. Letki, N.: Trust in newly democratic regimes. In: The Oxford Handbook of Social and Political Trust, vol. 335. Oxford University Press, New York (2018)
22. Schuppan, T.: E-Government in developing countries: experiences from sub-Saharan Africa. Gov. Inf. Q. **26**(1), 118–127 (2009)
23. Lallmahomed, M.Z., Lallmahomed, N., Lallmahomed, G.M.: Factors influencing the adoption of e-Government Services in Mauritius. Telematics Inform. **34**(4), 57–72 (2017)
24. Goddard, M.: The EU General Data Protection Regulation (GDPR): European regulation that has a global impact. Int. J. Mark. Res. **59**(6), 703–705 (2017)
25. Okong'o, K., Kyobe, M.: Empirical examination of e-Government in developing countries and its value in Kenya's public service. Electron. J. Inf. Syst. Eval. **21**(1), 35–45 (2018)
26. Mutimukwe, C., Kolkowska, E., Grönlund, Å.: Trusting and adopting E-government services in developing countries? Privacy concerns and practices in Rwanda. In: Janssen, M., et al. (eds.) EGOV 2017. LNCS, vol. 10428, pp. 324–335. Springer, Cham (2017). https://doi.org/10.1007/978-3-319-64677-0_27
27. Anderson, D., Wu, R., Cho, J.-S., Schroeder, K.: Introduction: global challenges in turbulent times: road to sustainable E-government. E-Government Strategy, ICT and Innovation for Citizen Engagement. SECE, pp. 1–10. Springer, New York (2015). https://doi.org/10.1007/978-1-4939-3350-1_1
28. Alzahrani, L., Al-Karaghouli, W., Weerakkody, V.: Analysing the critical factors influencing trust in e-government adoption from citizens' perspective: a systematic review and a conceptual framework. Int. Bus. Rev. **26**(1), 164–175 (2017)

A Cybersecurity Model for Electronic Governance and Open Society

Nuno Lopes[✉] and José Faria

United Nations University, Operating Unit on Policy-Driven Electronic
Governance (UNU-EGOV), Guimarães, Portugal
{lopes, faria}@unu.edu

Abstract. This paper starts by presenting the research landscape of the vulnerabilities of cyberspace; afterwards, it classifies the cyber vulnerabilities identified in the literature; finally, it proposes a cybersecurity model to tackle the cyberspace vulnerabilities found. The proposed model is grounded in three main pillars: a cybersecurity governance approach, cybersecurity capabilities, and cybersecurity best practices. The research methodology used to conduct this study is based on a quantitative and qualitative analysis of the literature on the field. The paper concludes that the model can be a useful tool for preventing and mitigating cyberattacks in public and private organizations.

Keywords: Cyberattacks · Cybersecurity · Model · Governance model ·
Vulnerabilities · Best practices

1 Introduction

Despite all the improvements made on software development frameworks, cybersecurity assessment, the inclusion of cybersecurity subjects in curricula, organization insights methodologies, and enforcement of special tools to protect our systems, the number and extension of cyberattacks seems to be increasing every year. The soaring number of users and personal devices connected to the Internet, the emergence of Internet of Things (IoT), the growing number of digital systems, such as electric stations, water stations, fuel pipelines, health facilities, etc., make the cyberspace increase every day and become more exposed than ever to cyberattacks.

An attack on an enterprise can be devastating, jeopardize the organization, and put their survival at risk. However, attacks on public services could affect not only a community, but an entire country.

In order to assure resilient and reliable public services, all cybersecurity stakeholders, specially the public entities, shall follow steady cybersecurity models and coordinate their efforts against cyberattacks.

Nowadays, it is almost impossible for a day to go by without cyber incidents [73]. Although detection systems and tools to protect systems are better than ever, with some of them already making use of dynamic tools to improve the capacity of reaction to unforeseen attack situations, and the fact that most of the new systems are more secure than in the past, there is still the need to reinforce cyberspace security with reliable

© Springer Nature Switzerland AG 2019
A. Chugunov et al. (Eds.): EGOSE 2018, CCIS 947, pp. 92–107, 2019.
https://doi.org/10.1007/978-3-030-13283-5_8

cybersecurity models, in order to prevent and mitigate cyberattacks. Cyberattacks are being propagated for different reasons and becoming more sophisticated every day.

This paper has four objectives: (1) raise awareness for the increasing number of cybersecurity incidents - Sect. 1; (2) showing the research landscape on the topic – Sect. 3; (3) organize the vulnerabilities identified in the literature by type – Sect. 4; (4) design a conceptual model capable of providing a holistic view on how to improve cybersecurity and mitigate cyberattacks – Sect. 5.

The remaining part of this work is organized as follows: Sect. 2 describes the methodology used to conduct the research work; Sect. 3 presents the research landscape of cybersecurity vulnerabilities in terms of publications growth, countries with more publications, percentage of disciplines contributing to this research area, and the percentage of research by the type of vulnerability; Sect. 4 presents a qualitative analysis of the reviewed literature resorting to conceptual maps; Sect. 5 proposes the conceptual model for cybersecurity based on three key pillars: a governance model, capabilities, and best practices; Sect. 6 finalizes the paper with the main findings and remarks of the research work.

2 Methodology

To achieve the four objectives mentioned in the previous section, four-step research activities have been conducted, which included: (1) data collection; (2) quantitative analysis; (3) qualitative analysis; (4) design of the model based on the previous three steps. Therefore, the research methodology used was a mix of quantitative and qualitative analysis of the reviewed literature, followed by a mapping of cyber vulnerabilities found in the literature by means of conceptual maps. The conceptual maps provided the basis and the input to build the key pillars of the model.

The data collection activity involved two sub-tasks: (1) determining data sources for identifying related work and (2) defining suitable keywords for obtaining relevant publications for conducting quantitative analysis to landscape the state of research. Three scientific databases were considered as data sources: Scopus (Elsevier 2015), Web of Science (Thomson Reuters 2015), and Google Scholar. Besides this, Scopus has been selected as the main data source due to its greater coverage of journal publications and hard sciences subjects. Google Scholar was also used to ensure that no relevant papers were left out of our study. The next step involved defining keywords to search for publications. The selected expression was "Cybersecurity and Vulnerabilities". The expression above was applied to Scopus on 8 August 2017 against article titles, abstracts, and keywords. As a result, a total of 246 publications were identified.

To conduct a detailed data analysis, the number of publications was narrowed down using a filter process – this process was reading the abstract of each paper to assess its relevance for this study. From this reading, 143 papers were selected, and 103 were rejected. The results are shown in Table 1.

Table 1. Number of publications

Criteria	Results
Publications	246
Not relevant or unavailable	103
Selected publications	143

The quantitative analysis was conducted based on the 143 publications identified at the outset of the data collection. Since the aim was to landscape the state of research, we applied descriptive statistics to analyse the following aspects: publication growth, country, type of publication, and discipline.

The qualitative analysis was conducted based on the selected 143 publications. Content analysis contributed to identifying findings related to the main attributes for the technical, behavioural, and physical vulnerabilities. Section 4 presents the definition and findings for each attribute. The analysis of the literature provided the basis to design the conceptual model for preventing and mitigating cyberattacks.

3   Quantitative Analysis

The following sections present major findings related to publication growth, countries, types of publications, the area of research, and their contribution to cyber vulnerabilities.

3.1   Publication Growth

The growth of cyber vulnerabilities research started in 2002 when the first paper on the topic was published. However, research remained scarce until 2009, with only 26 papers published over 7 years. Between 2010 and 2012, the research was steady: in average, 16 publications were released per year. Since 2012, the number of publications started to increase exponentially, reaching a total of 81 publications in 2016. In the last four years, the number of publications on cyber vulnerabilities increased more than five. The smaller number of publications in 2017 relative to the number of publications in 2016 is due to the search for this study having been conducted in August 2017. Probably, if the search was done at the end of 2017, the number of publications would be even higher than 2016. The annual growth of cyber vulnerabilities research between 2002 and 2017 is depicted in Fig. 1.

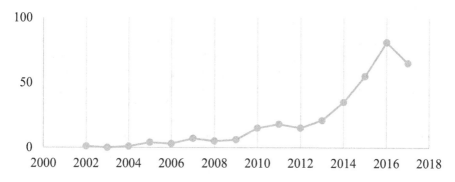

Fig. 1. State of research – publication growth

3.2 Countries

Based on institutional and researchers' affiliations, the leading countries that host more research on cyber vulnerabilities include the following: United States, United Kingdom, China, France, Spain, Australia, Italy, Canada, Israel, the Netherlands, South Africa, and the Republic of Korea. The results, including the number of publications produced per country, are depicted in Fig. 2.

The results show that the United States has, by far, the highest number of publications in relation to other countries. The second country in the list with more publications (United Kingdom) has tenfold fewer publications than the United States, and it is closely followed by China with 15 publications. Regionally, the leading countries are the United States (207) and Canada (5) in the Americas; the United Kingdom (23), France (12), Spain (9), Italy (8), and the Netherlands (5) in Europe; China (15), Republic of Korea (5), and Japan (1) in Asia; Australia (8) in Oceania; and South Africa (5) publishes the most in Africa. Concerning developing countries outside China, there are no publications in this research field.

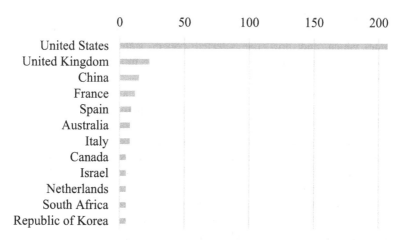

Fig. 2. State of research – countries

3.3 Disciplines

Based on the researchers' affiliations, the list of contributing disciplines and the percentages of researchers belonging to them are depicted in Fig. 3. Clearly, the area is dominated by Computer Science (37%) and Engineering (28%), therefore highlighting a strong technical focus for cyber vulnerabilities research, followed by Social Sciences (10%), Energy (5%), Decision Sciences (4%), and Mathematics (4%). The three dominant disciplines present in cyber vulnerabilities research highlights that this is a very technical domain. However, the social issues that arise with it are not left out either.

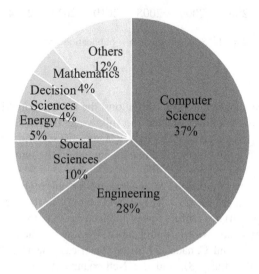

Fig. 3. State of research – disciplines

4 Qualitative Analysis

This section presents the results of qualitative content analysis of the 143 papers obtained from the final filtering of the data collection process. The analysis aimed at establishing which and how the selected papers address cyber vulnerabilities: (1) technical, (2) governance, and (3) behavioural. The following sections present the findings for each vulnerability.

A vulnerability becomes a threat if it is discovered and exploited. This weakness can be found at different levels, such as: software, hardware, firmware, operating system, every IoT device, network, and people and procedures [6].

Internally, each organization faces various challenges in terms of security and privacy, such as: former employees, external IT service providers that have any kind of access to the internal systems, ICT staff with insufficient skills, etc. Furthermore, it is possible to organize these vulnerabilities in three major classes: technical vulnerabilities, physical vulnerabilities, and vulnerabilities due to human behaviour.

The three types of vulnerabilities that were found are depicted in Fig. 4, where technical vulnerabilities show the highest number of research works.

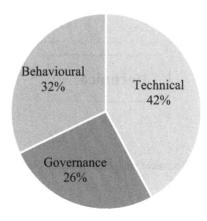

Fig. 4. State of research – type of vulnerabilities

4.1   Technical Vulnerability

This type of vulnerability refers to any kind of flaw based on intrinsic problems due to mis-development, intentionally provoked by malware or spyware, or even connectivity through heterogeneous software or architectures. As an example of the latter, the same protocol for a service could be implemented for different businesses. There are several vulnerabilities intrinsic to these different implementations, such as: protocol vulnerability, inappropriate protocol mapping and security service mapping, insecure configuration tool, insecure interconnection system, and design weaknesses [72].

The most common technical vulnerabilities result from software, as defined by DaCosta [20] "*A software vulnerability is a fault in the specification, implementation, or configuration of a software system whose execution can violate an explicit or implicit security policy.*" As expected, these vulnerabilities are not intentionally incorporated in the software [6] by the developer. The accumulated experience of the development team [59] and the training and enforcement of best practices and frameworks lead to better development and reduce the probability of technical vulnerabilities. Therefore, the development of software could take into consideration all scenarios and pitfalls to mitigate all vulnerabilities, but the misuse by the final user could overthrow such efforts.

The reviewed literature shows several technical vulnerabilities. The vulnerabilities referred in the literature have been classified in two main domains: software and hardware, as shown in Fig. 5. Table 2 shows the list of technical vulnerabilities found in the literature per domain and the respective bibliographic references.

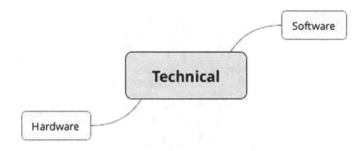

Fig. 5. Technical vulnerabilities conceptual map

Table 2. Technical vulnerability in Publications

Software	
Absence, fails or delays in updates	[7, 34]
Assessing software vulnerabilities	[1, 4, 9, 27, 39, 44, 45, 50, 51, 58, 63, 68]
Attacks to data integrity and privacy	[8, 16, 60]
Bug bounty program	[17, 42]
Exploit technical flaws: buffer overflow, XSS, etc.	[55, 69]
Inadequately tested software	[5, 19, 22, 34, 62]
Malware	[8, 30, 43, 44]
Open source software: lack of formal notification of vulnerabilities	[3, 5, 49]
Protocols vulnerabilities: design, mapping and interconnection	[2, 11, 17, 18, 31, 40, 43, 71]
Scanning software and network vulnerabilities	[5, 17, 21, 44, 48, 63]
Search and explore IRC, web, chats, data, etc. to identify threats and detect vulnerabilities	[14, 28, 38, 46]
Software vulnerabilities: impossible to verify all the code	[5, 37]
Software, hardware, network vulnerabilities, zero-day flaw	[5, 15, 17, 18, 22, 31, 34, 56, 57, 63, 64]
Technical vulnerabilities in the cloud for applications, IaaS, SaaS, and other platforms	[33, 47, 60]
Inadequate or under enforced of cybersecurity	[13, 34, 51, 66]
Hardware	
Defected devices, equipment or without cyber protections	[11, 18, 19, 25, 26, 29, 31, 38, 44, 70]
Technological innovations and IoT has expanded the entry points for cyber attacks	[35, 36, 49]
Technical flaws in IoT devices	[31, 35, 38]
Increase in inter-connectivity between medical devices with other systems increase the technical vulnerabilities	[31, 61, 65]
Security threats facing wireless devices	[24, 31, 32, 54, 61]

4.2   Governance Vulnerability

Governance Vulnerability refers to the management of communication devices. The Governance vulnerabilities referred in the reviewed literature have been classified into domains, as shown in Fig. 6. Table 3 shows the list of this sort of vulnerabilities per domain and the respective bibliographic references.

Fig. 6. Governance vulnerabilities – conceptual map

Table 3. Governance vulnerability in publications

Communication devices	
Device access: laptop, smartphone, etc.	[43, 61]
Exponential number of smartphones increase surface attack	[19]
Keyloggers, NFC, etc.	[55]
Weak design, development, counterfeit products, firmware and hardware	[60]
Communication protocols	
Open communication protocols (not encrypted)	[11, 22, 38, 68]

4.3   Behavioural Vulnerability

Vulnerabilities due to human behaviour are mainly based on actions or absence of actions by users. These actions compromise the system, whether intentionally or not.

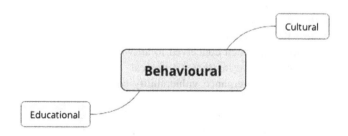

Fig. 7. Behavioural vulnerabilities – conceptual map

The Behavioural Vulnerabilities mentioned in the reviewed literature have been organized into two domains: Cultural and Educational, as shown in Fig. 7. Table 4 shows the list of this sort of vulnerabilities per domain and the respective bibliographic references.

Table 4. Behavioural vulnerability in publications

Cultural	
Users react to phishing, add-ons, etc.	[19, 55]
Insufficient funding and staffing, problems of governance	[12, 33]
After attacks, harden the systems and forget the human factor	[7, 23]
Use of unsafe WIFI to access emails, e-banking, etc.	[34]
Neglect updates by users	[25, 56]
Inappropriate behaviour on the use of mobile devices	[26, 34, 44]
Low security culture	[7, 44, 60]
Users and organizations do not share knowledge regarding flaws	[33]
Educational	
After attacks, harden the systems and forget the human factor	[23]
Use of unsafe WIFI to access emails, e-banking, etc.	[34]
Insufficient or under-enforced cybersecurity policies	[36]
Enforce several layers of defence without knowledge, and can develop a worst scenario them before	[67]
Operational deficiencies by operators	[31, 43, 44]
Focus on curricula on the graduate level curriculum in cybersecurity, training for ICT	[25, 53]
Schools teach defensive techniques, but we need to train offensive techniques as well	[69]
Cybersecurity education	[25, 52, 60]
Users react to phishing, add-ons, etc.	[19, 55]
Social engineering and shoulder surfing	[55]

5 Cybersecurity Model

A link between vulnerability types (i.e. technical, governance, and behavioural) and model components (i.e. capabilities, governance, and best practices) has been created to conveniently address the vulnerabilities.

Therefore, the model has been conceived to answer to the types of vulnerabilities found in the literature. This means that a technical vulnerability corresponds to the capability component; the governance vulnerability corresponds to governance component; and the behavioural vulnerability corresponds to the best practices component. Besides that, and given the multidisciplinary nature of the area, as it has been shown in Sect. 3, the model provides a holist approach on how to address the cybersecurity as a whole, that is, in an integrated way, which encompasses not only best practices, but also how to build capabilities and have a governance model to manage security.

Fig. 8. Cybersecurity conceptual model

Therefore, our proposal to leverage the resilience and robustness of any cyber-system is based on three strategic pillars: a cybersecurity governance model, cyber-security capabilities, and cybersecurity best practices. It is a paramount approach in order to ensure that all three pillars are coherent and act in coordination with each other, as shown in Fig. 8.

5.1 Cybersecurity Governance Approach

Data is the most important element in any information system, due to the fact that everything revolves around the use of data.

Governance could be viewed as: risk assessment, security measures, and collection of incident reports [41, 74].

Risk assessment: The activity of risk assessment must induce a strategic plan dedicated to identifying vulnerabilities and solve them, or if not possible, define what security measures should be taken to reduce the risk to the minimum. This activity should take place regularly.

Security measures: the implementation and management of a cyber-system must imply the enforcement of best practices shared between all actors. Because cyberse-curity is dynamic, all actors should exchange and foster discussions about new approaches to new problems and implement new best practices to improve security.

Incident reporting: this type of practice, regularly carried out, allows confrontation with the security measures enforced and this confrontation should stimulate and improve risk assessment, resulting in a strengthened security measure. This reporting also allows understanding the overall process of governance of our processes. More-over, without this reporting, it is impossible to understand what is happening inside and could, in fact, hinder a better contingency plan.

Therefore, every organization should devise a plan for data governance, with the purpose of framing all data and ensure each piece or group of data should be accessed only by whom it should be accessed. Regarding this plan, our proposal considers several aspects, such as:

- Organize the data in different classes, accordingly to the needs or purposes;

- Differentiate scenarios regarding data access by users and what privileges have every class of users;
- Ensure that the storage of data is done according to the regulations of the country or state the organization is located on, in case there is a need by the country or state legal authorities to access this data;
- Delineate a plan for recovery in case of data loss and develop a plan for backups;
- Devise a contingency plan for hardware, software, and data, and regularly enforce procedures to ensure data consistency;
- Regularly enforce audit procedures regarding access control and ensure that anyone has been accessed unduly;
- Define procedures to effectively delete data and its copies on every device or support, that is, ensure it is wiped properly;
- Ensure that the authentication and authorization system is robust;
- Ensure that all software used inside the organization is lawful and follows all procedures of a good development;
- Keep the ICT team committed with this plan and always updated regarding best practices.

This plan must be sponsored by top management and must be seen as a top priority.

This Data Governance Plan should encompass aspects of the organization and should regularly be revised to ensure compliance with the most recent best practices or include new technologies to improve cybersecurity.

5.2 Cybersecurity Capabilities

The recent attack perpetrated by ransomware, which took place due to a flaw in the protocol SMB, was a great lesson to everyone in the ICT field. Too many ICT teams have rushed to update their systems when the attack had already spread and only as a reaction to the news. Some big companies stopped their production due to this flaw, which should have been patched months ago.

All ICT team members must be well prepared and stimulated to improve their skills, because responsiveness is key in mitigating and stopping an attack, and preventing or reducing further damage. The team members should also be responsible for conceiving, ensuring, and compelling all users to fulfil the Data Governance Plan.

5.3 Cybersecurity Best Practices

User behaviour, regarding the use of the cyber-systems, is sometimes neglected by some organizations [10], whether they are a member of the ICT team or not.

We believe that rivalry between attackers and defenders is still taking place, but good practices can prevent a great number of problems. Hence, the ICT team should regularly promote sessions to refresh and upgrade the awareness and responsiveness of all users. Some of the best practices include:

- Weak passwords: highlight the importance to use strong passwords and change them regularly. It is tiresome for the user but can also thwart the attacker. Explain and enhance the important of using two-factor authentication when possible;

- Links: highlight the difference between the link you see, in an email for instance, and the link embedded, which is the real one. Explain the tactic usually used with links on fake emails - these links resemble the real one but point to another location;
- Software/plugins: clarify all the problems associated with the installation of software/plugins not checked or approved by the ICT team;
- External devices: use of external devices without a proper check;
- Access web sites: inform how to access web sites using secure connections and avoid the transmission of any valuable information over insecure connections;
- Personal copies: forbid any personal copies and any transfer of data to the outside;
- Bring Your Own Device (BYOD): clarify all potential problems induced by BYOD when using internal networks and accessing internal data. Explain how a BYOD could infect a system, as was the case of *WannaCry*, which propagates by itself when inside the network;
- Personal use: disallow, or even forbid, the use of the internal systems for professional and personal purpose. For instance, the use of the same browser to read personal email and access the internal applications could lead to a blend of personal and professional credentials, and create the opportunity for malware to capture valuable data;
- Sealed devices: under certain circumstances, and according to the importance of the data, access could be allowed only from devices prepared by the ICT team and sealed, which allow only a specific group of services to be run.

A group of users that is well prepared and aware can resist at least the most common charges by hackers and contribute to better cybersecurity.

6   Conclusions

The research conducted within this work shows that cybersecurity is a multidisciplinary area mainly studied by computer science, engineering, and social sciences. The vulnerabilities identified in the literature and classified as technical, governance. and behavioural showed to have a higher incidence in the technical aspect. Based on previous evidence, a conceptual model suitable to address those types of vulnerabilities has been designed. The model is composed by a governance component responsible for measuring, evaluation, and auditing the level of security, a capability component responsible for developing ICT skills in cybersecurity team, and a best practices component is responsible for promoting good behavioural to prevent and mitigate attacks.

The best approach to protect any system is to endow it with resilience regarding predictive acts and avoid any sort of vulnerabilities. The model can be used as a useful tool to address IT systems vulnerabilities. The recommended policies for each model component can be used as guidelines for the organizations to become more secure and safer. The model provides a holistic view of cybersecurity, highlighting the importance of simultaneously tackling all dimensions: Governance, Behavioural, and Practice. Solely addressing a unique dimension is not enough to ensure a strong security foundation. Although there is still a long away to go, as we are all in a learning process on how we could be better prepared for preventing and mitigating to ever-new cyberattacks, we think that our model is a good starting point to build more robust IT systems in the future.

Acknowledgment. This paper is a result of the project "SmartEGOV: Harnessing EGOV for Smart Governance (Foundations, methods, Tools)/ NORTE-01-0145-FEDER-000037", supported by Norte Portugal Regional Operational Programme (NORTE 2020), under the PORTUGAL 2020 Partnership Agreement, through the European Regional Development Fund (EFDR).

References

1. Abraham, S., Nair, S.: A novel architecture for predictive cybersecurity using non-homogenous markov models, vol. 1, pp. 774–781 (2015)
2. Abraham, S.M.: Estimating mean time to compromise using non-homogenous continuous-time markov models, vol. 2, pp. 467–472 (2016)
3. Achuthan, K., Sudharavi, S., Kumar, R., Raman, R.: Security vulnerabilities in open source projects: an India perspective, pp. 18–23 (2014)
4. Aissa, A.B., Abercrombie, R.K., Sheldon, F.T., Mili, A.: Defining and computing a value based cyber security measure. Inf. Syst. E-Bus. Manag. **10**(4), 433–453 (2011)
5. Allodi, L., Massacci, F.: Security events and vulnerability data for cybersecurity risk estimation. Risk Anal. **37**(8), 1606–1627 (2017)
6. Anand, P.: Overview of root causes of software vulnerabilities-technical and user-side perspectives. In: 2016 International Conference on Software Security and Assurance (ICSSA), pp. 70–74. IEEE (2016)
7. Anwar, M., He, W., Yuan, X.: Employment status and cybersecurity behaviors (2017)
8. Arabo, A.: Mobile app collusions and its cyber security implications, pp. 178–183 (2016)
9. Armstrong, R.C., Mayo, J.R.: Leveraging complexity in software for cybersecurity (2009)
10. Ashenden, D.: Information security management: a human challenge? Inf. Secur. Tech. Rep. **13**(4), 195–201 (2008)
11. Ashok, A., Sridhar, S., McKinnon, A.D., Wang, P., Govindarasu, M.: Testbed-based performance evaluation of attack resilient control for AGC, pp. 125–129 (2016)
12. Auffret, J.-P., et al.: Cybersecurity leadership: competencies governance, and technologies for industrial control systems. J. Interconnect. Netw. **17**(1), 1740001 (2017)
13. Baldwin, R., Hofecker, T., Carter, G.: Who's in control? Securing commercial unmanned aerial systems command and control a methodology and way ahead. J. Air Traffic Control **57**(4) (2015)
14. Benjamin, V., Li, W., Holt, T., Chen, H.: Exploring threats and vulnerabilities in hacker web: Forums, IRC and carding shops, pp. 85–90, August 2015
15. Biswas, B., Pal, S., Mukhopadhyay, A.: AVICS-Ecoframework: an approach to attack prediction and vulnerability assessment in a cyber ecosystem (2016)
16. Carter, W.A., Sofio, D.G.: Cybersecurity legislation and critical infrastructure vulnerabilities (2017)
17. Chatfield, A.T., Reddick, C.G.: Cybersecurity innovation in government: a case study of U. S. pentagon's vulnerability reward program, volume Part F128275, pp. 64–73 (2017)
18. Costello, P.J.: Identifying and exploiting vulnerabilities in civilian unmanned aerial vehicle systems and evaluating and countering potential threats against the United States airspace, pp. 761–762 (2017)

19. Dalton, W., Van Vuuren, J.J., Westcott, J.: Building cybersecurity resilience in Africa, pp. 112–120 (2017)
20. Mancoridis, S., Prevelakis, V., Dacosta, D., Dahn, C.: Characterizing the 'security vulnerability likelihood' of software functions
21. Flores, F., Paredes, R., Meza, F.: Procedures for mitigating cybersecurity risk in a Chilean government ministry. IEEE Lat. Am. Trans. **14**(6), 2947–2950 (2016)
22. Fox, S.J.: Flying challenges for the future: aviation preparedness – in the face of cyber-terrorism. J. Transp. Secur. **9**(3–4), 191–218 (2016)
23. Gisladottir, V., Ganin, A.A., Keisler, J.M., Kepner, J., Linkov, I.: Resilience of cyber systems with over and under regulation. Risk Anal. **37**(9), 1644–1651 (2017)
24. Goppert, J., Shull, A., Sathyamoorthy, N., Liu, W., Hwang, I., Aldridge, H.: Software/hardware-in the-loop analysis of cyberattacks on unmanned aerial systems. J. Aerosp. Inf. Syst. **11**(5), 337–343 (2014)
25. Graham, J., Hieb, J., Naber, J.: Improving cybersecurity for industrial control systems, pp. 618–623, November 2016
26. Herrera, A.V., Ron, M., Rabadao, C.: National cyber-security policies oriented to BYOD (bring your own device): systematic review (2017)
27. Hoffman, L.J., Rosenberg, T., Dodge, R., Ragsdale, D.: Exploring a national cybersecurity exercise for universities. IEEE Secur. Priv. **3**(5), 27–33 (2005)
28. Huang, H.-C., Zhang, Z.-K., Cheng, H.-W., Shieh, S.W.: Web application security: threats, counter measures and pitfalls. Computer **50**(6), 81–85 (2017)
29. Ismail, S., Sitnikova, E., Slay, J.: SCADA systems cyber security for critical infrastructures: case studies in the transport sector, pp. 425–433 (2015)
30. Jang-Jaccard, J., Nepal, S.: A survey of emerging threats in cybersecurity. J. Comput. Syst. Sci. **80**(5), 973–993 (2014)
31. Jillepalli, A.A., Sheldon, F.T., De Leon, D.C., Haney, M., Abercrombie, R.K.: Security management of cyber physical control systems using NIST SP 800-82r2 (2017)
32. Jøsang, A., Miralabé, L., Dallot, L.: It's not a bug, it's a feature: 25 years of mobile network insecurity, pp. 129–136, January 2015
33. Kamhoua, C., Martin, A., Tosh, D.K., Kwiat, K.A., Heitzenrater, C., Sengupta, S.: Cyber-threats information sharing in cloud computing: a game theoretic approach (2016)
34. Khatoun, R., Zeadally, S.: Cybersecurity and privacy solutions in smart cities. IEEE Commun. Mag. **55**(3), 51–59 (2017)
35. Khera, M.: Think like a hacker: insights on the latest attack vectors (and security controls) for medical device applications. J. Diabetes Sci. Technol. **11**(2), 207–212 (2017)
36. Kim, C.: Cyber-resilient industrial control system with diversified architecture and bus monitoring, pp. 11–16 (2017)
37. Kothari, S., Tamrawi, A., Mathews, J.: Rethinking verification: accuracy, efficiency and scalability through human-machine collaboration, pp. 885–886 (2016)
38. Lam, A., Fernandez J., Frank, R.: Cyberterrorists bringing down airplanes: will it happen soon? pp. 210–219 (2017)
39. Last, D.: Using historical software vulnerability data to forecast future vulnerabilities, pp. 120–126 (2015)
40. Liu, Z., Gupta, B.: A multifaceted assay on cybersecurity: the concerted effort to thwart threats, pp. 123–129 (2016)
41. Dekker, M.A.C.: Critical cloud computing-a CIIP perspective on cloud computing services —ENISA (2012)
42. McGraw, G.: Silver bullet talks with Katie Moussouris. IEEE Secur. Priv. **13**(4), 7–9 (2015)

43. Mejia-Miranda, J., Melchor-Velasquez, R.E., Munoz-Mata, M.A.: Vulnerability detection in smartphones: a systematic literature review [detección de vulnerabilidades en smartphones: Una revisión sistemática de la literatura] (2017)
44. Meszaros, J., Buchalcevova, A.: Introducing OSSF: a framework for online service cybersecurity risk management. Comput. Secur. **65**, 300–313 (2017)
45. Mtsweni, J.: Analyzing the security posture of South African websites, September 2015
46. Mtsweni, J., Shozi, N.A., Matenche, K., Mutemwa, M., Mkhonto, N., Van Vuuren, J.J.: Development of a semantic-enabled cybersecurity threat intelligence sharing model, pp. 244–252 (2016)
47. Murray, A., Begna, G., Nwafor, E., Blackstone, J., Patterson, W.: Cloud service security & application vulnerability, June 2015
48. Muñoz, F.R., Vega, E.A.A., Villalba, L.J.G.: Analyzing the traffic of penetration testing tools with anids. J. Supercomput. 1–16 (2016)
49. Nagurney, A., Shukla, S.: Multifirm models of cybersecurity investment competition vs. cooperation and network vulnerability. Eur. J. Oper. Res. **260**(2), 588–600 (2017)
50. Neuhaus, S., Plattner, B.: Software security economics: theory, in practice (2013)
51. Norris, D., Joshi, A., Finin, T.: Cybersecurity challenges to American state and local governments, pp. 196–202, January 2015
52. Ortiz, E.C., Reinerman-Jones, L.: Theoretical foundations for developing cybersecurity training. In: Shumaker, R., Lackey, S. (eds.) VAMR 2015. LNCS, vol. 9179, pp. 480–487. Springer, Cham (2015). https://doi.org/10.1007/978-3-319-21067-4_49
53. Pereira, T., Santos, H., Mendes, I.: Challenges and reflections in designing cyber security curriculum, pp. 47–51 (2017)
54. Rahman, S.S.M., May, Y.V.: Wireless security vulnerabilities and countermeasures for an airport, pp. 431–436 (2015)
55. Sabillon, R., Cavaller, V., Cano, J., Serra-Ruiz, J.: Cybercriminals, cyberattacks and cybercrime (2016)
56. Smeets, M.: A matter of time: on the transitory nature of cyber weapons. J. Strat. Stud. **41**, 1–28 (2017)
57. Song, J., Alves-Foss, J.: The Darpa cyber grand challenge: a competitor's perspective, part 2. IEEE Secur. Priv. **14**(1), 76–81 (2016)
58. Takahashi, T., Miyamoto, D., Nakao, K.: Toward automated vulnerability monitoring using open information and standardized tools (2016)
59. Tevis, J.-E.J., Hamilton, J.A.: Methods for the prevention, detection and removal of software security vulnerabilities. In: Proceedings of the 42nd Annual Southeast Regional Conference, ACM-SE 42, pp. 197–202. ACM, New York (2004)
60. Tweneboah-Koduah, S., Skouby, K.E., Tadayoni, R.: Cyber security threats to IoT applications and service domains. Wirel. Pers. Commun. **95**(1), 169–185 (2017)
61. Van Devender, M.S., Campbell, M., Glisson, W.B., Finan, M.A.: Identifying opportunities to compromise medical environments (2016)
62. Vassilev, A., Celi, C.: Avoiding cyberspace catastrophes through smarter testing. Computer **47**(10), 102–106 (2014)
63. Wang, Y., Yang, J.P.: Ethical hacking and network defense: choose your best network vulnerability scanning tool, pp. 110–113 (2017)
64. Watkins, L., Hurley, J.: Enhancing cybersecurity by defeating the attack lifecycle, pp. 320–327 (2016)
65. Williams, P.A.H., Woodward, A.J.: Cybersecurity vulnerabilities in medical devices: a complex environment and multifaceted problem. Med. Dev. Evid. Res. **8**, 305–316 (2015)
66. Wolff, J.: Perverse effects in defense of computer systems: when more is less. J. Manag. Inf. Syst. **33**(2), 597–620 (2016)

67. Wolff, J.: Perverse effects in defense of computer systems: when more is less, pp. 4823–4831, March 2016
68. Wu, W., Kang, R., Li, Z.: Risk assessment method for cybersecurity of cyber-physical systems based on inter-dependency of vulnerabilities, pp. 1618–1622, January 2016
69. Yang, J., Wang, Y., Reddington, T.: Integrate hacking technique into information assurance education, pp. 381–387 (2016)
70. Yang, Y., Xu, H.-Q., Gao, L., Yuan, Y.-B., McLaughlin, K., Sezer, S.: Multidimensional intrusion detection system for IEC 61850-based SCADA networks. IEEE Trans. Power Deliv. **32**(2), 1068–1078 (2017)
71. Yoo, H., Shon, T.: Challenges and research directions for heterogeneous cyber-physical system based on IEC61850: vulnerabilities, security requirements, and security architecture. Future Gener. Comput. Syst. **61**, 128–136 (2016)
72. Yoo, H., Shon, T.: Challenges and research directions for heterogeneous cyber–physical system based on IEC 61850: vulnerabilities, security requirements, and security architecture. Future Gener. Comput. Syst. **61**(Supplement C), 128–136 (2016)
73. Zetter, K.: Countdown to Zero Day: Stuxnet and the Launch of the World's First Digital Weapon. Crown Publishing Group, New York (2014)
74. Zissis, D., Lekkas, D.: Addressing cloud computing security issues. Future Gener. Comput. Syst. **28**(3), 583–592 (2012)

Data Science, Machine Learning, Algorithms, Computational Linguistics

Person, Organization, or Personage: Towards User Account Type Prediction in Microblogs

Ivan Samborskii[1,2], Andrey Filchenkov[1(✉)], Georgiy Korneev[1],
and Alex Farseev[1,3]

[1] ITMO University, 49 Kronverksky Pr., St. Petersburg 197101, Russia
{samborsky, kgeorgiy}@rain.ifmo.ru,
afilchenkov@corp.ifmo.ru
[2] National University of Singapore,
13 Computing Dr., Singapore 117417, Singapore
[3] SoMin Research, Singapore, Singapore
sasha@somin.ai

Abstract. During the past decade, microblog services have been extensively utilized by millions of business and private users as one of the most powerful information broadcasting tools. For example, Twitter attracted many social science researchers due to its high popularity, constrained format of thought expression, and the ability to react actual trends. However, unstructured data from microblogs often suffer from the lack of representativeness due to the tremendous amount of noise. Such noise is often introduced by the activity of organizational and fake user ac-counts that may not be useful in many application domains. Aiming to tackle the information filtering problem, in this paper, we classify Twitter accounts into three categories: "Personal", "Organization", and "Personage". Specifically, we utilize various text-based data representation approaches to extract features for our proposed microblog account type prediction framework "POP-MAP". To study the problem at a cross-language level, we harvested and learned from a multi-lingual Twitter dataset, which allows us to achieve better classification performance, as compared to various state-of-the-art baselines.

Keywords: Twitter · Social media · Profile learning ·
Natural language processing · Account type classification

1 Introduction

Web scientists use social media as a rich source of information about users' individuality, behavior, and preferences [9, 13, 15, 25]. It is used to recover user profile [3, 10, 12] and make targeted recommendation [11, 19]. The availability of these personal user attributes allows them to compete with traditional sociologists, epidemiologist and political experts in such tasks as voting outcome prediction [14, 24], disease outbreaks prediction [7, 17], or group population visualization [1]. However, the representativeness of the data in most of web science studies is extremely low due to the significant level of noise.

A. Chugunov et al. (Eds.): EGOSE 2018, CCIS 947, pp. 111–122, 2019.
https://doi.org/10.1007/978-3-030-13283-5_9

The noise in social media is often related to the fact that not all accounts represent a real human. For example, this can be caused by specific bots that mimic human behavior while being governed by an algorithm or another human. Many works are devoted to detecting such accounts [4–6, 26]. At the same time, some microblog accounts may not represent a person, but be related to something else: accounts of corporations (Adidas[1]), banks (DBS bank[2]), museums (The State Hermitage Museum[3]), animals (Grumpy Cat[4]), or personages (such as Harry Potter[5]). These accounts represent a certain subject that may or may not be equipped with the afore-mentioned personal user attributes (i.e. demographics). However, most of them are irrelevant to social studies.

Nevertheless, most of the existing social media analysis studies either do not perform irrelevant user account filtering [11, 12], perform it manually [16, 22], or do not utilize openly available user-generated data [20, 23]. For example, Tavares et al. [23] presented a method to classify personal and corporate accounts, which solved the problem with *84.6%* accuracy. However, the authors did not use user-generated content, which may result in a sub-optimal performance due to the lack of data representativeness. At the same time, Oentaryo et al. [20] utilized contextual, social, and temporal features, which allowed for achieving *91%* account type classification accuracy by gradient boosting algorithm. However, the employed data types are often not available for public use, which constrains the applicability of the proposed approach to real-world scenario.

Indeed, in our study, we perform the task of microblog user account type inference based on textual user-generated content only, which makes it applicable in the real-world settings. We assume that textual data is sufficient for achieving high classification performance and train our-proposed **"POP-MAP"** framework to perform "Person"-"Organization"-"Personage" Microblog Account Prediction.

2   On Microblog Account Typization

Microblog is a specific type of social media resource, which allows its users to share short status updates to their subscribers. One of the most well-known microblogs is Twitter, where messages (statuses) are publicly accessible in contrast to other big social networks, such as Facebook, and the length of message cannot exceed 140 symbols (280 since the end of 2017), which makes its posts standardized and rarely representing more than one topic [28].

According to Barone et al. [2], each Twitter account belongs to one of the following five types:

---

[1] http://twitter.com/adidas.

[2] http://twitter.com/dbsbank.

[3] http://twitter.com/hermitage_eng.

[4] http://twitter.com/realgrumpycat.

[5] http://twitter.com/arrypottah.

1. **Corporate Account**, which is typically a company news feed: Facebook[6], Google[7], Yandex[8], and VKontakte[9].
2. Corporate-led Persona Account, which is a corporate account that includes both personal and business sides. For example, an account of online shop Zappos[10] is Tony Hsieh's account, in fact.
3. Strictly Personal Account is an account representing an individual microblog user.
4. Business/Personal Hybrid Account is a mixture of the personal account and professional account types, where most of the tweets contain information about its user, but also a considerable number of tweets is dedicated to the user's professional interests. Accounts of famous people usually belong to this type, for example, Pavel Durov[11] or Jimmy Wales[12] accounts.
5. Personage Account, which is the personage-based account that typically is an animal, plant, or fictional hero.

In this paper, we adopt three most popular accounts types from the above categorization: organization account, personal account, and personage account. The other two hybrid types are considered to be a part of the selected ones, so that all the Corporate-led Persona Accounts are treated as organization accounts, while Business/Personal Accounts are considered to be personal accounts.

3 Feature Extraction

Classification algorithms strongly depend on features, which describe objects. Thus, feature engineering is a key step in solving most of the data mining problems. In this section, we de ne all the features we used to describe a Twitter account.

Words Frequency. Individual users typically use everyday vocabulary in their tweets, while organizations may adopt a domain-specific vocabulary that can be a good indicator of the organization account type. In accordance with this assumption, we use the following features:

– average word frequency among all words in tweet;
– average word frequency among all words in all user's tweets.

We utilized Sharov's Frequency Dictionary[13] and Word frequency data[14] for obtaining general usage frequency of Russian and English words respectively.

---

[6] http://twitter.com/facebook.

[7] http://twitter.com/google.

[8] http://twitter.com/yandex.

[9] http://twitter.com/vkontakte.

[10] http://twitter.com/zeppos.

[11] http://twitter.com/durov.

[12] http://twitter.com/jimmy_wales.

[13] http://dict.ruslang.ru/freq.php.

[14] http://www.wordfrequency.info.

Spelling Mistakes. It is well-known that individual user accounts tend to post more grammatical mistakes/misspellings as compared to properly-maintained organizational accounts. Inspired by this phenomenon, we utilized Language-Tool[15] to extract the number of mistakes/misspellings per account.

Hashtags. Hashtags are often used for grouping microblog messages and improvement of Twitter search. Personal accounts are characterized by extensive use of hashtags to express their thoughts, feelings, as compared to corporate accounts. We thus extracted the following hashtag-based features:

- average number of unique hashtags per account;
- average number of hashtags per tweet;
- average length of hashtag per tweet.

Users' Mentions. Similar to hashtags, user mentions spread in social networks. However, we cannot expect personage accounts to use them often due to the lower number of actual social ties between them and individual Twitter users. To incorporate this aspect, we extracted the following user mention features:

- average number of unique mentions per account;
- average number of mentions per tweet;
- average length of mention per tweet.

Tweet/Word Length. Many acronyms (i.e. "gotcha" meaning "I got you") widespread among users of social networks. The reason is that they are useful to t in more information into short twitter message. These acronyms, however, are not popular among organizational twitter accounts. Therefore, we extracted the following features representing text length:

- average length of word per account;
- average length of tweet per account.

Part of Speech (POS). To reflect different styles of language use, we included features related to words' POS. The following POS groups have been identified:

- noun;
- verb;
- personal pronoun;
- pronoun (others);
- adjective;
- adverb;
- preposition, conjunction, particle;
- adverb + adjective;
- adverb + adverb.

---

[15] http://languagetool.org.

For each group, we then calculated the following features:

- average number of groups per account;
- average number of groups per tweet;
- average number of negative particles per account.

Personal Words. Accounts belonging to people or personages can be easily identified by the so-called personal words. Inspired by this fact, we extracted "average number of personal words per account" feature.

Symbols. Similarly, to previous studies, for each symbol in Table 1, we calculated the following features:

- average number of signs per tweet;
- average number of unique signs per tweet;
- average number of tweets with a sign per account;
- average number of a sign per tweet;
- average number of tweets with signs per account;
- average number of unique signs per account.

Table 1. Symbols that are used to calculate features.

!	@	#	$	%	&	*	(
)	_	+	-	=	~	'	,
.	<	>	/	?	\	|	;
:	`	[	]	{	}	№	"

Emoticons. Similar to the symbol features, for each group of emoticons in Table 2, we calculated emotion features:

- average number of emoticons per tweet;
- average number of tweets with emoticon per account;
- average number of a emoticon per tweet;
- average number of unique emoticons per account.

Vocabulary Uniqueness. Organization accounts on Twitter are often created to be used for specific applications. For example, Yandex.Taxi[16] is designed to support taxi services, while Yandex.Market[17] is related to e-commerce services aggregation. Every specific usage domain reduces the diversity of words in organizations' microblog

---

[16] http://twitter.com/yandextaxi.

[17] http://twitter.com/yandexmarket.

Table 2. Emoticons groups that are used to calculate features.

:) :-) =)	:(:-(= (	;);-)
8) 8-) %) %-)	:') :'-) :,) :,-) = ') = ,)	:'(:'-(:,(:,-(= '(= ,(
:* :-* = *	O_o o_O = O = 0 0_0	:-b :-p :b :p = p = b;b;p
:D xD = D;D	:-[= [:3 > <	

accounts. Based on this assumption, we extracted the following vocabulary-uniqueness features:

– average number of unique words per account;
– average number of words not from a vocabulary per account.

Hyperlinks. Users often post URLs to third-party resources, such as events, pictures, etc. The URL usage can be a good indicator of individual user accounts. Based on this assumption, we extracted the features below:

– average number of links per account;
– average number of tweets with links per account.

Twitter-Specific Features. Organization accounts are often characterized by a large number of subscribers (followers), but a relatively small number of subscriptions (following). This is also the case of popular personage accounts. Also, it is worth mentioning that corporate accounts are often verified, which often does not hold for personal accounts, while personage accounts are almost never verified.

– number of subscribers;
– number of subscriptions;
– if the account is verified;
– average number of "favorite" tweets.

Overall, there we suggest *136* features for Twitter account type classification. It is worth mentioning that some of them (such as usage of hashtags, hyperlinks, and personal words) were never adapted before and, thus, they are one of the contributions of this study.

4   Experiment Setup

4.1   Data Collection

Due to the lack of publicly available datasets on Twitter account type inference, we collected our dataset. To do so, we developed a crawler for downloading last $n = 500$ tweets of each specified user, where the list of account names was created manually.

4.2   Utilized Machine Learning Methods

We employed the following commonly-utilized classification baselines that are implemented as part of WEKA[18] machine learning library: k-nearest neighbors, Naïve Bayes classifier, Support Vector Machines (SVM) classifier, Decision Trees (its C4.5 version), and Random Forest. These algorithms were applied to the profiles represented by our-extracted POP-MAP features that were presented in Sect. 3.

We used several feature selection (FS) algorithms [27] to select only representative features:

- dependency-based elimination, such as: CFS-BiS, CFS-GS, CFS-LS, CFS-RS, CFS-SBS, CFS-SFS, CFS-SWS, CFS-TS;
- consistency-based elimination, such as: Cons-BiS, Cons-GS, Cons-LS, Cons-RS, Cons-SBS, Cons-SFS, Cons-SWS;
- Significant algorithm, which is based on estimating feature "significance";
- ReliefF measures feature importance based on comparison to similar objects of the same class.

In addition, we utilized the well-known dimensionality reduction algorithm PCA that is also implemented in WEKA.

To evaluate the prediction performance by using the two well-adopted evaluation measures: accuracy and F-measure. We organized model evaluation using 5-fold cross validation.

5   Experiments on Russian Text Corpora

We have collected the sample consisting of *298* Russian personal accounts, *160* Russian organization accounts and *151* Russian personage accounts by the tool and method, described in the previous section.

5.1   Comparing Baselines

Since there are no existing solutions for the problem of microblog account type inference, we consider standard text classification techniques as our baselines:

- **Naïve Bayes** (*NB*) is a simple Naïve Bayes classifier with minor preprocessing (all hyperlinks are removed and letters are changed to lowercase) [8].
- **Classifier with stemmer** (*Stemmer*) is NB with Porter's stemmer applied [21].
- **Classifier with emoticons** (*Emoticon*) is the classifier from Lin [18] work, which determines chat users' age and gender based on emoticons in users' posts. To implement this method, we identified *500* different emoticons.

The baseline results are presented in Table 3. As we can see, stemming has expectedly improved *NB* but outperformed *Emoticon*. This is possibly due to organizations use less formal language in Twitter than we expected.

---

[18] http://www.cs.waikato.ac.nz/ml/weka/.

Table 3. Results of baselines for account classification for the Russian language.

Classifier	Accuracy	*F*-measure
NB	0.711	0.678
Stemmer	**0.749**	**0.702**
Emoticon	*0.511*	0.519

5.2   Comparing Approaches Trained POP-MAP Features

MAP without Feature Selection. We conducted experiments using the setup described in Sect. 4 on the collected dataset. The results are presented in Table 4. The best performance was shown by Random Forest, which is consistent with previous study [12] and can be explained by its feature selection ability.

POP-MAP with Feature Selection. To improve classification performance, we applied dimensionality reduction algorithms described in Sect. 4. First, we applied PCA. As we can see from Table 5, PCA did not improve the classification performance.

Then we picked the best feature selection algorithm for each classifier with respect to the resulting performance. The evaluation results are presented in Table 6. As it can be seen, feature selection improved performance of all the models. However, Random Forest kept its position of the best classifier, which can be explained by its additional built-in feature selection ability.

Table 4. Results for account classification for the Russian language without feature selection.

Classifier	Accuracy	*F*-measure
*k*NN	0.770	0.761
Naïve Bayes	0.645	0.688
SVM	0.490	0.219
Decision Tree	0.792	0.789
Random Forest	**0.862**	**0.858**
Best baseline (Stemmer)	0.749	0.702

Table 5. Results for account classification for the Russian language with PCA.

Classifier	Accuracy	*F*-measure
*k*NN	0.719	0.708
Naïve Bayes	0.495	0.547
SVM	0.820	0.815
Decision Tree	0.720	0.712
Random Forest	0.806	0.801
Best baseline (no FS)	**0.862**	**0.858**

5.3   Results Summary

From the Table 6, it can be seen that the best performance was achieved by Random Forest classifier on the CFC-TS-preprocessed data. The contingency matrix is presented in Table 7 shows us that the resulting classifier makes a small number of misclassifications, while the most complex task for it is to distinguish between personal accounts and personage accounts. This can be explained by the similar nature of these two types of accounts, which conforms well with manual comparison of such accounts.

We used mutual information (MI) measure to estimate feature importance. The most valuable features are average number of personal words per account (0.679), average number of personal pronouns per tweet (0.633), average number of personal words per tweet (0.472), average number of links per account (0.402), and a number of subscriptions (0.378). Among other features with MI greater than 0.2, seven are POS features, one is tweets with links per account, two are tweets length features.

Table 6. Results for account classification for the Russian language with feature selection.

Classifier	Accuracy	F-measure	FS algorithm	Number of features
kNN	0.799	0.792	CFS-RS	29
Naïve Bayes	0.795	0.790	ReliefF	44
SVM	0.639	0.616	Cons-SS	10
Decision Tree	0.813	0.808	CFS-BiS	23
Random Forest	**0.878**	**0.874**	CFS-TS	23
Random Forest	0.862	0.858	–	136

Table 7. Contingency table of the best classifier for the Russian language.

	Person	Organization	Personage
Person	55	1	6
Organization	1	32	1
Personage	3	0	23

As we can see, the most important features are related to personality and references. We may expect the same situation and for the English language.

6   Experiments on English Text Corpora

6.1   Dataset

To perform evaluation on English corpora, we have collected the sample consisting of 281 English personal accounts, 130 English organization accounts and 130 English personage accounts using the tool and method described in Sect. 3.

6.2   Results

In this setup, we tested only Random Forest since it has shown the ultimate performance for the Russian language. The best-achieved result was after applying Con-GS algorithm selecting *44* features and resulting in *0.894* of accuracy and *0.879* of F-measure. The contingency table is presented in Table 8. The resulting classifier also makes only a small number of mistakes. As we can see, the classifier for English corpora outperforms the best one for Russian corpora classifier.

Table 8. Contingency table of the best classifier for the English language.

	Person	Organization	Personage
Person	52	0	4
Organization	1	23	3
Personage	1	1	24

The most valuable features with respect to the MI are: number of subscriptions (*0.709*), average number of personal words per account (*0.516*), if the ac-count is verified (*0.479*), average number of tweets with links per account (*0.290*), average number of unique signs per account (*0.274*). Among other features with MI greater than *0.2*, four are symbol features, one is number of subscribers, one is average number of hyperlinks per tweet, and one is average length of tweets.

We can see that personal words are also the strong feature besides Twitter-specific features. However, POS-tagged features are not at the top as in Russia. Instead, symbol-specific features are useful for English.

6.3   Results for Binary Classification

We also compared our results with results, reported in [23], where authors classified microblog accounts only into personal and corporate types. To do so, we selected only personal and organization accounts from the initial datasets and run the best-built classifiers for English and Russian. The results of the comparison are presented in Table 9. As it can be seen, the POP-MAP results on both the Russian and English corpora are similarly high and significantly surpass the behavior-based approach.

Table 9. Results of baselines for account classification for the Russian language.

Algorithm	Accuracy	F-measure
User's behavior [23]	0.846	–
POP-MAP for English	0.975	0.947
POP-MAP for Russian	0.969	0.966

7   Conclusion

In this paper, we addressed the problem of Twitter account classification. We described *136* features, which we then used in different classification models. We run experiments on corpora of Russian and English tweets and achieve similarly high classification performance for both languages with the Random Forest model.

However, we discovered that there is a difference in text feature importance for two languages, while Twitter-specific features have the same importance. The only exception is a strong feature related to personal words that are useful in both English and Russian.

The research is supported by the Government of the Russian Federation, Grant 08-08.

References

1. Aramaki, E., Maskawa, S., Morita, M.: Twitter catches the flu: detecting influenza epidemics using twitter. In: Proceedings of the Conference on Empirical Methods in Natural Language Processing, pp. 1568–1576. Association for Computational Linguistics (2011)
2. Barone, L.: Which type of twitter account should you create? (2010). http://smallbiztrends.com/2010/02/types-of-twitter-accounts.html. Accessed 15 Apr 2016
3. Bartunov, S., Korshunov, A., Park, S.-T., Ryu, W., Lee, H.: Joint link-attribute user identity resolution in online social networks. In: Proceedings of the 6th International Conference on Knowledge Discovery and Data Mining, Workshop on Social Network Mining and Analysis. ACM (2012)
4. Boshmaf, Y., Muslukhov, I., Beznosov, K., Ripeanu, M.: Design and analysis of a social botnet. Comput. Netw. **57**(2), 556–578 (2013)
5. Cao, Q., Sirivianos, M., Yang, X., Pregueiro, T.: Aiding the detection of fake accounts in large scale social online services. In: Presented as Part of the 9th USENIX Symposium on Networked Systems Design and Implementation, NSDI 2012, pp. 197–210 (2012)
6. Chu, Z., Gianvecchio, S., Wang, H., Jajodia, S.: Who is tweeting on Twitter: human, bot, or cyborg? In: Proceedings of the 26th Annual Computer Security Applications Conference, pp. 21–30. ACM (2010)
7. Culotta, A.: Towards detecting influenza epidemics by analyzing twitter messages. In: Proceedings of the First Workshop on Social Media Analytics, pp. 115–122. ACM (2010)
8. Deitrick, W., Miller, Z., Valyou, B., Dickinson, B., Munson, T., Wei, H.: Gender identification on twitter using the modified balanced winnow. Commun. Netw. **4**(3), 1–7 (2012)
9. Farseev, A., Akbari, M., Samborskii, I., Chua, T.-S.: 360° user profiling: past, future, and applications. ACM SIGWEB Newslett, (Summer), Article no. 4 (2016)
10. Farseev, A., Chua, T.-S.: TweetFit: fusing sensors and multiple social media for wellness profile learning. In: Proceedings of the Thirty-First AAAI Conference on Artificial Intelligence. AAAI (2017)
11. Farseev, A., Kotkov, D., Semenov, A., Veijalainen, J., Chua, T.-S.: Cross-social network collaborative recommendation. In: Proceedings of the ACM Web Science Conference, p. 38. ACM (2015)
12. Farseev, A., Nie, L., Akbari, M., Chua, T.-S.: Harvesting multiple sources for user profile learning: a big data study. In: Proceedings of the 5th ACM on International Conference on Multimedia Retrieval, pp. 235–242. ACM (2015)

13. Farseev, A., Samborskii, I., Chua, T.-S.: bBridge: a big data platform for social multimedia analytics. In: Proceedings of the 2016 ACM Conference on Multimedia, pp. 759–761. ACM (2016)
14. Filchenkov, A.A., Azarov, A.A., Abramov, M.V.: What is more predictable in social media: election outcome or protest action? In: Proceedings of the 2014 Conference on Electronic Governance and Open Society: Challenges in Eurasia, pp. 157–161. ACM (2014)
15. Hendler, J., Shadbolt, N., Hall, W., Berners-Lee, T., Weitzner, D.: Web science: an interdisciplinary approach to understanding the web. Commun. ACM **51**(7), 60–69 (2008)
16. Kafeza, E., Kanavos, A., Makris, C., Vikatos, P.: T-PICE: Twitter personality based influential communities extraction system. In: 2014 IEEE International Congress on Big Data, pp. 212–219. IEEE (2014)
17. Lee, K., Agrawal, A., Choudhary, A.: Real-time disease surveillance using twitter data: demonstration on flu and cancer. In: Proceedings of the 19th ACM SIGKDD International Conference on Knowledge Discovery and Data Mining, pp. 1474–1477. ACM (2013)
18. Lin, J.: Automatic author profiling of online chat logs. Ph.D. thesis, Monterey, California. Naval Postgraduate School (2007)
19. Lin, J., Sugiyama, K., Kan, M.-T., Chua, T.-S.: Addressing cold-start in app recommendation: latent user models constructed from twitter followers. In: Proceedings of the 36th International ACM SIGIR Conference on Research and Development in Information Retrieval, pp. 283–292. ACM (2013)
20. Oentaryo, R.J., Low, J.-W., Lim, E.-P.: Chalk and Cheese in twitter: discriminating personal and organization accounts. In: Hanbury, A., Kazai, G., Rauber, A., Fuhr, N. (eds.) ECIR 2015. LNCS, vol. 9022, pp. 465–476. Springer, Cham (2015). https://doi.org/10.1007/978-3-319-16354-3_51
21. Porter, M.F.: An algorithm for suffix stripping. Program **14**(3), 130–137 (1980)
22. Schwartz, H.A., et al.: Personality, gender, and age in the language of social media: the open-vocabulary approach. PLoS One **8**(9), e73791 (2013)
23. Tavares, G., Faisal, A.: Scaling-laws of human broadcast communication enable distinction between human, corporate and robot twitter users. PLoS One **8**(7), e65774 (2013)
24. Tsakalidis, A., Papadopoulos, S., Cristea, A.I., Kompatsiaris, Y.: Predicting elections for multiple countries using twitter and polls. IEEE Intell. Syst. **30**(2), 10–17 (2015)
25. Varlamov, M.I., Turdakov, D.Y.: A survey of methods for the extraction of information from web resources. Program. Comput. Softw. **42**(5), 279–291 (2016)
26. Wang, A.H.: Detecting spam bots in online social networking sites: a machine learning approach. In: Foresti, S., Jajodia, S. (eds.) DBSec 2010. LNCS, vol. 6166, pp. 335–342. Springer, Heidelberg (2010). https://doi.org/10.1007/978-3-642-13739-6_25
27. Wang, G., Song, Q., Sun, H., Zhang, X., Xu, B., Zhou, Y.: A feature subset selection algorithm automatic recommendation method. J. Artif. Intell. Res. **47**, 1–34 (2013)
28. Zhao, W.X., et al.: Comparing twitter and traditional media using topic models. In: Clough, P., et al. (eds.) ECIR 2011. LNCS, vol. 6611, pp. 338–349. Springer, Heidelberg (2011). https://doi.org/10.1007/978-3-642-20161-5_34

Mining and Indexing of Legal Natural Language Texts with Domain and Task Ontology

Galina Kurcheeva[1], Marina Rakhvalova[2], Daria Rakhvalova[1], and Maxim Bakaev[1(✉)] (iD)

[1] Novosibirsk State Technical University, Novosibirsk, Russia
bakaev@corp.nstu.ru
[2] Siberian Transport University, Novosibirsk, Russia

Abstract. Today's legislation lags behind the needs and practices of the Internet, electronic governance and digital economy in general. It is widely believed that enhancement of the legal system with IT to facilitate law-making and law enforcement can contribute to improvement of business and social environment, as well as people's quality of life. Our paper is a study of foundations and means for building Legal Knowledge-Based Systems and transition to the so-called computational law. Particularly, we outline the application of legal and regulatory documents indexing technologies for legal language processing (LLP) and construct domain ontology for real estate legislation. The implementation of the approach may decrease the number of errors, overcomplexities and ambiguities in legal texts, allow automated search for relevant documents, and categorize complicated legal relations. These should save the practitioners from spending too much time on routine tasks, simplify decision-making in law enforcement and reduce the subjectivity, and ultimately contribute to creating uniform and consistent legislation.

Keywords: Computational law · Indexing · Document similarity · Full-text search · Law enforcement · Text analysis

1 Introduction

According to the *Strategy of scientific and technological development of the Russian Federation*, among the highest priorities are "transition towards leading digital and intelligent production technologies, robotic systems, new materials and construction methods, creation of systems for big data processing, machine learning and artificial intelligence", "capability for the Russian society to respond to major challenges involving interaction of human and nature, human and technologies, social institutions on the current stage of the global development, particularly through application of methods from the humanities" [1, paragraph 20].

The project activities department of the Russian Government has prepared proposals on digitalization of law-making and law enforcement to enhance the somewhat outdated legislation, which should aid in improving the business and social environments, as well as the quality of life indexes. The issues of automated law-making based

© Springer Nature Switzerland AG 2019
A. Chugunov et al. (Eds.): EGOSE 2018, CCIS 947, pp. 123–137, 2019.
https://doi.org/10.1007/978-3-030-13283-5_10

on artificial intelligence (AI) are being actively discussed, since this development direction was stated by the "Digital Economy" program asserted in July 2017 by the government. They also devise the actions plan for legal regulation in the digitalized economy, among which the development of machine-readable language for law-making and application of AI for analysis of legal acts.

The today's legal reality, shaped by the society's development needs, requires holistic legal regulation of social relations and, thus, consistent and unified law-making. Besides, it is necessary to follow all the principles and rules of the legal technique, binding for all the law-makers: the stability of legislation, advisability, timelessness, system analysis, completeness and concreteness of regulation, unambiguity of legal acts interpretation by all the legal relations subjects [2, p. 7], including the judicial authorities. At the same time, as noted by some researches, the persisting important problem in legal regulation is certain skewness in the legislation and lack of systematic vision for its development [3]. Ignorance and non-compliance with the legal technique inevitably cause errors in law-making that subsequently lead to imbalance in legislation. The harmoniousness of legislation must be ensured by rigorous application of the technique in every document's adoption, but at the same time imperfections of law-making are widely noted by both law theorists [4] and practicians from various branches of the law [5]. We, after many other researchers, lawyers and even politicians, argue that legal expert systems could significantly advance digitalization of the law-making and law enforcement.

The international legal practice has known software expert systems for solving individual tasks since the 1970s – more than 25 research projects in AI application in law has been carried out in USA, Germany and Great Britain. JUDITH (1975) developed by Heidelberg and Darmstadt Universities was one of the first legal expert systems that allowed the lawyers to obtain expert opinions on civil cases. The knowledgebase of the system contained prerequisites and executive files that indicate the relationships between the prerequisites; JUDITH could be also used for studying the legal reasoning [6]. Another example is Shyster system for consulting in case-based law [6]. There is currently ongoing development in creation [7] and integration [8] of legal ontologies and the so-called Legal Knowledge Based Systems that use them: e.g. for classification of cases based on natural language processing [9], or for structuring the selection of legal documents [10]. The "legal tech" industry in the USA and Europe is currently booming, and the "robotized" legal services are often cheaper and more efficient than the ones provided by humans. The exponential growth in popularity of new services is already reshaping the industry, and it's forecasted by *Deloitte* that in Great Britain alone computer algorithms will replace 114 thousands lawyers (39% of their total number) in the next 20 years.

However, since the semantic analysis technologies are language-dependent and legislations in different countries are very much diverse [11], the results and products from one country generally cannot be directly employed in another one, while the approaches and frameworks [12] can only be partially useful. In Russia, the most widely used legal systems are Consultant Plus and Garant, which are essentially legal assistance systems capable of finding relevant texts by keywords, thus allowing selection of legal materials. Also, reasonably popular are expert legal systems employed in forensic science and investigations, but their functionality is understandably limited. Most expert systems used in Russia are of management or technological domains, so the current practice suggests that the country is quite far from introduction of computational law [13].

Effectiveness of legal acts is the result of their enforcement, testifying the ability of legal norms to resolve the corresponding social and legal issues, considering the resources spent on the enforcement. The evaluation of the effectiveness is carried out during legal monitoring and it needs to also produce recommendations on how to implement the norms and make legal decisions in a more efficient way. One recognized way to increase this organizational quality is implementation and utilization of legal ontology-based intelligent systems. Developing such a system generally involves application of special juridical methods, construction of ontology for automated nat-ural- (or, rather legal-) language text processing and mining, choosing and applying vectorization models, semantic analysis of the texts with classical and heuristic algo-rithms, as well as general AI and machine learning methods, such as artificial neural networks, regression analysis, etc.

In our current work we focus on development of legal ontologies, specific for the legal texts mining and indexing tasks. The remaining of our paper has the following structure. In Sect. 2 we describe methods and tools in knowledge engineering that are relevant for the problem, and briefly justify the use of OWL as the knowledge repre-sentation format. In Sect. 3, we perform analysis in housing legislation with respect to relations between lexical and judicial terms and then provide description of demo OWL ontology module implementation in the popular Protégé editor. In Conclusions we summarize our contribution and outline directions for further work.

2   Methods and Tools

A formalized approach should be able to identify and overcome flaws in law-making and law enforcement, since legislation is the basis for law enforcement, which is in turn operationalization of the effective legal acts. One possible way to increase the effec-tiveness of legal regulation is monitoring of law enforcement [14] that is generally positively assessed by researchers [15, 16]. This legal monitoring is the systematic activities by the responsible governmental bodies, research community, society insti-tutions and organizations in evaluation, analysis, generalization and forecasting of the legislation status and enforcement practice. The monitoring of the law enforcement, particularly of legal proceedings, allows identification of effectiveness of various legal acts and selected legal norms, forecasting of the future state of social relations (both the ones regulated by the laws and the ones outside the legal system), making proposals on systematic improvement of laws and regulation, i.e. correcting the legal norms and the law enforcement practice [17].

We presume that the main directions for solving the above problems should be the analysis of pending and effective legal acts in the following aspects:

Identification of Legal Acts Regulating the Respective Social Relations for Introducing Coordinated Modifications. High intensiveness of law-making on various levels often causes the modifications to be fragmented and inconsistent, as the novelties lack unified logics. Some of the errors inflicted by the law-makers and the impossibility to incorporate the new law into the legislation are only found during law enforcement. There is currently lack of pre-emptive measures, but it is highly desired to identify all the related legal acts already during the new law's development stage, to make coordinated changes in all of them.

Identification of Gaps in the Legislation. The gaps in legislation are unavoidable, but a high number of them inevitably imply low level of legal regulation of social relations. Among the causes for the gaps are both objective factors, as legislation always lags behind the real life that brings on new forms of social relations, and subjective ones, related to the law quality of law-making. Law-related literature has quite a lot of research on individual gaps and the ways for overcoming them [18, 19], but there's lack of integral solutions that could allow avoiding the gaps during the legal act's development stage.

Identification of Collisions in the Legislation Legal science knows the concept of the legal collision and their types [20], but just as for the gaps, no pre-emptive technologies exist that could effectively detect the collisions. The developers of laws identify them "manually", generally relying on legal reference systems.

Unification of the Conceptual Apparatus Employed in the Legal Acts [21]. Ambiguity in lexical terms is always a serious challenge in such a complex domain as legal system. The growing specialization of knowledge increases the amount of scientific and technological terms, special expressions, etc. To attain the uniformness of legal terms, it is necessary to consistently use the same terms throughout the normative texts [22]. Meanwhile, the attempts to unify the legal terms, such as the one undertaken by the Russian Legal Academy of the Ministry of Justice in regard to the laws developed by the Federal executive power bodies [23, p. 56] have not so far gained wide application and did not resolve the problem.

Anti-corruption Inspection of the Legal Acts Drafts. According to the current legislation, the anti-corruption inspection is carried out on Federal, Regional and Municipal levels. The legal foundation for the inspection is laws and by-law documents [24, 25], while law-related literature contains quite a lot of works dedicated to the legal aspects of such inspection [26, 27]. However, its AI-based automation has drawn the researchers' attention just during the few last years, and there's clear lack of effective solutions in this field.

2.1 Technologies for Knowledge Representation and Reasoning

Semantic analysis, which is the prime technology for extracting meaning from texts, generally involves indexing – describing the text with a set of special terms extracted from the text or taken from a constrained (controlled) dictionary. Information retrieval systems perform indexing, formulation of query (user's information needs specified in a language understood by the system) and its comparison with the available (indexed) information. The most widely used technologies for creating indexes are [28]:

1. **Bag of words:** a set of unrelated terms (sometimes also called tags) that describe a certain object or information resource. Bag of words indexing/classification is currently widely applied to multidimensional objects such as audio, video or images, in data stores and recommender systems.
2. **Taxonomy:** when terms describing a domain form a hierarchy of categories, a taxonomy is a structure that generally has high clarity and is easy to comprehend due to the fact that only one semantic relation is used in such representation, that is, "parent – child". However, such choice of the relation imposes certain limitations.
3. **Thesaurus:** a collection of terms and word combinations grouped into units named concepts. They are organized either hierarchically or with semantic (associative) relations. The chosen relations form a pre-defined and fixed set which generally includes such relations as "parent – child", "part – whole", "cause – effect", or linguistic relationships.
4. **Ontology:** when a domain (field of knowledge) is formally described with concepts (classes), their attributes, relations between them, application axioms, and constraints, this description forms ontology. Thus, ontologies are more flexible than thesauri since ontology includes any kind of semantic relations, and at the same time permits a more detailed domain specification due to attributes, constraints, axioms, etc.

Since the 1990s, ontologies have been applied in Information Science for knowledge representation, management and integration; they are the key element in the Semantic Web concept. Currently, the following types of ontologies are identified based on their purpose: upper ontologies, domain-specific, and task-specific ontologies. The former aim to describe universal knowledge or codify the use of language (e.g., ontology specification language); perhaps, one of the most prominent examples is CYC, a common sense knowledge ontology. The scope of domain-specific ontologies is a certain domain of knowledge (e.g. LKIF for legislation [29]), while task-specific ontologies are even more concrete and generally built for a particular application. Another important advantage of ontologies that gained wide use since the 2000s, when several ontology libraries were created, is relative ease of integration. That is, domain ontology can be developed based on the concepts available in already existing upper ontology, even though finding a relevant ontology for integration or reuse [8] may involve additional research work.

So, the generally recognized benefits from using ontologies include:

- joint usage of common information structure by people and software agents;
- ability to re-use domain knowledge specified in ontologies;
- specification of explicit assumptions in the domain;
- possibility to formally analyze the domain knowledge.

All the above aspects are relevant for legal analysis, studies of juridical processes, legal acts development and decision-making. In the current work we will focus on ontology integration and analysis of the legal terms application, including improper usage, duplication, etc.

2.2 LKIF Core Ontology

In the quest for specifying the conceptualization in the legal domain, existing ontologies do provide some basis for reuse on the upper levels. However, the details differ on domain level, due to inconsistencies in national legislations and legislation systems, such as Anglosaxon vs. Continental laws. Task-specific ontologies, such as the ones for legal texts mining and indexing, generally have to be created anew for different languages and nations.

Let us illustrate this on the basis of Legal Knowledge Interchange Format (LKIF) ontology [29], which was created for the "translation of existing legal knowledge bases to other representation formats" and "has a firm grounding in commonsense". The authors seek to introduce architecture for developing legal knowledge systems and facilitate the exchange of knowledge between the existing systems. The overall structure of LKIF Core is presented in Fig. 1.

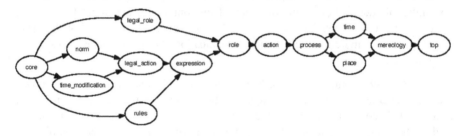

Fig. 1. Structure of LKIF (Core modules) [29].

Some modules need virtually no changes per various nations and legislation systems (example in Fig. 2). Some parts of the ontology under integration have to be closely examined for necessary changes and adaptations to national legislations (example in Fig. 3). The important technical issue in the ontology integration is the knowledge representation format. During the last decade, OWL (Web Ontology Language) prescribed by the W3C [30] is becoming the de-facto standard, even though certain modifications to it do exist.

2.3 OWL Ontologies and Protégé Editor

The general requirements towards ontology languages include [31]:

1. a well-defined syntax,
2. a well-defined semantics,
3. efficient reasoning support,
4. sufficient expressive power,
5. convenience of expression.

To address these requirements, some of which can be actually incompatible, the W3C's Web Ontology Working Group has devised Web Ontology Language (OWL), whose major family members currently include OWL Full, OWL DL, and OWL Lite.

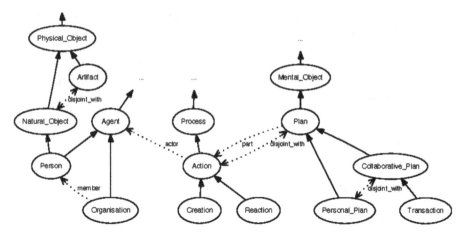

Fig. 2. Actions, agents and organizations in LKIF [29].

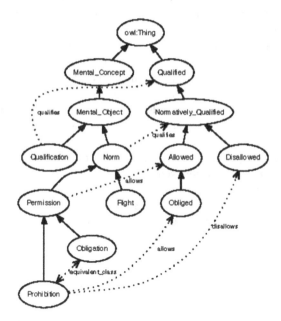

Fig. 3. Qualifications and norms in LKIF [29].

OWL has the highest level of expressivity compared to many other knowledge representation formats and the relations between classes in OWL ontology can be formally modeled based on description logics. Basically, it adds semantics to data schema and allows specification of many details about classes (concepts) and their properties. Another important advantage of OWL with respect to ontology integration is that it can be serialized in many languages and notations (RDF/XML, Turtle, etc.) and even stored in more traditional relational databases [32].

A popular tool for creating and managing OWL ontologies is free and open-source Protégé-OWL editor developed by Stanford University's Center for Biomedical Informatics Research (https://protege.stanford.edu/). It provides GUI interface, framework for adding extra components (e.g. for graphical representation of the ontology), supports names in different languages and encodings, allows OWL ontology export to several formats and has modular ontology support.

In the next section we first perform analysis of a legal branch domain with respect to relations between lexical and judicial terms and then describe the formal conceptualization as demo OWL ontology in Protégé editor.

3   Implementation

Development of a domain ontology involves the following principal steps:

1. **Defining the purpose and scope of the ontology.** Legal ontologies are the basis for legal intelligent systems that perform the tasks we previously outlined. In our current paper, we are developing an example ontology for a domain of limited scope – the housing legislation.
2. **Considering existing ontologies.** As we mentioned before, existing upper level legal ontologies can and should be used in the undertaking. However, particulars of national legislations generally make it impossible to re-use ontologies that conceptualize legislations of other countries and in different languages.
3. **Listing the relevant terms (concepts) and structuring them.** The list of the relevant terms and the relations between them in our work are provided by domain experts (practicing lawyers) who extracted them from existing legal documents. The structuring is mainly performed with a top-down approach.
4. **Specification of properties, allowed values (facets) and individuals.** Again, in our work these are specified based on the information extracted from domain experts and the acting legal documents. Based on the ontology goals, we are also introducing some semantic relations between the concepts.

3.1   The Housing Legislation

As an implementation example, in our current work we focus on housing legislation with respect to the following most urgent issues:

1. Identification of legal acts that contain the conceptual apparatus under analysis and can be subject to the modifications.
2. Identification of various types of collisions in the legislation.
3. Unification of the conceptual apparatus used in the legal acts.

The research has been done with the basic concepts in the housing legislation for the purpose of revealing the uniformity of their application in the normative legal acts of the constitutional, civil, housing, criminal and other branches of legislation, as well as the possibility of identifying the distinguishing features of the concepts under study. Together with the domain experts, we build ontology "module" with the terms that relate to the identified and classified problems that the authors found in the legislation, such as "premises" (помещение), "house" (жилище), "living premises" (жилое помещение) and "housing" (жильё). "Living premises" is the foundational concept in the housing legislation and *is a kind of* "premises". At the same time, Russian legislation in various domains also use the terms "house" and "housing" that do not always carry meaning. They are often used hierarchically and have ambiguous meaning, which contradicts to the legal technique requirements (resulting in collision) and decreasing both efficiency and effectiveness of law-making and law enforcement. The "living premises" term is used in a very large number of legal acts – in 700 just federal laws. However, some of them in quite a chaotic manner also contain the terms "house" and "housing", which unlike "living premises" are never explained in legislation or doctrine. Sometimes they are used as synonyms, but sometimes they contradict each other and the "living premises" term and alter the meaning of a legal regulation. According to the rules of logics, "living premises" must be a subset of "premises", but even this is not always respected. To make the issue even worse, the existing legal search systems (Consultant Plus and Garant) do not distinguish the terms and the search on "house" returns all the legal acts containing the terms with the same root.

Such an approach appears not just methodologically incorrect and complicating the application of legal acts, but also plain dangerous. According to the rules of logics, each concept has its own meaning that is expressed through certain terms – i.e. word or expression that is unambiguous for the term in all scientific fields. The reasoning behind the existing search engines is understandable – the search is performed based on associations (Fig. 1), and the above terms both have the same root and the same association with the place to live. With respect to legal search (that in this case offers virtually no means for refining the query), these additional results just cause the need for extra information processing – a mere inconvenience, – but in legal acts development it may lead (and actually does lead, as the analysis of legislation and the law enforcement suggests) to major errors. Consequently, the accurate implementation of rules prescribed by legal technique is essential in such situation.

Currently, the concept best detailed in Russian legislation and doctrine is "living premises", derived from the doctrinal concept "premises". The following are the attributes of the "premises":

1. Being a real estate object;
2. Seclusion – i.e. boundedness by a 3D perimeter, existence of a separate entrance.

Being a premise, the "living premises" inherit these attributes and also has its own qualifying attribute – fitness for permanent living. Besides, the additional qualifying attribute is the division between the living area and the supplement area (of support facilities). In the absence of the attributes allowing qualifying a premise as a living premise, it is considered non-living.

The analysis of Russian legislation allows concluding that by using the term "house", the law-maker implies both a living premise, a non-living premise, and objects that do not possess attributes of a premise at all. The same trend can be seen in international legal acts, including the practice of the European Court of Human Rights [33]. Examples of objects identified as "house" are an advocate's office or a trailer [34]. The problem would not be particularly adverse if each concept was qualified using the attributes stated above. So, if the law-maker intended to specify the object for the needs of criminal law – as the one intrusion to which is punishable – then it was unacceptable to borrow the inter-branch terms with accepted doctrinal and legal attributes without considering their relations. With the accepted classification, "house" should have been defined as "living premises, as well as other kind of building or premise used for temporary living, and a house where a citizen lives". Such a wording would allow avoiding the artificial mix-up of the conceptual apparatus elements.

Another term with the same root is "housing", which is currently understood per the following five meanings:

1. A concrete living premise;
2. A set of living premises (housing stock);
3. Objects from a group of premises;
4. Objects lacking the attributes of premises (sometimes very exotic ones, such as a boat cabin or a train conductor compartment, etc.);
5. Residential area.

If we are to analyze the relationships between them, we may note that the first four meanings duplicate the other existing legal concepts. So, it's unfeasible to use the pairs:

- "housing" – "living premises": since the attributes of the latter are well defined, these are synonyms;
- "housing" – "housing stock": since the concept and the types of the housing stocks are defined in art. 19 of the Housing Code of the Russian Federation [35], these are synonyms also;
- "housing" – "non-living premises": an associative relation is absent, common attributes are absent, the premise is not suited for living, but a citizen may reside there due to temporary reasons, e.g. staying in a hotel premise;
- "housing" – "objects lacking any attributes of a premise": also lacking associative relation, no common attributes.

Consequently, with respect to formal legal language and the conceptual identity rule, the only acceptable meaning is the fifth one: "housing" is the residential area.

3.2   The Housing Legislation Ontology Module

To operationalize the results of the above analysis of the housing legislation, we implemented the Housing Legislation legal ontology module in Protégé-OWL editor (version 5.2). The classes represented in Fig. 4 are the concepts (terms) covered by the analysis, initially with hierarchical relations only between "premises" – "living premises" and "premises" – "non-living premises". The *Disjoint with* relationship (that exists by default in Protégé-OWL) was specified between the "living premises" and "non-living premises" classes. The corresponding individuals (instances of the classes) mentioned in the analysis are presented in Fig. 5.

In Fig. 6 we show selected properties created in the ontology, corresponding to housing objects. Of particular interest are the *lexical synonymy* and the *legal equivalence* properties: the former reflects the actual use of two terms in legal documents,

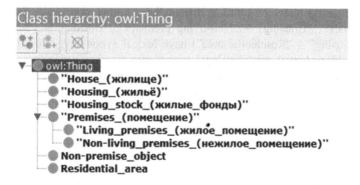

Fig. 4. Classes in the Housing Legislation ontology module.

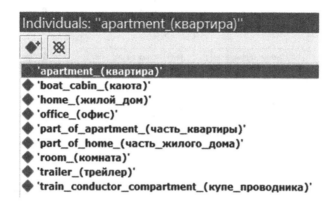

Fig. 5. Individuals in the Housing Legislation ontology module.

while the latter denote the proper state of affairs, corresponding to good legal technique as explained in the analysis.

Fig. 6. Properties in the Housing Legislation ontology module

So, all the five pairs of terms ("Housing" – "Living premises"; "housing" – "Housing stock"; "Housing" – "Non-living premises"; "Housing" – "Non-premise object"; "Housing" – "Residential area") have lexical synonymy, but only the pair "Housing" – "Residential area" has legal equivalence.

The overall structure of the Housing Legislation ontology module with the hierarchical relationships is shown in Fig. 7 (auto-composed with OntoGraf tool).

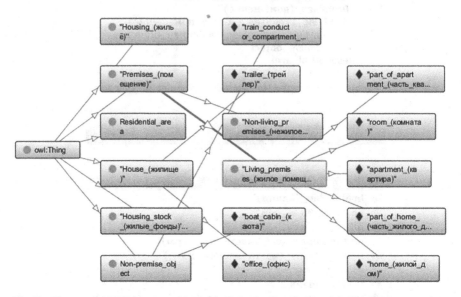

Fig. 7. The structure of classes and individuals in the Housing Legislation ontology module.

4 Conclusions

In our paper we illustrated one of the many contradictory aspects in the complex legal conceptual apparatus and the problems arising due to low quality of the regulatory material, caused in particular by modifying it without consideration of relations between the concepts, their scope and content. Lexical and terminological ambiguity is definitely a serious disadvantage of such a sophisticated system as legislation. For unification of juridical terms, each of them must be used consistently, denoting a certain concept in legal text. However, today when a new legal act draft is being prepared, the large amounts of related data are generally processed "manually", using just intelligence and time available for the developers. Accordingly, there are risks caused by their inability to process large datasets, inattention, fatigue, immense time costs, etc. Automation of selected processes in these activities could free significant amounts of human intelligence resources for their more efficient utilization and ultimately enhance the effectiveness of law-making and law enforcement in Russia.

In the current work we devised an OWL ontology module for such a popular law branch as housing legislation, which can be used for integration with a higher-level legal ontology, such as e.g. LKIF Core, which we considered as an example. The ontology implements the results of the analysis of the housing legislation with respect to lexical and legal-bounding terms, which was carried out by expert lawyers. Further implementation of the approach may decrease the number of errors, over-complexities and ambiguities in legal texts, allow automated search for relevant documents, and categorize complicated legal relations. These should save the practitioners from spending too much time on routine tasks, simplify decision-making in law enforcement and reduce the subjectivity, and ultimately contribute to creating uniform and consistent legislation.

As A. Ivanov noted, "The law has certain inherent properties that won't let fully entrust its making and enforcement to AI, i.e. the machines. The necessary discrepancy of legal norms with the formal logics rules – is one of the obvious reasons preventing its digitalization. Too many clauses and exceptions will have to be made when transforming the polysemantic terms into computers' language. Thus, the law itself would have to be transformed first, so that its terms have the same meaning in all the regulations. A titanic task!" [36]. Obviously, human mind won't be fully replaced by artificial intelligence, but the task could and should be resolved to a reasonable extent, by joining the efforts of researchers from various fields.

In our current paper we only provide illustrative example justifying the general need and approaches for the legal ontologies development. Our further research will involve implementation of larger scope legal ontologies, covering a whole group of social relations, and subsequently institutions and sub-fields of the law.

Acknowledgements. The reported study was funded by RFBR according to the research project No. 17-32-01087 a2 OGN.

References

1. Decree of the President of the Russian Federation dated 01.12.2016 № 642 "on the Strategy of scientific and technological development of the Russian Federation". 05.12.2016. No. 49. St. 6887
2. Kalina, V.F.: Legal Technique: Textbook for Applied Bachelor, 291 p. Yurayt Publishing House, Moscow (2015)
3. Andrichenko, L.V.: Legal mechanisms of social and cultural adaptation and integration of migrants in the Russian Federation. J. Russ. Law **10**, 5–18 (2015)
4. Vlasenko, N.A., Zaloilo, M.V.: Development of legal science school. J. Russ. Law **9**, 24–35 (2015)
5. Rueva, E.O.: Violation of the principle of fairness in the result of imperfections of the legal machinery of the criminal law. Russian investigator, No. 4, pp. 42–46 (2016)
6. Popple, J.: A Pragmatic Legal Expert System. – (Applied Legal Philosophy), pp. 24–25. Aldershot, Dartmouth (1996)
7. Griffo, C., Almeida, J.P.A., Guizzardi, G.: A systematic mapping of the literature on legal core ontologies. In: ONTOBRAS (2015)
8. Breuker, J., Valente, A., Winkels, R.: Use and reuse of legal ontologies in knowledge engineering and information management. In: Benjamins, V.R., Casanovas, P., Breuker, J., Gangemi, A. (eds.) Law and the Semantic Web. LNCS (LNAI), vol. 3369, pp. 36–64. Springer, Heidelberg (2005). https://doi.org/10.1007/978-3-540-32253-5_4

9. Capuano, N., De Maio, C., Salerno, S., Toti, D.: A methodology based on commonsense knowledge and ontologies for the automatic classification of legal cases. In: Proceedings of the 4th International Conference on Web Intelligence, Mining and Semantics (WIMS 2014), p. 27. ACM (2014)

10. Boella, G., Di Caro, L., Humphreys, L., Robaldo, L., Rossi, P., van der Torre, L.: Eunomos, a legal document and knowledge management system for the web to provide relevant, reliable and up-to-date information on the law. Artif. Intell. Law **24**(3), 245–283 (2016)

11. Molnár, B., Béleczki, A., Benczúr, A.: Application of legal ontologies based approaches for procedural side of public administration. In: Kő, A., Francesconi, E. (eds.) EGOVIS 2016. LNCS, vol. 9831, pp. 135–149. Springer, Cham (2016). https://doi.org/10.1007/978-3-319-44159-7_10

12. Gangemi, A., Sagri, M.-T., Tiscornia, D.: A constructive framework for legal ontologies. In: Benjamins, V.R., Casanovas, P., Breuker, J., Gangemi, A. (eds.) Law and the Semantic Web. LNCS (LNAI), vol. 3369, pp. 97–124. Springer, Heidelberg (2005). https://doi.org/10.1007/978-3-540-32253-5_7

13. Kurcheeva, G.I.: Comprehensive approach to smart urban development based on Big Data application. In: Journal of Physics: Conference Series: International Conference Information Technologies in Business and Industry, Tomsk, vol. 10015 (2018)

14. Decree of the President of the Russian Federation dated 20.05.2011 № 657 "on monitoring of law enforcement in the Russian Federation". Rossiyskaya Gazeta, № 110 (2011)

15. Alekseeva, M.V.: On the issue of the relevance of the Institute of legal monitoring for the constitutional law of the Russian Federation. Russian justice, No. 11, pp. 47–49 (2017)

16. Polukarov, A.V.: Administrative-legal regulation of anti-corruption monitoring in the social sector. Modern law, No. 2, pp. 28–35 (2017)

17. Khabrieva, T.Y., Lazarev, V.V., Gabov, A.V. et al. (eds.): Judicial practice in the modern legal system of Russia: monograph. Institute of legislation and comparative law under the Government of the Russian Federation, NORMA, INFRA-M, 432 p. (2017)

18. Klimov, A.A.: Activities of courts of General jurisdiction to identify gaps in criminal procedure law. Russian judge, No. 9, pp. 32–35 (2017)

19. Sharnina, L.A.: The problems of establishing gaps in the constitutional law. Constitutional and municipal law, No. 1, pp. 17–21 (2018)

20. Morozova, L.A.: Problems of typology of legal collisions (modern interpretation). Lex russica, No. 6, pp. 32–38 (2017)

21. Reutov, V.P.: Consistency of terminology as a manifestation of the culture of the language of the law. In: Akinfieva, V.V., Anan'eva, A.A., Afanasieva, S.I., et al. (eds.) Perm the Sixth Congress of legal scholars (Perm, 16–17 October 2015): Selected Materials, pp. 265–269. Statute, Moscow (2016)

22. Raw, V.M.: Law-Making in Russia. Theory and practice: collection of scientific articles Problems. In: Syry, V.M., Zanina, M.A. (eds.) Materials of Scientific-Practical Conference, № 3, pp. 147–148. Russian Academy of justice, Moscow (2010)

23. Berg, L.N.: Law enforcement activity in the aspect of system research. Russ. Law J. **1**, 56 (2011)

24. Federal law of 17.07.2009 № 172-FZ "on anti-corruption expertise of normative legal acts and draft normative legal acts". Rossiyskaya Gazeta, No. 133, 22 July 2009

25. Resolution of the Government of the Russian Federation of 26.02.2010 № 96 "on anti-corruption expertise of normative legal acts and draft normative legal acts". Rossiyskaya Gazeta, No. 46, 05 March 2010

26. Astanin, V.V.: Anti-corruption expertise in doctrine and practice. Russian justice, No. 8, pp. 5–9 (2016)

27. Alexeeva, L.G.: Anti-corruption expertise of normative legal acts. Legality, No. 9, pp. 14–16 (2017)
28. Bakaev, M., Avdeenko, T.: Indexing and comparison of multi-dimensional entities in a recommender system based on ontological approach. Computación y Sistemas **17**(1), 5–13 (2013)
29. Hoekstra, R., Breuker, J., Di Bello, M., Boer, A.: The LKIF core ontology of basic legal concepts. LOAIT **321**, 43–63 (2007)
30. World Wide Web Consortium (W3C): OWL web ontology language current status. https://www.w3.org/standards/techs/owl#w3c_all. Accessed 10 June 2018
31. Antoniou, G., van Harmelen, F.: Web ontology language: OWL. In: Staab, S., Studer, R. (eds.) Handbook on Ontologies. International Handbooks on Information Systems. Springer, Heidelberg (2004). https://doi.org/10.1007/978-3-540-24750-0_4
32. Astrova, I., Korda, N., Kalja, A.: Storing OWL ontologies in SQL relational databases. Int. J. Electr. Comput. Syst. Eng. **1**(4), 242–247 (2007)
33. Universal Declaration of human rights. Adopted at the third session of the UN General Assembly resolution a (III) of 10.12.1948. Rossiyskaya Gazeta, 10 December 1998
34. Haldeev, A.V.: On the concept of "housing" in the practice of the European court of human rights. Housing right, № 5, 6, 7 (2007)
35. Housing code of the Russian Federation of 29.12.2004 N 188-FZ. Rossiyskaya Gazeta, No. 1, 12 January 2005
36. Kondrashov, I., et al.: LegalTech and lawyers of the future. The Law, N 11, pp. 20–36 (2017)

Intellectualization of Knowledge Acquisition of Academic Texts as an Answer to Challenges of Modern Information Society

Aleksandra Vatian⬤, Sergey Dudorov, Natalia Dobrenko⬤,
Andrey Mairovich, Mikhail Osipov, Artem Lobantsev$^{(\boxtimes)}$⬤,
Anatoly Shalyto⬤, and Natalia Gusarova⬤

ITMO University, Saint Petersburg, Russia
alexvatyan@gmail.com, lobantseff@gmail.com

Abstract. Extracting knowledge from an increasing information flow is one of the main challenges of modern information society. The paper considers the possibilities and means for intellectualization of this process concerning such an important information source as the academic texts. In this case the user is faced with the task of finding fragments relevant to the subject of interest, within the vast textual documents often written in a foreign language. We experimentally investigated the comparative effectiveness of TS algorithms for extended coherent academic texts. The procedure of instrumental effectiveness evaluation was substantiated. The influence of the most significant characteristics of the text, including original language, structural organization (levels of heading), subjects of research (technique, information technologies and medicine) was considered. We have shown that for the intellectualization of knowledge acquisition from academic texts it is necessary to present to the reader the results of the TS fulfilled by different algorithms, in a complex. A system of complex visualization of TS results is proposed, and an appropriate software solution is developed. The visualization system for extended coherent texts explicitly demonstrates the semantic structure of the text, which allows the user to detect and analyze not the whole text, but only fragments corresponding to his current information needs and thus getting a complete idea of the subject of interest.

Keywords: Topic segmentation · Knowledge acquisition · Text structure · Information retrieval

1 Introduction

One of the main challenges that the modern information society is giving to each of its members is the need to process an ever-increasing information flow, presented primarily in the form of a variety of texts. Many information retrieval systems make this task easier for the user, allowing to get a response to a specific search query. Note that the above-mentioned term "to process" here is problem-oriented, and its meaning can vary greatly - from a superficial acquaintance with the theme of the text to mastering the subtle nuances of meaning that the author wanted to express.

© Springer Nature Switzerland AG 2019
A. Chugunov et al. (Eds.): EGOSE 2018, CCIS 947, pp. 138–153, 2019.
https://doi.org/10.1007/978-3-030-13283-5_11

The vast majority of modern information retrieval systems are aimed to find specific answers to short text inquiries or to identify specific facts in the text, but not to identify the semantic content of the text.

For example, in modern professional activities, the most relevant educational information is not contained in traditional textbooks, but in original scientific texts, primarily articles and monographs. Their content, as a rule, is an interlacing of a number of topics, i.e. the user is faced with the task of finding fragments relevant to the subject of interest, within the vast textual documents often written in a foreign language. Linguistic researches show that the semantic structure of such documents far from always can be represented by traditional search attributes, like the table of contents, meta tags or a set of keywords. As a result, in response to its search query in traditional information retrieval systems, the user receives either the entire document in which he is forced to manually perform a linear search, or the pages snatched out of context but having the maximum frequency of keywords. On them, the user can not form an overall view of the specific problem discussed in the document. In addition, he still has a doubt that some important aspects of the problem studied are not reflected in the pages shown.

To help the user work effectively within coherent text, it is necessary to solve the problem of automated division of the document into sub-themes taking into account internal features of the text and the user's goals. For the intellectualization of this process, topic segmentation (TS) [13] can be used, which allows the user to analyze not the whole document found, but only fragments containing relevant information.

The role of the TS in the study of textual material follows from a theoretical analysis of the structure and models of text comprehension [21]. According to [21], the author in writing the text forms its structure in the form of a hierarchy of macro and micro propositions, each of which corresponds to a separate segment (topic) of the text. The reader tries to reproduce the structure of topics that the author has provided, and to single out topics combination, correlated with his individual goals and situational models. In this case, the reader forms understanding (interpretation) of the text.

Obviously, effective TS should offer the reader the original structure of topics as a reference structure so that he can build his own interpretation with a minimum of resources - to choose what is needed for reading or to remove what is definitely not needed. This is especially important for texts in a foreign language for the author, where the improper allocation of the boundaries of the fragment being translated leads to a large expenditure of time and intellectual resources.

Since the division of text into topics is a semantic process, a theoretical topic definition that can be applied instrumentally does not exist [19, 22]. In this paper, we will, in accordance with [21], treat the topic as a semantically complete fragment of coherent text. Note that in the work on topic modeling, the term "topics" is used to refer to one of several themes that are present in the document as a whole. To avoid confusion in our work, in such cases the term "theme" is used.

To date, various algorithms of intellectualization of knowledge acquisition from texts have been proposed. In principle, all of them in one way or another provide approaches to solving the TS problem of extended coherent texts. At the same time, as our previous studies [3, 6] showed, on extended coherent texts each algorithm "behaves in its own way", highlighting meaningfully different fragments, which makes it difficult to interpret the results of TS.

Thus, in order to proceed to the real practice of the intellectualization of knowledge acquisition in extended coherent texts, it is necessary to carry out a comparative analysis of these algorithms based on the above-mentioned type of texts. To the best of our knowledge, such problem in the field of information retrieval from texts has not been considered before.

The work is organized as follows. Section 2 discusses the theoretical basis and algorithmic approaches to the TS. Section 3 describes the procedure for creating the experimental data set, as well as the algorithms of the TS selected for comparison. Section 4 presents the results of a comparative analysis of algorithms. Section 5 describes the method of visual composition of algorithms proposed by the authors as a means of intellectualizing of knowledge acquisition.

2 Background and Related Works

The object of the research in this work are texts related to the genre of academic texts, such as monographs, textbooks, scientific articles, the subjects of which are aspects of technologies of different subject areas. The solution of the TS problem with respect to these texts has its own specifics - a small sample size, a relatively long extension, a variety of original languages, a thematic unity with smooth transitions from one subject to another, a complex topic structure.

To model the structure of the text, a number of theories have been proposed, differing up to the conceptual apparatus [14, 21]. For example, in [14] the following methods of text structure formation are distinguished: (a) the hierarchy of topics, (b) the sequence of topics, (c) semantic returns, when the related subtopics in the text are not sequentially located, but are mentioned together with other subtopics.

The structural organization of the text is characterized by the concept of cohesion [10]. As shown in [7, 15, 17], academic texts mainly use four types of cohesion [10]:

- absolute cohesion – exact repetition of terms in adjacent sentences of text;
- synonymous cohesion – the use of terms that are similar in meaning in one context;
- substitute cohesion – the use of a pronoun or a term with a demonstrative pronoun to replace the meaning of the preceding sentence;
- parallel cohesion – a series of sentences that reveal the thesis of the text; the syntactic features of parallel cohesion are the parallelism of the structure.

This is the analysis of the characteristics of the text cohesion that is the basis for constructing the algorithms of the TS. To date, a wide range of approaches is proposed (see, for example, review [16]).

In our previous studies [3, 6] the problem-oriented investigation of TS algorithms for the academic texts was carried out. The most successful were three approaches to the TS, each of which corresponds to its own concept of the topic:

- TextTiling algorithm [11]. The text is considered as a linear sequence of word vectors for each topic, and the distance between these vectors is measured. The transition between the topics is considered only as a change in the vocabulary, that is, the "bag of words" model is realized in its pure form.

- LSA algorithm [9]. The text is considered as word-document matrix. The singular decomposition of the matrix allows to allocate in the text the most characteristic periodicity connected with the change of topic.
- LDA algorithm in combination with TextTiling algorithm (TopicTiling, [18]) is based on the generative text models. In the text, groups of fragment corresponding to a given number of themes are identified. It is assumed that each fragment contains the author's completed thought, that is, is a separate topic.

In this connection, in the present paper, these algorithms have been chosen as basic for a comparative evaluation. To improve the effectiveness of thematic modeling, we used LDA with regularizers, i.e. in the form of the ARTM algorithm [22].

The semantic connotation of the topic concept makes it difficult to organize a procedure for evaluating the effectiveness of the TS. Apparently, in the quest for objectification of measurements, practically in all works [16] the effectiveness of the TS is estimated using artificially created text concatenated from short, semantically unrelated fragments. But for extended texts, including for academic texts, this approach is not enough.

There is almost no application of TS to various text genres. The effectiveness of the vast majority of TS algorithms is evaluated on artificially created long texts compiled by concatenating individual sentences or short fragments from the texts of the news genre [18]). At the same time, the results of applying these algorithms to real scientific texts are scanty and often contradict each other (compare, for example, [11] and [3, 6]).

The most numerous group of TS algorithms considers the text as a linear sequence of nonoverlapping segments. Hierarchical TS tries to reveal the structure of interrelations between topics in the text. For example, the algorithm divSeg [20], calculating the measure of similarity between potential fragments of the text, iteratively segments the text in the form of a binary tree, however such a model of the text does not always correspond to reality [21]. Variants of a two-stage procedure are also proposed: separation of text into topics, as discussed above, and revealing their interdependence. For example, in [12], after separating text into topics for each topic on the basis of parsing, a term is defined that reflects the theme of the topic, and then these terms are organized into a hierarchy. In [23], for the second stage, agglomeration clustering is used. But the application of methods of hierarchical TS for real extended coherent texts has not been studied.

In this paper, we investigate the comparative effectiveness of TSs of extended texts of the genre of academic texts. The procedure of instrumental effectiveness evaluation is substantiated. The influence of the most significant characteristics of the text, including original language, structural organization (levels of heading), subjects of research (technique, information technologies and medicine) is considered. The necessity of visual composition of TS variants in order to facilitate the extraction of knowledge from extended coherent texts is justified, an appropriate software solution is proposed.

3   Method and Materials

3.1   Experimental Dataset Formation

When building the experimental dataset, we relied on the principles of sampling, presented in [2, 5]. Namely, among the texts relating to the genre of academic texts, we conducted stratification according to characteristics of importance for our research and selected the texts in such a way that each stratum in the dataset was represented by several samples, while in each text all the above-mentioned types of cohesion are presented. We do not set ourselves the task of a full-scale statistical study, therefore from the point of view of representativeness, such an approach seems quite legitimate [2]. For comparison with the existing methods, the data set also includes an artificially created text composed of concatenation of medical conclusions.

15 texts were selected with a total volume of 146,000 words, including 10 texts of technical subjects, 3 texts of medical subjects, 2 texts of information technology subjects. 2 texts were in French, 6 - in English, 7 - in Russian. The bibliographic and linguistic characteristics of some of the selected texts are presented in Tables 1 and 2 respectively. For 3 texts (2 – in French, on technical subject, 1 – in English, on medical subject), their professional translations into Russian are included in the data set.

Table 1. The bibliographic characteristics of texts chosen for dataset

Designation	Bibliographic description
T1	L' Art de la Marine, ou Principes et Préceptes Generaux de l'Art de Construire, d'Armer, de Manœuvrer et de Conduire des Vasseaux, par M. Romme, Correspondant de l'Academie des Sciences de Paris, et Professeur Royal de Navigation des Élèves de la Marine. La Rochelle, 1787. Chapitre VII
T2	Ibid, Chapitre VIII
T3	Lynne Wainfan, Paul K. Davis. Challenges in virtual collaboration: videoconferencing, audioconferencing, and computer-mediated communications. Santa Monica, Calif.: RAND, 106 p
T4	Aravind Shenoy Anirudh Prabhu. Introducing SEO: Your quick-start guide to effective SEO practices. Apress, 2016. 132 p
T5	Gordon Williamson. U-Boat Crews 1914–45. Osprey Publishing, 1995. 64 p
T6	Mathias Procop, Michael Galanski. Spiral and Multislice Computed Tomography of the Body. Stuttgart-N.Y., Thieme, 2001. 1104 p
T7	Ibid, Russian translation, 2011. V.1–416 p., V2. – 712 p
T8	Medical conclusions to computer tomograms (impersonalized and concatenated) – 20 items

As shown in the literature [3, 6, 8], although the boundaries of paragraphs are often subjective, the positions of the topic change in the text are in overwhelming majority of cases correlated with the boundaries of paragraphs. In the present paper, a paragraph is chosen as the terminal unit for the division of text, and not a separate sentence (like in [22]).

Table 2. The linguistic characteristics of texts chosen for dataset

Text	Language	Text size			Paragraph size (words)		Levels of heading
		Words	Paragraphs	Terms	Min	Max	
T1	French	20887	108	5163	13	764	1
T2	French	15160	78	3922	13	607	1
T3	English	13252	102	4825	30	290	3
T4	English	10710	123	4178	35	173	3
T5	English	10243	86	2693	18	198	2
T6	English	7338	131	5451	17	233	3
T7	Russian	7435	131	5453	12	161	3
T8	Russian	4096	100	3249	8	173	1

3.2   Text Markup and Segmentation Quality Metrics

As discussed above, the most common way to establish the validity of TS is comparison with human expert's results. All selected texts have author's markup of different levels (see Table 2). However, as studies [8] have shown, it does not always coincide with the structure of topics in the readers' view. In addition, in the scientific texts between the topics there may be a transitional zone in 1–2 paragraphs [3]. In this regard, we used the expert procedure [8] to form the reference markup of texts, according to which the reference boundary of the topic is fixed in the event that it was indicated at least 2/3 of the annotators.

16 annotators took part in the study, who randomly selected subgroups for specific texts. To assess the consistency of the annotation results, the Fleiss kappa was used. The average value was Fleiss kappa = 0,68, the maximum deviation of the boundary position was 2 paragraphs (for the texts T1 and T2 with 1 level of headings). For texts with levels of headings 2 and 3, the boundaries coincided with the author's markup with an accuracy of 1 paragraph.

To assess the quality of TS, traditional metrics were used, namely recall R, precision P and balanced F-measure (Eq. 1):

$$R = \frac{TP}{TP + FN}, \; P = \frac{TP}{TP + FP}, \; F = \frac{2PR}{P + R}, \tag{1}$$

where TP is the number of correctly defined partition boundaries, FP is the number of false boundaries, FN is the number of missing boundaries.

3.3   Text Preprocessing and Segmentation Algorithms Used

To optimize the work of TS algorithms, all texts were preprocessed. Various options for preprocessing the text were used separately and in combination with each other, including lemmatization, the removal of stop words, the removal of the most frequent words, the selection of terms, and the pairing of short paragraphs. Preprocessing was performed manually, or, where possible, frameworks pymorphy and nltk were used. For each text, an optimizing preprocessing set was identified and implemented. In particular, as the terms for texts T1–T6 we used only nouns, but for medical texts, this was not enough, and here the best results were shown by the selection of nouns and adjectives.

Table 3. The technical characteristics of the algorithms used

No	Algorithms	Implementation specificity
1	TextTiling	Implementation is self-written using python language
2	LSA	SVD is implemented using python's numpy. linalg.svd function, full_matrices parameter set to False. LSA is self-implemented using python language. As after SVD negative components of vectors could appear, it had been decided to shift a value of the cosine between neighbour vactors by adding 1 to the value and devide the result by 2, so that the measure was between 0 and 1
3	ARTM + TextTiling	The BigARTM framework was used. ARTM Regularizers used: Smooth and sparse regularizer of Phi and Theta matrices, Topic decorrelation regularizer, Topic selection regularizer. The number of iterations was 40

The technical characteristics of the algorithms used are shown in Table 3. To ensure comparability of the results, a cosine measure of lexical similarity is used as a measure of similarity between the compared fragments of the text obtained by different algorithms (Eq. 2):

$$\cos \varphi_i = \frac{\sum_n w_{n,i-1} w_{n,i}}{\sqrt{\sum_n w_{n,i-1}^2} \sqrt{\sum_n w_{n,i}^2}}, 0 \leq \cos \varphi \leq 1 \qquad (2)$$

where $w_{n,i}$ is weight of n-th term in i-th fragment. To adjust the cut-off level in the TextTiling-part of algorithms, we used additional heuristics proposed in [18].

4   Experimental Results and Discussion

The mean values and variances of the F-measure for the dataset are as follows: for the whole dataset $F = 0.60 \pm 0.09$; for the texts on technical subjects $F = 0.63 \pm 0.10$; for the texts on medical subjects $F = 0.59 \pm 0.05$; for the texts on IT-subjects $F = 0.54 \pm 0.08$; for the texts in English $F = 0.59 \pm 0.05$; for the texts in French $F = 0.70 \pm 0.03$; for the texts in Russian $F = 0.60 \pm 0.05$.

A picture of the effectiveness of individual TS algorithms for some texts is presented in Tables 4 and 5. Namely, Table 4 shows the values of the F-measure for all

Table 4. Balanced F-measures taking into account all levels of heading

Text	LSA	TextTiling	ARTM+ TextTiling	Mean
T1	0.70	0.68	0.69	0,69 ± 0.01
T2	0.72	0.66	0.75	0,71 ± 0.04
T3	0.67	0.62	0.48	0,59 ± 0.08
T4	0.52	0.48	0.47	0,50 ± 0.01
T5	0.51	0.47	0.52	0,50 ± 0.02
T6	0.64	0.52	0.58	0,58 ± 0.05
T7	0.61	0.54	0.62	0,59 ± 0.04
T8	0.57		0.67	0,62 ± 0.05

Table 5. The number of boundaries of the first level of the header, defined by each algorithm

Text	Number of boundaries of the 1st level marked by			
	Expert	LSA	TextTiling	ARTM+ TextTiling
T1	9	8	6	6
T2	11	8	8	11
T3	4	2	3	4
T4	3	1	2	3
T5	5	4	2	3
T6	2	1	2	0
T7	2	2	1	2
T8	19	8		16

allocated boundaries, regardless of the level of heading, and in Table 5 – the number of boundaries of the first level of heading only.

The above results for the whole dataset show that all the selected algorithms demonstrate sufficiently close values of the F-measure regardless of the subject of the text and the original language. Practically identical values of F-measure were obtained on real academic texts and on artificially formed (concatenated) text, which is an indirect confirmation of the representativeness of our methodology. These findings are clearly confirmed by a detailed analysis of individual texts, presented in Table 4.

Note that, despite the complex terminology base of medical texts, rather high quality segmentation is achieved for them without the use of external lexical resources or n-gram algorithms. This is an encouraging result, especially for the conditions of Russia, where the lexical resources of medical subjects are very poorly developed.

There is a pronounced dependence of TS efficiency on the structural organization of the text (texts T1 and T2 with a practically linear organization demonstrate the best F-measure). Comparison of Tables 4 and 5 confirms that the quality of segmentation taking into account all levels of structuring is better than taking into account only the upper level. This somewhat unexpected result contradicts the opinions [12, 20, 23], that were expressed on the basis of the study of artificial (concatenated) texts. At the same time, our research has shown that within the academic texts, the hierarchical structure of the table of contents can sufficiently weakly correspond to the real results of the TS.

The boundaries of topics selected by algorithms are graphically shown in Figs. 1, 2, 3, 4, 5, 6, 7 and 8 in comparison with the boundaries of topics that were presented in the authoring contents, as well as in the expert markup. The following legend is adopted in the figures: the header - the paragraph numbers, the line I – the author segmentation broken down by levels of heading (I.I, I.II, I.III), the line II – the segmentation by the LSA algorithm, the line III – the segmentation by the TextTiling algorithm, the line IV – the segmentation by the ARTM+ TextTiling algorithm; for the lines I–IV, the boundaries of the topics are indicated, for the line V, the shades of gray show the affiliation of the paragraphs to one of the themes according to ARTM + TextTiling algorithm: light gray – theme 1, medium gray – theme 2, dark gray – theme 3, black – theme 4, white – two themes are presented equally. The number of themes selected is automatically generated by the ARTM algorithm and ranges from 2 to 4 depending on text, 3 themes predominate.

In Figs. 9 and 10 presents a comparison of the top 10 words highlighted by the ARTM algorithm for original texts in English and their professional translations into Russian.

Fig. 1. Comparison of segmentation options for text T1.

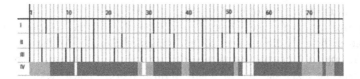

Fig. 2. Comparison of segmentation options for text T2.

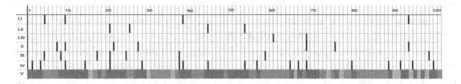

Fig. 3. Comparison of segmentation options for text T3.

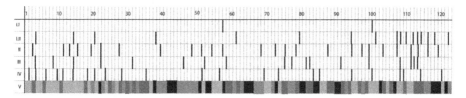

Fig. 4. Comparison of segmentation options for text T4.

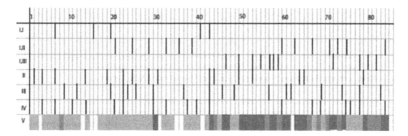

Fig. 5. Comparison of segmentation options for text T5

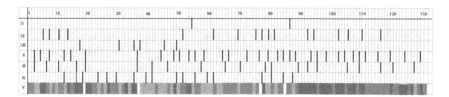

Fig. 6. Comparison of segmentation options for text T6

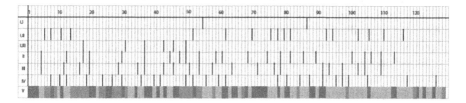

Fig. 7. Comparison of segmentation options for text T7.

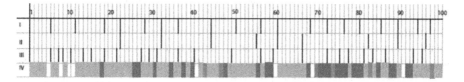

Fig. 8. Comparison of segmentation options for text T8

English:
topic 1 – year, pea, end, success, top, convoy, use, attack, vessel, man
topic 2 – shirt, color, service, parade, wire, cuff, sleeve, patch, survivor, dress
topic 3 – side, helmet, buckle, operation, ring, wear, device, Atlantic, leg, pair
Russian:
topic 1 – пуговица,образец,куртка,свастика,галун,пряжка,цвет,чин,клапан,якорь
topic 2 – командир,ранг,месяц,ряд,вступление,Великобритания,подлодка,субмарина,большинство, козырек
topic 3 – Германия,кокарда,тип,Кригсмарине,экипаж,фуражка,тулья,корона,борт,период

Fig. 9. Comparison of top-10 words for text T5 and it's Russian translation; matching terms are highlighted.

English:
topic 1 – involvement,diagnosis,morphology,benign,enhancement,biopsy,high,morphologic,sensitivity,size
topic 2 – pulmonary,usually,mm,mediastinal,lymphoma,chest,focal,small,cause,cell
topic 3 – **show,pneumonia,see,more,atelectasis,air,**central,**invasion,**lobe,**bronchi**
Russian:
topic 1 – случай,**воздушный**,лимфатический,пациент,лимфома,симптом,мм,**пневмония**,обычно,ткань
topic 2 – **бронх**,контрастный,стадия,плевра,часто,стенка,инвазия,процесс,трахея,усиление
topic 3 – узелок,редко,уплотнение,**ателектаз**,размер,метастаз,КТ_морфология,**обнаруживаться, наблюдаться, наиболее**

Fig. 10. Comparison of top-10 words for text T7 and it's Russian translation T8; matching terms are equally tinted.

The results of experiments for the original texts and their Russian-language "mirrors" show that the number and general structure of the themes submitted through the top-10 words are preserved. However, when translating, additional noise appears, which gives some offset of the segmentation positions for each algorithms (see Figs. 6 and 7, lines II and III) as a well as the distribution of themes by paragraphs (see Figs. 6 and 7, lines V). The noise of translation is also manifested in changing the list of the top 10 words as well as of their allocation within themes and their composition (see Figs. 8 and 9). This actually shows that when using the means of intellectual support of knowledge acquisition from academic texts, it is expedient first of all to analyze the original text.

Although, according to Table 4, all algorithms show approximately the same efficiency in the sense of the F-measure, but the analysis of Figs. 1, 2, 3, 4, 5, 6, 7 and 8 confirms that each algorithm fundamentally performs TS in different ways, highlighting one or other of the characteristic features of the structural organization of the text. For example, the TextTiling algorithm is characterized by boundary shift errors, and the ARTM algorithm – by small "blotches" (inclusions) in the current segment from other segments.

In general, all the algorithms, in spite of separate inclusions, demonstrate the actual distribution of themes in the texts (see lines V in all figures). But it was found that there are zones of frequent change of topics between adjacent paragraphs, i.e. separate topics of 1 paragraph size are formed. A detailed semantic analysis of the texts in comparison with the results of Figs. 1, 2, 3, 4, 5, 6, 7 and 8 shows that these zones are meaningfully consistent with the parallel type of connectivity. It can manifest itself directly in the form of list structures (for example, Fig. 3, paragraphs 18–33) or indirectly in the form of discussions of various aspects of the same thesis. For example, paragraphs 64–69 of text T3 (Fig. 3) list different aspects of the tendency of groups to differentiate "us" vs. "them" (where, why, how it happens), each of which is represented by its own set of words. Although, according to the cosine measure of lexical similarity, each such paragraph is a separate topic, but semantically it is a single topic, expressed through a parallel type of cohesion. As can be seen in Figs. 3, 4, 5, 6, 7 and 8, such zones connected with the parallel cohesion is very characteristic for academic texts. According to [21], such topics are to be regarded as fragments demonstrating the author's complete thesis. They need to be shown to the reader not separately but in combination with the results achieved by other algorithms.

5   Method of Visual Composition of Algorithms

The results discussed above show that different algorithms distinguish meaningfully different fragments of text, and the composition of algorithms in the classical form, i.e. by summarizing the results in order to single out the best one, seems to be wrong. At the same time, the simultaneous demonstration of several versions of the TS will allow the reader to obtain an overall and clear representation of the structure of the text, thereby facilitating the choice of an effective strategy for mastering the text. This is especially important for texts in a foreign language for the reader, where the unsuccessful allocation of the boundaries of the fragment to be translated leads to large expenditures of time and intellectual resources.

Thus, the problem arises of visualizing the results of the TS of the analyzed long text. Analysis of the literature [4] shows that visualization tools are now being increasingly used for intellectual support of various technological processes. Within the framework of our work, a TS text system has been developed, which includes a utility for visualizing the results of the TS. The system architecture in the UML notation as a deployment diagram is shown in Fig. 11.

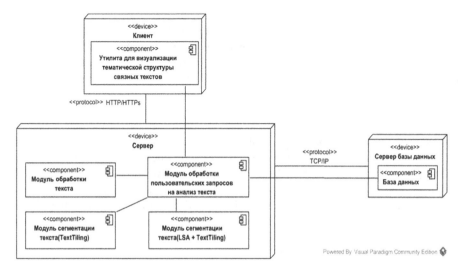

Fig. 11. The deployment diagram of the utility for visualizing the results of the TS

The service architecture is modular, which allows to add other TS algorithms. The server includes a dispatching module, a text preprocessing module, and an extensible set of text segmentation modules.

The dispatch module implements the functionality of the web server in the aspect of processing requests for text analysis and storing the results of the work of the text segmentation modules to provide them to users. The preprocessing module provides various options for preprocessing text, including lemmatization, removal of stop words, selection of nouns, merging of short paragraphs. The storage of the analyzed texts and the results of their processing takes place in the database. In the text segmentation module based on the LDA algorithm, the formation of the keyword topology is automatically performed, which is presented to the user in the keyword window, which makes it easier for the user to select the text fragments that interest him. When the text is segmented by other algorithms, a separate module can be provided for highlighting keywords (not shown in the figure).

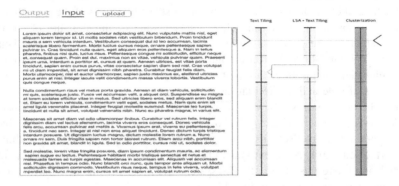

Fig. 12. The utility interface

Figure 12 provides an interface for visualizing the thematic structure of coherent texts. The utility considers the text not as an ACII sequence of characters, but as a sequence of letters as graphic symbols, which avoids converting source text into txt format. Each paragraph is represented as a rectangular object with a width of 500px and a height corresponding to the length of the paragraph as a text string. The current position in the text is set by the user by clicking on the text and calculated with the accuracy of the paragraph. For the initial drawing of the borders of the paragraphs of the text on the ruler, the proportions of all paragraphs are calculated, and the boundaries are drawn on the ruler of the static height. When a user clicks on a section of text, the cursor position data is stored in the global repository. All the lines, the number of which is unlimited, are realized using the technology of reactive programming. Each line drawing component is connected to the global repository, and when the cursor position is changed, the component redraws the cursor. Thus, a paragraph of text is represented as a rectangular object having a certain height on the screen, and to the right to it are attached the results of segmentation displayed on the rulers. This implementation of the visualization module allows you to associate the cursor position with the paragraph position, regardless of the scrolling of the text, i.e. The cursor moves along with the paragraph when the text is scrolled.

Thus, on the client side (on the visualizer screen), it becomes possible to display several segmentation results (as rulers) simultaneously for one text.

The operation of the system is organized according to the following scenario. The user loads the text to be segmented into the system, and selects the desired segmentation algorithms. The system performs segmentation and stores its results in the database. In the text window of the interface, the user is shown the selected text, which can be moved using the scroll bar. When clicking on the selected paragraph, the segmentation lines corresponding to the selected algorithms are activated, and the boundaries of the topics in which the selected paragraph is included are activated. This allows the user to more accurately select fragments of text to be studied. Moving text through the scroll bar, the user can extend the analysis area right up to the text boundaries. The analysis results are stored in the database and can be recalled repeatedly.

6   Conclusion

Extracting knowledge from an increasing information flow is one of the main challenges of modern information society. The paper considers the possibilities and means for intellectualization of this process concerning such an important information source as academic texts. In this case the user is faced with the task of finding fragments relevant to the subject of interest, within the vast textual documents often written in a foreign language.

We experimentally investigated the comparative effectiveness of TS algorithms for extended coherent texts in the genre of academic texts. The procedure of instrumental effectiveness evaluation was substantiated. The influence of the most significant characteristics of the text, including original language, structural organization (levels of heading), subjects of research (technique, information technologies and medicine) was considered. We have shown that for the intellectualization of knowledge acquisition from academic texts it is necessary to present to the reader the results of the TS fulfilled by different algorithms, in a complex.

A system of complex visualization of TS results is proposed, and an appropriate software solution is developed. The visualization system for extended coherent texts explicitly demonstrates the semantic structure of the text, which allows the user to detect and analyze not the whole text, but only fragments corresponding to his current information needs and thus getting a complete idea of the subject of interest.

Acknowledgement. This work was financially supported by the Government of Russian Federation, Grant 08-08.

References

1. LNCS homepage. http://www.springer.com/lncs. Accessed 21 Nov 2016
2. Atkins, S., Clear, J., Ostler, N.: Corpus design criteria. Literary Linguist. Comput. **7**(1), 1–16 (1992)
3. Avdeeva, N., Artemova, G., Boyarsky, K., Gusarova, N., Dobrenko, N., Kanevsky, E.: Subtopic segmentation of scientific texts: parameter optimisation. In: Klinov, P., Mouromtsev, D. (eds.) KESW 2015. CCIS, vol. 518, pp. 3–15. Springer, Cham (2015). https://doi.org/10.1007/978-3-319-24543-0_1
4. Aysina, R.: Survey of visualization tools for topic models of text corpora. Mach. Learn. Data Anal. **1**(11), 1584–1618 (2015)
5. Biber, D.: Representativeness in corpus design. Literary Linguist. Comput. **8**(4), 243–257 (1993)
6. Boyarsky, K., Gusarova, N.F., Avdeeva, N., et al.: Specifics of applying topic segmentation algorithms to scientific texts In: Proceedings of XVII International Conference on DAMDID/RCDL (2015)
7. Burrough-Boenisch, J.: Culture and conventions: writing and reading Dutch scientific English. Netherlands Graduate School of Linguistics (2002)
8. Cardoso, P.C., Taboada, M., Pardo, T.A.: Subtopic annotation in a corpus of news texts: steps towards automatic subtopic segmentation. In: Proceedings of the 9th Brazilian Symposium in Information and Human Language Technology (2013)
9. Choi, F.Y., Wiemer-Hastings, P., Moore, J.: Latent semantic analysis for text segmentation. In: Proceedings of the 2001 Conference on Empirical Methods in Natural Language Processing (2001)
10. Halliday, M.A.K., Hasan, R.: Cohesion in English. Routledge, London (2014)
11. Hearst, M.A.: Multi-paragraph segmentation of expository text. In: Proceedings of the 32nd Annual Meeting on Association for Computational Linguistics, pp. 9–16. Association for Computational Linguistics (1994)
12. Lloret, E.: Topic detection and segmentation in automatic text summarization (2009)
13. Martin, J.H., Jurafsky, D.: Speech and Language Processing: An Introduction to Natural Language Processing, Computational Linguistics, and Speech Recognition. Pearson/Prentice Hall, Upper Saddle River (2009)
14. Moens, M.F., Angheluta, R., De Busser, R., Jeuniaux, P.: Summarizing texts at various levels of detail. In: Coupling Approaches, Coupling Media and Coupling Languages for Information Retrieval, pp. 597–609. Le centre de hautes etudes internationales d'informatique documentaire (2004)
15. Myers, G.: Lexical cohesion and specialized knowledge in science and popular science texts. Discourse Processes **14**(1), 1–26 (1991)
16. Pak, I., Teh, P.L.: Text segmentation techniques: a critical review. In: Zelinka, I., Vasant, P., Duy, V.H., Dao, T.T. (eds.) Innovative Computing, Optimization and Its Applications. SCI, vol. 741, pp. 167–181. Springer, Cham (2018). https://doi.org/10.1007/978-3-319-66984-7_10
17. Randaccio, M.: Language change in scientific discourse. JCOM **3**(2), 1–15 (2004)
18. Riedl, M., Biemann, C.: Text segmentation with topic models. J. Lang. Technol. Comput. Linguist. **27**(1), 47–69 (2012)
19. Ries, K.: Segmenting Conversations by Topic, Initiative, and Style. In: Coden, Anni R., Brown, Eric W., Srinivasan, S. (eds.) IRTSA 2001. LNCS, vol. 2273, pp. 51–66. Springer, Heidelberg (2002). https://doi.org/10.1007/3-540-45637-6_5

20. Song, F., Darling, W.M., Duric, A., Kroon, F.W.: An iterative approach to text segmentation. In: Clough, P., et al. (eds.) ECIR 2011. LNCS, vol. 6611, pp. 629–640. Springer, Heidelberg (2011). https://doi.org/10.1007/978-3-642-20161-5_63
21. Van Dijk, T.A., Kintsch, W.: Strategies of discourse comprehension. Academic Press, New York (1983)
22. Vorontsov, K., Potapenko, A.: Additive regularization of topic models. Mach. Learn. **101**(1–3), 303–323 (2015)
23. Yaari, Y.: Segmentation of expository texts by hierarchical agglomerative clustering. arXiv preprint cmp-lg/9709015 (1997)

Mining of Relevant and Informative Posts from Text Forums

Kseniya Buraya[(✉)], Vladislav Grozin, Vladislav Trofimov,
Pavel Vinogradov, and Natalia Gusarova

ITMO University, 49 Kronverksky Pr., St. Petersburg 197101, Russia
ks.buraya@gmail.com

Abstract. In the modern world, the competitive advantage for every person is the possibility to obtain the information in a fast and comfortable way. Web forums occupy a significant place among the sources of information. It is a good place to gain professionally significant knowledge on different topics. However, sometimes it is not easy to identify the places on the forum, which contains useful information corresponding user demands. In this paper we consider the problem of automatic forum text summarization and describe the methods, which can help to solve it. We study the difference between relevance-oriented and useful-oriented query types. We will describe our dataset, that contains over 4000 of marked posts from web forums about various subject domains. The posts were marked by experts, by estimating them on a scale from 0 to 5 for selected query types. The results of our study can provide background for creation informational retrieval applications that will decrease the time of user's searching and increase the quality of search results.

Keywords: Text forums · Information retrieval · Relevant information

1 Introduction

The number of various informational resources is constantly growing nowadays. Upgrading knowledge in particular areas often becomes very time-consuming and difficult. Also, it is not so trivial to obtain basic knowledge in some new subject for the person who is not very competent in it. Thus, it is very important to have quick and comfortable access to information. First of all, it increases the possibility to obtain knowledge about the most important aspects of the area of interest.

Web forums are among the most important resources for the acquisition of professionally significant information. There people communicate with each other by creating the threads, that are dedicated to a specific topic, and lead the discussion by writing posts to them. Thus, a thread presents a well-formed user-discussion process on the declared subject.

As a resource of professionally significant information, compared to traditional educational resources and scientific publications, forum has the following advantages:

© Springer Nature Switzerland AG 2019
A. Chugunov et al. (Eds.): EGOSE 2018, CCIS 947, pp. 154–168, 2019.
https://doi.org/10.1007/978-3-030-13283-5_12

- the forum contains the most up-to-date information on a topic. Specific technological solutions are often formed in user's discussions, while the publication of the same information requires a long time;
- forum posts represent the experience of people who are directly using the specific technologies and have both positive and negative experiences. Such information is practically not available in the official documents;
- the information on a web forum is presented in a structured manner. It extends the capabilities of the informational search;
- the way of presenting information on a forum has more freedom in describing details, contains emotional evaluations and different types of visualization;
- the information on a forum reflects the collective opinion of the professional community.

At the same time, there are some disadvantages of using a web forum, as a source of professionally significant information:

- information redundancy – a large amount of repetitive, highly emotional and professionally irrelevant information;
- topics drift – changing the originally declared theme to others;
- the disadvantages of language – incomplete sentences, the differences in the understanding meaning of concepts in separate posts. This makes it difficult to analyze forums in foreign languages.

Consider the typical situation. Someone wants to learn about technology, which can be useful in his/her recent activities. Search query leads him/her to a forum, where the technology is discussed. The questions are: is there enough information on the forum for the detailed acquaintance with the area of interests? Which posts contain really professionally significant information?

It would be helpful to obtain the answers to these questions and then to study selected posts in details. This means that we have the problem of the automatic offline summarization of the most important posts, which contains professionally significant information. This task also becomes more meaningful when a forum is in unknown foreign language and available only through translation.

Authors of [3] proposed different approaches for text forums summarization. The most powerful methods for this task are the machine learning methods [5, 25]. However, there is a high number of different methods in machine learning, and the selection of the most efficient ones is a problem.

One of the main things in text and forum summarization is the extraction of keywords [2]. Keywords extraction methods are divided into two categories: selection of words from a predefined vocabulary or taxonomy by the document content, and extraction of keywords directly from the documents in analysis [16]. The methods of the second group are also divided into several categories [4, 32]: machine learning methods, linguistic methods, graph methods, statistical and heuristic methods. Statistical methods are based on the computation of different statistics of documents, including the frequency of word occurrences, tf-idf, n-grams and so on [25]. Heuristic methods [28] allow developing the structure of the document by using characteristics such as position of the word in the document, existence of formatting of the elements, document fragment length, etc. According to the article [3], the main tasks in forum summarization are sentiment-analysis, allocation of facts from the documents, analysis of user activity. However, at the same time, the problem of highlighting of professionally significant information is not presented even in its formulation.

Thus, in this paper, we consider the problem of automatic summarization of web forums. Our goal is to study the methods of selection forum posts, which contain professionally significant information.

2 Related Works

There are different approaches to the problem of text summarization. They can be divided into extraction-based and abstraction-based [26] summarization. Also, there are single-document and multi-document approaches. The majority of works in the area of forum summarization use extraction-based techniques and single-document approach [22]. Extractive forum summarization tasks are divided into generic summarization (obtaining a generic summary or abstract of the whole thread) and relevant query summarization, sometimes called query-based summarization, which summarizes posts specific to a query [12].

We found several types of research close to our work in literature. Authors of [11] studied reviews posted on the web assessing "Review Pertinence" as the correlation between review and its article. Authors of [29] considered the sentence relevance and redundancy within the summarized text. Their maximum coverage and minimum redundant (MCMR), text summarization system, computed sentence relevance as its similarity to the document set vector. This idea was also used in [30] for cross-lingual multi-document summarization.

Some articles [21, 30] were devoted to comparing system effectiveness and user utility. Authors of [20] compared traditional TREC procedure of batch evaluation and user searching on the same subject. Authors of [21] confirmed that test collections and their associated evaluation measures did predict user preferences across multiple information retrieval systems. They found that NDCG metric modeled user preferences most effectively.

To sum up, there are no articles with the in-deep study of the problem discussed in our article.

3 Methods

On the one hand, it is proposed to consider certain aspects of user's informational needs. The author of [24] has defined six possible assessment levels for information systems, where the first three were referred to measuring system performance (such as speed of the processing the query, matching the query and document content), the last three levels corresponded to user-oriented evaluation (including feedback, context, social and cognitive matching of query and document and etc.). The author of [14] uses the following measurements: (1) user's characteristics (gender, age, etc.); (2) the interactive parameters (the number of sent requests, the number of viewed documents, etc.); (3) the quantitative characteristics of query results (accuracy, completeness, NDCG, etc.); (4) the qualitative users characteristics (declared by experts).

On the other hand, there are some international projects [9, 13, 18, 25] for evaluation of information retrieval systems, based on the user's information needs. Each project contains an annotated collection of documents (mainly in the style of news), divided into groups of informational needs (tracks). The results of system performance are evaluated by laboratory experts following strong established and context-limited queries statements that limit the applicability of this approach to practical problems.

The analysis of this approaches shown, that the lower levels of classification that described by Saracevic [24] and Kelly [14] can be evaluated by traditional informational retrieval systems quality metrics (such as F-measure, NDCG, etc.). However, the possibility of using them for upper levels associated with the formulation of appropriate information request proposed to expert. In this case, to evaluate the efficiency of extraction of professionally significant information, we formulate information needs in the form of problem-oriented queries and use different contexts for their evaluation.

On the one hand, this approach is consistent with the structure of scaling requests adopted in TREC [9]. On the other hand, their contents cover the real user's informational needs when searching for professionally significant information.

So our target variables will be Informativeness and Relevance. Formal criteria for marking them up are listed in Table 1. It is obvious that binary evaluation of the quality of extraction of professionally significant information would be too coarse-grained. For expert marks of informativeness and Relevance, we use the six-level scale, constructed in a similar way, that described by Elbedweihy [9]. This allows us to consider the measured values as categorical or continuous in the interval [0, 5], depending on selected problem formulation: classification or regression. Also, our experts were given explicitly formalized instructions on how to mark up posts, using a strict and formal scale from Table 1. In order to avoid subjectivity and bias, we've involved several experts.

Table 1. Formal markup criteria

Parameter	Context	Value	Comment
Informativeness	Display posts that contains objective, interesting and professionally significant information on request	0	Post contains no useful information
		1	Post gives some useful information, but most of it is not useful
		2	Post gives a little amount of useful information
		3	Post contains useful information, but explanations and arguments are missing

(*continued*)

Table 1. (*continued*)

Parameter	Context	Value	Comment
		4	Post contains useful information, but explanations and arguments are incomplete
		5	Post contains a lot of useful information with rich explanations and arguments
Relevance	Display posts that contains semantically close information on request	0	Post is completely irrelevant to the query/topic
		1	Posts theme weakly intersects with query/topic
		2	Post contains mostly irrelevant information, but some parts of it are relevant
		3	Post contains mostly relevant information, but some parts of it are irrelevant
		4	Post is relevant to the query/topic, but contains some extending information
		5	Post is completely relevant to the query/topic

3.1 Quality Estimation

Widely used metrics such as F-score, recall/precision, and others are not applicable in our context. Although these measures are commonly used in both IR and semantic search evaluations, their main limitation is that they must be used with a binary scale. Because in our work we are using a non-binary scale, it makes more sense to follow the recommendations of the Elbedweihy [9] and use cumulative gain metrics to evaluate retrieval system quality. We used normalized cumulative gain, that is quality metrics, based on a comparison of the calculated position of the post with its position in the perfect sorting by expert marks. It's calculated using formula:

$$NDCG_N = \frac{DCG_N}{IDCG_N},$$

where

$$DCG_N = rel_1 + \sum_{i=2}^{N} \frac{rel_i}{log_2(i)}$$

N is the size of resulting set (how many documents to retrieve), rel_i is true value of target variable (relevance or informativeness) of i-th post in the retrieved set, and $IDCG_i$ is the maximum possible value of DCG_N for specified forum and for given N, i.e. DCG_N for an ideal algorithm.

To ensure model stability, we used bootstrap-like method. The data was resampled with replacement, then it was split into test and train sets. After that, models were fit, and model qualities were estimated. This process was repeated 200 times, and model qualities was averaged, and confidence interval was calculated:

$$StD_{NDCG} = \sqrt{\frac{\sum_{i=1}^{k} \left(NDCG_i - \overline{NDCG}\right)^2}{k}}$$

where k is the number of bootstrap splits, $\overline{NDCG}$ is the average of $NDCG$ values for k bootstrap steps, $NDCG_i$ that is the $NDCG$ value on the k-th iteration of bootstrap.

3.2 Features

There are various methods for feature extraction proposed in the literature [6, 19, 23, 27]. Based on our previous work, we have made problematic-based feature selection (Table 2). These features are divided into four groups: (1) the position of the author of the post among other users (his position in the social graph); (2) the position of the post in the thread; (3) text features; (4) the emotional evaluation of the post.

In our study, we used expert marks for evaluating the emotional component of posts.

We calculated the features from the first group in two ways to determine the possible relations between emotional evaluation and the values of the target variables for each post using weighted (sentiment graph) and unweighted (non-sentiment graph) graphs.

3.3 Models and Parameters

There are various machine learning methods and their algorithmic implementations nowadays. In the academic literature, there are different principles of their classification.

Also, there are constantly updated ratings, which are made by users and developers. As it was shown above, the result of extracting professionally significant information is determined by the context of the request and the type of evaluation metric, which is associated with the formulation of machine learning problem. So we used two classifying attributes for selection of methods and models of machine learning problem: the type of ML problem (classification/regression) and the target variable (informativeness/relevance).

Table 2. Features

Type	Feature and its meaning
Post author graph features	Betweenness, non-sentiment graph (Author's social importance)
	inDegree, non-sentiment graph (How many times author was quoted)
	outDegree, non-sentiment graph (How many times author quoted someone)
	Betweenness, sentiment graph (Author's social importance)
	inDegree, sentiment graph (With which sentiment author was quoted)
	outDegree, sentiment graph (Author's quotes sentiment)
Post author features	Number of threads author is participating in (Author activity)
Thread-based post features	Position in thread (Chance of off-topic)
	Times quoted (Post impact on forum)
Text features	Length (Number of arguments and length of explanations)
	Links (Number of external sources/images)
	Sentiment value, calculated using sentiment keywords (The emotional evaluation of post)
	Number of query keywords (Topic conformity)
	Most used topic keyword count (Topic conformity)

The selected machine learning algorithms and their parameters are listed in Table 3. For each algorithm we selected its regression and classification modes.

To analyze the impact of the query context on the quality of using machine learning methods we use the following models:

- Multiple Linear Regression (LM). Attempts to model the relationship between two or more explanatory variables and a response variable by fitting a linear equation to observed data. In connection with a sufficient amount of data and weak correlation between features, we use non-regularized model [8].
- Stochastic Gradient Boosting (GBM) which is a model capable of capturing non-linear dependencies. We used three CV folds to estimate the best amount of trees; a number of trees were capped to 2000, and shrinkage factor was 0.001. Indirection level value (number of splits for each tree) was set to 3 [10].
- Latent Dirichlet Allocation (LDA) that is robust interpretable model splits available posts into subsets (topics) according to their texts using bag-of-words approach. Each topic can be interpreted as a set of keywords, and we used the presence of these keywords to estimate target variables. Comparing the keywords sets in formed topics and texts of post we can distinguish the posts, which are corresponding to the specific query context [7].
- Cumulative link model (CLM). Also known as ordered logit model. This is modified ordinal version of multilogistic regression that makes use of the fact that we have several ordered classes [1].
- Word2Vec. This is a parametric model that are used to produce word embeddings. It assigns high-dimensional vector to each word in such way that words with similar meaning have similar vectors. In our experiments we use complete Russian

Table 3. Models Parameters

Model	Algorithm	
	Classification	Regression
	Logistic	Linear
	By default	By default
Support Vector Machine	LibSVM	LibSVM
	By default	By default
Decision Tree	J48	M5P
	Use reduced error pruning: true	Build regression tree/rule rather than a model tree/rule: true
K-nearest neighbors algorithm	IBk	IBk
	Neighbors number: 5; Weight neighbors: by the inverse of their distance; Neighbour's number selection: hold-one-out evaluation;	Neighbors number: 5;
		Weight neighbors: by the inverse of their distance;
		Neighbour's number selection: hold-one-out evaluation;
	Minimization parameter: mean squared error	Minimization parameter: mean squared error
Neural Network	MultilayerPerceptron	MultilayerPerceptron
	Learning Rate for the backpropagation algorithm: 0.001; Momentum Rate for the backpropagation algorithm: 0.001;	Learning Rate for the backpropagation algorithm: 0.001; Momentum Rate for the backpropagation algorithm: 0.001;
	Number of epochs to train through: 5000;	Number of epochs to train through: 5000;
	Percentage size of validation set: 20	Percentage size of validation set: 20
Naive Bayes/Gaussian model	NaïveBayes	GaussianProcesses
	Use kernel density estimator: true	By default

National Corpus model for Russian language and Google News Corpus for English. For each forum post, we do the following steps: split post and query into lexemes, and calculate semantic similarity between each lexeme and user query. After that we rank each post by sum of these similarities [17].

For more detailed analysis we also compare different methods of keywords extraction:

- Most Used Keywords. The model considers posts as a big set of words and selects the most frequent ones.
- Hclust. The model considers thread text as «Document-Term» matrix and forms a hierarchical classification of words. Clustering is the process of partitioning a set of objects into subgroups (clusters) according to proximity or some other criteria.

Formally the problem is posed as follows: let $X = \{x_1, x_2, \ldots, x_n\}$ be a finite set of objects; Y is a set of clusters. Then $\rho(x, x')$ is the distance function between objects x and x'. We are to partition the sample X into disjoint subsets (clusters) in such a way that each cluster consists of objects that are close according to the metric ρ, and object of different clusters are substantially different in this metric. Each object $x_i \in X_N$ is assigned with the corresponding cluster index y_j [15].

- K-means. The model considers thread's text as "Document-Term" matrix. Each word is then assigned to its closest cluster center and the center of the cluster is updated until the state of no change in each cluster center is reached [31].
- Expert. Selecting keywords for each thread by experts. Choosing the most semantically meaningful words based on the thread topic.
- Latent Dirichlet Allocation (LDA). See the description above.

3.4 Data Collection

To collect our data, we used the following steps:

- Select a forum and distinguish threads, which contain at least 400 posts.
- Define user query. Mostly we try the query to be the same as thread name.
- Collect all the posts from these threads with the following information: thread URL, post text, author, information about external sources in post.
- Mark down sentiment value, informativeness and relevance of each post by criteria, listed in Table 1.

The forums used in our work are listed in Table 4.

Table 4. The chosen Internet forums

Forum/URL	Thread title/Query
iXBT (Hardware forum) http://www.forum.ixbt.com/	Choosing of ADSL modem/How to choose ADSL router?
Fashion, style, health http://www.mail.figgery.com/	Diets for overweight people/How to lose weight?
Kinopoisk (cinema forum) http://www.forum.kinopoisk.ru/	"Sex at the city" series/How good is "Sex at the city" and why?
Housebuilding forum http://www.forumhouse.ru/	Building a house using 6×6 wooden planks/How to build a house using 6×6 wooden planks?
Velomania (bicycle forum) http://forum.velomania.ru/	Why are the pistons return to caliper?/Why are the pistons return to caliper?
Guitar players forum http://forum.velomania.ru/	All questions about guitar tuning/How to tune the guitar?
Evening dresses http://club.osinka.ru/	Wedding dresses/How to make the corset pattern?
Sewing the wedding\newline http://thesewingforum.co.uk/	Wedding dresses/Dress for friends wedding - tips for sewing satin/How to handle a silk dress?

3.5   Experiments

For each selected machine learning model we do the following steps:

1. Split data into the train (70\% of each forum) and test (30\%) sets.
2. For the selected model, train set for each target variable and apply it to the test set of each collected forum.
3. Sort posts by decreasing target variable approximation and take the N top posts.
4. Calculate *NDCG* for each selection using ground truth values for informativeness and relevance.

To ensure the model stability we used a bootstrap-like method. We resampled data for each iteration of steps 1–4, split it into train and test, fitted models and estimated quality. This process was repeated 200 times. Then we calculated the models average and its confidence intervals.

4   Results and Discussion

The Pearson correlation coefficient between informativeness and relevance on all forums is 0.36. This is an evidence of that these parameters are different, and query types expect IR system to do different things. Also, distribution of relevance is skewed towards 5 (see Fig. 1b), while the distribution of informativeness has the peak around 3 (see Fig. 1a). The skew of relevance is explained by the procedure of data collection: we choose posts from already relevant threads, so it is expected that most of the marked posts have high relevance. Distribution of informativeness shows that great portion of posts has moderate (2–3) informativeness, and only a small portion of posts have marginally high or low informativeness.

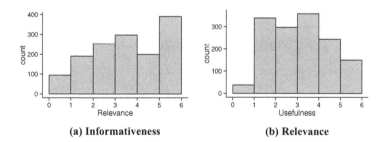

(a) Informativeness   (b) Relevance

Fig. 1. Distribution of target variables

Figures 2 and 3 shows the comparison of machine learning algorithms, that was listed in Table 3. There is not enough information there for selecting best algorithm for extracting professionally significant information. However, there is relatively high consistency (Kendall correlation coefficient was 0.73) among the six studied algorithms. Figure 4 shows the average quality for all algorithms of summarization for both target variables. As it can be seen, relevance is better described with regression methods, while in informativeness evaluation such dependence is weaker and backward. Also, as additional researches shows, the nature of nonlinearity depends on the specific features - there is a strong correlation between the length of the post and its informativeness (see Table 5).

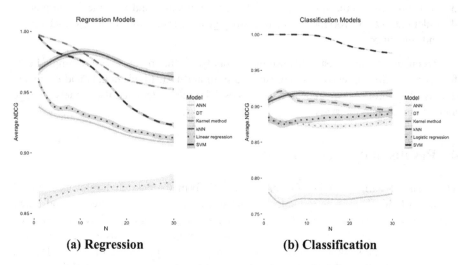

(a) Regression   **(b) Classification**

Fig. 2. Dependence of NDCG on informativeness and type of machine learning task type

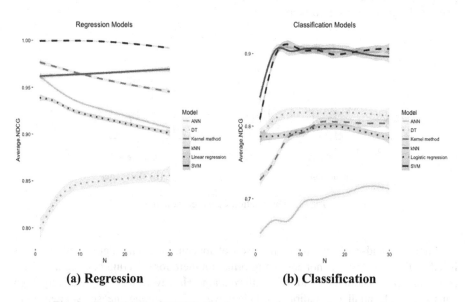

(a) Regression   **(b) Classification**

Fig. 3. Dependence of NDCG on relevance and machine learning task type

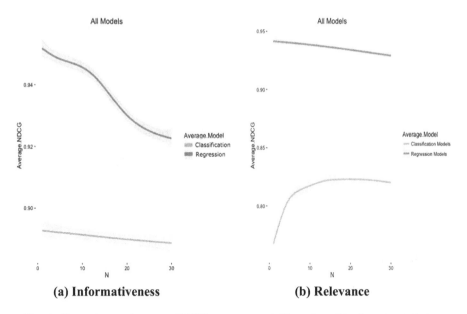

Fig. 4. Dependence of average NDCG on target variable and machine learning task type

Table 5 shows that keywords features are among first leading features in relevance evaluating. The Fig. 6 shows that informativeness is almost independent of keywords extraction method, while relevance is rather sensitive for its selection. Also, Most Used Keywords and Expert keywords are very similar in quality evaluation.

Comparison of Figs. 5 and 6 shows that LDA approach and word2vec model show the worst performance. These models use only textual features. Therefore, non-textual features have great impact on summarization performance.

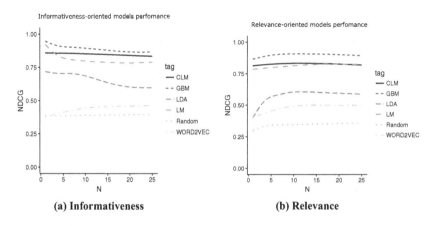

Fig. 5. Dependence of NDCG on target variable and model type

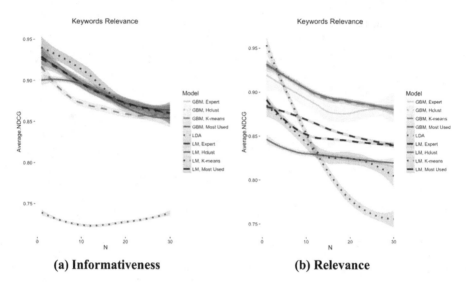

(a) Informativeness   **(b) Relevance**

Fig. 6. Comparison of keywords extraction methods

Regarding the results, our assumptions are the following: the relevance of posts is crucially determined by their lexical features, while the informativeness is related to the semantics of the forum in general and expressed in terms of the characteristics of the posts as a linguistic structure, as well as of the social graph of the forum. So the methods based on model "bag-of-words" such as classical search of keywords or topic modeling can be quite useful to highlight the relevant posts. At the same time, to extract informativeness posts, it makes sense to use specialized algorithms based on principals used in our work. The real interest to real information retrieval systems is the generalized extraction of information for the queries of different types.

Table 5. Best Features

Algorithm	Multiple Linear Regression	Gradient Boosting Model
Target Variable	Relevance	Informativeness
Best Features	Query Keyword Count	Length
	Most Used Keyword Count	Author outDegree
	Author inDegree	Author outDegree with Sentiment value
	Author inDegree with Sentiment value	Post position in thread

5   Conclusion

In this work, we consider the problem of automatic summarization of professionally significant information from web forums. We have collected a big dataset, which contains threads from web forums about different topics. We showed, that the context of query plays an important role in evaluating of information extraction from forums. The informativeness-oriented and relevance-oriented queries are different by nature and have a weak correlation of their target variables. Relevance is best described by a linear combination of features. Also, the method of keywords extraction plays a big role in model effectiveness, when the target variable is relevance. However, at the same time informativeness is better described by the non-linear combination of features and depends on the social graph of the forum and overall textual structure of the thread.

In our future work we want to investigate the practical use of the models, that were proposed in this paper.

Acknowledgements. This work was financially supported by the Government of the Russian Federation (Grant 08-08).

References

1. Agresti, A., Kateri, M.: Categorical Data Analysis. In: Lovric, M. (ed.) International Encyclopedia of Statistical Science. Springer, Heidelberg (2011). https://doi.org/10.1007/978-3-642-04898-2
2. Al-Hashemi, R.: Text summarization extraction system (TSES) using extracted keywords. Int. Arab J. e-Technol. **1**(4), 164–168 (2010)
3. Almahy, I., Salim, N.: Web discussion summarization: study review. In: Herawan, T., Deris, M.M., Abawajy, J. (eds.) Proceedings of the First International Conference on Advanced Data and Information Engineering (DaEng-2013). LNEE, vol. 285, pp. 649–656. Springer, Singapore (2014). https://doi.org/10.1007/978-981-4585-18-7_73
4. Beliga, S., Meštrović, A., Martinčić-Ipšić, S.: An overview of graph-based keyword extraction methods and approaches. J. Inf. Organ. Sci. **39**(1), 1–20 (2015)
5. Bishop, C.M.: Pattern recognition. Mach. Learn. **128** (2006)
6. Biyani, P., Bhatia, S., Caragea, C., Mitra, P.: Using non-lexical features for identifying factual and opinionative threads in online forums. Knowl. Based Syst. **69**, 170–178 (2014)
7. Blei, D.M., Ng, A.Y., Jordan, M.I.: Latent Dirichlet allocation. J. Mach. Learn. Res. **3**, 993–1022 (2003)
8. Bottenberg, R.A., Ward, J.H.: Applied multiple linear regression. Technical report, DTIC Document (1963)
9. Elbedweihy, K.M., Wrigley, S.N., Clough, P., Ciravegna, F.: An overview of semantic search evaluation initiatives. Web Semant. Sci. Serv. Agents World Wide Web **30**, 82–105 (2015)
10. Friedman, J.H.: Stochastic gradient boosting. Comput. Stat. Data Anal. **38**(4), 367–378 (2002)
11. Grozin, V., Dobrenko, N., Gusarova, N., Ning, T.: The application of machine learning methods for analysis of text forums for creating learning objects. Comput. Linguist. Intellect. Technol. **1**, 199–209 (2015)
12. Grozin, V.A., Gusarova, N.F., Dobrenko, N.V.: Feature selection for language independent text forum summarization. In: Klinov, P., Mouromtsev, D. (eds.) KESW 2015. CCIS, vol. 518, pp. 63–71. Springer, Cham (2015). https://doi.org/10.1007/978-3-319-24543-0_5
13. Harman, D.: Information Retrieval Evaluation. Synthesis Lectures on Information Concepts, Retrieval, and Services, vol. 3, no. 2, pp. 1–119 (2011

14. Kelly, D.: Methods for evaluating interactive information retrieval systems with users. Found. Trends Inf. Retr. **3**(12), 1–224 (2009)
15. Lomakina, L., Rodionov, V., Surkova, A.: Hierarchical clustering of text documents. Autom. Remote Control **75**(7), 1309–1315 (2014)
16. Lott, B.: Survey of keyword extraction techniques. UNM Education (2012)
17. Mikolov, T., Dean, J.: Distributed representations of words and phrases and their compositionality. In: Advances in Neural Information Processing Systems (2013)
18. Nenkova, A., McKeown, K.: A survey of text summarization techniques. In: Aggarwal, C., Zhai, C. (eds.) Mining Text Data, pp. 43–76. Springer, Boston (2012). https://doi.org/10. 1007/978-1-4614-3223-4_3
19. Nettleton, D.F.: Data mining of social networks represented as graphs. Comput. Sci. Rev. **7**, 1–34 (2013)
20. Oufaida, H., Nouali, O., Blache, P.: Minimum redundancy and maximum relevance for single and multi-document Arabic text summarization. J. King Saud Univ. Comput. Inf. Sci. **26**(4), 450–461 (2014)
21. Petrelli, D.: On the role of user-centred evaluation in the advancement of interactive information retrieval. Inf. Process. Manage. **44**(1), 22–38 (2008)
22. Ren, Z., Ma, J., Wang, S., Liu, Y.: Summarizing web forum threads based on a latent topic propagation process. In: Proceedings of the 20th ACM International Conference on Information and Knowledge Management, pp. 879–884. ACM (2011). Mining of relevant and informative posts from text forums 15
23. Romero, C., López, M.I., Luna, J.M., Ventura, S.: Predicting students' final performance from participation in on-line discussion forums. Comput. Educ. **68**, 458–472 (2013)
24. Saracevic, T.: Evaluation of evaluation in information retrieval. In: Proceedings of the 18th Annual International ACM SIGIR Conference on Research and Development in Information Retrieval, pp. 138–146. ACM (1995)
25. Schütze, H.: Introduction to information retrieval. In: Proceedings of the International Communication of Association for Computing Machinery Conference (2008)
26. Sizov, G.: Extraction-based automatic summarization: theoretical and empirical investigation of summarization techniques (2010)
27. Smine, B., Faiz, R., Desclés, J.P.: Relevant learning objects extraction based on semantic annotation. Int. J. Metadata Semant. Ontol. **8**(1), 13–27 (2013)
28. Sondhi, P., Gupta, M., Zhai, C., Hockenmaier, J.: Shallow information extraction from medical forum data. In: Proceedings of the 23rd International Conference on Computational Linguistics: Posters, pp. 1158–1166. Association for Computational Linguistics (2010)
29. Tang, J., Yao, L., Chen, D.: Multi-topic based query-oriented summarization. In: SDM, vol. 9, pp. 1147–1158. SIAM (2009)
30. Wang, J.Z., Yan, Z., Yang, L.T., Huang, B.X.: An approach to rank reviews by fusing and mining opinions based on review pertinence. Inf. Fusion **23**, 3–15 (2015)
31. Wartena, C., Brussee, R.: Topic detection by clustering keywords. In: 2008 19th International Workshop on Database and Expert Systems Applications, pp. 54–58. IEEE (2008)
32. Zhao, H., Zeng, Q.: Micro-blog keyword extraction method based on graph model and semantic space. J. Multimed. **8**(5), 611–617 (2013)

Text and Data Mining Techniques in Judgment Open Data Analysis for Administrative Practice Control

Oleg Metsker[1(✉)], Egor Trofimov[2], Sergey Sikorsky[1],
and Sergey Kovalchuk[1]

[1] ITMO University, Saint Petersburg, Russia
olegmetsker@gmail.com, sikorskiy.s@hotmail.com,
sergey.v.kovalchuk@gmail.com
[2] All-Russian State University of Justice, Moscow, Russia
diterihs@mail.ru

Abstract. This paper represents the study results of machine learning methods application for the analysis of judgment open data. The study is dedicated to develop empirical ways to identify the relationships and the structure of administrative law enforcement process based on semi-structured data analysis and give recommendations for improving the administrative regulation. The results of the research can be us ed for legislative, analytical and law enforcement activities in the field of governmental regulation. In the course of data analysis, the models based on decision trees and other machine learning methods is developed. In addition, the models for extracting information from semi-structured texts of court decisions is developed. Moreover, a predictive model of appeal outcome is developed. The effectiveness of the established methods are demonstrated in the recommendation cases for improving the current legislation by the example of administrative law for reducing the burden on public administration.

Keywords: e-government · Data mining · Text mining · Machine learning · Law · Modeling · Legaltech · Govtech

1 Introduction

The development of the data-driven modeling field of the law application practice is a catalyzing factor of e-government development. Most of the processes in the sphere of public administration refer to the execution of legislation. For this reason, the main purpose of the study is to identify the relationships and structure of the process of application of the legislation and to develop on this basis recommendations for improving the law with the use of intelligent methods of processing of multidimensional data. Data mining and modeling of administrative judicial control system processes allow identifying implicit connections, defining the structure and elements of the overall complex process, the interrelationships of the system components, and their relationship with scientific, technical, social, economic, political and cultural elements of the external environment. Besides, the issue of open data is one of the critical points

© Springer Nature Switzerland AG 2019
A. Chugunov et al. (Eds.): EGOSE 2018, CCIS 947, pp. 169–180, 2019.
https://doi.org/10.1007/978-3-030-13283-5_13

on the agenda of digitalization of the Government of the Russian Federation. The Decree of the President of the Russian Federation on May 7, 2012 No. 601 "On the main directions of improvement of the system of public administration" (sub-item "d" point 2) set the task to provide access to the Internet to open data, including those contained in the information systems of public authorities of the Russian Federation. The issues related to the modeling of the law enforcement processes on open data constitute an actual scientific and technical problem. With the right approach to knowledge extraction from open data, analytical capabilities of semantic approaches of intellectual analysis of processes are available to develop recommendations for improving the current legislation. At the same time, at the current level of the development of the jurisprudence, the limits and possibilities for using data mining and modeling processes of administrative and administrative regulation remain an unsolved scientific problem. Further, the second part of the article describes the problem, the link of this article with e-government and the background. The papers in this domain are poorly identified in the scientific community or belong to another legal system. Some close topics and experience are analyzed in the third part of this article. The empirical basis of the study is the data of judgments from the state information porta[1]. It described further in the fourth part of this article. The data covers most of the Russian regions and is randomly selected. The data reflect the process of prosecution on administrative law for 2016 and 2017. In the course of text mining and data mining it is possible to get the following contributions for the society: legislation optimization to save resources (time, human, financial, etc.); assessment of legislative initiatives related to changes in procedural regulation; assessment of prospects of appeal (protest) of acts of law enforcement; deviations identification for anticorruption, compliance service and/or to assess the professionalism of law enforcement officers. At present, the results obtained sufficient confidence about the feasibility detailed research about the identification of criminological characteristics. In the fifth part of this article describes cases for the improvement of the current legislation on the example of article 20.1 hooliganism.

2 Problem Definition

An important problem to be solved in this article is the creation of breakthrough solutions for e-government, supporting it infrastructure and adequate methods. It is necessary to take into account the existing retrospective experience and cost-effective analytics methods. From a scientific point of view, interdisciplinary studies are complicated, so their success requires solving several different tasks from different domains. It requires deep knowledge in these different domains. Communication of various highly focused specialists obtains the main contribution to such studies. This study covers several fields, including computer and legal sciences. It means that the results should be estimated accordingly. There is a problem of empirical based methods in law science based methods [1]. The methodological basis of the research in legal science is

---

[1] https://sudrf.ru/.

general and special scientific methods, including the systematic approach and formal legal method. These methods are conditionally empirical. The empirical analysis can provide valid estimates of what would have happened in comparison to what has already happened [2]. It is achieved by observing the outcomes that arise when new procedures are applied with results that occur in a similar context when a new procedure does not exist. Data analysis methods can provide new opportunities for lawmakers and scientists [3]. The social processes become more complicated with the introduction of modern methods and algorithms of information processing and storage [4]. Process administration supported by adequate methods becomes the necessary condition for quality management. The algorithms are well-known and widely used. For many decades they have been considered as the combined components of a computer program. Today, with advanced data analysis algorithms, a significant part of society's automation is being created, transforming many aspects of life. Therefore, it is essential to develop adequate methods of administration of such complex processes. E-government should be able to make empirical based predictions and create adequate predictive regimes not only in the military field, but also in the civil life. Administrative law is a critical e-government element in the prevention of more serious crimes. Of course, the legislator should not have such broad discretion in choosing the acts to be restricted. For the adoption of effective legislative acts, a correct understanding of the process of enforcing the law is necessary. Now the legislator relies on the opinion of experts, which can be subjective, and on statistics that are one-dimensional. Intellectual analysis provides much more opportunities for a correct understanding of the experience of law enforcement and the identification of shortcomings in the activities of the administration and courts. The large amount of data that computers analyze and the possibilities of machine learning make it possible to obtain a more accurate and objective knowledge of the operation of the law and the processes and interrelations that take place in this process. Today, the government does not have precise information about such processes and interrelationships. For example, over the years a "manual" analysis of administrative cases has led researchers to conclude that half of the hooliganism acts are committed by drunken persons. However, a computational analytical experiment of 19623 judicial acts in this category demonstrated that it is three times too high. However, the data problem affects a few points. First point is the growth of data amounts. The second important point is the growth of data complexity. The problem of extracting knowledge from semi-structured data is the third point. An equally significant problem is the correspondence of the data to the real process to be described. Typically, there is a gap between the query of the analytical community and the requirements that data warehouses providers fulfill. Using data mining and machine learning techniques it is possible to obtain an empirical basis for legal science and to provide an administrative practice with a predictive component. Thus, the authors of this article propose an effective method of analysis of large open data for e-government purposes.

3   Related Work

As a rule, the papers related to the analysis of administrative law enforcement practices involves judicial review of regulatory measures. If the appeal is applied correctly, it is possible to improve the regulatory impact [5]. The analysis of empirical data on claims reveals the structure of the process and the impact of courts on administrative bodies. As a result, it is possible to improve the analytical quality of decision-making by administrative authorities and to improve the quality of response of administrative services [6]. The data allows not only to analyze the current process better but also to predict [7]. The smart city concept is widely used for efficient use of resources [8]. The government and management in large cities have a positive experience of the use of intelligent methods of data analysis and machine learning to improve the efficiency of administration in various fields [9]. Decision support systems based on intelligent methods are developed in the following fields: healthcare [10] for quality control; nuclear emergency situation administration [11]; artificial neural networks, systems based on knowledge in the field of forest management [12]. A large number of papers are investigated text mining methods for data structuring and knowledge extraction [13]. The questions of data quality of the models used for learning are necessary, because the final results strongly depend on the data quality. Text mining, data mining and machine learning methods in particular are the basis of intelligent data-based systems. With the help of mining text methods, crucial predictive information is extracted, using templates [14] and machine learning. Machine learning algorithms have been successfully applied by the governments of large cities like Chicago for optimization administration, fire service [15], and rodents control [16]. The work on solving problems of optimization of a particular administrative process is explained but not the process of developing laws. Among other algorithms of data mining (tSNE [17], decision trees [18]), we can successfully solve the problems of classification, clustering and regression [19] to identify dependencies and better understand the processes. These are three main intelligent methods for solving the tasks. However, the application of data mining methods, as well as text mining and machine learning to improve administrative legislation is poorly identified. This fact makes a valuable contribution to this study.

4   Case Study

4.1   Preprocessing and Knowledge Extraction of Judgment Open Data

In the process analysis, the data describing the process should highly correspond to the specified process. Increasing the correspondence of data relating the real process is one of the critical tasks of data mining and text mining. Electronic data of judicial decisions consists of a set of various elements that contains structured and semi-structured information, as well as information represented in an unstructured form in the natural language (the contents of the rules, circumstances mitigating punishment, circumstances aggravating penalties, conclusion, etc.). The data represents a significant value for the analysis and the identification of process elements. Besides, the extraction of data from texts in natural language, is, in itself, an essential scientific task. The developed method of data structuring is based on analytical inquiries and hypotheses of representatives of the legal community. The method is based on patterns. The requirement for high accuracy causes the application of the method based on the patterns. By the primary method, a preliminary study of the subject area is carried out at the first stage. Applicable to the legal field are examined legislative acts, scientific articles, as well as reference and training in legal literature. As a result, of this preliminary research, hypotheses and problems of information identification are developed. To ensure the completeness of the data describing the judicial decision we extract information contained in the decisions of the first instance, the first revision, the second appeal in the descriptive and motivational part. Recent documents contain meaningful information about the circumstances of the case and are important data for further analysis. Then, according to the task of identification and extraction, algorithms are formed for teaching rules (templates) and selecting the necessary data for structuring. Typically, the templates for the first instance decisions differ from the appeal templates. For this reason, it is desirable to separate these documents during the preprocessing phase. Processed data is analyzed using a template. In case of an unsatisfactory result, the template is modified, and the data is processed again. The cycle of template modification and data processing continues until the required identification result is achieved. Later, these rules are divided into induction and probabilistic methods. Successful templates can be used for developing problem-oriented data processing libraries. Identified entities are written as attributes in datasets for analysis. When applying this method, errors in the data analysis, are often reduced to the wrong choice of the template or the analyzed part of the judicial document.

4.2   Common Open Data Analysis and Data Visualization

In the course of the study, the electronic data of 55,286 judgments courts of the different regions of Russia (Table 1) has been analyzed. The data was taken in random mode. These adjudications include 96.3% of sentencing orders and 3.7% of cancellation orders.

Administrative process relates to the field of traffic management, behavior in public places, fire safety, rules for the registration of lands, etc. Figure 1 shows the percentage of court records from dataset according to the laws.

The most common law is 20.1 for hooliganism entails a fine of 500 to 1,000 rubles or an administrative arrest of 1 to 15 days. Further, the distribution of fines under administrative laws (See Fig. 2).

This kind of visual data analysis identifies the distribution of the values of the attribute of a particular process. Medians and deviations deserve attention. From a practical point of view, the distribution can identify the fines that are not usually imposed but are in the law. This is applicable to the law improvement. Moreover, it allows to controlling the validity of the data. The given boxplots show emissions that can be compared with the fines borders. At this stage, the correctness of processing and extraction of knowledge is also controlled.

Table 1. The number of analyzed documents by Russia regions.

Region	Quantity
Southern Federal District	14637
Central Federal District	10878
Volga Federal District	9804
Siberian Federal District	7208
North-West Federal District	6107
Ural Federal District	3118
Far Eastern Federal District	2485
North-Caucasian Federal District	1049

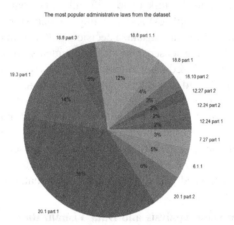

Fig. 1. The most popular administrative laws in the dataset for further deep analysis.

4.3   Correlation Analysis, Interpretation and Recommendation Hypotheses

At this stage of the study, correlation analysis and interpretation of the results were performed. For example, the most popular article from the sample was analyzing. In the course of the correlation analysis, the types of offenses extracted from the judgments by the methods of text mining were factorized. The analysis includes: the most popular article (20.1 part 1 or 20.1 part 2), the circumstances aggravating and mitigating the penalty, the duration of the arrest (See Fig. 3).

During the correlations analysis, the following conclusions have been made:

1. Fine per part of the article. Interpretation: it confirms the validity of the data as the penalty for part 2 is higher than for part 1.
2. Arrest correlates to the part of the article. Interpretation: the courts impose more severe sanctions on part 2, although in the law they are the same like part 1. Recommendation: amend the law for more severe punishment by judicial practice for part 2.

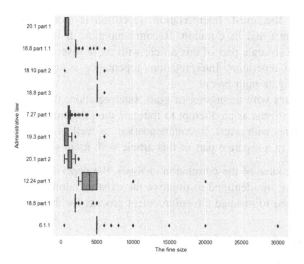

Fig. 2. Boxplot showing the distribution of fines applied as administrative process results.

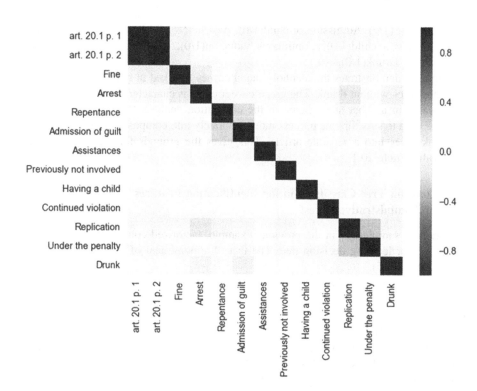

Fig. 3. An example of the correlation matrix in the visual analysis of electronic data in judicial decisions.

3. Repetition for the arrest. Interpretation: repetition is mostly correlated with the purpose of arrest and its duration. Recommendation: it is possible to propose a repetition in a separate part of this article with more severe punishment.
4. Repentance to repetition. Interpretation: repentance is used by violators as an attempt to mitigate punishment
5. Drunk correlates with admission of guilt. Interpretation: the admission of guilt is also used by citizens as an attempt to mitigate the punishment.
6. Drunk correlates with arrest. Recommendation: as well as in p. 3, it is possible to make a drunk in a separate part of this article with more severe punishment.

Thus, in the course of the correlation analysis, the dependencies and put forward several hypotheses are identified to improve the existing administrative process. This method can be used to manage the enforcement process for the e-government tasks.

4.4 Clusterization for Administrative Process Analysis

In the following experiment t-sne method of dimension reduction was used from sklearn[2] (See Fig. 4). This method is good for non-linear dependencies identifications and their visualization. As features were used: part of the article (20.1 part 1 or 20.1 part 2), Repair(1/0), Admission of child(1/0), Assistance(1/0), Previously not involved (1/0), Having a child(1/0), Continuous violation(1/0), Replication(1/0), Under the penalty(1/0), Drunk(1/0).

Figure 4 demonstrates the alcohol-related crimes (marked in red). The green color indicates cases without drunk. The green cluster cases is characterized by the first time crime cases in a sober state. Same in the correlation analysis (Fig. 3), it suggests a possible need to structure the process more accurately into compositions and separation of drunk cases into a separate article. This gives the grounds for the hypothesis to amend the article 20.1.

4.5 Decision Tree Classification for Identification Features of Administrative Arrest

The training samples, as in the previous example, factorized contents of crimes have been used for learning decision tree. The fact of appointment of arrest is used as the target (See Fig. 5).

This method of machine learning demonstrates the probability of the outcome of judgments depending on the circumstances of the case, based on the method of machine-learning training decision trees. This method shows the hierarchy of factors based on the Gini coefficient. It is worth noting that the decision tree gives significant results of the decision-making processes at the top levels. At these levels, the tree shows the importance of the circumstances of the case, which guides a judge in decision-making. At the lower levels of the tree shows the relationship of the various offenses (in part 1 or 2 of the article) criminological characteristics, which is beyond the scope of the process of qualification of the acts committed. The lower levels show the

---

[2] http://scikit-learn.org/.

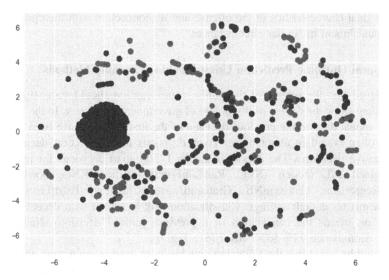

Fig. 4. An example of the method of reducing the dimension of multidimensional data by t-sne by sklearn

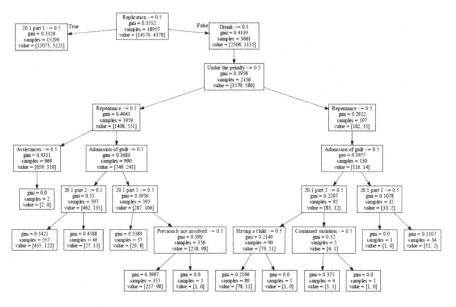

Fig. 5. The analysis of features using decision trees.

criminological characteristics of the offense and its connection with the choice of the type of punishment in similar circumstances.

4.6 Appeal Outcome Prediction Using Machine Learning Methods

It is believed that the reform of the public administration should start with appeals because they show the degree of discontent of government by society. In the following case, the appeal data on the previous decision of the first instance have been analyzed. Citizens often complain about higher court decisions to cancel court decisions and administrative decisions. The dataset based on 17500 court decisions for reconsideration trained ML models (SVC, RandomForestClassifier, KNeighborsClassifier, LogisticRegression, GaussianNB, GradientBoostingClassifier, ExtraTreesClassifier from sklearn) on default settings. Classification task is solved with decent accuracy (target class means the cancelation of a previous judicial decision). Naive Bayes classifier demonstrate 93% ROC cover (See Fig. 6).

It should be noted that the following data has been used as predictors: number and part of the article, forensic characteristics (aggravating circumstances, repetition, consent of guilt, repentance, the presence of children, drunk, fine size, type of administrative person). This model allows us to calculate the probability of cancellation of a court decision. Understanding the low probability can relieve the courts. High probability may indicate the need to change the management process.

4.7 Recommendations for Improvement of the Current Law

The results of the computational experiment allow to make the following theoretically and practically significant recommendations for bringing the current legislation in accordance with judicial practice: recommendation 1 about strengthening of sanctions of part 2 of article 20.1 of the administrative low of the Russian Federation according to the judicial practice (raising the lower limit of administrative arrest); recommendation 2 about isolation in separate part of article 20.1 of the administrative low of the Russian Federation of the new qualified (on the basis of repetition) sign of hooliganism; recommendation 3 about removal in separate part of article 20.1 of the administrative low of the Russian Federation of the new qualified (on the basis of drunk state) sign of hooliganism; recommendation 4 about need of revision of the list or the order of accounting of the circumstances mitigating administrative responsibility in connection with the practice of abuse of these circumstances from violators of public calmness.

The use of intelligent methods based on data mining allow to conclusions much more reasonable than is still accepted in legal science (using traditional manual and subjective methods of research). The legal practice data analysis is a new layer in the development of e-government. It moves law issues into the field of information technology that were previously solved only by experts and assessments. This skill is definitely necessary for the e-government administration.

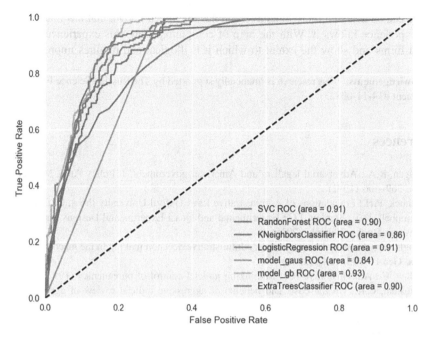

Fig. 6. ROC coverage of the model to predict the probability of a successful appeal.

5   Conclusion and Future Work

This study showed an objective, cost-effective, technological and easy method of big data analysis for e-government tasks. Among such tasks may be the optimization of the current legislation, analysis of legislative initiatives, optimization of the administrative process, reducing the cost of analysis. From the point of administrative and decision science view, empirical analysis of law enforcement practice has revealed a deviation in the decision-making process as it demonstrates the weak connection of some criminal characteristics of offenses with the process of making a court decision. The analysis of decision trees has been proved to be the most applicable and interpreter of the applied methods. Further research may focus on this point. Decision trees are the most interpreted view. An additional research is also needed for the syntactic structure of documents on court decisions regarding the importance of features. In the course of the study, a method of structuring for the subsequent analysis of data in the legal field has been developed. The efficiency of the developed method is proved in the course of experiments and the interpretation of the results in the form of recommendations for the improvement of administrative and tort legislation. Each of the considered areas of the possibility of improving the administrative regulation during the empirical study based on the data of judgments. Intellectual analysis and methods of machine learning can solve a complex problem, which still causes many disputes among legal experts. Now with the help of information technology it becomes possible to provide an empirical basis for the legislation and practice of its implementation, and all suggestions of experts can be assessed more objectively. It has long been known that law has no logic, only experience knows it. With the help of computing tools, this experience can take logical forms and show the extent to which it is illogical and requires improvement.

Acknowledgements. This research is financially supported by The Russian Science Foundation, Agreement #14-11-00823.

References

1. Kagan, R.A.: Adversarial legalism and American government. J. Policy Anal. Manage. **10** (3), 369–406 (1991)
2. Schuck, P.H.: Foundations of Administrative Law. Oxford University Press, Oxford (1994)
3. Campbell, D.T., Stanley, J.C.: Experimental and Quasi-Experimental Designs for Research. Ravenio Books, Helsinki (2015)
4. Coglianese, C.: Regulating by robot: administrative decision making in the machine-learning era. Geo LJ **105**, 1147 (2016)
5. Edley, C.: Administrative law: Rethinking judicial control of bureaucracy (1992)
6. Sunstein, C.R.: On the costs and benefits of aggressive judicial review of agency action. Duke LJ, 522 (1989)
7. Ryu, S.: Book review: predictive analytics: the power to predict who will click, buy, lie or die. Healthc. Inform. Res. **19**(1), 63 (2013)
8. Kitchin, R.: The real-time city? Big Data and smart urbanism. GeoJournal **79**(1), 1–14 (2014)
9. Choucair, B., Bhatt, J., Mansour, R.: How cities are using analytics to improve public health. Harv. Bus. Rev. (2014). https://hbr.org/2014/09/how-cities-are-using-analytics-to-improve-public-health
10. Fitzmaurice, J.M., Adams, K., Eisenberg, J.M.: Three decades of research on computer applications in health care: medical informatics support at the Agency for Healthcare Research and Quality. J. Am. Med. Inform. Assoc. **9**(2), 144–160 (2002)
11. Papamichail, K.N., French, S.: Design and evaluation of an intelligent decision support system for nuclear emergencies. Decis. Support Syst. **41**(1), 84–111 (2005)
12. Arrue, B.C., Ollero, A., Matinez De Dios, J.R.: An intelligent system for false alarm reduction in infrared forest-fire detection. IEEE Intell. Syst. Appl. **15**(3), 64–73 (2000)
13. Feldman, R., Sanger, J.: The text mining handbook: advanced approaches in analyzing unstructured data (2007)
14. Metsker, O., et al.: Pattern-based mining in electronic health records for complex clinical process analysis. Procedia Comput. Sci. **119**, 197–206 (2017)
15. Heaton, B.: New York City Fights Fire with Data, GOV'T TECH. http://www.govtech.com/public-safety/New-York-City-Fights-Fire-with-Data.html
16. Ash Center Mayors Challenge Research Team. Chicago's SmartData Platform, 8 January 2014. http://datasmart.ash.harvard.edu/news/article/chicago-mayors-challenge-367
17. van der Maaten, L., Hinton, G.: Visualizing data using t-SNE. J. Mach. Learn. Res. **9**, 2579–2605 (2008)
18. Friedl, M.A., Brodley, C.E.: Decision tree classification of land cover from remotely sensed data. Remote Sens. Environ. **61**(3), 399–409 (1997)
19. Weisberg, S.: Applied Linear Regression, vol. 528. Wiley, Hoboken (2005)

Digital Public Administration, Economy, Policy

Analysing Strategic Misalignment in Public Administration

Dóra Őri[✉] and Zoltán Szabó

Department of Information Systems, Corvinus University of Budapest,
Budapest, Hungary
{DOri,Szabo}@informatika.uni-corvinus.hu

Abstract. Problems concerning strategic alignment can manifest in several aspects and perspectives of an organisation. This paper presents public administration-specific organisational misalignment problems and propose a method for detecting the symptoms of the misaligned state in enterprise architecture models. The analysis follows the concept of strategic alignment perspectives, collecting typical misalignment symptoms and detection prospects along the four traditional strategic alignment perspectives. A case study in a public organisation demonstrates the usability of the proposed EAM-based misalignment assessment framework.

Keywords: Strategic alignment · Enterprise architecture management ·
Misalignment · Modeling · Alignment perspectives

1 Introduction

Rapid changes in technology, society and economy have strong impact on the public sector. Increasing complexity, volatility, uncertainty, and ambiguity push decision makers to explore the opportunities of digital transformation, but digitization is a great challenge for the sector. New technological trends enable completely new ways of interaction with society, emerging technologies have impact on how public services are organised and delivered to citizens. Growing expectations of the citizens for direct participation, transparency will also affect public services and organizations. These challenges enforce public sector organizations to implement innovative solutions, change organizational design, increase agility – that is why strategic alignment has increasing importance.

Strategic alignment was originally defined as concerning the inherently dynamic fit between external and internal domains, such as the product/market, strategy, administrative structures, business processes and IT [4]. Strategic alignment is based on the concept that strategic choices related to internal and external domains must be consistent. According to a generally accepted axiom organization's competitive position and supporting administrative infrastructure must be aligned, and consistency of decisions concerning external and internal domains is necessary. Organizational structure and competencies must be suited to implement strategy and to enable efficient and effective operations. On the other hand internal structure and capabilities can influence strategy. Traditionally IT had been playing internally oriented roles in an

© Springer Nature Switzerland AG 2019
A. Chugunov et al. (Eds.): EGOSE 2018, CCIS 947, pp. 183–197, 2019.
https://doi.org/10.1007/978-3-030-13283-5_14

organization. Recently, as IT has become a major enabler of organizational change and business innovations, it is a key factor in strategic planning.

The SAM model [4] can be referred to as the most cited alignment model in literature. The model has four key domains of strategic choice (a.k.a. alignment domains): (1) Business Strategy, (2) Organisational Infrastructure and Processes, (3) IT Strategy and (4) IT Infrastructure and Processes. The external axis of the model consists of the business and IT strategy domains, while the internal axis contains organisational and IT infrastructure and processes. Business axis refers to business strategy and business structure, while IT axis consists of IT strategy and IT structure. The model is based on two primary building blocks: (1) strategic fit and (2) functional integration. The strategic fit dimension means the need to align the external and internal domains of IT, while functional integration consists of the need to integrate business and IT domains. Organizational success depends on a complex coalignment of these domains. The objective is to build an organizational structure and internal processes that reflect the firm's strategy and the required IT capabilities.

The model is a complex coalignment of strategy, organization and management processes. The overall process involves a series of process stages, each concerned with one potential triangle. [4] argues that four from the eight possible combination are particularly important:

1. Alignment of the business strategy, organizational and IT infrastructure refers to the strategic execution.
2. Alignment of the business strategy, IT strategy and IT infrastructure refers to the technology transformation (or technology leverage).
3. Alignment of the IT strategy, business strategy and organizational infrastructure refers to the competitive potential (technology exploitation).
4. Cross-domain perspective that involves IT strategy, IT infrastructure, and organizational infrastructure and processes refers to the service level (technology implementation).

Our analysing approach is based on the framework of Henderson and Venkatraman [4], as it is the most widely accepted alignment model that fits to organizational design principles and also to the concepts of enterprise architecture management.

This study presents an alignment perspective-driven analysis of strategic alignment problems at public sector organisations, providing several typical misalignment symptoms and their detection and management suggestions. Furthermore, the paper proposes an enterprise architecture (EA) based method for misalignment symptom detection, which supports the management of these public sector specific symptoms. The usability of the proposed method is tested with a case study at a public administration organisation.

The rest of the paper is organised as follows: Sect. 2 presents the theoretical background for misalignment assessment, with special attention to EA-based misalignment analysis methods. Typical misalignment symptoms along the strategic alignment perspectives are assessed in Sect. 3. The proposed EA-based method as well as the case study are discussed in Sect. 4. The paper concludes with a discussion summary and some future research directions.

2   EA-Based Misalignment Assessment

To investigate the state of business-IT alignment in an organisation, two general perspectives can be considered, (1) to analyse its presence (alignment assessment) or (2) analyse its absence or deficiencies (misalignment assessment) [1, 2]. The common way of evaluating the state of business-IT alignment is alignment evaluation, which analyses the presence of this phenomenon. In the case of analysing its absence or deficiencies, misalignment assessment is conducted.

While organisations are continually trying to achieve alignment, they are suffering from difficulties which encumber the achievement of alignment. This observation points out the phenomenon of misalignment, which is referred to as the "opposite" of strategic alignment, i.e. when strategy, structure, processes and technology are not perfectly harmonised. Most traditional alignment studies deal with alignment achievement, while misalignment issues are scarcely covered in literature. However, organisations are in the state of misalignment as long as they achieve (or at least approach) the state of alignment. Misalignment analysis is an important step in achieving alignment since it helps to understand the nature and the barriers of alignment. In addition, it supports organisations in proposing certain steps to re-achieve alignment.

There are several misalignment models mentioned in literature. The very first mention of misalignment was conducted by Luftman [7], who collected a set of misalignment symptoms. The relevance of this work was twofold, (1) it declared that misalignment can be detected by its symptoms; (2) it stated that misalignment inhibits the achievement of alignment. The next relevant work on misalignment was conducted by Pereira and Sousa [9]. They gave a summary of key issues concerning Business-IT Alignment. In their work, they identified misalignment as one of the key alignment concerns. Additional frameworks on misalignment included different aspects regarding misalignment. Fritscher and Pigneur [6] proposed a business model ontology for misalignment identification. Zarvic and Wieringa [19] introduced the GRAAL framework (Guidelines Regarding Architecture Alignment). Strong and Volkoff [12] proposed a categorisation for misfit types. Carvalho and Sousa [1] proposed a model in which misalignment was introduced from a medical science perspective, using the analogy of detecting, correcting and preventing illnesses. Chen et al. [3] introduced an approach which dealt with business and IT architecture misalignment management. It was an engineering-principled misalignment detection and correction method which set up 12 steps to detect and correct misalignment.

Since misalignment is a non-desired state, organisations aim to eliminate it. Organisations can avoid this condition by detecting, correcting and preventing misalignment(s). The triad of (1) detecting, (2) correcting and (3) preventing misalignment(s) is the general process of handling the phenomenon [1, 3].

Problems, complicating factors and aggravating circumstances that occur while organisations are trying to achieve alignment are considered the indicators of misalignment. To classify these indicators, several approaches can be taken. Carvalho and Sousa [1] provide different classification schemes for the indicators of misalignment. Misalignment symptoms are considered evidence of inefficiencies, difficulties or inabilities that encumber alignment achievement. The existence of these symptoms demonstrates the state of misalignment in an organisation. Misalignment symptom detection deals with the identification of such indicators.

Several misalignment symptom collections have been proposed in recent literature on misalignment (e.g. [1, 10]). These collections contain different types of misalignment symptoms. Misalignment symptoms can be categorised via different approaches. Strong and Volkoff [12] provide a possible categorisation scheme by classifying misalignment symptoms into (1) Functionality, (2) Data, (3) Usability, (4) Role, (5) Control and (6) Organisational Culture misfit types. Saat et al. [11] propose a classification by IT system and business categories. The alignment perspectives of the SAM model [4] can also be used as a classification scheme for misalignment symptoms.

Enterprise architecture (EA) is the construction of an enterprise, described by its entities and their relationships [18]. EA is an organising logic for business processes and IT infrastructure in order to review, maintain and control the whole operation of an enterprise. This organising logic acts as an integrating force between business planning, business operations and enabling technological infrastructure. Enterprise architecture integrates information systems and business processes into a coherent map. Enterprise architecture supports IT strategy, IT governance and business-IT alignment It also helps to capture a vision of the entire system in all its dimensions and complexity [8, 14, 18]. The management of enterprise architecture results in increased transparency, documented architecture vision and clear architecture principles and guidelines. These factors contribute to efficient resource allocation, the creation of synergies, better alignment, and reduced complexity. In the end, better business performance can be achieved by using the enterprise architecture management (EAM) concept. EAM promotes the vertical integration between strategic directions and tactical concepts, design decisions, and operations. Additionally, it provides horizontal alignment between business change and technology. Enterprise architecture analysis types are methods that are capable of assessing EA models, e.g. evaluating dependencies, isolated objects, complexity or heterogeneity [8, 13, 17].

There have been many attempts to investigate reciprocal contributions between strategic (mis)alignment assessment and EA analysis [e.g. 15, 16]. Recently, there has been an increased interest in EA-based alignment assessment, especially in matching EA domains to evaluate the state of alignment in an organisation. The state of alignment can be examined via several methods. One of the main research methods of analysing alignment is enterprise architecture-based assessment [18]. This method assesses how IT is aligned with organisational goals. While earlier studies on alignment assessment primarily focused on strategic and holistic perspectives, the innate connection between business models and architectures have not been revealed [3]. Enterprise architecture describes the logical structure of the different architecture layers and links all levels from business strategy to IT implementation. In this sense, EA enables us to assess the alignment between business and IT. Undertaking an architectural assessment is a helpful way to determine the state of alignment and to identify re-architecture needs. Architecture assessment consists of sole architecture layer analysis, as well as fit analysis between the different layers. After architecture assessment re-alignment (or re-architecture) techniques are used [5]. Architecture alignment methods combine different alignment analysis types, alignment assessment frameworks, and EA analysis techniques to propose EA-based tools for alignment assessment.

3 Strategic Misalignment in Public Administration

This section presents public sector specific misalignment symptoms along the four traditional alignment perspectives of the SAM model. The proposed analysis is based on the work of [8] in which an alignment perspective-driven analysis approach was presented and used in detail. Alignment perspectives cover 3 out of 4 alignment domains to define directions for alignment domain analysis. Every alignment perspective consists of 2 alignment domain matches, a.k.a. perspective components. The following analysis presents typical misalignment symptoms to the alignment perspectives. Symptoms are also provided with EA models that possibly contain the symptom as well as EA analysis types that are able to reveal the symptoms in the EA models. Misalignment symptoms stem from misalignment symptom catalogs found in recent literature on the subject. Containing EA models and related EA analysis types also come from corresponding collections found in recent literature. For the justifications of the choices as well as the detailed catalogs from recent literature see [8].

The first perspective is concerned with strategy implementation. This cross-domain perspective involves the assessment of the implications of implementing the defined organizational strategy by appropriate organizational infrastructure and management processes (organizational design choices) as well as the design and development of the required IS infrastructure and processes. This alignment perspective is, perhaps, the most common and widely understood perspective as it corresponds to the classic, hierarchical view of strategic management.

Strategy Execution perspective deals with the supporting role of IT concerning organisational strategy-based organisational structure. Organisational strategy is translated into organisational processes and infrastructure to which IT processes and infrastructure provide appropriate support. The perspective is organisational strategy-driven, which means that if there is a change in strategy direction, organisational structure is changed accordingly. In this case, IT structure must be able to adapt to renewed organisational structure via modified supports.

Tables 1 and 2 presents typical misalignment symptoms to the corresponding perspective components of Strategy Execution perspective.

The first three symptoms are relevant in public sector: in large and complex organizations, providing a wide range of services, it is hard to define clear goals and to harmonize strategic thinking and management in the hierarchy. In public sector the number and influence of stakeholders creates a very complex socio-economic environment, where planning is difficult. These organizations are less agile as the structure, infrastructure and process (hard factors) and the knowledge, culture, beliefs, skills (soft factors) are very inflexible. As an impact of the high organisational inertia (inflexibility), the chance to misalignment in some aspects of the initiatives is high. On the other hand, the clear hierarchy makes responsibilities and reporting evident (although it is not generally true).

Table 1. Strategy Execution: Business Strategy and Business Structure matching.

Typical misalignment symptom	Containing EA artefact	Related EA analysis type
Undefined organisational mission, strategy, and goals	Driver/Goal/Objective Catalogue Business Footprint Diagram Goal/Objective/Service Diagram	Coverage analysis
Undefined business process goals, business process owners	Organisational Decomposition Diagram Driver/Goal/Objective Catalogue Role Catalogue Actor/Role Matrix Goal/Objective/Service Diagram	Coverage analysis
Lack of relation between process goals and organisational goals	Driver/Goal/Objective Catalogue Business Footprint Diagram Goal/Objective/Service Diagram	Dependency analysis, Network analysis
Undefined business roles or responsibilities	Organisational Decomposition Diagram Role Catalogue Actor/Role Matrix Business Use-Case Diagram	Coverage analysis
Undefined or multiple hierarchy or lines of reporting	Organisational Decomposition Diagram Role Catalogue Actor/Role Matrix Business Use-Case Diagram	Dependency analysis, Enterprise interoperability assessment

Business Structure and IT Structure matching related symptoms can be found in any organizations. Frequent changes in the organizational environment, client needs can make IT functionality obsolete. In many public sector organizations IT service management is not in a matured phase, so service levels are usually not professionally defined, resulting in poor performance and service quality.

The second perspective is technology transformation (technology leverage). This alignment perspective involves the assessment of implementing the chosen business strategy through appropriate IT strategy and the articulation of the required IS infrastructure and processes. In contrast to the strategy execution logic, this perspective is not constrained by the current organization design, but instead seeks to identify the best possible IT competencies through appropriate positioning in the IT marketplace, as well as identifying the corresponding internal IS architecture. Technology Transformation perspective is concerned with the organisational value of IT.

Table 2. Strategy Execution: Business Structure and IT Structure matching.

Typical misalignment symptom	Containing EA artefact	Related EA analysis type
Application functionality does not support at least one business process activity	Application Portfolio Catalogue Application/Function Matrix Process/Application Realisation Diagram	Dependency analysis, Coverage analysis, Heterogeneity analysis
Business process task supported by more than one application	Process Flow Diagram Application Portfolio Catalogue Application/Function Matrix Process/Application Realisation Diagram	Dependency analysis, Coverage analysis, Heterogeneity analysis
Critical business process does not depend on scalable and available applications	Application Portfolio Catalogue Application/Function Matrix Application Use-Case Diagram Process/Application Realisation Diagram Application/Technology Matrix	Dependency analysis, Coverage analysis
Undefined business service levels	Contract/Measure Catalogue	Coverage analysis, Enterprise coherence assessment

In this perspective, IT provides innovative solutions in response to the organisational goals. Innovative possibilities are divided into IT processes and infrastructure which enable the implementation of the innovative solutions. In this perspective, organisational structure does not constrain the implementation of the innovative solution.

Tables 3 and 4 presents typical misalignment symptoms to the Technology Transformation perspective, according to the two corresponding perspective components. Symptoms listed in Table 3 are especially true for public sector organizations, where IT is seldom considered as a strategic resource, and where HR shortages are common situations. Symptoms listed in Table 4 (structure matching) are also common in many public sector organizations, where the lack of the clear, market-driven orientation can result in poor service management.

Table 3. Technology Transformation: Business Strategy and IT Strategy matching.

Typical misalignment symptom	Containing EA artefact	Related EA analysis type
Insufficient IT resources	Software Distribution Diagram Platform Decomposition Diagram	Complexity analysis, Heterogeneity analysis
Lack of IT skills and competencies	Role Catalogue Organisation Decomposition Diagram	Network analysis, Coverage analysis, Complexity analysis
Lack of skills to develop or innovate certain types of products	Business Service/Function Catalogue Functional Decomposition Diagram	Coverage analysis
Poor IT planning and portfolio management	Functional Decomposition Diagram Application Portfolio Catalogue	Coverage analysis, Complexity analysis, Heterogeneity analysis

Table 4. Technology Transformation: IT Strategy and IT Structure matching.

Typical misalignment symptom	Containing EA artefact	Related EA analysis type
Poor IT planning and portfolio management	Functional Decomposition Diagram Application Portfolio Catalogue	Coverage analysis, Complexity analysis, Heterogeneity analysis
Under capacity infrastructure	Software Distribution Diagram Platform Decomposition Diagram	Network analysis, Coverage analysis
Lack or poor systems performance monitoring	Processing Diagram	Network analysis, Complexity analysis, Enterprise coherence assessment
Out of date technological infrastructure	Technology Portfolio Catalogue Platform Decomposition Diagram Processing Diagram	Coverage analysis, Interface analysis, Complexity analysis, Enterprise interoperability assessment, Heterogeneity analysis

The third perspective is competitive potential: this alignment perspective is concerned with the exploitation of emerging IT capabilities to impact new products and services (business scope), influence the key attributes of strategy (distinctive competencies), and develop new forms of relationships (business governance). This phase reflects the potential of IT strategy to influence key dimensions of business strategy. Unlike the previous perspective that considers business strategy as given, this perspective allows the adaptation of business strategy via emerging IT capabilities, reflecting the competitive role of IT, and it is concerned with the exploitation of emerging IT innovations to affect new products and services, and to influence the key attributes of strategy.

Competitive Potential perspective is about emerging information technologies which provide new possibilities to the organisation. These new concepts affect the organisational strategy, through which new organisational structure will be developed. In this perspective, IT provides new distinctive competencies to the organisation. Organisational strategy is built according to the potentials provided by IT. The perspective helps to exploit emerging IT capabilities to be able to develop new products and services.

Tables 5 and 6 presents typical misalignment symptoms to the Competitive Potential perspective, exhibited by the two corresponding perspective components.

Table 5. Competitive Potential: IT Strategy and Business Strategy matching.

Typical misalignment symptom	Containing EA artefact	Related EA analysis type
Lack of skills to develop or innovate certain types of business and products	Business Service/Function Catalogue Functional Decomposition Diagram	Coverage analysis
Poor IT planning and portfolio management	Functional Decomposition Diagram Application Portfolio	Coverage analysis, Complexity analysis, Heterogeneity analysis

Strategy matching symptoms related to competitive potential can be observed in many public sector organizations, where innovative thinking and sophisticated portfolio management approaches are not part of the standard managerial activities. Structure matching symptoms related to competitive potential are relevant in the public sector, as the agility of the typical organization is much less developed than the continuously stressed private companies.

The fourth perspective is service level: this alignment perspective focuses on how to build an appropriate IS service organization. This requires an understanding of the

Table 6. Competitive Potential: Business Strategy and Business Structure matching.

Typical misalignment symptom	Containing EA artefact	Related EA analysis type
Undefined organisational mission, strategy, and goals	Driver/Goal/Objective Catalogue Business Footprint Diagram Goal/Objective/Service Diagram	Coverage analysis
Undefined business process goals, business process owners	Organisational Decomposition Diagram Driver/Goal/Objective Catalogue Role Catalogue Actor/Role Matrix Business Footprint Diagram Goal/Objective/Service Diagram Business Use-Case Diagram	Coverage analysis
Lack of relation between process goals and organisational goals	Driver/Goal/Objective Catalogue Business Footprint Diagram Goal/Objective/Service Diagram	Dependency analysis, Network analysis
Undefined business roles or responsibilities	Organisational Decomposition Diagram Role Catalogue Actor/Role Matrix Business Use-Case Diagram	Coverage analysis
Undefined or multiple hierarchy or lines of reporting	Organisational Decomposition Diagram Role Catalogue Actor/Role Matrix Business Use-Case Diagram Organisation Decomposition Diagram	Dependency analysis, Enterprise interoperability assessment

external dimensions of IT strategy with corresponding internal design of the IS infrastructure and processes. This strategic fit for IT creates the capacity to meet the needs of IS customers. In this perspective, the role of business strategy is indirect and is viewed as providing the direction to stimulate customer demand. This perspective is often viewed as necessary (but not sufficient) to ensure the effective use of IT.

Service Level perspective deals with different ways through which IT can improve services, or IT can deliver the necessary capabilities to support products and services. Service Level perspective is intended for implementing an IT service-based organisation. Service levels are defined by collaboration between organisational areas and IT. The IT service centre operates according to the contracted service levels.

Tables 7 and 8 present typical misalignment symptoms to the Service Level perspective, according to the two constituent perspective components.

Table 7. Service Level: IT Strategy and IT Structure matching.

Typical misalignment symptom	Containing EA artefact	Related EA analysis type
Poor IT planning and portfolio management	Functional Decomposition Diagram Application Portfolio Catalogue	Coverage analysis, Complexity analysis, Heterogeneity analysis
Lack or poor systems performance monitoring	Processing Diagram	Network analysis, Complexity analysis, Enterprise coherence assessment
Technological heterogeneity	Technology Portfolio Catalogue Application/Technology Matrix Platform Decomposition Diagram Processing Diagram	Heterogeneity analysis
Out of date technological infrastructure	Technology Portfolio Catalogue Platform Decomposition Diagram Processing Diagram	Coverage analysis, Interface analysis, Complexity analysis, Enterprise interoperability assessment, Heterogeneity analysis

Symptoms listed in Tables 7 and 8 are related to poor IT service management practice, that is not evidently relevant for a big and IT dependent agency, but as a result of outdated organizational culture and lack of resources, are still common issues.

4   EAM-Based Method for Misalignment Detection

The following section provides an EAM based method to detect the symptoms of misalignment in EA models. This method – which description can be found in [8] in detail – used a strategic alignment perspective-driven approach and substantiated misalignment symptom queries with rule assessment techniques. The method is based

Table 8. Service Level: IT Structure and Business Structure matching.

Typical misalignment symptom	Containing EA artefact	Related EA analysis type
Frequent periods while applications are unavailable	Application and User Location Diagram Application Use-Case Diagram Application/Technology Matrix Processing Diagram	Complexity analysis, Enterprise coherence assessment
Information consistency or integrity problems	Data Entity/Data Component Catalogue Data Entity/Business Function Matrix Data Migration Diagram	Dependency analysis, Enterprise interoperability assessment, Enterprise coherence assessment, Heterogeneity analysis
Critical business processes are not supported by scalable and highly available applications	Application Portfolio Catalogue Application/Function Matrix Application/Technology Matrix	Dependency analysis, Coverage analysis

on three main steps: (1) Traditional alignment perspectives are connected to typical misalignment symptoms. (2) Relevant artefacts are recommended to the misalignment symptoms, i.e. the EA models which may contain the symptom in question. (3) Suitable EA analysis types are suggested to the misalignment symptoms, i.e. EA analysis types that are possibly able to detect the symptoms in the recommended containing artefacts.

Misalignment symptoms, containing architecture models and recommended EA analysis types come from catalogs that were presented in [8] and originally were based on recent literature. The method uses rule construction and rule testing approaches to detect the symptoms of misalignment in the XML exports of the EA models. Further details on the implementation of the proposed analysis method can be found in [8].

To test the applicability of the proposed method, a case study has been conducted. The empirical investigation deals with a public sector organization. The road management authority is a non-profit government corporation that manages matters relating to road safety, road traffic management, and transportation for around 32,000 km of a national public road network. The scope of activities spans from road operation and road maintenance over professional services to providing road information. In its actual form, the authority was set up in 2006 as a successor to a previous road management government authority. Its headquarters and three sites are located in Budapest, and the authority has approx. 170 branches around Hungary. The authority employs around 8,200 employees [8].

Road control initiative is a pilot project for setting up EA practice in the authority. The initiative is part of an integrated road network development project which aims to transform the internal operation as well as to optimise processes in order (1) to increase operational efficiency and transparency within the road management authority, (2) to achieve cost-efficient public task execution, (3) to provide a nation-wide integrated management system, (4) to increase access to management information, (5) to create the premises for standardised services, (6) to increase traffic safety. As part of the above introduced integrated road network development project, the road control project is concerned with the implementation of a traveling warrant system. The road control project was set up to outline the process of road control with EA methods over 2 sets of changes. The as-is state presents the actual state of road control activities. To-be No. 1 and To-be No. 2 phases deal with the changes in process execution, supportive applications, and underlying technological infrastructure. The study was carried out in the pilot EA model structure, showing the relevant EA models and artifacts to be modified during the progression of the project [8].

The analysis revealed problematic business-IT areas and alignment problems at the organization, which were detected in their EA models. Perceived misalignment symptoms in the case organisation included e.g.

- Undefined or multiple hierarchy or lines of reporting,
- Insufficient IT resources,
- Poor IT planning and portfolio management,
- Out of date technological infrastructure,
- Information consistency or integrity problems,
- Lack of data ownership,
- Lack of application interfaces.

These symptoms affected several EA domains and were located in different types of EA models: (1) Business Architecture - Undefined or multiple hierarchy or lines of reporting, (2) Data Architecture - Information consistency or integrity problems, Lack of data ownership, (3) Application Architecture: Lack of application interfaces, (4) Technology Architecture: Out of date technological infrastructure. EA analysis types that were able to detect these symptoms include: Dependency analysis, Enterprise interoperability assessment, Enterprise coherence assessment, Heterogeneity analysis, Coverage analysis.

The case study has demonstrated the utility and usability of the proposed framework by analyzing 21 problematic misalignment areas and detecting 7 different symptoms in their EA models. Thus, the method provided a compound framework for detecting misalignment symptoms in complex EA model structure. Misalignment problems in public sector organisations can also be considered as overwhelming issues. The case study confirmed that detecting, analysing and correcting misalignment support the public organisations in achieving better performance and value-adding potential by amending misaligned organizational areas.

5 Conclusion and Future Work

By the possibilities of IT, organisations have growing abilities to change the nature of their activities, to modify their relationships and to expand their capabilities. Organisational structure and competencies must be suited to implement strategy and to enable efficient and effective operations. Emerging new technologies and the growing expectations of the citizens push public sector organizations towards digitalization, while the application of technology-driven solutions for improving administration is still a major issue. Finding the right mix of organizational structure, processes, skills and IT based applications is a great challenge for the public sector. As a result of the unclear, sometimes undefined vision driving IT and organizational domains there are potentially numerous alignment problems in the public sector organizations.

The proposed analysis framework is based on EAM models to discover symptoms of misalignment. The method was tested in a public sector organisation, showing several misalignment issues related to the four main perspectives of strategic alignment (strategic implementation, technology leverage, technology exploitation, technology implementation). As part of future work, the framework needs further adjustments in terms of automation and analytic potential.

A systematic approach that help organizations to analyze not only application portfolio and technical issues, but also the complex interdependencies of the organizational and IT domain will provide a holistic view of the organization as a sociotechnical system. Decision makers and domain experts can use the presented analyzing model to discover actual or potential alignment issues within and between the EAM domains. Using the perspective based approach discussed in this paper organizations will be able to implement the alignment concept in practice.

Growing complexity requires more sophisticated management and planning practice in the public sector too. Finding the right configuration of organizational structure and IT solutions is still a major challenge, but the EAM based analyzing approach can facilitate exploration of the misalignment problems, and also high level and detailed planning for business and IT domains.

Acknowledgement.   Supported by the ÚNKP-17-4 New National Excellence Program of the Ministry of Human Capacities.

References

1. Carvalho, G., Sousa, P.: Business and Information Systems MisAlignment Model (BISMAM): an holistic model leveraged on misalignment and medical sciences approaches. In: Proceedings of the Third International Workshop on Business/IT Alignment and Interoperability (BUSITAL 2008). CEUR, vol. 336, CEUR-WS, Aachen, pp. 104–119 (2008)
2. Chan, Y.E., Reich, B.H.: State of the Art. IT alignment: what have we learned? J. Inf. Technol. **22**(4), 297–315 (2007)

3. Chen, H.M., Kazman, R., Garg, A.: BITAM: an engineering-principled method for managing misalignments between business and IT architectures. Sci. Comput. Program. **57** (1), 5–26 (2005)
4. Henderson, J.C., Venkatraman, N.: Strategic alignment: leveraging information technology for transforming organizations. IBM Syst. J. **32**(1), 4–16 (1993)
5. Enagi, M.A., Ochoche, A.: The role of enterprise architecture in aligning business and information technology in organisations: Nigerian government investment on information technology. Int. J. Eng. Technol. **3**(1), 59–65 (2013)
6. Fritscher, B., Pigneur, Y.: Business IT alignment from business model to enterprise architecture. In: Salinesi, C., Pastor, O. (eds.) CAiSE 2011. LNBIP, vol. 83, pp. 4–15. Springer, Heidelberg (2011). https://doi.org/10.1007/978-3-642-22056-2_2
7. Luftman, J.: Competing in the Information Age: Align in the Sand. Oxford University Press, London (2003)
8. Őri, D.: On exposing strategic and structural mismatches between business and information systems: Misalignment symptom detection based on enterprise architecture model analysis, Ph.D. thesis, May 2017
9. Pereira, C.M., Sousa, P.: Business and information systems alignment: understanding the key issues. In: Proceedings of the 11th European Conference on Information Technology Evaluation, pp. 341–348 (2004)
10. Pereira, C.M., Sousa, P.: Enterprise architecture: business and IT alignment. In: ACM Symposium on Applied Computing, pp. 1344–1345. ACM, New York (2005)
11. Saat, J., Franke, U., Lagerström, R., Ekstedt, M.: Enterprise architecture meta models for IT/business alignment situations. In: 14th IEEE International Enterprise Distributed Object Computing Conference, pp. 14–23. IEEE Press, New York (2010)
12. Strong, D.M., Volkoff, O.: Understanding organization-enterprise system fit: a path to theorizing the information technology artifact. MIS Q. **34**(4), 731–756 (2010)
13. Sunkle, S., Kulkarni, V., Roychoudhury, S.: Analyzing enterprise models using enterprise architecture-based ontology. In: Moreira, A., Schätz, B., Gray, J., Vallecillo, A., Clarke, P. (eds.) MODELS 2013. LNCS, vol. 8107, pp. 622–638. Springer, Heidelberg (2013). https://doi.org/10.1007/978-3-642-41533-3_38
14. TOG: The Open Group: TOGAF Version 9. The Open Group Architecture Framework (TOGAF) (2015). http://theopengroup.org/. Accessed 21 Jan 2015
15. van der Linden, D.J.T., Hoppenbrouwers, S.J.B.A., Lartseva, A., Proper, H.A.(Erik): Towards an investigation of the conceptual landscape of enterprise architecture. In: Halpin, T., et al. (eds.) BPMDS/EMMSAD -2011. LNBIP, vol. 81, pp. 526–535. Springer, Heidelberg (2011). https://doi.org/10.1007/978-3-642-21759-3_38
16. vom Brocke, J., Braccini, A.M., Sonnenberg, C., Spagnoletti, P.: Living IT infrastructures—an ontology-based approach to aligning IT infrastructure capacity and business needs. Int. J. Account. Inf. Syst. **15**(3), 246–274 (2014)
17. Wagter, R., Proper, H.A.(Erik), Witte, D.: A practice-based framework for enterprise coherence. In: Proper, E., Gaaloul, K., Harmsen, F., Wrycza, S. (eds.) PRET 2012. LNBIP, vol. 120, pp. 77–95. Springer, Heidelberg (2012). https://doi.org/10.1007/978-3-642-31134-5_4
18. Zachman, J.A.: A framework for information systems architecture. IBM Syst. J. **26**(3), 276–292 (1987)
19. Zarvic, N., Wieringa, R.: An integrated enterprise architecture framework for business-IT alignment. White Paper (2006)

Digital Law for Russia. Nearest Future or Only a Science Fiction?

Mikhail Bundin[1]([⊠]) [iD], Aleksei Martynov[1] [iD],
Nadezhda Biyushkina[1], and Pavel Kononov[2]

[1] Lobachevsky State University of Nizhny Novgorod (UNN),
Nizhny Novgorod 603950, Russia
mbundin@mail.ru, avm@unn.ru, asya_biyushkina@list.ru
[2] Saint-Petersburg University of MIA, Saint Petersburg 198206, Russia
pav.cononov@yandex.ru

Abstract. Continuous debates on the future of digital economy in the world has generated many issues connected not only with the creation of its infrastructure, but also on the creation of an adequate regulatory framework for its functioning and onward development. Modern researches rightly criticize the existing traditional legal constructs that are not suitable for the existing realities in the economy and require significant adaptation or creation of new legal concepts that are capable to meet the challenges of the new coming digital environment. Russia along with other countries have approached the issue of creating a special regulation for digital economy – a "digital law", which would become the backbone document containing the most important regulative principles for the whole digital sector. The adoption in 2017 of a number of digital policy documents and especially the Governmental Program "Digital economy" has given a new impulse and made a start to an open discussion on the perspective of recent adoption of a digital code. The authors seek to review existing regulation and doctrine in Russia to make suggestions on the content and structure of such a document.

Keywords: Digital economy · Legal aspects · Digital regulation · Digital law · Legal instruments · e-Democracy

1 Introduction

Digital development is now one of the main factors of world economic growth. By 2025 China could increase its GDP up to 22% due to introduction of Internet technologies. In the U.S. the expected growth of GDP caused by digital technologies, is even more impressive – by 2025 it could reach 1.6–2.2 trillion dollars [22, 31].

The development of digital sphere in Russia also has faced an unprecedented growth for the last five years. Smart technology, artificial intelligence, big data, blockchain, cloud computing, social networking, etc. have become part of everyday life. The people of Russia actively use now mobile applications and platforms [1] and have no less than two mobile phone numbers per person.

© Springer Nature Switzerland AG 2019
A. Chugunov et al. (Eds.): EGOSE 2018, CCIS 947, pp. 198–207, 2019.
https://doi.org/10.1007/978-3-030-13283-5_15

According to a one of recent analytical report made by McKinsey & Company, Russia ranks first in the number of Internet users in Europe and sixth in the world with more than 80 million users. The auditory of the main portal of public and municipal services (Gosuslugi.ru) is more than 40 million people that amounts to 30% of the population of Russia [8].

Potential economic effect of digitalization of the Russian economy would increase its GDP by 2025 up to 4.1–8.9 trillion (in 2015 prices) that is from 19 to 34% of the total expected GDP growth [8].

Regardless so positive tendencies Russia still could hardly be named among leaders in the development of digital economy especially due to the digital economy share in GDP. The share of digital economy in Russia's GDP is still about 3.9%, that is 2–3 times lower than in leading countries. However, it is already visible and the sector of the digital economy in recent years is growing rapidly. For example, the country's GDP from 2011 to 2015 increased by 7%, and the volume of the digital economy over the same period increased by 59% up to 1.2 trillion rubles in 2015 prices. Thus, in these five years, the digital economy accounted for 24% of total GDP growth [8].

This explains close attention to the problem of ensuring sustainable development of the digital economy sector in Russia. Recent policy documents such as the Federal Program "Digital Economy in Russian Federation" [11], Strategy for the Information Society Development 2017–2025 [28], and revised in 2016 Doctrine of Information Security [10] clearly demonstrate high attention to the problematics of digital economy in Russia, including the creation of an appropriate legal framework. The latter in most of cases presumes drafting a new specific law – a "digital law".

2 Methodology

The authors used quantitative and qualitative analysis of existing Russian and foreign publications in open sources in international and Russian science-citation databases. Taking into account the topic of the research, the main emphasis was made on publications indexed in the Russian scientific citation database (E-library[1]). To search for relevant publications taking into account the peculiarities of Russian morphology, we used such key words as "the codification of information legislation", "information code", "telecommunications code", "digital law", "regulation of the digital economy".

In addition to analyzing the state of modern scientific research, the authors used for qualitative analysis statistical data on digital economy in Russia and in the world, analytical reports (Digital McKinsey, OECD, World Bank), existing program and regulatory documents of Russia in the field of information society regulation.

---

[1] https://elibrary.ru.

3   Literature Review

Over the last decades in Russia appeared a number of studies with quite fair criticism of the existing regulation of information sphere. Most of them named the existing legal system too fragmentary to meet the realities of digital economy and general ICT growth [24].

Many researchers and practitioners have repeatedly expressed the idea of drafting more sustainable and profound document that could accumulate general principles for the whole information sphere in Russia and at the same time could be an appropriate basis for consecutive development of sub-legislation – a certain "digital law" or "digital code" of Russia [23].

It should be noted here, that this idea is not quite a new one. This issue was well treated by a group of scientists from the Institute of State and Law of Russian Academy of Sciences, which not only justified its necessity but also had prepared a draft version of a bill (Code of Information) for open discussion by the professional and political community [5].

A new impetus to the study of the problematics of systematization of the Russian legislation was given by the Government with adoption of the Federal Program "Digital Economy" [11]. The Program in itself and numerous comments from its creators named the problem of a new legal framework one of the key point on the way to digital economy. Surely, this led to continuous debates about the content and scope of a future "digital law". This resulted in appearance of new alternative bills and in creation under the auspices of the Ministry of Economic Development of Russia of numerous working groups of specialists in the areas of big data, information security, block chain, smart technologies, etc. – to discuss and work on its content [7, 32].

Another interesting initiative in this area announced initially even in 2009 and picked up recently in 2018 by Russian Media Communication Union is an idea of Infocommunication Code [3, 14, 16]. This bill, despite the more limited scope of application - telecommunications and media issues is still likely to have many similar and overlapping issues. Firstly, taking into account the fact that this document will have to replace the existing federal laws on communications and information as well as the fact that communication issues are too important in the regulation of the digital economy.

Worth to be noted that the idea of drafting an Information Code, or at least a serious intention to codify or streamline information legislation has recently been discussed in other EAEU countries, in particular in Belarus [26] and Kazakhstan [20].

It seems to be obvious that an idea of a significant and profound reform of Russian information legislation has deeply ripped and it is a high time for open discussion.

4   Current Regulation of Digital Sphere in Russia and Worldwide Practice

The international practice shows that an idea to create specific regulation for digital economy and its sectors is not quite new and has been discussing repeatedly. In practice, only UK had adopted it as a specific act in 2010 as Digital Economy Act [4, 12, 13, 15–18] that had been revised in 2017 [6].

To a certain extent, the systematization and harmonization of the rules on electronic commerce was held for a long time at the level of the European Union by adopting e-Commerce Directive 2000/31/EC [9]. The latter seems to be under question now as EU has announced new Digital Single Market Strategy seeking eventually to amend or revised it in order to define more appropriate e-commerce framework [27].

In Russia, as it was previously mentioned the idea of creating a new legal framework for IT sector has been discussing repeatedly since 2006 in differing forms and aspects [5, 24]. The Russian IT legislation is largely following global trends and is changing very dynamically. Over the past two decades the government has introduced more than 400 legislative acts concerning the issues of information exchange and information technology, sometimes very contradictory and non-systematically. As for sub-legislative acts of different levels there have been adopted more than 1500. This is not taking into account legislation, that somehow refers to the application of information technology or implicitly address the regulation of information interchange [2].

This all constitutes a continuous problem for Russian legislation and legal practice. The majority of modern Russian researchers name as the most acute problems of regulation of the Russian information sphere, the following [5, 21, 23, 24]:

- *irregularity*, when the same rules are duplicated in a large number of regulations, sometimes contradicting each other;
- *instability* of regulation, it is difficult to name an act that hasn't been amended or modified dramatically once a year.

According to some estimates, these reasons justify the need for a new general and more stable legal document with large scope, which would become the basis for the ongoing development of the digital economy in Russia.

5   Concept of Legal Framework for Digital Economy in Russia

Many of suggested issues to be included in the new digital law are well studied separately but the problematics of their systematization and balancing between together in one document has not been studied enough and the main question is not answered: 'What would be "digital law" and its content?'.

Currently, most commonly used term for its scope is the term of "digital economy", which could be interpreted in different ways [29, 30]. Generally, it could be understood in two ways – narrow and broad meaning. Narrowly, it is more close to the term of e-commerce or e-business – the sector of economy related to the ICT production, electronic goods and services. Broadly, it could be regarded as the idea and a concept of a new general economy changes caused by large implementation of ICT. The latter seems to be more appropriate for the description of the future "digital law" concept and its potential content.

Unfortunately, the Russian Digital Economy Program [11] (hereinafter – the Program) do not contain a specific meaning for "digital economy" and only name it as a main purpose for its introduction which are:

- creation of appropriate conditions for development of knowledge society in the Russian Federation,
- improving the welfare and quality of life by increasing the availability and quality of goods and services produced in the digital economy with the use of modern ICT technology,
- increasing awareness and digital literacy,
- improving access to and quality of public services for citizens as well as security within the state and abroad.

Eventually, there could be suggested also three main levels of digital economy:

- markets and sectors of the economy (industries), where the interaction of specific actors (suppliers and consumers of goods, works and services);
- platforms and technologies, which formed a competence for the development of markets and economic sectors (spheres of activity);
- environment that creates conditions for the development of platforms and technologies and effective interaction of market entities and economic sectors (fields of activity) and covers the regulatory framework, information infrastructure, personnel, and information security.

The Digital Economy Program covers two of the lower level of digital economy – the basic directions defining the goals and objectives of their development:

- key institutions forming the conditions for the development of the digital economy (regulatory framework, human resources and education, forming of research competence and technological capacity, etc.);
- main elements of the infrastructure of the digital economy (ICT infrastructure, information security, telecommunications).

The Program in general is focused on the following end-to-end digital technologies' issues:

1. Big data;
2. Neural networks and artificial intelligence;
3. Block chain technologies;
4. Quantum technologies;
5. New production technologies;
6. Internet of things;
7. Components of robotics and sensing;
8. Wireless technology;
9. Virtual and augmented realities.

Thus, considering the relationship of "digital economy" and "digital law", the latter intended to form legal regulation of "conditions for the development of platforms and technologies and effective interaction of persons of different markets and sectors of the economy". On this basis, the legal regulation for digital economy should include the above mentioned end-to-end digital technologies.

One of the officials of the Ministry of Economic Development Mr. S. Shipov distinguishes three stages in the development of digital legislation:

- to remove obvious barriers to the development of the digital environment (denial from paper labor contracts and labor history notes, which decrease the development of labor mobility);
- to treat more complex problematics, including big data and block chain technologies (special attention here should be paid for the usage of this technologies in public sector and for the elaboration of common approaches for this problematics);
- to develop more considerable and profound changes for Russian digital legislation [19].

All of these tasks should be fulfilled no later than in five upcoming years, otherwise it would make impossible to catch up after leading countries. At the same time, currently there is no any conceptual basis for the formation or development of digital legislation in Russia that could be seriously disputed or regarded as a coherent bill, taking into consideration that previously suggested bills are out of date as they do not include many nowadays issues [5]. The statement about the need for gradual replacement of legal regulation of digital spheres is hardly correct and justified. Digital law needs to have a monolithic foundation and its eminent goal is to the use of new ICT technologies for the whole economy. Another strong point to insist on is that inside all those relations should be a human being, his rights and freedoms. In this case ICT technologies should be only a mean to achieve public and private goals.

Thus, "digital law" should be regarded as a set of legal rules regulating social relations in sphere of creation, formation and use of digital infrastructure to meet private and public needs of a person by using ICT technologies.

It is also considered necessary to establish special legal framework for public and private sectors as the purpose of creation of digital infrastructure and use of ICT may be different in these two cases.

The other issue to be considered is a possibility to exclude a human being as a part of relations? Currently, the answer to this question can be only negative. It is the human intellect and his involvement in information technology relations provides global security of humanity and the whole world from uncontrolled machines.

6 Digital Law Reform

The structure of digital legislation should be ensured by its integrity. The existing practice of fragmentary introduction of digital legislation rules in sectoral legislation seriously damages the whole idea to create a sustainable and coherent regulation for digital economy. Various legal methods and means used in this case could affect 'digital law' as a monolithic structure with a stable set of principles and rules and could slow down its development and as a consequence of the whole digital economy.

That is why an incorporated digital law in the form of a new code of Russian Federation could be a right and reasonable solution.

The Program in its special chapter "Regulation" names the following areas (subgroups) to be treated by "digital law":

1. Legal restrictions;
2. Change Management;
3. LegalTech;
4. Integration regulation;
5. Electronic civil turnover;
6. Digital environment of trust;
7. FINTECH;
8. Big data;
9. Cyber-physical systems;
10. Intellectual property;
11. Antitrust regulation;
12. Special legal regimes;
13. Standardization;
14. Labour legislation.

In 2017, the Government Commission on the use of information technologies to improve the quality of life and conditions of doing business approved the Action Plan (hereinafter – the Action Plan) for "Digital Legislation" as a part of the Program [7]. The Action Plan provides for the creation of a special working group and a center of competence to work out the main branches of digital legislation [7]. In total, it seeks to amend or change more than 50 existing laws (telecommunications, IT, Internet, intellectual property, social networks, etc.) and to eliminate more than 250 existing administrative barriers affecting the normal development of the digital economy in Russia.

In addition, the Action Plan aims to introduce new or amend the existing national standards of the Russian Federation, such as:

– national standards in the field of information security, taking into account the requirements of security, compatibility and technological neutrality;
– national standards defining the requirements for registration, accounting, storage and exchange of digital (electronic) design and operational documentation and the digital model of the product at all stages of the product life cycle;
– national standards in the field of technology "Internet of things" and "Industrial (industrial) Internet of things";
– national standards in the field of technology "Smart production";
– national standards in the field of technology "Smart cities";
– national standards in the field of artificial intelligence and cyber-physical systems.

In order to ensure the uniformity of legislation in this area, it is proposed to adopt the Concept of comprehensive legal regulation of relations arising from the development of the digital economy, as well as to determine the Federal Executive body responsible for legal regulation in the digital economy.

It is worth to mention that all those changes are subject for harmonization inside the EAEU which should be ensured by preparing proposals on priority initiatives within the framework of the digital agenda of the EAEU, as well as the draft road map. Taking into consideration that other EAEU countries are also seeking for systematization and harmonization of their information legislation [20, 26].

It is important to understand that some issues of legal regulation in certain areas, including through the adoption of federal law, can hardly be called innovative and related to the digital economy, or to "digital law".

For example, the barrier-free toll collection system ("free flow") for the use of toll roads is well established in many countries, and applies to conventional transportation system of roads and is not worth considering to be a part of digital legislation.

On the other hand, the issue of translation of the law into computer-readable format to automate its execution, of language and tools to describe smart contracts is unexpectedly poorly treated there.

7   Conclusion

Thus, saying that currently Russia has developed a concept of a digital law could be rather early. On the one hand, we can underline a strong intention of the Government to change the present situation and create the necessary legal environment for the development and functioning of the digital economy, or, in other words, to create conditions for the further progressive introduction of ICT in all spheres of economy.

On the other hand, many of the steps taken can be considered rather hasty and more populist, without a real basis.

The existing alternative legislative proposals from professional and academic communities, which in themselves are interesting enough, generally are no longer relevant or most likely controversial with existing state policy.

The authors assume that the creation of a new Concept of legal regulation for the digital economy will require some more attention to the answers on more global issues related to the determination of the balance of interests of human, society and state in the use of ICT paying strong attention to information security issues.

It is obvious that the current proposals under the Action Plan are more focused on the answers to the today challenges and once again resemble ad hoc regulation or patching holes, but not the path to comprehensive and long-term concepts.

At the same time, the formed working groups on digital legislation has just begun their work and it is a bit early to assess the results and we could only make suggestions on but for which we will necessarily follow.

However, at the moment the legal environment for the digital economy is at the very beginning of formation and forecasts about the possibility of its finishing in the next 5 years look too optimistic. Already now, a lot of negative and reasonable critics could be found on the content of the Program and its implementation, including the legal framework issues [25].

References

1. Amelin, R., Channov, S., Komkova, G.: Problems of legal regulation of games with augmented reality (Example of the Russian Federation). In: Alexandrov, D.A., Boukhanovsky, A.V., Chugunov, A.V., Kabanov, Y., Koltsova, O. (eds.) DTGS 2017. CCIS, vol. 745, pp. 159–169. Springer, Cham (2017). https://doi.org/10.1007/978-3-319-69784-0_14
2. Amelin, R., Channov, S., Polyakova, T.: Direct democracy: prospects for the use of information technology. In: Chugunov, A.V., Bolgov, R., Kabanov, Y., Kampis, G., Wimmer, M. (eds.) DTGS 2016. CCIS, vol. 674, pp. 258–268. Springer, Cham (2016). https://doi.org/10.1007/978-3-319-49700-6_24
3. Balashova, A., Kolomychenko, M.: Code for the Largest ICT Companies: Why Russia Will Revise the Laws in the field of IT and Telecommunications. RB, Russia (2018). https://www.rbc.ru/technology_and_media/15/01/2018/5a58ccd99a79475bf73470c1. Accessed 23 July 2018
4. Barron, A.: 'Graduated Response' à l'Anglaise: online copyright infringement and the digital economy act 2010. J. Media Law 3(2), 305–347 (2015). https://doi.org/10.5235/175776311799280773
5. Concept for Information Code of Russian Federation. Institute of Law & State of Russian Academy of Science, Moscow, Russia (2014). https://cyberleninka.ru/article/n/2015-02-017-kontseptsiya-informatsionnogo-kodeksa-rossiyskoy-federatsii-ran-in-t-gosudarstva-i-prava-pod-red-i-l-bachilo-m-kanon-rooi. Accessed 23 July 2018
6. Digital Economy Act 2017. https://www.gov.uk/government/collections/digital-economy-bill-2016. Accessed 23 July 2018
7. Digital Economy Regulation – Skolkovo Community. http://sk.ru/foundation/legal/. Accessed 23 July 2018
8. Digital Russia Report 2017. Digital McKinsey (2017). https://www.mckinsey.com/~/media/McKinsey/Locations/Europe%20and%20Middle%20East/Russia/Our%20Insights/Digital%20Russia/Digital-Russia-report.ashx. Accessed 23 July 2018
9. Directive 2000/31/EC of the European Parliament and of the Council of 8 June 2000 on certain legal aspects of information society services, in particular electronic commerce, in the Internal Market ('Directive on electronic commerce'). http://eur-lex.europa.eu/legal-content/EN/ALL/?uri=CELEX:32000L0031. Accessed 23 July 2018
10. Doctrine of Information Security of Russian Federation. President of Russian Federation (2016). http://www.kremlin.ru/acts/bank/41460. Accessed 23 July 2018
11. Federal Program "Digital Economy in Russian Federation". Federal Government of Russian Federation (2017). http://static.government.ru/media/files/9gFM4FHj4PsB79I5v7yLVuPg u4bvR7M0.pdf. Accessed 23 July 2018
12. Garstka, K.: The amended digital economy act 2010 as an unsuccessful attempt to solve the stand-alone complex of online piracy. IIC Int. Rev. Intellect. Prop. Compet. Law 43(2), 158–174 (2012)
13. Goldstein, H.: Editorial: the digital economy act and statistical research. J. R. Statist. Soc. Ser. A (Statistics in Society) 180, 945–946 (2017). https://doi.org/10.1111/rssa.12317
14. Grishanova, E.M., Antipov, A.A.: Infocommunication Law. The need for codification of legislation on information, informatization, mass media, and communication in Russia. In: T-COMM Telecommunications and Transport, vol. 6, #12, pp. 12–13. Media Publisher (2012)
15. Rahman, M.I.: The doctrine of authorisation of copyright infringement and its influence on the terms and effect of the digital economy act 2010. Int. J. Private Law 7(4), 387–401 (2014). https://doi.org/10.1504/IJPL.2014.064930

16. Infocommunication Code Will Replace the Federal Law on Telecommunications, Solkovo, Russia (2009). http://sk.ru/foundation/legal/. Accessed 23 July 2018
17. Mansell, R., Steinmueller, W.E.: Copyright infringement online: The case of the Digital Economy Act judicial review in the United Kingdom. In: New Media & Society, vol. 15, no. 8, pp. 1312–1328. SAGE (2013). https://doi.org/10.1177/1461444812470429
18. Mendis, D.: Digital Economy Act 2010: fighting a losing battle? Why the 'three strikes' law is not the answer to copyright law's latest challenge. In: International Review of Law, Computers & Technology, vol. 27, no. 1–2, pp. 60–84. Taylor & Francis, UK (2013). https://doi.org/10.1080/13600869.2013.764137
19. Ministry of Economic Development Calls for Adoption of "Digital Law" in the Nearest 5 Years. TASS, Russia (2017). http://tass.ru/ekonomika/4479532. Accessed 23 July 2018
20. Muslimov, Sh.R.: To the question of systematization of information legislation of Kyrgyzstan. In: Problems of modern science and education, vol. 16(98), pp. 90–93 (2017). Problemy Nauki
21. Naumov, V.B.: Legal identification of subjects on the internet. In: Law and State: Theory and Practice, no. 5(137), pp. 148–152. Law and State Press (2016)
22. OECD Digital Economy Outlook 2017. OECD Publishing, Paris (2017). https://doi.org/10.1787/9789264276284-en
23. Parschukov, M., Perfilyeva, T.: Problems of codification of information legislation. In: Vestnik URFO. Security in Information Sphere, vol. 3(13), pp. 44–49, Chelyabinsk (2014)
24. Polyakova, T.: ICT Development and Systematization of Information Legislation. Zakonotvorcheskaya deyatelnost (2010). http://federalbook.ru/files/SVAYZ/saderzhanie/Tom%205/II/Polyakova.pdf. Accessed 23 July 2018
25. Romero-Moreno, F.: The Digital Economy Act 2010: subscriber monitoring and the right to privacy under Article 8 of the ECHR. In: International Review of Law, Computers & Technology, vol. 30, no. 3, pp. 229–247. Taylor & Francis, UK (2016). https://doi.org/10.1080/13600869.2016.1176320
26. Shalaeva, T.Z.: The Modern Realities of the Development of Belarusian Information Law: Theoretical and Methodological Approaches to Systematization. In: State and Law, #4, pp. 74-83. Nauka, Moscow (2015)
27. Shaping the Digital Single Market. https://ec.europa.eu/digital-single-market/en/policies/shaping-digital-single-market. Accessed 23 July 2018
28. Strategy for the Information Society Development in Russian Federation 2017-2030. Federal Government of Russian Federation (2017). http://static.government.ru/media/files/9gFM4FHj4PsB79I5v7yLVuPgu4bvR7M0.pdf. Accessed 23 July 2018
29. Urmantseva, A.: Digital Economy: How experts interpret this term. RIA, Russia (2017). https://ria.ru/science/20170616/1496663946.html. Accessed 23 July 2018
30. Vice Prime Minister Olga Golodets Told about Shortcomings in "Digital Economy Program". RIA, Russia (2017). https://ria.ru/economy/20171124/1509547271.html. Accessed 23 July 2018
31. World Development Report 2016: Digital Dividends. World Bank (2017). http://www.worldbank.org/en/publication/wdr2016. Accessed 23 July 2018
32. Zamahina, T.: State Duma Will Adopt the Bill on Digital Economy. RG, Russia (2018). https://rg.ru/2018/02/20/gosduma-primet-zakony-dlia-cifrovoj-ekonomiki.html. Accessed 23 July 2018

The Level of Readiness for Electronic Governance: Comparative Analysis of Armenian and Russian Societies

Anna Aletdinova[1](✉) and Ruben Elamiryan[2]

[1] Novosibirsk State Technical University, Novosibirsk 630073, Russia
aletdinova@corp.nstu.ru
[2] Russian-Armenian (Slavonic) University, Public Administration Academy of the Republic of Armenia, 19 Hrachya Kochar 17, Yerevan, Armenia
rub.elamiryan@gmail.com

Abstract. The development of electronic governance in any country is determined by cultural features, the level of education and information-communication infrastructure. The article comprehensively researches the readiness potential of Armenian and Russian societies for electronic governance. This choice is reasoned by the fact that, first of all, Russia and Armenia are members of the Eurasian Economic Union, which currently harmonizes digital transformation policies of the member-states. In this context the application of Hofstede's model and Inglehart-Welzel's cultural map allows to reveal that both Armenians and Russians are oriented towards struggle for survival at the expense of self-expression and strive to stability. The complex evaluation demonstrates low level for Power distance and Uncertainty. For Armenia it is 0.19 and for Russia - 0.06. This means that the level of technological conditions in a country does not necessarily lead to comprehensive technological penetration into a society. For instance, both Armenian and Russian societies have serious cultural barriers which impede the development of network interactions. The authors have calculated the readiness potential of the societies for electronic governance according to ICT access, ICT use, Government's online service, E-participation, grand coefficient of the coverage of population with higher education, Power distance and Uncertainty avoidance for the above mentioned period. Their values are fluctuating in the range of 36.40–38.57% for Russia and 22.39–27.71% for Armenia. Thus the readiness potential of the societies for electronic governance has serious potential to develop in the future.

Keywords: Society · Information and communication technologies · Electronic governance · Hofstede's culture model

1 Introduction

Electronic Governance (e-governance) provides simplification and support of management between various parties, including government structures, organizations and society, based on information and communication technologies. E-governance is often called digital, if the use of information and communication technologies is considered

A. Chugunov et al. (Eds.): EGOSE 2018, CCIS 947, pp. 208–220, 2019.
https://doi.org/10.1007/978-3-030-13283-5_16

to improve relations with organizations and society [1–3]. It provides greater opportunities to participate in democratic institutions and processes. In this context complex digital interactions of a society, government and organizations, as well as their coordination are possible only if the participants are ready for digital transformations and have a well-developed information and communication infrastructure.

Wide range of academic works research the development and readiness for electronic governance, as well as the relationship of national culture values and practice to e-Government readiness. The use of the term "e-government readiness" [4–6] necessitates the introduction of the notion of "Readiness for Electronic Governance." The latter demonstrates how well a society is ready for those changes.

At the same time while discussing the notion of readiness it is worth mentioning that in psychology it is viewed as a dynamic integrity of a person, an inner mindset for a certain behavior. In our case the readiness of a society for e-government means a mindset for interaction with a state through ICT.

At the same time on 11 October, 2017 the EEU Highest Economic Council approved the main directions of implementation of the EEU digital agenda till 2025 [7], which particularly includes development of e-governance.

Provided that both Armenia and Russia are EEU members the main objective of the research is to reveal in comparison the readiness of societies of the two countries to e-government as a component of digital transformations.

Moreover, the research is reasoned by the fact that Armenia and Russia are neighbor countries with deep ties of economic, cultural, and ICT cooperation. According to "Union of Armenians of Russia" the Armenian diaspora of Russia makes up more than 2.5 million. From this point view any transformation, particularly, digital, in any country may have deep and comprehensive impact on the other one.

The above determines the necessity of comparative research of readiness of the Armenian and Russian societies for e-government.

2 Related Work and Methods

2.1 The Factors Which Determine the Readiness of a Society for Electronic Governance

Electronic interaction between a society and a state will be implemented if both sides are ready for it, create the necessary conditions, as well as have the will. Scientists conducted a study proving the lack of confidence of citizens in electronic initiatives in the absence of knowledge and motivation for the use of electronic resources. The authors prove that open education helps to overcome public distrust of e-government [8].

Another research for Bangladesh, Canada and Germany demonstrates how cross-cultural differences impact consumers' perception of a mobile government adoption behavior [9]. Cultural differences in the adoption of e-government are also presented in the work [10]. The article tests 18 hypothesis of the relations of the national cultural values and e-governance readiness practice. It reveals positive and negative correlations [4]. The research shows that the education level of the employees impacts on the intensity of ICT use, while the rise of ICT influences on the development of the human capital [11].

In our view, the following groups of indicators can be applied to determine the readiness of a society for e-governance: indexes of culture, which characterize the level of acceptance of novelty and readiness to interact with the governmental bodies; the level of education among population; the current level of electronic interaction in the country; the level of development of information-communication infrastructure; as well as human resources to maintain and develop that infrastructure. The justification and analysis of the chosen factors to evaluate the readiness of the Armenian and Russian societies for e-government is presented below.

Indexes of Culture

Hofstede has developed a typology of cultural dimensions, which describes, on one hand, the impact of a society's culture on individual values of its members, and, vice versa, the influence of individual values on the behavior of a society. Initially, the Hofstede's model contained only four indicators. Later it was updated by Miknov [12–14]. As a result the model received six characteristics: power distance, which characterizes the fundamental issue of human inequality; individualism/collectivism, which explains the integration of individuals in the initial groups; masculinity/femininity connected with the distribution of emotional roles of men and women; uncertainty avoidance, which shows the level of public tension in wait of unknown future; long-term orientation/short-term orientation, it defines the choice of attention focus for human actions: future, present or past; indulgence/restraint, which resembles the satisfaction with basic human needs related to enjoying life or self-control [14].

The analysis of criteria for the Hofstede's model provides the values shown in Table 1 (formed on the basis of the following data [15, 16]).

Table 1. Comparative analysis of the Armenian and Russian cultures in the framework of the Hofstede's model

Criterion	Countries	
	Armenia	Russia
Power distance	76	93
Uncertainty avoidance	86	95
Individualism	26	39
Masculinity	28	36
Long-term orientation	No data	81
Indulgence	No data	20

Data on the last two indexes are not published for Armenia.

Power distance characterizes the level of acceptance and expectation of the unequal distribution of power by the members of organizations and institutionalized groups of a society (e.g., families). This parameter resembles inequality (on the scale "more vs. less") from the perspective of lower than higher level of a society. In Russia this index is a bit higher than in Armenia. Often state authorities take the responsibility to resolve conflicts and disagreements. This provides progress in the society. However, based on historical analysis, Armenian nation considers state interference fundamentally negative [17]. According to World Values Survey data, most Armenians are not interested in politics: 65% said they are either 'not very' or 'not at all' interested as compared to 35% who are either 'very' or 'somewhat' interested [17]. The research of the Institute of Sociology of the Russian Academy of Sciences demonstrates that the Russians tie the performance of state functions with the provision of social justice, creation of conditions for self-activity for people, establishment of an environment to develop long-term strategic solutions for their own problems, as well as creation of equal starting opportunities for the youth. At the same time more than one third of the Russian population believe that the state has to protect all the poor including those who appeared in that list not because of its own fault. Particularly, 14% of the respondents are convinced that in the framework of social protection the state has to support only those who can not work people (the elders, disabled people, and underage orphans) [18]. At the same time it is worth mentioning that the low level trust towards the government remains [19]. However during the last years the level of trust is increasing.

We consider the characteristic of power distance important to include in the calculation of potential of the society readiness for e-governance as it resembles, particularly, the attitude of a society towards the state.

Avoidance of uncertainties demonstrates how well the society perceives ambiguity of meanings, unregulated situations, which are new, unknown, unexpected, and different from ordinary stance [14].

The opposite type of culture, which allows uncertainties, is more tolerant to untypical and ambiguous opinions. They are often based on empirical experience and relativism, as well as allow different directions of thoughts to be next to each other. It means that people with this type of culture will be more tolerant to new technologies. This criterion is necessary to include in the calculation of the potential. Both for Armenia and Russia the indicators are rather high (86 and 95 respectively). This means that the societies have cautious acceptance of new ideas, methods and technologies.

Individualism as opposite to collectivism (which is viewed as not individual's, but society's characteristic) shows the level of integration of members of any society into groups. In individualistic cultures connections among individuals are not tight: everyone is responsible for himself/herself and the closest family.

In this regard the development of the modern Armenian society takes place in the framework of some polarization of value orientations among younger and elder generations. The process of transition of socio-cultural values is connected with some contradictions and even conflicts. Such "generation gaps" in Armenian society are reasoned by economic, social, cultural and ideological issues. The elder generation has experienced the process of socialization in the spirit of the Soviet ideology due to their "socialistic" background and past. The latter process of socialization was based on the development of socialistic values. The general orientation was based on promotion of education, achievement of long-term goals, social justice and equality (at least on declaration level).

On the other hand, the modern Armenian youth is much more oriented towards the values of individualism, fast achievement of material prosperity, hedonism, and competition [15]. Russia faces the similar situation. During the last years Russia faces atomization, which disintegrates the unity of the nation and, as a consequence, of the social solidarity. The results of sociological surveys show the developing tendency of destruction of traditional for Russian culture relations of mutual help [18].

Masculinity as opposite to femininity (as social, but not individual character) is related to distribution of values among gender groups. This, in turn, is also a fundamental problem of any society, which has many recipes to be solved. At the same time the characteristics of the Russian and Armenian cultures have many similarities.

Long-term/short-term orientation is a parameter to measure a culture on a scale, which encompasses tenacity, thrift, status hierarchy of relations, sense of shame towards mutual social responsibilities, respect towards traditions, personal resilience and stability.

Indulgence is common for societies, where the main and natural human needs (connected with enjoying life and receiving pleasure) are being satisfied rather easily.

Restraint characterizes a society where the satisfaction of needs is controlled and managed by strict societal norms.

These characteristics are removed from further research.

In the end of 20th century based on regular sociological polls, American political scientist Ronald Inglehart concluded that values of materialism are gradually being replaced by the values of post-materialism. Moreover he proved that massive and deep transformations of economic, political and social life change "political and economic goals, religious norms and family values. These changes, in turn, impact on temps of economic growth, on strategic settings of political parties, as well as on perspectives of development for democratic institutions" [20].

Other scholars joined his polls. Soon Inglehart and Welzel formed a cultural map of the world.

The evaluation of psychophysical characteristics, based on Inglehart-Welzel's map, demonstrates that high power distance and avoidance of uncertainties are specific for both for Russian and Armenian cultures [21]. The analysis results of cultures based on Hofstede's model proves this conclusion too. This means that orientation towards fight for self-preservation at the expense of self-expression is specific for both Armenians and Russians. At the same time both nations strive to stability.

The Level of Education

Another important characteristic, which affects the level of readiness of a society for e-governance, is the share of people with the higher education. The empirical research of the data on Russian regions, implemented by one of the authors, proves the interconnection between information-communication technologies and accumulation of human capital. The latter is expressed as an average quantity of years of study per one employed person in the region [11].

The research justifies the positive impact of the average education level on the quantity of employed personal computers in organizations for one hundred employees and the quantity of personal computers in organizations with access to the internet for one hundred employees. However this impact is decreasing during time.

A hypothesis was confirmed that introduction of information-communication technologies in industrial processes takes places more intensively in the territories with higher concentration of human capital. Thus, the level of education of population can be viewed as a characteristic, which influence the level of network interaction in the country.

In this regard the authors suggest considering the grand coefficient of the higher education coverage as a factor which defines the readiness of a society for e-government. The values of this index for Armenia and Russia are presented below in the Table 2 (it is based on the data from [22–26]).

Table 2. Tertiary enrolment ratio in Armenia and Russia, % gross

Countries	2013	2014	2015	2016	2017
Armenia	48.90	46.00	46.10	46.60	44.30
Russia	75.90	75.50	76.10	78.00	78.70

The grand coefficient of the higher education coverage can exceed one hundred per cent because of inclusion of data on students not typical for that age level.

The Table 2 demonstrates a tendency to increase coverage of population with higher education in Russia, while Armenia shows decline. The decrease in case of Armenia can be explained, particularly, by brain-drain, raising costs for the higher education, as well as restricted labor market for educated people.

The Development of Information-Communication Infrastructure

The information and communication infrastructure includes four indices developed by international organizations on ICT access, ICT use, online service by governments, and online participation of citizens. The Table 3 shows the values and their indexes in Armenia and Russia for the period of 2013–2017 (based on [22–26]).

Table 3. The indexes of information-communication infrastructure, Russia and Armenia, %

Variable	Countries	2013	2014	2015	2016	2017
ICT access	Armenia	40.70	45.20	56.40	60.80	65.70
	Russia	66.90	67.30	72.40	72.40	72.30
ICT use	Armenia	15.50	26.00	30.20	31.90	38.50
	Russia	39.70	43.40	49.70	55.20	58.70
Government's online service	Armenia	32.70	32.70	61.40	61.40	42.80
	Russia	66.00	66.00	70.90	70.90	73.20
E-participation	Armenia	0.00	0.00	52.90	52.90	52.50
	Russia	65.80	65.80	68.60	68.60	74.60

The above presented indicators were tested for further application in calculations of Global Innovation Index. Their maximal values can not exceed one hundred.

The analysis of indexes of information-communication infrastructure of Armenia demonstrates the enlargement of opportunities of network interactions for the Armenian nation for the last five years. The rising tendency was interrupted in 2017 only for the Government's online service index. Russia demonstrates stable increase in the development of information-communication infrastructure, which provides e-governance in the country.

2.2   The Assessment Method

The suggested method based on statistic formulas allows providing a general evaluation of the measure of achievement of the reference values for any group of indicators
with any units of measurement. This method is described in more details in the following work [27].

We suggest the following algorithm of calculation of the potential function to
assess the readiness potential of a society for electronic governance.

Let x_{ij} be the value of the j index in the year t_i of the research period. On the first
step we calculate the standard deviation of the j index (σ_j). Afterwards we define the
standardized values of the indexes according to the following formula:

$$Z_{ij} = \frac{x_{ij}}{\sigma_j}. \qquad (1)$$

The reference index values often are practically defined by experimental method.
However in our case, according to the Global Innovation Index calculation technique,
the maximal value (which is the reference one) will make up 100. Let us mark it as x_j^*.

The standardized values of the reference values can be defined by the formula:

$$Z_j^* = \frac{x_j^*}{\sigma_j}. \qquad (2)$$

The Weight of the indicators in the integral evaluation is defined by the formula:

$$\propto_j = \frac{Z_j^*}{\sqrt{\sum_{j=1}^{n}\left(Z_j^*\right)^2}}. \qquad (3)$$

In that case the values of a potential formula according to the years can be found
based on the formula:

$$y_i = \sum_{j=1}^{n} \propto_j Z_{ij}. \qquad (4)$$

At the same time the reference value of the potential formula can be calculated
according to the formula:

$$y^* = \sum_{j=1}^{n} \propto_j Z_j^*. \qquad (5)$$

The integral marks of the potential formula components according to the years are
calculated with the application of values, which are received with formulas (4) и (5):

$$C_i = \frac{y_i}{y^*} \cdot 100. \qquad (6)$$

If the indexes are permanent during the time frame, it is necessary to apply a different approach. Let x_j be the actual value of the index j. In that case the relative measure of the j to reach the goal value will be identified by the formula:

$$\beta_j = \frac{x_j}{x_j^*}. \tag{7}$$

If the actual value strives to a lesser reference, the formula (7) calculates the inverse value. The complex evaluation of the potential component is defined by the formula:

$$C^0 = \frac{1}{n}\sum\nolimits_{j=1}^{n} \beta_j. \tag{8}$$

The integral mark of the potential can be revealed as the average arithmetic from C_i and C^0, according to the formula:

$$C = \frac{1}{2}\left(C_i + C^0\right), \tag{9}$$

The application of this formula presumes the equal value of the evaluation components for the readiness potential of a society for e-governance. Further research of the significance of the evaluated factors will make it possible to change the weight coefficients in the proposed method. At the same time the opportunity of calculation for any index remains one of its main merits.

3 Results

The readiness potential of a society for e-governance will be calculated with the application of the following variables: power distance, uncertainty avoidance, grand coefficient of the higher education coverage, ICT access, ICT use, Government's online service, E-participation. For the first two indicators the reference value is the zero-value (according to the interpretation of values in the Hofstede's model). For the other variables let us establish reference values equal to 100. This is explained by the maximal possible values and calculation technique of the Global Innovation Index.

At the same time let us also accept the reference value for the grand coefficient of the higher education coverage equal to 100 despite the fact it can exceed this value (see details in the Sect. 2.1). The reference values and marks of dispersion and standard deviation are presented in the Table 4.

In that case the reference value of the potential function for Armenia will make up $y^* = 70.17$, while for Russia it is $y^* = 89.81$.

Below is the calculation of the standardized value of Z_{ij} for Armenia and Russia (Table 5).

Based on the Table 5, the formula (6) allows calculating the integral mark C_i of the first component of the readiness potential of a society for e-governance (Table 6).

Table 4. The subsidiary calculation of the readiness of the Armenian and Russian societies for e-governance (according to the 2013–2017 data)

Variable	Countries	σ_j^2	σ_j	x_j^*	Z_j^*	$\propto_j$
ICT access	Armenia	88.59	9.41	100	10.62	0.15
	Russia	19.89	4.46	100	22.42	0.25
ICT use	Armenia	57.93	7.61	100	13.14	0.19
	Russia	42.40	6.51	100	15.36	0.17
Government's online service	Armenia	167.63	12.95	100	7.72	0.11
	Russia	19.40	4.40	100	22.70	0.25
E-participation	Armenia	879.67	29.66	100	3.37	0.05
	Russia	17.06	4.13	100	24.21	0.27
Tertiary enrolment, % gross	Armenia	2.19	1.48	100	67.58	0.96
	Russia	1.61	1.27	100	78.90	0.88

Table 5. The standardized values of Z_{ij} for Armenia

Index	2013	2014	2015	2016	2017
$Z1_{(Arm)}$	4.32	4.80	5.99	6.46	6.98
$Z1_{(Rus)}$	15.00	15.09	16.23	16.23	16.21
$Z2_{(Arm)}$	2.04	3.42	3.97	4.19	5.06
$Z2_{(Rus)}$	6.10	6.66	7.63	8.48	9.01
$Z3_{(Arm)}$	2.53	2.53	4.74	4.74	3.31
$Z3_{(Rus)}$	14.98	14.98	16.10	16.10	16.62
$Z4_{(Arm)}$	0.00	0.00	1.78	1.78	1.77
$Z4_{(Rus)}$	15.93	15.93	16.61	16.61	18.06
$Z5_{(Arm)}$	33.05	31.09	31.15	31.49	29.94
$Z5_{(Rus)}$	59.88	59.57	60.04	61.54	62.09

Let us define the similar marks for such indicators, as Power distance and Uncertainty avoidance. It is necessary to take into consideration that these are constants

Table 6. The integral mark C_i for Armenia and Russia

Countries	Index	2013	2014	2015	2016	2017
Armenia	y_i	33.14	31.58	32.26	32.70	31.29
	C_i	47.23	45.01	45.98	46.60	44.59
Russia	y_i	65.48	65.32	66.65	68.12	69.21
	C_i	72.91	72.74	74.22	75.85	77.07

and hence the calculations are performed according to formulas (7)–(8). For Armenia the complex mark for the indicators of culture makes 0.19, while for Russia the mark is 0.06. The indicators are very low and characterize the presence of barriers in cultures of the Armenian and Russian nations. The latter impedes the development of e-governance.

The integral marks of the readiness of the Armenian and Russian societies for e-governance are calculated according to the formula (9) and presented in Fig. 1.

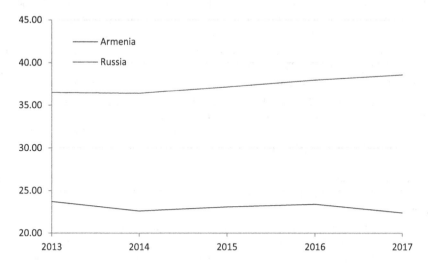

Fig. 1. The phase portrait of the readiness potential of a society for e-governance

The values of the readiness potential of the Armenian society for e-governance for 2013–2017 demonstrate fluctuations. The fluctuation coefficient made up five per cent without tendency to growth. The peaks of decrease for Armenia are reasoned by drop of Tertiary enrolment ratio in 2014, and drop of Tertiary enrolment ratio and Government's online service index in 2017. On the contrary, the readiness potential of the Russian society for e-governance for 2013–2017 demonstrates the growth tendency. The level of growth for the described period is 2.08%. The comparative analysis of the level of readiness of the Armenian and Russian societies for e-government for 2013–2017 demonstrates the tendency of rising gap among them. For instance, the level of readiness of the Russian society in 2013 was higher for 12.78%. In 2017 the gap increased to 16.18%. The gap between actual and reference values is high. It demands consistent solutions on the state-level.

4 Conclusions

The development of information-communication technologies has created the opportunity of distant participation in the process of electronic governance for all the interested stakeholders. However the success of application of those technologies varies for different cultures. At the same time based on their specificities societies have different level of trust to state power and desire to cooperate with it. The differences in value-orientations in societies are determined by political, ideological, spiritual, moral, economic and social transformations of social life.

The authors research the cases of Armenian and Russian societies as they have cultural similarities. The basic values of the Russian and Armenian societies are expressed in national traditions and customs, which allow to maintain the language and way of life, as well as to transfer social and labor experience. The analysis of the Hofstede's model clearly demonstrated that these cultures are characterized by power distance, avoidance of uncertainties, collectivism and femininity. There is no data on indulgence and short-term/long-term orientation for Armenia, but we can suppose that Armenia is close to Russia on this indicator. A recent research of one of the co-authors justifies this approach [28]. The analysis of the Hofstede's model is supplemented by the evaluation of psychophysical characteristics of Inglehart-Welzel cultural map. Armenians and Russians are oriented towards the struggle for survival at the expense of self-expression and strive to stability.

The article has chosen such indexes as Power distance and Uncertainty avoidance to calculate the readiness potential of a society for e-governance. However their joint mark was too low: for Armenia it is 0.19 and for Russia – 0.06. This clearly demonstrates that despite the establishment of any favorable condition in Armenia and Russia for the development of e-governance, the societies have clear cultural barriers which impede its development.

The rest of indexes, which are applied to calculate the level of readiness for e-governance, received higher marks. First of all, we analyzed the grand coefficient of the higher education coverage for Armenia and Russia for the last five years. Armenia has never demonstrated indicators higher than 48.9% with tendency towards decline. In Russia this index makes 78.8% with tendency towards rise. Its level is lower in Armenia than in Russia. This decrease in case of Armenia can be explained, particularly, by brain-drain, raising costs for the higher education, as well as restricted labor market for educated people. Secondly, the article has researched the indexes of the development of ICT infrastructure, such as: ICT access, ICT use, Government's online service, E-participation. Russia demonstrates stable tendency of increase of information-communication infrastructure. In Armenia the research observes the same tendency in the development of network interactions except the index for Government's online service, which interrupted the tendency in 2017.

The integral marks for indexes of education and development of information-communication infrastructure for 2013–2017 show fluctuation tendencies with tendency towards decrease in Armenia (from 47.23 to 44.59) and increase in Russia (from 72.91 to 77.07). The inclusion of the above mentioned indexes of culture into the integral mark allowed the authors to draw out the integral marks of the readiness of the societies for e-governance. For Armenia it made 22.39% (from possible 100) for 2017. In comparison to 2013 it demonstrated insignificant decrease for 1.32%. For Russia the readiness potential of the society for e-governance made up 38.57% in 2017 with 2.08% increase in comparison with 2013. For the period of 2013–2017 the research shows the tendency of rising gap between Russian and Armenian societies in readiness for e-government.

Thus it is worth mentioning that despite the level of development of the information-communication infrastructure in a country, this will not force its users to apply these technological innovations for the development of e-governance. The most important factor is education which develops the values of a society.

It is worth mentioning that the observed indicators do not cover all the aspects. This necessitates further research to include such characteristics, as political will, data privacy concerns and so on. In this article the authors outlined features based on wide range of academic works. However a correlation analysis of dependence of the development of the e-government from various cultural-psychological, political, technological and economic factors is necessary to reveal the most essential factors.

This will allow elaborating more precise leverages to govern them. Another issue in the context of this research is the verification of the received values based on application of wide range of data bases.

Thus the evolution of the readiness of a society for electronic governance is a complex task, which demands application of big missives of statistical data, sociological research, and well-developed methods, which take into account the country specifics for all countries.

As for the future work, it is worth to apply the below presented model to research the readiness level for other EEU members, such as Belarus, Kazakhstan and Kirgizstan. This will allow providing more effective digital transformations policy both for the EEU in general and for member-states in particular.

References

1. Kim, B.J., Park, S.: Why digital government not e-government? The paradigm shift of D. gov in Korea. In: Proceedings of The 17th International Digital Government Research Conference on Digital Government Research 2016, pp. 530–531. ACM (2016). https://doi.org/10.1145/2912160.2912233
2. Jun, C.N., Chung, C.J.: Big data analysis of local government 3.0: focusing on Gyeongsangbuk-do in Korea. Technol. Forecast. Soc. Chang. **110**, 3–12 (2016)
3. Veiga, L.: Digital government and administrative burden reduction. In: 9th International Conference on Theory and Practice of Electronic Governance (ICEGOV2016) 2016, pp. 323–326. Montevideo (2016)
4. Khalil, O.E.M.: E-government readiness: does national culture matter? Gov. Inf. Q. **28**(3), 388–399 (2011)
5. Koh, C.E., Prybutok, V.R., Zhang, X.: Measuring e-government readiness. Inf. Manage. **45**(8), 540–546 (2008)
6. Al-Omari, A., Al-Omari, H.: E-government readiness assessment model. J. Comput. Sci. **2**(11), 841–845 (2006)
7. Garant Homepage. https://www.garant.ru/products/ipo/prime/doc/71708158/. Accessed 01 Apr 2018
8. Platonova, I., Martynov, A., Bundin, M.: Trust in digital government as a result of overcoming knowledge access inequality and dissemination of belief in e-democracy. In: Proceedings of the 16th Annual International Conference on Digital Government Research 2015, pp. 309–311. ACM (2015)
9. Shareef, M.A., Dwivedi, Y.K., Laumer, S., Archer, N.: Citizens' adoption behavior of mobile government (mGov): a cross-cultural study. Inf. Syst. Manage. **33**(3), 268–283 (2016)
10. Carter, L., Weerakkody, V., Phillips, B., Dwivedi, Y.K.: Citizen adoption of e-government services: exploring citizen perceptions of online services in the United States and United Kingdom. Inf. Syst. Manage. **33**(2), 124–140 (2016)

11. Aletdinova, A., Koritsky, A.: The relationship of ICT with human capital formation in rural and urban areas of Russia. In: Alexandrov, D., Boukhanovsky, A., Chugunov, A., Kabanov, Y., Koltsova, O. (eds.) DTGS 2018. CCIS, vol. 859, pp. 19–27. Springer, Cham (2018). https://doi.org/10.1007/978-3-030-02846-6_2

12. Hofstede, G.: Dimensionalizing cultures: the Hofstede model in context. Online Readings Psychol. Cult. **2**(1), 8 (2011)

13. Minkov, M., Hofstede, G.: The evolution of Hofstede's doctrine. Cross Cult. Manage. Int. J. **18**(1), 10–20 (2011)

14. Hofstede, G., Minkov, M.: Long-versus short-term orientation: new perspectives. Asia Pacific Bus. Rev. **16**(4), 493–504 (2010)

15. Mkoyan, G.S.: National culture and ways of its preservation in a transforming society. Izvestiya of the St. Petersburg State Econ. Univ. **2**(98), 103–106 (2016)

16. G. Hofstede's model. https://www.hofstede-insights.com/country-comparison/russia/. Accessed 04 June 2018

17. Paturyan, Y.J., Gevorgyan, V., Badalyan, T., Grigoryan, N., Kojoyan, A.: Civic activism as a novel component of armenian civil society: new energy and tensions. Turpanjian Center for Policy Analysis (2015)

18. Gorshkov, M.K., Tikhonova, Ye, N.: Sotsiokul'turnyye faktory konsolidatsii rossiyskogo obshchestva: Informatsionno-analiticheskiy byulleten' Instituta sotsiologii Rossiyskoy akademii nauk=Information-analytical bulletin of the Institute of Sociology of the Russian Academy of Sciences **1**, 54 (2013). (in Russian)

19. Bowser, D.: Corruption, Trust, and the Danger to Democratization in the Former Soviet Union. Routledge, Berlin (2017)

20. Inglehart, R.: Postmodernization brings declining respect for authority but rising support for democracy. In: Norris, P. (ed.) Critical Citizens: Global Support for Democratic Government. Oxford University Press, Oxford (1999)

21. Inglehart, R., Welzel, C.: Changing mass priorities: the link between modernization and democracy. Perspect. Politics **8**(2), 551–567 (2010)

22. Dutta, S., Lanvin, B., Wunsch-Vincent, S. (eds.): The Global Innovation Index 2016: Innovation Feeding the World. Johnson Cornell University, Ithaca (2017)

23. Dutta, S., Lanvin, B., Wunsch-Vincent, S. (eds.): The Global Innovation Index 2016: Winning with Global Innovation. Johnson Cornell University, Ithaca (2016)

24. Dutta, S., Lanvin, B., Wunsch-Vincent, S.: The Global Innovation Index 2015. Effective Innovation Policies for Development. World Intellectual Property Organization, Geneva (2015)

25. Dutta, S., Lanvin, B., Wunsch-Vincent, S.: The Global Innovation Index 2014: The Human Factor in Innovation. WIPO, Geneva (2014)

26. Dutta, S., Lanvin, B.: The Global Innovation Index 2014: The Local Dynamics of Innovation. WIPO, Geneva (2014)

27. Shalanov, N.V., Aletdinova A.A.: Algorithm of taxonomy: method of design and implementation mechanism. J. Phys.: Conf. Ser. **1015** (2018). https://doi.org/10.1088/1742-6596/1015/3/032004

28. Elamiryan R.: Network society as the key factor for effective functioning of the Eurasian union. In: Proceedings of the International Conference on Electronic Governance and Open Society: Challenges in Eurasia (EGOSE 2016), pp. 83–92. https://doi.org/10.1145/3014087.3014114

Digital Services, Values, Inclusion

Exploring e-Services Development in Local Government Authorities by Means of Electronic Document Management Systems

Ingrid Pappel[1], Valentyna Tsap[1(✉)], Ingmar Pappel[2],
and Dirk Draheim[1]

[1] Tallinn University of Technology, Tallinn, Estonia
{ingrid.pappel,valentyna.tsap,dirk.draheim}@ttu.ee
[2] Interinx Ltd., Tallinn, Estonia
ingmar@interinx.com

Abstract. Estonia is a well-known example of a tech-savvy nation, especially when it comes to e-governance. Here, the government provides its citizens with public services online. Within a decade, the level of pervasiveness and technology acceptance reached a point where interaction between government and citizens is perceived to be a given. An integral part of the e-state is the digitalization of the public sector and, in particular, its basic routines that involve processing of documentation with an enormous amount of data. In this paper, we examine aspects, activities and outcomes of the development of e-services in local governments based on the use of electronic document and records management systems and their further co-existence. We provide an example of one of the Estonian local governments where the implemented conceptual interoperable framework has been validated. Moreover, we elaborate on interoperability solutions.

Keywords: e-services · EDRMS · Local government · e-government · Interoperability

1 Introduction

The foundation of any e-governance initiative presupposes the existence of a sufficient governance structure that operates within a transparent legal and policy framework. The governing entity has policies, processes, and procedures that enable electronic governance to take place – all supported by transparent laws. E-governance is relevant to many different areas such as e-democracy (including human rights, freedom of speech, freedom of information and knowledge) and e-commerce (building opportunities for the private sector). The focus of e-governance in this research is on the process of automating the delivery of efficient and effective government services to citizens. The main focus is on the digitalization of the internal processes of local governments by the implementation of appropriate technological tools that facilitate e-services delivery, increase their quality, cost- and time efficiency, and improve of e-government in general.

© Springer Nature Switzerland AG 2019
A. Chugunov et al. (Eds.): EGOSE 2018, CCIS 947, pp. 223–234, 2019.
https://doi.org/10.1007/978-3-030-13283-5_17

Technological solutions are an increasingly dominating factor in the move towards e-governance realizations. Electronic Document and Records Management Systems (EDRMSs) were among the first software platforms to facilitate the transformation of records management into a digital form. The use of EDRMSs allows to shift the processes inside the institution online and, therefore, is one of the most popular inter-governmental services in e-government projects [1–3]. Putting paperless management as the foundation of e-governance, the digitalization of the work processes of an organization should be an initial step in the transition process. This approach is expected, firstly, to increase the efficiency of work routines in local governments; secondly, to transform services and give current traditionally rendered services a new form; thirdly, to make it easier for organizations to adapt to technological changes.

This paper describes government processes that are digitalized by means of EDRMS tools, which in turn helps to create effective e-services. We will refer to good practices of e-government solutions in Estonia and its regions, where local governments have been successfully integrated into the digital environment by a conceptual implementation of EDRMSs. Within this setting, it will be shown that digitalization of public service activities is closely interconnected with electronic service provision. A concrete example of Estonian local government will serve as a summary of the most important key points and lessons learned.

Already in 2015, document exchange was digitalized to a degree of 97%. This has been the outcome of a survey that has been conducted in order to assess the acceptance of EDRMSs [4].

We proceed as follows. In Sect. 2, we draw the scene by explaining the prerequisites for EDRMSs. Section 3 givers an overview of existing local government EDRMS functionalities. Section 4 explains the importance of interoperability in the operation of governmental online systems by providing an example of EDRMS integration in Rapla County, Estonia. In Sect. 5, we describe the obstacles in the implementation process of EDRMSs. We continue the paper with a discussion in Sect. 6 and finish with a brief conclusion in Sect. 7.

2   Identifying Necessities for EDRMSs

The connection between information governance and the management of organization processes and workflows, along with digitalization, has been a clear trend in recent years. Electronic document management plays an important role in contemporary e-government applications and technologies. The main aim of it in the public sector is to store, manipulate, diffuse, and preserve knowledge in order to achieve the effectiveness of e-governance. Moreover, a flexible and adaptable document management system is needed in order to cope with the modern challenges that authorities and decision-makers are facing. These include issues such as increasing efficiency and quality while decreasing the duration of government processes and providing structure and organization in documentation and related activities of authorities [5]. Document management systems are also used to ease the communication between different parties: citizens, officials, contractors, decision-makers, and others [6].

There is a significant importance of defining standards and regulations in this field in order to maintain the efficiency and transparency of administration activities. Estonia's Government Office has defined regulations on standards, procedures, methods, and products to assist the modern IT-evolution processes [7]. These standards are set to ensure the development of wholesome, authentic and reliable document management and information systems. In addition to Estonian regulations, the European Union project, "Model Requirements for the Management of Electronic Records" (MoReq) defines basic requirements for document management [8]. The list of requirements is very detailed and based on the ISO 15489 standard [9]. In addition to the requirements, MoReq defines criteria for document functions, e.g., workflows, email and electronic signatures. In the case of Estonia, there are many regulations (Public Information Act, active since 2001; Personal Data Protection Act, active since 2003; General Procedural Actions Act, active since 2001; Administration Procedure Act, active since 2002 [10–13], which coordinate the use of electronic document management systems.

It is necessary to mention that now, with the introduction of EU GDPR and the eIDAS regulation, countries are obliged to take necessary measures in order to comply with new rules. This, in turn, directly affects the sphere of electronic document management and related elements and requires a thorough revision of the entire process of data gathering, processing, exchanging, storing, etc. It is expected from all involved parties to align their policy, legislation, rules, and procedures to these regulations; which is expected to lead to the creation of the digital single market, a harmonization of data privacy laws.

2.1 Using EDRMSs for Facilitation of e-Services Delivery

As a part of the transition to e-government, shifting public services to the digital environment has undoubtedly been an integral process. Going further, paperless management provides transparency to both transition processes and decision-making processes. Linking the development of e-services with the work processes of EDRMSs has been a logical step, as according to the Public Information Act, all authorities have to maintain their documents registries electronically. In recent years, EDRMSs have become more important as an informational environment for activities and decisions of organizations. In our Estonian example almost, all cases of service provision presuppose the preparation of an administrative legislation for a specific application [14]. In the past, decisions for a service provision request have been made entirely outside the EDRMS, so that only the final decision could be submitted and notified, e.g., the issuance of a building permit. Today, the entire request processing, from initiation to completion, is handled within an EDRMS.

While moving towards e-services and paperless management, the traditional ways of providing public services to citizens should remain available, as we will never reach a level of full digitalization where citizens communicate with authorities exclusively online. Multiple ways of accessing services from the government should be offered. However, if we yet again speak about delivering a service to a citizen offline, the part of the process that is being carried out on the side of the government should be digitalized.

Looking at e-services in a wider perspective that captures not only the public but also private sector, a difference in the approach to the design, implementation and delivery of services can be discovered. The digital environment has opened an enormous range of opportunities for service providers and manufacturers to bring services and products along with a new quality, value and experience. The domain of customer relations and customer satisfaction has come in front as an essential factor of influence. Shankar et al. defines two types of customer satisfaction both for online and offline environments, which are service encounter satisfaction and overall satisfaction. The first one is transaction-specific and the second one refers to a relation-specific one, mainly having a cumulative nature [15]. Both of the types are applicable in the sphere of public e-service provision and each attribute of service delivery will reflect on the overall level of citizens' satisfaction and in turn will have a long-term effect on the success of e-government.

2.2   Re-engineering Business Processes in Local Governments

The aim of a process optimization is to resolve complex challenges and improve a product, service or a process [16]. Relatively little is known about the application of business process modeling concepts in the public sector as there is so far not much attention in this area of research. However, there are findings, for instance, reported by Gulledge and Sommer, that confirm positive effects of process optimization in public sector based on documenting the existing processes, managing them by means of measuring and optimizing, and improving the products or services itself [17].

In this perspective, using the vocabulary and terminology of the domain of process optimization, e-government services are usually thought of within the strategy discipline of operational excellence that is focused on efficiency, streamlined operations, supply chain management and high volume [18]. The choice of such value discipline is seemed to be evident as the product in case of the public sector is the service which is standardized, and not customized, required to be provided continuously.

The process of paperless management implementation entails a wide variety of business processes that ideally fit the purpose of continuous improvement carried out in phases. Moreover, embedding technologies and innovative solutions like EDRMS and e-government, in general, serves as a driving force for organizational changes and justifies the necessity of re-engineering business processes into more time- and cost-effective models. It is essential to ensure that while the processes will be re-engineered and updated, the internal change is also going to be thought through. Not only acceptance of technologies matters on the side of end-users, i.e. citizens, but also public-sector workers. Here, officials on the one hand are a part of the process that is being improved, and on the other, are users of technologies as well.

However, it should be taken into account that it is not always the case that each and every procedure has to be transferred to digital environment. For instance, if one application is submitted on the citizen end, in order to process this request on the government end electronically, it may require a chain of multiple queries to be executed and forwarded to multiple entities' databases [4]. That way, it should be realized that there can be easy and difficult implementations, and several options to improve those processes can be used for that purpose.

3   Overview of a Local Government EDRMS

75% of Estonian local governments use EDRMSs. The most commonly used EDRMS is Amphora by Interinx Ltd.

To date, most of the public services are electronic and linked to EDRMSs.

Submission of a service request can be performed via different channels and environments, but regardless of form of request, all processes and activities related to handling this request start in EDRMSs that facilitate efficient workflows.

Before EDRMSs have been rolled out, records management in local governments was mainly paper-based.

The development of the EDRMS Amphora started in 1998. Its main goal was to develop software that would enable public sector organizations to implement paperless document management. First steps towards it consisted of developing a software that would allow for implementation of paperless management in public sector authorities, and this proved to be a challenging task as the efficiency and realization of the system were constrained. EDRMSs have started to spread out rapidly in 2006–2007 when the primary rules and principles for implementation of paperless management were introduced. This brought EDRMSs to many other projects at the state level allowing to become also interoperable with other EDRMSs due to the opening of Estonian Document Exchange Center (DEC). Moreover, the EDRMSs, in particular Amphora, were integrated with the Estonian Citizen Portal (a one-stop-shop portal of public e-services). This was a beginning of electronic applications usage as a part of e-services in Estonia.

3.1   e-Services Used in Estonian Local Governments Based on EDRMS Functionalities

Next, we will delve into an example of e-services provision based on an EDRMS used in one of the counties of Estonia, i.e., Rapla. The case presents the application of e-services linked to the EDRMS and Citizen Portal, and the development of assessment criteria for measuring the digital performance of the local government where the mentioned functionality operates.

The entire process of implementation and integration of the EDRMS has been carried out on the basis of the e-LocGov model, a framework for the implementation of e-government solutions in local governments. The e-LocGov model consists of a technological part and a (change) management part. The technological part includes EDRMS with the required integration for implementing local government systems. The management part includes a methodology of how to carry out the transformation into a new platform. The e-LocGov model addresses: (1) state-level readiness; (2) organizational readiness; (3) transition methodology; and (4) assessment of feedback, statistics, and impact, which are an imperative part of the framework for the transition of local governments into e-governance.

As already mentioned in Sect. 2.1, when handling a request for service provision, a set of administrative legislation documentation is presupposed. In order to ensure proper implementation of an EDRMS, the first decision to make was identifying what e-services should be linked to the system. Hence, a total of 24 most important e-forms has been developed and implemented in Rapla County. In cooperation with the workgroup from the local government, the necessary data descriptions for each selected service were prepared and created as forms. This process was coordinated with the representatives of local governments who approved the final dataset. The main shortcoming was the lack of a common repository for describing the services. Moreover, the entire process of evaluation and description was relatively time-consuming (Table 1).

Table 1. List of developed e-forms

Name of the application	Fields before	Fields after	Integration with state registries
Application for childbirth	21	19	Yes
Application for the admission to 1st grade	16	16	Partial
Application for the kindergarten	25	23	Partial
Application for freeing of property tax	21	19	Partial
Application for property excavation	18	17	Partial
Approval for positioning drill hole location	27	27	Partial
Application for guardianship	32	32	Partial
Application for placement in nursing home	24	22	Yes
Application for detail planning of property	31	29	Partial
Application for public event organisation	22	20	Partial
Withdrawal of organised waste transportation	16	16	Partial
Application for funeral benefit-support	15	12	Yes
Application for compensation of travel expenses	24	23	Partial
Application for building planning	29	24	Partial
Application for registering a pet	25	22	Partial
Application for nursing compensation	23	23	Partial
Application for school attendance	20	16	Partial
Request for information	11	11	Partial
Application for project initiation	21	21	Partial
Application for land/property division	24	21	Partial
Application for social benefits	18	17	Partial
Application for property tax exemption	19	19	Partial
Application for advertising space	17	15	Yes
Application for compensations of recreational activities	18	16	Partial

After the project, the citizens had the opportunity to obtain the necessary applications from the Citizen Portal or through the website of the local government. After filling in and submitting the application, it was received in the implemented EDRMS where further procedural processes were initiated.

4   Interoperability as a Basis for Seamless e-Service Provision

An EDRMS cannot exist as a central system that provides services to an organization as an independent unit. In order to ensure a complete paperless management, the internal and external systems of an organization have to communicate based on an interoperable solution [19]. In Estonia, the integration of EDRMS with other IT solutions has been a growing trend. The exchange of data between software helps to save money and time that is otherwise spent on preparing transcripts, copies, and reconfiguring data. Information management in a common system with the cross-usage of data allows for better monitoring of the procedural steps.

The cross-usage of data between different systems is an important future perspective that allows re-using data and optimizes the time spent on data entry. EDRMS must be able to offer the intermediation of such communication because the dataset inserted there is essentially the same as the data in the main state registries. While running various projects aimed for establishing paperless systems in local governments, the interoperability of the EDRMS system has been the main focus for offering an interface for intermediating communication (automatically generating the requested data into the document form) with different state databases. In order to integrate EDRMS Amphora with other systems, it is possible to use diffcrent protocols and technologies: http, https, get, post, WebDav, SOAP, XML-RPC, Twain, IMAP, POP3, SMTP, SSL, LDAP, etc.

4.1   Managing Business Processes via Interoperability Functionalities

This subsection is ought to give an understanding of the role of interoperability when it comes business processes where the involved parties operate based on heterogeneous technologies.

Over several years, numerous integrations have been developed on the basis of EDRMS, e.g. interfaces with national registries, financial software and personnel software, etc. Information management in a common system and cross-usage of data allows for better monitoring of the procedural steps.

Figure 1 depicts a concrete example of a workflow and cross-usage of data carried by multiple organizations.

The information moves between the systems on the basis of a set of agreed-upon rules of metadata in the XML format. In this case, the scheme shows how an interface functions and enables interaction between EDRMS and a finance management software (among the solutions that are aimed at local governments).

A unified finance management software has been used by more than half of the local governments in Estonia. For verifying the data descriptions, the e-invoice

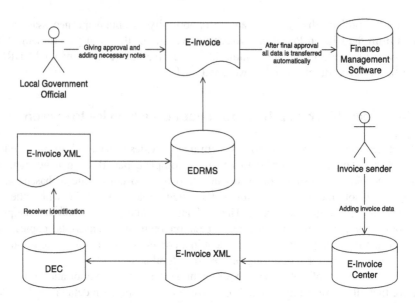

Fig. 1. The invoice handling process between finance management software and EDRMS

standard developed by the Bank of Estonia is used, and the items of the invoices are transmitted between the systems.

There is also an interface with a finance management software, wherein the interface is still based on the XML-invoice that conforms to the Estonian e-invoice standard. It was adapted to the finance management software's invoice base, in order to enable exporting the XML-output that conforms to the Estonian e-invoice standard and importing it to the finance management software's databased. The communication between the systems is carried out in both directions – EDRMS is being updated with regard to the dimensions and suppliers of an invoice, and EDRMS sends the items of an invoice to the finance management software's database. This functionality permits to digitalize all incoming invoices and process them in the digital form. Analogous practices can be found where digital invoices are used in the public sector elsewhere in the world. A data exchange channel that has been developed in EDRMS is the interface for communicating with national registries where gateway functionality facilitates creating different get and post requests when using web services and linking those to other systems. Inside an institution, there are several information systems where the organization-related information is managed. In addition, there was a need to develop an interface in EDRMS for communicating with a personnel software Persona, whereby a document that is registered in Persona is sent with its content and metadata to EDRMS. Many smaller local governments can manage the personnel-related documents directly in EDRMS and the financial software. In addition to the above-mentioned interfaces, EDRMS communicates with DEC and Service of Official Documents (SOD) that permit a fully electronic exchange of documents between local governments and citizens. The re-use of already existing data is inevitable in order to save time when processing the information and eliminating the data entry mistakes.

It is necessary to mention once again the eIDAS regulation that in this context is also relevant and urges to introduce necessary changes to enable as well the cross-border interoperability of e-services.

5   Obstacles to EDRMS Implementation

Although various technological solutions have been developed, several shortcomings still hinder their wider use. One of the main shortcomings is implementing the new solutions as their application requires a significant amount of financial and human resources. It has become evident that all technological solutions (not only EDRMSs) targeted for local governments should be described on the basis of a harmonized format and methodology. The solutions applied in local governments need to be described by employing consistent principles. It is important to consider communication and interoperability with other systems. This would ensure cooperation between the various local government and state systems. The integration of government information resources and processes, and ultimately, the interoperation of an independent government information system appear essential [20].

Another issue related to interoperability of involved entities is the excessive complexity of administrative business processes (Sect. 2.2). In addition, developing new duplicating systems should be avoided. A more efficient integration of existing solutions would entail resource savings for all parties. This creates an increased necessity for integrating the various IT solutions employed in the work of the institutions upon the transformation from one governance model to another. That in turn changes the existing work processes from the perspective of handling surrounding information and knowledge, amongst others. Given that e-government services extend across different organizational boundaries and heterogeneous infrastructures, there is a dire need to manage the knowledge and information resources stored in these disparate systems [21]. A customized and thorough knowledge management strategy is required. In this sense, knowledge management also serves as an important component when it comes to optimization of business processes (Sect. 2.2) that ensures effective use of information and resources within organization creating added value. Distinguishing and understanding business processes allows for description of information architecture, business process models and working procedures. Consequently, it becomes then possible to describe also roles and responsibilities of employees, apply efficiently their skills, knowledge and experience.

6   Discussion and Related Work

The developments of the information society over the past decade have resulted in inevitable changes. The decision-making processes that have often been static and unwavering have had to evolve and adapt in the light of new principles. Expanded social networks have reformed the interaction between local governments and citizens which are now infinitely more interactive. Digital channels are open for interaction, which could not have been foreseen years ago. The administration of a local government or the use of services by citizens from any corner of the world is becoming a reality. Along with ICT, the tendency in the last few years has been to develop and apply a competence-based governance model. The most widespread approach is the creation of the ICT capacity and competence base, employing people and their knowledge as software.

As mentioned above, in the past there were no appropriate IT solutions for launching paperless management. Today, however, major parts of IT systems for supporting transition into e-governance have been developed.

Citizens can use different e-services and participate in the decision-making processes of local governments. They are more aware of the possibilities of how to monitor the work procedures of local governments. Conditions have been and are being created for citizens to use services and obtain information from local governments by using different channels. Extensive use of EDRMS gives the opportunity to move communication to a faster level of consuming services and information. Nevertheless, the extent of that use is left to be decided by the local governments: whether to follow the legislation with its minimum requirements, or to create opportunities for implementing the participatory democracy on a larger scale.

The growth of citizen satisfaction is tied to the growth of the digital performance of local governments. The higher the digital performance of a local government, the more possibilities the citizen has to take advantage of the services. According to Accenture eGovernment Report, the goal for e-government now is to tailor service delivery to meet the needs of the citizens, as opposed to approaching it from the government side [22]. During the application of e-governance possibilities, there are contradictions between requirements arising from rules and standardized work routines, and from using progressive ICT tools. The implementation of paperless management and digital document work proceedings has to be facilitated by the rules and instructions described on the state level wherein several problems still require solutions in order to reach a wider assessment of the synergies and cooperation between local governments and the state.

The application itself does not only entail learning the software components. It is also necessary to change one's thinking by implementing renewed work routines. User acceptance of intergovernmental services is an important factor [2]. People are afraid of changes and becoming replaceable. They are not confident about the accessibility of the technology. On the one hand, according to Bannister and Connoly [23], the expectation that technology-enabled change has the ability to increase the trust of the citizens, thereby transforming government, may be too high. However, having a solid foundation provides a good start for bridging that trust gap [24].

Coming back to the case of Estonia where public sector is successfully functioning online and has gained citizens' trust, it is planned to bring public service provision to next level. A proactive and automated service provision is expected to be beneficial to government in terms of improvements in workflows of organizations, cost- and time efficiency.

7 Conclusion

As a part of the transition to e-government, paperless management can enable the creation of e-services that allow for fully digitalized digital interaction between citizens and local governments. The case of Rapla County in Estonia and its results proves the potential of EDRMSs for improving the technological and organizational performance of local governments, which in turn facilitates better service provision to the citizens. Upon its implementation and further development, the developed framework leads to a more effective local government and increases the efficiency of cooperating with citizens and enterprises. However, in order to ensure the success in establishing such systems, a huge implementation effort is needed. In case of Estonian local governments, a systematic implementation methodology was used. We consider that the most important lessons that can derived from Estonian experience are: development and utilization of interoperability solutions that enable communication and data exchange between entities, continuous improvement of processes as well as continuous feedback.

References

1. Ngoepe, M.S.: An exploration of records management trends in the South African Public Sector: a case study of the Department of Provincial and Local Government (2008). http://uir.unisa.ac.za/handle/10500/2705. Accessed 15 Oct 2012
2. Hung, S.Y., Tang, K.Z., Chang, C.M., Ke, C.D.: User acceptance of intergovernmental services: An example of electronic document management system. Gov. Inf. Q. **26**(2), 387–397 (2009)
3. Yaacob, R.A., Sabai, R.M.: Electronic records management in Malaysia: a case study in one government agency. In: Asia-Pacific Conference On Library & Information Education & Practice 2011 (A-LIEP2011): Issues, Challenges and Opportunities, 22–24 June 2011, Pullman Putrajaya Lakeside, Malaysia (2011)
4. Draheim, D., Koosapoeg, K., Lauk, M., Pappel, I., Pappel, I., Tepandi, J.: The design of the Estonian governmental document exchange classification framework. In: Kő, A., Francesconi, E. (eds.) EGOVIS 2016. LNCS, vol. 9831, pp. 33–47. Springer, Cham (2016). https://doi.org/10.1007/978-3-319-44159-7_3
5. Deloitte. Document Management in Local Government: Finding the real savings (Report) (2011). http://www.deloitte.com/assets/Dcom-UnitedKingdom/Local%20Assets/Documents/Industries/GPS/UK_GPS_DocumentManagementinLocalGovernment.pdf. Accessed 11 Nov 2013
6. Sar, H.K., Wong, T.Y.C.: Web-based document management systems in the construction industry. In: Construction Economics and Managements I, Working Paper, Rome, Italy, 6–10 May 2012 (2012). http://www.fig.net/pub/fig2012/papers/ts01c/TS01C_wong_5393.pdf. Accessed 11 Nov 2013
7. Government Office. Requirements for electronic document management systems' functionality. Available online in Estonian: Nõuded elektrooniliste dokumendihaldussüstemide funktsionaalsusele (2002). http://valitsus.ee/UserFiles/valitsus/et/riigikantselei/dokumendihaldus/dokumendihaldusest/noudedelektrooniliseledokumendihaldusele/FNoue_rk1.pdf. Accessed 11 Nov 2013

8. DLM Forum Foundation. Modular Requirements for Records Systems – MoReq2010 (2011). http://moreq.info/index.php?option=com_jotloader&view=categories&cid=40_4e47 a2abad7422897e078fd469dd9933&Itemid=129&lang=en. Accessed 17 Nov 2013
9. International Organization for Standardization – ISO. Information and documentation – Records management, ISO 15489–1:2001 (2001). http://www.iso.org/iso/catalogue_detail? csnumber=31908. Accessed 15 Oct 2012
10. Riigi Teataja. Public Information Act. Available online in Estonian: Avaliku teabe seadus (2001a). https://www.riigiteataja.ee/akt/12766090. Accessed 11 Nov 2013
11. Riigi Teataja. General Procedural Actions Act. Available in Estonian: Asjaajamiskorra ühtsed alused (2001b). https://www.riigiteataja.ee/akt/840660. Accessed 11 Nov 2013
12. Riigi Teataja. Administration Procedure Act. Available online in Estonian (2002). https:// www.riigiteataja.ee/akt/686696?leiaKehtiv. Accessed 11 Nov 2013)
13. Riigi Teataja. Personal Data Production Act. Available online in Estonian (2003). https:// www.riigiteataja.ee/akt/748829. Accessed 11 Nov 2013
14. Pappel, I., Pappel, I.: Methodology for measuring the digital capability of local governments. In: Proceedings of the 5th International Conference on Theory and Practice of Electronic Governance, Tallinn, Estonia, 26–28 Sept 2011, pp 357–358. ACM, Tallinn (2011c)
15. Shankar, V., Smith, A.K., Rangaswamy, A.: Customer satisfaction and loyalty in online and offline environments. Int. J. Res. Mark. 20(2), 153–175 (2003)
16. Bhatt, G.D., Troutt, M.D.: Examining the relationship between business process improve-ment initiatives, information systems integration and customer focus: an empirical study. Bus. Process Manage. J. 11(5), 532–558 (2005)
17. Gulledge Jr., T.R., Sommer, R.A.: Business process management: public sector implications. Bus. Process Manage. J. 8(4), 364–376 (2002)
18. Jain, A.K., Jeppe Jeppesen, H.: Knowledge management practices in a public sector organisation: the role of leaders' cognitive styles. J. Knowl. Manage. 17(3), 347–362 (2013)
19. Pappel, I., Pappel, I.: Implementation of service-based e-government and establishment of state IT components interoperability at local authorities. In: The Proceedings of the 3rd IEEE International Conference on Advanced Computer Control (ICACC 2011), Harbin, Hiina, 18–20 Jan 2011, pp 371–378. Institute of Electronics and Computer Science, Singapore (2011a)
20. Scholl, H.J., Kubicek, H., Cimander, R., Klischewski, R.: Process integration, information sharing, and system interoperation in government: a comparative case analysis. Gov. Inf. Q. 29(3), 313–323 (2012)
21. Iyer, L.S., Singh, R., Salam, A.F., D'Aubeterre, F.: Knowledge management for Government-to-Government (G2G) process coordination. Electron. Gov. Int. J. (EG) 3(1), 18–35 (2006)
22. Accenture. E-Government Leadership Report: Engaging the Customer (2003). http://nstore. accenture.com/acn_com/PDF/Engaging_the_Customer.pdf. Accessed 15 Oct 2012
23. Bannister, F., Connolly, R.: Trust and transformational government: a proposed framework for research. Gov. Inf. Q. 28(2), 137–147 (2011)
24. Tsap, V., Pappel, I., Draheim, D.: Key success factors in introducing national e-identification systems. In: Dang, T.K., Wagner, R., Küng, J., Thoai, N., Takizawa, M., Neuhold, E. (eds.) FDSE 2017. LNCS, vol. 10646, pp. 455–471. Springer, Cham (2017). https://doi.org/10. 1007/978-3-319-70004-5_33

Areas of Habitation in the City: Improving Urban Management Based on Check-in Data and Mental Mapping

Aleksandra Nenko[(✉)], Artem Koniukhov, and Marina Petrova

ITMO University, 14 Birzhevaya line., 199034 St. Petersburg, Russia
Qullab.spb@gmail.com

Abstract. In this paper we present a study on areas of habitation in St. Petersburg, Russia, which are actively used and perceived by city dwellers as coherent units. The motivation behind the study is to define generic urban areas formed by actual user experience and different from administrative division to improve urban management of the city territory. We employ mixed methods approach to account both for users' practices in urban space, based on analysis of check-in data, and users' perception of urban space, based on analysis of mental maps. The clustering algorithm is based on spatial and social proximity indexes and has been validated through the results of the mental mapping survey. The dataset of check-ins is retrieved from VKontakte social network, the most popular one for St. Petersburg and for Russia, and comprises 6128 venues with 763079 check-ins collected for December 2017–February 2018 time period. The mental mapping has been conducted within 39 users of different age and gender, representing different areas of the city under study. We compare the borders of the areas of habitation with the map of administrative division, consider functional load of the areas in different areas of the city, define environmental factors which form the borders, give suggestions on how knowledge on areas of habitation could inform and improve urban management practice.

Keywords: Areas of habitation · LBSN · Check-in data · Mental mapping · Mixed methods · Urban management

1 Introduction

Starting from Chicago school one of the continuous queries of urban researchers is detecting and defining urban communities and milieus where they concentrate and develop certain lifestyles. People tend to form spatial communities and zones of concentrated human activity [1]. Administrative division of the city does not always reflect such generic clusters of urban life. Mapping areas of activity allows to improve urban management in view of urban polycentricity and service sufficiency.

The motivation behind the study is to define "areas of habitation" formed by actual user experience and different from administrative division to improve urban management of the city territory. We define areas of habitation as parts of the city which are actively used on daily basis and perceived by city dwellers as coherent units. Well developed areas of habitation coincide with high level of quality of life in the city [2].

© Springer Nature Switzerland AG 2019
A. Chugunov et al. (Eds.): EGOSE 2018, CCIS 947, pp. 235–248, 2019.
https://doi.org/10.1007/978-3-030-13283-5_18

In these areas residents can satisfy their daily needs with minimal time and financial costs. They also form communities of practice united by similar style of life taking place in shared urban venues.

We suggest that defining areas of habitation should be based on the numerous data coming today from location-based social networks (LBSNs), while it is user-generated, illustrates people behaviours in urban venues and is voluminous and highly accessible. To supplement analysis of users behaviours in space with knowledge of space perception, we employ sociological methods. We put the following research questions: what are the areas of habitation in St. Petersburg? Do they coincide with municipal division of the city? What are the functional characteristics of these areas? What are the environmental factors which form these areas? The case study taken for this paper is St. Petersburg, Russia, the second largest city in Russia (almost 5 mln people), with active use of LBSNs.

2 Literature Review

Defining areas in urban space where people concentrate and which they regularly use on everyday life basis is a challenge for urban management practice which aims at better decision targeting, cost reduction, and service placement effectiveness. Uncertainty of urban boundaries arises from a combination of factors such as administrative, religious, social, and physical artifacts [3]. Administrative boundaries typically do not physically manifest themselves in urban space, but their existence influences perception of the city. At the same time, administrative artifacts are overlain by a variety of factors, such as the built structure, land use, transport accessibility, service distribution, social (in)homogeneity, population density, and housing systems [4]. The interplay of these factors gives rise to different conceptions and actual boundaries of the neighborhoods defined by the residents which may differ fundamentally from administrative definitions and are in constant transition [3]. Such neighborhoods are considered in [5] as the sub-places making up the place of the city where end users consume services and products. In urban management practice there is a real need to develop methods to define and explore such regions.

K. Lynch has proposed the concept of imaginability to define the perceived structure of the city space and imaginary borders of the city units. Lynch has proved that conceived clearness or vagueness of the boundaries in urban space could be explained by physical properties of the urban territory [6]. He has also proposed a mental mapping technique to define the perceived areas of their city and their borders: during an interview a person was asked about her memories and emotions of a place which were analyzed as a system of subjective landmarks, borders, and routes inside the area.

This study is positioned within the field of vernacular or naive geography which considers how people delimit space in everyday use [7]. Vernacular geography deals with regions which are typically not represented in formal administrative division and which are often considered to be vague. Vernacular geography adds to developing information systems based on non-expert users' notions of space rather than the traditionally administrative geography.

Exploring "organic" areas of the city and their generic usage requires data which reflects vernacular features of urban space. A data source of great assistance here is the so called user generated content (UGC) or, more specifically, volunteered geographic information (VGI) [8]. Both UGC and VGI are uploaded to the web by individuals through different channels, location-based social networks (LBSNs) check-ins, images and tags.

LBSNs data is nowadays actively applied by researchers for a number of tasks, conjugate with rethinking of the socio-spatial structure and boundaries of the city based on knowledge of real life practices of the citizens. These tasks include defining regions in the city based on networks of human interactions [9]; creating maps of aggregate activities and defining predominant land use [10]; extracting patterns of social mobility in the city [11, 12]; defining urban points-of-interest (POIs) [13]; allocating generic toponyms and correspondent conceived borders of the areas [4, 14]; detecting spatio-temporal communities [15].

The methodologies most often used are based on statistical analysis of network properties, in particular, community detection with Newman-Girvan algorithm, defining distance-decay effects [9, 12, 15]; probabilistic models of topic occurrence [4, 14]; clustering analysis of spatial data, e.g. DBSCAN [16]; Principal Component Analysis (PCA) [10, 17]; gravity models [4]; analysis of spatial distributions of tags and check-ins [11]; dynamic sequential analysis of spatio-temporal patterns [18]. The data used for these studies includes LBSNs data Twitter posts [14], Flickr photos and tags [4, 11] as well as telecommunication and mobile-phone datas [9–11, 15], bank or other transaction records. The applied value of these studies for urban management lies in creating recommendation systems for designing transportation system and pedestrian routes, for service provision and crowd management, for urban planning of public spaces in the city, etc.

Analysis based solely on LBSNs or telecommunication data is somewhat constrained due to the level of aggregation of the data used as well as the scarcity or somewhat banality of the social properties of the data analyzed. The reliability of LBSNs data is nowadays more and more questionable: are still such services as Twitter or Foursquare popular with users, do they really represent the behaviours of all users? Telecommunications data is more precise but is predominantly used as aggregated and does not allow to make finely grained conclusions on social properties of agents. These studies could benefit from the mixed methods research approach which we are presenting in this study. Mixed methods approach combines subjective interpretations given by people to their activities, trips and communities, which are derivable from qualitative and quantitative sociological surveys, with objective parameters, which can be explored on the level of big user-generated data.

3 Methodology

To define areas of habitation we employ mixed methods approach: we account for users' practices in urban space based on analysis of check-in data and for users' perception of urban space based on analysis of mental maps of a sample of citizens in line with K. Lynch technique. Below we present the sequence of the methodological procedure: first, the results of the initial clustering algorithm applied to check-in data, second, validation of the algorithm with mental mapping results and, third, refinement of the computational algorithm.

3.1   Initial Computational Algorithm

The computational algorithm we are applying is based on the "Livehoods Project" conducted by Cranshaw et al. 2012 [19]. The Carnegie Mellon University team has proposed a spectral clustering model for a city-scale of Pittsburgh, PA, US, based on a dataset of 42787 check-ins of 3840 users at 5349 venues collected from a location-based online social network. They have called the received clusters "livehoods". To define them the researchers have introduced the social proximity index which accounts for the distance between the neighboring venues and also for the similarity of the users who have check-ined there. The index is calculated as a cosine similarity of the vectors representing the venues.

The data source used in this study is the most popular social network in Russian speaking countries VKontakte (VK). The dataset was retrieved via API and contains around 6128 venues parsed located in administrative borders of St. Petersburg city, with the total number of check-ins is 763079 created by 128406 users during December 2017–February 2018. For our dataset we have appointed V to be a set of n_V VK venues and for each $i, j \in V$ we have computed Euclidean distance $d(i, j)$. To compute geographical distance between the venues we have transformed lat/lng coordinates to UTMZone36V projection. We have also appointed U as the set of n_U VK users and C as the set of these user's geolocated messages (check-ins) in the venues which make up the set V. Each venue $v \in V$ is represented as a "bag of check-ins" to v. The uth component of the vector c_V is the count of users' check-ins in v. For this matrix we have computed social similarity index $s(i, j)$ between each pair of venues $i, j \in V$.

$$s(i,j) = \frac{c_i \cdot c_j}{||c_i|| \cdot ||c_j||} \tag{1}$$

Based on the social similarity index values we compiled affinity matrix $= (a_{i,j})_{i,j=1,\dots,n_V}$. For a venue v the $N_m(v)$ is the m closest venues according to the $d(v, \cdot)$.

$$a(i,j) = \begin{cases} s(i,j) + \alpha & \text{if } j \in N_m(i) \text{ or } i \in N_m(j) \\ 0 & \text{otherwise} \end{cases} \tag{2}$$

where α is a small constant that blocks venues from having no connections to any others.

The received graph $G(A)$ (see Fig. 2a) was subjected to the following spectral clustering algorithm presented in the "Livehoods project" (Fig. 1).

Data: V, A, G(A), k_{min}, k_{max}, τ
Results: Clusters $A_i, \ldots, A_k$

1. Compute the normalized Laplacian matrix L_{norm}.
2. Let $\lambda_1 \leq \cdots \leq \lambda_{k_{max}}$ be the k_{max} smallest eigenvalues of L_{norm}. Set $k = max_{i=k_{min},\ldots,k_{max}-1}\Delta_i$ where $\Delta_i = \lambda_{i+1} - \lambda_i$
3. Find the k smallest eigenvectors $e_1, \ldots, e_k$ of L_{norm}.
4. Let E be an $n_v \times k$ matrix with e_i as columns.
5. Let the $y_1, \ldots, y_{n_v}$ be the rows of E and cluster them into $C_1, \ldots, C_k$ with k-means. This induces a clustering on $A_1, \ldots, A_k$ by $A_i = \{j | y_j \in C_i\}$.
6. For each A_i, let $G(A_i)$ be the subgraph of $G(A)$ induced by vertices A_i. Split $G(A_i)$ into connected components. Add each component as a newcluster, removing $G(A_i)$.
7. Let b be the area of bounding box containing coordinates in , and b_i be the area of the box containing A_i. If $b_i/b > \tau$, delete cluster A_i, and redistribute each $v \in A_i$ to the closest A_j under single linkage distance $d(v, A_j)$.

Alg. 1. "Livehoods project" spectral clustering algorithm.

Fig. 1. The map of clusters in St. Petersburg received with the initial clusterization algorithm.

For this paper $m = 10$, $\alpha = 0.001$, $k_{min} = 30$, $k_{max} = 30$, $\tau = 0.4$.

3.2 Validation of the Initial Algorithm

Parallel to analysis of big urban data we have conducted a qualitative sociological survey to map the mental borders of the areas for city residents living or working at different areas of St. Petersburg. The survey was conducted from mid-March till mid-April 2018. The methodology used was semi-structured interviews, 39 interviews were collected in total. The respondents were representing 2 age groups - 20–30 and 40–50 years old - who have been selected as the most active consumers of the city space due to their regular study and/or work practices and whose mental maps might represent the areas of habitation most fully. The interviewees chosen were residing and working in central, semi-central and peripheral city districts in equal proportions.

During the interviews respondents were asked to describe their everyday life practices and to draw their mental maps - everyday routes and venues they visit close to the place they live in or work at. The interviewees also commented on the emotional perception of their mental area, places they like and dislike, attractors and barriers. The interviews have shown that the areas of habitation mapped by respondents do not correspond or correspond only partly to the ones defined by the initial clustering algorithm (Algorithm 1). Based on sociological survey we have discovered a number of environmental factors influencing formation of the area of habitation the algorithm did not account for: (a) barriers created by the built environment (industrial zones, motorways, railways); (b) natural barriers (Neva river, channels); (c) pedestrian accessibility.

Besides sociological validation we have discovered that the k-nearest neighbor algorithm proposed by "Livehoods project" is not working for our dataset, while the graph $G(A)$ had only 493 ties with weight more than α out of 54798 ties. To test this we have clustered the unweighted 10-nearest neighbour graph and have received almost similar results. This means that the social similarity of venues was not grasped by the k-nearest neighbor algorithm for our dataset.

3.3 Refinement of the Computational Algorithm

To account for environmental barriers and to form a graph of venues with more social proximity we have refined the clusterization algorithm by introducing a metrics of pedestrian accessibility. The social proximity index is calculated for a pair of neighboring objects, which are located at a 5 min distance from each other, which in spatial terms is defined as 500 m radius around each venue.

We have computed a new affinity matrix $E = (e_{i,j})_{i,j=1,\ldots,n_V}$. For a given venue v, $N(v, \varepsilon)$ is the set of venues which distance from v is smaller than ε.

$$e(i,j) = \begin{cases} s(i,j) + \alpha & \text{if } j \in N(i, \varepsilon) \text{ or } i \in N(j, \varepsilon) \\ 0 & \text{otherwise} \end{cases} \tag{3}$$

New similarity graph $G(E)$ was constructed by connecting each venue node by undirected edge with venues in ε meters radius. The weight of the edge between venues i, j is set according to $s(i,j)$.

The walkable distance between the venues in non-central areas of the city is often more than 500 m, so the received graph is unconnected, while spectral algorithm requires a graph consisting of one connected component. To receive the connected graph we define an affinity matrix $C = UNION(A, E)$. The resulting graph $G(C)$ (see Fig. 2b) has 15496 ties with weight more than α out of 54798 ties.

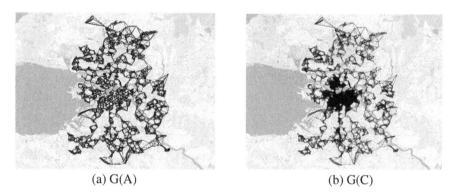

(a) G(A)   (b) G(C)

Fig. 2. Representation of similarity graphs on St. Petersburg map.

We have applied the spectral clustering algorithm (Algorithm 1) without the last two post-processing steps and have set the following parameters: $\varepsilon = 500$, $m = 10$, $\alpha = 0.001$, $kmin = 30$, $kmax = 250$. The new number of clusters received was 155. The results of the new clusterization represented in Fig. 4 [1]. For the clusters the median check-in count is 28, the minimal number of check-ins in a venue is 10, maximal is 3103.

4   Results

After refining the computational algorithm according to mental mapping results we have received UGC-based and mental areas of habitation which collocate in the city space. Such collocation signifies that these areas are reflecting both practices of users and their perceptions. There is no full correspondence in the UGC-based and mental areas: the latter are bigger than the former, especially in the non-central locations. Such a result might be explained by the nature of the check-in data, which reflect the users' behaviours only partly: the check-ins are made mostly in urban venues where people want to demonstrate themselves to be, and does not account much for the rest of everyday life practices. The comparison of a sample of 7 mental areas and check-in clusters is shown at Fig. 3.

---

[1] Results can be accessed online at spblivehoods.github.io.

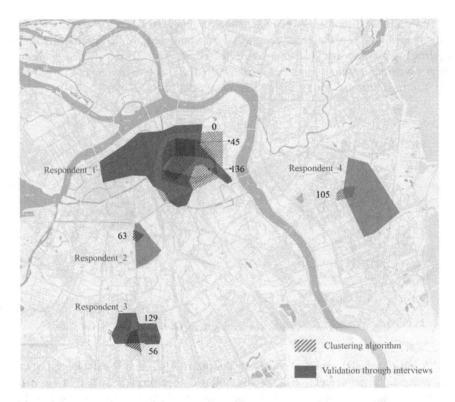

Fig. 3. Borders of clusters based on check-ins and of areas based on mental maps.

The borders of the check-in clusters do not coincide with the municipal division of St. Petersburg: the central areas intersect several municipal districts, the non-central areas are much smaller than one municipal district (see Fig. 4). The possible interpretation is that central areas are much more developed in terms of public life which forms clusters of its own, while non-central public life is underdeveloped and shrinks to the zones closer to the subway stations. Such division informs us that St. Petersburg development is biased in direction of the historic centre and that the non-central areas are underdeveloped. However there are clusters that can be managed as new centers and the main condition for their formation as for now is the availability of a subway station nearby.

Further we have defined the nature of the central and non-central clusters in terms of their functional load. We have analyzed the character of the sampled clusters based on the functional layout of the venues which they consist from and in connection to the city area they are located in. The functions of the venues were defined based on data from Google and were collected via Google Places API text search, which allows receiving the venue title by geolocation. For a more detailed account, we have chosen 3 clusters representing different areas of the city with a various typology of the built environment, namely a central city area, a former industrial territory, and a sleeping quarter.

Fig. 4. Cluster borders VS. borders of St. Petersburg municipal areas.

The centre of St. Petersburg is illustrated here by clusters "0", "45" and "136", which are "nested" within each other (see Fig. 5). "0" cluster is the largest one in the city center and intersects the borders of seven municipal districts. It is formed by Suvorovsky avenue and Kirochnaya street in the North-East, Aleksandra Nevskogo Square in the East, Obvodny channel embankment and Bagrationovskaya square in the South, and Gostiny Dvor subway station in the West. The cluster is centered on Vosstaniya Square (which is also a subway station). The cluster includes 625 venues, the least popular venue has 10 check-ins, the most popular one - 826 check-ins. The main functions here are food (157 venues), bars (66 venues), shopping (56 venues), art (46 venues) and points of interest (33 venues), entertainment and nightlife (53 venues) and others. This distribution indicates the concentration of leisure, tourism and cultural practices in the central area.

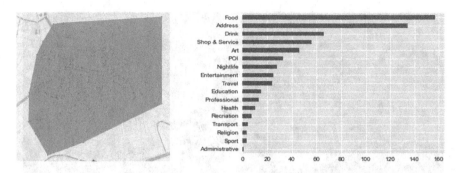

Fig. 5. "0" city center cluster borders and functional load.

St. Petersburg urban transformation is characterized by the redevelopment of the vast industrial territories which form the "grey belt" around the city center. In the late 90 s with the collapse of the Soviet Union, the majority of the factories has stopped running. Nowadays the former industrial territories undergo the process of lengthy redevelopment mostly as residential areas with a small share of public functions. A typical cluster in this area "63" is located along Moskovsky avenue and is bordered by Frunzenskaya subway station in the North and by the intersection of Kiyevskaya street and Moskovsky avenue in the South. Compared to the central clusters, "63" has a very limited number of venues - 7, the least popular venue has 13 check-ins, the most popular one - 144 check-ins. Functional load of the venues is food, transport (subway station) and residential function (address) (Fig. 6).

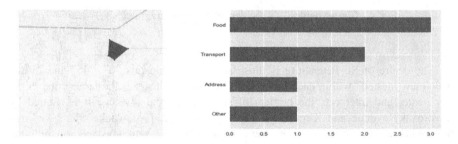

Fig. 6. "63" industrial area cluster borders and functional load.

St. Petersburg is a rapidly growing city with new residential complexes appearing at the city periphery as well as in the historical but remote areas. "139" cluster is located next to Ozerki subway station, where multi-storied residential buildings are being actively built. "139" has a bigger number of venues than the "63" - 12, the least popular venue has 10 check-ins, the most popular one - 83 check-ins. Activity here is also centered on "food" function represented by cafes with a small average check. However, there is a bar and a shop, unlike in "63" cluster (Fig. 7).

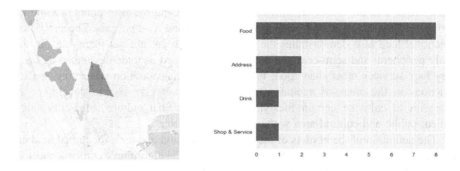

Fig. 7. "139" sleeping quarter cluster borders and functional load.

Areas of habitation in the city center are bigger than the ones in the non-central areas. This can be explained by the fact that the city center has a bigger number of venues which are visited and check-ined by people. They also overlap with each other demonstrating different "lifestyles" formed by different social groups visiting central venues. Analysis of the functional load of the central clusters shows that they have a more distinguished leisure character. The non-central clusters are smaller and more dispersed in urban space, they tend to form closer to the subway stations. Their functional load reflects their residential character. The utmost function which is present in all of the check-in clusters is food - cafes, restaurants, bistros form the core of the public life in each area of habitation of St. Petersburg. This might be interpreted both as a feature of the Northern city with priority on indoor leisure and as a consequence of city's underdeveloped infrastructure for more variable public activities.

5   Conclusion

This study presents an approach to define generic areas of habitation as the potential city centers based on UGC and mental mapping. The borders and the localization of the areas of habitation presented in the paper differ quite heavily from the administrative city division. The concept of areas of habitation can improve practice of urban management by introducing knowledge on the actual behaviors of the citizens, the places they concentrate in, and the character of urban service consumption. The mixed methods approach helps to define the areas of habitation which reflect both citizens practices in space and their perception of space. The map of areas of habitation is important for studying the quality of urban life and targeting urban management efforts. First, such a map is illustrating the (in)equality of development of different city areas. The study shows that in the centre of St. Petersburg areas of habitation are bigger than the ones in the non-centre. Second, the map is giving basis for managing urban polycentricity. In the given study the new possible centers of the city in semi-central and peripheral areas are the transport (subway stations) hubs. Third, the analysis of the functional load of the areas of habitation gives an overview of the specific needs of the consumers inside the clusters so that the appropriate urban policies can be formulated. Based on the results of this study the central areas of habitation in St. Petersburg are recommended to be addressed with inclusive cultural and touristic policies while the peripheral clusters are in more need of transportation and food policies. The analysis of functional load also demonstrates the functions which are not yet there: e.g., in this study peripheral and semi-central clusters can be defined as underdeveloped as far as they lack services other than food, residential and transportation. Detecting specific functions in the areas of habitation or their parts can give rise to developmental strategies to cultivate certain lifestyles, for example, bar culture area, educational milieu, public and cultural area within a sleeping quarter.

The definition of the borders of the areas of habitation and their functional load has benefitted from the mixed methods approach. The initial algorithm to process check-in data has been reconsidered based on the mental mapping results: the borders of the clusters were redefined with more account for accessibility which makes people perceive the area in a different way. The qualitative survey also gives possible explanations on the difference in the size of clusters in the city centre and periphery: subjectively the central clusters are bigger while people living and working there use more diverse services, enjoy walking by feet and are not strictly attached to one subway station, as well as there are more landmarks and routes to take.

The study also outlines a number of environmental factors which form the areas of habitation, such as the natural and built environment barriers which make up the borders of the cluster and pedestrian accessibility within the cluster. The analysis of the environmental factors has also benefited from the mixed methods approach: the environmental barriers were defined based on the results of the mental mapping and then incorporated into the clustering procedure for check-in data.

6 Discussion

Interpretation of the areas of habitation should be done carefully with account for the nature of LBSNs data, which represents demonstrative behaviour rather than everyday life routines. People are willing to signify those places which have a specific cultural and social status, and these are rather public spaces (e.g., cafes and museums) than everyday life places (e.g., supermarkets and drugstores). For this reason the areas of habitation defined in the centre of St. Petersburg with more venues for cultural and leisure consumption are bigger than the ones at the city periphery.

The areas of habitation built with the refined algorithm are showing more alignment with the results of the sociological survey, however not full correspondence: the mental areas are bigger than the clusters, especially in the non-central locations. This might be explained by the nature of the data as well: the mental maps include more venues and places which people visit than the check-in data. This obvious difference in check-in and mental borders as well as in public vs. everyday life behaviours should undergo further sociological exploration.

The results of the check-in data clustering received for our dataset differs from the results obtained by [19] with non-overlapping small units in the central area of the city of Boston and several bigger ones in the city periphery. In our case the central clusters are bigger and overlap while the peripheral ones are smaller and more numerous; this configuration aligns more with the mental mapping results. The difference in the results deserves further investigation both from methodological and analytical points of view. Study on environmental factors which form the borders of the areas of habitation should be developed further. In particular, for this paper we have incorporated the measure of pedestrian accessibility defined as the 500 m radius from the venue. In further research the pedestrian accessibility might be better defined through isochrones, which provide a more accurate account on the actual time needed to walk a specific distance in a given graph of pedestrian routes.

Acknowledgements. This research is financially supported by The Russian Science Foundation, Agreement #17-71-30029 with co-financing of Bank Saint Petersburg.

References

1. Hanson, J., Hillier, B.: The architecture of community: some new proposals on the social consequences of architectural and planning decisions. Architecture et Comportement/ Architecture and Behaviour **3**, 251–273 (1987)
2. Westerink, J., Haase, D., Bauer, A., Ravetz, J., Jarrige, F., Aalbers, C.B.E.M.: Dealing with sustainability trade-offs of the compact city in peri-urban planning across European city regions. Eur. Plan. Stud. **21**, 473–497 (2013)
3. Campari, I.: Uncertain boundaries in urban space. Geog. Objects Indeterminate Boundaries **2**, 57–69 (1996)
4. Hollenstein, L., Purves, R.: Exploring place through user-generated content: Using Flickr tags to describe city cores. J. Spat. Inf. Sci. **2010**, 21–48 (2010)
5. Davies, C., Holt, I., Green, J., Harding, J., Diamond, L.: User needs and implications for modelling vague named places. Spat. Cogn. Comput. **9**, 174–194 (2009)
6. Lynch, K.: The Image of the City, vol. 11. MIT Press, Cambridge (1960)
7. Egenhofer, M.J., Mark, D.M.: Naive geography. In: Frank, A.U., Kuhn, W. (eds.) COSIT 1995. LNCS, vol. 988, pp. 1–15. Springer, Heidelberg (1995). https://doi.org/10.1007/3-540-60392-1_1
8. Goodchild, M.F.: Citizens as sensors: the world of volunteered geography. GeoJournal **69**, 211–221 (2007)
9. Ratti, C., et al.: Redrawing the map of Great Britain from a network of human interactions. PLoS ONE **5**, e14248 (2010)
10. Reades, J., Calabrese, F., Ratti, C.: Eigenplaces: analysing cities using the space–time structure of the mobile phone network. Environ. Plan. **36**, 824–836 (2009)
11. Girardin, F., Calabrese, F., Fiore, F.D., Ratti, C., Blat, J.: Digital footprinting: uncovering tourists with user-generated content (2008)
12. Liu, Y., Sui, Z., Kang, C., Gao, Y.: Uncovering patterns of inter-urban trip and spatial interaction from social media check-in data. PLoS ONE **9**, e86026 (2014)
13. Ying, J.J.-C., Lu, E.H.-C., Kuo, W.-N., Tseng, V.S.: Urban point-of-interest recommendation by mining user check-in behaviors. In: Proceedings of the ACM SIGKDD International Workshop on Urban Computing (2012)
14. Ferrari, L., Rosi, A., Mamei, M., Zambonelli, F.: Extracting urban patterns from location-based social networks. In: Proceedings of the 3rd ACM SIGSPATIAL International Workshop on Location-Based Social Networks (2011)

15. Gao, S., Liu, Y., Wang, Y., Ma, X.: Discovering spatial interaction communities from mobile phone data. Trans. GIS **17**, 463–481 (2013)
16. Schoier, G., Borruso, G.: Individual movements and geographical data mining. clustering algorithms for highlighting hotspots in personal navigation routes. In: Murgante, B., Gervasi, O., Iglesias, A., Taniar, D., Apduhan, B.O. (eds.) ICCSA 2011. LNCS, vol. 6782, pp. 454–465. Springer, Heidelberg (2011). https://doi.org/10.1007/978-3-642-21928-3_32
17. Eagle, N., Pentland, A.S.: Eigenbehaviors: identifying structure in routine. Behav. Ecol. Sociobiol. **63**, 1057–1066 (2009)
18. Huang, Y., Zhang, L., Zhang, P.: A framework for mining sequential patterns from spatio-temporal event data sets. IEEE Trans. Knowl. Data Eng. **20**, 433–448 (2008)
19. Cranshaw, J., Schwartz, R., Hong, J., Sadeh, N.: The livehoods project: utilizing social media to understand the dynamics of a city. In: Sixth International AAAI Conference on Weblogs and Social Media (2012)
20. Shelton, T., Poorthuis, A., Zook, M.: Social media and the city: Rethinking urban socio-spatial inequality using user-generated geographic information. Landscape Urban Plan. **142**, 198–211 (2015)
21. Phung, D., Adams, B., Venkatesh, S.: Computable social patterns from sparse sensor data. In: Proceedings of the First International Workshop on Location and the Web (2008)
22. Ferrari, L., Mamei, M.: Discovering daily routines from Google latitude with topic models. In: 2011 IEEE International Conference on Pervasive Computing and Communications Workshops (PERCOM Workshops) (2011)
23. Farrahi, K., Gatica-Perez, D.: Discovering routines from large-scale human locations using probabilistic topic models. ACM Trans. Intell. Syst. Technol. (TIST) **2**, 3 (2011)

Creating Public Value Through Public e-Services Development: The Case of Landscaping and Public Amenities in St. Petersburg

Anastasia A. Golubeva[ID] and Evgenii V. Gilenko[(✉)][ID]

Graduate School of Management, St. Petersburg State University,
Saint Petersburg, Russia
{golubeva, e.gilenko}@gsom.spbu.ru

Abstract. Development of public e-services as part of the e-government strategy is a trend in recent decades. Public e-services (from informational to transactional ones) transfer and develop in various spheres of citizens' inter-action with authorities (from obtaining information to participation in voting). This provides broad advantages for government authorities, individual users, and society as a whole - from reducing transaction costs to increasing public trust in the government. Benefits from public e-services implementation have been widely discussed in scientific literature. However, in recent years, inte-grated solutions for benefits assessment have become increasingly important, allowing to cover systematically various possible effects from public e-services introduction.

One of these approaches is the concept of public value, which was formulated in the 1990s, and has been widely applied in public sector only from the beginning of 2000. Public value describes the value that the government makes to the society. In this research, the possibility of applying of the public value concept to assessment of potential benefits from public e-services implemen-tation is illustrated by the example of citizens' claims on landscaping and public amenities, which are provided by local authorities.

Keywords: Public e-services · Public value ·
Landscaping and public amenities · Econometric analysis

1 Introduction

Public e-services development is a trend in recent decades. From informational to transactional ones, they modify citizens' interaction with public authorities in various spheres – from obtaining information to participation in voting. This provides broad advantages for the government, individual users, and the society at large, such as reducing transaction costs, public services' quality improvement, increasing public trust in the government, etc. (see, for example, [1]).

Benefits from public e-services implementation have been widely discussed in the scientific literature (see, for example, [2, 3]). However, in recent years, integrated

© Springer Nature Switzerland AG 2019
A. Chugunov et al. (Eds.): EGOSE 2018, CCIS 947, pp. 249–264, 2019.
https://doi.org/10.1007/978-3-030-13283-5_19

solutions for benefits' assessment have become increasingly important, allowing to cover systematically various possible effects from public e-services introduction.

One of these approaches is the concept of public value, which was formulated in the 1990s. Public value describes the value that the government provides to the society. Public value and values of society are interrelated, therefore public value is a cumulative representation of public understanding of what they consider valuable (see [4]). There are three main areas in which public authorities create public value, namely: public services quality and efficiency, public policy outcomes and public trust (see [5]).

In this research, the possibility of applying the public value concept to assess potential benefits from public e-services implementation is illustrated by the example of public service, provided on a local level. There are several key prerequisites for using local public services as an object for research in this case:

- public values and preferences for local public goods and services can be identified most fully and reliably on the local level;
- local public services' quality (and its potential change due to transition to the electronic interaction) can be assessed by citizens fairly objectively;
- the results of the activities of the local administration are fairly easily measurable (in comparison with higher authorities' work);
- the overall quality of interaction and, as a consequence, the general level of public trust is as fully liable as possible on the local level.

For our research we chose the local public service of filing applications *about landscaping and public amenities*. This sphere is one of the most significant among the local issues in terms of both public attention and the amount of public finance expenditures, with complaints on the quality of landscaping and public amenities being among most frequent public complaints.

As the most socially active public services customers, the citizens of *retirement age* were chosen for this research. Usually, they are most aware of the acute local problems and more actively than other categories of the population interact with the local administration.

Based on the above-mentioned prerequisites, in this study we address the following principal question: what are the prospects for creating public value for the considered category of citizens by transferring applications to the electronic format through:

- better service quality (a simpler, faster and more convenient format for interaction);
- improved service effectiveness (greater responsiveness of the local authorities)?

The rest of the paper is organized as follows. Section 2 provides the public value theoretical framework. Section 3 discusses the directions of impact of e-government on public value creation. Section 4 describes the methodology of this research. Section 5 gives calculation results. Section 6 concludes.

2 The Public Value Framework

The era of New Public Management (NPM) movement was characterized by attempts to quantify the effectiveness and efficiency of public administration with the help of quantitative indicators. Such a narrow approach to evaluation was widely criticized in the 1990s. It is obvious that interaction between the state and the society is not limited to provision of public services and there are many other criteria that characterize governance quality. For instance, under increasing importance of democratic values, government openness, transparency, accountability, which are difficult to assess objectively, should also be taken into account. A more universal methodology was required that would allow analyzing a wide range of results and benefits of reforms emerging on different levels of government (federal, regional and local).

In contrast with NPM, the public value concept takes a broader view on what matters and what works, without diminishing the value of performance measures (see [5, 6]). In the modern scientific research, the concept of public value is widely used for analysis and evaluation of government activities in general, as well as public sector organizations in particular (in healthcare, education, housing and communal services, transportation, etc.). It also became a methodological basis for developing new quality standards of public services delivery (see, for example, [7–9]). Nowadays, the concept can be considered as an inclusive framework for evaluating the effectiveness and efficiency of public services.

Generally speaking, *public value* describes the value that the government contributes to the society. It is an equivalent of the shareholder value in public management (see [5]). Therefore, taken from public individual and collective experience of interaction with the government, public value represents the evaluation of how needs and preferences of the society are met and satisfied.

Considered in terms of public value, the ideal and value of any public sector organization or public administration in general should be measured primarily by the extent to which their activities are focused on maximizing public value. Therefore, public value characterizes their strength, significance, and ability to produce socially desirable results. In this regard, results of any reforms in the public sector should be evaluated through the lens of changes in the ability to produce public value.

Public value and public services are closely related. Creation and maximization of public value is possible only in those areas, which reflects true values and needs of the citizens.

Kelly et al. (see [10]) identified three main sources of public value creation: public services, public policy outcomes, and public trust.

1. Public services. Public services is one of the key sources of public value produced by public administration. Kearns (see [11]) specified five principal factors that influence the perception of public services value by citizens: availability, customer satisfaction, perceived importance, fairness in provision, and the costs of obtaining them.

In accordance with the Accenture Public sector value model (see [12]), government agencies maximize public services value in two dimensions (see Fig. 1). On the one hand, service delivery should be optimized in terms of cost-effectiveness. The lower the cost of the output corresponding to the specified (or legally established) quality standards, the higher is the value of public services. On the other hand, the second dimension of public services value is related to external evaluation of their quality and reflects the customer's view on the process and on the results of this process.

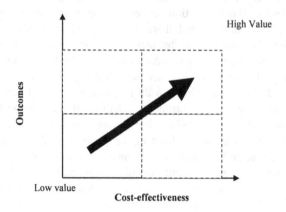

Fig. 1. Public services value model [12].

Qualitative characteristics of a service cannot be measured in monetary terms, but they have a direct impact on the perceived quality of the service and on the degree of customer satisfaction. They include:

- perceived quality of the service;
- number of possible channels of public service delivery;
- availability, completeness and accuracy of information about the service;
- transparency of the process;
- complexity of the service (number of organizations involved);
- customer support, etc.

The efforts of public administration to increase the level of citizens' satisfaction should be based on clear understanding of the relative importance (or value) of various service characteristics, affecting this satisfaction.

2. Public policy outcomes. The performance of a public administration is assessed not only by the experience of individual citizens, but also by its' ability to provide a number of socially desirable and significant outcomes. These results are derived from the objectives of the public policy in certain functional areas.

Unlike individualized public services, public policy outcomes are more likely to have the characteristics of pure public goods: results in areas such as law and order, health, social security, environmental improvement, expansion of educational services, etc. are consumed by society collectively. Obviously, public policy outcomes are more difficult to evaluate in terms of public value rather than individual public services. The reason is not only the collective nature of consumption but also the problem of "many hands", when many public sector organizations take part in production of the certain outcome. Anyway achieving better results in line with the values adopted by society should be associated with a higher level of public value produced by the public administration.

3. Public trust. Trust makes it possible to achieve community goals that would not be achievable in its absence [13, 14]. This statement is confirmed by the fact that the level of trust positively correlates with social stability, which includes economic, social and psychological well-being of the society [15].

Trust in the institutions of government can be considered as an example of results of public administration activity. However, other results perform primarily a service function, while trust is a consequence of the collective experience of citizens [16].

Grimsley et al. showed a positive correlation between the degree of satisfaction with public services and trust in public administration [15–18]. In addition, the study found that trust and satisfaction with public services largely depend on how the experience of interaction with public authorities affects the citizens' perception of their own awareness, possibility of personal control and impact on the processes. Therefore government can increase public value through improving public trust using levers as openness, transparency, accountability, responsiveness.

The relationship between three sources of public is illustrated in Fig. 2.

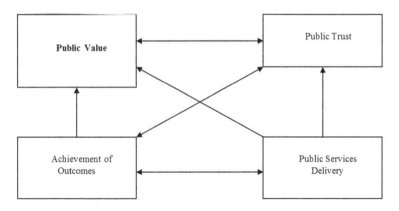

Fig. 2. Interrelation of public value elements [19].

3 The Impact of e-Government on Public Value Creation

In a broad sense, e-government is defined as a way for governments to use the most innovative information and communication technologies, particularly web-based Internet applications, to provide citizens and businesses with more convenient access to government information and services, to improve the quality of the services and to provide greater opportunities to participate in democratic institutions and processes (see [20]).

E-government is seen as an instrument to achieve broad objectives of improving governance quality, such as government effectiveness, public services quality, greater government openness, and so on.

Obviously, being a public project, the evaluation of IT investments into government-society interaction should include broad benefits and results of this transformation. For this reason, recent studies have emerged that use the public value paradigm to comprehend broader outcomes of e-government strategy [21–24].

For the first time this approach was proposed by Kearns (see [11]). Since the primary goal of ICT use is to improve governance, e-government can be considered as a means to improve the production of public value. As a consequence, e-government policies in general and public e-services in particular can be assessed by their ability to increase the capacity of public administration to increase public value (see [25]).

Improving *quality and efficiency of public services* through their transfer to the electronic format has been widely discussed in the scientific literature and is proved by numerous empirical studies (see, for example, [26–28]). This is achieved through process simplification, multi-channel service delivery, overall speed and convenience improvement. A public service customer gets an opportunity to receive the service at any time and in any convenient place, which in turn increases their satisfaction with the service and overall trust in public authorities.

E-government development strategy provides a whole range of effects on the *outcomes of government policies* in various functional areas. The mechanisms of positive changes here are reduction of administrative barriers, raising awareness of the population, reducing corruption through greater transparency of processes, etc. The contribution of e-government to achievement of greater results at the same cost levels is due to a wide range of synergistic effects that are becoming possible due to the change in the format and quality of interaction between the state and the society. Many studies confirm positive effects of e-government on economy, poverty, health, education, community and social services, etc. (see, for example, [29, 30]).

Public trust is largely a result of a cognitive attitude to information about the work of the government. Thus, the level of individual trust can depend not only on the actual quality of government's work, but also on the interpretation of information about government's activities by the individuals. In this regard, the level of information openness (transparency), intensity and quality of information exchange affect the level of public trust (see [31]). The spread of information technologies in the society and the overall increase in the flow of the government information along with e-participation development can play a significant role in overcoming information gaps between the state and the society, thus, correcting public perception of the government activities and increasing government responsiveness and public trust.

It is worth noting that the implementation of e-government services alone is not capable of increasing public value, it only creates/enhances the <u>potential</u> for its' production. Broad positive effects from e-government directly depend on the level of public e-services adoption by public services customers. There are several factors, crucially influencing that (see [32]):

- access;
- trust in electronic way of interaction;
- benefits recognition, which directly affects the motivation to use electronic services.

Access to e-government services is determined by three main components: access to new technologies (Internet network and electronic communication means - computer, smartphone, etc.), availability of sufficient ICT skills, and customer awareness of the existence of electronic services.

Trust in new technologies is based, as a rule, on the previous experience of the user. In addition, the overall level of trust in the government is positively related to the trust in innovations offered in the public sector (see, for example, [33]).

Individual assessment of the *benefits* from e-services' use depends on many factors. They include expectations regarding the quality of services in the electronic format in comparison with the traditional format, the user's initial experience in accessing electronic services and their actual quality (see Fig. 3).

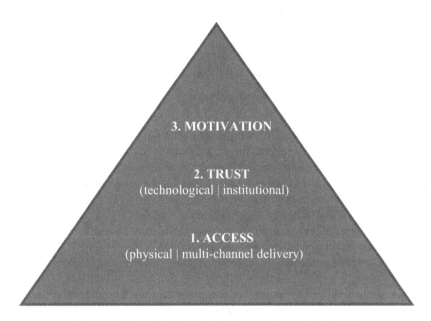

Fig. 3. Hierarchical model of public e-services adoption [32].

In general the positive effect on public value production is higher, the greater the number of customers becomes loyal (permanent) users of public e-services.

4   Research Methodology

4.1   Research Design and Data

According to the above-mentioned considerations, in this research we study the perceived value of provision of public services on landscaping and public amenities (as being most concerning to the majority of people) via the electronic format. The target group of people are citizens of the retirement age. As it was mentioned above, traditionally this category of citizens is the most socially active of the population.

Figure 4 presents the general scheme along which the public value of landscaping and public amenities services is created.

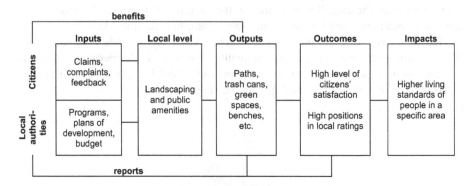

Fig. 4. Enhancement of the public value of landscaping and public amenities services.

Thus, the **aim** of this research is to give an illustration on how to apply the public value concept to analysis of expected (potential) benefits (outcomes) of implementation of the electronic interaction of state authorities with consumers (citizens) of public services for a specific case of public services (landscaping and public amenities).

In order to try to find empirical support to the questions to be discussed below, we developed our own questionnaire and collected a sample of 100 responses of aged (from 47 to 83 years old) citizens of the Krasnogvardeyskiy District of St. Petersburg. The survey was run in person in April and May, 2018.

The questionnaire consisted of four principal parts, covering the following principal aspects.

Part 1: socio-demographic portrait of the respondent (age, gender, education, level of income, marital status, access to the Internet, etc.).

Part 2: questions on the respondent's knowledge about the district's administration activity.

Part 3: questions on the respondent's attitude towards the electronic format of interaction with the district's administration.

Part 4: questions on potential intentions of the respondent to use the electronic format in interaction with the district's administration to solve landscaping and public amenities problems.

For the majority of the questions the respondents were asked to provide answers in a 5-grade Likert scale, from 1 being "completely disagree" to 5 being "completely agree".

To achieve the aim of the research, it is important to address the following issues:

- people's perception of public value of a public service itself;
- citizens' expectations regarding the characteristics of the public service;
- enhancement of citizens' trust in the local authorities' activities via better public services provision.

Issue 1. The Value of a Public Service

For the consumers (citizens) of a public service, determine the value of the public service at large and the value of its different quality characteristics in particular. In our case, the both things are important: landscaping and public amenities services provision in general, and ways and means of citizens' communication with the local authorities in particular.

It is important to emphasize that the way of the communication itself is also a public service, and it is exactly what we study in this research. Thus, *the subject of our research how the new (electronic) way of interaction between the citizens and local authorities can enhance public value of a public service* (in our case, landscaping and public amenities provision).

To capture the attitudes of the respondents towards the electronic way of communication with the local authorities, we can use Part 4 of the questionnaire. The details on the variable of this part are given in Table 1.

Table 1. Part 4 of the questionnaire: variables description.

Variable	Description	Mean value
EFuse	Would you use the electronic format to interact with district's administration to solve landscaping and public amenities problems?	4.03
EFcomfort	Would the electronic format make the process of claim submission more **simple** and **comfortable** to you?	4.08
EFoften	Would the electronic format make you submit your claims to the administration more **often**?	3.74
EFopen	Would the electronic format make the process of interaction with the administration more open and **transparent**?	3.85
EFtrust	Would the electronic format increase your **trust** in administration's activity?	3.46

All the variables are measured in the Likert scale with 1 – completely disagree to 5 – completely agree. Cronbach's alpha on this is **0.91** which strongly speaks in favor of excellent consistency of the survey.

The results provided in Table 1 mean the following. The majority of respondents do consider the electronic way of claim submission to the administration as an effective way to solve landscaping problems of Krasnogvardeiskiy district. The mean value of EFuse is above 4 which means that people rather would agree to use this way of communication with the administration.

As for the related characteristics of the electronic format for the public service (such as simplicity, comfort, and transparency), they all have the mean value of at least higher than 3.7, which also speaks in favor of people's appreciation of these characteristics.

As a result, from the provided descriptive analysis, we can preliminary state that the electronic way of communication with the local authorities can indeed potentially increase the public value of the landscaping public service.

Issue 2. Public Service Consumers' Expectations

Elaborating the previous issue and discussing the potential for increasing the public value of a public service, it is important to keep in mind that such potential will also strongly depend on the expectations of public service consumers about the quality characteristics of the public service, specifically in the context of transferring the interaction with the local authorities to the electronic format.

Public value of e-services, broadly speaking, is related to something which is important to the citizens when interacting with the administration. In the questionnaire there is a specific question on which aspects are most important to the respondent when interacting with the administration. And the distribution of responses is as follows:

- speed of administration' reaction to the problem (41%);
- transparency of the interaction process (15%);
- politeness of administration's employees (18%);
- convenience of submission of the claim (26%).

It can be seen that second most important aspect of citizens' interaction with administration is the *convenience* of the process of claim submission (more than 25% of respondents set it as a first priority). Informally speaking, this means that if the way of interaction of citizens with local authorities is inconvenient, this may strongly deteriorate the public value of the corresponding public service.

Thus, by establishing the link between convenience of the interaction process and potential readiness to use the electronic format of interaction, we could demonstrate that improvement of the electronic means of communication with citizens may increase the public value of the corresponding public service.

So, we formulate the following research hypothesis.

RH1. Adoption of the electronic format of interaction of citizens with district's administration (in our case, on the landscaping and public amenities problems) can increase the public value of such services through improvement of the convenience of such interaction.

Issue 3. Enhancement of Citizens' Trust

As a final step, we need to consider the potential of influence of the public service provision improvement on citizens' trust in local authorities' activities and find the interrelation between citizens' trust and the intensity of their interaction with the local authorities which indirectly may point at potentially higher results to be achieved in this sphere.

The principal scheme here is as follows: *higher level of administration's openness and transparency will improve citizens' trust in their activities, thus making people to strengthen interaction with the administration* (in our case, by providing more information on the landscaping and public amenities problems). As a result, the administration will be able to provide more outcomes to the people, thus improving the living standards of people in the area (see Fig. 4).

Speaking about trust in administration's activity, the respondents were asked about their opinion on whether the electronic format would be of help in making interaction with the administration more open, transparent, and clear to the citizens. The distribution of their responses has the following structure:

- 67% agreed that it would make interaction more transparent;
- 26% disagreed;
- 7% had difficulties answering this question.

This allowed us to state the following research hypothesis.

RH2. Higher transparency of the process of citizens' interaction with the administration should also increase the trust of citizens in administration's activity.

Finally, the respondents of our survey were also asked on their opinion on whether adoption of the electronic format of interaction is able to strengthen their trust and readiness to cooperate with district's administration. The distribution of their responses was as follows:

- 59% believed that the electronic format of interaction is able to increase trust in administration's activity;
- 20% didn't believe that;
- 21% had difficulties answering this question.

As it can be seen, the majority of respondents relate trust in administration's activity to the electronic format.

From the side of the administration, it should mean that increasing trust in their activity will also increase the willingness of people to interact with them (to submit claims on landscaping and public amenities problems more often). The administration would definitely benefit from it, since that would mean better understanding of the situation in the district and more accurate planning of their activity.

This allowed us to formulate the following hypothesis.

RH3. Growing trust in administration's activity should motivate people to submit their claims more actively.

5   Empirical Results

In this section we consider the results of empirical analysis of the respondents' answers by apply the principal components analysis to test the above-given research hypotheses. But before doing this, we first have to check where the necessary pre-conditions for electronic format adoption were met for the surveyed people (see the concluding part of Sect. 3).

5.1   Pre-conditions for Public e-Services Adoption

The descriptive analysis allows address the pre-conditions to public e-services adoption. As it was mentioned above (see Sect. 3), the three principal factors that influence such adoption are *access*, *trust* and *benefits*.

Access to Public e-Services. Recalling the components of access to e-government services, the descriptive analysis of our sample showed the following.

Speaking about *physical access* to the Internet, the distribution of responses is as follows:

- 49% of the respondents had mobile and fixed (stationary) access to the Internet;
- 36% had only fixed (stationary) access to the Internet;
- 13% had only mobile access to the Internet;
- only 3% didn't have access to the Internet.

As for the ICT skills of the citizens, the distribution of the responses looks like this:

- 8% of the respondents didn't have ICT skills at all;
- 28% had a beginner's level in ICT;
- 49% had a level of an intermediate user (were able to use MS Office applications);
- 15% had an advanced level in ICT.

As for the citizens' awareness of the existence of an electronic service of claim submissions on landscaping and public amenities problems, the respondents provided the following answers:

- 64% of the respondents didn't know about such service;
- 36% knew about the service.

Based on this statistics, we can definitely say that for the greater majority of the surveyed aged citizens' physical access to the Internet and the presence of the necessary ICT skills are of no big problem. A slightly greater problem here is the unawareness of the existence of the corresponding electronic service. Still, it means that the first pre-condition to adoption of public e-services is fulfilled to a certain degree.

Trust in the Electronic Way of Interaction. As it was mentioned above, this kind of trust is based both on (1) the user's experience and (2) their perceived (potential) readiness to prefer the electronic way of communication with the administration over the traditional way.

To reflect aspect (1), the respondents were asked whether they had fear to make financial transactions over the Internet. The distribution of the responses here is as follows:

- 51% were afraid of making such transactions;
- 44% were not afraid of that;
- 5% were not sure.

The answers to the question related to aspect (2) are as follows:

- 62% of the respondents would be ready to trust and to prefer the electronic way of interaction over the traditional way;
- 26% had difficulties in answering that question;
- 13% would not be ready to trust the electronic way.

From the perspective of these results, it can be stated that at least a half of the respondents would be ready to adopt and prefer the electronic way of interaction with the administration. This means that at least partially the second pre-condition is also fulfilled.

Perceived Benefits. The final pre-condition for public e-services adoption is related to the expected benefits from usage of such services. In the survey the respondents were asked both about their knowledge of the advantages of electronic format, and about their expectations to have higher chances to achieve their aim by using this format.

For the knowledge of the advantages of electronic format, the fractions of the responses were as follows:

- 54% of the respondents were aware of the advantages of electronic format;
- 21% were not aware of them;
- 25% had difficulties answering this question.

About their expectations to have higher chances for success with their claim when using the electronic format, the respondents provided the following answers:

- 67% of the respondents indeed expected an increase of their chances;
- 12% didn't expect such an increase;
- 21% had difficulties answering this question.

As a result, it can be stated that, in the opinion of the people, the electronic way of interaction with the administration can indeed improve their chances in solving their landscaping and public amenities problems.

Summary. To sum up the results provided in this subsection, we can conclude that, to a quite high degree, the necessary pre-conditions for public e-services adoption were fulfilled for the surveyed group of citizens.

5.2 Empirical Study Results

We applied the principal components analysis (PCA) the corresponding 5 variables (given in Table 1) to reveal the latent structure of the attitudes of the citizens towards the electronic format of citizens' interaction with the administration. As a result, a *biplot* of the PCA result was constructed (see Fig. 5).

In the graph, the projections of the original variables on the coordinate system of the two first principal components are presented. To interpret this graph, we will need to look at which projections go together and which are orthogonal to each other. Thus, this figure allows indicating a number of peculiarities and supporting or disproving our research hypotheses.

Specifically, *Research Hypothesis 1 finds its support*. Indeed, the intention to use the electronic format (variable EFuse) is co-directed with how convenient people feel about submission of their claims to the administration (variable EFcomfort).

Unfortunately (and, surprisingly) *Research Hypothesis 2 is not supported* by the calculations. This is reflected by the fact that trust in administration's activity (variable EFtrust) and the expected greater openness of administration's activities (variable EFopen) are actually not correlated (they move in different directions). This may stem from the fact that for the older people trust in authorities is associated with factors, other than comfort and openness. They perceive the results of authorities' activities, not just an improved (in terms of openness and comfort) process of claim submission. In order to increase their trust in administration, the latter has to show actual outcomes (specific results of activity).

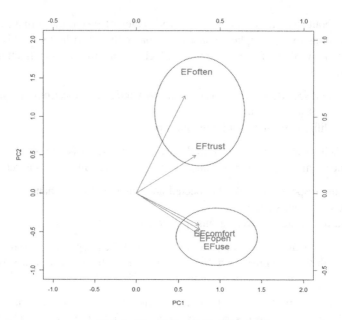

Fig. 5. The biplot of the PCA.

Research Hypothesis 3 is supported by the PCA. Indeed, the expected increase in trust (variable EFtrust) as a result of the electronic format adoption, goes along with the potential intention of people to submit their claims to the administration more often (variable EFoften). So, growing trust in administration's activity should motivate people to submit their claims more actively.

6 Conclusions and Recommendations

Our analysis allows to make several important conclusions.

Firstly, it is definitely worth further teaching the aged people working with new information technologies, since, as our analysis revealed, these people are quite loyal to the opportunity of employing the new (electronic) format of interaction with district's administration.

Secondly, for the administration it is important to continue improving the convenience of the submission process (i.e., the electronic form of claim application), since people would be more loyal to a more user-friendly electronic way of interaction. This may also influence the responsiveness of the administration itself, thus increasing the trust in administration's activity.

Thirdly (and this may seem surprising), the potential wider openness and transparency of the claim submission process due to the switching the electronic format is not correlated with trust in administration's activity for this (aged) group of people. On the one hand, this may be a reflection of the fact that this group of people is quite unpretentious and are ready just to be heard, without further monitoring of the problem solving process. They are more interested in the ability to effectively submit a claim itself, and in the speed of administration's reaction.

On the other hand, this may also indicate that to develop trust from the part of the older people, the administration has to regularly show some actual results of its activity, not just simplification of the claim submission process.

Overall, the obtained results may be used by local authorities to improve and enhance communication with the local population of the retirement age. Taking account of the findings of this research may increase the public value of the public service of landscaping and public amenities.

References

1. OECD. Trust and Public Policy: How Better Governance Can Help Rebuild Public Trust, OECD Publishing (2017). https://www.oecd.org/gov/trust-and-public-policy-9789264268920-en.htm
2. Alston, R.: E-Government Benefits Study, Australian Government Department of Finance (2003). https://www.finance.gov.au/agimo-archive/__data/assets/file/0012/16032/benefits.pdf
3. Gilbert, D.: Barriers and benefits in the adoption of e-government. Int. J. Public Sect. Manage. 17(4), 286–301 (2004)
4. Talbot, C.: Paradoxes and prospects of public value. In: Paper presented at Tenth International Research Symposium on Public Management, Glasgow (2006)
5. Moore, M.: Creating Public Value – Strategic Management in Government. Harvard University Press, Cambridge (1995)
6. Benington, J.: From private choice to public value. In: Benington, J., Moore, M.H. (eds.) Public Value: Theory and Practice, pp. 31–49. Palgrave Macmillan, Basingstoke (2011)
7. Best value in public service. Guidance to accountable officers, Smarter Scotland, Scottish executive (2006). http://www.scotland.gov.uk/Publications/2006/05/16142759/1
8. Creating value: findings from public service innovation focus groups, NZIER, February 2004. http://www.treasury.govt.nz/innovation/nzier-cv.pdf
9. Improving public services: evaluation of the best value pilot program, Local government centre, Warwick Business school, University of Warwick (2001)
10. Kelly, G., Mulgan, G., Muers, S.: Creating public value. An analytical framework for public service reform, Strategy Unit, Cabinet Office, UK (2004). http://www.cabinetoffice.gov.uk/strategy/downloads/files/public_value2.pdf
11. Kearns, I.: Public Value and E-Government, Institute for Public Policy Research, London (2004). http://www.ippr.org.uk/uploadedFiles/projects/Kearns_PublicValueandeGovenrment_ippr.pdf
12. Jupp, Y.: A value model for the public sector. Accenture Outlook 1, 16–21 (2004)
13. Coleman, J.: Foundations of Social Theory. Harvard University Press, Cambridge (1990)
14. Fukuyama, F.: Trust: The Social Virtues and the Creation of Prosperity. Free Press, New York (1995)
15. Green, G., Grimsley, M., Stafford, B.: The Dynamics of Neighbourhood Sustainability. Joseph Rowntree Foundation, York Publishing Services, York (2005)
16. Grimsley, M., Meehan, A., Tan, A.: Promoting Social Inclusion: Managing Trust-Based Relations Between Users and Providers of Public Services. European Academy of Management, St. Andrews, UK (2004)

17. Grimsley, M., Meehan, A., Sen Gupta, K.: Evaluative design of e-government projects: a public value perspective. In: Proceedings of the Twelfth Americas Conference on Information Systems, 4–6 August 2006, Acapulco, Mexico (2006)
18. Grimsley, M., Meehan, A.: e-Government information systems: Evaluation-led design for public value and client trust. Eur. J. Inf. Syst. **16**(2), 134–148 (2007)
19. Golubeva, A.A.: Evaluation of regional government portal on the basis of public value concept: case study from Russian Federation. In: ACM International Conference Proceeding Series, vol. 232, pp. 394–397 (2007)
20. Fang, Z.: E-Government in digital era: concept, practice, and development. Int. J. Comput. Internet Manage. **1**, 1–22 (2002)
21. Chatfield, A.T., Al Hujran, O.: E-Government evaluation: a user-centric perspective for public value proposition. In: International Conference on E-Learning, E-Business, Enterprise Information Systems, and E-Government, pp. 53–59 (2007)
22. Hui, G., Hayllar, M.R.: Creating public value in E-Government: a public-private-citizen collaboration framework in web 2.0. Aust. J. Publ. Admin. **69**(s1), S120–S131 (2010)
23. Karunasena, K.: An Investigation of the Public Value of e-Government in Sri Lanka. RMIT University Melbourne, Australia (2012)
24. Sivaji, A., et al.: Measuring public value UX-based on ISO/IEC 25010 quality attributes: case study on e-Government website. In: 3rd International Conference on User Science and Engineering (i-USEr) 2014, pp. 56–61 (2014)
25. Castelnovo, W., Simonetta, M.: The public value evaluation of e-Government policies. Electron. J. Inf. Syst. Eval. **11**(2), 61–72 (2007)
26. Syed, F.: Assessing e-government service delivery (government to citizen). Int. J. eBusiness e-government Stud. **4**(1), 45–54 (2012)
27. OECD, Denmark: Efficient e-Government for Smarter Public Service Delivery (2010)
28. Zemblyt, J.: The instrument for evaluating e-service quality. Procedia Soc. Behav. Sci. **213**, 801–806 (2015)
29. Harris, R.: Information and communication technologies for governance and poverty alleviation: scaling up the successes. IT Dev. Ctries. **13**(1), 15–17 (2009)
30. Bhatnagar, S., Singh, N.: Assessing the impact of E-government: a study of E-government projects in India. Inf. Technol. Int. Dev. **6**(2), 109–127 (2010)
31. Mutz, D.C., Flemming, G.: How good people make bad collectives: a social-psychological perspective on public attitudes toward congress. In: Cooper, J. (ed.) Congress and the Decline of Public Trust. Boulder. Westview Press (1999)
32. Gilenko, E., Golubeva, A.: Perception of public e-services by Russian citizens: a Pilot study in St. Petersburg. Russ. Manage. J. **15**(3), 289–302 (2017)
33. Fledderus, J., Brandsen, T., Honingh, M.E.: Restoring public trust through the co-production of public services: a theoretical elaboration. Public Manag. Rev. **16**(3), 424–443 (2014)

Potential for Improving Public Services by Exploring Citizens' Communication to Public Organizations

Eriks Sneiders[1(✉)], Lasith Gunawardena[2], Said Rutabayiro Ngoga[3], Rasika Darayathna[4], and Jean Claude Byungura[1]

[1] Department of Computer and Systems Sciences, Stockholm University, Stockholm, Sweden
{eriks,byungura}@dsv.su.se
[2] Department of Information Technology, University of Sri Jayewardenepura, Nugegoda, Sri Lanka
lasith@sjp.ac.lk
[3] College of Science and Technology, University of Rwanda, Kigali, Rwanda
nrutabayiro@ur.ac.rw
[4] University of Colombo School of Computing, Colombo, Sri Lanka
rnd@ucsc.cmb.ac.lk

Abstract. While the purpose of public organizations is to serve citizens, the citizens themselves are not always consulted in order to develop better public services. We argue that the direct communication from citizens to public organizations contains a wealth of information on how the organizations could improve their services, and this information is worth exploring. In order to prove our argument, we have interviewed 19 public organizations in Rwanda and Sri Lanka, identified 26 issues raised by the citizens, and mapped these issues into four solution domains: availability and timeliness of information, policy development, business process development, availability and design of e-services.

Keywords: Citizen-centered E-government · Participatory governance · Bottom-up policy making · Co-creation of public services

1 Introduction

Traditionally, public services have been perceived as something designed and implemented by public organizations for the rest of the society to consume. Osborne et al. [1], however, claim that public services cannot exist without being co-produced together with citizens, where the citizens' involvement is voluntary or involuntary. The concept of e-participation has reinforced the co-producer's role of a citizen: the citizen can be an explorer who identifies the needs, an ideator and a designer who co-develops ideas and co-designs the services, a diffuser who facilitates adoption of the services by the society and monitors them working [2–4]. Advancing technology (e.g., collaboration platforms, AI and big-data analysis) facilitates the "do-it-yourself" government and citizens' self-organization [3, 5].

© Springer Nature Switzerland AG 2019
A. Chugunov et al. (Eds.): EGOSE 2018, CCIS 947, pp. 265–280, 2019.
https://doi.org/10.1007/978-3-030-13283-5_20

In reality, however, the engagement of ordinary citizens is likely to be obscure, in particular in policy making where the rules and public services for the society are being designed. There are numerous approaches to bottom-up policy making (see Sect. 7); still, published results of such policy making are hard to find. A recent study [6] shows that public organizations in Rwanda rely primarily on input from domain experts, governmental and non-governmental organizations, and companies. Some government officials in Sri Lanka confirmed, in private communication, the same situation in their country. The lack of published results on citizens' involvement in decision making suggests that the situation is not specific to these two countries.

The framework of this research is the direct communication generated by citizens, addressed to public organizations, and how this communication can be used in order to improve public policies and services. Two questions arise: is the content of the communication actionable; is the volume of the communication sufficient to make it actionable? In order to answer both questions, we interviewed 19 public organizations, estimated the volume of the communication, identified 26 issues raised by the citizens, and mapped these issues into four solution domains. The answer to both questions is affirmative.

2 Method

There are two kinds of communication between citizens and public organizations. The first kind is well-structured and formal: registration of people, property, credentials, and issuing related certificates. The second kind is more ad hoc: the citizens ask questions, report problems. We are interested in the second kind of communication as the input to knowledge mining in order to improve public services. In order to demonstrate the opportunities, we interviewed 19 public organizations – 7 in Rwanda, 12 in Sri Lanka – and asked about (i) the channels that citizens use to contact the organization, (ii) communication volume by channel, (iii) the frequent inquiries, and (iv) archiving of the communication from citizens.

The respondents were selected by the snowball sampling process; we interviewed public organizations that had enough volume of ad hoc communication with citizens. In each organization, one person was interviewed for about 20–30 min. The typical duties of the interviewees were the head or vice-head of the unit, public relations officer, officer who communicates with the citizens. During the interview, notes were taken. After the interview, a summary was sent to the interviewee; six interviewees replied with "ok" or minor comments.

In Rwanda, the organizations were happy to reveal their identity. The organizations were Rwanda Public Procurement Authority, City of Kigali, Ministry of Justice (MINJUST), High Education Student Loans Department at Rwanda Education Board (HESLD/REB), Rwanda Governance Board (RGB), Consumer Protection Unit at Rwanda Utilities Regulatory Authority (CPU/RURA), and Admission Office of the University of Rwanda (AO/UR).

In Sri Lanka, the organizations preferred to remain anonymous. The respondents were municipalities as well as governmental organizations active in education, management of natural resources, economic development, transportation, foreign affairs, and management of civil servants.

3   Issues That Citizens Raise

We asked each of the 19 organizations about frequent inquiries from the citizens (not formal registration procedures) and identified, in total, 54 such inquires. We summarized the inquiries, as well as two own observations while visiting the organizations, into 26 issues and 10 problem domains displayed in Table 1.

The fourth column ("N") shows the number of organizations that reported the issue relevant. Table 1 summarizes joint results from Rwanda and Sri Lanka because this is not a comparative study and we want to avoid unintended conclusions. Also, joint results increase anonymity.

Table 1 demonstrates that the direct communication from citizens to public organizations contains signals that call for improvement of the provided services. In order to show that such improvement is realistic, the last column in Table 1 maps each issue into one or several solution domains; the mapping comes from the analysis in the next section. A solution domain is a realm of development activities in order to improve the services. Table 2 lists four solution domains, which were identified by analyzing the issues in the next section, as well as the number of issues from Table 1 that are linked to each solution domain. The solution domains are following:

- *Availability and timeliness of information*, i.e. information provided where and when it is needed, is a basic utility that reduces the hassle with using a service without the need to change the service itself.
- By *policy development* we mean developing the utility of the service, its input and output, eligibility requirements, as well as the legal basis for the service.
- By *business process development* we mean first of all improving the user experience when the citizens interact with the service; to a lesser extent internal optimization which leads to a better service, such as respecting the deadlines.
- *Availability and design of e-services* is an important part of business process development, so important that it got a separate solution domain.

4   Reasoning Towards Improvement

Analysis of the direct communication from citizens to public organizations can fuel the development of e-services, business processes, policies, and information supply. We demonstrate it in this section by analyzing the issues and possible solutions, which leads to the solution domains in the last column of Table 1. The analysis and selected solution domains are subjective opinions of the authors; they are based on the interviews, our observations while visiting the organizations, common sense, and previous research. The analysis has not been confirmed by the respondents. We would like to emphasize that the goal of this section is not to state universally valid solutions but

Table 1. Issues raised by the citizens, their problem domains and solution domains.

Problem domain	Issue	Comments	N	Solution domains
Information supply	Requests for personal data	Forgotten login credentials. Non-standard certificates being issued. State employees may have personal files outside their direct reach	4	eS
	Telephone inquiries about the status of the interaction	"What is the status of my application?" "Have you received my letter?" A phone call prior to a visit	3	Inf, eS
	Inquiries about eligibility for a service	Eligibility for getting subsidized loans, scholarships, economic support	3	Inf, eS
	Requests for clarification regarding a service	Confirmation of previously published information. "Which one of the related services is most relevant for me?" "Which documents are required for the application?" "How do I calculate the period of employment?"	6	Inf, eS
	People do not know where to seek help	Then they visit the local municipality	1	Inf
	Platform between information provider and information consumer	Announced vacancies. Changes in the lecture schedule at a university	2	Inf, eS
Data update	Non-standard update of standard personal data	Citizens try to register their address different from where they live	1	PD
	Update to the personal file	State employees may have personal files outside their direct reach	1	PD, eS, BP
Service update	Negotiated update of an existing service	Increased amount of the scholarship. Pension transferred to the spouse of a late husband or wife, or recalculated because of a part-time job	3	PD, BP
Bad user interface	Difficulty to use a web-based information system	Citizens do not understand online forms or interpret them incorrectly	3	Inf, eS, BP

(*continued*)

Table 1. (*continued*)

Problem domain	Issue	Comments	N	Solution domains
Bad service	Complaints about delays in the service	Case that is supposed to take a few days takes more than a few days	4	BP
	Complaints about interruptions in the e-service	Poor contact between dependent e-services	1	eS
	Wrong/missing data needs to be corrected	After an application has been received, some supporting documents are found missing and need to be added. A property has wrong data in the registry; the error needs to be corrected after it is discovered	2	eS
	Complaints that the service does not deliver the expected outcome	Job seekers do not find vacancies. A public procurement process does not result in product/service offers	2	PD, BP
	Unfriendly service	Citizens use intermediaries for registration of property and receiving certificates because dealing with the service directly takes too much time and hassle	1	PD, eS, BP
Material claims	Economic support to poor citizens	Subsidized housing, home infrastructure, public transportation	4	PD, BP
	Compensation for nationalized property	State acquires land for public infrastructure	3	PD, BP
	Support in case of a natural disaster	People need clean water; water pumps and cleaners in case of draught	1	PD, BP
Jobs	Professional and business development	Vocational training, advice and networking for small businesses	2	PD, BP
Conflict management	Disputes regarding ownership of real estate	Family members and neighbors dispute the ownership of property/land	1	eS
	Complaints from citizens about unfair distribution of economic support	"The neighbor got more help than me, it's unfair"	1	PD, BP

(*continued*)

Table 1. (*continued*)

Problem domain	Issue	Comments	N	Solution domains
	Consumer complaints	Transportation and sanitation service providers disrespect regulations	1	PD, Inf, BP
	Mediation in case of mismanaged funds and internal conflicts in churches and NGOs	Complex interaction between organizations lies outside the scope of this research	1	
Land management	Land requested for private or business use	Land management is a piece of science itself; we leave it to the professionals	1	
Infrastructure	Insufficient infrastructure for the service	Staff members at an educational establishment request better infrastructure	1	
	Service not available nearby	Parents cannot find a school place for their child	1	
	Paper files	Paper files are still the prevailing information carrier in Sri Lanka		

Table 2. Solution domains, the number of and the share of linked issues.

Solution domain	Abbreviation	Number of linked issues
Availability and timeliness of information	Inf	7 (17%)
Policy development	PD	11 (27%)
Business process development	BP	12 (29%)
Availability and design of e-services	eS	11 (27%)

rather to demonstrate that the content of the communication from the citizens to the public organizations is actionable. We present our reasoning by problem domain.

Information Supply. Retrieving personal data is best done by an e-service where the user enters his or her credentials and the e-service delivers the requested information. Inter-organization e-services eliminate the need for paper certificates.

Telephone inquiries about the status of one's interaction with the organization signal inefficient communication. One interviewed organization had half of its phone calls from the citizens with only one question: "What is the status of my application?" Another organization mentioned that the citizens often call to confirm whether their paper letter has been received. A third organization mentioned that citizens usually call before they come for a face-to-face visit. E-services and clear information could save most of these calls, and people's time and stress.

Right placement of the information, user experience while they navigate through the information, readability and completeness of the information help people satisfy their information need in a self-service mode. Interactive information seeking systems [7], which guide the user through the information flow, can help with the navigation problem; analysis of the logs [8] of the information system can help with the completeness problem.

AO/UR has compiled Frequently Asked Questions (FAQ) on its website, but people do not read them. Maybe people do not find them; maybe people do not care to look for them. If people write an email-style text message requesting information that is readily available, then an email-answering system [9] can automate the interaction.

If citizens do not know where to seek help, then comprehensive web-based information may provide guidance. Google is an effective, time- and cost-efficient solution for the citizens who are willing to google.

The aforementioned solutions assume that public information is available online and the citizens are comfortable with self-service when they contact public organizations, instead of dedicated personnel answering their questions. Sri Lanka, for example, has a strong tradition of face-to-face interaction between citizens and local government through the institution of grama niladhari ("village officer"), as well as overcrowded receptions of public organizations. The respondent at one divisional secretariat (municipality) mentioned that 90% of their interaction with citizens is face-to-face; the remaining 10% are phone calls. Research shows that an important e-governance adoption factor is trust, which may be undermined by the technology-created spatial and temporal distance between a citizen and the government [10].

In non-western countries, some local traditions may bypass the western-style governance altogether. Abunzi ("mediators") are traditional Rwandan judges who know people's needs. If a legal dispute is worth less than 3 million Rwandan Francs, the case is judged by Abunzi who do not report to the official legal system. No information online, no self-service.

Data update is most efficient by using an e-service, if the data storage is digital, which may not always be the case. Self-service needs policies on which data the citizens may update themselves, and which update requires a prior approval. The e-service may span across organization borders, which affects the business processes in the participating organizations. User authentication and digital signature require an appropriate legal basis and infrastructure.

If the data update still requires face-to-face interaction between citizens and public organizations, then the organizations may invest in minimizing two problems – overcrowded receptions and visits to a range of officials, often across organization borders, in order to collect approvals and certificates.

Service update needs policies and business processes for smooth implementation of the update.

Bad User Interface. Three interviewed organizations mentioned that citizens contact the organization because they cannot fill in an online form – the citizens either do not understand it, or they fill in wrong data and get stuck. The remedy in such a case could be comprehensive explanation of the requested input (see "information supply"), usable design of the form itself [11], or eventually a well-designed e-service that guides the user through the step-by-step application process. The level of how intuitive the information system is has a direct impact on the learning abilities of its users; the design of the information system should take into account the diversity of the users' age, language skills, cultural diversity, and computer literacy [12].

If use of a public service requires skills that ordinary citizens do not normally possess, trained intermediaries may help [13]. In Rwanda, all lawsuits are filed through an Integrated Electronic Case Management System. If a case is not filed in the system, it is not a court case. Many citizens use Internet cafés in order to file their court cases; hiring a private legal representative is expensive. Without prior experience, a citizen may ask the manager of the Internet café for help, and they both make mistakes. MINJUST responded to the problem by training the managers of Internet cafés to file court cases.

Bad Service. If an organization cannot keep its deadlines, it should redesign its business processes. Faulty e-services need to be fixed; interoperability across organization borders is a challenge [14]. Manual collecting of citizens' data will always be subject to human error, which can be reduced by letting a "smart" e-service collect and validate the data. If a service continuously does not deliver what it promises, well, some research suggests that more resources and better management may help [15], but the service needs to be redesigned anyhow.

If citizens avoid contacting an unfriendly service because the service is time consuming and unpleasant to deal with, and pay intermediaries to do business with the unfriendly service instead, then the public-private partnership [16] may be institutionalized and developed quality-wise, or the business processes and interaction with the service should be redesigned to meet the citizens' needs.

Material Claims. Poverty reduction requires effort in at least two dimensions: income and access to services such as health care, education, sanitation, infrastructure, and security [17]. Therefore economic support to poor citizens is likely to fuel the development of policies and business processes in both dimensions.

The subject of material claims lies outside the scope of this research; still, we believe there must be space for learning the citizens' needs and subsequently improving the relevant policies and business processes.

Jobs. Professional development of the citizens is closely related to the economic growth of the country. The government may invest in vocational training and career guidance, as well as help small businesses with advice (e.g., certification, marketing, enterprise development) and networking (e.g., contact with supermarkets, export organizations, financial institutions), as the respective public organizations in Sri Lanka do. This is an ongoing process of learning the needs, opportunities, solutions, and collaboration with established businesses and their lobby organizations.

Conflict Management. Disputes regarding ownership of real estate are best resolved with the help of rigorous cadastral records and associated e-services. In order to deal with citizens' complaints regarding unfair distribution of economic support, the authorities must learn what causes these complaints, and then implement the lessons in policies and business processes. Consumer protection depends on informed complaining consumers [18], channel management [19], and effective law enforcement procedures. On a positive note, consumer complaints may lead to innovation [20].

The infrastructure of public services needs financial investment; financial investments lie outside the scope of this research.

There exists a piece of public infrastructure that has utmost influence on public services and the entire society. It is paper files as the information carrier. Paper files make e-services impossible, face-to-face interaction and queueing for the services mandatory. Paper files are likely to make services suffer from faulty data because of human error, and business processes around paper files will notoriously be slow and miss their deadlines.

There is another important aspect of paper files. During a visit at one Sri Lankan municipality, we observed some 10–15 persons in a room, mostly women, browsing through files, reading, sorting, and stapling the papers. There are about 1.5 million civil servants in Sri Lanka (the figure given by one interviewed organization), and about 12.6 million people in the age group 15–54 [21], which means that civil servants are about 12% of the working population. Because public organizations work with data and information, paper files as the information carrier are an important employer (as well as a burden on tax payers and a competitor of other publicly funded services such as education and healthcare). Paper files give jobs to many women and low-skilled (by western standards) workers, two types of employees who are disadvantaged on the labor market [22], as well as to middle management who makes sure that the employees are always occupied. State is an attractive employer in Sri Lanka because of job security and guaranteed pension. Removing paper files from the job market also removes attractive jobs, and jobs for underprivileged job seekers. It certainly requires new job opportunities, training, education, employment opportunities for women (e.g., hotel and restaurant industry is not a widely-accepted employer for women in Sri Lanka, although the country is a popular tourist destination), business development. Job market is a complex ecosystem, and ill-considered changes in the ecosystem may lead to political instability in the country.

This is the end of our reasoning upon the 26 issues. We have demonstrated that public organizations may learn a lot from their direct communication with citizens in order to improve their services. If so, why did we not observe much of the learning outcome at the interviewed organizations? This is a good question; it is our future research question.

Well, it is not accurately true that there were no learning outcomes at all. As mentioned earlier, MINJUST in Rwanda trained the managers of Internet cafés to file legal cases. AO/UR has compiled FAQs on their website. Furthermore, AO/UR considers introducing a chat system that allows, in asynchronous mode, forwarding inquiries to different units and following the status of these inquiries – solved or not solved. HESLD/REB publishes announcements on their website as a response to suddenly frequent inquiries. CPU/RURA makes quarterly reports with recommendations to the management (we do not know how the management uses the reports).

Both Rwanda and Sri Lanka invest in developing good governance. "Rwanda Governance Scorecard 2016", the latest edition by RGB, reports on governance practices and achievements in the country. Sri Lanka Institute of Development Administration works on acquiring research-based evidence for policy makers. Both countries seek to develop their governance practices; analysis of the citizens' direct communication to public organizations is an opportunity yet to be utilized.

5   Frequent Inquiries in the Flow of the Communication

While the content of the direct communication from citizens to public organizations is most interesting, the volume and the structure of the communication allow us to estimate the significance of the issues in Table 1. Of the 19 interviewed organizations, 14 could estimate the total number of inquiries received from citizens within a certain period of time. Figure 1 illustrates the total number of inquiries per channel, normalized per five-day business week, for 12 organizations. Two organizations had extreme numbers and were not included in the chart.

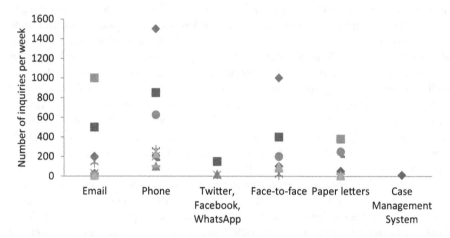

Fig. 1. Estimated number of inquiries per channel per five-day business week, 12 organizations. Individual channels are not used by all the organizations.

Almost the same 13 organizations could estimate the share of frequent inquiries among all the inquiries. Four organizations reported 100% of the communication flow covered by frequent inquiries (apparently minor issues were ignored). Three organizations had 70–90%, four organizations had 50–69%, and two organizations had 20–30% of the communication flow covered by frequent inquiries.

Furthermore, 8 organizations could estimate the share of individual frequent inquiries among all the inquiries, see Fig. 2. For example, the fifth organization from the left had three frequent inquiries and the distribution of these inquiries was estimated 60, 5, and 4% of the flow.

We conclude that the volume of the communication and the share of the frequent inquiries in the communication flow substantiate the use of the issues in Table 1 as a source to develop and improve public services.

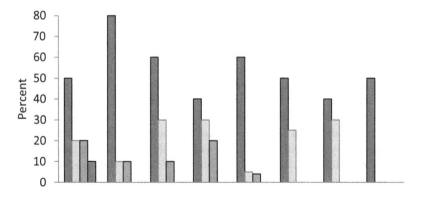

Fig. 2. Share of individual frequent inquiries among all the inquiries, 8 organizations.

6 Archiving the Communication

We asked the organizations how they archive their communication from citizens; the means of archiving affect the opportunities for knowledge mining. We summarize the archiving methods by communication channel; the number in parentheses shows how many organizations use the particular archiving method. In Rwanda:

- *Email.* Stored in the inbox indefinitely (5) or deleted when the inbox is full (1). Filed on paper (1).
- *Telephone calls.* No record (4). Notes filed on paper (2). Summary of today's issues sent to the management (1).
- *WhatsApp* messages on the personal phone; most interesting ones are kept, the rest is deleted (1).
- *Twitter, Facebook* messages stay indefinitely (1).
- *Face-to-face meetings.* Notes filed on paper (1). The meeting is registered in a book (1). No record (1). In the other organizations, the citizens meet individual officials or local units who do not report individual meetings.
- *Paper letters* are archived by 2 organizations.
- *Case Management System* keeps the messages indefinitely (2).

In Sri Lanka:

- *Email.* Stored in the inbox indefinitely (2). Filed on paper (3). Included in a personal paper file (2). Printed and forwarded internally, not archived (1).
- *Telephone calls.* No record (5). Updates made in a personal paper file (2). Notes filed on paper (3). The call is registered in a book (1). The call is forwarded without any record (1).
- *Face-to-face meetings* (we do not consider formal registration procedures). Notes filed on paper (1). Updates made in a personal paper file (2). Complaints, issues, and their solutions filed on paper (2). Citizens have to formulate their needs as a letter (2). In the other organizations, the citizens meet individual officials or local units who do not report individual meetings, or there are no face-to-face meetings.

- *Paper letters* are archived by 8 organizations.

In Sri Lanka, the citizens may dial 1919 and call the Government Information Center which distributes information on behalf of many public organizations; hence, these organizations are not fully aware of the details of the inquiries.

In order to have a more aggregated view, we counted the number of organization-channel instances (the same communication channel for different organizations counts as different organization-channel instances), classified the archiving methods into archiving types as shown in Fig. 3, and calculated the distribution of the organization-channel instances by archiving type. Please observe that 100% means 23 organization-channel instances for Rwanda and 35 organization-channel instances for Sri Lanka. Also, please observe that Fig. 3 does not illustrate the amount of communication, i.e., busy and not so busy organization-channel instances are counted equally.

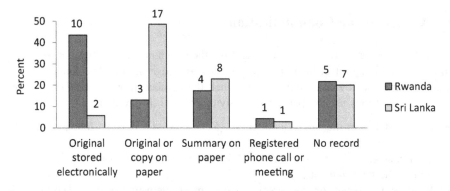

Fig. 3. Number of organization-channel instances (on top of the bar) per archiving type and the share of the archiving type (the bar) for the country.

In Rwanda, ICT-based text communication channels are significant, which allows electronic archiving of the original content. In Sri Lanka, much of the communication is archived on paper – either the original documents, or printed emails, or summaries. In both countries, around 20% of the organization-channel instances do not archive the communication.

Despite the differences between Rwanda and Sri Lanka regarding communication channels and archiving methods, the organizations in both countries possess the aggregated knowledge about the issues that the citizens raise. This aggregated knowledge does not seem to be well-documented, though; our method of knowledge mining was interviews with the management.

7 Learning from the Citizens

Surveys and polls are probably the most common form of soliciting feedback, used also to obtain citizens' input in policy making [23]. Surveys and polls are not initiated by the respondents, and low response rate may be a problem.

Charalabidis et al. [24] distinguish three generations of e-participation tools: (i) official government websites with predefined topics and discussion options; (ii) government establishes its presence in social media; (iii) government uses advanced technology for opinion mining, sentiment analysis, crowdsourcing in social media a.k. a. citizen-sourcing, social media monitoring, open innovation – these are different names for related activities to obtain citizens' input for developing more socially rooted policies.

The goals of social media adoption by public organizations are (i) increasing citizens' participation and engagement in the policy development and implementation, (ii) promoting transparency and accountability, reducing corruption, (iii) co-production of public-services, (iv) exploiting public knowledge and talent to develop innovative solutions to complex societal problems [25]. Social media trigger a governance paradigm shift because they facilitate bottom-up participation and self-organization of citizens [26], as well as facilitate openness and transparency, rationalize the actions of civil servants and policy makers, promote direct democracy [27]. Our own solution domains in Table 2, compared with the ambitions of the social media adoption, seem more modest and oriented towards solving operational challenges at hand.

While studying the literature on social media adoption by public organizations, we observed that opinion mining in social media is not regarded as a successor of opinion mining in the citizens' direct communication to public organizations. Opinion mining in the direct communication has never really existed. Arguably, the following three phenomena make social media different from the direct communication, which has triggered the social media adoption: (i) public organizations cannot control the communication in social media, at least not in the western countries; (ii) social media facilitate the aforementioned self-organization of citizens which cannot be ignored by public organizations; and (iii) the e-participation tools and technologies – visualization and argumentation, voting and deliberation, opinion mining, simulation, serious games, big-data analysis, etc. [28] – have managed to arrive just in time.

Four Dutch case studies [26] show symptomatic applications of social media monitoring by public organizations. In 2007, the ministry of education was surprised by a student revolt; in order to be better prepared for the future surprises, the ministry commissioned social media monitoring, i.e., an early warning system. In 2009, the ministry of environment felt threatened by a political scandal around climate research. The ministry commissioned monitoring of "who, where, how often, and what" was discussed. Eventually, the ministry invited the sceptics of the government's climate policy to meet the officials. Thus, both ministries used social media monitoring in the context of policy making. Two other governmental agencies monitored the image of the organization, questions and problems posted by the citizens. Answering questions in an online community is more efficient than answering individual phone calls. Thus, both agencies used social media monitoring in the context of service delivery.

These Dutch case studies are among the best examples of social media adoption by public organizations; there are hardly any published examples of policies and services co-designed by the citizens. There exist two evaluation frameworks that help measuring social media interactions in the public sector [25, 29, 30], but the actual evaluations did not include any final "product".

Another Dutch research [31] sheds some light on why this final "product" is often missing. Politicians consult citizens; the role of citizens is mainly to provide information and ideas. Other actors, such as social and professional organizations and entrepreneurs, are more important in the policy making process itself. Civil servants are the decisive actors. 73% of the surveyed entrepreneurs believe that citizens lack the necessary knowledge to participate in policy making, and civil servants are highly critical about the value of the information and suggestions provided. Also Sneiders et al. [6] suggest that public organizations rely primarily on input from domain experts, governmental and non-governmental organizations, and companies.

8   Conclusions

This research explores the direct communication generated by citizens, addressed to public organizations, and how this communication can be used to improve public policies and services. We have interviewed 19 public organizations in Rwanda and Sri Lanka, identified 26 issues raised by the citizens, and mapped these issues into four solution domains: availability and timeliness of information, policy development, business process development, availability and design of e-services (Table 1, Sect. 4). Furthermore, we show that the volume of the communication is sufficient to substantiate the importance of the issues (Sect. 5). Therefore we conclude that the citizens' feedback embedded in their communication to public organizations is actionable and can be used to develop and improve public policies and services. We collected our data in two countries; still, we believe our conclusions are valid for most countries.

There exists a substantial amount of research in co-production of public services. Still, published results of citizens' involvement in developing public policies and services are rare.

Our own results and those of the related research suggest a conflict between the wealth of governance-related information generated by citizens on one side, and reluctance of public organizations to act upon this information on the other side. Therefore we propose the future research that identifies the barriers inside public organizations that hinder more direct involvement of citizens in governance, investigates how the barriers could be lifted, and whether the barriers should be lifted at all.

Acknowledgements. The authors would like to express their gratitude to the people in Rwanda and Sri Lanka who made this research possible. Thanks a lot to Sri Lanka Institute of Development Administration, without you we would never reach those 12 organizations.

References

1. Osborne, S.P., Radnor, Z., Strokosch, K.: Co-production and the co-creation of value in public services: a suitable case for treatment? Public Manag. Rev. **18**(5), 639–653 (2016)
2. Nambisan, S., Nambisan, P.: Engaging Citizens in Co-creation in Public Services: Lessons Learned and Best Practices. IBM Center for the Business of Government (2013)
3. Linders, D.: From e-government to we-government: defining a typology for citizen coproduction in the age of social media. Gov. Inf. Q. **29**(4), 446–454 (2012)
4. Scherer, S., Wimmer, M.A., Strykowski, S.: Social government: a concept supporting communities in co-creation and co-production of public services. In: Proceedings of the 16th Annual International Conference on Digital Government Research, pp. 204–209. ACM, New York, USA (2015)
5. Raikov, A.: Accelerating technology for self-organizing networked democracy. Futures (2018). https://doi.org/10.1016/j.futures.2018.03.015
6. Sneiders, E., Byungura, J.C., Henkel, M., Perjons, E.: Potential of language technology to support public organizations and their communication channels in a developing country. In: Proceedings of the 10th International Conference on Theory and Practice of Electronic Governance, pp. 236–244. ACM, New York, USA (2017)
7. Ruthven, I., Kelly, D. (eds.): Interactive Information Seeking, Behavior and Retrieval. Facet Publishing, London (2011)
8. Pabarskaite, Z., Raudys, A.: A process of knowledge discovery from web log data: systematization and critical review. J. Intell. Inf. Syst. **28**(1), 79–104 (2007)
9. Sneiders, E.: Review of the main approaches to automated email answering. New Advances in Information Systems and Technologies. AISC, vol. 444, pp. 135–144. Springer, Cham (2016). https://doi.org/10.1007/978-3-319-31232-3_13
10. Warkentin, M., Gefen, D., Pavlou, P.A., Rose, G.M.: Encouraging citizen adoption of e-government by building trust. Electron. Mark. **12**(3), 157–162 (2002)
11. Seckler, M., Heinz, S., Bargas-Avila, J.A., Opwis, K., Tuch, A.N.: Designing usable web forms: empirical evaluation of web form improvement guidelines. In: Proceedings of CHI 2014, pp. 1275–1284. ACM, New York, USA (2014)
12. Pappel, I., Pappel, I., Saarmann M.: Digital records keeping to information governance in Estonian local governments. In: Proceedings of i-Society 2012, pp. 199–204. IEEE (2012)
13. Weerakkody, V., El-Haddadeh, R., Al-Sobhi, F., Shareef, M.A., Dwivedi, Y.K.: Examining the influence of intermediaries in facilitating e-government adoption: an empirical investigation. Int. J. Inf. Manag. **33**(5), 716–725 (2013)
14. Scholl, H.J.: Interoperability in e-Government: more than just smart middleware. In: Proceedings of HICSS 2005, pp. 123–123. IEEE (2005)
15. Boyne, G.A.: Sources of public service improvement: a critical review and research agenda. J. Public Admin. Res. Theor. **13**(3), 367–394 (2003)
16. Skelcher, C.: Public-private partnerships, pp. 347–370. Oxford University Press, Oxford (2005)
17. Karnani, A.: Fighting Poverty Together: Rethinking Strategies for Business, Governments, and Civil Society to Reduce Poverty. Springer, New York (2016). https://doi.org/10.1057/9780230120235
18. Crié, D.: Consumers' complaint behavior: taxonomy, typology and determinants: Towards a unified ontology. J. Database Mark. Cust. Strat. Manag. **11**(1), 60–79 (2003)
19. Lee, S., Cude, B.J.: Consumer complaint channel choice in online and offline purchases. Int. J. Cons. Stud. **36**(1), 90–96 (2012)

20. Meik, J., Brock, C., Blut, M.: Complaining customers as innovation contributors: stimulating service innovation through multichannel complaint management. In: Proceedings of SRII Global Conference 2014, pp. 125–132. IEEE (2014)
21. CIA: The World Factbook. Sri Lanka. https://www.cia.gov/library/publications/the-world-factbook/geos/ce.html. Accessed 02 May 2018
22. Fields, G.S.: Working Hard, Working Poor: A Global Journey. Oxford University Press, Oxford (2012)
23. Robbins, M.D., Simonsen, B., Feldman, B.: Citizens and resource allocation: improving decision making with interactive web-based citizen participation. Public Admin. Rev. **68**(3), 564–575 (2008)
24. Charalabidis, Y., Triantafillou, A., Karkaletsis, V., Loukis, E.: Public policy formulation through non moderated crowdsourcing in social media. In: Tambouris, E., Macintosh, A., Sæbø, Ø. (eds.) ePart 2012. LNCS, vol. 7444, pp. 156–169. Springer, Heidelberg (2012). https://doi.org/10.1007/978-3-642-33250-0_14
25. Ferro, E., Loukis, E.N., Charalabidis, Y., Osella, M.: Policy making 2.0: from theory to practice. Gov. Inf. Q. **30**(4), 359–368 (2013)
26. Bekkers, V., Edwards, A., de Kool, D.: Social media monitoring: responsive governance in the shadow of surveillance? Gov. Inf. Q. **30**(4), 335–342 (2013)
27. Stamati, T., Papadopoulos, T., Anagnostopoulos, D.: Social media for openness and accountability in the public sector: cases in the Greek context. Gov. Inf. Q. **32**(1), 12–29 (2015)
28. Kamateri, E., et al.: A comparative analysis of tools and technologies for policy making. In: Janssen, M., Wimmer, M.A., Deljoo, A. (eds.) Policy Practice and Digital Science. PAIT, vol. 10, pp. 125–156. Springer, Cham (2015). https://doi.org/10.1007/978-3-319-12784-2_7
29. Mergel, I.: A framework for interpreting social media interactions in the public sector. Gov. Inf. Q. **30**(4), 327–334 (2013)
30. Loukis, E., Charalabidis, Y., Androutsopoulou, A.: Promoting open innovation in the public sector through social media monitoring. Gov. Inf. Q. **34**(1), 99–109 (2017)
31. Michels, A., De Graaf, L.: Examining citizen participation: local participatory policy making and democracy. Local Gov. Stud. **36**(4), 477–491 (2010)

Accessibility of Italian E-Government Services: The Perspective of Users with Disabilities

Maria Claudia Buzzi[1][(⊠)] [iD], Marina Buzzi[1] [iD], and Fiorella Ragni[2]

[1] IIT-CNR, v. Moruzzi, 1, 56127 Pisa, PI, Italy
{claudia.buzzi,marina.buzzi}@iit.cnr.it
[2] Department of Law, University of Pisa, Pisa, Italy
f.ragni@tiscali.it

Abstract. The advent of the Internet has shaped our life in every field including study, work, social interaction, free time, and politics. In the sector of Public Administration (PA) and services delivered to citizens, benefits include better access to a vast amount of information, saving time, simplified services, and increased transparency. However, PA services should also be easy to use for people with disabilities, including those who interact through assistive technology. This paper offers the results of an online survey of people with disabilities accessing Italian PA services. Results from the sample highlight the need to improve service accessibility and usability, and the request for increasing their number and set of functions.

Keywords: Accessibility · Usability · Public Administrations · People with disabilities

1 Introduction

E-government involves the use of electronic communication devices, computers and the Internet to provide public services to citizens in an efficient and cost-effective way. Thanks to the Web, anyone with an Internet connection can easily access a wide choice of services 24 h/day. The number of e-government services increases every day; examples are demographic certificates (such as marital status or address changes), tax payment, licensing, school enrollment, property forms, and so on. It is important for such services to be accessible to people with disabilities in order to ensure inclusive access and equity.

Both literature and accessibility experts confirm that incorporating accessibility and usability guidelines at the phase of website design can help guarantee the high efficiency and efficacy of the service, thus increasing user satisfaction. In recent years, public administrations have acknowledged this aspect, but usability and accessibility issues still prevent the effective use of e-government services by everyone. Several recent studies have noted the poor accessibility of governmental websites [1, 3, 10, 13, 14]. Unfortunately, all these studies are performed by using automatic tools, such as aChecker (https://achecker.ca/) or WebAim (https://webaim.org/) and do not consider the actual experience of users with disabilities.

© Springer Nature Switzerland AG 2019
A. Chugunov et al. (Eds.): EGOSE 2018, CCIS 947, pp. 281–292, 2019.
https://doi.org/10.1007/978-3-030-13283-5_21

The 2011 report "Monitoring eAccessibility in Europe", funded by the European Union, indicates that only one-third of the content generated by public administrations in the EU was accessible and highlights how the adoption of WCAG 2.0 guidelines is a slow and fragmented process (http://www.eaccessibility-monitoring.eu/). Understanding the current difficulties of people with disabilities when interacting with e-government services is the first step in identifying where to intervene.

Older persons (age 65 years or over) in Europe represent 19.4% of the population, with an increasing trend [5]. Specifically, Italy has the highest percentage of people aged 65 or older, (i.e., 22.3% of the total population) [5].

Prevalence of disabilities is increasing due to population aging: e.g., in developed countries studies have shown that up to 40% of people over 65 years suffer from a chronic illness or disability that limits their daily activities [8]. Considering the increasing digital process occurring in the PAs and the aging of the European population, it is urgent to implement best practices to guarantee web accessibility and usability for all, thus increasing autonomy and empowering every individual.

This paper presents a study that sheds light on Italian public administration (PA) accessibility via an online survey answered by 68 people with disabilities from Tuscany, accessing PA services in Italy. The paper is organized as follows: after the related works, the study's methodology is presented in Sect. 3; results and discussion follow in Sects. 4 and 5 respectively, while conclusions and future work end the paper.

2   Related Work

Every person has the same rights and opportunities, and there should be no discrimination against people with disabilities, according to the 1948 Universal Declaration of Human Rights (UN). With the advent and growth of the internet over the last 20 years, most countries have approved laws to encourage and guarantee equal opportunities for all to access digital resources; accessibility of web sites and services is important for everyone but it is crucial for people with disabilities, since their interaction can require more time and effort. The concept of web accessibility implies that both the website and the services it contains are accessible.

The Web Accessibility Initiative (WAI) of the World Wide Web Consortium (W3C) is a group of international experts who work together to develop accessibility Web standards. Among these, the Web Content Accessibility Guidelines (WCAG) has the goal of providing a single shared standard for web content accessibility that meets the needs of individuals, organizations, and governments internationally. This standard is generally used as a reference point and adopted by several national governments to guide the eGovernment accessibility process. In this area, the European Union (EU) for instance specifically approved:

- 2010–11: ratification of the United Nations Convention on the Rights of Persons with Disabilities (UNCRPD)[1] by the EU in January 2011. Specifically, Article 9

---

[1] http://ec.europa.eu/social/main.jsp?catId=1138&langId=en.

concerns the duties of stakeholders in the accessibility field to ensure equal access for persons with disability.

- 2014: The European standard on accessibility requirements for public procurement of ICT products and services was adopted in February 2014[2]: EN 301 549 V1.1.1 (2014-02) Accessibility requirements suitable for public procurement of ICT products and services in Europe
- 2016: On 26 October 2016, the European Parliament approved the Directive (EU) 2016/2102 of the European Parliament and of the Council on the accessibility of the websites and mobile applications of public sector bodies[3].

In December 2015 the European Accessibility Act was proposed, aimed at improving the functioning of the internal market for accessible products and services by removing barriers created by divergent legislation. However, legislation is not enough to guarantee accessibility. Indeed, Europe has had to postpone the original objective of reaching 100% PA website accessibility by 2010 to 2020.

Many studies have been carried out to evaluate the accessibility and usability of PA websites. In the following, we cite just some recent examples. In 2016, Galvez and Youngblood examined 132 state and local e-government websites in Rhode Island, using a combination of code inspection, heuristic evaluation, and automated analysis, to determine the effects of templates on accessibility, usability, and mobile readiness. The results suggested that while best-practice-based templates may be helpful in improving usability, accessibility, and mobile readiness, it is crucial for designers to receive training in these areas and crucial for governments to monitor state and local Web sites being compliant with standards [6]. In a previous work, Youngblood and Mackiewicz used e-government and corporate usability benchmarks to compare municipal government websites in Alabama. The study reveals substantial problems with municipal website usability, including accessibility. The authors highlight, and we agree, that such problems could erode a municipality's web credibility [16]. In 2015, Coelho Serra et al. presented a study on the manual evaluation of four Brazilian e-government mobile applications using WCAG 2.0. Numerous accessibility issues were detected. Results showed that many elementary accessibility problems widely known by HCI researchers were encountered extensively in the applications evaluated. This highlights the importance of furthering research in accessibility design and evaluation of mobile applications, in order to provide more inclusive access to essential applications used by all citizens, such as e-government services [4]. In 2018, Alcaraz-Quiles et al. investigated the impact of e-government implementation on the transparency, accessibility and usability of Spanish Regional Government websites, observing that the transparency of analyzed websites is inversely related to accessibility since the information is available but could require considerable time to find it [2]. In 2015 Ismailova performed an accessibility test on 55 Kyrgyz Republic e-government websites using several automatic evaluation tools. Results showed that about 70% of government websites have accessibility errors thus requiring the application of accessibility guidelines such as WCAG [9]. In 2016, Kesswani and Kumar analyzed

---

[2] https://www.etsi.org/deliver/etsi_en/301500_301599/301549/01.01.01_60/en_301549v010101p.pdf.

[3] https://eur-lex.europa.eu/legal-content/EN/TXT/?uri=uriserv:OJ.L_.2016.327.01.0001.01.ENG.

the accessibility of Top Universities and educational websites in the UK, Russia, China, Germany and India with respect to the WCAG 2.0. In most of these cases, despite legislation imposed by governments, educational websites follow less than 50% of the guidelines; thus, much greater effort is required to satisfy the accessibility guidelines [11]. A 2011 study investigated the accessibility of Malaysia e-government websites by using the WCAG v. 1.0. The evaluation process revealed several issues, thus the authors provided a few recommendations to further improve the usability and accessibility of e-government website [15].

Some eGovernment accessibility studies have been performed in emerging countries as well. In 2016, Adepoju et al. evaluated the accessibility and performance analysis of state government websites in Nigeria by using two online-automated tools to test for their conformance with the Web Content Accessibility Guidelines [1]. Results show that none of the websites evaluated totally conform to WCAG 2.0 standards. In 2014, Karkin and Janssen analyzed previous literature in order to develop a set of criteria used for evaluating the websites of sixteen Turkish local governments. The websites performed relatively well on traditional indicators, but not satisfactory at providing platforms for citizen engagement, responsiveness and dialogue [10]. Patra and Das in 2014 analyzed the factors that have an impact on the accessibility of e-Governance services, especially in rural India in order to improve their accessibility and to help achieve the mandate of inclusive e-Governance. [14].

Regarding the Italian situation, an analysis performed 5 years ago highlighted that many Italian institutional websites were still poorly accessible. Specifically, more than 950 pages covering the Italian administrative areas (20 regions) were automatically checked and data analyzed, showing that none were fully compliant with Italian legal requirements (Law decree n. 04/2004 and updates) [7].

Most accessibility studies were carried out using automatic measurements of accessibility, thus representing an approximation since some criteria require human inspection to be verified. Martínez et al., comparing results of automatic vs manual evaluation of web accessibility, showed that only 73% of the manually checked results were correctly predicted by automatic evaluation tools [12]. Furthermore, human inspection is usually done by accessibility experts and not by users.

Considering that eGovernment websites and services evolve quickly, that automatic evaluation of web accessibility is an approximation, and wishing to understand the point of view of users, our study aims to complement related studies investigating the current degree of accessibility of Italian e-government websites as experienced/perceived by users with disabilities.

3 Methodology

3.1 Description

An online survey was created using Google Form, a component of Google Drive. Google Form allows one to automatically aggregate collected data, presenting them in graphics. Moreover, it offers a good degree of accessibility, especially for individuals using a screen reader. A long survey would be very demanding in terms of cognitive effort and time required, thus discouraging people who interact via assistive technology, so the questionnaire is short. As the main objective of this study is to understand the accessibility of services provided by PAs, we focused on the access to a service, the service's completion and the interaction.

The largest and most important organizations of persons with disabilities (visual, motor, hearing, intellective and autism) were contacted by phone, asking the coordinator or the president's secretary to distribute the questionnaire's address to their associates.

3.2   The Survey

The questionnaire was in Italian since the survey was conducted in Italy. There were ten questions, nine being closed questions and the last a text box for suggestions. The first four questions characterize the sample while the last six investigate the participants' usability experience with online PA services.

The questionnaire's content and language were assessed by two accessibility experts and modified according to the provided suggestions. Next, the online version was checked by a totally blind person who verified its accessibility via screen reader.

3.3   Participants

A total of 68 people filled out the questionnaire. The sample is not very large, it is not easy to involve people with disabilities without rewards, but it is quite varied and could provide an initial set of issues to further investigate in the future. The age distribution is shown in Fig. 1, left. Only the age range 18–29 years is under-represented. However, due to their youth, these users probably use PA services less and have fewer problems interacting with mobile devices/assistive technology than do older participants. Regarding gender, the sample is well-distributed with 53% male and 47% female, as shown in Fig. 1, right.

Most participants were visually impaired but all the main disabilities are present, although intellectual/developmental disability is under-represented. This is probably due to the difficulties they encounter in autonomously accessing online services, which generally require complex interaction (Fig. 2).

Figure 3 shows the distribution of participants by job. More than half of participants (54%) are employees of a PA; Italian law requires PA offices to recruit a percentage of people with disabilities. Nineteen participants (i.e., 28% of the sample) are retired since Italian law allows people with disabilities to retire earlier. One participant is a student. Five people (i.e., 7% of the sample) are practitioners. Two housewives (3%) and four unemployed people (6%) complete the sample.

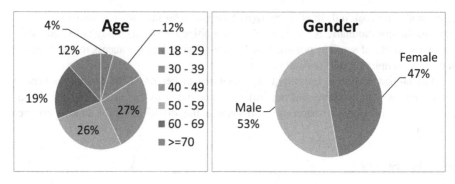

Fig. 1. The sample characterization: age and gender

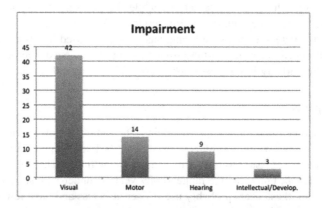

Fig. 2. Sample characterization: disabilities. Most of the participants are visually impaired, followed by motor-impaired people.

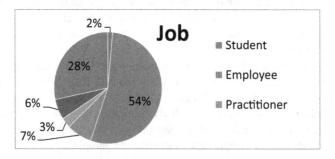

Fig. 3. Sample characterization: job

4 Results

4.1 Evaluating Online PA Services

The main objective of this study was to understand the accessibility of eGovernment services as perceived by participants, in terms of ability to

- Access PA services
- Complete the services
- Evaluate the interaction.

Concerning the frequency of Internet use, most participants use Internet daily, seven users weekly and only one seldom (Fig. 4). This reflects the importance of the Internet for people with disabilities, not only for working and studying but also for participating in social life and carrying out everyday tasks (e.g., booking hotels and holidays, buying products, contacting friends, organizing meetings, and so on). For instance, many PA services, if fully accessible via Web, can be performed remotely and autonomously, avoiding the need for the help from accompanying persons in order to arrive at the office and fill out paper forms – a great leap in personal autonomy.

As reported in Fig. 5, the sample users consult many PA services in different areas. Health, Local Administration, Job services and tax are the most frequently requested. In Italy the process of digitalization of PA services is quite fragmented but in recent years much has been done to fulfill e-government aims. People can access information on medical tests performed in public health structures and more generally on the electronic health records; many taxes can be paid online and the National Institute for Social Security offers many services such as checking the current pension situation, management of insurance against accidents at work, training offered to employees of public administration, etc.

Regarding accessibility issues encountered by the sample, a first point concerns the participants' experience in accessing the online PA services. In order to better understand collected data, one should bear in mind that unskilled people having problems accessing online services often blame the failure on themselves – as unable to act correctly in a digital environment – instead of considering the cause as due to poor usability design.

Most users (88%) declared they have experienced some issues: 68% of participants had problems sometimes and 20% many times, as shown in Fig. 6. Concerning the ability to successfully complete a PA service, which reflects the effectiveness of the service, 11% of participants declared they were always able to successfully complete it, while for 30% it was only "often". More than half of the sample (i.e., 51%) was successful only "sometimes", and two participants "never" (Fig. 7). Despite the small sample, these are very bad results and Italian PAs should improve their services to better guarantee web accessibility and usability for all. A very frequent issue encountered was related to the difficulty of finding the information or service the user was looking for. For this kind of issue, a more usable reorganization and presentation of web content could be beneficial to improving user orientation and usability on the whole.

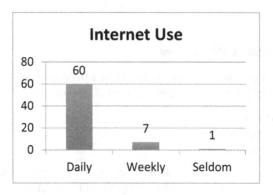

Fig. 4. Participants' internet use

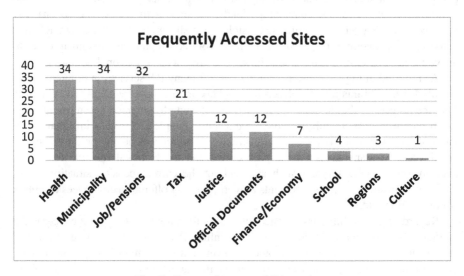

Fig. 5. Frequently accessed PA services

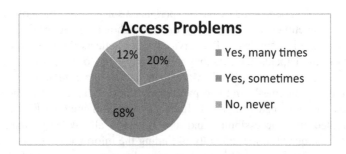

Fig. 6. Frequency of problems detected when accessing online PA services

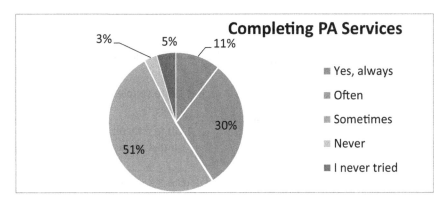

Fig. 7. Completing online PA services

Regarding the simplicity of user interaction, most participants evaluated the interaction as simple (46% as "Quite simple in most cases" and 9% as "Always simple") but considerable difficulties were still encountered by 45% participants: 9% of them judged the interaction as "Always difficult" and 36% as "Quite difficult in most cases" (see Fig. 8). The majority of the sample found the interaction easy but 45% of the users encountering difficulties is however a very high percentage and again it suggests the need to revise and simplify PA websites and services to improve their usability.

Aiming to verify user satisfaction, one of the main usability issues, we proposed the explicit question "Are you satisfied with your interaction with PA websites?" The answer was rated on a 5-item Likert scale (1 = Completely unsatisfied to 5 = Completely satisfied). Figure 9 shows that most participants were in the middle with 47.1%, not satisfied users were 22% (with 4.4% very unsatisfied) and satisfied users were 31% (with only 5.9% very satisfied). In this case, data might not represent the real picture of the user satisfaction, because as previously mentioned, unskilled people having problems accessing online services often blame the failure on themselves instead of considering the cause as due to poor usability design.

Many users' suggestions have been collected regarding what online PA services need to be improved. Most users ask for increased service usability, e.g., the interaction's simplicity (62.1%), or adding new services (22.7%). Additional requests include:

- Make it easier to find what you are looking for
- Improve interface usability, simplifying complex interfaces, structuring better content and main information, etc.
- Add an online real-time customer care service, a chat service (textual, and better still with sign language translation) for assistance/help
- Improve video accessibility using a sign language interpreter (SLI) or subtitling.

The last points are related to the need to increase/strengthen the communication channels with the PAs. The user sample thus highlighted a high degree of citizen engagement; indeed, citizen engagement can be measured in terms of gathering proposals for improving public services, citizen satisfaction questionnaires, live

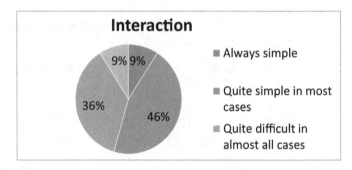

Fig. 8. Interaction in accessing online PA services

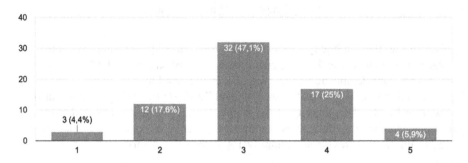

Fig. 9. User satisfaction when accessing online PA services

broadcasting, direct communication addresses by the city Mayor/Coordinators and connection to social network groups [10].

The main limitation of this study is the low cardinality of the sample. Although it is not possible to generalize findings, since 68 individuals is not representative of the Italian population with disabilities, it can offer an overview of some of the problems detected. The questionnaire did not require evaluating specific websites or services: users answered according to their experience with e-government services so no comparison could be made. Despite this, the Italian PA services are very different and range from delivering information to exploiting dynamic social, health, educational or economic services. In this sense, the results can represent a subjective evaluation of Italian e-government quality. Furthermore, the under-representation of citizens aged 18–29 could be also a problem and can cause bias, since this age group is more likely to use technology. For future work, we plan to organize a future study to increase the sample (to reach more than 500 users) and to contact the Student Services of the Italian universities to reach out to students with disabilities (age 19–25 or over).

5   Conclusion

This study attempts to better understand the experience of people with disabilities when accessing online PA services. In countries such as Italy, the main social services such as hospitals, schools and municipalities are part of the PA, and online procedures are increasing day by day. If the accessibility of such services is inadequate, equal opportunities would not be guaranteed for everyone and there would be a risk of cutting off people with disability from the advantages of the Digital Age.

Results seems to confirm previous studies highlighting that usability is still neglected in the design of online PA services for citizens. Studies on usability of PA websites conducted in Europe [13], Turkey [10], India [14], Nigeria [1], and Saudi Arabia [3], showed the need to further improve the accessibility and usability of PA services.

Great effort is necessary to increase accessibility and usability of governmental web sites and applications. To this aim, a multi-stakeholder approach is needed: simple authoring tools helping website creators to create accessible websites, the availability of accessible but pleasant and rich templates for popular Content Management Systems, translating examples and reusable portions of code published by the WAI group of the W3C into every language (most resources are in English, creating linguist barriers), and legislative and economic actions of governments are all necessary components. Finally, the involvement of users with disabilities in the design and test of PA websites and services should be encouraged to become a best practice. We hope a multi-stakeholder approach will favor access for all, according to Tim Berners-Lee, W3C Director and inventor of the World Wide Web, who said: "The power of the Web is in its universality. Access by everyone regardless of disability is an essential aspect".

References

1. Adepoju, S.A., Shehu, I.S, Bake, P.: Accessibility evaluation and performance analysis of e-government websites in Nigeria. J. Adv. Inf. **7**(1) (2016). www.jait.us/uploadfile/2016/0204/20160204021203295.pdf
2. Alcaraz-Quiles, F.J., Urquia-Grande, E., Muñoz-Colomina, C.I., Rautiainen, A.: E-government implementation: transparency, accessibility and usability of government websites. In: International E-Government Development, pp. 291–306. Palgrave Macmillan, Cham (2018)
3. Al-Khalifa, H.S., Baazeem, I., Alamer, R.: Revisiting the accessibility of Saudi Arabia government websites. Univers. Access Inf. Soc. **16**(4), 1027–1039 (2017)
4. Coelho Serra, L., Pedroso Carvalho, L., Pereira Ferreira, L., Belimar SilvaVaz, J., Pimenta Freire, A.: Accessibility evaluation of e-government mobile applications in Brazil. Procedia Comput. Sci. **67**, 348–357 (2015)
5. Eurostat: Statistics Explained. Population Structure and Ageing. http://ec.europa.eu/eurostat/statistics-explained/index.php/Population_structure_and_ageing. Accessed 18 July 2018
6. Galvez, R.A., Youngblood, N.E.: e-Government in Rhode Island: what effects do templates have on usability, accessibility, and mobile readiness? UAIS **15**(2), 281–296 (2016)

7. Gambino, O., Pirrone, R., Di Giorgio, F.: Accessibility of the Italian institutional web pages: a survey on the compliance of the Italian public administration web pages to the Stanca Act and its 22 technical requirements for web accessibility. Univers. Access Inf. Soc. **15**(2), 305–312 (2016)

8. Hutton, D.: Older people in emergencies: considerations for action and policy development. World Health Organization, Geneva (2008). www.who.int/ageing/publications/Hutton_report_small.pdf

9. Ismailova, R.: Web site accessibility, usability and security: a survey of government web sites in Kyrgyz Republic. Univers. Access Inf. Soc. **16**(1), 257–264 (2017)

10. Karkin, N., Janssen, M.: Evaluating websites from a public value perspective: a review of Turkish local government websites. Int. J. Inf. Manag. **34**(3), 351–363 (2014). https://doi.org/10.1016/j.ijinfomgt.2013.11.004

11. Kesswani, N., Kumar, S.: Accessibility analysis of websites of educational institutions. Perspect. Sci. (2016). https://doi.org/10.1016/j.pisc.2016.04.031

12. Casado Martínez, C., Martínez-Normand, L., Olsen, M.G.: Is it possible to predict the manual web accessibility result using the automatic result? In: Stephanidis, C. (ed.) UAHCI 2009. LNCS, vol. 5616, pp. 645–653. Springer, Heidelberg (2009). https://doi.org/10.1007/978-3-642-02713-0_68

13. Olsen, M.G.: How Accessible is the Public European Web? http://citeseerx.ist.psu.edu/viewdoc/download?doi=10.1.1.661.9048&rep=rep1&type=pdf

14. Patra, M.R., Das, R.K.: Accessibility of e-governance in rural India: a critical view point. In: Proceeding of ICEGOV, pp. 375–378. ACM, New York (2014). https://doi.org/10.1145/2691195.2691218

15. Rahim, W.A., Suhami, M.R., Safie, N., Semsudin, S.S.: Assessing the usability and accessibility of Malaysia e-government website. Am. J. Econ. Bus. Adm. **3**(1), 40–46 (2011). ISSN 1945-5488

16. Youngblood, N.E., Mackiewicz, J.: A usability analysis of municipal government website home pages in Alabama. Gov. Inf. Q. **29**(4), 582–588 (2012). https://doi.org/10.1016/j.giq.2011.12.010

Digital Democracy, Participation, Security, Communities, Social Media, Activism

Evaluation of an eParticipation Project Against eParticipation Success Factors

Hans-Dieter Zimmermann[(⊠)]

FHS St. Gallen University of Applied Sciences, St. Gallen, Switzerland
hansdieter.zimmermann@fhsg.ch

Abstract. (e)Participation, as a characteristic of open government, is gaining more and more public attention recently. Therefore, it is important to be able to evaluate eParticipation projects against a sound framework to look into the projects' impact on society. As several evaluation frameworks focus on quantitative measures only, such as cost-benefit analyses, only a very few provide qualitative measurements. In this paper, we evaluate a concrete eParticipation project from Switzerland, which has not been systematically evaluated before. As an evaluation framework, a list of 23 success factors, which has been developed based on extensive research, has been applied. The results are two-fold: first, the evaluation process triggered a systematic ex post reflection of the project; second, it was discerned that the used framework is highly useful and applicable for the evaluation of eParticipation projects; some suggestions for the further development of the framework are being discussed as well. Both results contribute to the body of knowledge in the area of eParticipation in general.

Keywords: eParticipation · Success factors · Evaluation

1 Introduction

In most countries of the Western world, we can observe a fundamental development in societies, which is regarded as "open government". Since the beginning of the 1990s, government agencies on all federal levels tend to be more open. The "new public management" philosophy can be characterized by less bureaucracy and more efficiency, citizen orientation, as well as transparency of public actions. In this context, Open Societal Innovation "refers to the adaptation and subsequent sustainable use of appropriate open innovation approaches from business, adapted and utilized by state and society to solve societal challenges" (von Lucke et al. 2012). Citizen participation can be understood as an involvement of citizens in democratic processes on different levels (Arnstein 1969). Nowadays, an increasing citizen engagement can be achieved by ICT-enabled formats of eParticipation: "eParticipation involves the extension and transformation of participation in societal democratic and consultative processes, mediated by information and communication technologies (ICTs)" (Sanford and Rose 2007).

It can be assumed that political participation formats applying ICT means are especially suited to include youth into participatory processes as youth are generally acquainted in using digital devices and social media platforms to communicate and

© Springer Nature Switzerland AG 2019
A. Chugunov et al. (Eds.): EGOSE 2018, CCIS 947, pp. 295–307, 2019.
https://doi.org/10.1007/978-3-030-13283-5_22

interact. Rexhepi et al. consider "the youth as one of the most crucial stakeholders and primary special interest groups in terms of sustainable development" within local communities (Rexhepi et al. 2018, 115). In their paper, the authors also introduce a four-step process to promote youth eParticipation; the fourth step is called "Evaluating the obtained added values on both personal and community level" (Rexhepi et al. 2018, 118).

Although there are several sources from practitioners as well as scholars describing and discussing eParticipation projects, we can hardly find models or frameworks which provide measurements for a systematic evaluation of those initiatives and projects. Applying quantitative cost-benefit analyses to eParticipation projects is not satisfactory as this hardly considers the non-quantitative benefits, such as the results of citizen participation on democratic processes, which may contribute to the quality of life of a community and its citizens.

Macintosh and Whyte developed a framework for eParticipation in 2008 arguing "that there is a need for coherent evaluation frameworks employing such perspectives and methods, to better understand current eParticipation applications and learn from these experiences" (Macintosh and Whyte 2008). The authors presented a layered eParticipation framework based on a case study addressing three perspectives: democratic, project, and socio-technical criteria comprising 20 single criteria in total.

Drobnjak and Trean developed a "five-level participation model, which takes into account the advantages of the Social Web or Web 2.0, together with a quantitative approach for the evaluation of eParticipation projects." (Teran and Drobnjak 2013, 77) The proposed framework allows a quantitative evaluation of eParticipation projects based on three components: web evolution, media richness, and communication channels.

In 2013, the United Nations' Public Institutions and Digital Government Department of Economic and Social Affairs proposed METEP: Measurement and Evaluation Tool for Citizen Engagement and e-Participation (United Nations Department of Economic and Social Affairs (UNDESA) 2013). In addition, a self-assessment questionnaire has been provided accordingly[1].

All mentioned evaluation approaches focus rather on the political as well as the ICT-related dimensions of an eParticipation project, but less on the issues concerned with the concrete implementation and execution of such a project, especially on the local level.

Panopoulou et al. published a very comprehensive study identifying success factors for designing eParticipation projects in 2014 (Panopoulou et al. 2014). In their study, the authors not only made an in-depth literature study but also conducted qualitative interviews with practitioners. Based on both inputs, they presented a framework comprising 23 success factors, including specific activities associated with each factor.

In this experience paper, we will apply the framework developed by Panopoulou et al. to a specific eParticipation project in order to evaluate it. We have chosen this framework as it is based on a very comprehensive and relatively recent literature study as well as practitioners input. The framework comprehensively covers the success

---

[1] workspace.unpan.org/sites/Internet/Documents/UNPAN94222.pdf.

Table 1. List of eParticipation success factors based on (Panopoulou et al. 2014)

1	Vision/strategy	13	User needs and expectations
2	Scope and goals	14	Value for citizens
3	Policy and legal environment	15	Value for government/organization
4	Support from government/management	16	Digital divide, disabled and desired target groups/user training
5	Management and planning	17	Employee training
6	Funding	18	Participation process, policy making stage and roles
7	Organizational structures, processes, and data	19	Change management
8	Integration and compliance	20	Leader/champion
9	Security and privacy	21	Promotion plan
10	Technology advances/constraints	22	Monitoring and evaluation plan
11	Good practice	23	Sustainability
12	Organizational culture and collaboration		

factors. To our knowledge, there is no further framework of success factors for eParticipation initiatives available in literature which is approximately as comprehensive as the chosen one.

In this paper, we will not discuss the methodological approach of the applied framework, but we will apply it as published. Furthermore, it is not the intention of the paper to evaluate or discuss the critical success factors as such, neither to add others or reduce the list, but simply to apply them as they have been published. Furthermore, as the goal of the paper is to evaluate the given project against given success factors, we won't discuss the issue of alternative methodological approaches. Nevertheless, we will briefly discuss the practicability of the applied framework.

In the following, we will briefly introduce the given eParticipation project before applying the success factors to the project. The goals are twofold: (1) to evaluate the given project ex-post, and (2) to gain experiences about the usefulness and applicability of the framework, as well as to contribute to the youth eParticipation literature in general through a discussion of project against the evaluation framework. As we apply the identified success factor of the framework to a concrete project, we will be able to assess the applicability of the success factors which have been originally identified as success factors for designing such projects.

2   eParticipation Project

The eParticipation project was conducted in 2014 to 2017 in a Swiss community with approximately 7,000 inhabitants. The project focused especially on youth participation through applying ICT means and was called *JugendMachtPolitik*, which can be translated as *Youth Does Politics*, although the German term *Macht* also translates to *power*.

The project was initiated by the government of the local community in cooperation with researchers from a regional university. It was mainly funded through a program of the Federal Social Insurance Office (FSIO) based on a national law supporting (political) youth activities[2]. The project had two major goals: 1. to implement a concrete youth eParticipation project in the community and 2. to develop general guidelines based on the experiences drawn from the project and the existing research. The target group of the project was students from the local school between the 5th and the 9th grade (approximately 10 to 15 years of age). In total, the target group comprised 444 students according to the official statistics of the canton of St. Gallen 2014[3].

The project was not a scientific nor a research project, but an activity based on the community's strategic agenda. Nevertheless, the project was accompanied by two university researchers who served as experts during the setup phase of the project. The two researchers had a background in social work and information systems. Throughout the project duration, the researchers took an observing role collecting data from the project activities. Based on the concrete observations as well as the existing literature, the researchers developed some general guidelines intended to support further communities in Switzerland when setting up such eParticipation project. The guidelines are published in (Arnold et al. 2017).

The project preparations started in early 2014. Before, it was decided by the municipality to put a focus on children and adolescents. In addition, the community participated in the Swiss UNICEF initiative, Kinderfreundliche Gemeinde[4], the Swiss adoption of UNICEF's Child Friendly Cities Initiative[5]. As one result of the analysis, it has been identified that the community offers structural prerequisites for youth participation – a youth commission, a special youth association - but lacks respective processes.

Based on a survey presenting five different scenarios developed by the project group, the students of the target group were asked to vote for their preferred application in May 2014. Based on the result, a mobile eParticipation platform facilitating an idea exchange was developed by students of a vocational school located in a city nearby.

In mid-August 2015, at the beginning of the school year, the application was rolled out. All students of the target group got their personal ID, including an initial password through the school. The first phase lasted until mid-October 2015.

During this initial project phase of approximately eight weeks, more than 40 ideas and topics have been captured on the platform by a total of 25 identified different authors. Entries got up to 15 feedbacks (comments) each. The different posts have been liked or commented by maximum of 25 students for each posting. Thus, 5.6% of the students have actively contributed to the platform, whereas the silent majority was not active at all. These figures roughly correspond to the so called '90-9-1 principle' (Carron-Arthur et al. 2014).

Further details of the project have been presented in (Zimmermann 2016).

---

[2] (Kinder- und Jugendförderungsgesetz, KJFG) (www.admin.ch/opc/de/classified-compilation/2009 2618/index.html).

[3] www.statistik.sg.ch/content/statistik/home.html.

[4] www.unicef.ch/de/so-helfen-wir/in-der-schweiz/kinderfreundliche-gemeinde.

[5] childfriendlycities.org.

3   Evaluation of eParticipation Project

In this section, we will go through each of the success factors as presented in Table 1 and apply the experiences we gained from the project accordingly. The original source of the 23 success factors provides a more detailed explanation (Panopoulou et al. 2014, 204–205).

1. Vison/strategy
   The project was initiated by the local community's government based on a long-term strategy focusing on strengthening the role and general involvement of kids and young people in the community. Among other activities, the community participated in the UNICEF program *"Kinderfreundliche Gemeinde"*, the Swiss adoption of UNICEF's Child Friendly Cities Initiative as mentioned earlier. Although the community waived the certificate, some of the program's feedback lead directly to the eParticipation project. Thus, in 2013, the community expressed the vision of focusing on the youth's needs, including their inclusion to partici-patory processes within the community's administration. Within the scope of this political agenda, the eParticipation project has been launched and executed. Nevertheless, it must be indicated that a political agenda is often made for a legislative period and depends on the distribution of power between political parties and groups, as well as on crucial people, such as the major or the responsible members of the executive authority within the community. As politics shows, political priorities can change over time, especially after elections.

2. Scope and goals
   The goals of the project have been defined very clearly as well as realistically, also from an ex-post perspective. The main goal was to develop and to deploy a concrete eParticipation tool or platform in order to enable the youth's stronger involvement in the community's political processes. In doing so, the community wanted to gain valuable practical experiences. The goals of the project were in line with the community's strategic agenda at that time.

3. Policy and legal environment
   In terms of ICT policies and standards, the Swiss regulation, e.g., in terms of data protection, has been considered when setting up the mobile eParticipation platform. Furthermore, all activities were planned to be compliant with the existing legal frameworks as well as the administrative processes in Switzerland. Following the rules, regulation, and laws must be a matter of course in such project.

4. Support from government/management
   The project was initiated by the community's government and was based on the vision and strategy of the community (see 1.). In the setup phase as well as during the project's runtime, the support from the administration as well as the executive authority of the community was broad and very strong. The project manager was one of the members of the executive authority of the community's government, and another one was also part of the project team. Furthermore, the local school as well as the official youth work were part of the project team.
   Although this kind of official support can be seen as a crucial success factor, one has to take into account that government representatives are elected for a legislative

period, and it is not guaranteed that the people will stay in their position throughout the course of the project as well as that they will be re-elected (see 1.). Consequently, the support of such project may change unpredictably.

5. Management and planning

As mentioned above, a government executive was appointed as the responsible project manager. By profession, this person had no record in project management. Overall, this situation did not turn out as a disadvantage to the project at all. The experiences show that it is rather crucial to have all involved stakeholders of the project participating in the project team from the very beginning. In this respect, the project manager was well-connected within the community, which was a clear advantage for the project because he was able to bring together all relevant stakeholders from the very beginning.

For the project management, beyond some simple instruments for planning and managing the meetings as well as enabling the necessary communication among the project members, no specific tools or frameworks have been applied. From an ex-post perspective, this did not cause any problems during the project.

Before the project was launched officially in August 2015, the planning phase took approximately 18 months. A sound planning has been considered as a critical and crucial success factor of such a project, which was also mentioned in the derived guidelines (Arnold et al. 2017). Especially in the context of a youth eParticipation project, the school holiday calendar has to be considered. As the local school was a major player within the project, it was decided to start the project right after the summer break in 2015.

Furthermore, in terms of planning the project's schedule, it should be mentioned that the project's term should be not *interrupted* by elections too early as the elections' results might result in a shift of strategy and priorities, including available funds and persons involved as well.

Providing resources in terms of available time has been a challenge, as in most Swiss communities, even executives don't work fulltime for the community and instead, have other jobs as their main occupation. Furthermore, for all the other involved persons, the project was on top of their regular job-related activities. Therefore, the available labour resources can be considered as a bottleneck in such context.

6. Funding

In terms of financial resources, on one hand, the community provided a certain budget mainly in the form of personal hours for the involved persons from the administration and the community's government; on the other hand, the project mainly benefited from the funding by the Federal Social Insurance Office (FSIO) based on a specific funding program focusing on community development in terms of youth participation as well as the canton of St. Gallen.

In conjunction with '1. Vison/strategy', it has to be pointed out that any implementation of a strategy has to be backed by respective funds, which have to be planned ahead of time. Otherwise, strategic intentions will just stay mere *lip services*.

In the present project, it was clear from the very beginning that without external funding, the project would not be possible as the internal funds would not have been sufficient to implement the intended project.

7. Organizational structures, processes, and data

As already mentioned, the core project team involved all relevant stakeholders. In addition, a group of students from the local school managed the moderation of the online platform, led by a person from the official youth work of the community, who was advised regarding the role of a moderator during a briefing session.

All involved groups and persons agreed on a clear organizational structure, comprising a description of the respective roles, tasks, responsibilities as well as working processes, which was captured in a document. Clear organizational structure helps keep the project management tasks lean and minimize the necessary communication among the involved project members during the phases of the project.

8. Integration and compliance

It was decided to develop a mobile platform from scratch. The system was designed as a standalone system. Therefore, integration/compatibility with other systems and standards has not been an issue.

9. Security and privacy

The system's development was done by students of a nearby school providing vocational education ("Berufsschule") and was led by a teacher who is a professional software developer. After long discussions, it was decided to develop the mobile platform as a closed and standalone system. The developed platform had no connections to other services, such as social media platforms, etc. A main motivation was to comply with the data protection regulation in Switzerland. Today, requirements in terms of data protection and privacy would be even higher after the introduction of the General Data Protection Regulation (GDPR) within the EU[6].

As no social login was feasible, only participants with valid IDs were allowed to access the system; an ID had to be issued by the community's school administration based on their records, and it was distributed to students of the target group (5th to 9th grade) through the school. Not using an already-known and accepted ID or a social login required students to remember another new ID, including the respective password. As the password recovery function of the developed platform was not user-friendly and inconvenient, this led to lower acceptance of the system as the students' feedback suggested.

The eParticipation platform as such was hosted in a professional environment complying with all the legal regulation in terms of data protection, etc.

10. Technology advances/constraints

As the eParticipation platform was targeted at young persons, it was decided to develop an online platform optimized for use on mobile devices. Although this step seems to be logical in today's world, the project team conducted a survey in the local school in order to find out which devices and platforms are mostly used and preferred by the students. So, the platform decision was not only made on some general assumptions but on the concrete situation within the target

---

[6] www.eugdpr.org.

group. Furthermore, it was decided to not develop dedicated mobile apps as the resources of the project did not allow this at all.

The user interface design was done by students who developed the platform as well, but no specialists had been involved due to budget restrictions. From an ex-post perspective, this was a disadvantage as the UI was less appealing compared to professional (social media) platforms used by the target group on a regular basis. This also applies to further issues such as platform functionalities, etc.

As the platform was developed by students as part of a regular course, there were basically no resources to further enhance and develop the platform, including fixing bugs throughout the duration of the project.

11. Good practice

In the preparation phase of the project, several technical solutions have been evaluated and considered, including using existing social media platforms. None of the existing platform looked at by the team met the requirements (e.g., in terms of data and privacy protection or desired functionalities) and constraints (e.g., in terms of budget). As no good practice could be identified, it was decided to build a new platform from scratch.

12. Organizational culture and collaboration

As mentioned earlier, the main goal during the setup phase was to involve all the stakeholders in the project from the very beginning. Therefore, no cultural challenges or organizational conflicts have turned up throughout the duration of the project.

13. User needs and expectations

In order to meet the users' needs, the project team conducted a survey during the setup phase, as mentioned previously. Beyond the use of technical platforms and devices, the young persons have been asked what kind of eParticipation tool they were willing to use. As they didn't know the term eParticipation and so the project team developed several scenarios describing several platform options representing different forms and levels of participation and involvement. In the end, majority voted for an idea exchange platform. Other scenarios have been, for example, a simulation game-like platform or a rather traditional online forum.

As the survey's result also showed the project team that the majority of students would like to use the platform through their smartphones, some implicit expectations in terms of usability and interface design could be derived.

As already said, the system developed was not that appealing as it could have been due to limited resources, especially in terms of time and knowledge, including experiences in mobile software development. As it was developed by a class of students within one semester, there was a lack of sustainability in general.

It also tuned out, that a non-existing *help desk* caused some challenges for the users and for the project team, which also led to a reduced acceptance of the platform, as students' feedback suggested.

14. Value for citizens

Overall, the value of the platform for the citizens, the young persons of the community in this case, was given. However, as only a minority of the students participated actively by using the platform, the value must be relativized. Nevertheless, some expectations have not been met.

Especially in the beginning of the project, the users' usage of the platform is relatively intense. On the idea platform, users could either post their own ideas or comment and vote on others' ideas; they could also discuss and comment on topics given by the editorial team. With this twofold strategy, the project team wanted to assure a high level of contribution and interaction.

It turned out as a crucial challenge that users expected a rather immediate reaction on their inputs, firstly at least some kind of acknowledgement, but secondly a content-related feedback as well. While the first part can be achieved relatively easy, e.g., as the task of a moderation team, it must be said regarding the second aspect that government processes, even in a small community, are much less responsive; they are not made for immediate and spontaneous inputs and feedbacks. It is a lesson learned from the project that a rather quick feedback must be guaranteed. Users want to know what is going to happen with their ideas and feedbacks.

Another lesson learned is that participation always means a (smart) combination of different online and offline means. At least in one concrete case when users could comment on a topic online, a well-attended half day face-to-face workshop was set up physically to discuss and to further develop results.

Both lessons learned confirmed experiences from other projects and related research.

Although the level and frequency of participation and interaction was relatively high in the beginning of the project, it was rather limited towards the end. Beyond the technical limitations of the platforms which were previously mentioned, one of the overall findings is that participation doesn't work just because of available tools – which also confirms previous findings in the research. Young people as well as adults have to learn that they are able to contribute and to participate, but they also have to accept that resources, such as time and knowledge, are necessary prerequisites in order to actively participate in debates. As the users were not really educated in participation, it was one of the findings of the project that active participation in public and societal issues has to be addressed in school much more actively.

15. Value for government/organization

As said before, for the local community government, the project fit into the strategic agenda. It was not the goal to address effectiveness of processes but to involve young people, who are not allowed to vote yet, into the community's processes. To reiterate, it must be learned that active participation needs personal investment and thus, it takes time.

The biggest value for the community's administration and executive authority was the very concrete experiences the project delivered. They learned the topics that the students are interested in, be it locally, like a new opportunity to go for a swim in the community (so far, the community has no outdoor pool), be it the unrealistic demands for a railway station in the community or for a Starbucks coffee shop (which tells about mobility or entertainment issues of the students) or even rather global environmental issues. The second major learning was about the design of participatory processes: eParticipation platforms have to be integrated in the regular administrative processes, which means that people should get a feedback about their contribution in participation. Furthermore, on behalf of the executives responsible for the community's school, it became clear that eParticipation has to be addressed in school.

Regrettably, shortly after the end of the official project, the executive authority changed after elections. Also, the project manager got a new position with the community's administration. Thus, the new executives decided to not continue the previous strategy any longer. Therefore, it can be said that during the course of the project, the government as well as the administration gained some real interesting insights, but there won't be a long-term effect in this case.

Unfortunately, a change in strategy and targets can happen any time in a democratic setting, therefore – and due to other reasons - long-term impacts are hard to estimate.

16. Digital divide, disabled and desired target groups/user training

The project was targeted at all young persons of the community from 5th to 9th grade. To not exclude anybody, the school played an important role initiating the official project. IDs were distributed through the school, students got an introduction in class, and eParticipation as a topic was addressed in class as well (although way too short). Students without any access to a computer or smartphone at home had the opportunity to access the eParticipation platform through the school's computers. Therefore, 100% of the intended target group could be reached at the start of the project.

The technical decision to develop an online platform optimized for mobile devices also contributed to the goal to enable students without a smartphone or tablet to access the platform through a web browser on a PC at school or at home.

17. Employee training

As already said, all members of the project team contributed on the basis of their existing experiences and competencies; there was no additional training. Only the editorial team of students, who moderated the platform, got an introduction in terms of how to moderate.

18. Participation process, policy making stage, and roles

All actors and stakeholders have been involved from the very beginning. There was a clear organizational structure, including communication and decision processes in place.

Overall, the necessary effort to keep the involvement level high has been underestimated. The project decided to ask an editorial team, comprising of students, to moderate the platform. Although they got an introduction into the task of moderation, it turned out that the editorial team had some challenges as they were not used to work as a moderator and were unsecure about their role and task.

It can be deduced from this that future projects clearly have to develop clear strategies and to provide resources in manpower and knowledge, including training, as moderation can be seen as a crucial success factor for eParticipation platforms.

As the number of contributions was manageable, it was decided to not apply any sophisticated tool to capture and analyze data. The analyses made were based on very simple methods of counting entries, replies, etc.

As mentioned, the feedback process also has to be defined and a quick feedback should be guaranteed.

19. Change management

Based on the scale of the project and its available resources, an explicit change in management was not considered at all.

In general, to achieve sustainable results, appropriate measures for the change in management have to be planned and implemented. For a sustainable eParticipation process, it will be necessary to educate and train all members of the administration accordingly. It has to be learned that the consideration and integration of external sources in the community's political processes has to be self-evident in an open government culture.

20. Leader/champion

The initiator of the project, who was also the overall project manager, could be considered as the leader or champion who drove the project's ideas during the course of the project internally. Outside the core team, the two university researchers in particular promoted the initiative in (academic as well as non-academic) publications, presentations, meetings, and social media.

21. Promotion plan

The project had no specific promotion plan beyond several information events at the local school and some more general events within the community to present the initiative.

The accompanying publicly-funded project had the goal of a further and broad promotion, such as to develop the general guidelines for eParticipation projects within communities in Switzerland which is now available online for free (Arnold et al. 2017).

22. Monitoring and evaluation plan

The project was observed and monitored by the two university researchers during its duration in order to derive some general findings in order to prepare the guidelines. A detailed evaluation plan was not part of the project.

23. Sustainability

As mentioned earlier, the project was discontinued after the official end. The main reason for the discontinuity was the major changes in the local government after local elections. Also, the *champion* of the project filled a different position within the community's administration after the election and although he wanted to continue and further develop the initiative, the experiences made the community's executives decide to discontinue it. Therefore, sustainability could not be achieved.

4 Discussion and Research Directions

In this paper, we pursued two main goals. The first was to systematically evaluate a concrete given eParticipation project, which has been conducted in a Swiss community, as the project was not formally evaluated before.

Applying the scientifically developed framework of success factors for designing eParticipation initiatives by (Panopoulou et al. 2014) to the project resulted in a systematic ex-post reflection of the project. Evaluating the results and experiences of a concrete eParticipation project against a sound framework of success factors contributes to the body of knowledge in the field of eParticipation in general, as outcomes of the project are being made tangible. In addition, it also adds value to the project and its participants.

During the process of the project evaluation, it turned out that the framework's 23 success factors, which have been applied as evaluation criteria, are well-suited to evaluate a real-world project in general and are highly practicable. Nevertheless, the analysis revealed some limitations as well. The study by Panopoulou et al. had the main aim "to determine a concrete set of success factors to be considered when designing an eParticipation initiative." (Panopoulou et al. 2014, 195) However, it was not the goal of their study to come up with a methodological approach applying the success factors for evaluation. So, going through the 23 criteria and applying them to a concrete project as we did in this paper disclose some valuable insights about the project. But what is missing is some kind of weighting of the factors addressing the question which are the critical and decisive success factors for designing and evaluating any eParticipation project. It also could be discussed whether some of the 23 factors identified might be grouped. Applying the factors to just one project reveals some relevant insights. But as governments spend (tax) money for numerous eParticipation projects, it would be helpful to be able to compare the success of those projects. Therefore, it would be necessary to not only weigh the factors but also to provide some kind of measurement scale, similar to the METEP framework (United Nations Department of Economic and Social Affairs (UNDESA) 2013). Although in our view, a qualitative evaluation of eParticipation projects is highly relevant in the light of open government and eDemocracy, public administrations and governments also would need quantitative analyses in order to learn about the effectiveness of such investment from a merely financial perspective.

To summarize, we achieved our second goal to contribute to the validation of the framework by confirming its usefulness and applicability in the area of eParticipation initiatives as well as by outlining some shortcomings and future research directions.

Matching the guidelines developed for practitioners based on the projects experiences as well as respective literature (Arnold et al. 2017) against the success factors of the framework, it can be said that they are congruent with no contradicting conclusions. Consequently, we can assume that the success factors of eParticipation projects discussed and applied in this research are robust enough to serve for future initiatives in this area.

References

Arnold, R., Girardet, L., Zimmermann, H.-D.: JugendMachtPolitik/Innovative Formen der Partizipation mit neuen Medien von Kindern und Jugendlichen auf Gemeindeebene, Grabs/St. Gallen (2017). http://doi.org/10.13140/RG.2.2.28369.53604/1

Arnstein, S.R.: A ladder of citizen participation. J. Am. Inst. Planners 35(4), 216–224 (1969). https://doi.org/10.1080/01944366908977225

Carron-Arthur, B., Cunningham, J.A., Griffiths, K.M.: Describing the distribution of engagement in an Internet support group by post frequency: a comparison of the 90-9-1 Principle and Zipf's Law. Internet Interv. **1**(4), 165–168 (2014). https://doi.org/10.1016/J.INVENT.2014. 09.003

Macintosh, A., Whyte, A.: Towards an evaluation framework for eParticipation. Transforming Gov.: People, Process Policy **2**(1), 16–30 (2008). https://doi.org/10.1108/175061608108 62928

Panopoulou, E., Tambouris, E., Tarabanis, K.: Success factors in designing eParticipation initiatives. Inf. Org. **24**(4), 195–213 (2014). http://www.sciencedirect.com/science/article/pii/ S147177271400027X

Rexhepi, A., Filiposka, S., Trajkovik, V.: Youth e-participation as a pillar of sustainable societies. J. Clean. Prod. **174**, 114–122 (2018). https://doi.org/10.1016/J.JCLEPRO.2017.10. 327

Teran, L., Drobnjak, A.: An evaluation framework for eParticipation: the VAAs case study. Int. J. Soc., Hum. Sci. Eng. **7**(73) (2013). https://waset.org/publications/5553/an-evaluation-framework-for-participation-the-vaas-case-study

United Nations Department of Economic and Social Affairs (UNDESA): Measuring and Evaluating e-Participation (METEP): Assessment of Readiness at the Country Level (2013). http://workspace.unpan.org/sites/Internet/Documents/METEPframework_18Jul_MOSTLAT ESTVersion.pdf

von Lucke, J., Herzberg, J., Kluge, U., vom Brocke, J., Müller, O., Zimmermann, H.-D.: Open Societal Innovation – The Alemannic Definition (2012). https://esocietybodensee2020. wordpress.com/publikationen/open-societal-innovation-the-alemannic-definition/

Zimmermann, H.-D.: Youth e-participation: lessons learned from an ongoing project in Switzerland. In: Versendaal, J., Kittl, C., Pucihar, A., Mirjana, K.B. (eds.) Proceedings of the 29th Bled eConference, Bled, pp. 588–596 (2016). http://aisel.aisnet.org/bled2016/5

E-Participation Social Effectiveness: Case of "Our Petersburg" Portal

Lyudmila Vidiasova[✉] and Iaroslava Tensina

ITMO University, Saint Petersburg, Russia
bershadskaya.lyudmila@gmail.com,
tensina.yaroslava@mail.ru

Abstract. The issues of involving citizens in political management are becoming more and more relevant all over the world. Many different platforms are being created, where residents can express their ideas, proposals, complaints and leave their voices. From a scientific point of view, the issue of estimating the effects that these platforms result in remains unresolved. The paper presents the results of developing a methodology for assessing the social effectiveness of e-participation portals. In the paper results of its' approbation for social effectiveness estimation of a portal for urban problems in Petersburg (Russia) are demonstrated. According to collected data, the portal "Our Petersburg" referred to the medium level of social effectiveness development. The portal has demonstrated a great progress in organizational dimension indicators and less success in technical and socio-economic ones.

Keywords: E-Participation · Social effectiveness · Citizens' engagement · Urban development · Saint Petersburg

1 Introduction

The issues of involving citizens in political management are becoming more and more relevant all over the world. Many different platforms are being created, where residents can express their ideas, proposals, complaints and leave their voices. However, the issue of social effects assessment stands almost untouched. In the scientific community and in the political arena there are discussions about new opportunities for a deliberal democracy based on the use of advanced platforms. However, it becomes obvious that the creation of platforms is not a panacea for the effective citizens' involvement in governance. In his book, Stephen Coleman emphasizes the importance of four types of "democratic capabilities people need if they are to be free to act confidently and efficaciously within the seriously flawed political democracies" [1, p. 89]. This justification suggests that there are certain parameters and conditions for achieving effective e- participation.

In this paper, the authors propose an approach to assessing e-participation portals social effectiveness, which makes it possible to evaluate this phenomenon in three dimensions: organizational, technological and social. The paper is structured as follows. First, it provides a literature review on e-participation assessment, effectiveness and efficacy categories and their indicators. Second, it outlines the methodology

A. Chugunov et al. (Eds.): EGOSE 2018, CCIS 947, pp. 308–318, 2019.
https://doi.org/10.1007/978-3-030-13283-5_23

developed for e-participation social effectiveness assessment, the system of indicators and data collection tools. The next section provides the results of "Our Petersburg" portal assessment. These are followed by a discussion of findings and conclusions.

2 Literature Review

The scientific background is full of examples of e-participation research. But regardless of whether a new methodology is being considered for conducting a comparative analysis [2–4], or a separate case-study is being conducted [5], researchers agree that this phenomenon is complex and ambiguous.

In the international practice presented, there is a separation of different types of e-participation tools. In the traditional UN methodology [3] e-information, e-consultation and e-decision-making are detected. In the concept of Terán and Drobnjak [6] these types expand into 5 level: eInforming, eConsulting, eDiscussion, eParticipation, eEmpowerement. According to the main research purpose of the current paper, the authors consider e-decision-making tools as the most preferred for evaluate the social effects.

A classic study of Macintosh underlines "evaluating e-participation as making sense of what has or has not been achieved, understanding how to assess the benefits and the impacts of applying technology to the democratic decision-making processes" [7]. Perez-Espes et al. [8] stressed the need to build new models of e-participation with ability to respond to the new challenges (transparency, participation, control etc.). The authors suggested the following criteria for participation efficacy evaluation: motivation, information, communication, transparency, quality.

Researchers determine the following building blocks being critical for e-participation development: e-participation portal, transparency features, engagement features, collaboration features, open government data features, targeting specific groups [9]. Much attention in scientific work is paid to the role of institutional factors: the lack of political will and commitment of decision-makers is a serious obstacle to the effective implementation of the e-government reform program [10–12]. Also, this political background could not act without the proper legislation [13] and legitimation [14] as well.

Agbabiaka underlines the necessity to collect citizens' estimates and perceptions of new services, as well as the emerging public values [15]. Zolotov agrees that "the influence of competence, meaning and habit of continuing the intention led to a significant value, being the habit of the strongest predictor" [16].

Technological side also matters. Literature review found out the specific attention to usage level, usability [17], multichannel accessibility [18] and their influence on the portals' popularity and trust in e-participation mechanisms [19]. Researchers also note transparency as one of the key elements of effective electronic participation [20].

As research shows, social media also form the environment for uniting supporters on specific issues. They can unite individual social groups, form real communities [21]. The actions of these communities can be a serious support for the promotion of petitions and ideas on e-participation portals, and in turn influence their effectiveness [22].

The literature review conducted have demonstrated researchers' attention to the e-participation evaluation at the angle of the technological, organizational and social dimension. In the works presented there are attempts to systematize indicator systems, but a complex view does not reach maximum completeness. This paper suggests a methodology attempting to combine these dimensions to assess e-participation social effectiveness.

3 Research Design

In this research we applied several methods using a multi-method approach that could focus on e-participation effectiveness as a complex phenomenon and benefit form the use of multiple disciplines [23]. In the methodology we consider "e-participation as a set of methods and tools that ensure electronic interaction between citizens and authorities in order to consider the citizens' opinion in terms of decision making at state and municipal level" [24]. From this point of view, its social effectiveness is the ability to realize publicly stated goals, achieve results that meet the needs of the population and are accessible to those who are interested in them.

In the research we paid attention to those e-participation tools that lead to decision-making. Based on this, the evaluation of social effectiveness was presented as a measurement of the implementation of a complete decision-making cycle, consisting of 5 stages [25]. The literature review revealed the need to pay attention to three dimensions of e-participation effects. Accordingly, the proposed methodology included indicators for three dimensions for each stage. The sequence of stages is determined by the following logic. At "Agenda setting" the prerequisites for citizens' contribution collection is organized. The "Policy preparation" stage means aggregation of different opinions and voices as well as involvement of new users. The layout of citizens' ideas and their transfer to the responsible authorities occurs at the third stage. The "Policy execution" considers authorities' response on citizens' applications, voting etc., implementation of decisions adopted. And, finally, "Policy monitoring" shows the decisions' implementation and citizens' feedback on the outcomes. The methodology developed is schematically presented in Fig. 1.

The three dimensions on Fig. 1. present a complex of organizational, technical and socio- variables suitable to evaluate the availability, effects and outcomes of e-participation. The organizational dimension shows the scale of legitimation, political values creation, power and deliberation. The technological dimension addresses the issues of portals' operation and functionality. Finally, social dimension indicates the effectiveness of the submitted applications/initiatives/petitions, as well public values development.

The methodology developed counts 27 indicators for e-participation social effectiveness assessment. According to the methodology, for each indicator the estimated portal can receive from 0 to 1 points. Table 1 presents the set of indicators for the assessment.

Fig. 1. Methodology for assessment e-participation social effectiveness

In the survey the following research methods were applied:

- Automated monitoring of e-participation portals via the information system created by the authors;
- Automated research of network communities formed around e-participation portals;
- Official statistic collection (ICT indicators);
- Keyword search;
- Web analytics (measurement the presence of specific indicators on the portal);
- Expert evaluation (measurement of the qualitative indicators).

The majority of indicators were collected with the use of the automated monitoring of e-participation portals system. The system was created in 2014 by the authors and colleagues from the ITMO University. The system allows to collect data on citizens' petitions and claims published at the specific portal in a real time. For each portal a special programming module is created. For the research task, a specialized module for data collection and processing was designed for the "Our Petersburg" portal.

An automated research of network communities formed around e-participation portals was conducted with the use of a web-crawler configured to collect data on the relationships between users of communities. The web-crawler collected data on pairs of communications between users in the community and recorded them in the database.

All indicators presented were reduced to a single scale from 0 to 1. To calculate the level of social effectiveness for each portal, the integral estimates for each dimension were calculated with the final indicator of social effectiveness being as an integral measure of the three dimensions (additive function).

The evaluation of the *dimension* is defined as the ratio of the sum of the indicators in stage n to the maximum possible number of indicators for stage n, multiplied by 100%. In its turn, the score for each *stage* is calculated as the arithmetic sum of the measurement estimates with a 1/3 coefficient for each dimension.

As an integral evaluation (eParticipation social effectiveness), the arithmetic sum of estimates of parameters is taken (taking into account coefficient k for each stage).

Table 1. System of indicators for assessing e-participation portals' social effectiveness

Stage	Dimension	Indicators	Social effects
1 Agenda setting	Organizational	Legitimacy, regulation framework	Openness Citizens' awareness with participation opportunities
	Technological	Internet usage Easy search of the portal	
	Social	Registration in ESIA (single inf.system for the Russian citizens) Information sharing about the portal	
2 Policy preparation	Organizational	Possibilities of deliberation	Active citizens' involvement Sense of community
	Technological	Users' support at all stages Opportunities for participation people with disabilities Multichannel participation Links with other tools and resources	
	Social	Citizens' activity in publications Growth of network activity Nature of citizens' contribution	
3 Inclusion of citizens' contribution in decision	Organizational	Officials' responsibility for a response Obligation to the inform public on citizens' contribution analysis	Democratic values generation
	Technological	Usability and interface Personal data security	
	Social	Voting activity Additional tools for citizens' opinions collection	
4 Policy execution	Organizational	Problem solving/petition's support	Justice and fairness of decision-making Transparency
	Technological	Publication of review's history	
	Social	Users' satisfaction	
5 Policy monitoring	Organizational	Transparency of results and G2C interaction Confirmation of influence on political decisions	Trust in government Citizens' satisfaction
	Technological	Ranking of citizens and their input Access to archiving	
	Social	Time saving for G2C interaction	

The coefficients for calculating the final indicator are set for each stage: 0.1 – for the first stage, 0.2 – for the 2 and 3 stages, 0.25 – for the 4 and 5 stages.

The result obtained on a scale from 0 to 100% was transferred to the averaged 5-level scale indicating a "Very Low" level at 0–24, 9%, "Low" level at 25–49, 9%, "Medium" level at 50–69, 9%, "High" level at 70–89, 9%, and finally "Very high" level at 90–100%. As the results of social effectiveness assessment, the portal could find its' place at the appropriate level according to achieved points. The separation into levels could provide a background for a meaningful comparison between different portals.

4   Findings

The portal "Our Petersburg" (https://gorod.gov.spb.ru/) was selected for social effectiveness assessment. This portal was developed in 2014 for collecting citizens' proposals and suggestion for urban issues. In order to submit a request, the user must register through the Public Services Portal or by using a personal account in the social network VKontakte. The portal provides the following opportunities for citizens' e-participation in urban governance issues:

- to post messages on city problem with photo- detection,
- to follow the problems' solutions,
- to receive information on city urban programs, their activities and results,
- to get access to technical and economic passports of apartment buildings in St. Petersburg and get information about the organizations that serve them,
- to follow rankings of management companies and city services.

Messages sent through the portal "Our Petersburg" must compulsorily receive a response from the authorities in a strictly defined time. The indicators on the portal were assessed using web portal analytics, automated portal monitoring, automated analysis of network communities in social networks, official statistic and expert assessments. For web-analytics the detected indicators were registered in the form of screenshots of the pages on which the sought feature was found. To analyze the portals, a monitoring system for e-participation portals, created at the ITMO University (http://analytics.egov.ifmo.ru), was used. The monitoring system allows real-time downloading of data on submitted initiatives/petitions/appeals and monitoring the collection of votes.

During the research period, the monitoring system collected 75820 messages published on the portal. The most popular categories of citizens' initiatives were landscaping, maintenance of the apartment houses, facade of buildings, violation of the rules for using common property and violation of land legislation (Fig. 2).

The analysis of the number of initiatives demonstrates the citizens' growing interest to the portal for the entire period of its functioning (Fig. 3). Some decrease have been noticed at the period of traditional summer vacation (June–August) or winter national holidays (January) when citizens are involved in celebrations and do not pay much attention to urban issues.

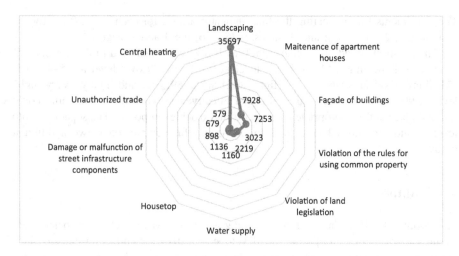

Fig. 2. Number of initiatives on the portal "Our Petersburg" by categories, 2014–2017

The analysis of proposal' statuses demonstrates that the majority of citizens' messages remain satisfied (44%), while the number of non-satisfied decisions remains insignificant (less than 1%). The rest of them were in the process of getting a response or decision-making.

The results of web-analytics show that one of the features of the portal is the availability of special categories for active users. The most active users can receive the special status "Public controller" that gives the opportunity to leave feedback on each appeal, confirming or refuting the solution of the problem. The qualitative analysis of the petitions on the portal demonstrates that only 130 complaints were repeatedly evaluated by a "Public Controller", which is 0.17% of the number of initiatives on the portal.

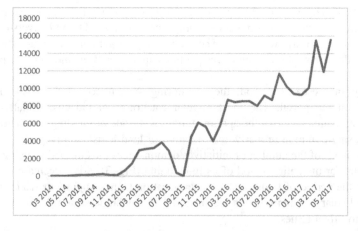

Fig. 3. The number of initiatives on the portal "Our Petersburg", 2014–2017

According to the methodology proposed, the portal "Our Petersburg" got 52.6 out of 100% and demonstrated the medium level of social effectiveness development. Figure 4 presents the results of calculating indicators for the stages of political decision-making. The survey shows that the portal does not provide opportunities for collective discussions on city problems, collecting opinions from citizens. However, we need to take into account the specificity of the portal: detecting a problem and fixing it.

The portal "Our Petersburg" received high scores for all stages, except for the analysis of the contribution of the public (11.4%), where the lowest indicators were obtained in the social dimension. Figure 5 demonstrates the results of dimensional assessment. According to collected data, the great progress has achieved in organizational dimension. The highest indicators were obtained by the indicators of legitimacy, the convenience of resource search, the legally fixed responsibility of the authority, the usability of the portal, the rating of users, and the saving of time spent on interaction with authorities.

The lowest values were obtained by indicators informing users, the possibility of deliberation, providing opportunities for participation of special categories of citizens, the nature of the contribution of citizens, the availability of additional mechanisms for collecting citizens' opinions.

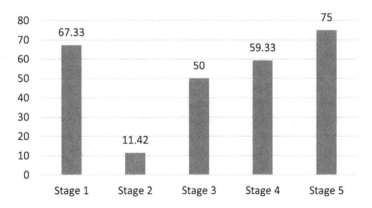

Fig. 4. Scores for "Our Petersburg" social effectiveness assessment, by stages

The analysis of specific indicators allows us to conclude that the portal is mostly effective in terms of the legitimacy of the resource. It provides an opportunity to solve problems in a shorter period of time compare to traditional methods of G2C interactions. In terms of usability, the portal is simple and convenient to use. The process of creating a petition is intuitively understandable and contains successive stages. Nevertheless, the portal doesn't provide an opportunity to contribute to citizens in the discussion of individual petitions as well it's not sufficiently focused on expanding the potential audience of users. Thus, the final value allows to refer the portal to the medium level of social effectiveness.

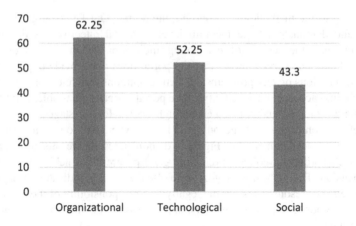

Fig. 5. Scores for "Our Petersburg" social effectiveness assessment, by dimensions

5   Discussion

We compared the results with the data of the city residents survey conducted at the end of 2017 by authors. In the online survey, 421 respondents took part (simple repetitive sampling, 95% accuracy, confidence interval 5%). The survey results showed interesting trends, which were reflected in the use of e-participation portals.

First, the share of inactive citizens is high. According to the study, over a third of residents do not react to problems in the city. According to the research, 22% use electronic portals to solve urban problems. Also 10% call the authorities to report about a problem and 8% use the state telephone service.

Secondly, there is a positive attitude to electronic channels of communication with government representatives among residents. 57% of respondents consider e-portals to be the most effective way to solve problems. Popularization of the portal can increase the number of Public controllers, and, accordingly, citizens' satisfaction from solving problems.

Also, the citizens' survey revealed the prevalence of optimistic people in the city, and 77% of them believed in real influence on political decisions through e-participation portals. Another, positive trend was presented by the readiness of 91% of the respondents to participation in the city management. That is also an indicator of an active community development being able to produce more effectiveness to e-participation activities.

6   Conclusion

The results of the study showed the operability of the presented methodology. Using open access data (portals, official statistics, social networks), data were obtained that characterize the social effectiveness of the portal for solving urban problems. Based on the research data, we consider socio-economic indicators as the most significant to be developed at the studied portal.

According to the results of the conducted research accompanied with the citizens' opinion poll, it can be concluded that the evaluated portal has the potential for increasing the social effectiveness by attracting new users to a portal from a group of active, non-indifferent citizens. The presented methodology should be tested on various types of portals, including portals of electronic petitions, public discussion etc., in order to fully evaluate the relevance of the indicators for each group of portals presented.

Further research steps could be addressed to develop the proposed methodology for difference e-participation portals types counting e-petitions, online deliberation platforms, urban issues portals, crowdsourcing etc. Each of these types could provide specific data sets that allow to measure some other sides of social effectiveness.

Acknowledgements. This work was conducted with the support of RFBR grant No. 16-36-60035, "The research of social efficiency of e-participation portals in Russia".

References

1. Coleman, S.: Can the Internet Strengthen Democracy?. Polity Press, UK (2017)
2. Measuring and Evaluating e-Participation (METEP): Assessment of Readiness at the Country Level. UNDESA Working Paper (2013). http://workspace.unpan.org/sites/Internet/Documents/METEP%20framework_18%20Jul_MOST%20LATEST%20Version.pdf
3. UN E-Government Survey (2016). https://publicadministration.un.org/egovkb/en-us/reports/un-e-government-survey-2016
4. Zheng, Y.: The impact of E-participation on corruption: a cross-country analysis. Int. Rev. Public Adm. **21**(2), 91–103 (2016). https://doi.org/10.1080/12294659.2016.1186457
5. Schroeter, R., Scheel, O., Renn, O., Schweizer, P.: Testing the value of public participation in Germany: theory, operationalization and a case study on the evaluation of participation. Energy Res. Soc. Sci. **13**, 116–125 (2015). https://doi.org/10.1016/j.erss.2015.12.013
6. Terán, L., Drobnjak, A.: An evaluation framework for eParticipation: the VAAs case study. Int. Scholary Sci. Res. Innov. **7**(1), 77–85 (2013)
7. Macintosh, A., Whyte, A.: Towards an evaluation framework for e-Participation. Transforming Gov. People Process Policy **2**(1), 16–30 (2008). https://doi.org/10.1108/17506160810862928
8. Perez-Espes, C., Wimmer, M., Jimenez, J.M.M.: A framework for evaluating the impact of E-participation experiences. Innov. Public Sect. **21**, 20–29 (2014). https://doi.org/10.3233/978-1-61499-429-9-20
9. Millard, J., Thomasen, L., Pastrovic, G., Cvetkovic, B.: A roadmap for e-participation and open government: empirical evidence from Western Balkans. In: Proceedings of the ICEGOV 2018 (2018, in press)
10. Chugunov, A.V., Kabanov, Y., Misnikov, Y.: Citizens versus the government or citizens with the government: a tale of two e-participation portals in one city - a case study of St. Petersburg, Russia. In: ACM International Conference Proceeding Series, Part F128003, pp. 70–77. ACM (2017)
11. Raoelson, H., Rakotonirina, V.: E-government: factor of public administration efficiency and effectiveness. Case of the ministry of higher education and scientific research in Madagascar. In: Proceedings of the ICEGOV 2018 (2018, in Press)

12. Vidiasova, L., Dawes, S.S.: The influence of institutional factors on e-governance development and performance: an exploration in the Russian Federation. Inf. Polity **22**(4), 267–289 (2017). https://doi.org/10.3233/IP-170416
13. Gil-Garcia, J.R., Pardo, T.A., Sutherland, M.K.: Information sharing in the regulatory context: revisiting the concepts of cross-boundary information sharing. In: ACM International Conference Proceeding Series, 01–03 March 2016, pp. 346–349. ACM (2016)
14. Civil Participation in Decision-making Processes: An overview of standards and practices in Council of European Member States. European Center for Not-for-profit Law. European Center for Not-for-profit Law (2016)
15. Agbabiaka, O.: The public value creation of e-Government: an Empirical study from citizen perspective. In: Proceedings of the ICEGOV 2018 (2018, in Press)
16. Zolotov, M.N., Oliveira, T., Casteleyn, S.: Continued intention to use online participatory budgeting: the effect of empowerment and habit. In: Proceedings of the ICEGOV 2018 (2018, in press)
17. Hagen, L., Harrison, T.M., Uzuner, Ö., May, W., Fake, T., Katragadda, S.: E-petition popularity: do linguistic and semantic factors matter? Gov. Inf. Q. **33**(4), 783–795 (2016). https://doi.org/10.1016/j.giq.2016.07.006
18. Kawaljeet, K.K., Amizan, O., Utyasankar, S.: Enabling multichannel participation through ICT adaptation. Int. J. Electron. Gov. Res. **13**, 66–80 (2017). https://doi.org/10.4018/IJEGR.2017040104
19. Jho, W., Song, K.: Institutional and technological determinants of civil e-Participation: Solo or duet? Gov. Inf. Q. **32**, 488–495 (2015). https://doi.org/10.1016/j.giq.2015.09.003
20. Reggi, L., Dawes, S.: Open government data ecosystems: linking transparency for innovation with transparency for participation and accountability. In: Scholl, H., et al. (eds.) EGOV 2016. LNCS (LNAI, LNB), vol. 9820, pp. 74–86. Springer, Heidelberg (2016). https://doi.org/10.1007/978-3-319-44421-5_6
21. Harrison, T.M., et al.: E-Petitioning and online media: the case of #bringbackourgirls. In: ACM International Conference Proceeding Series, Part F128275, pp. 11–20. ACM (2017)
22. Picazo-Vela, S., et al.: The role of social media sites on social movements against policy changes. In: ACM International Conference Proceeding Series, Part F128275, pp. 588–589. ACM (2017)
23. Gil-Garcia, R., Pardo, T.: Multi-method approaches to digital government research: value lessons and implementation challenges. In: Proceedings of 39th Annual Hawaii International Conference on System Sciences (HICSS-39) (2006)
24. Vidiasova, L., Tensina, I., Bershadskaya, E.: Social efficiency of E-participation portals in Russia: assessment methodology. In: Alexandrov, D.A., Boukhanovsky, A.V., Chugunov, A.V., Kabanov, Y. (eds.) DTGS 2018. CCIS, vol. 858, pp. 51–62. Springer, Heidelberg (2018). https://doi.org/10.1007/978-3-030-02843-5_5
25. Van Dijk, J.A.G.M.: Participation in policy making. Study of social impact of ICT (CPP № 55 A- SMART №2007/0068). Topic Report, pp. 32–72 (2010)

Challenges of E-Participation: Can the Opinions of Netizens Represent and Affect Mass Opinions?

Chungpin Lee[✉]

Department of Public Administration and Policy, National Taipei University,
New Taipei City, Taiwan
cplee@gm.ntpu.edu.tw

Abstract. This paper aims to understand the representativeness of online public opinion and the influence of online public-issue discussions on mass opinion. By analyzing three survey datasets from Taiwan, the findings show that online civic participants are not representative of the general population; moreover, online discussions of public issues do not directly affect general public opinion. According to these findings, this paper recommends that online public opinions are used with caution as they are not necessarily representative of general public opinion.

Keywords: Sentiment analysis · Public opinion poll · E-participation · Representativeness

1 Introduction

With the Internet having become an integral part of people's daily lives, governments at various levels have used it as a means to understand people's needs in order to tailor services to meet those needs. For this purpose, various tools have been employed, including online polls and the analysis of the sentiments of netizens. Technology optimists even believe such online methods will substitute traditional offline public opinion surveys, as they are more effective in ascertaining the up-to-date opinions of the majority of the population. These methods have not only affected public policy decision, but also facilitated e-democracy development. In Taiwan, the media often cites online opinions when criticizing public policies; moreover, it is not uncommon for the government to change its policy decision in response to online criticisms or the outcomes of online polls. In other words, online opinions have influenced the direction of public policies.[1]

---

[1] There are several examples that illustrate this; for instance, in June 2018, the Taiwanese government made "a big U turn regarding its childcare policy" due to a citizen proposal being endorsed by "thousands of netizens" (https://www.thenewslens.com/article/98742, visited on 2018/7/12). In addition, in 2016, "four thousand people left angry messages on Hualien County governor Shih's Facebook homepage"; this resulted in the governor changing his previous decision to calling off school and work in Hualien due to the typhoon (http://www.peoplenews.tw/news/2dbd589c-2958-450e-a1b4-0964c42ad959, visited 2018/7/12).

© Springer Nature Switzerland AG 2019
A. Chugunov et al. (Eds.): EGOSE 2018, CCIS 947, pp. 319–333, 2019.
https://doi.org/10.1007/978-3-030-13283-5_24

Does such a situation represent the maturity of online democratic governance or the creation of chaos much like opening up Pandora's box? To date, what role have online opinions played? What is the nature of online opinions? How should we respond to such opinions? The answers to these questions are diverse in academia, with some scholars believing that the collection and analysis of online opinions are conducive to obtaining a better understanding of the views of the general population; they even believe that such opinions are helpful in forecasting election outcomes. It is a low-cost and efficient method that has great potential as both a substitute and supplement for traditional polling (e.g., O'Connor et al. 2010; DiGrazia et al. 2013; Bermingham and Smeaton 2011; Beauchamp 2017; Ceron et al. 2014). However, other scholars doubt the credibility and effectiveness of the online method, due to the existence of multiple factors causing unpredictable bias (e.g., Gayo-Avello 2011, 2013; Mislove et al. 2011).

This paper aims to answer the following three questions by examining the empirical data on the Internet and public policies in Taiwan: (1) Along with the popularity of the Internet, are there more and more online political participants? Have they become increasingly representative of the opinions of the general population? If the answers are positive, it will be much more feasible and legitimate for online opinions (e.g., online sentiment analysis, online polls, and messages received on a politician's Facebook page) to substitute traditional off-line public-opinion polls (e.g., telephone surveys). (2) Will the positive or negative sentiment of online texts affect mass public opinion? (3) Do online opinions affect the attitude of individuals towards public policies? The answers to these questions will affect the manner in which we utilize online opinions, namely, whether we use them as key references in decision making or treat them as being less significant in the process.

In the second section, the paper will review the results of existing studies on the relationship between online opinions and public opinions uncovered by traditional polls. This will be followed by an explanation of the data analysis in the third section and an analysis of the results and discussion in the last two sections.

2 The Relationships Between Opinions of Netizens and Mass Public Opinions: Optimists and Pessimists

An increasingly important question in the public administration and political science fields is whether opinions obtained in the virtual world, including social media activity and netizens' emotions (sentiment analysis), can be used to assess offline public opinion. The current research findings regarding this issue have been vigorously debated.

The optimists argue that affordable and ubiquitous online mechanisms have great potential to provide new means for the flow of ideas, the formation of opinions, and the exchange of ideas among citizens; they also argue that it is a valuable real-time source for public managers to measure public attitudes. DiGrazia et al. (2013) used American elections as a case study to show that there was a statistically significant association between the tweets that mentioned a candidate and the votes that the candidate subsequently received. The political behavior of American citizens could be extracted and predicted from social media (Beauchamp 2017; O'Connor et al. 2010). In Germany,

Tumasjan et al. (2011) used a sentiment analysis of over 100,000 messages containing political issues and found, similarly, that the tweets' sentiment corresponded closely to voters' political preferences. Bermingham and Smeaton (2011) used an Irish general election as a case study and Ceron et al. (2014) used evidence from elections held in Italy and France. All of them found a similar result. The sentiment analyses are predictive, demonstrating a significant correlation between social media and the results of traditional mass surveys. Ceron et al. (2015) analyzed data from the USA and Italy and concluded that Twitter analysis has the ability to "nowcast" as well as to forecast electoral results.

Given that the e-civilian is considered to be a highly biased/non-uniform group of the general population, how can these aforementioned findings be justified? According to Ceron et al. (2015), this can happen only if we accept the logic that Internet users act like opinion makers/elites who are able to influence the preferences of a wider audience under the broader media. In this light, social media discussions are able to reproduce all public opinions. According to Prichard et al. (2015), conducting online discussion research presents low-level risks in terms of human research ethics, principally because the information derived is unlikely to lead to the identification of each individual. People are more willing to speak out online; therefore, online sentiment analysis becomes a useful new tool for assessing and knowing public opinion.

However, not all studies harbor such optimism. For example, since online users are a very biased sample, Gayo-Avello (2011) warned that social media may become another "Literary Digest" poll case. Mislove et al. (2011) found that social media users are significantly overrepresented by a limited group of the general population, are predominantly male, and represent a highly non-random sample of the overall race/ethnicity distribution. Regarding the effect of online political deliberation, Conover et al. (2011) demonstrated that the network of political retweets exhibits a highly segregated partisan structure with extremely limited connectivity between left- and right-leaning users. In other words, there is a political polarization trend in the social media world. This is not what people hope to see from the virtual world.

By collecting a whole body of research regarding electoral prediction from Twitter data and conducting a meta-analysis, Gayo-Avello (2013) concluded that the research findings are overly optimistic. Current research has not yet provided strong evidence to support the notion that the analysis of online activities can replace traditional polls. Using online text data to correlate with or to predict electoral results is still problematic as core problems are not addressed. Most existing works have not addressed the sampling bias; they have simply applied data mining algorithms without an understanding of the representativeness of the user population.

In sum, more research is required in order to understand the online world. In particular, the issues listed below cannot be ignored (Gayo-Avello 2011): (1) big-data fallacy: large sums of data do not make such collections statistically representative samples of the overall population; (2) demographic bias; (3) naïve sentiment analysis: researchers should avoid noisy instruments and always check whether they are using a random classifier; (4) silence speaks volumes; (5) (a few) past positive results do not guarantee generalization. Researchers should always be aware of the file-drawer effect.

3 Data

To add more evidence-based information, this paper aims to understand the relationship between netizens' political opinion and mass opinion by answering the following three questions: (1) Have online political participants become more and more representative of the general population? (2) Will public opinion presented online affect mass opinion in general? (3) Do online opinions affect the attitudes of individuals towards public policies? Datasets from three studies are used in answering the three aforementioned questions:

A. Data for question one: care for the underprivileged and the provision of fair digital opportunities have been a focus of government efforts in constructing the information and communications infrastructure and improving the availability of government services. Since 2004, the Taiwanese government has implemented many policies in order to ensure fair digital opportunities in various regions, groups, and industries. Such policies include the "Narrowing Digital Divide Plan," "Creating Fair Digital Opportunities Plan," "Digital Outreach Project," and "Universal Digital Application Project for Remote Areas." In order to obtain a comprehensive understanding of the digital development status in Taiwan, the National Development Council has been conducting annual surveys on individual/household digital opportunity (SDO) since 2004. This annual survey features phone interviews with Taiwanese citizens aged 12 or older, selected randomly via the Computer-Assisted Telephone Interviewing System (CATI). The sample sizes and sampling errors are listed below (Table 1).

B. Data for question two: the Taiwan E-Governance Research Center has been conducting an annual longitudinal study, named "Public Value in E-Governance (PVEG)," since 2013. The 2017 survey was conducted from September 1 (Friday) through September 30 (Saturday) via phone interviews with Taiwanese citizens aged 15 and above that were randomly selected. There were 7,530 valid samples, with the sampling error being ±1.15% at 95% confidence level. Two policy-related questions were included in the survey to measure mass opinion: "Do you support the Labor Standards Act?" and "Do you agree with the Railway Policy recently passed by the Legislative Yuan?" In addition to the phone survey, the 2017 PVEG project also collected online textual data on these two policy issues (the Labor Standards Act and the Railway Policy) for the online sentiment analysis during the same time frame. These textual data were analyzed and compared with the results from the phone survey.

C. Data for question three: the 2016, or the fourth, PVEG project with a longitudinal (panel) design focused on two policy issues (the legalization of same-sex marriage and the licensing of the Uber operation). It examined the influence of the online world on changing public opinion (differences in attitude between Time-1 and Time-2) (Table 2).

Table 1. Results of Taiwan's annual individual/household digital opportunity survey

Year	Sample size	Sampling errors	Internet user (%)	Mobile internet user (%)
2004	14,120	±0.83%	61.1	–
2005	26,622	±0.6%	62.7	–
2006	26,702	±0.6%	64.4	–
2007	15,007	±0.8%	65.6	–
2008	16,131	±0.8%	68.5	–
2009	16,133	±0.8%	67.6	41.9
2010	16,008	±0.8%	70.9	53.0
2011	13,272	±0.9%	72.0	70.4
2012	13,257	±0.9%	73.0	77.3
2013	3,079	±1.8%	76.3	76.6
2014	13,262	±0.9%	78.0	91.5
2015	8,493	±0.9%	78.0	90.2
2016	23,465	±0.6%	79.7	91.7
2017	9,337	±1.0%	82.3	97.4

Table 2. Design and results of the 2016 PVEG project

Method \ Time	Time-1 (2016/July)	Time-2 (2016/August)	Population	Questionnaire
House-hold phone survey	Successful samples: 1,300	Panel samples: 382	Citizens aged 15 or above throughout Taiwan	1. Do you agree with 「A」? 2. What are the major sources of information influencing your view on the issue (approval or disapproval), be they TV, radio broadcasts, newspapers, online news, online discussions, friends, own judgment, or others? 3. Have you recently partaken in any online discussions on issue A or viewed any online discussions? Note: "A" in the questionnaire is one of two policies.
Mobile phone survey	Successful samples: 1,310	Panel samples: 391		

4   Findings: What Is the Role Played by Online Opinions?

The core objective of this paper lies in understanding netizens' opinions on public issues, including their representativeness for and relationship with mass public opinions. Answers to the three questions with empirical data follow.

4.1   Are Online Political Participants Representative of Overall Population?

The first question addresses the representativeness of online participants with regards to public issues. Theoretically, with Internet access having become ever more popular, every individual is likely to become a netizen. This means that the number of netizens has the potential to equal that of the population; consequently, this may augment the representativeness of online opinions. However, does Internet access undeniably lead to online public participation? Or is online participation in public issues confined to a specific group of people?

This paper analyzed data from the annual SDO survey for seven years (2008, 2010, 2012–2016), out of a total of 12 years. The studied questionnaires contained a common question: "Did you express opinions online on current politics, social events, or public policies?" The paper extracted "online civic participants" (those with a "yes" answer to this question) from valid samples as sub-samples and then compared their attributes (gender, age, education) with those of general citizens.

The comparison found that males continually have a higher share in the makeup of online civic participants, with the minimum share standing at 57% in the 2015 survey. That is seven percent higher than the minimum share standing in the general population, underscoring a higher male participation (Fig. 1).

In order to analyze the representativeness of every age group, the paper compared the distribution of the shares of online political participants in various age groups with the distribution of shares of corresponding age groups in the population. In cases where the value is >0, online civic participants in the age group are seen as over-representative; in cases where the value is <0, they are seen as under-representative; when the value equals 0, their online representativeness is the same as it is in the general population.

Data showed (Fig. 2) that between 2008 and 2016, the share of online civic participants in the age group of 20–40 was invariably higher than the corresponding share in the general population. In addition, the share of online civic participants aged 61 and older was lower than the corresponding share in the general population, underscoring its under-representativeness, while online civic participants in the age groups of 12–20 and 41–60 were over-representative in some years but under-representative in others. It is clear that the popularity of the Internet has yet to render online civic participants as being representative of the general population.

Using the same analysis, the paper found (Fig. 3) that online civic participants with a college or higher education were invariably over-representative in contrast with those with a senior high school or lower education who were under-representative.

In sum, regarding question one, the paper concludes that despite the increasing popularity of the Internet and the gradual formation of a broader Internet-access

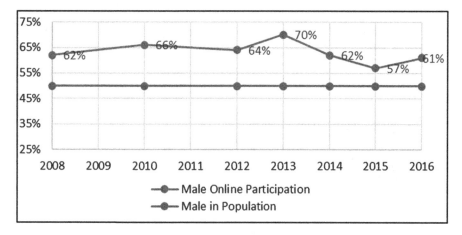

Fig. 1. The representativeness of online civic participants—in relation to males

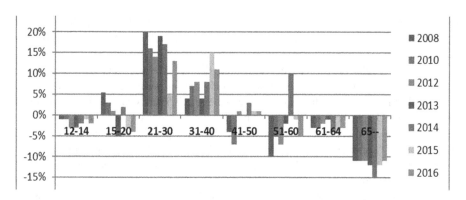

Fig. 2. The representativeness of online civic participants–age

environment in Taiwan, the distribution of people expressing opinions on public issues online is still uneven in comparison to that of the general population. Hence, online civic participants are a group with insufficient representativeness for the general population.

4.2 Correlation Between Online Sentiment and Public Opinion: An Aggregate Level Analysis

In the wake of the thriving development of the Internet in recent years, many studies have asserted that with online opinions becoming ever "louder" and "influential," the general public, especially the silent majority, will inevitably be influenced by their opinions. As a result, the sentiment analysis of online discussions and posts has

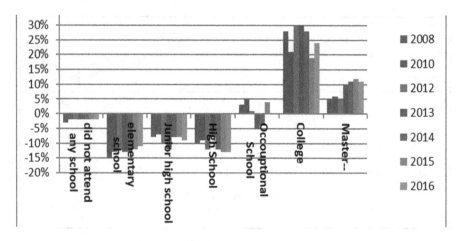

Fig. 3. The representativeness of online civic participants–education level

received higher regard in the field of e-democracy; this is due to the belief that it not only facilitates the fast grasp of public opinion but can also forecast or even manipulate public opinion.

This paper subsequently used the second dataset to verify the narrative of the relationship between online opinions and public opinion in the general population. To begin with, the paper split the valid samples from the 7,530 Taiwanese interviewees of the 2017 PVEG survey into 29 sub-sample groups on a daily basis during the survey period (2–20 September 2017). The shares between the pros and cons in relation to the two policies—"Labor Act" and "Railway Policy"—in the sub-sample groups were then calculated. The results of the phone polls (Figs. 4 and 5) showed a steady trend, with the share of the interviewees supporting the legal revision of the Labor Act policy standing at around 30% throughout the entire period, except on September 3rd, when the supporting rate reached nearly 50%. Regarding the Railway Policy, results of the

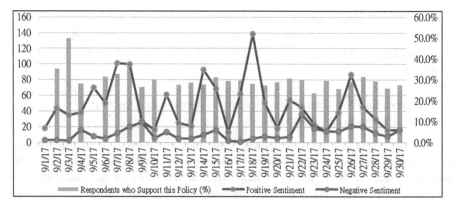

Fig. 4. Trend of sentiment analysis vs. results of daily phone surveys–"Labor Act" policy

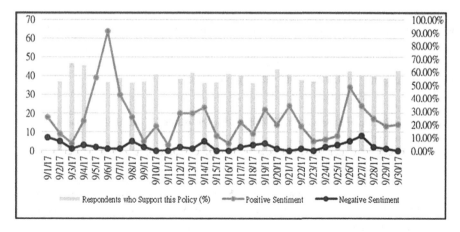

Fig. 5. Trend of sentiment analysis vs. results of daily phone surveys–"Railway" policy

daily polls were also quite steady, with supporters accounting for 50%–60% of the valid samples. In both cases, the outcomes were in sharp contrast with the wildly fluctuating support and opposition of the two policies among netizens, as shown in the results of the sentiment analysis of the online posts.

As shown in the two figures above, the "wild fluctuation" in online sentiment, as opposed to the "steady trend" of public opinion in the general population, is clearly visible. This paper then analyzed the relationship between the poll results of the daily sub-sample groups and their corresponding online sentiment, either positive or negative. The results showed that public opinion in the general population, as shown in the phone poll results for nearly one month (n = 27), had virtually no relationship with the outcome of the analysis of online sentiment on the same day (the D day).

Regarding the casual relationship between online opinion and mass opinion, there are two hypotheses. One asserted that public opinion in the general population is formed first before being posted online (if this is true, we would see a positive correlation between the D− days of the survey results and the online sentiment analysis). The other claimed that online opinions subsequently affect public opinion (if this is true, we would see a positive correlation between the D+ days of the survey results and the online sentiment analysis).

This paper found no clear relationship between the two, in either way, as shown in (1) the comparison of online sentiment on a specific day (D day) with the results of the phone poll during the previous five days (D − 5 day) or the previous day (D − 1 day), and (2) the comparison of online sentiment on a specific day (D day) with the results of the phone poll one day after (D + 1 day) or five days after (D + 5 day).

Among all the analyses, only the positive online sentiment toward the Railway Policy had a significant positive relationship with the phone poll results of public opinion two days before (r = .55) and one day before (r = .661), as well as a significant negative relationship with the phone poll results of public opinion two days after (r = −.429). However, since the majority of the cells of the correlation analysis (Table 3) were insignificant and the direction (positive/negative) of the only three significant relationships was not consistent, there was likely no clear correlation between online opinions and general public opinion. The results thus suggest that they are independent from each other. Of course, in order to obtain a more convincing argument, we still need further studies to determine how the cause-effect transpires between netizens' sentiments and mass public opinion.

Table 3. Pearson correlation coefficients between the results of the daily phone survey and sentiment analysis (n = 27)

Supporter (Positive) in Survey Respondents (%)	Positive Sentiment— Labor Act	Negative Sentiment— Labor Act	Positive Sentiment— Railway Policy	Negative Sentiment— Railway Policy
Mass opinion (D-5 day)	0.093	-0.151	-0.388	-0.054
Mass opinion (D-4 day)	0.037	-0.259	-0.293	-0.026
Mass opinion (D-3 day)	-0.009	-0.205	-0.076	-0.132
Mass opinion (D-2 day)	-0.229	-0.021	.550**	0.016
Mass opinion (D-1 day)	0.048	0.130	.661**	0.276
Mass opinion (D day)	0.363	-0.019	0.245	-0.122
Mass opinion (D+1 day)	0.122	-0.297	-0.281	-0.098
Mass opinion (D+2 day)	0.051	-0.059	-.429*	0.379
Mass opinion (D+3 day)	0.201	-0.219	-0.200	0.372
Mass opinion (D+4 day)	-0.172	-0.027	0.004	-0.221
Mass opinion (D+5 day)	-0.317	-0.151	0.092	-0.049

** $p < 0.01$, * $p < 0.05$.

4.3   Online Public vs. the General Public: An Individual Level Analysis

To answer the last research question, the paper analyzed data from the 2016 PVEG survey. The phone polls were based on both household phones and mobile phones, followed by a tracking poll (T2) of nearly 400 surveyed subjects one month after the completion of the previous poll (T1), in order to detect changes in the attitudes of the samples (change difference = T2 − T1). The data enabled us to ascertain the influence of online discussions on public opinion.

1. Legalization of same-sex marriage.

Regarding the "legalization of same-sex marriage" policy, Tables 4 and 5 show that approximately 14.9% of the subjects (6.8% + 8.1%) of household-phone polls and 14.6% of the subjects (8.4% + 6.2%) of mobile-phone polls changed their attitudes (including positive and negative changes), with their "own judgment" being the largest factor, followed by the influence of "TV". Online opinions had an insignificant influence, as only one subject with an attitude change participated in online discussions on the topic.

Table 4. Cross-table of attitude change, sources of change, and the experience of online public participation–household phone survey

| Difference between T1-T2 | Source of Information Causing Attitude Change | | | | | | | | Joined/Read Online Discussion Forums | | |
	TV	Newspaper	Internet News	Interne Forums	Friends	Own Judgment	Broadcasts	Total	Yes	No	Total
Changed to Agree	6 (28.6)	3 (14.3)	1 (4.8)	1 (4.8)	2 (9.5)	8 (38.1)	0 (0.0)	21 (6.8)	1 (6.7)	14 (93.3)	15 (8.0)
Changed to Disagree	3 (12.0)	1 (4.0)	1 (4.0)	1 (4.0)	1 (4.0)	18 (72.0)	0 (0.0)	25 (8.1)	0 (0.0)	9 (100.0)	9 (4.8)
No Change	43 (16.3)	8 (3.0)	20 (7.6)	11 (4.2)	13 (4.9)	167 (63.3)	2 (0.8)	264 (85.2)	6 (3.7)	158 (96.3)	164 (87.2)

Table 5. Cross-table of attitude change, sources of change, and the experience of online public participation–mobile phone survey

| Difference between T1-T2 | Source of Information Causing Attitude Change | | | | | | | | Joined/Read Online Discussion Forums | | |
	TV	Newspapers	Internet News	Internet Forums	Friends	Own Judgment	Broadcasts	Total	Yes	No	Total
Changed to Agree	5 (16.7)	0 (0.0)	2 (6.7)	4 (13.3)	3 (10.0)	16 (53.3)	0 (0.0)	**30 (8.4)**	1 (3.8)	25 (96.2)	**26 (8.9)**
Changed to Disagree	4 (18.2)	0 (0.0)	1 (4.5)	2 (9.1)	2 (9.1)	12 (54.5)	1 (4.5)	**22 (6.2)**	0 (0.0)	16 (100)	**16 (5.5)**
No Change	39 (12.8)	3 (1.0)	25 (8.2)	33 (10.9)	16 (5.3)	187 (61.5)	1 (0.3)	**304 (85.4)**	7 (2.8)	244 (97.2)	**251 (85.7)**

2. Legalization of Uber.

The share of subjects with attitude change toward the legalization of Uber was higher, reaching 38% in the second-round of household phone polls as shown in Table 6. The most significant factor causing attitude change was "own judgment" (37.5% and 45.57%), followed by "TV" (35.7% and 37.1%). Similarly, online opinions had scant influence, as over 90% of the subjects did not take part in online discussions on the topic. In the T2 follow-up mobile phone poll, as shown in Table 7, 28.1% of the subjects changed their attitudes; again, the two main factors causing the attitude change was "own judgment" and "TV." The influence of the Internet was minimal.

Table 6. Cross-table of attitude change, sources of change, and the experience of online public participation–household phone survey

Difference between T1-T2	Source of Information Causing Attitude Change								Joined/Read Online Discussion Forums		
	TV	Newspapers	Internet News	Internet Forums	Friends	Own Judgment	Broadcasts	Total	Yes	No	Total
Changed to Agree	20 (35.7)	7 (12.5)	4 (7.1)	2 (3.6)	2 (3.6)	21 (37.5)	0 (0.0)	56 **(23.4)**	1 (2.3)	42 (97.7)	43 **(24.7)**
Changed to Disagree	13 (37.1)	1 (2.9)	2 (5.7)	1 (2.9)	1 (2.9)	16 (45.7)	1 (2.9)	35 **(14.6)**	0 (0.0)	19 (100.0)	19 **(10.9)**
No Change	52 (41.9)	8 (6.5)	15 (12.1)	4 (3.2)	4 (3.2)	40 (32.3)	1 (0.8)	124 **(51.9)**	4 (4.1)	94 (95.9)	98 **(56.3)**
Other	10 (41.7)	1 (4.2)	1 (4.2)	0 (0.0)	2 (8.3)	10 (41.7)	0 (0.0)	24 **(10.0)**	0 (0.0)	14 (100.0)	14 **(8.0)**

Table 7. Cross-table of attitude change, sources of change, and the experience of online public participation–mobile phone survey

Difference between T1-T2	Source of Information Causing Attitude Change								Joined/Read Online Discussion Forums		
	TV	Newspapers	Internet News	Internet Forums	Friends	Own Judgment	Broadcasts	Total	Yes	No	Total
Changed to Agree	8 (21.6)	0 (0.0)	4 (10.8)	4 (10.8)	2 (5.4)	19 (51.4)	0 (0.0)	37 **(11.3)**	4 (12.9)	27 (87.1)	31 **(11.1)**
Changed to Disagree	22 (40.0)	1 (1.8)	7 (12.7)	1 (1.8)	2 (3.6)	21 (38.2)	1 (1.8)	55 **(16.8)**	0 (0.0)	42 (100.0)	42 **(15.0)**
No Change	42 (20.1)	2 (1.0)	27 (12.9)	20 (9.6)	14 (6.7)	102 (48.8)	2 (0.8)	124 **(63.9)**	18 (9.6)	169 (90.4)	187 **(66.8)**
Other	7 (26.9)	2 (7.7)	1 (3.8)	0 (0.0)	1 (3.8)	15 (57.7)	0 (0.0)	26 **(8.0)**	0 (0.0)	20 (100.0)	20 **(7.1)**

The results showed that TV is the main source of information affecting citizens' attitudes regarding policy issues. Contrary to the expectation of many, the results showed no evidence regarding the influence of online discussions on public opinion. Traditional media continues to play a critical role on citizens' perceptions of public policy.

5   Discussion and Preliminary Conclusion

Can the opinions of netizens represent and affect mass public opinions? The results of this research suggest that the answer to this question is no. This paper sought to understand whether online public opinion is representative of the general population and to assess the influence of online public policy discussions on mass opinion. To begin with, the paper analyzed past data on online civic participants, finding that despite the widespread use of the Internet in Taiwan, online opinions are quite different from those of the general population. Specifically, the majority of online civic participants are male, educated at the college level or higher, and aged between 21 and 40.

The paper also analyzed the relationship between online sentiments and the outcomes of traditional polls to ascertain whether there is a correlation between online opinions and general public opinion. A significant relationship between the two was not found. In other words, they are independent from each other, as general public opinion on public policies was found to be quite stable and generally not influenced by online sentiments. This finding was affirmed by a follow-up analysis of the PVEG data as a means of ascertaining the influence of online discussion/participation and online news on opinion formation. The results showed that some people would change their stance on some matters of public policy, however, mostly due to their own judgment as a result of collecting relevant information by themselves, or the influence of TV media. The results showed that the Internet only exerted minimal influence.

Despite the results, the author asserts that while online discussion on public issues does not directly affect general public opinion, it still possibly has an impact given that the interaction between traditional media and online opinions has become quite common. Many traditional media in Taiwan cite online information as the basis for their reporting or commentary, which in turn often becomes the basis for online discussions. Therefore, despite the lack of representativeness, online opinions could still influence public opinion via the citation of/been reported by traditional media (Fig. 6). The online discussion on public issues indirectly affects general public opinion. However, this trend is worrisome, given the lack of the representativeness and uniformity of online opinions, and their ability to reach a broad audience via the traditional media. It

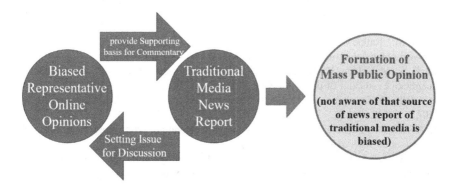

Fig. 6. The interactive effects between online opinions, traditional media, and public opinion

would be detrimental to the development of e-democracy, should online opinions be allowed to augment their influence on public opinion or the decision making of public administrators.

Some scholars have proposed substituting online-opinion analysis for traditional polls on public opinion (please see the section two of this paper). This paper holds a more conservative stance, in view of the independence of online opinions from public opinion. They need the intermediary of traditional media to connect them. However, if traditional media cannot play the role of a neutral, fair and objective third party, it would be impossible to execute the vision of a mechanism capable of collecting real-time public opinion via quality direct civic participation and communication online. Traditional media would still dominate the power to dictate the agenda of public issues. In practice, public administrators should utilize online opinions with caution, avoiding an overreliance on them, as the "loudest voices" online are not necessarily the most authentic or representative of the general population.

This study has a number of limitations, which future studies ought to avoid. For example, different sampling errors may have caused dissimilar correlations due to the varying daily sample sizes pertaining to question two of the analysis. In addition, this study used self-reported assessment of influence sources in PVEG 2016 survey; as a result, this may have caused problems regarding reliability. In the sentiment analysis part, different keyword settings may have produced different results; consequently, a keyword sensitivity analysis is needed to solve this problem.

References

Beauchamp, N.: Predicting and interpolating state-level polls using Twitter textual data. Am. J. Polit. Sci. **61**(2), 490–503 (2017)

Bermingham, A., Smeaton, A.: On using Twitter to monitor political sentiment and predict election results. Paper presented at the Proceedings of the Workshop on Sentiment Analysis where AI meets Psychology (SAAIP 2011) (2011)

Ceron, A., Curini, L., Iacus, S.M., Porro, G.: Every tweet counts? How sentiment analysis of social media can improve our knowledge of citizens' political preferences with an application to Italy and France. New Media Soc. **16**(2), 340–358 (2014)

Ceron, A., Curini, L., Iacus, S.M.: Using sentiment analysis to monitor electoral campaigns: method matters—evidence from the United States and Italy. Soc. Sci. Comput. Rev. **33**(1), 3–20 (2015)

Conover, M., Ratkiewicz, J., Francisco, M.R., Gonçalves, B., Menczer, F., Flammini, A.: Political polarization on Twitter. ICWSM **133**, 89–96 (2011)

DiGrazia, J., McKelvey, K., Bollen, J., Rojas, F.: More tweets, more votes: social media as a quantitative indicator of political behavior. PLoS One **8**(11), e79449 (2013)

Gayo-Avello, D.: Don't turn social media into another 'Literary Digest' poll. Commun. ACM **54**(10), 121–128 (2011)

Gayo-Avello, D.: A meta-analysis of state-of-the-art electoral prediction from Twitter data. Soc. Sci. Comput. Rev. **31**(6), 649–679 (2013)

Mislove, A., Lehmann, S., Ahn, Y.-Y., Onnela, J.-P., Rosenquist, J.N.: Understanding the demographics of Twitter users. In: ICWSM 2011, no. 5, p. 25 (2011)

O'Connor, B., Balasubramanyan, R., Routledge, B.R., Smith, N.A.: From tweets to polls: linking text sentiment to public opinion time series. ICWSM **11**(122–129), 1–2 (2010)

Prichard, J., Watters, P., Krone, T., Spiranovic, C., Cockburn, H.: Social media sentiment analysis: a new empirical tool for assessing public opinion on crime. Curr. Issues Crim. Just. **27**, 217 (2015)

Tumasjan, A., Sprenger, T.O., Sandner, P.G., Welpe, I.M.: Election forecasts with Twitter: how 140 characters reflect the political landscape. Soc. Sci. Comput. Rev. **29**(4), 402–418 (2011)

Exploring the Connection Between the Existence of Local Web Communities and Civic Activity: St. Petersburg Case Study

Sergei Kudinov[(⊠)], Ekaterina Ilina, and Ekaterina Grekhneva

Institute for Design and Urban Studies, ITMO University,
Birzhevaya Liniya 14, 199034 Saint Petersburg, Russia
{sergei.kudinov,ilinaer,eagrekhneva}@corp.ifmo.ru

Abstract. Active development of information and communication technologies
in recent decades has significantly affected modern life in cities. Civil society
has obtained e-participation tools, such as tools for sending electronic appeals on
problems of the urban environment to the authorities to initiate their solving. At
the same time, local web communities have emerged and are now widely spread
due to social media. Within the framework of the research, it was suggested that
the number and concentration of appeals on problems of the urban environment
in individual local areas could be directly related to the existence of active web
communities of residents in these territories. To test this hypothesis, appeals sent
by residents of St. Petersburg for 2 years were analyzed. As a result, zones of
high and low civic activity were identified, and local communities existing
within the boundaries of these zones were studied. The hypothesis regarding the
connection between the existence of local web communities in a certain urban
area and civic activity was confirmed. At the same time, no clear correlation was
identified between the headcount of local web communities and the number of
appeals sent by residents of the territories to which these local communities
belong. Further studies using alternative sources of appeals and new territories
as examples will make it possible to supplement the existing data and to obtain a
more accurate assessment of the relationship of the described factors.

Keywords: Electronic participation · Electronic appeal ·
Local web community · Civil society · Civic activity ·
Urban environment quality

1 Introduction

In recent years, the number of people actively using modern communication technologies has been growing rapidly. Thus, in April 2018, the number of unique mobile
phone users exceeded 5 billion, having increased by 100 million people since April
2017, and the number of Internet users in April 2018 was 4.087 billion, showing an
increase of 276 million people compared to the data for April 2017 [1].

The driver of active development and increasing the availability of mobile and
Internet technologies is their relevance and application in people's everyday life [2, 3,
4]. Modern technology helps people choose the best route when planning trips around

A. Chugunov et al. (Eds.): EGOSE 2018, CCIS 947, pp. 334–347, 2019.
https://doi.org/10.1007/978-3-030-13283-5_25

the city or between cities, remotely receive a wide range of services, for example, make a purchase in an online store; it enables you to work remotely, and find almost any necessary information, including city services and organizations.

Thus, the development and existence of cities in the digital age is accompanied by a close interaction between city residents and urban information systems. In many cities, the Smart City concept is being actively implemented, in which information technology is used to manage cities and to organize and optimize existing urban processes [5]. In particular, Smart City collects data for analyzing and predicting the behavior of residents [6], modeling urban processes, optimizing the use of resources [7].

An important component of the Smart City concept is the mechanisms of citizens' interaction with authorities and urban systems and services through information technology [8]. Such interaction can be based on legal mechanisms established by the state through official or public specialized e-participation services [9]. In recent years, there has been a tendency to integrate urban services for the population into social media, providing convenient opportunities for residents to obtain certain services in a familiar communication environment [10].

At the same time, social media have opened up new opportunities for unification and self-organization of urban communities, including local ones [11]. This helped to increase residents' awareness about events in their neighborhoods, as well as their involvement in urban and local events and activities [12].

One of applications of civic activity is urban environment quality control, which implies detecting disrepair, poor quality of roads and communal services and drawing the attention of the administration to the problems identified. The emergence of such e-participation tools, e.g. sending official electronic appeals to the authorities, gives the population a simple way to initiate the elimination of urban problems. Civic activity of individual residents can be reinforced by involving local communities in problem solving, thus increasing the demand of entire population groups for a high-quality urban environment.

The existence of machine-readable data on electronic appeals on urban environment issues, as well as information on local web communities allows for a quantitative analysis of civic activity and a search for the connection between civic activity and local web communities in the city.

In this article, we explore data on electronic appeals by residents and local online communities in a popular social network, connected with territories and citizens' places of residence, using the city of St. Petersburg, Russia, as an example. Zones of different concentration of residents' appeals are revealed, a comparative analysis of territories with a similar development typology but different concentration of appeals is conducted, and the activity of local communities in these territories is investigated in this article.

2 Background

2.1 The Role of IT in Civil Society Development

Information technology becomes an important part of life in modern states, not only for individuals, but for the entire civil society as a whole. On the one hand, the capabilities of online resources are used in a conservative way – to obtain information and publish news. On the other hand, new ways of using web resources arise: creating web communities, attracting like-minded people, sending official electronic appeals to government bodies, creating electronic petitions, attracting attention to problems of civil society. The above ways enable the civil society to act more effectively [9].

Thus, social media, which were initially created as entertainment, have recently become a full-scale resource for informing, holding discussions, manifesting civic activity and uniting citizens [13]. Social media are a tool that makes it possible to significantly simplify ways of active participation in the public life of a country or a city, such as searching for and sharing information, attracting like-minded people, planning and coordinating actions [14].

For example, in the event of a significant problem affecting the interests of residents of an urban area or a street, one of the first actions is to discuss the problem in social media in the corresponding group if it already exists, or to create a new group whose main goal is to solve this particular problem.

Nowadays e-petition platforms are a popular and effective way to express your civic position [15]. These online resources enable any person to petition the decision-makers for a particular problem, and also facilitate information sharing on the web through automatic sharing in the most popular social networks or forwarding the petition's electronic address directly to any addressee, from a friend to electronic media.

In addition to social media and petition platforms used by civil activists, there are independent tools that simplify the process of applying to the authorities for certain types of violations in the urban environment. One of the first tools of this kind was FixMyStreet which emerged in the UK in 2007. It allows to promptly send appeals on urban issues to the city authorities [16]. Then similar services were created in other countries, one of the most famous is the US-developed SeeClickFix [17].

In addition to the above-mentioned online resources, electronic media also play a significant role in the life of a modern civil society. News services not only report on the events in the city, the country and the world, but also actively share information on the issues raised by citizens, enabling high-speed information transfer and attracting attention of responsible officials and organizations due to significant reach. The popularity of electronic media is growing, while the number of people receiving information from traditional media is decreasing [18].

In Russia, a new round of civic engagement took place in 2011–2012 in the wake of protest actions of urban, regional, and federal levels [19, 20, 21]. This helped socially active population of Russia to acquire modern communication technologies and start using new tools for civic engagement [22]. Social media started to be used to organize and coordinate protest actions. However, along with the event-based use, e-petition platforms, social media, and specialized services began to be used in everyday civic activities not related to protest events.

2.2 Development of Electronic Participation in Russia

The goal of the Smart City urban development concept, popular in many countries around the world, is to ensure the highest quality of life for citizens [23]. The concept sees the development of a city as a sustainable ecosystem which has a number of characteristics, including the involvement of citizens in the use of information technology, in particular for interacting with government bodies. In Russia, the set of legally approved official channels of interaction between citizens and the authorities was widened in 2010 with the opportunity to interact using information technology as a result of a number of amendments to Federal Law No. 59-FZ [24]. As a result of the amendments, a clarification was added on the possibility of receiving and the process of handling citizens' applications in electronic form, as well as on the way for the authorities to send responses and requests to citizens by electronic means.

Thus, citizens obtained an alternative way of sending requests and appeals to the authorities in addition to paper letters sent by mail, and personal visits. The new method proved to be more convenient for citizens using information technology for communication, because less resources and time are required to send the appeal, and the delivery time is significantly shorter.

The next step towards the application of modern information technologies to the process of interaction between citizens and authorities was the implementation of the Information Society state program [25], within which a single portal of state and municipal services was developed, and electronic reception rooms were created on the websites of authorities. This reduced the likelihood of sending requests to an incorrect or nonexistent email address.

At the same time, resources appeared for sending electronic petitions to the authorities, in particular change.org became one of the most popular in Russia [26]. The Russian Public Initiative was created by the state. This online resource was designed for citizens of the Russian Federation to start public initiatives and vote on them. Unlike the independent resource change.org, RPI petitions are of legal importance.

At the next stage of the development of electronic channels for citizens' interaction with authorities, online resources similar to the previously mentioned FixMyStreet and SeeClickFix were developed. Among them, we can mention both the resources created by initiative groups of citizens and non-profit organizations (RosYama, Beautiful Petersburg, Angry Citizen), and official electronic services of authorities – electronic reception rooms and services for interaction between city residents and authorities (Our City portal in Moscow, Our St. Petersburg portal). These services are designed to receive messages from citizens on such problems of the urban environment as pits on the roads, violation of parking rules, equipment defects on children's playgrounds and sports grounds, etc.

2.3 Social Media Becoming the Field of Action for Local Communities

Virtual social media play a crucial role by influencing people's lives and activities in different ways and differing from former social media by the interaction mechanism only. In the virtual world, interaction takes place with the help of web technologies, while in the early social media it occurred directly during real communication [27]. In recent years, the emergence of social media has become another potential communication channel for simplifying the activities of local communities. Social media allow communities to create platforms for quickly launching any campaigns and sharing information with a wide audience [14]. At the turn of the 20th and 21st centuries some social scientists believed that the Internet weakened intergroup relations, and that the desire to spend time and communicate in virtual reality would eliminate the need and desire to spend time together [28]. At the same time, there is an opinion that the transition to a "virtual society" expands the boundaries for communication from the local community to the scale of the whole world. Even the Internet emerged, in 1962, the Canadian philosopher Marshall McLuhan said that with the emergence of modern communication tools, humanity was becoming a "global village" united by connections and information around the world [29].

Studies have shown [30] that providing a local community with constant Internet access and an online discussion platform transforms and strengthens the ties between neighbors. The Internet not only allows maintaining neighborly relations, but also facilitates discussions and engages the population into local issues. In addition, the introduction of ICT specifically designed to facilitate communication and information exchange in residential areas can reverse the trend of non-interference in the activities of local communities. Using online networks at the local level can improve information exchange and help expand local social networks, create a high level of social capital, reduce costs and increase the speed of attracting people to take part in the community life [31].

2.4   Summary and the Hypothesis

The widespread use of virtual social media, not only for entertainment but also for information exchange in local communities, and the growing popularity of sending applications to the authorities using electronic resources suggest the existence of a correlation between these phenomena. In this paper, the hypothesis that the number and concentration of appeals on problems of the urban environment can be directly related to the existence of an active online community of residents of the corresponding local urban area is explored.

The study of such mechanisms will help to find ways to increase the effectiveness of civic participation in certain areas of cities by involving local communities in these processes through modern technologies.

3   Methodology and Experiment

The subjects of this study are citizens' appeals on the problems of urban environment quality and local web communities. The study was conducted on the territory of St. Petersburg, the second largest city in the Russian Federation, with a population of more than 5 million people [32].

3.1   Initial Data

At the time of the study, three e-participation platforms on urban quality issues were most actively used in St. Petersburg. Two of them provide services for sending e-appeals to the city administration – the Electronic Reception of the Administration of

St. Petersburg [33] and the web resource of the Beautiful Petersburg public movement [34]. The third one, Our St. Petersburg portal [35], receives messages on violations in the urban environment that are not formally located within the legal boundaries of Federal Law No. 59-FZ, but are considered by the authorities after passing a preliminary moderation.

Access to information from requests sent through the Electronic Reception is limited. There are no open mechanisms for obtaining the database of Our St. Petersburg either. For this reason, in the framework of this study we used the data of Beautiful Petersburg, access to whose database was granted to us.

Resources for sending appeals developed by Beautiful Petersburg are a website and a mobile application called Beautiful World. The tools work in the following way: the user needs to indicate the address of the violation in the urban environment on the map or in a text form and, if possible, upload a picture illustrating the problem. Next, you need to select the type of violation from the list, after which the text of the message will be automatically generated, which the user can edit, if necessary, and instantly send using the service.

To analyze citizens' complaints on the quality of the urban environment, the downloaded database was used with the following data fields: ID (unique appeal identifier), x (x coordinate), y (y coordinate), uID (unique identifier of the user who generated the appeal), date (appeal creation date). The array of appeals is a csv file.

For studying local web communities, VK was chosen, which is the most popular social media not only in Russia as a whole [36, 37], but also in St. Petersburg [38].

3.2 Defining the Areas for Research

To test the hypothesis within the framework of this stage of the study, it was decided to identify two pilot areas that are similar in their town-planning characteristics but differ in the conditional level of civic activity, which in this case is defined by us as the total number of sent complaints on the problems of the urban environment over the territory for a certain period.

As for the period, a sample of applications created within two years from March 22, 2015 to March 21, 2017 was used. The data was uploaded to QGis 3.0.2, resulting in the formation of a vector layer in which each appeal is represented by a single point on the map.

Since the service for application sending developed by Beautiful Petersburg also works in other regions of Russia, the data was additionally filtered by the coordinates within the administrative boundaries of the city of St. Petersburg, using the Intersection tool of the fTools QGis plug-in.

Based on the prepared layer with data on appeals, an appeal concentration map was constructed. To do this, in QGis, a rendering with the Heatmap style was configured for the appeal layer with the following parameters: gradient from transparent to dark red, radius of 2000 map units, maximum value chosen automatically, no point weighting. The result is shown in Fig. 1.

The area of the highest concentration of appeals is evident when the map is analyzed visually. For further research in this area with increased civic activity, a territory

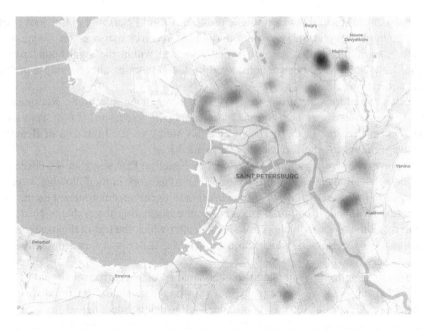

Fig. 1. Heatmap of appeal concentration in the territory of St. Petersburg (Color figure online)

was chosen that was limited to several quarters of the same development typology. The territory is located in the historical district Grazhdanka.

At the next step, it was necessary to select a territorial antipode – a second territory featuring a low civic activity but similar to the first territory by its area, number of inhabitants, years and typology of development. For this, territories outside the zones of increased civic activity having a similar urban planning typology were investigated by means of expert analysis. A suitable area was discovered in the historic district of Rzhevka.

The selected areas have similar city planning characteristics, but they differ significantly in the level of civic activity measured by the number of applications sent by residents (Table 1).

Table 1. Comparative features of selected territories.

Feature	Territory 1	Territory 2
District	Grazhdanka	Rzhevka
Number of residents	78,969 people	94,389 people
Area	2.67 km²	2.68 km²
Years of development	1970–1980	1970–1980
Type of development	Microdistrict and infill	Microdistrict and infill
Number of appeals	2,482	691

3.3   Selecting Local Communities

Local web communities can be described as self-organized groups of people of different sizes, united by extensive family, work, friendly ties, by interests or by place of residence, formed for communication, support and management [30].

The analysis of the research methods for local web communities has shown that the main ways to identify them are automated search for keywords – crawling [39] and manual search (Center for Applied Urban Studies) [40]. At this stage, due to time limits and the small area of research represented by two limited territories, a manual search of local web communities was applied.

To identify local web communities of certain territories, the toponyms of the city were used as keywords, which can be divided into the following categories: District, Microdistrict, Municipality (Russian "MO"), Historical name, Street, Colloquial names, Housing estate. For the territories selected earlier, the following keywords were highlighted: Krasnogvardeysky and Kalininsky (districts); Grazhdanka, Rzhevka, Murinsky, Malinovka (historical names); MO Prometey, Porokhovye (municipalities); Lunacharskogo, Svetlanovsky, Industrialny, Entuziastov (streets), etc.

As a result of the search on VK, web communities were found which can be considered local on a territorial basis. Search for communities was made by keywords chosen earlier for the considered territories mentioned in the community name, as well as by analyzing publications that include links to other online communities, and then checking if the community found belongs to the selected territory using Open-StreetMap's open resource data.

The typology of local web communities was stated as follows:

- By scale: from a point-type community (for example, a residential building) to a territorial (district) community
- By topics: from communities that unite residents to communities of interest

For the first territory, with a high concentration of appeals, 95 communities were found; for the second territory, with a lower concentration of appeals, 212 communities were found. Further, commercial communities and communities in which there were no publications for the considered time period were excluded from the sample. As a result, 67 communities were left for the first territory and 59 for the second territory (Table 2).

Table 2. Communities of the selected territories.

Community type	Territory 1	Territory 2
Point-type community of residents	23	31
Point-type community of interest	8	1
Territorial community of residents	29	23
Territorial community of interest	7	4
Total	67	59

3.4   Correlation Between Appeals and Local Web Communities

In the course of further research, it was necessary to determine the coverage of local communities. Sensual perception is one of the biological foundations of human activity, behavior and communication in urban space, while vision is the most developed of human senses. In the context of urban planning, where the relationship between senses, communication and measurement is very important, we can talk about the social field of vision. According to the studies of the Danish architect Jan Gehl, the limit of the social field of vision of a person is 100 m, and from this distance the observer is able to observe what is happening in the territory as a whole [41]. This value was chosen as the radius of coverage for the point-type community.

For territorial communities, the coverage area is determined by the territory at which the community operates – for example, for a district community, the coverage area is the area of the district.

Since the territorial communities of the territories under consideration are fairly large (district, municipality) and, accordingly, have significant coverage areas, the correlation between the presence of local web communities and the concentration of appeals was checked for point-type communities only.

To perform the check, a map of the coverage areas of point-type local web communities was created, and rendering was configured in such a way that the color of the coverage area was defined as the gradient from transparent to dark red, depending on the size of the community – the larger the community, the darker its color. To assess the correlation, data on the messages sent on the territory was added to the map (Fig. 2).

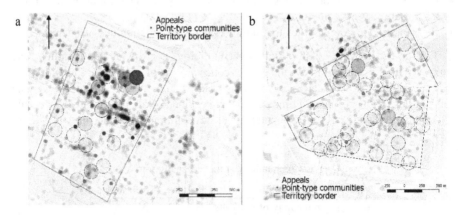

Fig. 2. Map of overlapping coverage areas of local point-type web communities and appeals for (a) Territory 1; (b) Territory 2. (Color figure online)

During the analysis of the received maps for each coverage zone of the web community, the number of appeals within the zone was counted. In case when the appeals were located at the intersection of several community coverage areas, they were assigned to the community with the largest number of people. Appeals were processed in a similar way in the special case when the coverage areas of several communities were completely the same. Based on the obtained data, charts illustrating the obtained correlations between the headcount of local web communities and the number of appeals belonging in their coverage areas were created for each of the considered territories (Figs. 3 and 4).

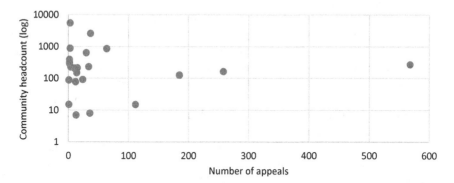

Fig. 3. The correlation between the community headcount and the number of appeals for Territory 1.

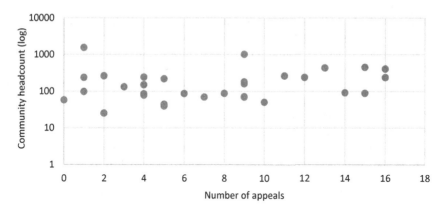

Fig. 4. The correlation between the community headcount and the number of appeals for Territory 2.

The created charts allow for the conclusion that there is no explicit correlation between the local web communities headcount and the number of appeals sent by residents of the territories to which these local communities are related. At the same time, the hypothesis that the number of appeals on problems of the urban environment can be directly related to the existence of an active online community of residents on the local urban area in question is confirmed. Thus, in Territory 1, where there is higher civic activity, 57.6% of appeals are in the coverage areas of local web communities, while in Territory 2, where there is a lower level of civic activity, 34.4% are in the coverage areas of local web communities.

4   Conclusions

In the conducted research, the concentration of appeals for violations in the urban environment in St. Petersburg, obtained from the Beautiful Petersburg database for the period from March 22, 2015 to March 21, 2017, was analyzed. A territory with increased civic activity was identified, and a territory with similar development characteristics but reduced civic activity was found using expert analysis.

For the two territories under consideration, a different number of local web communities were found on VK.com (212 for Territory 1 and 95 for Territory 2), but after commercial and inactive communities were excluded from the sample, their numbers became comparable (67 and 59 respectively). Communities were classified by scale (point-type vs. territorial) and by subject (communities of residents vs. communities of interest); only point-type communities were studied in detail (31 for Territory 1 and 32 for Territory 2). The coverage area of the point-type communities was defined by a coverage radius of 100 m.

On the basis of the data obtained, maps of the community coverage area overlapping and the coordinates of appeals for violations in the urban environment were created, and the results obtained were analyzed.

The hypothesis regarding the connection between the existence of local web communities on a local urban territory and civic activity was confirmed by the proportion of appeals that fell within the coverage of local web communities – for the territory with increased civic activity, 57.6% of appeals were within the coverage areas of local web communities, while for the territory with a reduced civic activity, the share of such appeals was 34.4%.

The revealed absence of a direct connection between the concentration of electronic appeals on a certain territory and the number and headcount of local web communities associated with this territory may be due to both the unique features of the territories chosen for the study, and the existence of unrealized potential of local communities. Active local communities, whose participants are informed about the ways of manifesting their civic activity to solve problems of the urban environment, can encourage citizens to use the methods of electronic participation. The growth of civic activity can provide public benefits, initiating a dialog between residents and the city administration, and improving the ways the authorities address the problems of the urban environment.

Further work includes comparison of the results obtained against results of similar research done by other methods. Apart from that, we plan to get access to alternative sources of data on citizens' appeals, as well as to analyze other urban territories with an increased civic activity. To study a large sample of territories, automatic data collection methods will be used, including automatic search for web communities by a list of key words describing the territory in question (toponyms, geonyms, etc.) and automatic filtering of the resulting community list which will help exclude communities of purely commercial or advertising nature using a special word list (stop list). In addition, we plan to automate the processing of data on local web community activities, in particular, to study how communities inform their members of electronic civic participation methods, as well as to perform an in-depth analysis of arrays of appeals on urban environment violations.

Studying appeal data from alternative sources together with data of Beautiful Petersburg for more territories using automated collection and analysis methods will help us increase the accuracy of the results, adjust the hypothesis, and state more detailed conclusions on how much local web communities influence civic activity.

Acknowledgment. This research is financially supported by The Russian Science Foundation, Agreement #17-71-30029 with co-financing of Bank Saint Petersburg.

References

1. Social media use jumps in Q1 despite privacy fears. http://wearesocial.com/blog/2018/04/social-media-use-jumps-in-q1-despite-privacy-fears. Accessed 10 May 2018
2. Tsatsou, P.: Why Internet use? A quantitative examination of the role of everyday life and Internet policy and regulation. Technol. Soc. **33**(1), 73–83 (2011)
3. Haythornthwaite, C.: Introduction: The Internet in everyday life. Am. Behav. Sci. **45**(3), 363–382 (2001)
4. Kilpeläinen, A., Seppänen, M.: Information technology and everyday life in ageing rural villages. J. Rural Stud. **33**, 1–8 (2014)
5. Nam, T., Pardo, T.A.: Conceptualizing smart city with dimensions of technology, people, and institutions. In: Proceedings of the 12th Annual International Digital Government Research Conference: Digital Government Innovation in Challenging Times, pp. 282–291. ACM, USA (2011)
6. Schaffers, H., Komninos, N., Pallot, M., Trousse, B., Nilsson, M., Oliveira, A.: Smart cities and the future internet: towards cooperation frameworks for open innovation. In: Domingue, J., et al. (eds.) FIA 2011. LNCS, vol. 6656, pp. 431–446. Springer, Heidelberg (2011). https://doi.org/10.1007/978-3-642-20898-0_31
7. Dirks, S., Gurdgiev, C., Keeling, M.: Smarter cities for smarter growth: How cities can optimize their systems for the talent-based economy. IBM Global Services, USA (2010)
8. Bakıcı, T., Almirall, E., Wareham, J.: A smart city initiative: the case of Barcelona. J. Knowl. Econ. **4**(2), 135–148 (2013)
9. Linders, D.: From e-government to we-government: defining a typology for citizen coproduction in the age of social media. Gov. Inf. Q. **29**(4), 446–454 (2012)
10. Bertot, J.C., Jaeger, P.T., Hansen, D.: The impact of polices on government social media usage: issues, challenges, and recommendations. Gov. Inf. Q. **29**(1), 30–40 (2012)
11. Beaudoin, C.E., Thorson, E.: Social capital in rural and urban communities: testing differences in media effects and models. J. Mass Commun. Q. **81**(2), 378–399 (2004)
12. Serageldin, I., Grootaert, C.: Defining social capital: an integrating view. In: Social Capital: A Multifaceted Perspective, vol. 1, pp. 203–218 (2000)
13. Gladarev, B., Lonkila, M.: The role of social networking sites in civic activism in Russia and Finland. Eur.-Asia Stud. **64**(8), 1375–1394 (2012)
14. Williamson, W., Ruming, K.: Using social network analysis to visualize the social-media networks of community groups: two case studies from Sydney. J. Urban Technol. **23**(3), 69–89 (2016)

15. Lindner, R., Riehm, U.: Electronic petitions and institutional modernization. International parliamentary e-petition systems in comparative perspective. JeDEM - eJournal eDemocracy Open Gov. **1**(1), 1–11 (2009)

16. King, S.F., Brown, P.: Fix my street or else. In: Proceedings of the 1st International Conference on Theory and Practice of Electronic Governance - ICEGOV 2007, pp. 72–80. ACM Press, USA (2007)

17. Mergel, I.A.: Distributed democracy: SeeClickFix.Com for Crowdsourced issue reporting. SSRN Electron. J. (2012). https://doi.org/10.2139/ssrn.1992968

18. Koganuramath, M.M., Angadi, M.: Print media vs internet media. Nagpur University, India (1999)

19. Koesel, K.J., Bunce, V.J.: Putin, popular protests, and political trajectories in Russia: a comparative perspective. Post-Sov. Aff. **28**(4), 403–423 (2012)

20. Petrov, N., Lipman, M., Hale, H.E.: Three dilemmas of hybrid regime governance: Russia from Putin to Putin. Post-Sov. Aff. **30**(1), 1–26 (2014)

21. Robertson, G.: Russian protesters: not optimistic but here to stay. Russ. Anal. Digest **115**, 2–7 (2012)

22. Alexanyan, K., et al.: Exploring Russian Cyberspace: Digitally-Mediated Collective Action and the Networked Public Sphere, 2012-2, 3. Berkman Center Research Publication (2012)

23. Caragliu, A., et al.: Smart cities in Europe. In: 3rd Central European Conference in Regional Science, pp. 45–59. VU University Amsterdam (2009)

24. About the order of consideration of appeals of citizens of the Russian Federation (in Russian). http://pravo.gov.ru/proxy/ips/?docbody=&firstDoc=1&lastDoc=1&nd=102106413. Accessed 03 May 2018

25. About the approval of the state program of the Russian Federation "Information society" (2011–2020) (in Russian). http://pravo.gov.ru/proxy/ips/?docbody=&nd=102349623&rdk=&backlink=1. Accessed 03 May 2018

26. Sokolov, A., Verevkin, A.: Digitalization and evolution of civic engagement: new ways of participation in public policy. In: Chugunov, A.V., Bolgov, R., Kabanov, Y., Kampis, G., Wimmer, M. (eds.) DTGS 2016. CCIS, vol. 674, pp. 269–274. Springer, Cham (2016). https://doi.org/10.1007/978-3-319-49700-6_25

27. Papageorgiou, T.: Crawling Facebook, a social network analysis. Master thesis (2011)

28. Nie, N.H., et al.: Internet and society. a preliminary report. Society **1**(1), 275–283 (2002)

29. McLuhan, M.: The Gutenberg galaxy: the making of typographic man, p. 293. University of Toronto Press (1962)

30. Hampton, K., Wellman, B.: Neighboring in Netville: How the Internet supports community and social capital in a wired suburb. City Community **2**(4), 277–311 (2003)

31. Hampton, K.: Place-based and IT Mediated 'Community". Plan. Theory Pract. **3**(2), 228–231 (2002)

32. Population of St. Petersburg as of January 1, 2017 (In Russian). Web document. http://petrostat.gks.ru/wps/wcm/connect/rosstat_ts/petrostat/resources/4e67d90040bd4afc874f87a3e1dde74c/СПб+числ+на+01.01.2017+по+MO.pdf. Accessed 03 May 2018

33. Electronic reception – Administration of St. Petersburg (in Russian). http://gov.spb.ru/gov/elektronnaya-priemnaya-pre/. Accessed 03 May 2018

34. Beautiful Petersburg (in Russian). http://красивыйпетербург.рф/. Accessed 03 May 2018

35. The Portal "Our St. Petersburg" (in Russian). http://gorod.gov.spb.ru/. Accessed 03 May 2018

36. Alexa.com: Vk.com Traffic, Demographics and Competitors. http://www.alexa.com/siteinfo/vk.com. Accessed 26 May 2017

37. Top social networks in Russia: latest trends, winter 2015–2016. http://www. russiansearchtips.com/2016/03/top-social-networks-in-russia-latest-trends-in-winter-2015-2016/. Accessed 26 May 2017
38. The distribution of authors in social networks in the Russian region (in Russian). https://br-analytics.ru/statistics/am?hub_id=3&date=201704&period_type=month. Accessed 26 May 2017
39. Gjoka, M., et al.: Practical recommendations on crawling online social networks. IEEE J. Sel. Areas Commun. **29**(9), 1872–1892 (2011)
40. Environment for people (in Russian). https://sredaforpeople.ru/. Accessed 03 May 2018
41. Gehl, J.: Cities for People, p. 269. Island Press, Washington, D.C. (2010)

Online Activity of Deputies and Public Policy Effectiveness: Moscow Local Authorities' Case

Galina Nikiporets-Takigawa[1,2(✉)], Olga Popova[3],
and Victor Kazanin[2]

[1] University of Cambridge, Sidgwick Avenue, Cambridge CB3 9DA, UK
gn254@cam.ac.uk, nikiporetsgiu@rgsu.net
[2] Russian State Social University,
Vilgelma Pika St. 4, 129226 Moscow, Russian Federation
victor@kazanin.cc
[3] Saint Petersburg State University, University Embankment 7/9,
199034 Sankt-Petersburg, Russian Federation
o.popova@spbu.ru

Abstract. The paper discusses the growing potential of the social networks to get transparency of the political process which is enhanced through the transformation of one-way broadcasting into the interactive communication and involvement of the citizens to the policy making, and then assess the practice of this communication and involvement based on the mapping of the usage of the social networks for the communication of the deputies of the local authorities of the sixteen districts of the largest Moscow okrug with the local citizens. The methodology of the study comprises the assessment of the political communication of the deputies in social networks based on three factors: coverage, activeness and involvement. In view of the worldwide practice, theoretical premises and the up to date Russian legislation we qualify the online professional behavior of the local authorities representatives as violation of the regulation and the effective public policy. Finally, recommendations how to deal with the low level of the online activity of the politicians in view of the effective public policy making are offered.

Keywords: Social networks · Public policy · Public sphere · Political process · Information technology · Local self government

1 Introduction

By early 2018, 53% of the world's population - 4.021 billion people began to use the internet, 43% use social networks. In North America, users of the World Wide Web are 88%, in Eastern Europe - 90%, in Northern Europe - 94%, in East Asia - 57%, in West Africa - 39%. The average user spends 6 h a day on the internet [9]. The development of the information society, the spread of new technologies of mass information and communication, including social networks and messengers, affect all spheres of human life: social, economic, political, making changes in the process of socialization of people and their political and social behavior [2, 8, 23].

© Springer Nature Switzerland AG 2019
A. Chugunov et al. (Eds.): EGOSE 2018, CCIS 947, pp. 348–360, 2019.
https://doi.org/10.1007/978-3-030-13283-5_26

First social networks, which were created as a tool for communication between students for nearly a decade turned into influential sources of information, a means of political mobilization, a catalyst for evolutionary transformation within the political process, a trigger of protest movements, a generator of public opinion, a necessary component of the implementation of the state policy, as well as of the election campaigns [10, 16, 19, 22, 31, 34].

The use of the political ads for the shaping of the public opinion on the key issues of the political agenda is not an innovation of the 21st century. At the end of the last century, political advertising was widely used on television, radio and the printed media. However, only from the second decade of the new millennium there was a trend of using social media as a platform.

According to investigators from the Federal Bureau of Investigation and Facebook specialists, over 3000 advertisements were created on the platform during the 2016 pre-election period aiming to polarize public opinion on the wide scale of social and political issues from the problem of openly carrying of firearm to the Black Lives Matter movement[1] [18]. The reports submitted by the company to the U.S. Senate said about 10 million users who have seen such ads and these ads could significantly affect this result and the elections.

The opportunities that Facebook and other social media can offer are much superior to traditional media. They allow interactivity, high speed of information dissemination, easy communication, targeting people on strictly specified parameters, extraterritoriality (the geographical factor has ceased to have any impact on communication capabilities), which help to get any audience locally and internationally and mobilize them quickly, unite like-minded people and coordinate their actions [33].

The possibilities for political mobilization online are extremely broad, they are associated not only with the increase in the appearance for the election or the change in the number of people intending to vote for a particular candidate, but they allow activating the participation of citizens in signing petitions, in public events, both constructive and destabilizing [24].

The internet and social networks form unique models of the organization of the political space in which horizontal links contribute to the development of civic activity, function more efficiently than the hierarchy and exert a strong influence on the significant political events of recent years: the Moldovan 'Twitter-revolution' of 2009, the Green revolution in Iran same year, the Arab Spring [17], the Russian Winter protests [26], the Ukrainian events in 2013.

In political science, there are three approaches in research regarding social networks that can be conditionally designated as 'cyber-optimistic', 'instrumental', and 'cyber-

---

[1] Black Lives Matter opposes to the using of violence against African-American communities. The start of the movement is linked to the #BlackLivesMatter Hashtag, widespread in social networks in the summer of 2013, after George Zimmermann, the murderer of the African American teenager, Treyvon Martin, was acquitted. The movement became massive after street demonstrations in 2014, caused by the death of two more African Americans. At present, there are no specific leaders in the organization, but they manage to organize mass protests throughout the country and in other countries. Such a scale of mobilization is the result of the implementation of the hashtag on social networks, as well as other online advertising tools [11].

pessimistic'. Within the first approach, social networks are positioned as a factor for the democratization of political process, since any individual can make a rational choice by obtaining an extremely broad stream of information free from the control by political actors [35]. Within the framework of this approach, it is noted that every citizen can identify his/her civil position and take part in the discussion; politicians get the chance of direct communication with potential voters without regard to the will of controlling structures or restricting access to online space. Such a view corresponds to Dahl ideas of the possibility of total penetration of information [7] and optimistic conviction of Habermas in the possibility of creating a discourse free from coercion as a direct road to democracy [13].

According to the instrumental approach, the internet, along with social networks cannot create a new quality of political processes because the internet is just one additional communication tool, built on a more advanced technological mechanisms [28]. The apologists of this approach argue that while the internet become a part of life of the ordinary people, this not resulted in a deeper involvement of the voters in politics, neither the growth of civic consciousness, absenteeism decries, getting rid of irrationalism in reaction to political events, political decisions, etc. [27], or the increasing popularity of the democratic ideas [15].

The third, pessimistic view, considers that the internet contributes to the spread of 'post-truth' in social networks [1], when citizens believe not in the reality, but in what the majority believes, looking at the constantly updated news, sometimes overwhelmed with the fake. Personal information about users on the social net-works allows using Big Data not only to set up advertising mechanisms so that people are forced to take not rational decisions, but also gives the opportunity to manipulate people offline.

Some researchers appeal to much more stringent examples; this concerns, for example, the work of the analytical algorithm Cambridge Analytica, which is called the culprit for the slowdown in the growth of the UK economy and the significant cause of Brexit [4]. They confirmed the possibilities of using social networks for authoritarian and totalitarian regimes against their citizens. An example is the so-called 'digital dictatorship' technology in the 'Social Credit System', which the Chinese government uses to determine the rating of a citizen influencing the social and financial possibilities of a citizen based on the indicators of his activity in social networks [21]. Shneiderman and Berners-Lee and co-authors rightly drew attention to the 'digital footprints' left by participants in social networks and other internet platforms [3, 32].

Whichever approach scientists choose, they agree that the internet creates a unique communicative environment that significantly changes the political process. Research of network communications in public policy provides ample opportunities to choose a 'framework' theory for explaining the processes and assessing the quality of participation of government representatives in networked communities and positioning their activities on official websites and personal pages in the 'World Wide Web.' The most popular are the theory of the network society, the theory of political mobilization online, the concept of transition from the internet model Web 1.0 to Web 2.0 and now to Web 3.0 within the framework of the 'digital divide'. The network logic of the interaction of participants in political process ('networkization' of civil society) and the complication of the mechanism of public policy through the expansion of the management space offer new challenges for politicians.

Since political communications in the modern world are understood as the form and the content of politics, as well as political relations, this allows to say that politics is no longer conceivable without information technology. The evolution of information technology brings the concept of publicity beyond the limits of current political system. The architecture of interaction between civil society and the system of state and municipal government is no longer constrained by the framework of traditional bureaucratic procedures, and the internet is a simplification of the existing order of political communication.

The creators of the theories of political systems G. Almond and D. Easton adhered to such ideas. In their works, they argued that political communication was a technical function of the political system. Each subsystem is a section of the communication network in which information flows are coordinated. Through political communications, information flows are distributed throughout the political system, thereby indirectly developing all elements and the institutions of political power.

Habermas writes about similar characteristics of communication. Expanding his theory of the «public sphere», he uses as an example the reading rooms and libraries of the late 18th century, which existed in Germany and were parts of a dense network of public communication [14: 11]. The emergence of such networks determined the further development of public communications: readers per capita increased in line with the emergence of the new publishing houses, bookshops, reading clubs, educational associations and so on. This evidence allows us to speak about emergence of any network structure having its own communication channels and tools of communication.

However, then the French Revolution caused a politicizing shift in the public sphere, which was formed based on the literary discussions. The resulting policy of censorship in Germany in the middle of the 19th century in relation to published literature contributed to the politicization of the public sphere. Public opinion, previously based on rational discussion, on the principles of transparency and sincerity of the opinions of all its participants, acted as an 'authoritative guardian'. Nevertheless, because of democratic changes, the 'authoritative guardian' turned into a state guardian, thus consolidating the concept of «public sphere» over the political space.

The philosopher divided power into two main types: power born in the process of communication and administratively applied power arguing that the use of administrative power alone sooner or later leads to a crisis of its legitimacy [12: 33–34, 20]. Thus, Habermas emphasizes that the sphere of public policy is vitally necessary as a permanent condition for the existence of a political system in democratic states.

Based on the belief that communications are the basis of public policy, he develops the theory of social dialogue through that we can achieve the mutual understanding of the political decision and to meet the political demands of all subjects of the public policy. The result of this approach is the conclusion that communication is a mechanism for coordination. Such a mechanism allows solving problems, on which civil society is focused, and which require a political decision. For effective functioning of the mechanism, several requirements must be met: all participants in the discussion have the right to participate; all should have equal rights to make claims; all participants must be able to accept the claims of others; the socio-political status of the participants in the discussion does not matter; and any manipulations in order to achieve hidden goals should be avoided.

This set of requirements is met in the social networks communication. Participants in communication are not related to each other and have only one goal - to reach a consensus solution on the given problem. Some researchers insist that reaching a solution is not the ultimate goal of discussions on the internet, and self-presentation, rather than discussion, is the driving motive for the active use of social networks. However, this conclusion is not relevant to the case of politicized discussions, which we are discussing here.

The 'public sphere', which Habermas described as the structure of secular European society in the middle of the 19th century, in the 21st century transformed in a transnational space, where the media are a key tool for the formation of public policy. At the same time, traditional media give their leading positions to the new media, namely social networks.

For civil society, the existence of a communication channel with the authorities is of paramount importance. Moreover, the use of this channel should become a priority in government policy, and explicit evasion of such tools can be regarded as deliberate abandonment of the democratic path of development and consolidation of authoritarian practices. Ancient Roman politician Cicero argued, 'The disruption of political communication, interaction, ultimately leads to the erosion of power or to powerlessness' [6]. At the present stage, the idea can be interpreted in view of the national interests of the state, which include the development of civil society institutions, an open electoral process, and a transparent political process. Any doubts in this regard put the political system under stress and allow us to talk about the illegitimacy of the existing government. Here comes that the development of political communication and its contributing tools is a task of the state.

This paper proposes to evaluate the practice of implementing this task and the level of use of the newest technologies of communication with the masses in the form of social networks by representatives of local authorities.

2   Method

According to VTSIOM[2], by the summer of 2017 the internet in Russia has come close to TV in terms of audience coverage [30]. There is a decline in the number of people using Central TV as a main source of information – from 78% to 69% in 5 years since 2012 to 2017. Similar statistics is observed with Regional TV, where the analysts observe a decline from 52% to 44% over the five-year period, even though this calendar period was mainly associated with the regional political agenda, due to the absence of Federal election till 2016. The internet in general and the social networks and messengers in particular strengthened their positions: over the past year there has been an increase of 15% and 11% respectively [29].

The printed media and radio have been left behind, only by joint efforts reaching the result of 25% and 20% (against 41% for social networks). The only increase for the

---

[2] All-Russian center for public opinion research, VTSIOM (until 1992—all-Union) - the oldest Russian research organization, regularly conducting sociological and marketing research based on public opinion polls.

printed media is currently observed for the foreign magazines, but only in the large cities with the population of more than one million. However, this is temporary tendency as the printed media has been transformed to the digital format very quickly and threatens the existence of even the most elite segment of printed media in the form of well-known magazines.

The level of 'networkization' of Russian residents, especially in large industrial cities, is quite high. Conducted by the Levada Center in September 2016, the survey 'The internet use in Russia' [36] showed that 73% of Russians use the internet; including 47% of respondents do it every day. There are intergenerational differences in the use of the internet. According to the Omnes of the Gesellschaftfur Konsumforschung Group in January 2017 'Internet penetration in Russia: the results of 2016', the 96% of young people aged 16 to 29 years used the internet. In the age group of 30–54-year-old Russians, this figure is 82%, but among Russian citizens aged 55 and over - so far only 29%. However, experts predict the increase in using social networks of people from the older age groups.

The social networks become increasingly popular among all strata of the Russian society. Vkontakte is used by 42% of internet users, most of whom are young people under 34 years, while Odnoklassniki is used by 27% of the internet users with the users over 60 build the majority. Among other popular Russian social networks are Instagram, Facebook, Moy Mir, Twitter, LiveJournal. According to other source involved in the social networks traffic monitoring and analysis, the audience of the video hosting service YouTube in Russia is equal to that of the Odnoklassniki [37]. The only difference is age, since video blogging and streaming (related to the organization of live broadcasts on video hosting as Twitch and YouTube) is dominated mainly by the younger generation of users from 18 to 49 years [38].

Conducted in the St. Petersburg State University (about 70% of students - people from different regions of Russia) study 'Factors behind student youth absenteeism in a Russian megacity (St. Petersburg case)' [39] showed a different level of students' interest in social networks and messengers. The most popular networks are: Vkontakte (88.9%) - the leader; followed by YouTube (66.1%), Instagram (59.7%), WhatsApp (58.9%), Telegram (55.5%), with a significant margin followed by Skype (43.3%), Facebook (32.3%), Viber (27.9%), Twitter (24.7%). Mass media outsiders are Tumblr (7.7%), My World (5.5%), LinkedIn (4.4%), Classmates (3.6%), Flickr (1.7%). In the results obtained, the indicators of the use of Twitter and Facebook were unexpectedly low. The multidimensional scaling procedure showed a high frequency of sharing of various internet resources and communication channels by students: Vkontakte is often used in conjunction with YouTube and Skype, and Facebook with Viber; most commonly shared are WhatsApp, Telegram, Instagram.

The arrival of the politicians in these networks is quite expected as they target young people. Thus, within the framework of our research in view to discuss the online political communication of the representatives at the level of the local administration with the citizens, we choose as the material the social networks, broadly understanding it as a fundamentally new platform for discussion that can influence the qualitative and quantitative composition of political participation, contribute to the effective political communication and increase its influence.

The methodology of the study is centered on the assessment of the political behaviour of the local administration representatives (deputies) in social networks based on three factors: coverage, activity and involvement.

Coverage refers to a deputy's presence in various social networks, which is of priority importance for our study considering the fact that the audience of social media differs, as was shown earlier on the example of statistics. Deputies get the maximum result of 3 points if they use a diversity of social networks, including photo- and video-hosting.

Activity is counted by how frequently this deputy posts the information, which is directly related to the professional duties. Deputies get the maximum result of 3 points if they report on their activities at least once a week.

Involvement is measured by the accuracy of the deputy in addressing the comments about the local problems, challenges and concerns, which are posted, by the local citizens, and the quality of the answer and problem solving. Deputies get the maximum result of 3 points if they do not ignore incoming appeals and show their interest via the discussion in the comments.

The overall result is an arithmetic mean between the three categories and provides an overall picture of the use of social media by municipal district members in their professional activities.

Data analysis is performed on a three-point scale based on the criteria described above (Table 1).

Table 1. The methodology of assessing the activities of local self-government deputies by category.

Points	Coverage	Activity	Involvement	Common result
0	The total absence of personal accounts in social networks	Updates less often than once a quarter	Limited ability to leave comments on the Deputy's page	Extreme form of online absenteeism
1	The possession of the only personal account	Information appears at least once in three months	Ignores incoming user comments	Low culture of using social media
2	The possession of at least two personal accounts in different social networks	Highlights the most important events during the month	Responds to user comments selectively	Local self-government is interested in working with the population in a new format
3	The usage of a diversity of social networks, including photo- and video ho stings	Weekly report on its activities	Actively leads the discussion	Social networks are the main tool for working with citizens

The research sample includes 343 social networks' and messengers' accounts of 187 deputies who took the mandates of representative bodies of local self-government of the sixteen districts of the Southern Administrative Okrug[3] of Moscow following the elections of September 10, 2017. Links to accounts on social networks are taken from free access in the Internet, search error can be no more than 10 accounts for the entire sample. The spread on social media in the number of accounts is: Facebook - 142, Vkontakte - 67, Instagram - 51, Twitter - 37, Odnoklassniki - 29, Moy Mir - 10, YouTube - 4, LiveJournal - 2, Periscope - 1.

3 Results

The most popular thematic communities in the social networks are groups of a humorous nature (43% of user views), related to health (41%), and to politics (41%). Men and older generations are more interested in what is happening in the country and the world in comparison to women and younger internet users. The various studies prove that the political figures and famous politicians form key topics of interest of internet users. This global trend has been already used by representatives of both the legislative and executive branches of government and many political leaders, GPs, mayors, deputies, NGOs heads and other top political managers have their personal accounts in the social networks and messengers. According to 'Medialogia', the company responsible for monitoring and analysing media and social media, in the period from May to October, Russian politicians such as Moscow mayor Sergei Sobyanin, Maria Zakharova, Ramzan Kadyrov, Sergey Aksenov every month lead the ranking of the TOP 15 most-quoted bloggers [40].

The active involvement in the politician's online communication in form of comments to their posts appears as the very effective and often unique way to get the attention of the politician to a certain local issue. In comparison with the traditional media, in this sense social networks have certain advantages.

Firstly, with the help of notifications, a comment or a post which is addressed to a politician will get to the addressee and will not be lost in bureaucratic schemes.

Secondly, the traditional media imply some special conditions for the information perception: the printed media require the purchase of a newspaper or a magazine (if the source does not have an electronic version), TV or radio requires the allocation of the addressee messages to certain time and place. Internet enabled communication, on the contrary, allows the user to choose the time and place when and where s/he is ready to communicate with a politician and set up only requirement - access to the internet.

Thirdly, to adjust Russian administration system to the Open Government doctrine requirements, all administrative bodies are obliged to create a special communication channel with the masses. All of them have enthusiastically or just under the pressure of the regulations created this channel and reassured local citizens that this

---

[3] Okrug – in Russian means a territorial area which is larger than district but less then region. For instance, Moscow is divided into 12 okrugs, which further are divided into 125 disctricts.

channel serves exactly for the communication (that is for a dialogue) rather than just to convey the information.

How the deputies use the channel? Our research answers this question and the results are summarized in Table 2.

Table 2. The results of the analysis of the online activity of the deputies of the Southern administrative Okrug of Moscow.

Rating	Area	Coverage	Activity	Involvement	Common result
1	Birulevo Zapadnoye	2.6	1.9	1.5	2.00
2	Nagatinskiy Zaton	1.8	2.4	1	1.73
3	Chertanovo Centralnoye	1.8	2	1.3	1.70
4	Donskoy	2.3	1.4	0.9	1.53
5	Birulevo Vostochnoye	1.73	1.4	1.07	1.40
6	Tsaritsyno	1.5	1.4	1.2	1.37
7	Nagornuy	1.9	1.1	0.9	1.30
8	Moscvorechye-Saburovo	1.9	0.9	0.8	1.20
9	Orehovo-Borisovo Yuzhnoye	1	1.6	0.73	1.11
10	Chertanovo Yuzhnoye	1.4	1.2	0.73	1.11
11	Brateevo	1.3	1.1	0.8	1.07
12	Orehovo-Borisovo Severnoye	1.33	1.07	0.8	1.07
13	Nagatino-Sadovniki	1.3	0.9	0.9	1.03
14	Chertanovo Severnoye	1.4	0.7	0.5	0.87
15	Danilovskiy	0.75	0.67	0.83	0.75
16	Zyablikovo	0.87	0.33	0.47	0.56
	SAO	1.56	1.25	0.90	1.24

The result of each category, which was used during the research, is calculated as the arithmetic mean between the numbers of deputies of each district and the results they gained during the analysis of their performance. Common result is the arithmetic mean between three categories of the research.

As for coverage, according to the results of the analysis, the majority of the local deputies use one-two social networks targeting the youth and business audience.

However, the average activity is one post in three months. Based on the frequency of the meetings which are mandatory for all deputies in the local administration (normally, two per calendar month), as well as the frequency of the weekly mandatory face-to-face meetings with the local audience, the results evidence the lack of deputies' activities in social media.

The average value for the involvement points that deputies ignore the incoming appeals.

Considering the obtained data, it is quite natural that the result indicates the low culture of using social media in professional public and political activity of Deputies of local government in Moscow.

4 Discussion

The principle of publicity is laid in the foundation of local self-government as the institution of power which is the closest to the masses [25, 81]. The effectiveness of such institutions depends directly on the level of openness and transparency. In the age of information technologies and widespread social media, the presumption of publicity in Russia alongside with the worldwide practices is established by Law, namely the Article 6 of the Federal Law of 09.02.2009 №8-FZ (ed. from 09.03.2016) 'On ensuring access to information on the activities of state and local self-government bodies'.

The Law determines that the local government must place the information about its activity on the internet to ensure the open access to the information. According to the Law, the departments of the local administrations in all municipal districts (okrugs) must create the official websites and place the information as soon as the new information appears. The other regulation ensures the interactivity and force the local administration to establish online communication with the local citizens. This online activity including website, its content, the speed of the information flow, the feedback option and other options for the communication with the masses – is an object of control and the base for ranking, promotions, elections and other competitions between the councils and its representatives.

However, the only and purely official website cannot be considered an effective way to meet the government openness requirements. The lack of the interactivity, abrupt news, headache for the internet users who try to find some information on the local administration websites while the majority of links go nowhere, or point to the error 444 and the search engines cannot distinguish the links from the official websites from those on the bogus websites – are characteristic to the official websites of the local administration.

Given such a poor performance on the website, the social networks and personal online activity of the deputies appear to be an innovative and highly effective way to communicate with the local citizens and to answer all of their questions and concerns. But the results of an empirical study of the online activity of municipal deputies at the level of the local administration on the example of the sixteen districts of the Southern Administrative Okrug of Moscow confirm the lack of such activity as intentions and willingness to satisfy the information and communication needs of their constituents.

This evidence of avoiding activity in the social networks as an integral part of the internet leads to the conclusion that the political behaviour of the deputies can be qualified as the violation of the Article 6 of the Federal Law of 09.02.2009 №8-FZ. It can be caused by the lack of the legally fixed deadlines and other regulations about the consideration of the public appeals incoming via social media. Currently, only regulation is written in the Article 7 of the Federal Law of 02.05.2006 No. 59-FZ (second edition on 03.11.2015) 'About the order of consideration of appeals of citizens of the Russian Federation'. It says that an online appeal should be answered electronically only by e-mail. Such ambiguous regulation means in practice a brief, automatically formed response informing the citizen that his/her appeal has been received and the answer will follow. It is often followed by an even more formal answer, which comes very late when the citizen has already forgotten, in what occasion and to whom s/he addressed the appeal.

5 Conclusion

Social networks can increase the transparency of the political process, transforming the unilateral broadcasting of ideas and programs by the elites to the masses in public policy, in the development of which all citizens actively participate. They can develop at the appropriate level 'a new culture of relations between government and citizens', 'a new quality of feedback and involvement of citizens and business in the making of the most important state decisions both at the federal and especially at the regional and municipal level', as required by the program of the 'Open Government', implemented in 2012, the results and development prospects of which until 2024 we are discussing today[4]. Policymakers who use social networks directly to perform their functions are much more effective, and their activities are much more citizen-oriented than the activities of their colleagues who ignore the demands of the information society.

This opportunity appears especially important for representatives of the legislative power at various levels. Deputies, being representatives of the people, should be guided in the activity by inquiries and requirements of the citizens who gave them the vote. Since a significant proportion of citizens' appeals are related to the local social, political, economic life concerns and problems, for local legislative assemblies, such appeals and any feedback from the local citizens, settlements and other local divisions is the sense-forming element of all political activity.

There is a clear request for a transparent and open political process in the global political space. The response to this request is information technology, which has become widespread because of its easy access, speed and interactivity. The new information and communication technologies change political process, political institutions, political culture and behaviour. The public sphere has evolved and is now developing not only vertically, but also horizontally, contributing to the political mobilization and enable a highly active political participation at all level of the society internet and social network sites play no longer an instrumental, but the dominant role in the political process.

Nevertheless, the local and regional politics perform very low level of the understanding of the new perspectives of the political landscape of the 21st century avoiding not only communication with the citizens, who are the voters and whose opinion are crucial during the elections and in the daily political activity. They also very modestly inform the public about their activities. The lower the level of the local administration, the fewer representatives use social media in their professional activities.

To overcome the further regression of political publicity, it is necessary to amend the legislative framework and to oblige the deputies and other representatives of the local administrations to fully address the appeals received through personal messages or comments on social media accounts.

Although internet technologies and online communication of political actors with the masses and citizens are already a routine of political and, in particular, election campaigns, the Russian segment of the internet become used for this purpose somewhat

---

[4] The results of the implementation of the Open Government system and perspectives till 2024. http://report.open.gov.ru.

later than in Western countries [5], and in Russia the possibility of forming a political agenda via the internet is still insufficiently estimated.

The academic community needs to continue research of both social science and technical nature, in the field of transformation of the public policy into the internet space, in the field of technologies that contribute to the development of political transparency, as well as on the issues of the online-absenteeism in the political process, which is evident among the local government and at the level of regional and Federal authorities. Political actors need to raise the cultural level of the use of information technologies to increase the efficiency of their professional activities, thereby contributing to the formation of a transparent democratic process and the rejection of the authoritarian practices of the 21st century.

References

1. Americans' trust in mass media sinks to new low. Gallup.com. http://www.gallup.com/poll/195542/americans-trustmass-media-sinks-new-low.aspx. Accessed 06 Mar 03 2018
2. Arceneaux, K., Johnson, M., Murphy, C.: Polarized political communication, oppositional media hostility, and selective exposure. J. Polit. **74**, 174–186 (2012)
3. Berners-Lee, T., Hall, W., Hendler, J., O'Hara, K., Shadbolt, N., Weitzner, D.: A framework for web science. Found. Trends Web Sci. **1**(1), 1–130 (2006)
4. Cambridge Analytica: ex-director says firm pitched detailed strategy to Leave.EU. The Guardian. https://www.theguardian.com/uk-news/2018/apr/17/cambridge-analytica-brittany-kaiser-leave-eu-brexit. Accessed 06 Mar 2018
5. Chadwick, A., Anstead, N.: Parties, election campaigning, and the internet. In: Chadwick, A., Howard, P. (eds.) Routledge Handbook of Internet Politics, pp. 56–76. Routledge, London, UK (2009)
6. Cicero, M.T.: On the State. MYSL, Moscow (1999)
7. Dahl, R.: On Democracy. Yale University Press, New Haven (1998)
8. Deuze, M.: Media life and the mediatization of the lifeworld. In: Hepp, A., Krotz, F. (eds.) Mediatized Worlds: Culture and Society in a Media Age, pp. 207–220. Palgrave Macmillan, London (2014)
9. Digital in 2018: world`s internet users pass the four billion mark. We are social. https://wearesocial.com/blog/2018/01/global-digital-report-2018. Accessed 05 May 2018
10. Foot, K., Schneider, S.: Web Campaigning. MIT Press, Cambridge (2006)
11. Guynn, J.: Meet the woman who coined #BlackLivesMatter. USA Today, 03 April 2015
12. Habermas, J.: Democracy. Mind. Morality. Nauka, Moscow (1992)
13. Habermas, J.: The Inclusion of the Other: Studies in Political Theory. Polity Press, Cambridge (1999)
14. Habermas, J.: Structural Change of the Public Sphere. Ves' Mir, Moscow (2016)
15. Hindman, M.: The Myth of Digital Democracy. Princeton University Press, Princeton (2008)
16. How Facebook could help swing the US election. NewScientist (2012). http://www.newscientist.com/article/dn22261-how-facebook-could-help-swing-the-us-election.html. Accessed 03 Jan 2014
17. Howard, P., Duffy, A., Freelon, D., Hussain, M., Mari, W., Mazaid, M.: Opening closed regimes: what was the role of social media during the Arab Spring? Project on Information Technology & Political Islam (PITPI) (2011). www.pITPI.org. Accessed 15 Sept 2017

18. Isaac, M., Shane, S.: Facebook's Russia-linked ads came in many disguises. The New York Times, 10 February 2017
19. Ivanov, I.S., Zueva, O.O.: The internet-technologies use in electoral campaign (the case of the Moscow mayoral electoral campaign 2013. Locus: People Soc. Cult. Mean. **3**, 66–72 (2015)
20. Kazakov, M.Y.: 'Public sphere' by J. Habermas: implementation of the online-discourse. Vestnik Nizhegorodskogo universiteta **3**(31), 125–130 (2013)
21. Kovachich L.: Big brother 2.0. How China build digital dictatorship. Moscow Carnegie Center. http://carnegie.ru/commentary/71546. Accessed 06 Apr 2018
22. Lilleker, D.G., Vedel, T.: The Internet in campaigns and elections. In: Dutton, W.H. (ed.) The Oxford Handbook of Internet Studies, pp. 401–420. Oxford University Press, Oxford (2013)
23. Margolis, M., Resnick, D.: Politics as Usual: The Cyberspace 'Revolution'. Sage Press, New York (2000)
24. Mazzoleni, G., Schulz, W.: Mediatization of politics: a challenge for democracy? Polit. Commun. **16**(3), 247–261 (1999)
25. Mikheev, D.S.: Transparency in local government through the prism of the constitutional provisions. Eurasian Advocacy **4**(5), 81–83 (2013)
26. Nikiporets-Takigawa, G.: Protest 2:0: through networked consolidation to participation: why Russian Manezhka cannot become Ukrainian Maidan. Russ. J. Commun. **6**(3), 246–259 (2014)
27. Norris, P.: Preaching to the Converted? Pluralism, participation and party websites. Party Polit. **9**(1), 21–45 (2003)
28. Papacharissi, Z.: The virtual sphere: the internet as a public sphere. New Media Soc. **4**(1), 9–27 (2002)
29. Press release No. 3388. Social networks: who goes there and why? https://wciom.ru/index.php?id=236&uid=116254. Accessed 28 May 2018
30. Press release No. 3435. TV vs internet: a dispute of generations. https://wciom.ru/index.php?id=236&uid=116341. Accessed 20 May 2018
31. Sabato, L.: The Year of Obama: how Barack Obama Won the White House. Logman, New York (2010)
32. Shneiderman, B.: Web science: a provocative invitation to computer science. Commun. ACM **50**(6), 25–27 (2007)
33. Sokolov, A.V., Solovieva, A.V.: Mobilization in sociopolitical campaigns. Vlast' **21**(11), 55–58 (2013)
34. Stanton, J.: The man behind Obama's online election campaign. Web 2.0 convergence (2009). http://www.digitalcommunitiesblogs.com/web_20_convergence/2009/04/the-man-behind-obamas-online-e.php. Accessed 06 Sept 2018
35. Trippi, J.: The Revolution Will Not Be Televised: Democracy, the Internet and the Overthrow of Everything. Harper Collins, New York (2004)
36. http://www.levada.ru/2016/09/29/ispolzovanie-interneta-2/. Accessed 06 May 2018
37. http://gs.seo-auditor.com.ru/socials/2017/. Accessed 28 May 2018
38. http://twitchadvertising.tv/audience/. Accessed 28 May 2018
39. Factors behind the student youth absenteeism in a Russian megacity (St. Petersburg case) project № 106-9131-879 (2017)
40. http://www.mlg.ru/ratings/socmedia/blogers/. Accessed 28 May 2018

Social Media Discourse Analysis

Information Streams for Inter-ethnic Relations in Crimea and Sevastopol: SMA and Discourse Analysis of Posts in Social Networks of Runet

Elena Brodovskaya[1], Anna Dombrovskaya[2(✉)], and Irina Batanina[3]

[1] Financial University Under the Government of RF, 125993 Moscow, Russia
brodovskaya@inbox.ru
[2] Moscow State Pedagogical University, 1199911 Moscow, Russia
an-doc@yandex.ru
[3] Tula State University, 300012 Tula, Russia
batanina@mail.ru

Abstract. The article is devoted to the results of the Social Media Analytics study of dynamic, technological and substantial markers of social media Russian-writing flows on interethnic and inter-religious relations in Crimea and Sevastopol. The study assessed the extent of the social media Russian-writing messages representing the forming of negative interethnic and inter-religious attitudes among Crimean and Sevastopol inhabitants. The logic of study leads from the development of social and cultural contexts to shaping of digital patterns of interethnic and inter-religious relations and from accumulating of relevant social media streams to the analysis of metrics of information flows. The authors consider Russian state policy on inter-ethnic and inter-religious relations and publication activity of social media leaders of mass opinion the main factors of changes in the proportion of social media documents concerning on the interactions between ethnic Russians and Ukrainians, and between ethnic Russians and Crimean Tatars. The main prospect of the study is the development of digital markers for the automatic uploading Ukrainian-writing and Crimean Tatar-writing streams to compare their characteristics, reflecting the inter-ethnic and inter-religious relations in Crimea and Sevastopol.

Keywords: Inter-ethnic relations · Inter-religious relations ·
Socio-cultural integration of crimean society · Social media ·
Internet communication · SMA-study · Digital markers · Discourse analysis

1 Introduction

The processes of social and cultural integration of the Crimean society, determined by the reunification of Russia, Crimea and Sevastopol, are facing serious challenges associated with the aggravation of the inter-ethnic issue in the transition period for the socio-economic, socio-political and socio-cultural spheres of the new subjects of the Russian Federation. In the process of studying the problems of inter-ethnic and inter-religious relations in Crimea and Sevastopol, a special role belongs to the methods of social computing—an interdisciplinary field researches, including the study of social

© Springer Nature Switzerland AG 2019
A. Chugunov et al. (Eds.): EGOSE 2018, CCIS 947, pp. 363–373, 2019.
https://doi.org/10.1007/978-3-030-13283-5_27

behavior and social context by means of computer systems (computational systems) and the development and use of information technologies, which have important social or political context. The use of intellectual search of digital markers in the framework of this study allows to identify markers of intensity and markers of the content of the discourse of interethnic and inter-religious relations in the Crimea and Sevastopol. Intensity markers provide statistical and structural analysis of messages, revealing the scope of discussion of the problem of interethnic and inter-religious relations in the Crimea and Sevastopol. In turn, substantial markers give an idea of the semantic content of circulating messages about the analyzed subject.

A body of science studies is in the theoretical foundation of this research: the theory of discourse (Laclau and Mouffe [17], Van Dijk [8], Fairclough [11], Edwards [10], etc.), the theory of metaphors (Lakoff and Johnsen [18]), the epistemology method (Sériot [29], the theory of collective representations (Lebon [19], Marcuse [22], Durkheim [9], Gamson [13], Howard [16]), framing theory (Takeshita [31], Wu [36], McCombs [24], etc.), the theory of the agenda (Lippman [21], Reynolds [24]), theory of resource mobilization (McCarthy and Zald [23], etc.), the concept of relative deprivation (Merton [25], etc.), the concept of factors of socio-political destabilization (Golstone [14], Howard [17], etc.), theories and concepts of network political participation (Jenkins [12], Castells [6], Alexander [1], Smith [30], Tilly [32]), the concept of creating collective political content (Toffler [34], Noveck [26], etc.), the concept of communicative determinism of political participation (Livingstone [20], Polat [28], Weber [35], Bergman [4]), theory of social and political conflicts (Simmel and Koser [33]), theories and concepts of social, ethnic and interethnic attitudes (Allport [2]), concepts and theories of identity system and ethnic identity (Lukman and Berger [3]).

2   Methodology and Method

The research methodology is based on the following approaches: historical institutionalism, network and cognitive approaches, Data Mining, Text Mining, Predictor Mining, Social Computing (Brodovskaya and others [5]), comparative analysis.

Historical institutionalism allows to take into account the historical aspects of the attitudes of inter-ethnic and inter-religious relations in Crimea (Skocpol [27], etc.). The network approach makes it possible to investigate the relationship between the mobilization of political action and the network activity of Internet users (Green [15], Howard [17], etc.). Cognitive approach focuses on the analysis of processes of subjective formation of inter-ethnic and inter-religious peace, the subjective perception and interpretation of messages transmitted in the social media space (Dalton [7], etc.). Data Mining is used in the study, due to the fact that it is an interdisciplinary field that arose at the intersection of applied statistics, artificial intelligence, database theory, etc., which includes a system of methods of detection of previously unknown data and available interpretation of knowledge necessary for modeling and forecasting of socio-political processes (Data Mining, Text Mining, Predictor Mining, Social Computing) [5].

The comparative analysis is applied to compare the substantial, dynamic and technological features of information flows in social media regarding interethnic and interreligious relations in the Crimea and Sevastopol.

The strategy of applied research is hybrid, based on a combination of quantitative and qualitative methods used to analyze the features of perception of inter-ethnic and inter-religious relations in the virtual environments of the Crimea and Sevastopol.

The empirical model of the study includes: discourse analysis of social media users' messages; automated cyber-metric analysis (kind of SMA) of information flows relevant to the research topic with the online service of social media monitoring IQBuzz.

The automated accumulation of social media Russian-writing posts was made with special tool – the service for social networks monitoring "iqbuzz"; the size of uploading social media massages amounted to 600 000 messages, the accumulated documents dated from 01.09.2013 to 28.12.2017, the following social media were used: http://livejournal.com, http://vk.com, http://twitter.com, http://mirtesen.ru, http://www.odnoklassniki.ru/, http://www.youtube.com, http://instagram.com, http://tut.by, http://ursa-tm.ru, http://my.mail.ru, http://www.facebook.com, http://fkiev.com, http://www.kharkovforum.com, http://www.yaplakal.com/forum, http://altyn-orda.kz, http://meta.ua, http://www.tks.ru/forum, http://cofe.ru, http://kob.su/forum, http://mypage.ru, http://opolshe.ru/, http://www.doneckforum.com, http://www.e1.ru, http://www.forum-tvs.ru, http://www.littleone.ru, http://www.pkforum.ru/board/, http://www.prado-club.su/forum, https://aftershock.news.

The basis for the development of digital markers for automated search is the contexts of such significant for the forming of inter-ethnic and inter-religious events in the Crimea and Sevastopol, as the follows:

- Recognition of the Mejlis as an extremist organization;
- Victory of the Ukrainian singer at Eurovision-2016 with a song about the deportation of Crimean Tatars in 1944;
- Protest mass actions in May 2015 and 2016 related to the deportation of Crimean Tatars in 1944;
- UN resolutions on violation of the rights of Crimean Tatars adopted in 2017;
- pardon the leaders of the Majlis on October 26, 2017.

Preparatory work allowed to set the following keywords (digital markers) to upload the relevant social media documents: "the Oppression of the Crimean Tatars"|"Invaders of the Crimea"Resolutie"|"Occupation of Crimea"|"the Deportation of the Crimean Tatars"|"Eternal suffering of the Crimean Tatars"|"Genocide of the Crimean Tatars"|"Crimean Ukraine|Crimea is not Russia"|"the Crimean Tatars-the owners of the Crimea"|"Glory to Ukraine", {("Crimean Tatar"|"Crimean Tatar people"|"the Crimean Tatar population"|"Majlis|Cemil|Chubarov)& ("Russia|Russian|occupation|"the Russian Empire"|occupiers|deportation|genocide"|"mass repression"|"massacre"|Stalin|"Soviet"|"the Stalinist regime").

The basic characteristics of the accumulated social media massive are the following:

- the share of social media massages reflecting the discussion on the problems of interethnic relations in Crimea and Sevastopol;
- activity of public opinion leaders and blogs containing discussion of the problem of interethnic relations in Crimea and Sevastopol;

- semantic core of information flows reflecting discussion of the problem of interethnic relations in Crimea and Sevastopol;
- discursive practices that form users' attitudes about inter-ethnic relations in Crimea and Sevastopol.

The discourse analysis was focused on the markers – elements of discourse practices: the attitudes of Crimean Tatars towards Russians, the attitudes of Russians towards Crimean Tatars; the assessment of Crimean Tatars of the living prospects in Russia, the key problems of Crimean Tatars adaptation in RF. The technique of discourse analysis is based on the identifying the way of semantic representation of the matter markers in relevant social media messages.

3   Research Result

Specific weight and dynamics of information flows.

According to the data of accumulated social media streams, there are two main information flows in the space of documents on interethnic relations in Crimea: massages, in which the reunification of Crimea and Russia is presented as a factor of interethnic discord between ethnic Russians and Ukrainians and messages, which are focused on the negative perception of Russian policy towards Crimean Tatars.

The ratio of the specific weight of these information flows is 79.6% (streams concerning on interethnic relations between Ukrainians and Russians); 20.4% (streams concerning on inter-ethnic relations between Crimean Tatars and Russians) (in total, 600,000 documents are accumulated).

Publication activity of leaders of public opinion and blogs.

20 leaders of public opinion were identified. They are forming inter-ethnic social attitudes in the Crimea and Sevastopol, having several thousands user audience, and therefore significant impact on the mass consciousness of the Crimean and Sevastopol users. A qualitative analysis of the names and nicknames of these public opinion leaders reproduces a pattern associated with significantly less representation in social media of the problems of the relationship between the Crimean Tatars and ethnic Russians in comparison with the representation of contradictions between ethnic Ukrainian and Russian ethnic communities.

Thus, according to Table 1, all public opinion leaders who construct attitudes towards interaction between the peoples of the Crimean Peninsula and have an audience of more than 10,000 users, are focused on discussing the crisis in the South-East of Ukraine, forming a negative perception of the reunification of Crimea and Russia, as well as the positioning of the point "Crimea belongs to Ukraine". The leaders, who focus on the problems of relations between the Crimean Tatars and ethnic Russians, have statistically insignificant audiences, and do not have a significant impact on the public consciousness of social media users. At the same time, we draw attention to the fact that the present study is focused on the analysis of Russian-writing flows about the inter-ethnic relations between the Crimean Tatars and ethnic Russians, which can largely explain the narrow coverage of the user audience by the leaders of public opinion, forming the attitudes on the interaction between the Crimean Tatars and ethnic

Russians, and predetermine the prospects for the analysis of Crimean Tatar-writing social media flows about interethnic relations in Crimea and Sevastopol.

Table 1. The activity of the leaders of public opinion, reflecting the discussion of the problem of interethnic relations in Crimea.

Name and nick	Media	Size of audience
Reports from the militia of Novorossia (South – East of Ukraine) (club57424472)	VKontakte	447834
Information resistance (club70774335)	VKontakte	88962
NFORMATION warfare (club4121067)	VKontakte	56356
CRIMEA – UKRAINE (club2311758)	VKontakte	34770
SaveDonbassPeople	(club43806582)	VKontakte	32288

The most numerically represented audience belongs to the news media blogs, which determines their high potential in developing the agenda related to inter-ethnic relations and the construction of behavioral attitudes towards the interaction between ethnic groups. Notice that the three blogs that were among the most impressive ("Antimaidan", "Typical Donetsk", "Reports from the militia of Novorossiya") are related to the discussion of the crisis in the South-East of Ukraine and contain dialogues about the importance of reunification of Russia, Crimea and Sevastopol in the development of inter-ethnic relations on the Peninsula. This means that in the information space of social media, the most powerful background that stimulates the circulation of messages about attitudes towards inter - ethnic harmony or disagreement is a topic related to the events in the Donetsk and Luhansk Republics. A notable fact of the reporting statistics of the service "iqbuzz" is that all these blogs are related to the blogohosting "Vkontakte". Thus, it is this social media that retains the status of a leader in the dissemination of values and meanings about inter-ethnic relations in Crimea and Sevastopol. Tag cloud analysis. The analysis of the tag cloud showed the dominance of such words in the texts of the uploaded messages on inter-ethnic relations in Crimea and Sevastopol, which reflect geographical concepts: "Ukraine", "Kiev", "Country", "Russia", "Sevastopol", "Simferopol", "Donbass", etc., as well as the words united by the meaning associated with the reunification of Russia, Crimea and Sevastopol: "2014", "to return", etc. (see Table 2), as semantically reflecting the militaristic dimension: "War", "Front line", as well as the mention of the historical event of 1944- the deportation of the Crimean Tatars,

The semantic core of the unloaded social media documents on the problems of inter-ethnic relations in Crimea and Sevastopol shows that the semantics of dialogues can be combined by such a logical chain: the accession of Crimea and Sevastopol to Russia forms the opposition of "Russia, Russian – Ukraine, Ukrainian" and is the background for the discussion of the crisis in the South-East of Ukraine and the ethnic Russian state policy towards the Crimean Tatars.

Discourse analysis of online group messages.

Table 2. Key words of unloading messages reflecting discussion of the problem of interethnic relations in Crimea and Sevastopol.

Tegs (key words)	Frequencies
Ukrain, Ukrainean	4463
Kiev	3747
Russia, Russian	4284
2014	2643
War	2752
Battle-line	2063
Putin	1483
Sevastopol	1385
Simferopol	1090
Donbass	978
Take (back)	831
1944	1072

Analyze the results of discourse analysis of accumulated messages allowed to analyze the meanings and values of discursive practices of uploaded content (total analyzed 1,000 documents selected by the method of the target sample according to the criterion of the highest content). The study identified three basic types of discursive practices on inter-ethnic and inter-religious relations in Crimea and Sevastopol in the online communities of the "VKontakte" network. As a rule, these types of online groups have a strong association with the ethnicity of their participants. The first type of discursive practices is represented by ideas about the oppression of the Crimean Tatars in Crimea and Sevastopol, their critical statements about the situation of the Crimean Tatars in Crimea and Sevastopol, and forms the semantic core of the negative information flow, reflecting the negative attitude of the Crimean Tatars to the reunification of Crimea and Russia and the acuteness of problems of inter-ethnic and inter-religious interactions in the Peninsula. Online groups, united by a name that includes an indication of the ethnicity of the participants, in this case, the Crimean Tatars, are deliberately focused on their social distance from other nations, on isolation and disintegration. Examples of the names of such groups are: "Crimean Tatars – the only strength of Crimea. We will always be together!!!" (https://vk.com/club82500334), "Crimean Tatars are the pride of Crimea" (https://vk.com/club82148811), "Crimean Tatars in Islam" (https://vk.com/crimean_islam), "Crimean Tatars are the indigenous people of Crimea" (https://vk.com/public73551522) etc. Many of the online communities of the Crimean Tatars are closed, examples of the names of these groups: Crimean Tatars all over the World - UNITE!!! (https://vk.com/club1713475), "Crimean Tatars of Sevastopol" (https://vk.com/sevas_tatar), "Crimean Tatars of St. Petersburg" (https://vk.com/crimeantat) and others. The closeness of these groups (the inability to freely join the number of its participants) together with the stressed national identity indicates the orientation of these communities to social distance and isolation within the ethnic community. The thematic palette of the discourse, formed mainly by representatives of Crimean Tatar nationality in these online communities, is quite wide:

from the victory of the singer Jamala at the international contest "Eurovision" with a song about the deportation of Crimean Tatars in 1944 to the abolition of the Mejlis and the recognition of its extremist organization; from the discussion of the activities of M. Dzhemilev to assess the actions of R. Chubarov as an expert on the problems of Crimean Tatars in Crimea and Sevastopol, and many others. The rhetoric of disagreement with the reunion of Crimea and the Russian Federation is manifested in the following statements in online chats:

"...the land of my ancestors and I can't let those (Russians) to be masters here.....I will never surrender" (https://vk.com/club82500334), "Crimean Tatars are the only owners of Crimea" (https://vk.com/public73551522). These fragments contain at least two connotations: the construction of the idea of "capture" and annexation of Crimea by Russia, as well as the expression of conviction in the sole right of Crimean Tatars to own the Peninsula. Most often such statements are accompanied by visualization of the Ukrainian and Crimean Tatar flags with the emphasized unity of the color scheme, which along with discursive practices reflects the idea of returning the Crimea to Ukraine.

The content forming the concepts of negative state identification and negative historical memory of Crimean Tatars in the negative discourse of inter-ethnic relations on the Peninsula is quite common in the analyzed online communities. Examples of posts and reposts of such content: *"The eternal pain of the Crimean Tatars: the deportation of the Crimean Tatars from the Crimea by Catherine II, the deportation of the Crimean Tatars from Crimea Alexander III, the deportation of the Crimean Tatars from Crimea by order of the state Committee of defense, 2014 is the intention to recognize the Mejlis of the Crimean Tatar people the observational organization. What? Are we waiting for the next deportation?"*(https://vk.com/club82500334). Those messages make Crimean Tatars to develop fear, negative expectations and anxiety about their future in the Russian Crimea.

A separate semantic block of the discourse under consideration contains statements expressing a negative attitude towards the Russians, the Russian authorities and the ethnic Russians. Here are fragments of this kind of posts:

"Tatar, believe, it will rise, captivating star of happiness..... and on the wreckage of the Russian Empire will write Your names!"(https://vk.com/club82500334).

"Thank God that I am not Russian!" (https://vk.com/club82148811).

"Tatars drive!" (https://vk.com/club82148811).

Summurising the charactaristics of the matter discourse, notice the folowing ones:

- the authorship of discursive practices belongs to the opinion leaders – representatives of the Crimean Tatar people, who have the purpose to form the attitudes of social distancing;
- the addressees of these types of discourse is the Crimean Tatar community and primarily the Crimean Tatar youth, socialized in Ukraine and considers Ukraine as their homeland;
- the speech techniques of discourse - emotional and rational steretipization, the use of terms - ideologies aimed at the development of interethnic contradictions.

The second type of discursive practices is formed, as a rule, by users who have Russian nationality. These are the discourses constructed around the idea of the

Crimean Tatars' lack of grounds for a negative attitude towards Russia and the Russians. This discourse has several dimensions. The first aspect is related to the expression of critical attitude of users, as a rule, belonging to the Russian national group, towards the Crimean Tatars and their life strategy. Fragments of the discursive practices are the follows: *"They (Crimean Tatars) have no reasons to complain…"* (https://vk.com/krimskybunt*).* "They *(about the Crimean Tatars) are owners of the Crimea as well as other ethnic groups…"* (https://vk.com/public73551522).

In these quotations the attitudes of representatives of the Russian national group on criticize of behavior of the Crimean Tatars, the attitude towards them as to the possessors and the passive recipients of the facilitation and aid.

In the next group of statements, the discourse of the need to oppose the information flows aimed at the formation of protest attitudes towards Russia and ethnic Russians among the Crimean Tatars is constructed.

An example of this type of message is the materials that call into question the official statements of Crimean Tatar public figures about the oppression of Crimean Tatars in Crimea, the disregard of their rights, etc.:

"Chubarov told about the oppressed life of the Crimean Tatars… in a parallel universe. Every day, throughout life, cold and prudent, purposeful and loyal to personal interests, Refat Chubarov blatantly lies… to the Crimean Tatar people…." https://vk.com/club2378378.

The analyzed discourse has the following characteristics:

– the authors of this discourse are Russian bloggers aimed at categorical attitude to the claims of the Crimean Tatar people;
– the addresses of these type of discourse are the user audience of Russian and Crimean Tatar nationality;
– the main speech technique of the discourse is discrediting aimed at the development of interethnic contradictions.

Another facet of the discourse under discussion is reflected in the messages addressed to the Crimean Tatars considering Russia the best state in which the Crimean Tatar ethnic group could be well: *"Ukraine would have evicted the Crimean Tatars. The Tatars have only one homeland Kazan, Russia is building a second home for the Tatars in the Crimea!"* (https://vk.com/club2378378).

A significant dimension of the discourse concerning to the need to counter the information infusions aimed at forming a negative attitude of the Crimean Tatars to anything ethnic Russian are semantic concepts presented in the following online groups messages: *"The current situation with the Crimean Tatars is somewhat similar to the "Maidan". Again a large mass of people set up to fight. Again, the media increasingly cover their right cause, trying to attract as many like-minded people from around the world. And again these people are pushed to arms, due to inaction of political methods"* (https://vk.com/club2378378).

This type of messages is aimed at forming a strong belief in the importance of maintaining social stability, positive inter-ethnic relations in the Crimea and the importance of awareness of the Crimean Tatars of the possibility of using certain political power in their interests the difficulties of the transition period associated with the reunification of Crimea and Russia.

4   Conclusion

The most intensive formation of public opinion of Russian-speaking users about inter-ethnic and inter-religious relations in Crimea and Sevastopol is carried out by blogs, which reflect diametrically opposed positions regarding the discussion about the justice and injustice of the reunification of Russia, Crimea and Sevastopol. Despite the absolute dominance and great influence of blogs aimed at designing positive attitudes towards the Peninsula's accession to the Russian Federation, a significant user audience of blogs focused on condemning this event calls for the need to counter these flows, which strengthen the social and cultural distance between the peoples of Crimea, the socio-cultural disintegration of the Peninsula's. In the information space of social media, the most powerful background that stimulates the circulation of messages about attitudes towards interethnic consent or disagreement is the topic related to the Russian state policy towards the Crimean Tatars. Discursive practices in this information flow contain three main semantic structures: the discourse of the oppression of the Crimean Tatars; the discourse of the unreasonableness of the claims of the Crimean Tatars; discourse warning of the Crimean Tatars from the internalization of anti-Russian rhetoric. The dynamics of the share of social media reports is also largely determined by the aspects related to the Russian state policy towards the Crimean Tatars.

5   Research Perspectives

1. Creation of markers dictionaries for the implementation of Ukrainian-language and Crimean Tatar-language unloading to compare the characteristics of the Russian-language array with markers of social and media flows on interethnic and interreligious relations in Crimea and Sevastopol.
2. Based on the results of scientific research, development of technologies to counteract information flows aimed at aggravating interethnic and interreligious relations in Crimea and Sevastopol.

Acknowledgment. The study is implemented with the funds of the grant of Russian Foundation for Basic Research "Ukrainian information flows in the Crimean segment of social media: risks and technologies to overcome the negative effects of anti-Russian rhetoric in the online environment (№ 18-011-00937 for 2018-2020).

References

1. Alexander, J.: On smart frameworks of "Strong Program". Sociol. Rev. **9**(2), 5–10 (2010)
2. Allport, F.H.: Social Psychology. Routledge, London (1924)
3. Berger, P.L., Luckmann, T.: The Social Construction of Reality: A Treatise in the Sociology of Knowledge, Garden City (1966)
4. Bergman, M.L., Kasper, G.: Perception and performance in native and nonnative apology. In: Kasper, G., Blum-Kulka, S. (eds.) Interlingua Pragmatics, pp. 82–107. Oxford University Press, Oxford (1993)

5. Brodovskaya, E.V., Dombrovskaya, A., Karzubov, D.: Online mobilization of mass protests in Ukraine, Moldova, Armenia, and Kazakhstan (2013–2016.): the results of comprehensive comparative empirical study. In: Proceedings of the International Conference on Electronic Governance and Open Society: Challenges in Eurasia St. Petersburg, Russia, 04–06 September 2014, pp. 32–36. ACM, New York (2017). http://dl.acm.org/citation.cfm?id=3129764&dl=ACM&coll=DL&CFID=813102647&CFTOKEN=10709015. –Accessed 21 Jan 2018

6. Castells, M.: The Rise of the Network Society. The Information Age: Econimy, Society and Culture, vol. 1, 2nd edn. Wiley-Blackwell, Hoboken (2009). New Preface edition

7. Dalton, R.J., Cain, B.E., Scarrow, S.E.: Democratic public and democratic institutions. In: Cain, B.E., Dalton, R.J., Scarrow, S.E. (eds.) Democracy Transformed? Expanding Political Opportunities in Advanced Industrial Democracies, pp. 250–275. Oxford University Press, Oxford (2003)

8. van Dijk, T.: Ideology and Discourse. A Multidisciplinary Introduction. English version of an Internet course for the Universitat Oberta de Catalunya (UOC) (2000)

9. Durkheim, E.: The rules of sociological method. In: Solovay, S.A., Mueller, J.M. (eds.). Collier-Macmillan Limited, New York (1964)

10. Edwards, D., Potter, J.: Discursive Psychology. Sage, London (1992)

11. Fairclough, N.: Analysing Discourse: Texstual Analysis for Social Research. Routledge, London (2003)

12. Jenkins, H.: Convergence: Where Old and New Media Collide. NYU press, New York (2006)

13. Gamson, W., Croteau, D., Hoynes, W., Sasson, T.: Media images and the social construction of reality. Ann. Rev. Sociol. **18**, 373–393 (1992). http://links.jstor.org/sici?sici=0360-0572%281992%2918%3C373%3AMIATSC%3E2.0.CO%3B2-Z. Accessed 25 Mar 2018

14. Goldstone, J.A.: Revolution and Rebellion in the Early Modern World. University of California Press, Berkeley (1993)

15. Green, S.: Twitter and Russian protest: memes, networks and mobilization. In: Gurr, T. (ed.) Why Men Rebel. Princeton University Press (1974). http://www.newmediacenter.ru/ru/2012/05/22/. Accessed 14 Apr 2018

16. Howard, P.N., Parks, M.R.: Social media and political change: capacity, constraint and consequence. J. Commun. **62**, 359–362 (2012)

17. Laclau, E., Mouffe, C.: Hegemony and the Socialist Strategy. New York (1985)

18. Lakoff, G., Johnsen, M.: Metaphors We Live By. The university of Chicago press, London (2003)

19. Lebon, G.: Psychology of the Masses and Peoples. Social and Human Sciences. Domestic and Foreign Literature. Episode 11: Sociology. Abstract J. **2**, 166–189 (1995)

20. Livingstone, S., Couldry, N., Markham, T.: Youthful Steps towards civic participation: does the internet help? In: Loader, B. (ed.). Young Citizens in the Digital Age. Political Engagement, Young People and New Media, pp. 21–34. Routledge, New York (2007)

21. Lippmann, W.: Public Opinion. New York (1922)

22. Marcuse, H.: On Concrete Philosophy. In: Marcuse, H., Abromeit, J., Wolin, R. (eds.) Heideggerian Marxism. University of Nebraska Press, Lincoln (2005)

23. McCarthy, J.D., Zald, M.N.: Resource mobilization and social movements: a partial theory. Am. J. Sociol. **82**, 1212–1241 (1977)

24. McCombs, M., Reynolds, A.: News influence on our pictures of the world. In: Bryand, J., Zillmann, D. (eds). Mahwah "Media Effects" (2002)

25. Merton, R.K.: Social structure and anomie. Am. Sociol. Rev. **3**, 672–682 (1938)

26. Noveck, B.S.: Wiki Government: How Technology Can Make Government Better, Democracy Stronger, and Citizens More Powerful. Washington (2009)

27. Pierson, P., Skocpol, T.: Historical Institutionalism in Contemporary Political Science in Political Science: The State of the Discipline. In: Katznelson, I., Milner, H. (eds). Norton, New York (2002)
28. Polat, R.K.: The internet and political participation: exploring the explanatory links. Eur. J. Commun. **20**, 435–459 (2005)
29. Sériot, P.: Structure Et Totalité: Les Origines Intellectuelles Du Structuralisme En Europe Centrale Et Orientale. Presses universitaires de France, Paris (1999)
30. Smith, A.D.: National identity and vernacular mobilization in Europe. Nat. Nationalism **17** (2), 233–248 (2011)
31. Takeshita, T.: Exploring the media's roles in defining reality: from issue-agenda setting to attribute agenda setting. In: McCombs, M.E., Shaw, D.L., Weaver, D.H. (eds). Communication and Democracy. Mahwah (1997)
32. Tilly, C., Giugni, M.: How Social Movements Matter. University of Minnesota Press, Minneapolis (1999)
33. The Significance of Simmel's Work ex: In: Koser, L. (ed.) Masters of Sociological Thought: Ideas in Historical and Social Context, 2nd edn. Harcourt Brace Jovanovich, New York (1977)
34. Toffler, A.: Previews and Premises: An Interview with the Author of Future Shock and The Third Wave. Black Rose Books, Montreal (1987)
35. Weber, L., Loumakis, A., Bergman, J.: Who Participates and Why? An Analysis of Citizens on the Internet and the Mass Public. Soc. Sci. Comput. Rev. **21**, 26–42 (2003)
36. Wu, H.D., Coleman, R.: Advancing agenda setting theory: the comparative strength and new contingent conditions on the two levels of agenda-setting effects. J. Mass Commun. Quarter. **86**(4), 775–789 (2009)

Battle in Twitter: Comparative Analysis of Online Political Discourse (Cases of Macron, Trump, Putin, and Medvedev)

Radomir Bolgov[1]($\boxtimes$), Igor Chernov[1], Igor Ivannikov[1],
and Dmitry Katsy[2]

[1] Saint Petersburg State University, Saint Petersburg, Russia
{rbolgov,ivannikov-1968}@yandex.ru,
igor_chernov@mail.ru
[2] Bonch-Bruevich Saint - Petersburg State University of Telecommunications,
Saint Petersburg, Russia
dmitrikatsy@hotmail.com

Abstract. This case study is an example of interdisciplinary research, which couples the linguistic aspects with the study of public political discourse in social media. The purpose of the study is to identify how "realism" terms and national/global agenda are represented in Twitter discourse of leaders of countries which claim to be global powers today. Obviously, it is impossible to claim a high status in the modern world without participation in global discussions (including the level of influence on public opinion in Twitter). We collect data from official accounts of the U.S. President Donald Trump, France's President Emmanuel Macron, Russia's President Vladimir Putin, and Russia's Prime Minister Dmitry Medvedev. Then we propose a research method developed by us which contains 5 stages. The main method of research is traditional content analysis, not only selective (under this or that theory), but also "frontline" one. We are interested in the subject matter (key, most frequent vocabulary) that dominates the considered texts. We separate the same amounts of text (approximately 33 000 words) in the content of the Twitter pages of Trump, Macron, Putin and Medvedev. Then we quantify the words and identify the key concepts which are specific for political realism and political idealism. We perform a "frontal" general analysis of all the most frequently used concepts. We make a quantitative assessment of the nature of the use of political leaders' key concepts (this stage of analysis is divided on several sub-stages). Finally we compare the frequency of concepts' use by leaders of the West and Russia.

Putin-Medvedev pair has obvious coincidences with Trump at the external level, but a significant divergence in the base level, i.e. this is another picture of the world, another choice of subjects, in contrast to Trump-Macron pair. Russian leaders are focused on domestic problems of the country. Global agenda is not sufficiently represented in Twitter accounts of Russian leaders. Trump and Macron discuss common (global) themes herewith they have different ideological preferences.

Keywords: Twitter · Social media · Political discourse · Content analysis · Comparative analysis

© Springer Nature Switzerland AG 2019
A. Chugunov et al. (Eds.): EGOSE 2018, CCIS 947, pp. 374–383, 2019.
https://doi.org/10.1007/978-3-030-13283-5_28

1   Introduction

Social networks play an increasing role in the modern world. The social network of Twitter has registered more than 330 million users around the world, and therefore it is not surprising that its information capabilities are used by such world leading politicians as US President D. Trump, Russian President V. Putin and French President E. Macron. In conditions of rapid development of information and communication technologies and the social and political changes that they cause (global informatization of the world) it is impossible to achieve their political goals without using these tools.

If the efficiency of Twitter's use of D. Trump is sufficiently obvious, then the effectiveness of the use of Twitter by Russian leaders needs expert interdisciplinary evaluation. In this study, the content of Russian leaders is not considered in the evaluation key, but in the quantitative one, i.e. we analyze how much this content on its subject (terminology) coincides with the content of Western leaders.

The purpose of the study is to identify how "realism" terms and national/global agenda are represented in Twitter discourse of leaders of countries which claim to be global powers today. Obviously, it is impossible to claim a high status in the modern world without participation in global discussions (including the level of influence on public opinion in Twitter).

2   Discourse and Social Media

We follow to the concept of discourse explicated by van Dijk, which means social interaction based on linguistic communication. The key aspect of the discourse is not the fact of "live" communication and not the specific linguistic parameters of the produced text. The most important component of texts construction and perception is the judgments of social situations behind them and their cognitive representation [7: 122].

The notion of the final understanding of discourse as verbally mediated social interaction was developed by Habermas, who proposed to consider communication and discourse not just as the interaction of at least two able to speak and act subjects entering (through verbal and non-verbal means) in interpersonal relationships [11: 11], but the interaction that takes place on important public and political issues.

Discourse in social media is a collection of open (accessible for change and expansion), verbally mediated discussions on certain topics, and conducted by peer-to-peer actors. However, a full part of the public discourse is only those discussions that are devoted to important for the whole society problems that have already fallen into the public sphere. Discourse in social media is a part of the general public discourse, with the difference that any subject can become its actor in social media [6].

The computer semantic analysis of the discourse of social networks and media today is one of the most actively developing areas of computer linguistics and, in particular, computer semantics. A significant contribution to the development of this direction is made by numerous modern studies of methods of using automatic linguistic processing of texts to effectively solve such problems as automatic classification of messages, recognition of named entities, data mining, sentiment analysis, automatic referencing and other tasks, the main difficulty of solving them is due to the multi-valued and multivariant nature of language. As a separate direction, it is worth noting the analysis of online discourse (not necessarily political) within the framework of applied linguistics [15], for example, the sentiment analysis in speech communication.

The analysis of political discourse has long included content analysis, operational coding, cognitive mapping etc. A number of works are devoted to the discourse analysis, in particular, [5, 6]. It is worth noting in-depth content analysis of political realism and political idealism [4]. These authors even announced the beginning of a rhetorical turn in international relations. Also there is a set of works on the discourse of Donald Trump, for example, [21]. In addition, some researchers analyze the experience of political leaders in a comparative perspective, in particular [1]. Tregubov makes an attempt to compare the discourse of V. Putin and D. Medvedev [17].

3 Political Discourse in Twitter

Twitter is designed to publish 140-character texts on the Internet [12]. Twitter has a default function that displays the number of followers on each user's page. This feature allows to evaluate the audience and popularity of Twitter accounts. While Twitter was created as a platform for the exchange of non-political information [13, 14], today it is widely used as a platform for online communication on a variety of politically [20] and socially significant topics [22]. Twitter has become a frequently used channel of political discourse [18]. Politicians and public persons have their own Twitter accounts, where they publish their messages [9, 12]. Twitter is used in political discourse to spread political views and opinions, as well as to maintain online presence [16].

Twitter, as one of the social networks, can be conceptualized as a public online sphere. Baumer and colleagues [3] indicate that the political microblogging on Twitter has increasingly become influential and democratizing source of news and information. Government officials who have their own Twitter accounts have the same publishing rights with non-public Twitter users. It is noteworthy that politicians in Twitter adhere to the same ethical principles as all other Twitter users. Twitter triggers an egalitarian type of online discourse that is democratic, user-friendly and multimodal [10, 23]. The Twitter discourse has unique characteristics, such as linking messages with users, hyperlinks to external Internet sources and hashtagging [2]. The style of the discourse in Twitter includes fluidity of meaning, innovation and creativity [10], along with consciously controlled and fixed users' views of the outside world [12]. In addition, the discourse on Twitter is extremely dynamic due to the speed with which the texts are published on Twitter [22]. Presumably, such a discursive space includes Twitter-specific ways of political discourse, in particular, foreign policy discourse.

The choice of Twitter as a social-network platform of discourse is due to its openness to all participants, the conciseness of messages, as well as the ease of sharing and tagging information. In addition, participants often repeat information in all social media to increase the audience reach. Therefore, the analysis of only this platform seems to be sufficient for analyzing the discourse in social media. In previous studies, the authors also preferred Twitter as a platform, in particular, for researching social movements, protests and election campaigns [8, 19]. So, S. Hong and D. Nadler studied the technology of using social media by candidates for presidency. In particular, the authors studied the number of mentions of a candidate in Twitter. The results of the conducted research showed that with the advent of social media, the number of channels for broadcasting information to the audience increases. It turned out that the high level of activity of candidates in social media, as a result, has a minimal impact on the level of public attention in the online environment.

4   Methods of Research

The main method of research is traditional content analysis, not only selective (under this or that theory), but also "front-line" one. We do not just single out the terms that are characteristic of realists/idealists, but we also study all the content. And we do not build cognitive maps. In this case, we are only interested in the subject matter (key, most frequent vocabulary) that dominates the texts under consideration. The study can be divided into the following stages:

1. We separate the same amounts of text (approximately 33 000 words) in the content of the Twitter pages of Trump, Macron, Putin and Medvedev.
2. We quantify the words and identify the key concepts which are specific for political realism and political idealism.
3. We perform a "frontal" general analysis of all the most frequently used concepts.
4. The final stage of the content analysis of the texts involves a quantitative assessment of the nature of the use of political leaders' key concepts. Following N. Tregubov, this stage of analysis is divided on several sub-stages: (1) expert quantitative evaluation of the nature of the use by political leaders of units of analysis; (2) determination of average values of estimates for each case of using units of analysis; (3) checking the relevance of the obtained average values using the methods of descriptive statistics and correlation analysis, correcting irrelevant data; (4) changing the marks of the scale rating to the opposite (inverting) taking into account the context of the use of certain units of analysis; (5) the construction of a single list of scale estimates of all cases of using the concepts of realism with a range of values from 1 (the most negative attitude of the actor to realism) to 9 (maximally positive); (6) analysis of obtained quantitative results.
5. We compare the frequency of concepts' use by leaders of the West and Russia.

While conducting a quantitative evaluation of mentioning the units of analysis we took a survey of 6 experts from St. Petersburg State University. The main task was to determine in what value (negative, neutral or positive), leaders use these or other key concepts of realism (see Table 1). As a result, we obtained 6 independent expert evaluations of all cases of using the units of analysis (see Table 2).

Table 1. Expert survey form.

Character use notions	Maximum negative (1)	Empha-tically negative (2)	Negative (3)	Neutral negative (4)	Neutral (5)	Neutral positive (6)	Positive (7)	Emph-atically positive (8)	Maxi-mum positive (9)
Please determine in which meaning (negative, neutral or positive) the text uses the key concepts of realism. The results of the evaluation are displayed in the table.									
Sequence number of approval									

Table 2. Results of expert survey

Cases of use	Experts						Average value	Standard deviation
	1	2	3	4	5	6		
1	5	6	7	6	5	5	5,666,667	0,816496581
...								

However, the procedure for checking the reliability of intercoding (calculation of the linear correlation coefficient (Pearson's r) of scale scores issued by each two researchers) allowed talking about the achievement of a significant level of consensus between experts. Of the 15 correlation coefficients obtained, 12 exceeded 0.6, which may indicate a satisfactory level of consensus among experts on the evaluation of this set of cases. Therefore, for these cases of using units of analysis as the final scale score, it was considered to be the arithmetic mean of the assessments of the consensus experts (see Table 3). The remaining 3 cases of using the concepts by the actors required additional processing. In particular, the main error of some experts was revealed, leading, in our opinion, to the irrelevance of the assessment of these cases. This error is due to the fact that in a number of cases the experts evaluated not the character, but the context of the use of this or that concept. For cases of this kind, the final scale score was taken to be the arithmetic mean of the assessments of experts located in the "right", from our point of view, range of values.

Table 3. Correlations between expert estimates

	Expert 1	Expert 2	Expert 3	Expert 4	Expert 5	Expert 6
Expert 1	1					
Expert 2	0.77	1				
Expert 3	0.68	0.75	1			
Expert 4	0.71	0.82	0.65	1		
Expert 5	0.33	0.33	0.65	0.75	1	
Expert 6	0.67	0.42	0.72	0.74	0.81	1

When carrying out the procedure for inverting a series of scores obtained as a result of an expert survey, we proceeded from the hypothesis that idealistic and realistic concepts used in tweets of actors can be considered as antonyms and, consequently, a positive evaluation by the actor of the notion of "interest" (or its individual components) means, in this particular case, a negative attitude towards law and morality, and vice versa. The most general results of the expert evaluation of the nature of actors' use of concepts can be described in the form of a set of obtained limiting and average values of the corresponding scales. Thus, according to the results of the analysis, Vladimir Putin's most "idealistic" case of using the concepts received an average score of 1.6 points (between the most negative and emphatically negative values) and the most "realistic" - 8.3 points (positive). In this case, the arithmetic mean of all scale estimates of Putin's use of concepts are 5.4 points (between neutral and neutral-positive values), and the standard deviation is 2.3 points. In turn, Dmitry Medvedev's most "idealistic" case of the using the units of analysis was estimated by experts at 2.2 points (emphatically negative value), and the most "realistic" - at 8.3 points (emphatically positive value). In this case, the average value of all scales of Medvedev's use of the units of analysis is 5.0 points (neutral value), and the standard deviation is 1.9 points.

5   Results of Research

5.1   Macron-Trump

At once it is possible to note, that the President of the USA and the President of France both are active Twitter users. They publish records daily on time and repeatedly. Unofficial style is specific for their tweets. In addition, there is an active response to current political information.

For comparative analysis of the pages of Trump and Macron on Twitter, we chose the parts of the content that were the same in size and allocated in the same time. But since Macron was somewhat more active than Trump on Twitter, the content of Trump's Twitter page was taken from November 1, 2017 by January 24, 2018, and Macron's Twitter pages are from November 28, 2017 by January 24, 2018 (approximately in 33,000 words).

As a result of the traditional analysis of the actors' using the characteristic concepts of political idealists and realists, the following results were obtained (Table 4):

Table 4. Key concepts of realism in the tweets of Macron and Trump.

	Trump	Macron
Nation	43	43
Multilateralism	0	4
Security	24	19
Terrorism	10	18
Military (militaire)	37	15
War (guerre)	3	8
Power (force)	6	13
Interest (interet)	7	0

We can see the division on the realism/idealism, but it is not always clear. We can talk about some balance, because common themes are used, which means existence of general vocabulary. But in the case of Trump, the focus is even on vocabulary for "interest" and against "versatility." Thus, Trump is a political realist, Macron is a political idealist.

Then we conduct a general analysis. We share the content on the domestic, international and universal (global) subjects (Table 5).

Table 5. Domestic, international and global topics in tweets of Macron and Trump.

	Trump	Macron
USA/America/American (for Trump), France/francais (for Macron)	154	128
World (monde)	21	27
Global	3	3
Human rights (droits d' hommes)	4	6

If we extend the database and analyze all the content ("front-line" content analysis of phrases), it is obvious that these two actors have more common features than differences with common topics used.

5.2   Medvedev-Putin

At once it can be noted that the President and the Prime Minister of Russia are quite active users of Twitter, but the content is more official than personal. In fact, this is a record of meetings and speeches.

For a comparative analysis of the pages of Putin and Medvedev in Twitter, the same volume (coinciding with the volume of the analyzed material of Trump and Macron) was singled out parts of the content which are same by number of words and allocated in the same time. But since Putin was somewhat more active than Medvedev in this social network, the content of Putin's Twitter page was taken from December 20, 2016 by January 24, 2018, and Medvedev's Twitter page from March 21, 2014 to January 24, 2018 (approximately 33 000 words) (Table 6).

Table 6.   Key concepts of realism in tweets of Putin and Medvedev.

	Putin	Medvedev
Nation (national) + people + state	3 + 5 + 19 = 27	3 + 10 + 6 = 19
Multilateral	0	0
Safety (security)	5	5
Terrorism (terrorism)	1	5
Military	8	4
War	1	7
Strength + power	0 + 0	4 + 3
Interest	2	3

We can note that there are some general topics and often use of the same vocabulary, with exception of cases "Power-strength-war", since Putin does not actually use this lexicon. Both actors are realists. Putin is a realist on all other indicators.

Then we conduct a general analysis. Just as for analysis of a pair "Macron-Trump", we share content on domestic, international and universal (global) subjects (for example, taking only four words) (Table 7).

Table 7. Domestic, international and global topics in tweets of Putin and Medvedev

	Putin	Medvedev
Russia/Russian	93	94
World (world)	6	10
World/world/global	0	8
Human rights	1	0

We can make a conclusion that Twitter discourses of Putin and Medvedev (the second is taken to check the objectivity of the result) are similar in that they do not pay proper attention to the external "global" agenda.

6   Conclusions

Putin-Medvedev pair has obvious coincidences with Trump at the external level, but a significant divergence in the base level, i.e. this is another picture of the world, another choice of subjects, in contrast to Trump-Macron pair. Russian leaders are focused on domestic problems of the country. In other words, Trump and Putin talk about different things while Trump and Macron talk about the same thing.

Following on the results of the content analysis we can note that global agenda is not sufficiently represented in Twitter accounts of Russian leaders despite the claiming of Russia to be a great power. However, obviously, it is impossible to claim a sufficiently high status in the modern world without participation in global discussions (including the level of influence on public opinion in social media). The use of new online platforms is often of a formalistic nature. Moreover the quality of Twitter content is a subject of many questions (only the official information), although it is translated into English. Trump and Macron discuss common themes herewith they have different ideological preferences.

References

1. Aharony, N.: Twitter use by three political leaders: an exploratory analysis. Online Inf. Rev. **36**(4), 587–603 (2012). https://doi.org/10.1108/14684521211254086
2. Ausserhofer, J., Maireder, A.: National politics on Twitter. Inf. Commun. Soc. **16**(3), 291–314 (2013). https://doi.org/10.1080/1369118X.2012.756050

3. Baumer, E., Sinclair, J., Irvine, B.: 'America is like metamucil': fostering critical and creative thinking about metaphor in political blogs. In: CHI 2010: Expressing and Understanding Opinions in Social Media, pp. 1437–1446 (2010). https://doi.org/10.1145/1753326.1753541
4. Beer, F., Balleck, B.: Realist/idealist texts: psychometry and semantics. Peace Psychol. Rev. 1(1), 38–44 (1994)
5. Bodrunova, S.S., Litvinenko, A.A., Gavra, D.P., Yakunin, A.V.: Twitter-based discourse on migrants in Russia: the case of 2013 bashings in Biryulyovo. Int. Rev. Manage. Mark. 5, 97–104 (2015)
6. Bolgov, R., Filatova, O., Tarnavsky, A.: Analysis of public discourse about Donbas conflict in Russian social media. In: Proceedings of the 11th International Conference on Cyber Warfare and Security, ICCWS 2016, pp. 37–46 (2016)
7. van Dijk, T.A.: Cognitive situation models in discourse production: the expression of ethnic situations in prejudiced discourse. In: Forgas, J.P. (ed.) Language and Social Situations. Springer Series in Social Psychology, pp. 61–79. Springer, New York (1985). https://doi.org/10.1007/978-1-4612-5074-6_4
8. Doroshenko, L., Schneider, T., Kofanov, D., et al.: Ukrainian nationalist parties and connective action: an analysis of electoral campaigning and social media sentiments. Inf. Commun. Soc. 1–20 (2018). https://doi.org/10.1080/1369118X.2018.1426777
9. Fischer, E., Reuber, R.A.: Social interaction via new social media: (how) can interactions on Twitter affect effectual thinking and behavior? J. Bus. Ventur. 26, 1–18 (2011). https://doi.org/10.1016/j.jbusvent.2010.09.002
10. Gillen, J., Merchant, G.: Contact calls: Twitter as a dialogic social and linguistic practice. Lang. Sci. 35, 47–58 (2013). https://doi.org/10.1016/j.langsci.2012.04.015
11. Habermas, J.: Relationship to the world and rational aspects of action in four sociological concepts of action. Sociol. obozrenie (Sociol. Rev.) 7(1) (2008). [in Russian]
12. Marvick, A., Boyd, D.: I tweet honestly, i tweet passionately: Twitter users, context collapse, and the imagined audience. New Media Soc. 13(1), 114–133 (2010). https://doi.org/10.1177/1461444810365313
13. Munson, S., Resnik, P.: The Prevalence of Political Discourse in Non-Political Blogs (2010)
14. Page, R.: The linguistics of self-branding and micro-celebrity in Twitter: the role of hashtags. Discourse Commun. 6(2), 181–210 (2012). https://doi.org/10.1177/1750481312437441
15. Potapova, R.K.: Social network discourse as an object of interdisciplinary research. In: Proceedings of the 2nd international conference "Discourse as social activity: priorities and prospects", pp. 20–22 (2014). [in Russian]
16. Spina, S., Cancila, J.: Gender Issues in the interactions of italian politicians on twitter: identity, representation and flows of conversation. Int. J. Cross-Cult. Stud. Environ. Commun. 2(2), 147–157 (2013)
17. Tregubov, N.A.: Articulation of ideas about political modernization in rhetoric of Putin and Medvedev: an attempt of comparative content analysis. Vestnik Permskogo universiteta. Seria: Politologiya 3(11), 69–81 (2010). [in Russian]
18. Tumasjan, A., Sprenger, T., Sandner, P., Welpe, I.: Election forecast with Twitter: how 140 characters reflect the political landscape. Soc. Sci. Comput. Rev. 29, 1–17 (2010). https://doi.org/10.1177/0894439310386557
19. Woolley, J., Limperos, A., Oliver, M.: The 2008 presidential election, 2.0: a content analysis of user-generated political Facebook groups. Mass Commun. Soc. 13(5), 631–652 (2010). https://doi.org/10.1080/15205436.2010.516864
20. Xifra, J., Grau, F.: Nanoblogging PR: the discourse on public relations in Twitter. Public Relat. Rev. 36, 171–174 (2010). https://doi.org/10.1016/j.pubrev.2010.02.005

21. Yakoba, I.A.: Deconstruction of Donald Trump's discourse (cases of his 2016 elections speeches). Diskurs Pi **1**(26), 164–169 (2017). [in Russian]
22. Yardi, S., Boyd, D.: Dynamic debates: an analysis of group polarization over time on Twitter. Bull. Sci. Technol. Soc. **30**(5), 316–327 (2010)
23. Zappavigna, M.: Enacting Identity in microblogging through ambient affiliation. Discourse Commun. **8**, 1–20 (2013). https://doi.org/10.1177/1750481313510816

Social Media as a Display of Students' Communication Culture: Case of Educational, Professional and Labor Verbal Markers Analysis

Natalia E. Shilkina[1] , Anna V. Maltseva[1(✉)] ,
Olesya V. Makhnytkina[2] , Marina V. Titova[3] ,
Elina V. Gubernatorova[3] , Igor A. Katsko[4] ,
Farida I. Mirzabalaeva[5] , and Svetlana V. Shusharina[6]

[1] Saint-Petersburg University, Saint-Petersburg, Russia
{st803519, st801923}@spbu.ru
[2] Saint-Petersburg University, ITMO University, Saint-Petersburg, Russia
olesyamahnitkina@yandex.ru
[3] Altay State University, Barnaul, Russia
{tltova.marine, gub-ilina}@yandex.ru
[4] Kuban State Agrarian University, Krasnodar, Russia
ingward@mail.ru
[5] Plekhanov Russian University of Economics, Moscow, Russia
faridamir@yandex.ru
[6] ITMO University, Saint-Petersburg, Russia
svetlana_shu@bk.ru

Abstract. Social media are the source reflecting the linguistic situation and modern trends that have emerged in the language of a virtual society with incredible precision. Texts of students' messages allow us to analyze vocabulary in the linguistic and cultural aspect, model a linguistic and cultural field and create a linguacultural commentary on those lexical units that represent the dominating story of youth culture at the current stage of language and society development.

The article presents the results of the research of student youth verbal markers in relation to professional and labor intentions, the methodology of their linguacultural study, comparative analysis and classification of lexical units. Tag names have been revealed based on expert analysis of the messages of the "VKontakte" social media in accordance to the frequency of the selected tags occurrence record. Words-markers are being highlighted in the context of students' professional and labor intentions as well as bigrams/triplets with words-markers. The article reveals the peculiarities of linguistic and social situation in the linguacultural and social aspects. It stresses the lexemes that form the core of the linguacultural field as well as the features of the linguistic and social situation in the linguacultural and social aspects. In the paper the role of researching the features of virtual communication in the aspect of language and culture interaction on the example of labor and professional intentions has also been stated.

© Springer Nature Switzerland AG 2019
A. Chugunov et al. (Eds.): EGOSE 2018, CCIS 947, pp. 384–397, 2019.
https://doi.org/10.1007/978-3-030-13283-5_29

Keywords: Social media · Verbal markers · Linguacultural commentary · Language and culture · Tags · Bigrams · Students · Secondary analysis · RuNet

1 Introduction

The study of virtual communication in the aspect of language culture is currently being relevant and significant. Social media are the source, reflecting the linguistic situation and modern trends that have been emerging in the language of a virtual society with incredible accuracy. They are also a necessary part of the modern social space. The spread of information technologies is associated with positive results of this process, namely when active users gain a wide access to useful information that increases their mobility, competence and competitiveness in educational, professional, employment and other spheres. However, negative consequences are not excluded. They are related to the potential threat of undergoing manipulation, assimilating negative behavioral practices that are detrimental to social adaptation. Consumers of social media content involuntarily absorb various value and behavioral settings and implement them in educational and work activities as well as daily interaction. The scale of content increase in the Internet, the growth of social media popularity, time consumption by users while taking part in Internet communications - all this leads to the urgent necessity to search for new approaches of collecting and analyzing data on behavioral patterns of active social media users. The texts of youth's messages are the most relevant reflection. They are open for the analysis of vocabulary in a linguistic and cultural aspect aimed at modeling a linguistic and cultural field and creating a linguistic and cultural commentary on those lexical units that represent the basic theme of youth culture at the present stage of language and society development.

2 Related Works

Contemporary research demonstrates that social media are the source, reflecting the linguistic situation with incredible accuracy alongside with modern trends that have arisen in a virtual society language. At the same time social media are the source of knowledge about alterations not only in the language but culture in general. The analysis of educational, professional and labor verbal markers of student youth is a further step in the study of social media, revealing their significance in reflecting socially significant intentions of an individual and a group.

Researchers are interested in the changes of the national language [1, 2]; the emergence of a new speech culture [3]; the formation of a new communicative speech etiquette [4] and even the birth of a new virtual language [5]. Most of the works related to the analysis of communication focus on social networks both of Russian and global Internet space. The works of Gavra [6], Pocheptsov [7], Kashkin [8], Nakhimova [9], Lowery [10], Guo [11] and others [12, 13] constitute the foundation of the social media research. The description of new media, their properties as well as the features of network communication is contained in the research of Bykov [14]. While studying "social media", these authors suggest comprehending social media as a kind of online media where each person can act both as an audience and as an author.

The software being used for this purpose allows anyone to post, comment, move, edit information and create communities without any special knowledge in the field of encoding [14]. Thus, the concept of "social media" is used as a single name for all varieties of Internet entities operating in accordance with the web 2.0 principle. In addition to performing the functions of exchanging opinions, supporting communication and receiving information by their participants, social media can become the objects and means of information management and the platform of information confrontation. According to D. A. Gubanov, "social media contributes, firstly, to the organization of social communication among people and, secondly, to the realization of their basic social needs." Gubanov argues that such platforms play a significant role in spreading opinions that affect the actions of network users [3, 4, 15].

In spite of a rather long period of analyzing the facts that have arisen as a result of modern technologies, the issue of adapting materials obtained through the analysis of social media in a scientific discourse still remains urgent in a significant number of topical studies of linguistic, sociological, political and interdisciplinary nature. The authors of this paper offer their case as a design for the social media research. So, the present research focuses on describing the outcomes of the approbation of original methodology for obtaining scientific knowledge out of massive volume of unstructured information provided by social media, as an example of evaluating the culture of communication among students within the RuNet.

3   Research Problem

The article presents verbal markers of student youth in relation to professional and labor intentions. It also conveys the methodology of verbal markers' linguacultural research, comparative analysis and classification of lexical units. Tag names have been revealed based on expert analysis of the messages of the "VKontakte" social media on the frequency of the selected tags occurrence. Words-markers are being highlighted with respect to professional and labor intentions alongside with bigrams/triplets. The article reveals the triple of the linguistic and social situation in linguacultural and social aspects, the lexemes that form the core of the linguacultural field. It focuses on the importance of researching the features of virtual communication in the aspect of language and culture interaction on the example of labor and professional pursuits.

The goal of the research is to generalize the features, qualitative and quantitative characteristics of lexical units that represent the language picture of modern community world vision.

The main difficulty in analyzing the social media content is the unstructured information. In this connection, an important stage is the compilation of dictionaries containing the words-markers characterizing the negative and positive styles of thinking and behavior of social media users, which can be obtained as a result of studying the opinions of a wide range of experts including sociologists, psychologists, teachers, law enforcement officials etc. The next step is the selection of software to accomplish the research task. Typically, such software tools include programme counters that allow you to automatically record the indicators of websites' content or the implementation of any actions. Another tool is log analyzers that are internal local programmes installed on the computer owner of the Internet resource, through which extensive information about visitors and their actions on a particular website is accumulated. Blog analyzers are one more source which belongs to online analysis services for social media that monitor the appearance of certain previously set keywords in the blogosphere [16].

A further crucial step is to solve the problem of data consolidation. It should be stressed that with an inefficient organization of this stage, the data collection and analysis may never end. The methods that can be used to analyze the content of social media, on the one hand, depend on the research tasks, and, on the other hand, on the data itself, the features of which have been described above. The range of methods by which processing, and analysis are performed includes preliminary visualization, calculation of standard descriptive statistics, and further modeling of research hypotheses on this basis that are verified by more sophisticated methods [17].

The final stage is the conceptualization of the results of social media content analysis aimed at identifying the facts of the formation and distribution of behavioral patterns that are different in sentiment.

4   Research Methodology

Empirical data for this study from the original research project of the authors based on the analysis of educational, professional and labor intentions have been taken.

The concept of the linguistic picture of the world goes back to the ideas of Wilhelm von Humboldt, who was one of the first linguists to notice that "every person has a subjective image of an object that does not completely coincide with the image of the same subject of another person." The word thus carries a burden of subjective representations, the differences of which are within certain limits, since their carriers being members of the same language group, have a certain national character and consciousness [18].

In the thirties of the twentieth century, Weisgerber introduced the term "language picture of the world" (sprachliches Weltbild) into science, noting that a concrete community spiritual content and treasure of knowledge live and act in the language, which is rightly called the picture of the world of a specific language [19].

There are a large number of definitions of the language picture of the world in modern science. However, the definition that meets the requirements for identifying the features of subjective images of the virtual world as a means of representation of the results of linguistic and mental activity most of all may be given as follows: these are the ideas about reality that form a unified system of views.

So, the language picture of the world is the reality reflected in the language, the linguistic division of the world, information about the world being transmitted through the units of language of different levels [20].

VKontakte (vk.com) is one of the most popular social media in Russia. About 380 million users are already registered on the site and the 40% are not elder than 25 years. The social network users can join groups based on specific interests; for instance, there are groups almost in every university that discuss topics connected with the events related to it. The majority of members of these groups are students or university entrants.

The source of data has been the "Overheard in..." groups of the VKontakte social network website encompassing more than one hundred universities throughout the all Russian Federation federal districts. There has been considered classical, technical, pedagogical and medical universities. The empirical base is formed using the system of monitoring and analysis of media Beensaid [21]. The procedure of message filtering has been carried out. Only the messages, reflecting the educational, professional and labor intentions of users have been included in the sample. For this purpose, a set of common tag-markers has been determined on the basis of an expert survey of specialists in the organization of work with young people, teachers, sociologists and linguists, which includes 693 words-nouns. In all filtered message tags have been allocated, i.e. words-nouns. As the messages have not been of a large volume, as a rule, up to 10 tags have been allocated in each message, on the basis of which the bigrams and triplets have been modelled further on.

It becomes possible to imagine a language picture of the world in the "VKontakte" through messages, comments, which highlight the most popular hashtags in the community today. A hashtag (a symbol is #) is a word or phrase, preceded by this symbol. Users can be united into a group of posts on a topic using hashtags - words or phrases starting with # symbol. For example: #exam, #student, #university, #education etc. This service allows you to trace the urgent words-topics, as well as questions that concern the representatives of this or that Internet community. Thus, we can distinguish the nuclear units of the VKontakte user's worldview, which are of significant value, both for a separate linguistic personality, and for a given lingua-cultural community as a whole.

In general, tags form the types of communicative competence of a virtual linguistic personality, among which there may be distinguished the following three groups:

1. general competence, including the ability to understand and interpret lexical units that are comprehensible and clear to all speakers of the Russian literary language, mainly related to stylistically neutral vocabulary;
2. professional competence, combining the ability to understand words which meanings are clear to people who participate in common professional activities;
3. social competence is based on the ability to absorb and interpret lexical material, comprehendible only to representatives of a particular social group.

So, the vocabulary of educational process analyzed in the virtual communication ("University education and employment intentions") contains several lexical groups such as a session, a diploma, a university (university), and training. Microgroups have been identified based on the technical process of teaching students. The corresponding lexical units and their variants have been included into each subfield.

The "session" word group (523) from the number of frequency tags encompasses such units as "exam" (1491), "question" (1213) etc. Research of bigrams allows to build the "Exam" microgroup within the "Session" subfield. It has become possible due to the most frequently found tags. Thus, this microgroup includes lexical units representing the basic concepts associated with the process of preparation, organization, implementation and examination pass.

Open data from the "VKontakte" social media directly refers to the public ones, which allows to be handled without restrains. When a person posts his or her data to a social media, a user accepts the terms of the "VKontakte" site use and, therefore, agrees that his personal data become publicly available, depending on the selected privacy modes. In this case, additional user consent to the collection and processing of such publicly available personal data is not required [22].

It should be noted that some tools to search for the target audience on social media make the collected data impersonate. Since after selecting the required characteristics: topic, gender, age, geographic location, etc. a list of id pages is created, excluding any possible personal data [23].

5 Empirical Material for the Research of Verbal Educational, Professional and Labor Verbal Markers

Empirical data for this study from the original research project of the authors based on analysis of educational, professional and labor intentions have been taken. The analyzed empirical database [24] contains samples of verbal markers most widely spread among student youth from the Internet sources. Messages (phrases), words-markers, bigrams/triplets with words-markers, sentiment of messages in relation to events, their evaluation, forecasts or emotional appeal of youth representatives are considered.

According to the original research design the empirical material was distributed into 4 sections such as "Tags", "Analysis of messages", "Bigram", "Triplets".

The "Tags" section contains tag names (nouns) that were identified based on expert analysis as the most important verbal markers about the professional and labor intentions of academic youth. In total, 693 tags have been allocated, which can be divided into groups:

1. the process of learning and evaluation of learning outcomes (tags - exam, question, lecture, semester, assessment, debt, etc.);
2. tags that allow affiliation with the educational institution, training areas (university, faculty, specialty, profile, etc.);
3. tags that define specific disciplines, areas of knowledge (mathematics, law, biology, etc.);
4. tags that define the specialty, the profession of students (psychologist, software developer, sociologist, doctor, etc.);
5. tags - labor markers (work, employment, wages).

As we have already mentioned the data consists of messages posted in the "Overheard in ..." groups, the "Vkontakte" social media, opening the opportunity to conduct linguacultural analysis (frequency of occurrence, sentiment, common tags/bigrams/triplets) of basic educational and professional labor markers, i.e. tags.

The analysis of messages allows you to trace the following specific attributes for online communication:

1. the period of the topic life is determined by the urgency of the events occurring off-line;
2. each message remains relevant during the topic life;
3. the messages contain specific symbolic ways of transmitting emotional expression - smiles, caps lock, underscore, strikethrough etc.;
4. the message contains tags, i.e. the most important verbal markers of its key content;
5. the message has a "creation time", i.e. the information about the date and time of message posting on the Internet;
6. there can be identified several tags in the topic, united in bigrams and triplet tags.

Thus, the analyzing elements are the text of the message, the message category, the sign of the message emotional sentiment, the exact time of its creation, the message tags, bigrams and triplets.

The "Bigram" section contains all possible pairs of tags, one of which is a tag identified based on expert analysis as the most important verbal marker about the professional and labor intentions of academic youth. This table contains 78057 bigrams. The most common bigrams are presented in Table 1.

Table 1. Bigrams

Tag 1	Tag 2	Frequency
Job	Price	129
Exam	Course	120
Exam	Question	110
Course	Competition	106
Job	Course paper	105
Job	Payment	105

The "Triplets" table contains phrases with three tags, one of which is a tag, identified on the basis of expert analysis as the most important verbal marker on professional and labor intentions of academic youth.

6 Results

All results below present different groups of tags with similar means along with ties between them. The selection of individual subfields is based on the identification of dominant tags and can be represented in the following way:

- exam 1491
- question 1213
- course 1203
- job 936
- faculty 804
- student 607

- session 523
- diploma 503
- document 485
- educational establishment of higher professional education 409
- specialty 382
- major 381
- faculty staff 345
- help 340
- training 319
- mathematics 313
- Master's studies 302
- university 288
- language 264
- education 253.

6.1   Subgroup "Education"

An "applicant", using the certificate obtained after secondary school completion, the results of the Unified State Examinations, including the profile exams scores, selects a university in order to get higher professional education. If the minimum admissible enrollment score is exceeded and a "threshold" is reached, the applicant is enrolled into the training in the chosen "specialty", thus, the applicant becomes a "student".

At the end of the "semester", a "session" starts, during which each student can receive an "automatic" assessment, i.e. assessment of knowledge, competences and skills obtained within a discipline without a testing examination procedure. To prepare for the exam, a student has to learn answers to "questions" in accordance to the training "course" syllabus, make "notes", attend a "consultation" before an examination, then, according to the "schedule", take an "exam" and get an "assessment" in accordance with the "requirements". An exam that will not be passed on time is a "debt" that poses a big "trouble" and deprives a student of the opportunity to receive a "scholarship", then a student is given a sheet of paper, i.e. a "document for admission or non-admission" to the rest of the exams, and if he or she takes the bottom ranking position, a student becomes a candidate for "expel". Thus, extralinguistic information, in particular, a description of the fragment of reality, confirms the division of vocabulary based on the identified tags into the subfields and microgroups.

Paradigmatic in this subfield is represented by an antonymic relationship ("expel-admission", "student-applicant", "automatic assessment-debt", optional relations ("university-uni"), hyponymic relations ("session-examination", "consultation", "question").

Observations over systemic links and relationships of all analyzed subfields made it possible to find out that the paradigmatic is represented by synonymous (in all groups of words), antonymic (in two groups) and variant relations (in each of the following subfields: university, diploma, training, session). Hyponymic relationships can also be identified.

The following (503) lexical units are included into the "diploma" word-group: "document" (485), "graduation", "graduate" (university, faculty), "certificate of award", "diploma award ceremony", "project defense" (diploma paper) and "job" (936).

Next group entitled "university" (288) encompasses such lexical units as higher educational "establishment" (409), "faculty" (804), "student" (607), "faculty staff" (345), "help" (340).

Among the text messages of the academic youth community the "training" group (319) has become one of the most numerous. It includes the "education" (253) microgroup – "document", "stamp", "faculty", "specialty", "signature", "assessment", "job", "employer", and "specialty" microgroup (382). The mentioned microgroup includes a list of some specialties such as "mathematics" (313), "language" (264) as well as some general notions, e.g. "degree" (381), "master's studies" (302), "course" (1203).

6.2 Subgroup "Student"

The composition of the "student" tag group is of interest. The lexeme "medic" is fixed in the meaning of "a medical university student" while the lexeme "freshman" is represented in the research text field in the meaning of "a student studying in the first year". By contrast, there is a lexeme "chap" with the opposite meaning. There have also been marked distinctive features of the philology specialty and of the pursuing academic degree such as a "Bachelor's" one.

The construction of the "Studenthood" field not only as a semantic but also as a linguacultural model has become possible because the material collection strategy at the very initial research stage has been oriented to obtaining exhaustive data on each group of words in close connection with the virtual culture of this community. This technique of data processing includes several important steps. First of all, it was necessary to study a group of dominant (in terms of frequency of use) tags, among which the most recurring tags have been distinguished (from 1491 - the most common tag "exam", to "education" - 253 times) the features of displacement (if such a phenomenon took place in history) units. It was vital to note in connection with what occurred crucial and culturally significant events in the student and applicant enrollment environment (for example, the introduction of a new threshold value in scores for passing the enrollment procedure based on the Unified State Examinations results). Then follows the second stage of the presented vocabulary analysis, aimed at identifying the lingua-cultural component in the meaning of the word, i.e. a detailed study of the change in the analyzed concept, the development and the current state of the activity or reality. The third stage is a data comparison of realities and information about the development of individual subfields for each presented tag group. Thus, the peculiarities of the language picture of the world formation are revealed in connection with the marked events (actions, problems) and the sociocultural situation of a single community (Studenthood/social group of students). For a detailed analysis of lexical material, interpretation and classification of its results, the following methods of modern linguistics are comprehensively used in the research paper:

- descriptive method, which presupposes observation, generalization and classification of the material;
- comparative method;
- method of organizing a semantic field as a specific union of lexical units, the basis for the separation of which is the "semantic unity" of lexical units, and the essential features of the field can be considered the link of its elements and "the essential nature of these links [25];
- method of linguacultural interpretation, based on the "integrative approach to the word" with the mandatory involvement of background information (historical, cultural) that make up the cultural context [26].

6.3   Linguistic Comparative Analysis of Lexical Units

There have been noted different tag groups in the texts of the analyzed messages, such as (Table 2):

Table 2. The results of a comparative analysis of the lexical units' data with the meanings of these words, fixed in the dictionaries of the modern Russian literary language

Tags (1019)	Borrowings from the other languages	Identity (form + meaning)	Abbreviated forms (tying, truncation, abbreviation)	Identity of forms but differences in semantics
%	7%	61%	4%	28%
Count	71	621	40	285

1. shortened forms: "academ" (the lexeme is come across in the meaning of "academic leave"), Eng, "basket", "budget", "dep.", "histfac", "lab", "philfac" etc.
2. names of courses and disciplines: "ethics", "ecology", "economics", "biology", "biochemistry", "finance", "regional studies", "programming", "neurology", "Latin", "informatics" etc.
3. names of higher educational establishments (e.g., there can be come across the following abbreviated names: "BSPU", "BelSU", "DGPU", "DonSTU", "SGMU"). Other tags are also allocated to semantic categories:
    a. names and family names;
    b. forms borrowed from the English language;
    c. positions in the educational establishment of higher professional education;
    d. titles of academic and administrative departments in the university;
    e. professions (labor intentions).

The features of student communication culture with the help of social media are most vividly manifested while conducting comparative analysis of the same student audience without the media means involvement. Such a comparison becomes possible while using three parameters that are the most meaningful in the study of the given material. First, to achieve the ultimate goal of communication a speaker uses stable phrases such as clichés, aimed at obtaining a concrete expected programmed outcome.

In contrast to the case of direct communication, the construction of speech patterns is more variable, which is explained by the immediate reaction of the person receiving the information. Second, the analysis of the material within the framework of this study made it possible to single out a "fragmentation-integrity" criterion as one of the main criteria. All in all, communication in a real-time format without the use of information technology (social media) is an exchange of whole structured constructions in accordance with the purpose of an utterance.

An object, reflecting the author's position and reasoning are usually being stated. In most cases communication of users in general and representatives of the student environment in particular are of fragmentary nature in social media. It can only be either the statement of the issue, or the given argument, or the conclusions. Third, in the process of communication through social media there is no greeting or reference to as an element of communicative culture. More often than not such words as "people", "friends" and less often forms associated with the time of day - "night owls"; with a professional group - "biologists", "lawyers" etc.; with gender differences - "a young man", "a girl" come across. While in direct communication, a greeting as a structural unit makes a higher percentage in a percentage ratio even without its own syntactic meaning. Thus, the linguistic methods of arranging a comparative analysis of direct (in real communication) and mediated (through social media) communication made it possible to identify significant differences in both the process of the communicative act and the evaluation of the final output.

7 Conclusions and Research Prospects

Studying the vocabulary of virtual communication of Russian students presents a significant interest for linguacultural research, as it allows to identify the characteristic features of language culture in the space of a particular communicative Internet group.

First, there are formal differences in the attributes of online and offline communications. Online communications are more time-consuming and, as a rule, last at least 24 h. Messages on educational, professional and labor topics remain relevant until the completion of the discussed event. Each message has the value of a written text, because it is not deleted from the communication as an oral message and contains information about the date and time of its appearance. The emotional component of the message is significantly coarsened and transmitted morphologically, syntactically, punctuated, but almost never stylistically. Compared to oral offline speech messages are reduced to the volumes required for the transfer of key content. In general, online messages are informative, evaluative, analyzing, complicated by ideological, political, social and ideological predilections [27].

Second, we are talking about the features of meanings attributed to lexical units used in online communications. At the same time, lexemes, namely educational, professional and labor markers can be used without changes or acquire forms that are not fixed in dictionaries. The identity of lexical units in online messages with the meanings of these words, fixed in the dictionaries of the contemporary Russian literary language [28] comprises 61% of cases. These are the lexical units such as "postgraduate studies", "archive", "argument", "accreditation" etc. Along with the literary Russian expressions lexical borrowings from the English language are used, for example, "ask", "share", "use", "go", "top", "jam", "boys", however, these words are written in the Russian language, thus, distorted. The same is attributed to the professional IT-terminology – "drivers", "motherboard", "pixel", "bug" (7%). These terms are used by the youth representatives who are connected with the IT sphere as well as by those who use these lexical units on the level of general competencies. Moreover, these lexemes are abbreviated in Russian. They sound as slang expressions. Alongside with the mentioned lexemes other abbreviated forms of words are used, i.e. contraction, truncation, abbreviation. All of them are of the Russian origin, e.g. "laba", meaning laboratory works; "vyshka", meaning higher mathematics; "terver", meaning probability theory; "abiture", meaning applicants to educational institutions (4%). Lexemes with numerous semantic changes with the unchanged form make up 28%, e.g. "transfer along the chain", "crack", etc.

Educational, professional and labor markers are found both among the identical lexical units of dictionaries, and among borrowed, distorted and abbreviated lexemes. This allows to assume that the words for which up-to-date convenient simplifying transcripts have not been found so far are neither shortened nor changed.

Virtual communication is an objective reflection of the linguistic and cultural orientation of socialization in educational and public activities. In this respect, certain features of the formation of the cultural socialization of young people in modern education environment, among the speakers of the Russian language, can be formulated. A linguistic component forms the language picture of the world which is an intertextual basis of mutual understanding and accurate interpretation of the younger generation texts.

The virtual communication system reflects the language picture of the world of the contemporary Russian youth, while using the grounding plots of the material and spiritual culture of modern society, representing the names of objects and phenomena of real reality, i.e. an extralinguistic component.

Forms of communication in the Internet communities, found in contexts, can be considered as a linguistic and cultural field where the most frequent and popular tags form the nuclear part of lexical subgroups - subfields.

The language picture of the world of the nation is fixed in the native language, and the peculiarities of one's own vision and analysis of events, objects, phenomena in the life of the younger generation are reflected by the indicated units in the youth slang. Considering the youth language of virtual communication as a reflection of the picture of the world of its speakers, it becomes clear that, despite the changes in values, ideals, views, interests and needs of the younger generation, the tendency to various types of abbreviations in speech, a large number of expressively colored vocabulary and direct translation from other languages is being preserved.

Changes in the world vision of modern youth are reflected in the semantics of slang units, in the development of paradigmatic relations and in the use of new word-formation models.

The modern language of the virtual community demonstrates a tendency to expand the boundaries of the linguacultural field, as it represents the most important fragments of reality (education process) in the youth language picture of the world. In this regard, the lexical composition (tags) is a kind of reflection of the modern youth mentality.

The phenomena of modern youth language culture in the student community are analyzed through the facts of their reflection at social media communication places, and also by means of interpretation of linguistic facts through an extralinguistic component (description of real actions, processes, subjects). As a rule, each language contains features related to national specifics. Thus, the third element, i.e. "community" appears in the formula "language and culture". This phenomenon can be considered as a development of the thought about the interaction of all the components of the "language-culture-nation" row, which stimulated the Sapir-Whorf's linguistic relativity hypothesis, the main thesis of which is that language determines the type of thinking of people speaking on it, and, therefore, differs "by the language picture of the world" [29].

This study proves the idea that the language picture of the world is a scheme of perception of reality fixed in the language and specific for the given language community.

The obtained results provide the basis for conceptualizing data on stereotypes, expectations and requirements of academic youth for professional and labor activities, identifying diversity of views and value systems, assessing messages in terms of their cognitive simplicity or complexity, integrity or fragmentation, integrality or differentially, emotional saturation or indifference, positive or negative coloration.

In the research perspective, it is possible to create a classification of virtual linguistic personalities, a description of the language picture of the virtual world and participants of virtual communication, as well as a deep analysis of linguacultural concepts existing in the minds of virtual subculture representatives in terms of "distant" etymology.

Acknowledgements. The reported study was funded by RFBR according to the research project № 18-011-00477A.

References

1. Efremova, E.S.: On the impact of the Internet on the development of French youth argo. Lang. Cult. 1(29), 5–15 (2015). https://doi.org/10.17223/199961995/29/1. (in Russian)
2. Mironova, N.I.: Internet communication as a section of the course "Russian language and culture of speech." In: Problems of Modernization of Current Higher Education: Linguistic Aspects of the III International Scientific and Methodical Conference, pp. 55–59. Ippolitov Press, Moscow (2017). (in Russian)
3. Ucanova, O.G.: Dialogue program "speech communications": the linguistic demand for modern society. Mod. Probl. Sci. Educ. 3, 230–234 (2012). (in Russian)
4. Mironova, N.I.: Speech aggression and "language of hostility" as sections of the modern course "Russian language and culture of speech" in the university. In: Language Personality and Effective Communication in the Modern Multicultural World. Collection of Articles on the Results of the III International Scientific and Practical Conference, pp. 10–16. BGU Press, Minsk (2018). (in Russian)
5. Kurbatov, V.I.: Virtual communication, virtual network thinking and virtual language. Humanitarian S. Russ. 4, 56–68 (2013). (In Russian)

6. Gavra, D.P.: Fundamentals of the Theory of Communications. Piter, St. Petersburg (2011). (in Russian)
7. Pocheptsov, G.G.: Media: Theory of Mass Media. Nauka, Moscow (2008). (in Russian)
8. Kashkin, V.B.: Introduction to Communication Theory. AST, Moscow (2013). (in Russian)
9. Nakhimova, E.A., Chudinov, A.P.: Foundations of the Theory of Communication. AST, Moscow (2013). (in Russian)
10. Lowery, S.A., DeFleur, M.L.: Milestones in Mass Communication Research. Longman, New York (1988). https://doi.org/10.1080/08821127.1988.10731159
11. Guo, Ts.: Theory of Communication. China Academy of Social Science Publishing House, Beijing (1999). (in Chinese)
12. Kastels, M.: Information Age: Economics, Society and Culture. Higher School of Economics, Moscow (2000)
13. McLuhan, M.: Understanding the Media: External Expansions of Man. Canon Press, Moscow (2003)
14. Bykov, I.A., Filatova, O.G.: Technologies web 2.0 and public relations: a paradigm shift or additional opportunities? Bull. St. Petersburg Univ. **2**, 226–236 (2011). (in Russian)
15. Gubanov, D.A., Novikov, D.A., Chkhartishvili, A.G.: Social Networks: Models of Information Influence, Management and Confrontation. Fizmatlit, Moscow (2010). (in Russian)
16. Korytnikova, N.V.: Online Big Data as a source of analytical information in online research. Sociol. Res. **8**, 14–24 (2015). (in Russian)
17. Gandomi, A., Haider, M.: Beyond the hype: big data concepts, methods, and analytics. Int. J. Inf. Manag. **35**, 137–144 (2015). https://doi.org/10.1016/j.ijinfomgt.2014.10.007
18. Humboldt, B.: Language and Culture. Progress, Moscow (1985). (in Russian)
19. Weisgerber, J.: Muttersprache und Geistesbildung. Editorial, Moscow (2004). (in Russian)
20. Lutovinova, O.V.: Lingvocultural Characteristics of Virtual Discourse. Peremena, Volgograd (2009). (in Russian)
21. Beensaid LLC. https://www.beensaid.in/. Accessed 19 Feb 2018
22. Frolov, A.: Roskomnadzor banned free processing of data from "VKontakte": what is the threat to the business (in Russian). https://vc.ru/25542-rkn-vk-rules. Accessed 19 Feb 2018
23. Klimin, A.I.: Features of the target audience coverage while placing advertising on the internet. Sci. Tech. Pap. SPbSPU **2**(2), 220–224 (2012). (in Russian)
24. Maltseva, A., Makhnytkina, O., Shilkina, N., Mirzabalaeva, F., Ilinykh, S.: Data base of verbal markers about professional and labor intentions of students' youth (LabExp). Official J. "Comput. Programs. Data Bases. Integr. circ." (of the Agency for Pat. Trademarks (ROSPATENT) 3 (in Russian). http://www1.fips.ru/fips_servl/fips_servlet?DB=DB&Doc Number=2018620499&TypeFile=html. Accessed 16 June 2018
25. Karaulov, J.N.: General and Russian Ideography. Science, Moscow (1976). (in Russian)
26. Kosharnaya, S.F.: Myth and Language: An Experience of Linguacultural Reconstruction of Russian Mythological Picture of the World. BelGU, Belgorod (2002). (in Russian)
27. Solganik, G.Y.: About a text modality as a semantic basis of the text. In: Structure and Semantics of the Art Text. Papers of the VII-th International Conference, pp. 364–372. SportAcademPress, Moscow (1999). (in Russian)
28. BAS - Dictionary of the Modern Russian Literary Language, vol. 17. Publishing House of the USSR Academy of Sciences, Moscow (1950–1967). (in Russian)
29. Whorf, B.L.: Language, Thought and Reality: Selected Writings of Benjamin Lee Whorf. The Technology Press of Massachusetts Institute of Technology, New York (1956)

Digital Data, Policy Modeling

Using Open Data for Information Support of Simulation Model of the Russian Federation Spatial Development

Aleksandra L. Mashkova[1,2,3]([envelope]) [ID], Olga A. Savina[1,3] [ID],
Yuriy A. Banchuk[3] [ID], and Evgeniy A. Mashkov[1] [ID]

[1] Orel State University Named After I.S. Turgenev, Komsomolskaja St. 95,
302026 Orel, Russian Federation
aleks.savina@gmail.com
[2] Central Economics and Mathematics Institute Russian Academy of Sciences,
Nakhimovsky Av. 47, 117418 Moscow, Russian Federation
[3] Belgorod National Research University, Pobedy St. 85, 308015 Belgorod,
Russian Federation

Abstract. In this paper we present a model of spatial development of the Russian Federation and principles of integrating open data into it. Our study is interdisciplinary and combines methods of computer modeling, artificial intelligence, demographic, financial and economic analysis. The proposed approach has significant differences from currently used mathematical and computer models of the economy, as it allows to reflect the spatial aspect of economic dynamics, integrate large arrays of accumulated data, take into account structural interrelationships of economic agents, influence of administrative mechanisms and institutional environment. The model is agent-based and consists of several modules, representing demographic, economic, financial processes, employment and consumption, educational and administrative institutions. Acting subjects in the model are artificial agents capable of interaction with each other and social environment. For the information support of the model large amounts of data on economic interrelations and spatial structure of the Russian economy are formed, including Federal State Statistics Service yearbooks and official information on the websites of the ministries.

Keywords: Computer model · Open data · Spatial development ·
Computational Experiment · Agent-based modeling · Statistics

1 Introduction

Due to the territorial peculiarities of the Russian Federation, ensuring sustainable growth requires taking into account spatial aspects, including infrastructure, production capacity, human resources and living standards in different regions. To analyze multiple factors, it is necessary to use big data, including both open statistical information, results of sociological surveys, monitoring of federal programs, and private data from ministries, departments, social networks and search systems. The processing of these data requires special methods and tools, so integration of methods of computer

© Springer Nature Switzerland AG 2019
A. Chugunov et al. (Eds.): EGOSE 2018, CCIS 947, pp. 401–414, 2019.
https://doi.org/10.1007/978-3-030-13283-5_30

modeling, artificial intelligence, distributed computing and analysis of big data is an urgent task to create tools for forecasting socio-economic and spatial development of the Russian Federation and assessing effectiveness of state and regional policy.

Problems of regional economy were investigated by academician A. Granberg on the basis of systemic modeling of the national economy, interregional and inter-sector optimization models. Currently, one of the main research directions in this area is a new economic geography in which uneven spatial development is explained by size of local markets and availability of external markets, density of economic activity, transport costs, etc. [12, 18, 28]. The models are based on general equilibrium models and assume monopolistic competition, increasing returns to scale and transport costs, which greatly simplifies the actual processes and reduces predictive capabilities of this approach.

A significant number of works in the new economic geography is devoted to empirical studies based on statistical data [4, 6, 19]. Structural modeling is based on econometric estimation of the factors, included in existing theoretical models, and does not take into account other factors. An alternative approach (modeling in the reduced form) allows to evaluate a variety of factors and to reveal new connections between them, but the results are not connected with theoretical models and consequently poorly interpreted.

We have chosen agent-based modeling as a main method in this study, since it allows to reflect dynamics of a macro-system as a result of the interaction of micro-level objects. Agent-based modeling process is inductive. Theoretical premises of agent-based modeling arise from complex systems, collective behavior and game theories. Central ideas are agents as objects, emergence and complexity. On the basis the agents' interactions higher-order patterns and complex behavior might emerge. In contradistinction to analytic methods, which assume equilibria of a system, agent-based models allow the possibility of generating those equilibria. The concept of agent-based modeling was proposed in the 1990s [7] and since then has been widely disseminated in the analysis of economic, financial, social and environmental processes [1–3, 5, 8, 9, 14, 22, 26]. The complexity of agent-based models has risen along with advances in computing power and information resources, resulting in larger models with complex interactions and whose inputs require sophisticated analytical approaches. Similarly, the increasing use of data in agent-based models has further enhanced the complexity of their outputs [13, 17].

The aim of our research is constructing an agent-based computer model of the Russian Federation spatial development, which reflects age and sex structure and resettlement of population, composition of households, regional economic structures, administrative and educational institutions. For information support of the model we use federal statistical yearbooks and official information on the websites of the ministries and propose an algorithm for integrating aggregated open data with detailed information of regional administration and organizations. At the current research stage, we present concept of the model, sources and methods of data processing for its information support.

2   Research Methodology

Forecasting processes of spatial development of the Russian Federation a is a complex
task and requires an interdisciplinary research that integrates methods of computer
modeling, artificial intelligence, demographic, financial and economic analysis and big
data analysis. The principles and methods used in our study are presented in Fig. 1.

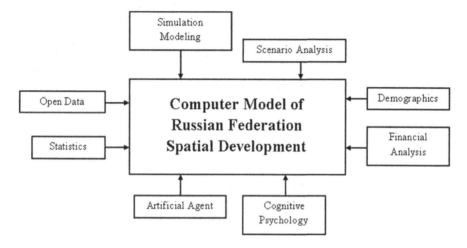

Fig. 1. Interdisciplinary scheme of the research.

The core of the research is an agent-based computer model of an artificial society,
reflecting sex-age structure, composition of households and spatial distribution of
Russian population; infrastructure, production capacities, educational and administrative institutions in different regions. Application of agent-based approach allows to
analyze influence of macro-level administrative decisions on the behavior of micro-
level objects [16]. In the model there are actors who can make decisions and change
their behavior: agents, households, organizations and public administration. Modeling
of demographic and production processes takes into account spatial location, economic
and personal relationships.

Scenario analysis is used to study simulation results. When performing scenario
calculations, various combinations of environmental parameters are set, which are
uncontrollable and unpredictable. After a series of calculations, consequences of various control actions in conditions of different scenarios are evaluated (Fig. 1, above).

Methods of demographic and social analysis are used to reproduce dynamics of the
population and migration processes among regions (Fig. 1, on the right). Demographics is important in forecasting spatial development, since individuals are participants in various socio-economic relations, acting as labor, consumers, taxpayers,
students. Interactions between organizations are reflected using methods of accounting
and financial analysis.

The Open Definition defines open data as a piece of data which is open if anyone is free to use, reuse, and redistribute it [27]. In the context of the presented research we consider open government data as a main open data source for information support of the model, including Federal State Statistics Service yearbooks, 2010 All-Russian Population Census reports and reports of the Economic Development Ministry [20]. Open data is used to create the initial generation of agents, organizations and administrative institutions; to set their regional location and interrelations between them (Fig. 1, on the left). Statistical methods are used to collect and present statistics in the model.

To reflect decision-making procedures of agents, methods of artificial intelligence and cognitive psychology are used. An important contribution to the study is made by the concept of bounded rationality: decision-making procedures are based on subjective preferences and information limitations of agents.

Our methodology for research of spatial development of the Russian Federation includes the following steps:

1. Reconstructing current territorial and demographic structure of population, administrative and economic system of the Russian Federation in the agent-based computer model.
2. Modeling dynamics of the system through decision-making procedures and behavior of agents and organizations.
3. Setting scenario parameters and alternative control actions for the system.
4. Conducting a series of experiments, statistical processing and analysis of the results.

In the following paragraphs we will consider methods used for the first step in more detail.

3   Structure and Algorithms of the Model

The developed model includes a number of interconnected modules reflecting various aspects of an artificial society: Demographics, Education, Employment, Production & Service, Consumption & Saving, Finance and Administration (see Fig. 2). Each module corresponds to the spatial structure of the Russian Federation, which means that each region has its own population, production and educational system corresponding to other regions and state administration.

State administration determines structure of the budget, taxation scale, transfer payments, the interest rate and other parameters. Regional administrations implement their functions through educational, medical, social security and defense budgetary organizations.

The module "Demography" reflects maturation, birth and death of agents in each region. New households are formed after marriages and divorces. Population of the regions also changes due to migration processes. We consider interregional migration in the model, connected with differences in educational opportunities, employment and living standards. Agents might decide to migrate after comparing these parameters in different regions on the basis of available information. These issues are discussed in more detail in [15, 21].

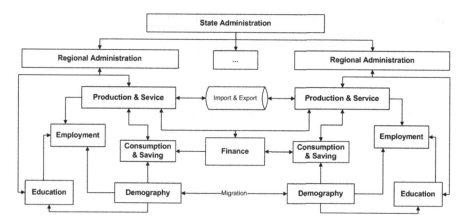

Fig. 2. Interrelation between modules of simulation model of the Russian Federation spatial development.

Agents act as labor, taxpayers, consumers, creditors and students, thus interacting with the environment and with each other. To reproduce behavior of agents as acting subjects of socio-economic processes in the model we use methods of artificial intelligence and cognitive psychology. Environment in the model is complex and diverse, so agents need a special architecture to interact with it [10, 11, 24]. Direct use of artificial agents' architectures in agent-based models is difficult due to several reasons. First, artificial agents' architectures are focused on solving technical problems, rather than reproducing social behavior. Secondly, use of complex multi-level architectures limits the number of active agents [23, 25]. The cognitive model TOTE, proposed in the 1960s by Miller, Galanter and Pribram, is the basis of the agent architecture used in the model. TOTE (Test – Operate - Test- Exit) model describes the cycle of achieving a goal in interaction with the environment. The application of this architecture makes it possible to realize the concept of bounded rationality by using fuzzy logic functions and reflecting information constraints of agents. These issues are discussed in more detail in [15].

Acting subjects of the model, along with individual agents, are organizations. The model includes three types of organizations: commercial organizations, financial (regional banks and the Central bank) and budgetary (organizations of the public sector). Organizations conducting production and service are considered commercial, except from educational and medical organizations that are at most budgetary in the Russian Federation. Public sector also includes administrative, military and defense organizations. Since most of state-run enterprises have been privatized after 1990s, we do not consider them as a separate type; instead commercial organizations with the state participation allocate a part of their income to the state budget. Each type of organization has its own accounting system, which is a simplified version of the system adopted in the Russian Federation. Economic transactions and mutual settlements of organizations are reflected in their accounting; financial results for a year are calculated in a balance sheet; for commercial organizations, a profit and loss statement is also constructed. Workplaces are linked with organizations; each agents-employee is assigned to a workplace.

Organizations permanently interact with each other. Figure 3 illustrates interactions of a commercial organization with counterparties during manufacturing process, which includes the following operations: wage and taxes payment; payment for materials and equipment; calculation of amortization; sale of the product; loans refund; calculating financial result for the period. After analysis of financial results organizations decide whether they need to change volume of production, hire or fire of employees, launch investment programs or take a credit.

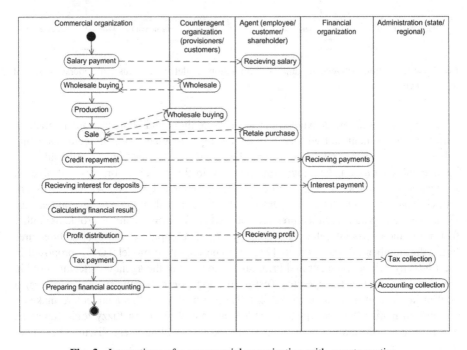

Fig. 3. Interactions of a commercial organization with counterparties.

Consumption and saving is connected with production. On the one hand, agents get wages (is they are employees) and profits (if they are businessmen); on the other – they spend their incomes on goods and services. The surpluses are invested to the regional bank; lack of cash might be compensated by a credit. The consumer in the model is not an individual agent, but a household. Members of a household have a common budget and property; they share their incomes (wages, profits, pensions and other transfers). Income, expenditure and property of households is accounted, which makes it possible to assess financial state of a household during a simulation (e.g. when a household applies for a credit) and calculate statistics on structure of income and consumption of households after the simulation.

Financial system in the model includes the Central Bank and regional financial organizations that accept deposits and credit organizations and households (module "Finance").

Educational system turns students into qualified graduates. This function is realized through the recruitment of students, transferring them to the following courses and assigning them a specialty at the end of the educational institution (module "Education"). Graduates are assigned to the employment center, which selects vacant jobs, corresponding to their qualifications (module "Employment"). In the module "Employment" graduates are assigned to the employment center, which selects vacant jobs, corresponding to their qualifications.

The model is based at a certain number of limits and assumptions in demographics, economics, finance and other related spheres. There are several reasons for setting these assumptions. Firstly, dealing with real-world complexity requires aggregating of objects and processes. Production, for example, is a technologically complicated process, but in the model it is simplified to converting supplies into products within one operation; another examples are unifying different types of credits between financial organizations and omitting operations on the stock exchange. Secondly, we lack detailed information about financial and economic processes, which results in strict aggregation of organizations (discussed in part 4). Thirdly, there are limits of computing power, due to which we aggregate agents in order to reduce their number (100 to 1 at the current stage). And finally, forecasting social dynamics requires reproduction of decision making processes of millions of people in different spheres, from structure of daily expenses to marriages and divorces. Each decision is an issue for a separate research, that's why we concentrate on three types of decisions, connected with economic reasons: where to live, study and work, while prognosis of other decisions is based on statistics.

We collect statistics in the model using accounting methods. Modeling results after a simulation include the gross national and regional product, structure of import and export, dynamics of regional human resources and standards of living of the population. The model of the Russian Federation spatial development is realized as a computer program. We enter arrays of initial modeling data on the input interface; the output interface presents modeling results in the form of statistical tables, maps and graphs.

4   Information Support of the Model

Information support of the model of the Russian Federation spatial development is a database; structure and relationships between the objects are presented in Fig. 4. Objects of the model refer to regions, which are assigned to the map of the Russian Federation through the coordinates. Agents live in regions and belong to households; they are linked with workplaces and educational places. Workplaces are connected with organizations; educational places are assigned to educational institutions.

For the information content of the model it is necessary to download and process initial data on demographic structure of the population, spatial distribution of production and infrastructure, economic links, financial state of organizations and

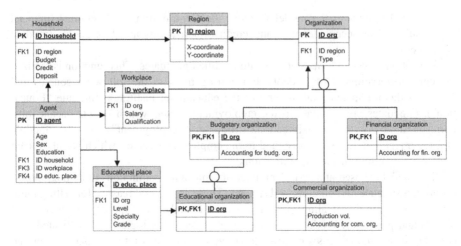

Fig. 4. Structure of information support of the model.

households. This information is presented in a large array of data sources: official statistical collections, results of sociological surveys, monitoring the implementation of federal targeted programs etc. Above all, there is private data of ministries, departments and commercial organizations, social networks and search systems, access to which is impossible without special permission.

Due to the disparity of the initial data, a method of step-by-step specification is proposed for their integration into information support of the model.

1. Aggregated objects of the model are formed on the basis of official statistical tables.
2. Information about the regions, whose administration would provide access to selective resources, is detailed.
3. Information about the organizations that provided relevant information and residents, who participated in special surveys, is detailed.

The initial modeling data is presented in the form of tables exported from Excel files to the model through the input data interface. For the current research stage, we use open data of Federal State Statistics Service 2010 All-Russian Population Census and reports of the Economic Development Ministry [20]. There are tables of initial modeling data for each module.

Interface tables for the module "Demography" contain information on the demographic structure of the population, including number of population by age groups in each region and their affiliation to households. For the module "Production" we enter gross regional product and its sector structure, input-output tables, export and import structure. Module "Finance" requires information about credits and deposits of households and organizations. For the module "Employment" interface tables are Labor force size and composition, Unemployment by age groups and educational attainment, Average monthly nominal wages of employees of organizations by economic activity [20].

Further we consider a specification algorithm that refines spatial and sector structure of production based on the available data at each stage (Table 1). Basic information on the sector structure of the economy, cross-sector interrelations, export and import is presented in the input-output tables formed by the Federal State Statistics Service and available on the official website [20]. These tables, however, do not reflect the spatial aspect of production. Regional production structure is presented in the table "Gross added value of the regions by sectors of the economy" in the statistical yearbook, but direct comparison of data of these two tables is impossible for two reasons. First, calculation of the gross regional product differs from calculation of the gross domestic product, as a result of which the total gross regional product is less than the gross domestic product. Secondly, information on regional production is presented in the form of economic activity types, which implies less detail in comparison with the sector structure (for example, 37 sectors are classified as one economic activity type "manufacturing activities").

Table 1. Data sources for the module "Production".

Stage	Table	Data	Source
1	Input-output table	x_{ij} - cross-sectoral deliveries V_s - added value in sector s Exp_s - export in sector s Imp_s - import in sector s	Federal State Statistics Service website
	GDP structure	V_a - added value of economic activity a in Russia	Federal State Statistics Service yearbooks
	Regional product structure	v_{ra} - added value of economic activity a in region r	
2	Regional production sectoral structure	v_{sr} - added value of sector s in region r	Data sources of regional administration
3	Production of organizations	$v_{org\text{-}sr}$ - added value of organization org, belonging to sector s in region r	Public accounting documents; private data sources of organizations

Thus, spatial representation of production in the model requires matching initial statistical information and its detailing by additional sources. Necessary calculations are presented in stages:

Stage 1. Harmonization of statistical data from different sources.

    1.1. Calculation of share of each sector in the corresponding type of economic activity on the basis of the input-output table.

$$d_{sa} = V_s / V_a \tag{1}$$

d_{sa} – share of sector s in economic activity type a, V_s – gross product of sector s, calculated by method of added value, V_a – gross product of economic activity type a, calculated by method of added value; sector s belongs to economic activity type a.

1.2. Correction of the table of output of economic activities in regions, taking into account the difference in the domestic product and total amount of regional products in separate economic activities:

$$k_a = V_a / \sum_{r=1}^{90} v_{ra} \tag{2}$$

$$v_{ra}^k = v_{ra} \cdot k_a \tag{3}$$

k_a – correction coefficient of economic activity type a; V_a – gross product of economic activity type a; v_{ra} – product of economic activity type a in region r, presented in statistical tables; v_{ra}^k – corrected product of economic activity type a in region r.

1.3. Completion of the table of output of sectors in regions:

$$v_{sr} = v_{ra}^k \cdot d_{sa} \tag{4}$$

v_{sr} – product of sector s in region r; sector s belongs to economic activity type a.

Stage 2. Specification of data on sector structure of regional production.

2.1. Calculation of gross product of sectors in regions that provided detailed information about sector structure of regional production:

$$V_s^{det} = \sum_{r=1}^{u} v_{sr}^* \tag{5}$$

V_s^{det} – gross product of sectors in regions that provided detailed information about sector structure of regional production; u – number of regions that provided detailed information about sector structure of regional production; v_{sr}^* - product of sector s in region r that provided detailed information.

2.2. Calculation of gross product of sectors in regions that did not provide detailed information about sector structure of regional production:

$$V_s^{ost} = V_s - V_s^{det} \tag{6}$$

V_s^{ost} – gross product of sectors in regions that did not provide detailed information about sector structure of regional production.

2.3. Correction of share of each sector in corresponding economic activity type:

$$\widehat{d_{sa}} = V_s^{ost} / \sum_{r=u+1}^{90} v_{ra} \tag{7}$$

$\widehat{d_{sa}}$ – corrected share of sector s in economic activity type a in regions that did not provide detailed information about sector structure of regional production; sector s belongs to economic activity type a.

2.4. Completion of the table of corrected output of sectors in regions:

$$\widehat{v_{sr}} = \begin{cases} v_{sr}^*, & r \in [1, \ldots u] \\ v_{ra}^k \cdot \widehat{d_{sa}}, & r \in [u+1, \ldots 90] \end{cases} \tag{8}$$

$\widehat{v_{sr}}$ – corrected product of sector s in region r; u – number of regions that provided detailed information about sector structure of regional production.

Stage 3. Specification of data on organizations.

3.1. Creation of agents-organizations that provided detailed information on their production.

3.2. Calculation of gross product of organizations in the regions that did not provide information about their production:

$$v_{sr}^{ost} = \widehat{v_{sr}} - \sum_{org=1}^{c} v_{org-sr}^* \tag{9}$$

v_{sr}^{ost} – gross product of organizations in sector s in region r, that did not provide information about their production; c – number of organizations that provided information about their production; v_{org-sr}^* – product of organization org in sector s in region r, that provided information about their production.

3.3. Creation of an agent-organization aggregating information about organizations in the regions that did not provide detailed information on their production.

Information objects of the model are created on the basis of initial data and are being changed in accordance with program algorithms and individual decisions of agents. Reconstruction of the modeled society is carried out in the base year of modeling. The first step is to set the geographical structure of the object; in this case it is regional structure of the Russian Federation. After that the original generation of agents is created, distributed among households and resettled by regions; after that, the financial state of households is initialized. For generating organizations, we set their type - commercial, financial or budgetary, and initialize values of their accounts. Agents are distributed to workplaces in accordance with their qualifications and employment structure in each economic sector of the region. Educational institutions are associated with sets of educational places for various groups of specialties and levels of education: school, secondary professional education; bachelor's, master's or postgraduate courses. For educational places, agents of the appropriate age are assigned. The generated society is stored in a database (Fig. 4) for later use in a series of scenario calculations.

5   Perspectives of the Study

In the presented research methodology, we integrate open data into the simulation model of the Russian Federation spatial development, which would allow to obtain detailed predictions based on the results of computational modeling. As controlled parameters of the model we set alternative spatial development programs, while unmanageable scenario parameters are exchange rates, volumes and prices of exported goods and services and significant factors of the international economic and political situation. After loading initial data sets, the model would provide assessments of management decisions consequences and their influence on the economic system in a spatial context, taking into account existing production capacities, infrastructure and human resources of the regions.

The proposed approach can be applied to a wide range of studies at the level of regions, the country and the global economic system as a whole. The modular structure of the model allows, on the one hand, to detail considered processes and institutions, and on the other - to expand the range of studied phenomena, including social stability in the Russian Federation, involvement of population in political processes and long-term economic dynamics connected with structural and technological changes. An important direction is also further development of decision-making procedures of artificial agents that present population of the Russian Federation in the model by increasing their ability to receive and analyze information and take into account irrational aspects of behavior.

Acknowledgement. The reported study was funded by RFBR according to the research project № 18-29-03049.

References

1. Barros, J.: Exploring urban dynamics in Latin American cities using an agent-based simulation approach. In: Heppenstall, A., Crooks, A., See, L., Batty, M. (eds.) Agent-Based Models of Geographical Systems, pp. 571–589. Springer, Dordrecht (2012). https://doi.org/10.1007/978-90-481-8927-4_28
2. Benenson, I., Omer, I., Hatna, E.: Entity-based modeling of urban residential dynamics: the case of Yaffo, Tel Aviv. Environ. Plan. B: Plan. Des. **29**, 491–512 (2002)
3. Bonabeau, E.: Agent-based modeling: Methods and techniques for simulating human systems. Proc. Nat. Acad. Sci. U.S.A. **99**(Suppl 3), 7280–7287 (2002). https://doi.org/10.1073/pnas.082080899
4. Combes, P.-P., Mayer, T., Thisse, J.-F.: Economic Geography. The Integration of Regions and Nations. Princeton University Press, Princeton (2008)
5. Conte, R., Castelfranchi, C.: Understanding the effects of norms in social groups through simulation. In: Gilbert, N., Conte, R. (eds.) Artificial Societies: the Computer Simulation of Social Life, pp. 213–226. UCL Press, London (1995)
6. Davis, D.R., Weinstein, D.E.: Bones, bombs, and break points: the geography of economic activity. Am. Econ. Rev. **92**(5, Dec), 1269–1289 (2002). https://doi.org/10.3386/w8517

7. Epstein, J.M., Axtell, R.: Growing Artificial Societies: Social science from the bottom up. Brookings Institution Press, Washington, DC (1996)
8. Epstein, J.M.: Modeling civil violence: an agent-based computational approach. Proc. Nat. Acad. Sci. U.S.A. **99**, 7243–7250 (2002)
9. Feitosa, F.F., Le, Q.B., Vlek, P.L.G.: Multi-agent simulator for urban segregation (MASUS): a tool to explore alternatives for promoting inclusive cities. Comput. Environ. Urban Syst. **35**(2), 104–115 (2011)
10. Gilbert, N.: When does social simulation need cognitive models? In: Cognition and Multi-Agent Interaction: From Cognitive Modeling to Social Simulation, pp. 428–432. Cambridge University Press, Cambridge (2006)
11. Holland, J.H., Miller, J.H.: Artificial adaptive agents in economic theory. Am. Econ. Rev. Pap. Proc. **81**, 365–370 (1991)
12. Krugman, P.: Development, Geography, and Economic Theory, 4th edn. The MIT Press, Cambridg (1998)
13. Lee, J.S., et al.: The complexities of agent-based modeling output analysis. J. Artif. Soc. Soc. Simul. **18**(4), 1–4 (2015)
14. Macy, M., Willer, R.: From factors to actors: computational sociology and agent-based modeling. Ann. Rev. Sociol. **28**, 143–166 (2002)
15. Mashkova, A.L., Demidov, A.V., Savina, O.A., Koskin, A.V., Mashkov, E.A.: Developing a complex model of experimental economy based on agent approach and open government data in distributed information-computational environment. In: Proceedings of International Conference Electronic Governance and Open Society: Challenges in Eurasia (Saint-Petersburg), pp. 27–31. ACM, New York (2017)
16. Mashkova, A.L., Savina, O.A., Lazarev, S.A.: Agent model for evaluating efficiency of socially oriented federal programs. In: Proceedings of the 11th IEEE International Conference on Application of Information and Communication Technologies (Moscow), vol. 2, pp. 217–221. V. A. Trapeznikov Institute of Control Sciences of Russian Academy of Sciences, Moscow (2017)
17. Moss, S.: Alternative approaches to the empirical validation of agent-based models. J. Artif. Soc. Soc. Simul. **11**(1), 1–5 (2008)
18. Ottaviano, G., Thisse, J.-F.: New economic geography: what about the N? Environ. Plan. A **37**(10), 1707–1725 (2005)
19. Redding, S.J.: The empirics of new economic geography. J. Reg. Sci. **50**(1), 297–311 (2010)
20. Russian Federation Federal State Statistics Service Homepage. http://www.gks.ru/wps/wcm/connect/rosstat_main/rosstat/en/main/. Accessed 26 Mar 2018
21. Savina, A.L.: Algorithmic aspects of constructing an agent model of migration flows. In: Proceedings of the Fifth All-Russian Scientific and Practical Conference on Simulation Modeling and its Application in Science and Industry, vol. 1, pp. 260–264. CTCC, Saint-Petersburg (2011). (in Russian)
22. Semboloni, F., Assfalg, J., Armeni, S., Gianassi, R., Marsoni, F.: CityDev, an interactive multi-agents urban model on the web. Comput. Environ. Urban Syst. **28**(1), 45–64 (2004)
23. Sun, R., Naveh, I.: Social institution, cognition, and survival: a cognitive–social simulation. Mind Soc. **6**, 115–142 (2007)
24. Sun, R.: Prolegomena to integrating cognitive modeling and social simulation. In: Sun, R. (ed.) Cognition and Multi-Agent Interaction: From Cognitive Modeling to Social Simulation, pp. 3–28. Cambridge University Press, Cambridge (2006)
25. Sun, R.: The CLARION cognitive architecture: Extending cognitive modeling to social simulation. In: Sun, R. (ed.) Cognition and Multi-Agent Interaction, pp. 79–102. Cambridge University Press, New York (2006)

26. Tesfatsion, L.: Agent-based computational economics: growing economies from the bottom up. Artif. Life **8**(1), 55–82 (2002)
27. The Open Definition website. https://opendefinition.org/. Accessed 26 Mar 2018
28. Thisse, J.F.: Economic geography. In: Handbook on the History of Economic Analysis, vol. III, pp. 133–147. Chapters, Edward Elgar Publishing, November 2016. Chap. 11

A Universal Model of a Subject Area for Situational Centers

Fedor Georgievich Maitakov$^{(\boxtimes)}$ ⓘ,
Alexander Alekseevich Merkulov ⓘ,
Evgeny Vladimirovich Petrenko ⓘ,
and Abdurashid Yarullaevich Yafasov ⓘ

Kaliningrad State Technical University, Kaliningrad, Russian Federation
maitakov@mail.ru, vsmcenose@mail.ru,
petrenkoe@hotmail.com, yafasov@list.ru

Abstract. Situational centers are becoming a key element of digital economy, facilitating decision-making for managers of different levels (country, constituent region, municipality, etc.). In order to accelerate decision-making, improve their quality, and also to communicate the decisions made to executors, it is necessary to unite separate situational centers into a single system – a system of distributed situational centers. Since each particular situational center is built on the basis of the model of its subject area, and, accordingly, its database structure, there arises a problem of information interaction of situational centers among themselves. The purpose of the work is to create a universal model of the subject area and to implement it in a relational database, independent of the scope of activity, level and complexity of the organization. The model has been tested when creating software products line "Open Budget" situational center, "Electronic Budget" situational center, "Municipality" universal virtual situation center, etc. and has showed significant acceleration of database design and resource saving.

Keywords: Situational center · Data model · Subject area ·
Management levels in economic systems ·
Quality control of management processes

1 Introduction

At present, creation of situational centers (SCs) capable of providing additional flexible methods of monitoring and management is an urgent problem of digitalization of both the economy and management [1]. Integration of SCs of different levels (country, constituent region, municipality, etc.) into a single system – a system of distributed SCs – will allow managers to accelerate decision making, improve decision quality, and speed up communication of decisions made to performers.

Mainstreaming of SCs is hampered by the unique character of the product and, as a result, high time expenditures, development efforts and, as a consequence, high cost.

The unique character is determined by the scope of the organization, its level, complexity, etc. However, in each specific case a unique model of the subject area and, accordingly, database (DB) structure and user interface are created.

© Springer Nature Switzerland AG 2019
A. Chugunov et al. (Eds.): EGOSE 2018, CCIS 947, pp. 415–423, 2019.
https://doi.org/10.1007/978-3-030-13283-5_31

To facilitate the design of the DB structure, developers most often use CASE-tools [2] or ORM-tools [3]. CASE-tools substitute writing scripts with "drawing" in the designer [2]. ORM-tools create DB objects from an object-oriented application code (the so-called "Code First" method) [4]. Generated by these tools, databases contain hundreds of tables, have low performance, and are extremely difficult to maintain.

At the same time, integration of separate SCs into a distributed SCs system is becoming an intractable challenge: ensuring information interaction of one unique SC, having its unique DB structure, with another unique SC, similarly having its unique DB structure, is also a unique problem. When developing software, the need to take into account the application orientation of each individual SC excludes the possibility of using standard solutions or simple replication of software products, which significantly increases the cost of the project. The following problems associated with the development of SC are identified [5]:

- the situational centers market is limited;
- SCs of municipal government have regional-sectoral specifics;
- it is necessary to modify the SC.

All this complicates the development of the SC, increases its cost, requires a wide range of specialists. One way to solve this problem may be to use unified models that are customizable for a particular application [6].

Creation a separate SC based on the universal model of a subject area, and, accordingly, having a standard DB structure and a unified configurable user interface, will allow replicating SC in organizations of different level, complexity and scope of activity. The typical DB structure of a separate SC will, in this case, make it possible to unify information interaction between individual SCs and unite them into a distributed SC system. This will allow a breakthrough in electronic control.

This paper considers a universal model of the subject area for situational centers and its implementation in a relational DB.

2   The Model of a Subject Area for Situational Centers

Most often when developing a database for the SC, a relational data model [7, 8], an object-relational data model [9], a universal data model [10] and a matrix universal object-relational database [11] are used. The use of a relational model and object-relational model will require developers to completely redesign it [12] when moving to another subject area. Two other data models have the following disadvantages [10].

- complex queries;
- low speed;
- absence of declarative integrity constraints.

A different approach is proposed, which was developed in the course of many years of experience in creating SCs in various subject areas. It consists in the fact that the model of an abstract subject area is described in a relational database. This model was called the "Categories of Operations, Entities and Links" (COEL) [13]. Its basic concepts are *Categories*, *Operations*, *Entities* and *Links*. *Entities* are units of information, *Links* define relationships between two or three *Entities*, *Operations* are any procedures that change the *Links* between *Entities*, the *Entities* themselves or their properties.

Entities, *Operations* and *Links* are divided into categories.

The categories of *Entities* in the subject area include: *Subjects*, *Objects*, *Territories*, *Reasons*, *Actions*. These concepts are universal for all subject areas. Depending on the specific character of the subject area, the number of categories can be increased as required. Each category of *Entities*, in turn, is divided into types, for example, *Subjects* are divided into *Individuals*, *Juridical persons*, etc.

Operations and *Links* also is divided into categories defined by the categories of the entities being merged, and have their own type, for example, an *Invoice*, a *Waybill*, a *Provider*, a *Student*, to *Include*. A *Student* is a *Link* between an *Individual* (for example Ivanov Ivan) and a *Juridical person* (for example Kaliningrad State Technical University).

When implementing the COEL model in the relational DB, all *Entities* of the subject area (*Subjects*, *Objects*, *Territories*, *Reasons*, *Actions*, etc.) are stored in one table *Entities* with their common fields (*ID*, *Category*, *Type*, *Code*, *Alias*, *Name*, *From*, *UpTo*). The clustered key of this table is the field set *Category*, *Type*, *ID*. This allows you to quickly select all *Entities* of the given *Category* and *Type* (for example all *Entities* that have the *Subject* category and the *Individual* type). Other category-specific fields are stored in expansion tables corresponding to categories.

3   Elements of the COEL Model Database

We will consider only the main tables and their interrelations in the COEL model database within the framework of this paper.

The main tables of the COEL model database are:

1. *Categories*
2. *EntityTypes*
3. *Entities*
4. *LinkTypes*
5. *Links*
6. *DocumentTypes*
7. *Documents*
8. *UoMs*
9. *Operations*.

The records of the first five tables (*Categories/EntityTypes/Entities* and *LinkTypes/ Links*) are the entities of the subject area and the relationships between them.

The last four tables (*DocumentTypes*, *Documents*, *UoMs* and *Operations*) represent operations of the subject area. For any operation it is necessary to issue a document (each document has its own type, for example, a waybill, an act of issuing finished products, etc.). Each document combines several operations.

The diagram of the relationship of the main tables (with their approximate structure) of the implementation of the COEL model in the relational DB is shown in Fig. 1.

In this figure, the key symbols opposite the names of the columns mean that in this column a unique numeric value is stored for each row. Logical relation between the tables is shown by a broken line that has the key symbols at one end and infinity (∞) at the other, and means "one-to-many" or "1:N" relationship.

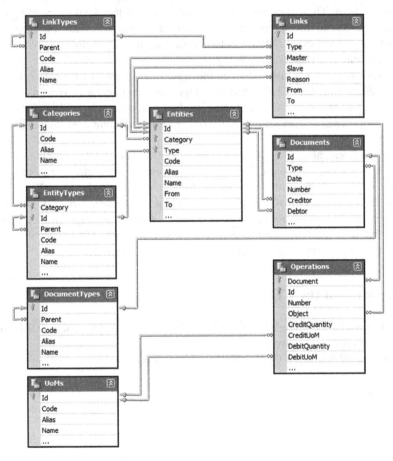

Fig. 1. Interrelations of the main tables of the implementation of the COEL model in the relational database.

The *Links* table entries have three references to the *Entities* table entries – the master, the slave and the reason. The master and slave entities are mandatory, the reason is optional.

The *Documents* table entries and the *Operations* table entries also have references to the *Entities* table entries (the *Documents* table entry has two ones, the *Operations* table entry has one). The *Entities* table entries referenced by the *Documents* table entries are the subjects of the operation, and the entries in the *Operations* table are its object.

The provider (creditor) and the recipient (debtor) are the subjects of the operation. If they are the same (i.e., the provider is equal to the recipient), then this means that the operation is performed by one subject.

Each subject of the operation (both the provider and the recipient) has its own quantity and unit of measure for each operation object (*CreditQuantity/CreditUoM* and *DebitQuantity/DebitUoM*, respectively). If the subjects of the operation are different, then, usually, the quantities and measurement units of the operation object are the same. If the subject of the operation is certain, then, usually, the quantities and units of measurement of the operation object are different. The first case, as a rule, is the operation of changing the owner of the object (changing the *Links*), the second is the operation of changing the object of the operation itself (changing the properties of the object), and, usually, the document groups several operations.

The presence of operations in the COEL model makes it possible to take into account the dynamics of interaction between the entities of the subject area, which is significant for many information systems and especially for situational centers.

Thus, the *EntityTypes* table will contain the names of the object types of the subject area, the *Entities* table will contain the objects of the subject area and the *Links* table will contain the relations between the objects of the subject area.

For example, in the *Education* subject area the *EntityTypes* table will contain records: *Educational organization, Faculty, Department*, etc. The *Entities* table will contain the educational organizations themselves, faculties, departments, etc. When the subject area is changed, the structure of the database remains unchanged, and only the contents of its tables change.

Since in the relational database implementing the COEL model information is stored about the objects of the subject area, the objects of the subject area themselves and the links between them, it allows us to use clustered indices, declarative integrity constraints of data. This ensures the reliability of data storage and the database high speed.

Let us introduce the following notation for a formal description of the COEL model:

p_{ij} – the j-th property of the i-th entity/link;

$P_i = \{p_{i1}, p_{i2}, \ldots, p_{in}\}$ – set of properties of the i-th entity/link;

e_i – i-th entity;

$E_i = <e_i, P_i> = <e_i, \{p_{i1}, p_{i2}, \ldots, p_{in}\}>$ – i-th entity with n properties;

r_i – i-th link;

$R_i = <r_i, P_i> = <r_i, \{p_{i1}, p_{i2}, \ldots, p_{im}\}>$ – i-th link with m properties;

$E_i R_l E_j$ – l-th link, establishing the interrelationship between the two entities – i-th и j-th;

$E_i R_l E_j R_l E_k$ – l-th link, establishing the interrelationship between the three entities – i-th, j-th и k-th.

Then the t-th operation O_t is a transformation from a set of n-entities (and their properties) and m-links (and their properties) into a set of k-entities (and their properties) и l-links (and their properties):

$$<E_1, E_2, \ldots, E_n, R_1, R_2, \ldots, R_m> \xrightarrow{O_t}$$
$$<E_1, E_2, \ldots, E_k, R_1, R_2, \ldots, R_l>$$

4 Implementation of the COEL Model in the "Open Budget of the Kaliningrad Region" Situational Center

The proposed approach had implemented in the development of SC in state authorities of the Kaliningrad region of the Russian Federation. Let us consider the result of using the COEL model when creating the "Open Budget of the Kaliningrad Region" situational center (available on the Internet at https://sc.gov39.ru).

The *Subjects* of the regional budget process are:

- the high-ranking officials (of the constituent region and of the municipalities);
- legislative and representative authorities (of the state authority and of the local self-government);
- executive authorities (of the state authority and of the local self-government);
- the Central Bank of the Russian Federation;
- the state and municipality fiscal control bodies;
- the management bodies of state extra-budgetary funds;
- the chief administrators and the administrators of budgetary funds;
- the chief administrators and the administrators of budget revenues;
- the chief administrators and the administrators of budget deficit financing sources;
- the recipients of budget funds.

etc.

The following entities are *Objects* of the regional budget process:

- the tax revenues (the land tax, the property tax, the personal income tax, etc.);
- the gratuitous income (the grants, the subsidies, the subventions, etc.);
- the income from the use of property;
- the fines (for violations of the law);
- the budgetary allocations (for rendering state or municipal services, for social security of the population, for servicing state or municipal debt, etc.);
- the budget loans (to the constituent region, to the municipality, etc.);
- the objects of capital construction (the buildings, the structures, etc.);
- the infrastructure facilities (industrial, social, transport, engineering, etc.).

etc.

The *Reasons* of the regional budget process are:

- the normative legal acts (laws, codes, regulations, etc.);
- the contracts;
- the obligations (of the state and local government bodies).

etc.

The *Operations* are:

- the amendments to normative-legal acts;
- the documents confirming the occurrence of monetary obligations (the acts of work performed, the acts of acceptance, etc.);
- the documents of purchase and sale (the invoices, the cash orders, etc.).

etc.

In the COEL model, all entities are entries of the *Entities* table of the *Subject* category and following types: *Governor, Head of the Municipality, Ministry, Agency* and others listed above. Each *Subject* of the budget process can have its own set of properties and states, for example, *Municipalities* have the following properties: *Population size, Area of territory*. All *Objects* are also entries of the *Entities* table, but the *Object* category and following types: *Land tax, Grant, Subsidy*, and other. Similarly to the *Subjects*, each *Object* of the budgetary process can have its own set of properties and states, for example, *Buildings* and *Structures* have the following properties: *Area, Cost*. All *Reasons* are also entries of the *Entities* table, but the *Reason* category and following types: *Law, Code, Decree* and others. Similarly to *Subjects* and *Objects*, each *Reason* can have its own set of properties and states, for example, *Law* has the *Entry into force effective date* property.

Subjects, Objects, and *Reasons* can form hierarchies. In the COEL model, these hierarchies are represented the entries of the *Links* table and have type which is named *Include*. In these entries, the *Master* entity is a whole, and the *Slave* entity is a part (see Fig. 1).

When implementing COEL model in a relational database we will consider the *Operations* using the example of such notion of a subject area as *Applications for Amendments to the Budget Law*. The entries in the *Documents* table of the *Application* type represent this notion. In the case when the *Application* comes from the recipient of budget funds, the *Creditor* field indicates *Ministry of Finance*, and the *Debtor* field indicates the recipient of budget funds. The budget allocations indicated in the application in question are an entry in the *Operations* table, in which the *Object* field contains a reference to the *Entity* of the *Object* category, such as the *Recipients of budget funds*. The *CreditQuantity, DebitQuantity, CreditUoM* and *DebitUoM* fields contain the number and unit of the budget allocations (see Fig. 1).

It is not necessary to make significant changes to the structure of the database of the COEL model, comparing the notions of the "Open Budget of the Kaliningrad Region" subject area with the concepts of the COEL model in this way. It is enough just to fill some tables (*Categories, EntityTypes, LinkTypes, DocumentTypes* and others) with the entries required for the given subject area.

As a database management system for the implementation used Microsoft SQL Server 2014. The number of main tables is 20, the volume of database now is 2.5 GB, the number of entries in the *Entities* table is 130 thousand, the number of entries in the *Links* table is 250 thousand, the number of entries in the *Documents* table is 145 thousand, and the number of entries in the *Operations* is 3.6 million. Time of submission of the requested output information for OLAP-cubes containing up to 10 thousand entries does not exceed 5 s.

5 Summary

The proposed universal model of the subject area (COEL) and its implementation in the relational DB allow us to unify the structure of the database of a separate SC. This will make it possible to replicate SCs, mainly changing only the contents of the database tables, as well as to unify the information interaction between separate SCs and integrate them into a system of distributed SCs.

The use of the COEL model in the design of the DB of the "Open Budget of the Kaliningrad Region" SC allowed us to improve the system performance due to the simplicity of the database architecture. The main labor input in the development of this SC was the organization of data import from other information systems used in the budget process. Changes in the functioning of the SC are to adjust the content of the database tables, with changes in its structure is not required, which greatly simplifies the modification.

6 Conclusion

The COEL model has been tested when creating a software products line for governmental management:

- the "Open budget" configuration for the VSM Cenose WEB situational center [14];
- the "Electronic budget" situational center [15];
- the "Municipality" universal virtual situational center [16].

As a result, the design of the database has been significantly accelerated.

According to the Federal State Statistics Service in the Russian Federation at the beginning of 2017, there were 22,327 municipal entities of various levels, more than 270 thousand small enterprises (the number of employees – 16–100 people), 20.6 thousand – medium enterprises (101–250 people), and almost 52 thousand medium and large enterprises and organizations. First of all, medium and large enterprises and organizations and 2,600 top-level municipal entities will require situational centers as a first step towards the creation of Smart City, Smart Municipality, Smart Enterprise. Thus, there is a growing need for situational centers for state structures. At the same time, acceleration of design and saving of resources are the main requirements for public procurement.

Acknowledgments. The work was carried out within the framework of the grant "Development of NTI-II", contract number: 151GRNTIS5/35877 dated July 21, 2017, the topic Distributed intellectual system for management of coastal infrastructure facilities and territories on the basis of situational center technologies.

References

1. Kostrikova, N.A., Merkulov, A.A., Yafasov, A.Y.: Technology of synthesis of distributed intellectual control systems as an instrument of sustainable development of territories and complex objects. Mar. Intell. Technol. **3**(37), 135–141 (2017)
2. Vendrov, A.M.: Proektirovanie programmnogo obespecheniya ehkonomicheskih informacionnyh sistem: Uchebnik. – 2-e izd., pererab. i dop. Finansy i statistika, 544 s. (2005)
3. Noubl, D., Anderson, T., Braithwaite, G., et al.: Flex 4. Cookbook. – Per. s angl, 706 s. BHV-Peterburg, Saint Petersburg (2011)
4. Lerman, J., Miller, R.: Programming Entity Framework: Code First, 196 s. O'Reilly Media, Sebastopol (2012)
5. Biryal'cev, E.V., Minnihanov, R.N.: Situacionnyj centr glavy regiona Rossijskoj Federacii v paradigme cifrovoj ehkonomiki. Materialy V Mezhdunarodnoj nauchno-prakticheskoj konferencii «Sovremennye problemy bezopasnosti zhiznedeyatel'nosti: intellektual'nye transportnye sistemy i situacionnye centry», Rossiya, Kazan', 27–28 fevralya 2018, CH. II, S. 3–11 (2018)
6. Zacarinnyj, A.A.: Tekhnologii situacionnogo centra kak oblachnye uslugi. Materialy V Mezhdunarodnoj nauchno-prakticheskoj konferencii «Sovremennye problemy bezopasnosti zhiznedeyatel'nosti: intellektual'nye transportnye sistemy i situacionnye centry», Rossiya, Kazan', 27–28 fevralya 2018, CH. II, S. 24–31 (2018)
7. Kogalovskij, M.R.: EHnciklopediya tekhnologij baz dannyh. Finansy i statistika, 800 s. (2005)
8. Ramakrishnan, R., Gehrke, J.: Database Management Systems, 2nd edn, 930 c. McGraw-Hill Higher Education, New York City (2000)
9. Stonebraker, M., Moore, D.: Object-Relational DBMSs: The Next Great Wave. Morgan Kaufmann Publishers, Burlington (1996)
10. Musa-Ogly, E.S., Bessarabov, N.V.: Universal Data Models. Programmer's Town, pp. 51–55 (2011)
11. Miklyaev, I.A.: Universal application of the matrix universal object-relational database of data. In: Proceedings of the I International Scientific and Practical Conference Object Systems, Russia, Rostov-on-Don, 10–12 May 2010, pp. 34–39 (2010)
12. Date, C.J.: An Introduction to Database Systems, 8 edn, 1328 s. Per. s angl. Izdatel'skij dom "Vil'yams" (2005)
13. Merkulov, A.A., Dmitrovskij, V.A., Maitakov, F.G.: Model' dannyh «Kategorii operacij, sushchnostej i svyazej». Materialy V Mezhdunarodnogo baltijskogo morskogo foruma, S. 1632–1639 (2017)
14. Maitakov, F.G., Merkulov, A.A., Petrenko, E.V., et al.: Konfiguraciya situacionnogo centra VSM Cenose WEB "Otkrytyj byudzhet". Rospatent sv. 2015612041 (2015)
15. Maitakov, F.G., Merkulov, A.A., Petrenko, E.V., et al.: Situacionnyj centr «EHlektronnyj byudzhet». Rospatent sv. 2015612058 (2015)
16. Yafasov, A.Y., Merkulov, A.A., Petrenko, E.V., et al.: Universal virtual situational center Municipality. Rospatent sv. 2013661281 (2013)

Exploring Influence of State Economic Policy on Political Preferences of Population Using Agent Modeling

Aleksandra L. Mashkova[1,2,3]([envelope]) [ID], Ekaterina V. Novikova[1] [ID],
and Olga A. Savina[1,3] [ID]

[1] Orel State University Named After I.S. Turgenev, Komsomolskaja St. 95,
302026 Orel, Russian Federation
aleks.savina@gmail.com
[2] Central Economics and Mathematics Institute Russian Academy of Sciences,
Nakhimovsky Av. 47, 117418 Moscow, Russian Federation
[3] Belgorod National Research University, Pobedy St. 85, 308015 Belgorod,
Russian Federation

Abstract. In this paper we present a model of dynamics of political preferences considering current economic situation and expected changes. The model is agent-based and represents demographic structure and economy of the Russian Federation. Political system in the model is democratic, consisting of Legislative and Executive. Legislative is multiparty; each party proposes a pre-election program to attract voters. Agents are grouped into clusters that are homogeneous in political preferences. Belonging to the cluster determines issues of pre-election programs that are important for the agent. Agents implement concept of retrospective economic voting, for this they keep a record of their subjective estimates of living standards in previous periods. After elections Legislative and Executive are formed. Legislative proposes laws and approves structure of the state budget. Executive implements measures of state social, monetary and economic policy that affect organizations and population.

Keywords: Economic policy · Retrospective voting · Agent-based modeling · Political activity · Social tension

1 Introduction

Development of methods and models for prediction of social dynamics is an urgent task in modern economic and political studies. Problem of integration of knowledge about economic and social processes is of great importance since both economic results and social consequences of taken measures need to be considered when developing state economic policy. Underestimation of these consequences leads to increasing social tension and reinforcement of discontent with the current authorities. Application of populist measures aimed at attraction of voters in economic policy could lead to negative economic effects, e.g. budget shortage, inflation increase, which in its turn could lead to aggravation of social situation in a long term.

© Springer Nature Switzerland AG 2019
A. Chugunov et al. (Eds.): EGOSE 2018, CCIS 947, pp. 424–435, 2019.
https://doi.org/10.1007/978-3-030-13283-5_32

Integration of studies of economic and political processes is substantiated in the institutional theory in works by North [18, 19], Stiglitz [23, 24], Mau [17] and others. However, models, methods and tools for analysis and prediction in these fields develop independently.

In economics, both on the level of regions and countries and during analysis of world economy at a whole large-scale econometric models (LEM) are used. The main disadvantage of LEMs is the fact that these models do not reflect the structure of economy and connections among economic subjects; prediction in this case is based on extrapolation of past observations. So, LEMs show good results only given relatively stable conditions of economic functioning; in case of a global crisis such predictions are unreliable.

Computable general equilibrium (CGE) models are widely used to study macroeconomic processes. There are static and dynamic CGE models: static models descript economic structure in more detail, however, make only short-term predictions; dynamic models, on the contrary, are used for long-term predictions, however, describe economy in a simpler form which limits their applicability to estimate measures of state economic policy [14].

Simulation models are alternative to LEM and CGE models as prediction tools for macroeconomic processes. Agent-based computational economy models (ACE) are a modern tendency in simulation modeling used for analysis of macroeconomic processes [25]. Methodology of ACE matches the evolutionary economics theory by Richard R. Nelson and Sidney G. Winter and is based on John Holland's paradigm of interacting adaptive agents. Economic complexity is a field closed to ACE and connected with investigation of institutional effects' and bounded rationality of participants' influence on dynamics of complex social and economic processes.

Field of application of models of political processes is relatively wide, they are used for election program planning, prediction of political situation, estimation of social consequences of administration's decisions. Models-concepts, mathematical and simulation models are in this case tools of analysis. Models-concepts are logical models represented as cognitive schemes and describe interaction between some factors that affect historic process.

Mathematical models are based on the game theory approach and describe a class of social processes without details about economic and social conditions in every specific case. Downs's democracy model, in particular, is based on two premises: every government tries to maximize political support and every resident tries to rationally maximize usefulness of the result of their action [7]. Further research of political processes based on tools of game theory include consideration of interest of voters in participation in voting, candidates' support of specific ideology and a number of other parameters, however, influence of change in the economic state on electorate's choice is not considered [6].

Computational models take into account the dynamic character of political processes, large number of significant parameters and carry multivariate calculations. Among other methods of simulation modeling agent-based modeling appears the most appropriate to study social and economic processes with many participants [15, 16]. Agent-based modeling provides possibility of computational prediction of dynamics of political activity of the population. There are several models of elections based on agent approach. Kollman, Miller and Page studied the relationship between voters' preferences and the responsiveness of adaptive parties [10]. In the model of electoral competition by Makarov and Dankov [13] the parties search for a political platform that would be acceptable for the major of the voters. While the voters have certain preferences in economic policy, the models lack economic environment, so the agents can't evaluate consequences of their decisions. In the model by Kollman, Miller and Page, as well as in the model of electoral competition, agents are perfectly rational, they use the same behavioral models and don't have any informational constraints. The review showed that, despite its advantages, agent approach has yet not been applied to real data in political studies [10, 13, 15].

In this paper we propose methodology and tools for complex analysis and prediction of political preferences of population considering current economic situation and implemented measures of state economic policy. Agent-based modeling has been chosen as the main method of the present study, as it is capable of exploring dynamics of a complex system as a result of decisions and interactions of micro level agents. To determine the procedures of decision-making we use method of cluster analysis, which allows to identify groups that are homogeneous in terms of political interests and preferences. Agent's choice is based on the concept of retrospective economic voting. Integration of these methods is aimed at predicting behavior of various electoral groups in different social and economic conditions.

2 Structure of the Model

The model is designed as an artificial society, which is a computer program that reproduces demographic structure of the population and its geographic distribution among the regions of Russia. Agents in the model correspond to the population of the Russian Federation; their main characteristics are living standard and political preferences. Apart from agents and parties, who are usually considered as acting subjects of election models, we also include organizations, which embody economy of the Russian Federation. This allows to present wages, profits, taxes and employment in different sectors and regions. These factors influence living standard of the agents directly, along with budgetary transfers. Political parties present programs with proposals of different measures; agents evaluate programs and candidates depending on their current economic state and expectations. After the elections, Legislative and Executive are formed; they determine new state policy. Thus elections provide a feedback function, as a result of them socio-economic policy might be adjusted.

The developed model includes a number of interconnected modules reflecting various aspects of social dynamics: 'Population', 'Economy', 'Education', 'Voting', 'Legislative' and 'Executive' (see Fig. 1).

In the module "Population" social and demographic structure of the population and its geographic distribution among the regions of Russia is reproduced; maturation, birth and death of agents in each region is reflected. These issues are discussed in more detail in [22]. Agents act as labor, consumers, students and voters, thus interacting with other modules.

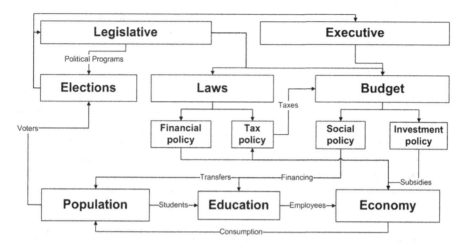

Fig. 1. Structure of the agent model of political preferences dynamics.

For an adequate estimation of the economic policy, social and economic environment of the model has to reflect implementation of these measures. Economy in the model is considered in the context of sectors and regions, as both these factors are significant in assessing living standards of the population, implementation of investment projects and government support programs. The model reproduces industries in the form of enlarged regional enterprises, jobs and products, associated with them. Population is connected with the economy through employment on the one hand, and consumption on the other. The quantitative and qualitative composition of the labor force affects productive capacities of the economy; development of the economy, in turn, influences on living standards of the population.

Political system in the model is democratic and multiparty. We assume that it is simplified and consists of two institutions: Executive and Legislative. Based on the accepted assumption, we omit possible contradictions between the President and the Government, treating them as a united institution of executive power. Executive determines structure of the budget, taxation scale, transfer payments, the interest rate and subsidies to different sectors of the economy. These functions are implemented through educational, medical, social security and defense budgetary organizations. Taxation scale is regulated by Legislative; it also approves structure of the budget. Since the aim of this research is to study influence of economic policy on the political preferences of the population, other aspects of foreign and domestic policy are not considered in the framework of the model.

3 Elections in the Model

Elections in the model reproduce adopted in the Russian Federation procedures in a simplified form. Elections of Legislative are carried out once in 5 years, Executive elections - once in 6 years. Candidates submit their electoral programs; population evaluates them and votes for the selected candidates. According to the election results, distribution of mandates in Legislative is determined or the Executive is appointed.

3.1 Political Programs

In the model both Legislative and Executive are elective. The Legislative is multi-party; parties in the model correlate with leading parties in Russia. At the moment, the number of officially registered parties in Russia is about 75 (this number is constantly changing), but composition of the State Duma remains stable. According to the election results, four parties occupied their place in the State Duma of 4-7 convocations: United Russia (UR) [26]; Communist Party of the Russian Federation (CPRF) [5]; Liberal Democratic Party of Russia (LDPR) [12]; A Just Russia Party (JR) [1]. Since 1999, United Russia has taken the role of the ruling party, obtaining an absolute majority of votes in the elections.

To attract the voters, parties present programs that reflect interests of certain electoral groups. Ideologies of political parties are right, left or center oriented; some parties take an intermediate position: right-centrism or left-centrism [11]. Programs of political parties are grouped into issues in which parties consider it necessary to make changes. The most important issues in political pre-election programs are: improving the living standards of the population; development of the economy, including agriculture and industry; support of business, construction and housing services; financing of health care and education. Table 1 compares political programs of parties belonging to the State Duma of 4-7 convocations, as well as the Civic Platform [4], Rodina [21] and Yabloko party [27]. The position of the party for each item is marked:

Table 1. Comparison of pre-election programs of political parties in Russia.

Issue	UR	CPRF	LDPR	JR	CP	Rodina	Jabloko
Social transfers	L	L	L	L	L	L	L
Medicine	L	L	L	L	L	L	L
Education	L	L	L	L	L	L	L
Industry support	L	L	L	L	L	L	L
Housing construction support	R	N	L	L	L	N	R
Housing services support	R	L	L	L	L	N	L
Business	R	R	R	R	R	R	R
Tax system	R	L	L	L	R	N	R

L - if the proposed concept refers to the left position in the traditional sense (social equality achieved through active income redistribution);

R - if the proposed concept refers to the right position in the traditional sense (market freedom and inequality);

N - if the concept for this issue is not indicated in the program.

Comparative analysis of pre-election programs of the parties shows that, despite their official left or right position, their proposals on certain issues are very similar. For example, all parties, including CPRF, support business, which traditionally refers to the right ideology. Public funding for education and health is also observed in all programs, including the right party Yabloko. Thus, a fairly general concept in political programs of different parties is a market economy with powerful elements of a social state, which is close to the Keynesian model of state economic policy.

Similarity is also observed in socio-economic issues in political programs of the presidential candidates. In the presidential elections, however, the personal authority of the candidates and the general assessment of the current administration by the voters are of greater importance.

The model includes 7 parties: United Russia, CPRF, LDPR, A Just Russia, Yabloko, Civic Platform and Rodina. The parties Yabloko Party, Civic Platform and Rodina, although not included in the State Duma of 4-7 convocations, have differences in political programs from other parties, and therefore may attract some voters in the long term. Party programs in the model include the main issues of socio-economic policy presented in Table 1.

3.2 Voting

We use method of cluster analysis for identification of groups that are homogeneous in political preferences and have similar electoral behavior. The main criteria for clustering are sphere (budgetary or commercial organizations, military and defense sector), type of employment (employees, businessmen, self-employed) and level of income. Students, pensioners, unemployed people and person on maternity leave are distinguished as separate clusters.

An agent can belong to several clusters, for example, be a working pensioner or a self-employed student, in this case its political preferences are combined. For each cluster, it is possible to select issues of pre-election programs that are of special interest to them (Table 3). Thus, pensions and benefits are critical for pensioners and persons on maternity leave; tariffs for housing and communal services - for persons with low incomes (pensioners and employees with minimal wage); tax policy - for businessmen and self-employed.

Ownership to a certain cluster determines political preferences of the Agent. Businessmen and self-employed would gravitate toward candidates with a right attitude to tax policy and business (market freedom and low taxes), while low-income individuals would choose candidates with a left attitude in social policy.

Analysis of party programs (Table 1) shows that most parties in the Russian Federation combine both these positions in election campaigns, so in this situation, evaluation of real results of the ruling party and the President becomes very important. In the model agents implement concept of retrospective economic voting [2, 20] and for evaluation of the authorities they keep a record of their subjective estimates of living standards in previous periods.

When making an electoral decision, agents compare political programs of parties and choose the one that represents interests of their cluster. If the candidate was in

Table 2. Clusters of electorate.

№	Cluster
1	Students
2	Pensioners
3	Unemployed
4	Person on maternity leave
5	Employees, minimal wage
6	Employees, budgetary org., military & defense
7	Employees, budgetary org., other sectors
8	Employees, commercial org.
9	Self-employed
10	Businessmen

Table 3. Political preferences of electorate clusters.

Political program parameter	1	2	3	4	5	6	7	8	9	10
Social transfers	L	L	L	L	L	L				
Medicine		L		L	L		L			
Education	L			L	L		L			
Industry support			L					L		
Housing construction support			L	L	L					
Housing services support		L	L		L					
Business									R	R
Tax system					L				R	R

power in previous periods, and the agent's living standard remained low, he will make a protest vote, even if the candidate's program formally promotes his interests (Fig. 2).

Protest voting can be expressed both in the choice of opposition parties and in refusal to participate in elections. Increase of protest voting is a sign of social stability disruption and threatens to cause acts of protest targeted by destructive political influence.

3.3 Formation of the Authorities

After the election procedure its results are summed up. In the Executive election, the winner is determined by a majority of votes; the policy fixed in the pre-election program becomes the current state policy. The composition of the Legislative is determined in proportion to the number of votes for each party that has overcome the 5% barrier.

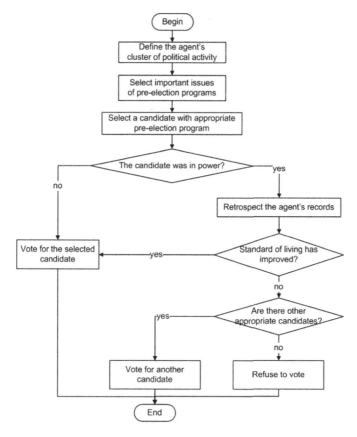

Fig. 2. Algorithm of voting in the model.

4   State Administration

4.1   Legislative

Legislative power in the model is represented by one elected body. The legislative process is an algorithm of actions from the legislative initiative to its endorsement in the form of law (Fig. 3).

The right of legislative initiative in the Russian Federation is enjoyed by the President, the Federation Council, the State Duma, the Government of the Russian Federation, legislative bodies of the constituent entities; in the model this function is assigned to the parties that join the Legislative. The legislative proposal is submitted to the State Duma for consideration. Normally, the legislative proposal passes three readings. In the first reading, the general provisions of the legislative proposal, the need for its adoption, the important details should be discussed and analyzed. As a result, the legislative proposal may be rejected, adopted finally or adopted with corrections. The main work in the second reading falls on the discussion of the amendments. At the end of the second reading, the legislative proposal may be adopted or rejected. In the third

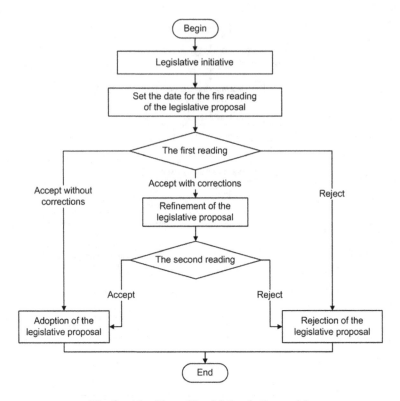

Fig. 3. Algorithm of Legislative in the model.

reading, it is decided to accept or reject the legislative proposal. The legislative proposal is adopted if the majority of the deputies of the State Duma voted for it. In the model, this process is simplified to two readings, and before the second reading the legislative proposal is finalized taking into account comments of all parties included in Legislative.

The process of approving the legislative proposal in the model is also simplistic. The legislative proposal is approved by the Executive if its content corresponds to the current state policy, otherwise it is vetoed. The approved law comes into force ten days after its approval.

4.2 Executive

The program of Executive is implemented through a set of measures of tax, social, investment and monetary policy. The main tool for implementing social and investment policies is the state budget. In the model, the state budget is presented in aggregate form (Table 4). The expenditure part determines social transfers, investment in developing sectors (agriculture and industry), science, military and defense. The amount and structure of military and defense spending is classified, so in our study these issues are not addressed in detail; employees in this sector are grouped to a separate cluster of political activity (Table 2). Budget filling is made by tax proceeds, revenues from the state property and financial assets. Structure of the budget is approved by Legislative, this process in the model is also simplified to two readings.

Table 4. Structure of the state budget in the model.

Revenues	Expenditure
Taxes	Financing of budgetary organizations
Individual income tax	Medicine
Unified social tax	Education & Science
Corporate income tax	Administration
Other taxes	Culture
Revenues from the state property	Military & Defense
Revenues from financial assets	Social transfers
Other revenues	Pensions
	Maternity leave transfers
	Unemployment benefits
	Other transfers
	Investments in economy sectors
	Science
	Agriculture
	Industry
	Other

Monetary policy is implemented through the discount rate of interest and lending to financial organizations by the Central Bank of the Russian Federation.

The model makes reflects the influence of economic policy measures on the standard of living of various categories of population. The influence of social policy is direct, it changes incomes of pensioners, unemployed and persons on maternity leave. Investment and financial policies affect the standard of living indirectly, through development of business and production in different sectors, which in turn leads to increased employment and higher incomes in the long run.

Tax policy is often a matter of debate, because increasing taxes can hamper business development, and their reduction - lead to budget deficits, cuts in social and investment spending. In recent years, high prices for products of the fuel and energy complex have made it possible to avoid increasing taxes in other industries. However, in case situation on foreign markets changes, this issue may become relevant, then computational experiments on the model would help to assess the impact of alternative changes in tax policy on different groups of population and the economy as a whole.

4.3 Perspectives of the Study

Upon completion of the program realization and procedures of informational filling of the model, a series of computational experiments aimed at forecasting political activity of the population in various scenarios is planned. Scenarios are formed from a number of uncontrollable factors that could have significant influence on social and political situation in Russia: currency rate, oil prices and international sanctions. Results of the statistical analysis of the numerical data would help to predict vote distribution depending on dynamics of life standard indicators, employment, inflation, that are expected during implementation of state economic policy, and estimate efficiency of measures taken in order to support social and political stability. Analysis of results of retrospective and prognostic modeling identifies existing patterns between the rate of economic inequality and electoral support for different parties; completeness and diversity of pre-election programs and political activity of the population; fulfillment of electoral promises and future electoral support. The developed model could also be used for prediction of a long term dynamics of economic inequality and its political consequences and for development of social institutes providing effective public distribution system.

Acknowledgments. Modeling of state economic policy realization was funded by RFBR according to the research project № 18-310-00185.

References

1. A Just Russia Political Party official website (in Russian). http://www.spravedlivo.ru/7634910. Accessed 15 Feb 2018
2. Anderson, C.J.: Economic voting and political context: a comparative perspective. Electoral Stud. **19**, 151–170 (2000)
3. Axelrod, R.: The Complexity of Cooperation: Agent-Based Models of Competition and Collaboration. Princeton University Press, Princeton (1997)
4. Civic Platform Political Party official website (in Russian). http://праваяпартия.рф/3591. Accessed 23 Feb 2018
5. Communist Party of the Russian Federation official website (in Russian). https://kprf.ru/party/program. Accessed 15 Feb 2018
6. Davis, O., Hinich, M., Ordeshook, P.: An expository development of a mathematical model of the electoral process. Am. Polit. Sci. Rev. **2**(64), 426–448 (1970)
7. Downs, A.: Economic Theory of Democracy. Harper & Row, New York (1957)
8. Epstein, J.: Modeling civil violence: an agent-based computational approach. Proc. Natl. Acad. Sci. U.S.A. **99**(Suppl. 3), 7243–7250 (2002)
9. Epstein, J.M., Axtell, R.: Growing Artificial Societies: Social Science from the Bottom Up. Brookings Institution Press, Washington, DC (1996)
10. Kollman, K., Miller, J., Page, S.: Adaptive parties in spatial elections. Am. Polit. Sci. Rev. **86**(4), 929–937 (1992)
11. Lebedev, S.V.: Left and right in the history of Russian political thought. In: Russia: Past, Present, Future. Materials of the All-Russian Scientific and Practical Conference, St. Petersburg, 16–19 December 1996, C. 72. Publishing House of BSTU, St. Petersburg (1996). (in Russian)
12. Liberal Democratic Party of Russia official website (in Russian). https://ldpr.ru/party/Program_LDPR/. Accessed 15 Feb 2018
13. Makarov, V., Dankov, A.: Regional and Electoral Competition: a comparative analysis of the impact of political institutions. RES, Moscow (2002). (in Russian)

14. Mashkova, A.L., Demidov, A.V., Savina, O.A., Koskin, A.V., Mashkov, E.A.: Developing a complex model of experimental economy based on agent approach and open government data in distributed information-computational environment. In: Proceedings of International Conference Electronic Governance and Open Society: Challenges in Eurasia, Saint-Petersburg, pp. 27–31. ACM, New York (2017)
15. Mashkova, A.L., Novikova, E.V., Savina, O.A.: Agent model for evaluating influence of tax policy on political preferences. In: Proceedings of International Conference Electronic Governance and Open Society: Challenges in Eurasia, Saint-Petersburg, pp. 258–261. ACM, New York (2016)
16. Mashkova, A.L., Savina, O.A., Lazarev, S.A.: Agent model for evaluating efficiency of socially oriented federal programs. In: Proceedings of the 11th IEEE International conference on application of Information and Communication Technologies, Moscow, vol. 2, pp. 217–221. V. A. Trapeznikov Institute of Control Sciences of Russian Academy of Sciences, Moscow (2017)
17. Mau, V.: Russia's Economy in an Epoch of Turbulence: Crises and Lessons. Routledge, Abingdon, Oxon, New York (2018)
18. North, D.C.: Institutions. Institutional Change and Economic Performance. Cambridge University Press, Cambridge (1990)
19. North, D.C.: Understanding the Process of Economic Change. Princeton University Press, Princeton (2005)
20. Powell, G.B., Whitten, G.D.: A cross-national analysis of economic voting: taking account of the political context. Am. J. Polit. Sci. 391–414 (1993)
21. Rodina Party official website. http://nwrodina.ru/programma/. Accessed 23 Feb 2018
22. Savina, O.A., Mashkova, A.L., Sarapkina, S.V.: Program implementation and assessment of the adequacy of the module "Demography" of the computational model of experimental economy. Informatsionnye sistemy i tekhnologii 6(92), 32–38 (2015). (in Russian)
23. Stiglitz, J.E.: The Price of Inequality: How Today's Divided Society Endangers Our Future. W.W. Norton & Company, New York (2012)
24. Stiglitz, J.E., Greenwald, B.C.: Creating a Learning Society: A New Approach to Growth, Development, and Social Progress. Columbia University Press, Columbia (2015)
25. Tesfatsion, L.: Agent-based computational economics: Growing economies from the bottom up. Artif. Life 8, 55–82 (2002)
26. United Russia official website (in Russian). http://er.ru/program/#25. Accessed 15 Feb 2018
27. Yabloko Party official website (in Russian). http://www.yabloko.ru/program. Accessed 23 Feb 2018

Digital Government, Administration, Communication

Data-Centricity as the Key Enabler of Digital Government: Is Russia Ready for Digital Transformation of Public Sector

Yury Akatkin🆔 and Elena Yasinovskaya$^{(\boxtimes)}$🆔

Plekhanov Russian University of Economics,
36 Stremyanny per., Moscow 117997, Russia
{u.akatkin, elena}@semanticpro.org

Abstract. The leaders of digitalization are developing digital government as a platform that stimulates public-private partnerships in the creation of innovative applications and services. The primary and permanent core of this platform is data, and it is the data ready for the information sharing and the provision of seamless public services. Growing digital world has formed the culture of interaction between government and society based on Open Data. The great importance has the ability of consumers to understand the meaning (semantics) determined by the provider, which is essential for the publication of Linked Open Data. The application and dissemination of data models serve for adequate semantic interpretation during information sharing and aim to achieve semantic interoperability. Both data-centric and model-oriented approaches are fundamental for the digital transformation of public administration. In this paper, we give a brief review of the leading countries digitalization experience and use it to outline the criteria characterizing the implementation of a data-centric paradigm. We have conducted the study showing if Russian e-government is ready for the digitalization in terms of the following areas: (1) the practice of information sharing; (2) the preconditions for the shift to a data-centric and model-oriented paradigm; (3) the regulatory barriers of digital transformation. We believe that the lack of data-centricity can become a serious obstacle to fulfill the plans of the "Digital Economy of Russian Federation" program. Therefore, we give some recommendations to introduce the data-centric approach that would enable the use of disruptive digital technologies and support the development of digital government in Russia.

Keywords: Digital government · E-government · Digitalization · Interoperability · Semantic interoperability · Data-centricity · Model-oriented approach · Information sharing

1 Introduction

Digital transformation of public sector, which characterizes Digital Government as a new stage of e-Government (e-Gov) development, has the following distinctive features [1]:

© Springer Nature Switzerland AG 2019
A. Chugunov et al. (Eds.): EGOSE 2018, CCIS 947, pp. 439–454, 2019.
https://doi.org/10.1007/978-3-030-13283-5_33

1. *Changing the priorities:* in order to meet the expectations of the new "digital generation", which is accustomed to the convenience, mobility and speed that have become traditional for the services offered by business sector. The provision of shared and seamless services by public administrations, various business entities and the non-profit organizations.
2. *Expanding the scope of innovative social technologies:* to increase citizens' involvement and participation by using social media, specialized resources for civic initiatives, online voting, legislative and policy-making activities etc.
3. *Introducing new digital technologies* such as Data Mining, Big Data, Deep Learning, Decision Making and others.

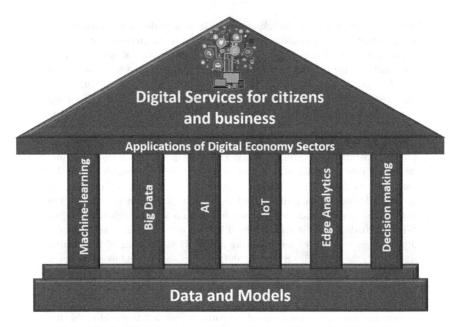

Fig. 1. Digital government as a platform: data-centric view

Over the last 10 years, in the modern digital world, the use of Open Data (OD) ready for information sharing has formed *the culture of interaction between the government and society.* It is not sufficient just to open the data, but there is also the need to provide them with an adequate interpretation on the consumer side, the movement towards *Linked Open Data* (LOD) has become one of the priorities for the digital government development in many countries.

Digital Government (DG) is developing as a platform (Fig. 1). According to O'Reilly, government as a platform provides a common set of core systems that enable government departments to share digital services, technology and processes [30]. The basis of this platform is data. The documents, in their turn, are secondary, derived from data, and the applications and services built on the latest digital technologies rely on data as well. Unlike the document- or application-centric [15] paradigms, *data-centricity* contributes to the growth of innovations, the creation of new services and applications, destroys barriers that public-private partnership meets.

Digital government systems are heterogeneous. They have a variety of stakeholders; their development is going synchronously in the frames of life cycles. The interaction of these systems occurs in dynamically expanding heterogeneous environment. Therefore, the interoperability and the priority of information sharing, which eliminate the duplication of information and fix responsibility areas, are crucial for the effective interaction of DG systems. The use of data models [42] holding the domain knowledge, which is essential for *the model-oriented approach*, is the basic tool to achieve semantic interoperability. The application of model-oriented approaches in the socio-technical system of systems (and Digital Government in particular) [4] is becoming one of the important tasks in cross-agency, cross-border and international interaction.

The roadmap of the "Digital Economy of the Russian Federation" program, adopted in July 2017, focuses on the development of innovations and the use of disruptive digital technologies, although it has not fully defined the ways of their implementation and dissemination. At the same time, it underlines the need to create "the conditions for the development of digital economy in Russia, in which the data in digital form is a key factor of production" [39]. However, Russian strategic papers do not adequately reflect *the data-centricity and model-oriented approach, which are dominant in digitalization all over the world.* This can become an obstacle to the public sector digitalization, the modernization of administrative procedures and the large-scale use of disruptive digital technologies. To implement these tasks successfully in such a short term (up to 2025), we need to lay a significant groundwork and prepare the data and models for sharing, describing knowledge about the data as well as the subject area of their use.

Digital transformation has a short, but already established and successful practice in many countries. Based on the review of this practice we have identified the criteria characterizing the application of data-centricity in digitalization and carried out a comparative analysis of the scientific and technological level achieved in order to answer the question put in the title: is Russia ready for digital transformation of public sector.

2   Methods

When reviewing academic resources and the strategic documents of the leading countries in the development of digital government, we pursue two goals: (1) to study and represent the existing experience in public sector digitalization; (2) to identify the criteria that characterize the application of data-centric and model-oriented approach.

Based on these criteria, we have conducted the study in the following areas:

1. *The practice of information sharing.* We used the 5-star model suggested by Tim Berners-Lee [6] to determine the level of Open Data published on Russian Open Data Portal[1].

2. *Preconditions for the shift to the data-centric and model-oriented paradigm in digital government.* Guided by the fact that such prerequisites are usually reflected either in scientific research (at the initial stage) or in the practical application of innovations:

   a. We have searched for scientific research papers published over the past two years and related to innovations in the field of digital transformation of public administration in Russia and abroad, using the keywords chosen in accordance with the selected criteria.

   b. We have surveyed the systems of Russian e-government in order to understand if they are ready for the information sharing and cross-agency interaction in a heterogeneous environment with a variable number of participants. We used materials published in open access, including descriptions of information systems, methodological and regulatory documents, as well as the systems themselves via the Internet.

3. *Regulatory barriers.* We have considered the practice of open data standards and models applying for information interaction in Russia and in the world.

Section 3 of this paper represents the review of academic sources and strategic documents. Section 4 describes the results of the conducted study and Sect. 5 gives the conclusion and authors' recommendations.

3   Review

Digital transformation of the government goes far beyond automation of administrative procedures and the creation of various applications (web sites, portals, mobile apps etc.) for the provision of public services. The basis for this transition is a *new, data-centric paradigm* in which applications become the same data consumers as other interested participants [10]. The possibility of unimpeded and open use of data (taking into account the semantics) leads to a rapid growth of digital channels of interaction (primarily mobile), provides the realization of big data and decision-making systems using artificial intelligence.

Digitization all over the world is developing fast due to advanced analysis, powered by intensive computing systems, which provides unprecedented opportunity to unleash the value of interconnected data [5]. At the same time, the openness of data, which enables their transparency, simultaneously affects the growth of innovations, as developers create such applications that reuse government data in unexpected ways [30].

Back in 2010, the idea of implementing the Government as a platform (GaaP) appeared [30]. It had the aim of encouraging the private sector to build applications that

---

[1] https://data.gov.ru/.

government did not consider or did not have the resources to create. Open Data became a powerful tool for the realization of this objective. According to O'Reilly, platforms that generate the highest economic activity are the ones that are the most open, where decentralization and low entry barriers for participation make it easy for users and developers to add value to the existing platform, while open standards encourage innovation. Open standards allow interoperability between different services and products which in turn consolidates openness of each service and product [30].

The United Kingdom is pursuing the GaaP vision [25] principally through the Government Digital Service [18], a central agency that since 2015 has specific responsibility and resources for its realization [17]. The principles of open standards the UK recognizes as one of the powerful tools that unlocks the transformative power of open source software to open up government and gives the possibility for the smallest supplier to compete with the largest [32]. The Government Transformation Strategy (2017) highlights data as a priority. It proposes the appointment of a new Chief Data Officer, and the creation of 44 potential new registers [20].

The United States has shown the capability to create digital government in a very short time. In 2012, this country adopted the Strategy of Digital Government [12] and managed to implement it within 12 months [12]. This became possible, because of ten years of enormous work spent to reorganize state information resources, to form and disseminate architectural models and exchange models of interaction, to introduce (not without problems and errors) an architectural approach at all stages of the creation and modernization of e-Government, to ensure interoperability at all levels of information systems interaction.

The basis for digital transformation was laid down in 2007 as part of the US National Strategy for information sharing [29] which then continued in 2012 under the motto "information is a national asset" [28] and in general led to the active development and dissemination of National Information Exchange Model[2].

The US Digital Government Strategy [12] committed to progress from managing documents to managing discrete pieces of open data and promoted shared platform approach, which was devoted to collaboration both within and across agencies, to reduce costs, streamline development and apply consistent standards. Customer-centric approach as one of the fundamental principles influenced the methods of data creation, managing, and providing by anyway (through websites, mobile applications, raw data sets, and other modes of delivery), that allowed customers to shape, share and consume information, whenever and however they want it [12]. OMB[3] Memorandum "Managing Information as an Asset" [26] established the priority of open standards that ensured the possibility of widespread use of government data, products and services; stimulated the growth of innovations and supported the implementation of open data principles[4].

European "eGovernment Action Plan 2016–2020. Accelerating the digital transformation of government" is now in the phase of active implementation [9]. Digital

---

[2] National Information Exchange Model, https://www.niem.gov/.

[3] Office of Management and Budget.

[4] https://project-open-data.cio.gov/open-standards/.

transformation in EU is based on the promotion of interoperability within the ISA[2] program, [11] as well as the share and reuse of interoperability solutions in accordance with the recommendations presented in the European Interoperability Framework (EIF) [8]. EIF has the objective to enable seamless interaction of public administrations of different countries for the provision of pan-European services to citizens and businesses, to minimize digital fragmentation of services and data, and to support the EU's digital single market to work smoothly.

The creation, sharing and reuse of semantic models such as Core Vocabularies[5] plays a significant role in the development of European interoperability solutions. Core Vocabularies are simplified, re-usable and extensible data models that capture the fundamental characteristics of an entity in a context-neutral fashion. Public administrations can use and extend the Core Vocabularies in the following contexts: (1) Development of new systems; (2) Information exchange between systems; (3) Data integration; (4) Open data publishing [13]. The creation of an open data ecosystem is maintained with the use of open standards built around the DCAT-AP specification, which has currently become a de facto open data standard in Europe with a number of countries and portals adopting or extending it [7].

The application of data models in e-government systems [33] is the subject of numerous studies. For example, an extensive literature review [36] describes how the generic data models support the interoperability of public administration in subdomain, national and global level. The "Comparative analysis of metadata models on e-government open data platforms" [27] stresses that they contribute to the formation of an adequate environment, for the consumption of data released on these platforms.

A very important initiative for digital transformation of e-government is the transition from open government data to Linked Open Data (LOD)[6]. In 2011 W3C has set up a Government Linked Data working group [19], at the same time Tim Berners Lee suggested *the 5 star model,* which not only rates datasets, but also *provides a roadmap for moving from open to linked data* [6].

The implementation of LOD to publish structured and interlinked data in open formats and combine content from various sources is one of the key indicators on some of e-government maturity models [24].

Consulting companies reflect the priority of data-centricity in their recent publications. In 2017, Gartner [16] suggested identifying data-centricity as a new e-government maturity stage. Its key performance indicators are the degree of data openness and the number of applications built on open data [16].

However, the openness of the data itself is not sufficient for the digital transformation of government. Transition to a data-centric paradigm changes the approach to the organization of information systems: it is not the application that becomes the source of open data (upload-publish-use), it's the data, accessible and prepared for sharing, that stimulates the creation of new innovative applications.

The effective use of disruptive digital technologies important for digital government such as Data Mining, Big Data, Deep Learning and Decision Making, depends on

---

[5] https://ec.europa.eu/isa2/solutions/core-vocabularies_en.

[6] EU Linked Open Data Project, https://okfn.org/projects/lod2/.

processing of large volumes of raw data. That requires changing the approach to creating and maintaining government information resources.

Government data should be provided for processing "as is" with the help of new digital technologies, but not after their preliminary processing via the applications of data provider, which is typical for document-centric state systems. Formation of the output document (interface) on the supplier's side helps public administration to transfer the zone of its responsibility from the data itself to the output forms. That is, of course, simpler. The problem is that this archaic procedure takes a lot of time, causes an implicit interpretation of data by provider's applications, and possibly its employees.

In fact, for the application of digital technologies in the public sector, it is necessary to move from document-centric to data-centric systems, in which public administration is responsible for primary data, and documents are formed from retrieved data according to clearly defined rules. Besides, the supplier must also provide data models (standards) for correct machine processing of data (Fig. 2).

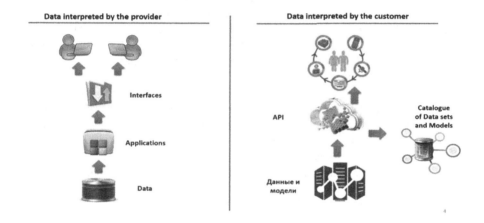

Fig. 2. Transition to data-centricity and model-orientation

This approach together with the use of object-oriented models is essential for OD initiatives and SDMX-datahubs [37], and with the use of semantic models for more precise interpretation of data in domain context is basic for LOD initiative[7]. These international projects are the drivers of a data-centric paradigm, allowing public administrations to acquire the experience of digital transformation and creating the basis for the application of new digital technologies.

The experience of digitalization leaders shows that the achievement of success in digital transformation requires many years of dedicated work to form the necessary basis – government data prepared for sharing in public administration exchange and open data for unlimited use. This data groundwork, as well as the development and

---

[7] http://lod-cloud.net/.

implementation of data-centric strategies and processes is the key enabler for the realization of digital government potential in the shortest possible time.

Studying academic sources and conceptual/strategic documents allows us to offer the following key criteria that characterize the implementation of the data-centric and model-oriented approaches in the course of digital transformation:

1. Linked open government data publication (use of semantic models).
2. Application of information exchange models to achieve semantic interoperability.
3. Use of open data model standards.

4   Results and Discussion

4.1   Practice of Information Sharing in Russia

Information sharing demands data to be accessible, open and presented in such a format that the maximum number of consumers could use it without losing the meaning laid by the provider. Berners-Lee, the inventor of the Web and Linked Data initiator, proposed a 5-star deployment scheme for Open Data [6]. We use his model to assess the possibility of sharing for the datasets published on the Open Data Portal of Russian Federation (See footnote 1).

Table 1 represents the statistics of Open Data publication (*criterion 1*) collected from the Open Data Portals of Russia, USA[8] and EU[9]. The comparison shows that the total number of datasets published in Russia is next smaller than the quantity of datasets published by the other countries. Open Data in Russia is catastrophically not "available on the web (whatever format)". From this point of view, Russian e-government is not open enough and can hardly get the first star (see Fig. 3).

Table 1. Open data portals statistics (Russia, USA, EU)

Format	Russia		USA		EU	
	Number of data sets	% of data sets	Number of data sets	% of data sets	Number of data sets	% of data sets
Total	20 309		280 593		866 207	
PDF	n/a	n/a	92 335	32.91	45 427	5.24
CSV	12 187	60.01	18 128	6.46	104 201	12.03
XML	6 397	31.50	31 601	11.26	15 122	1.75
JSON	973	4.79	13 612	4.85	46 364	5.35
ZIP	71	0.35	40 706	14.51	56 340	6.50
XLS	55	0.27	2 136	0.76	25 542	2.95
XLSX	32	0.16	1 564	0.56	11 062	1.28
GZ	31	0.15	n/a	n/a	n/a	0.00
RDF	5	0.02	9 379	3.34	3 559	0.41

---

[8] https://www.data.gov/.

[9] https://www.europeandataportal.eu/en/homepage.

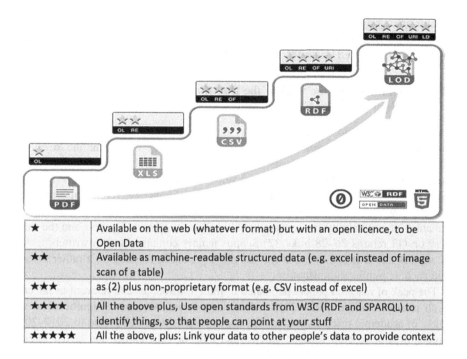

★	Available on the web (whatever format) but with an open licence, to be Open Data
★★	Available as machine-readable structured data (e.g. excel instead of image scan of a table)
★★★	as (2) plus non-proprietary format (e.g. CSV instead of excel)
★★★★	All the above plus, Use open standards from W3C (RDF and SPARQL) to identify things, so that people can point at your stuff
★★★★★	All the above, plus: Link your data to other people's data to provide context

Fig. 3. 5* open data

On the other hand, 60% of Russian datasets are in CSV format, but only few hundredths of a percent use RDF. Accordingly, we can say that OD is mostly published in non-proprietary formats and this is correspondent to the third stage of the 5-star model.

In addition, during the study, we have found that many of datasets published on data.gov.ru are in fact not available or were updated 2–3 years ago. Among the ten models recommended under the "Government" tag, only two were updated at the end of 2017, the update of the rest took place in 2016. At the same time, data structure is filled just for a few datasets and does not provide a description of the data contained, but gives only a formal description of field types (string, date, number, etc.).

Even a cursory analysis confirms the doubt that such Open Data can be accessible, machine readable and "linked". Nevertheless, The Government Commission for the Coordination of the Open Government in Russia considers the transition to LOD as one of the important objectives [31]. Item 3.4 of the "Open Data of the Russian Federation" Action Plan required the implementation of pilot projects for the publication of linked open datasets with the possibility of visualization in June 2016 [38]. However, in May 2018, we have not found any of them.

It is obvious that moving from OD to LOD causes considerable difficulties. At first, this is due to the lack of an information sharing culture. Data provider is concerned with the task to publish Open Data and does not care how consumers can interpret it. Moreover, LOD is a rare topic in Russian research papers, there is no practice of Linked Open Data creation, and it is difficult to find qualified specialists. Domestic tools for linking do not exist, and foreign ones are not implemented. Public sector does not show the intention to develop, maintain and use Catalogues of domain data models, which can provide LOD with the semantic description.

4.2 Preconditions for the Shift to the Data-Centric and Model-Oriented Paradigm in Digital Government

Academic studies and research precede the development and implementation of innovations. We use the *criteria (1–3)* selected in our review to define the keywords and detailed search phrases to clarify queries and to avoid irrelevant results. We prefer to use Google Scholar (GS) for the search due to the following assumptions: (1) Russian Scientific Electronic Library[10] does not contain references to foreign materials and produces fewer sources for the same requests in Russian. For example, the query "semantic interoperability in e-government" in Russian gives 1–3 papers and the same query on GS returns 26–28 links; (2) Scopus mainly contains English-written resources, so it is not practical to use it for searching papers in Russian on a rather narrow topic such as public administration.

The peak of research papers published in foreign resources and relevant to selected search phrases came in 2010–2014, when these issues were more significant to the subject of academic research abroad. We have limited the search period to 2017–2018 in order to capture both Russian studies that did not exist earlier and actual foreign works reflecting not only theoretical approaches but also the practice of their implementation. Column 3 of Table 2 shows GS search results.

Search engines display all the publications that contain words from the search query. Expert evaluation of first 30 links in the search results let us determine the proportion of papers that accurately matched the topic of discussion and selected criteria. Column 4 of Table 2 presents the results of evaluation.

As we can see from Table 2, there are very few Russian studies related to data-centricity and model-oriented approach in the field of digital transformation in public sector. Academic research papers, confirming the prerequisites for the application, implementation or actual use of LOD, data models and open data standards in the Russian e-government, are not published yet or probably not available at all.

We have also studied the practice of LOD (*criterion 1*), data models (*criterion 2*) and open data standards (*criterion 3*) implementation in the current information systems of the e-government in Russia (e-Gov IS). We used information (descriptions, project documentation, and presentations) retrieved from the Internet and published on the websites of the responsible authorities, because the systems themselves have external access. Conducted analysis shows that the surveyed e-Gov IS have no focus on information sharing. We have found no trace of data models publication as well as the distribution for further reuse. We can point to only one mention of a unified data model noted in the draft of the System Project of the Russian Federation e-government modernization until 2020 [35] but this document did not pass the agreement and was sent to revision in 2017.

---

[10] https://elibrary.ru/elibrary_about.asp.

Table 2. Google Scholar search results and relevance evaluation

	Search query	Total since 2017		% relevant from first 30	
		en	ru	en	ru
Open standards	Open standards in digital government	17900	1100	100%	83%
	Open standards in e-government experience	5100	2040	100%	16%
Data models, semantics, ontologies	Domain ontology in digital government	7680	82	70%	50%
	Domain data models in e-government	4870	2030	73%	16%
	Semantic interoperability in e-government	5120	26	70%	50%
Linked open data	Linked open data in e-government	4700	415	90%	13%
	LOD e-government	77	27	100%	10%

Among Russian e-Gov IS there is no federal or regional system responsible for ensuring interoperability at all levels and stimulating the community of experts to create, disseminate and reuse domain data models and open data standards.

4.3   Open Data Standards for Breaking Regulatory Barriers

We can confidently assert that the use of data exchange standards has already become a global practice at the international and national levels as well as in the exchange of information between enterprises.

Data standards, as a rule, belong to the category of open standards, especially in the systems where the number of participants is dynamically changing during the lifecycle. In this case, they can be de jure standards, such as the "Electronic health record communication" [21] and "Product data representation and exchange" [34], or de facto standards that are developed and maintained by sustainable groups of companies or organizations. Most of the applied data models belong to the second category, although some of them can obtain official status after completion of development such as SDMX [22].

The use of "de facto" data standards developed and supported with the direct participation and maintenance of the government is rather usual for the organization of cross-agency interaction in variety of countries.

Our own research (e.g. [3]), as well as many years of practice and expert work in the public sector give us the basis to analyze the use of data standards and models[11] for

---

[11] A detailed review of models and standards, as well as examples of their application, we wil represent in the future monograph "Digital Transformation of the Government. Data-centricity and Semantic Interoperability".

interaction at the domain, national or international levels. Here we have to state that the practice of data models' application in Russia has an episodic nature.

The implementation of an early version of Statistical Data and Metadata eXchange [22] in the Unified Interdepartmental Information and Statistical System [40] is one of such examples. Another example of the system based on international standards is the Unified State Information System on the Environment in the World Ocean [41]. It applies ISO/TC 211 group "Geographic Information/Geomatics" [23]. The data model of this system is open and available to the participants of information exchange. Another well-known data standard is the "Aeronautical Information Exchange Model" [2], which is used in Russian aviation.

As a rule, the deployment of data standards in Russia takes long time, brings many difficulties and is often performed with a great delay. For example, the plan of the Central Bank of the Russian Federation to implement eXtensible Business Reporting Language [14] is designed for 8 years (2016–2022)[12]. However, the practical adoption of this standard started in 2008 (USA), and now it has already covered about 50 countries.

Russia does not have its own open standards. Programmers and scientists develop data models, but the state level does not apply them. This situation is a systemic problem for digitalization of economics and public sector in particular within such short timeframes, as standardization process takes extremely long time. The development and application of open standards, supported by the expert community, ensures the reduction of regulatory barriers based on the application of national standards.

5   Conclusion and Recommendations

This paper presents the results of the study of Russia's readiness for digital transformation of public sector. We have conducted a brief analysis of the academic sources and strategic documents issued by the leaders in digital government development (UK, USA, EU). The given review proves that both data-centricity and model-oriented approach are essential for the current international practice of digitalization. In order to determine whether there are prerequisites for the transformation in Russia, we identified three main criteria: (1) publication of linked open government data (use of semantic models) (2) application of information exchange models to achieve semantic interoperability and (3) use of open standards and data models.

Based on these criteria and Berners-Lee's 5-star deployment scheme we have made an insight into information sharing practice via Open Data and have determined that OD in Russia is at the initial levels of development (1–3).

The study of Russian and foreign academic resources along with the practice data models and open standards application and dissemination, have shown that

---

[12] https://www.cbr.ru/finmarket/projects_xbrl1/.

prerequisites for the moving towards the data-centric and model-orientated paradigm in Russia have not yet been created. That minimal list of published papers shows that the work this direction is unsolicited. The ideas presented in them have little chance to break through the bureaucratic barriers and become a driver for future changes. Data models of information systems are not available for cross-agency information exchange participants, and the data is not available for sharing and reuse. OD is published "as is" (e.g. European DCAT is not used for the description of datasets) and consumers interpret OD "as they can".

International standards and models are used in e-Gove IS only when cross-border cooperation is required. Russia does not have its own open standards. IT specialists and domain researchers develop data models autonomously, but at the state level, there is no common practice of application.

Therefore, we conclude that Russia now makes no effort to move towards data-centric paradigm. Moreover, we cannot trace the intention to lay this groundwork from the government as well as from responsible ministries and committees. This can be a serious obstacle to the implementation of Digital Economy program, at least in the public sector. One of the important reasons for that is the absence of background that allows the promotion of disruptive digital technologies and the transition to a digital government.

We believe that for a successful digital transformation of the public sector in Russia, it is necessary to develop the following areas:

- Cross-agency interaction based on information sharing and the construction of a single digital environment certainly is a significant result for the validity and quality of government decisions, which we expected from the digital transformation of e-government. However, this result itself is also important for the development of seamless public services, shared by state departments, various business entities and non-profit foundations such as volunteer, charitable and other organizations.
- Building Digital Government as an ecosystem of shared public services, i.e. open platform that provides the conditions for the provision, innovative development and the dissemination of integrated services. This will allow achieving socially signif-icant goals and reveal the potential of Linked Open Government Data to stimulate innovation and transformation of public services.
- Developing the culture of information sharing and the arrangement of seamless interagency cooperation determine the responsibility of the Provider (agency) for the data provided as well as the possibility of unambiguous reading and under-standing, by both people and machines.

To implement these directions, the road map for digital transformation of e-government on Russia's should include actions that ensure the transfer to data-centric and model-orientated paradigm and provide interoperability at all levels: legal, orga-nizational, semantic and technical.

References

1. Accenture: Digital at Depth for Government Innovation (2015). https://www.accenture.com/t20150523T033713Z__w__/us-en/_acnmedia/Accenture/Conversion-Assets/DotCom/Documents/Global/PDF/Dualpub_9/Accenture-Digital-at-Depth-for-Government-Innovation.pdf. Accessed 06 June 2018
2. Aeronautical Information Exchange Model, AIXM. http://www.aixm.aero. Accessed 06 June 2018
3. Akatkin, Yu.M., Drozhzhinov, V.I., Konyavskiy, V.A.: The data model standards for the information sharing as the import substitution tool for strategic information systems. In: The Technologies of Information Society in Science, Education and Culture: Digest of Articles for the XVII « Internet and Modern Society » (IMS-2014) Conference, Saint-Petersburg, November 2014, p. 356. SPb: ITMO University (2014). (in Russian). ISBN 978-5-7577-0488-3
4. Akatkin, Yu.M., Yasionvskaya, E.: Digital transformation of the government. Data-centricity and Semantic Interoperability, p. 48. DPK Press (2018, preprint). (in Russian), ISBN 978-5-91976-108-2, http://csi.semanticpro.org/_data/library/215/tsifrovaya_transformatsiya_gosudarstvennogo_upravleniya.pdf. Accessed 06 June 2018
5. Berman, S.J., Bell, R.: Digital transformation: creating new business models where digital meets physical. IBM Global Business Services, IBM Institute for Business Value (2011). https://www-07.ibm.com/sg/manufacturing/pdf/manufacturing/Digital-transformation.pdf. Accessed 06 June 2018
6. Berners-Lee, T.: 5-Star Open Data. http://5stardata.info/en/. Accessed 06 June 2018
7. Carrara, W., et al.: Towards an open government data ecosystem in Europe using common standards. JOINUP (2017). https://joinup.ec.europa.eu/sites/default/files/inline-files/dcat_ap_carrara_dekkers_dittwald_dutkowski_glikman_loutas_peristeras_wyns_v3.5.pdf. Accessed 06 June 2018
8. Communication from the Commission to the European Parliament, the Council, the European Economic and Social Committee and the Committee of the Regions European Interoperability Framework – Implementation Strategy (2017). https://eur-lex.europa.eu/legal-content/EN/TXT/?uri=COM:2017:134:FIN. Accessed 06 June 2018
9. Communication from the Commission to the European Parliament, the Council, the European Economic and Social Committee and the Committee of the Regions, EU eGovernment Action Plan 2016–2020, Accelerating the Digital Transformation of Government, (2016). https://eur-lex.europa.eu/legal-content/EN/TXT/?uri=CELEX:52016DC0179. Accessed 06 June 2018
10. Data-Centric Manifesto. http://datacentricmanifesto.org/principles/. Accessed 06 June 2018
11. Decision (EU) 2015/2240 of the European Parliament and of the Council of 25 November 2015 Establishing a Programme on Interoperability Solutions and Common Frameworks for European Public Administrations, Businesses and Citizens (ISA^2 Programme) as a Means for Modernising the Public Sector. https://eur-lex.europa.eu/legal-content/EN/TXT/?uri=CELEX%3A32015D2240. Accessed 06 June 2018
12. Digital Government, Building a 21st Century Platform to Better Serve the American People (2012). https://obamawhitehouse.archives.gov/sites/default/files/omb/egov/digital-government/digital-government.html. Accessed 06 June 2018
13. e-Government Core Vocabularies, SEMIC.EU. https://joinup.ec.europa.eu/collection/semantic-interoperability-community-semic/core-vocabularies. Accessed 06 June 2018
14. eXtensible Business Reporting Language. https://www.xbrl.org/. Accessed 06 June 2018

15. Fernández, A.: Putting value at the core of your business: data-driven vs Data-centric. Stratio (2018). http://www.stratio.com/blog/datadriven-versus-datacentric/. Accessed 06 June 2018
16. Gartner: 5 Levels of Digital Government Maturity (2017). https://www.gartner.com/smarterwithgartner/5-levels-of-digital-government-maturity/. Accessed 06 June 2018
17. Government as a Platform, GOV.UK. https://www.gov.uk/government/policies/government-as-a-platform. Accessed 06 June 2018
18. Government Digital Service, GOV.UK. https://www.gov.uk/government/organisations/government-digital-service. Accessed 06 June 2018
19. Government Linked Data (GLD), Working Group. https://www.w3.org/2011/gld/wiki/Main_Page. Accessed 06 June 2018
20. Government Transformation Strategy, Cabinet Office, London (2017). www.gov.uk/government/uploads/system/uploads/attachment_data/file/590199/Government_Transformation_Strategy.pdf. Accessed 06 June 2018
21. ISO 13606-1:2008: Health informatics – Electronic Health Record Communication. Part 1: Reference Model. https://www.iso.org/standard/40784.html. Accessed 06 June 2018
22. ISO 17369:2013: Statistical Data and Metadata Exchange (SDMX). https://www.iso.org/standard/52500.html. Accessed 06 June 2018
23. ISO/TC 211 Geographic Information/Geomatics. https://www.iso.org/committee/54904.html. Accessed 06 June 2018
24. Janowski, T.: Digital government evolution: from transformation to contextualization. Gov. Inf. Q. **32**(3), 221–236 (2015). https://doi.org/10.1016/j.giq.2015.07.001, https://courses.edx.org/asset-v1:DelftX+OG101x+1T2016+type@asset+block/Paper_Tomasz_-_pre_publication_version.pdf. Accessed 06 June 2018
25. Margetts, H., Naumann, A.: Government as a Platform: What can Estonia Show the World. Oxford Internet Institute, University of Oxford. https://www.politics.ox.ac.uk/materials/publications/16061/government-as-a-platform.pdf. Accessed 06 June 2018
26. Memorandum for the Heads of Executive Departments and Agencies (2013). https://obamawhitehouse.archives.gov/sites/default/files/omb/memoranda/2013/m-13-13.pdf. Accessed 06 June 2018
27. Milic, P., Veljkovic, N., Stoimenov, L.: Comparative analysis of metadata models on e-government open data platforms. IEEE Trans. Emerg. Top. Comput. (2018). https://doi.org/10.1109/tetc.2018.2815591. https://ieeexplore.ieee.org/document/8315058/. Accessed 06 June 2018
28. National Strategy for Information Sharing and Safeguarding (2012). https://obamawhitehouse.archives.gov/sites/default/files/docs/2012sharingstrategy_1.pdf. Accessed 06 June 2018
29. National Strategy for Information Sharing (2007). https://georgewbush-whitehouse.archives.gov/nsc/infosharing/. Accessed June 2018
30. O'Reilly, T.: Government as a platform. In: Lathrop, D. (ed.) Open Government: Collaboration, Transparency, and Participation in Practice, 26-p. O'Reilly Media, Sebastopol (2010). https://www.mitpressjournals.org/doi/pdf/10.1162/INOV_a_00056. Accessed 06 June 2018
31. Open Data Council: The Governmental Commission for the Coordination of the Open Government Activities, Meeting Protocol, No. 1, Methodical Recommendations on the Organization and Planning of Activities in the Field of Open Data (2018). (in Russian). http://opendata.open.gov.ru/opendata/documents/. Accessed 06 June 2018
32. Open Standards Principles, Policy Paper, Cabinet Office (2018). https://www.gov.uk/government/publications/open-standards-principles/open-standards-principles. Accessed 06 June 2018

33. Peristeras, V., Tarabanis, K., Goudos, S.K.: Model-driven government interoperability: a review of the state of the art. Comput. Stand. Interfaces **31**, 613–628 (2009)

34. Product Data Representation and Exchange, ISO/TC 184/SC 4. https://www.iso.org/committee/54158/x/catalogue/p/1/u/0/w/0/d/0. Accessed 06 June 2018

35. Russian Federation e-Government System Project. E-government 2020 – Ministry of Communications, p. 122, August 2016. (in Russian). http://www.tadviser.ru/images/6/6c/K_конференции_TAdviser_СП_ЭП2020.doc. Accessed 05 June 2018

36. Ryhänen, K., Päivärinta, T., Tyrväinen, P.: Generic Data Models for Semantic eGovernment Interoperability: Literature Review. https://www.diva-portal.org/smash/get/diva2:993528/FULLTEXT01.pdf. Accessed 06 June 2018

37. SDMX Architecture for Data Sharing and Interoperability, Organisation for Economic Cooperation and Development (OECD) Statistics Directorate (2010). https://www.unece.org/fileadmin/DAM/stats/documents/ece/ces/ge.50/2010/wp.10.e.pdf. Accessed 06 June 2018

38. The Government Commission for the Coordination of the Open Government Activities, Action Plan, Open Data in Russian Federation, Meeting Protocol 25.12.2014 No 10. (in Russian). http://rulaws.ru/goverment/Plan-meropriyatiy-Otkrytye-dannye-Rossiyskoy-Federatsii/. Accessed 05 June 2018

39. The Government of the Russian Federation: The Digital Economy of the Russian Federation Program, Approved by the Government of the Russian Federation in its resolution No. 1632-r (2017). (in Russian). http://static.government.ru/media/files/9gFM4FHj4PsB79I5v7yLVuPgu4bvR7M0.pdf. Accessed 06 June 2018

40. Unified Interdepartmental Statistical Information System, Guidance. (in Russian). https://www.fedstat.ru/tools/storage/file?id=2. Accessed 06 June 2018

41. Unified State Information System on the Environment in the World Ocean (ESIMO). (in Russian). http://portal.esimo.ru/portal/portal/esimo-user/metadata. Accessed 06 June 2018

42. Wahlin, R.: Data-centric architectural best practices: using DDS to integrate real-world distributed systems. Mil. Embedded Syst. http://mil-embedded.com/articles/data-centric-real-world-distributed-systems/. Accessed 06 June 2018

Micro-level Assessment of Health of e-Governance Projects Using Kite Model

Ajay Adala

Bengaluru, India

Abstract. The success/failure of e-governance projects is normally assessed by their outcome and impact on efficiency of government working. The e-governance project which is successful is known to have a significant impact in government working, transformation of its processes and improving its reliability, accountability and transparency. Several models exist today for assessing e-governance projects. The methodologies adopted in these models vary depending on the objective of assessment and likely availability of quantitative and qualitative data. It has been observed that the general objective of e-governance assessment studies is to assess the impact of the project and realization of project objectives viz., cost-saving, process cycle time etc. While the existing models of assessment provide insights on project outcome, it may be necessary to adopt models which can assess the inherent strength of the entire eco-system of e-governance project. The Kite Model is one such model which considers various intrinsic and extrinsic factors for diagnosing the health of e-governance projects. The assessment of various components assigned to each factor provides a basis for a macro-level analysis. In order to carry out micro-level assessment of e-governance projects, an attempt has been made to derive various sub-components within each component and evaluate them based on assessment points applicable for each component. This paper provides insights on micro-level assessment of each component and proactively identify areas which can be prioritized for ensuring the health of e-governance projects.

Keywords: Kite Model · Micro-analysis · Assessment

1 Introduction

The general objective while evaluating e-governance projects has largely been to measure its impact on reliability, accountability and transparency on comparison with traditional model of governance. The objectives defined while conceptualizing e-governance projects are often considered as a basis of assessment. Most of such studies tend to be survey-based recording the perception of various stakeholders with regard to realization of intended benefits. The studies also gather information on the various issues which are likely to influence efficient usage of the system. The conclusions derived from such additional data, which may be treated as bye-products of the main study, are also considered important inputs for ensuring proper alignment of the system to its goals.

© Springer Nature Switzerland AG 2019
A. Chugunov et al. (Eds.): EGOSE 2018, CCIS 947, pp. 455–468, 2019.
https://doi.org/10.1007/978-3-030-13283-5_34

On the other side, some assessment studies focus on savings achieved post implementation of e-governance projects [6]. These savings may be quantified in terms of monetary, approval turn-around time, time and effort, ease and convenience, physical storage spaces, data retrieval etc. The conclusions resulting from such studies are often considered as critical inputs for scaling/replication/continued operation of projects.

It may be worthwhile to assess the inherent strength of the entire eco-system of e-governance project in an effort to diagnose the health of the project. Such an exercise focuses on internal state of affairs, techno-operational aspects and other administrative provisions which can ascertain whether the necessary level of preparedness and readiness is achieved for successful implementation of e-governance projects [1]. This requires collection of data which is related to the project, implementation agency, service provider and other stakeholders. Such data can be used to appropriately assess whether the e-governance project would be capable of successfully deploying and sustaining its activities in technical, operational, administrative, financial, legal, and institutions (toefil) aspects.

2 Why Kite Model?

As per literature review, several assessment frameworks related to e-government implementation exist today. The methodologies adopted vary depending on the objective of assessment and likely availability of quantitative and qualitative data. The key findings of literature review as follows.

- The e-government assessment framework designed by Indian Institute of Management, Ahmedabad (India) focused on two core ideas emphasized by each of the frameworks reviewed earlier—measuring the total value delivered by a project to different types of stakeholders and identifying multiple components of the value that would need to be measured in different ways, reflecting a variety of outcomes experienced by each type of stakeholder [4].

- As per Fitsilis, Anthopoulos and Gerogiannis, an "ideal" e-government assessment framework should combine five different and concrete perspectives namely: project organization perspective, project processes perspective, project results perspective, social and economics perspective, citizen satisfaction perspective. Most of the e-governance assessment frameworks focus on multiple e-Government stakeholders and on their different points of view for project quality. They recognize strategic goals as important parameters for project evaluations [6].

- The DeLone and McLean Information System Model has just three components: the creation of a system, the use of the system, and the consequences of this system use. Each of these steps is a necessary, but not sufficient, condition for the resultant outcome(s) [5].

- Five Elements of Successful E-Government Transformation are process reform, leadership, strategic investment, collaboration, civic engagement. Further, strong leadership can ensure the long-term commitment of resources and expertise and the cooperation of disparate factions. Leadership can also articulate a unifying theme that can propel the e-government initiative through all the necessary steps [7].

- It is important to note that effective institutional coordination through e-government and integration in service delivery at the policymaking level requires a profound shift that is generally difficult in practice. This represents a paradigm shift towards a connected and people-centred government, where agencies and levels of government share objectives, data, processes and infrastructures across organizational boundaries [9].

- e-Government involves interplay between various e-Government actors viz., political organizations, administrative bodies/public sector, business organizations/ associations, training & research organizations and citizens/civil societies [1].

- The 6-i framework (Institutional Framework, Internal Process Re-engineering, Internal Capacity Building, Innovations, Investment Model (Business Model), Infrastructure (Core)) was used to assess whether e-Governance projects have an overall balance of all critical factors in order to achieve a progressive state [8].

- The feasibility of having a successful e-government is directly depended on the governments' overall ability and readiness to spend on the necessary information technology and related costs [3].

In order to address the deficiencies on existing assessment frameworks and ensure use of a single framework to assess e-governance projects at any stage of implementation, the author has designed a framework and named it as Kite Model. It primarily focusses on various factors which can assess the inherent capability of e-governance projects to successfully deploy, operate or sustain.

The Kite Model is an attempt to easily understand the factors responsible for successful implementation of e-governance projects and conveniently diagnose them to indicate their health [2]. The factors resemble the essentials required to fly a Kite and maintain its flight. The "Infrastructure Readiness" provides major support and considered as the backbone. The "Sustainability Sureness" gives shape and considered as an arc which is always in stressed condition. The "e-Governance Champion" ensures appropriate propelling and guidance, particularly in turbulent condition. The "Political Will" ensures enough breeze which can gently lift the Kite and keep it flying [2] (Fig. 1).

The model assesses the following factors and assigns index to each of them.

(i)   Infrastructure Readiness
(ii) Sustainability Sureness
(iii) e-Governance Champion Capability
(iv) Political Will.

The intrinsic factors viz., "infrastructure readiness" and "sustainability sureness" are assessed based on how well they are addressed on procedure (P), documentation (D), compliance (C) and audit (A). The grading of P, D, C and A is based on 6-point scale as mentioned in Table 1. The points corresponding to the grade are then multiplied with the assigned weight mentioned in Table 2. The index for each component

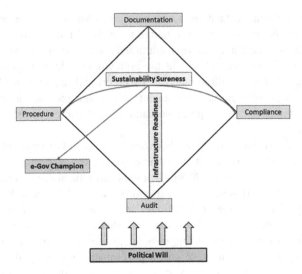

Fig. 1. Kite Model

(on a scale of 5) is obtained by adding the weighted points. The factor-level index is the simple average of indices calculated for each component.

Table 1. Grading table

Grading	Points
Poor	0
Fair	1
Average	2
Good	3
Very Good	4
Excellent	5

The weights for P-D-C-A are mentioned in Table 2.

In case of extrinsic factors viz., the "e-Governance champion capability" and "political will", the components are graded as per Table 3. Thereafter, the points are multiplied with the weights assigned for each component. The factor-level index is arrived by adding the weighted points calculated for each component.

The list of various components under each of the intrinsic factors and extrinsic factors, as defined by the Kite Model [2] are mentioned in Table 3.

The weightage of components under extrinsic factors are mentioned in Tables 4 and 5.

The indices arrived for the various factors of Kite Model indicate their health as per health rating mentioned in Table 6. The higher the index, the healthier the factor.

Table 2. Weights assigned to PDCA

Parameter	Weightage
Procedure (P)	1
Documentation (D)	3
Compliance (C)	4
Audit (A)	2
Total	10

Table 3. Factors and their components

Intrinsic factors		Extrinsic factors	
Infrastructure readiness	Sustainable sureness	e-Governance champion	Political will
Physical infrastructure	Financial sustainability (Govt.)	Technology orientation	Legal backing
Hardware infrastructure	Financial sustainability (Vendor)	Acceptance in government	Government agenda
Network infrastructure	Application support	eGov leaders	Dashboard services
Software infrastructure	Incident handling	Decision-making powers	
Security infrastructure	Reforms management	Collaborative mindset	
Manpower infrastructure	Change management		
Institutional infrastructure	Real-time monitoring		
Training infrastructure			
SLA monitoring infrastructure			

Table 4. Component weights for e-Gov champion capability

Components of e-Gov champion capability	Weightage
Technology orientation	1
Acceptance in government	3
eGov leaders	1
Decision-making powers	3
Collaborative mindset	2
Total	10

Table 5. Component weights for political will

Components of political will	Weightage
Legal backing (L)	4
Government agenda (G)	4
Dashboard services (D)	2
Total	10

Table 6. Assessment table

Index	Status
>4	Healthy
3–4	Caution
2–3	Risky
<2	Dangerous

3 Micro Level Analysis Using Kite Model

The component-level assessment for intrinsic and extrinsic factors results in diagnosing e-governance projects at a macro level. It may be essential that each component be assessed in detail. In order to ensure such micro-level assessment, each component is further divided into sub-components. This means that the sub-components are assessed first which are then consolidated to indicate the health of the component and subsequently the consolidation of components to arrive at factor-level index.

In case of intrinsic factors, these sub-components are assessed on how well they are addressed on procedure (P), documentation (D), compliance (C) and audit (A). In case of extrinsic factors, these sub-components are assessed on weighted grading. An equal weightage to all sub-components has been considered to arrive at component-based grading.

Based on the ground-level experiences shared by several experts on implementing e-governance projects, the likely sub-components within each component have been arrived. These are elaborated in following sub-sections.

3.1 Infrastructure Readiness

The various sub-components under each component of "Infrastructure Readiness" have been derived based on field-level experience and audit exercises. These are listed in Table 7.

3.2 Sustainability Sureness

The various sub-components under each component of "Sustainability Sureness", which have been derived based on practical experience and feasibility exercises, are listed in Table 8.

Table 7. Sub-components for infrastructure readiness

Components	Sub-components (Micro-level parameters)
Physical infrastructure	1. Data centre
	2. Disaster recovery centre
	3. Work premises
	4. Office equipment and stationery
Hardware infrastructure	1. Servers (Web Application, database, content etc.)
	2. Data storage
	3. Backup media
	4. Desktops
	5. Peripherals (Printers, Scanners, reading devices etc.)
Network infrastructure	1. Routers, Switches, Hubs
	2. Internet bandwidth
	3. Internal LAN
	4. External WAN
Software application	1. Software design
	2. software code
	3. Software deployment
	4. Application versioning
	5. Technologies
Security infrastructure	1. Firewall
	2. Anti-Virus solutions
	3. Threat detection
	4. Access to Hardware, Network and Software application
	5. Physical security
	6. Access to user-credentials, keys, documents, files
	7. Application vulnerability
Manpower resources	1. Ground staff (on-site)
	2. Operational staff
	3. Technical, functional and legal consultants
	4. Government staff
	5. System administrators
Institutional infrastructure	1. Nodal implementing agency
	2. Committees, Advisory groups and Discussion forums
	3. Technical, functional, legal and operational teams
	4. Communication channels
	5. Information repository
Training infrastructure	1. Well-equipped training facility
	2. Training programs
	3. Training manuals
	4. Training teams
	5. On-screen training facility
	6. Helpdesk facility
SLA monitoring infrastructure	1. Tools to measure service levels
	2. Generation of SLA reports

Table 8. Sub-components for sustainability sureness

Components	Sub-components (Micro-level parameters)
Financial sustainability (Government)	1. Budgetary allocation, Grant, Loan
	2. Transactional revenue
	3. Fees by user entities
	4. Interest on deposits
	5. Penalties on vendor
	6. Advertisement revenue
Financial sustainability (Vendor)	1. Timely vendor payments
	2. Quantum and periodicity of payments
	3. Financial strength of the vendor
Application support	1. Handholding to users
	2. Helpdesk activities
	3. Deployment of patches
	4. Execution of scripts
Incident detection and handling	1. Tools to detect issues
	2. Incident reporting process
	3. Root cause analysis
	4. Mitigation of risks
Reforms management	1. Process reforms
	2. Support from vendor to implement reforms
	3. Readiness of government to compensate vendor
Change management	1. Review of change management strategies
	2. Constitution of expert committee
	3. Initiatives to change mindset and attitude of users
	4. Engagement of external consultants
Real-time monitoring	1. Automated tools/application to monitor SLAs
	2. Real-time reporting of issues and breaches

3.3   e-Governance Champion Capability

The various sub-components under each component connected with "e-Governance Champion Capability" have been derived based on survey and interviews. These are listed in Table 9.

3.4   Political Will

The various sub-components under each component of "Political Will" are listed in Table 10. These sub components have been derived based on interview questionnaires and field study.

Table 9. Sub-components for e-Governance champion capability

Components	Sub-components (Micro-level parameters)
Technology orientation	1. Able to embrace and understand technologies
	2. Awareness on various hardware, software and network aspects
	3. Appreciate the role of technology, its dependencies and its limitations
	4. Attempt to understand the issues and suggest solutions
Acceptance in government	1. Professional relations with political executives and government officials
	2. Convincing ability within and outside government
	3. Capability to present and justify proposals
Availability of e-Governance leaders	1. Motivated and tech-savvy government officials at project operation level
	2. Training of government officials
	3. Building a team of techno-managerial professionals
Decision-making powers	1. Financial and Administrative powers
	2. Capability to revise powers based on necessity
	3. Powers to reform workflows and approval process
	4. Independence in decision-making and handling day-to-day activities
Collaborative mindset	1. Exhibit team-work
	2. Facilitating joint decisions on critical issues
	3. Ensure harmonious working between various stakeholders, including government teams

Table 10. Sub-components for e-Governance champion capability

Components	Sub-components (Micro-level parameters)
Legal backing	1. Acts specific to e-governance projects
	2. Rules, Regulations, bye-laws etc. supporting e-governance projects
	3. Orders/notifications/circulars guiding e-governance activities
Government agenda	1. Mandatory review of e-governance projects within departments
	2. Involvement of political executives in discussion forums
	3. Project evaluation activities by government agencies
Dashboard services	1. Customized MIS dashboard for political executives
	2. Alert services in case of major achievements and benefits
	3. Real-time information in case of major disruptions in services

3.5   Points of Assessment

The most important aspect while assessing each sub-component is to arrive at the various points of assessment for each component that are used as a basis to carry out the assessment studies. Based on the literature review and work group discussion, the likely points of assessment are listed in Table 11.

Table 11. Points of assessment for each component

Components	Points of assessment
Infrastructure readiness	
Physical infrastructure	Finalisation of requirements and setting up of physical infrastructure
Hardware infrastructure	Methodology adopted in finalising requirements, procurement and installation of hardware infrastructure
Network infrastructure	Estimation of network and bandwidth requirements and their provisioning
Software application	Adherence to standard policies and practices during software design and development and adoption of technologies
Security infrastructure	Framing and adoption of appropriate policies and strategies to ensure security of application, data, hardware, content, resources and equipment
Manpower resources	Estimation and deployment of skilled manpower
Institutional infrastructure	Sufficiency of institutional structures for ensuring implementation and continuity of projects
Training infrastructure	Provision to conduct various types of training programs including their justification and extent of coverage
SLA monitoring infrastructure	Methodology and tools to capture SLA data, measure service levels and generate SLA reports
Sustainability sureness	
Financial sustainability (Government)	Strategies and available funds to meet financial expenditure during implementation and maintenance phases of the project
Financial sustainability (vendor)	Financial capability of the vendor to implement and sustain the project
Application support	Quality of providing support for effective use of the application
Incident detection and handling	Mechanism to handle incidents and ensure non-recurrence
Reforms management	Readiness of the system to incorporate process reforms and re-engineering
Change management	Handling change management issues and requests
Real-time monitoring	Deployment of a system for efficient monitoring and reporting
e-Governance champion	
Technology orientation	Capability to understand and visualise theoretical and practical aspects of technologies
Acceptance in Government	Comfort level in handling administrative activities in a manner which helps projects
Availability of e-Governance Leaders	Capability to build and nurture a team of e-governance skilled resources
Decision-making powers	Institutional structure and policies favouring smooth functioning of e-Gov champions
Collaborative mindset	Attitude to encourage participative working environment with collective responsibility
Political will	
Legal backing	Readiness of political machinery to give legal backing to e-governance projects
Government agenda	Inclusion of e-governance projects as common agenda of government
Dashboard services	Willingness of political executives to view critical project information

4   Case Study: e-Procurement Project, Govt. of Karnataka, India

The author has undertaken a study of the unified end-to-end e-Procurement project implemented in the State of Karnataka (India) and assessed the health of the project at a micro-level using the Kite Model. The details are as follows.

4.1   Brief Details

The State of Karnataka (India) has implemented unified end-to-end e-Procurement system for automating the entire cycle of procurement from Indent/Estimate creation stage till final payment to the supplier/contractor. This Government-to-Business (G2B) project was conceptualized in the year 2005 and commenced its operations in the year 2007. The software application is developed, deployed and maintained by a Service Provider. The engagement with Service Provider is on Public Private Partnership model with transaction-based revenue model. The payment to Service Provider is based on SLAs. The project is operational till date. The system kept evolving by incorporating new features commonly used by several procuring entities. Currently, more than 300 procuring entities are using the platform which publish around 100,000 tenders every year.

4.2   Micro-level Assessment

The various sub-components under each component of intrinsic and extrinsic factors have been assessed. The basis of assessment was on available documents, surveys and interviews. The results are tabulated in Tables 12, 13, 14 and 15 below.

Table 12. Micro-level assessment of infrastructure readiness

Infrastructure readiness	1	2	3	4	5	6	7	Average
Physical	4.8	0.4	3.2	3.5				3.0
Hardware	3.9	2.9	2.7	3.9	3.9			3.5
Network	4.5	5.0	3.5	3.5				4.1
Software	3.6	3.2	3.9	4.2	2.3			3.4
Security	4.8	4.8	4.2	3.8	4.5	3.5	3.0	4.1
Manpower	4.4	4.4	4.1	4.1	3.8			4.2
Institutional	3.9	4.2	3.4	4.2	2.6			3.7
Training	3.8	4.1	3.8	3.5	0.4	3.2		3.1
SLA monitoring	4.3	4.5						4.4
							Index	3.70

Health status: Caution

Table 13. Micro-level assessment of sustainability sureness

Sustainability Sureness	1	2	3	4	5	6	Average
Financial sustainability (Govt.)	5.0	5.0	5.0	4.3	5.0	NA	4.9
Financial sustainability (Vendor)	3.4	3.8	4.9				4.0
Application support	3.9	3.4	3.5	3.1			3.5
Incident handling	2.4	2.3	2.3	2.3			2.3
Reforms management	3.4	2.6	2.7				2.9
Change management	2.2	3.4	2.3	3.1			2.8
Real-time monitoring	4.2	0.4					2.3
						Index	3.20

Health status: Caution

Table 14. Micro-level assessment of e-Gov champion capability

e-Gov champion capability	1	2	3	4	Average	Weighted points
Technology orientation	5.0	4.0	4.0	5.0	4.5	0.45
Acceptance in government	2.0	3.0	4.0		3.0	0.90
e-Gov leaders	1.0	3.0	4.0		2.7	0.27
Decision-making powers	2.0	2.0	4.0	3.0	2.8	0.83
Collaborative mindset	4.0	4.0	4.0		4.0	0.80
					Total	3.20

Health status: Caution

Table 15. Micro-level assessment of political will

Political will	1	2	3	Average	Weighted points
Legal backing	5.0	4.0	4.0	4.3	1.73
Government agenda	2.0	2.0	3.0	2.3	0.93
Dashboard services	1.0	1.0	0.0	0.7	0.13
				Total	2.80

Health status: Risky

4.3   Results

The indices derived for each of the major factors indicates that the e-Procurement project is in the right direction except for the "political will" which has been observed to be in "risky" area. However, the level of risk is not high as the index is near to 3.0 ("caution" level). On analyzing the micro-level indicators, it has been observed that several sub-components fall in "danger" zone. These are listed below, along with the respective component.

   (i)   Disaster Recovery (Physical Infrastructure)
  (ii)   On-screen training facility (Training Infrastructure)
 (iii)   Real-time reporting of issues and breaches (Real time monitoring)
 (iv)   Motivated and tech-savvy government officials at project operation level (Availability of e-governance leaders)
  (v)   Customized MIS dashboard for political executives (Dashboard Services)
 (vi)   Real-time information to political executives in case of major disruptions in services (Dashboard Services).

The analysis also brings into focus those sub-components which fall in "risky" zone. Some of these are as follows.

   (i)   Application of Technologies (Software Application)
  (ii)   Information repository (Institutional Infrastructure)
 (iii)   Incident reporting process (Incident Detection and Handling)
 (iv)   Review of Change Management Strategies (Change Management)
  (v)   Financial and Administrative Powers (Decision-making Powers)
 (vi)   Mandatory review of e-governance projects within departments (Government Agenda).

5 Conclusion

The assessment of various components constituting the intrinsic factors ("infrastructure readiness" and "sustainability sureness") and extrinsic factors ("e-governance champion" and "political will") of the Kite Model is considered an exercise at a macro level. It is likely that some aspects may not outcrop during such assessment, which may be critical and require careful attention. To avoid such situations, the components need to be subjected to micro-level assessment. The paper has been successful in listing an elaborate list of sub-components for each component, which when assessed, will bring into light the unhealthy areas of implementation. This will also help in preparation of a detailed health-chart indicating the status of various health check-points (sub-components) at any point of time. Such information becomes very useful in mitigating the unseen risks and improve the overall health of the project.

The micro-level assessment need to be a continuous exercise as the indices vary with changes in work practices/policies/regulations. The components and its sub-components substantiating the factors of Kite Model can be further enhanced and expanded to improve the comprehensiveness. Such an attempt will further strengthen the micro-level assessment, which can aid decision makers to initiate preventive and corrective measures for ensuring good health of e-governance projects.

References

1. Adala, A.: Formulation of empirical factor relations influencing e-government preparedness. In: International Conference on e-Government, ICEG 2008, 23–24 October 2008, Melbourne, Australia, pp. 17–26 (2008)
2. Adala, A.: Assessing the health of e-governance projects - a Kite model. In: e-CASE & e-Tech 2018, 1–3 April, Osaka, Japan, vol. 12, no. 1, pp. 109–128 (2008)
3. Basu, S.: E-government and developing countries: an overview. Int. Rev. Law Comput. Technol. **18**(1), 109–132 (2004)
4. Bhatnagar, S.C., Singh, N.: Assessing the impact of e-government: a study of projects in India. Inf. Technol. Int. Dev. **6**(2), 109–127 (2010)
5. Delone, W., McLean, E.: The DeLone and McLean model of information systems success. J. Manag. Inf. Syst. **19**, 9–30 (2003)
6. Fitsilis, P, Anthopoulos, L, Gerogiannis, V.C.: Assessment frameworks of e-government projects: a comparison. In: PCI 2009 Conference Proceedings (2009)
7. Information for Development Program: e-Government Handbook for Developing Countries. A project of InfoDev and the Centre for Democracy and Technology, November 2002
8. Ravindran, D.S.: Unified End-to-End e-Procurement Project: Presentation to World Bank, Centre for e-Governance, Government of Karnataka (2012). https://eproc.karnataka.gov.in/documents/world_bank_ppt
9. United Nations Department of Economic and Social Affairs: United Nations E-Government Survey (2016). https://publicadministration.un.org

The Development of Digital Economy and Public Administration Education

Sergey Semenov[1] and Olga Filatova[2]([envelope])

[1] The Russian Presidential Academy of National Economy and Public Administration, Vernadsky Prospect, 82, Building 1, 119571 Moscow, Russia
[2] RUDN-University, Miklukho-Maklaya Street, 6, 117198 Moscow, Russia
filatova_ov@rudn.university

Abstract. The article analyzes the extent of conformity of actual Russian regulation in public service and federal education standards in public administration to the goals of the development of digital economy. For this purpose the authors analyze the following topics. First - the actual strategic documents in the field of the digital economy, including the main risks of the development of information technologies on the public service. Second, the present situation with higher and postgraduate education of public servants, regulation of public service and requirements for some positions connected with the information technologies. Third, the digital competences of the graduates of the public administration education programs from the federal education standards of bachelor and master level. The authors come to the conclusion that education standards in public administration pay little attention to the skills in information technologies, as well as the actual regulation of public service and public administration education needs in the digital economy. As possible ways of adaptation the authors suggest integration of competences for digital economy in education standards and creation of courses and education programs of bachelor, master and postgraduate levels corresponding to the goals of the development of digital economy.

Keywords: Digital technologies · Public administration education · Public service

1 Introduction

The digital economy, its perspectives, its risks, and problems are widely discussed not only as an independent sphere but also how it impacts other areas of the public sphere. E-government research indicates that its development depends on three elements: technologies, management, and governmental institutions [2]. Digital technologies (including e-government) change the organization of work of public administration, public policy making, and the communications between government and business, government and noncommercial organizations, government and citizens.

Digital technologies in public administration consist of a number of directions including e-government, the development of information infrastructure, Smart city, information security, digital health care and education [5]. All of them form and change

A. Chugunov et al. (Eds.): EGOSE 2018, CCIS 947, pp. 469–480, 2019.
https://doi.org/10.1007/978-3-030-13283-5_35

public administration. For example, the following four aspects of e-government influence public administration: One, citizen-centered service, information as a public resource, new skills and relations, and accountability and management models [2]. Two, basic changes take place in the functioning of state bodies and in the interaction among political actors [4]. Three, digital technologies simplify the communications between the citizens and the government [8]. Four, the development of e-government governments can serve citizens more quickly and with much lower costs (from public information to renewal of the documents) [3]. All the changes demand adaptation of the principles of public service, the principles of communication between the citizens and the government, and changes in the public policy making. Big Data has special role in the digital discourse in the way of working with information as a public resource. Big Data can be used for public policy making to create the Smart city. Some authors mention that Big Data demands special skills of collecting relevant information, using the technology, and analyzing and interpretation of data and visualization of the results [6, 7, 9]. New directions in digital technology demand the adaptation of work of the civil service, because they are responsible for the projects of the implementation of the digital technologies in the practice of public administration. This also means that public administration education programs must change to provide the appropriate skills and competencies to public servants. We suppose that current public administration education does not adequately prepare students for working in digital economy because it does not pay much attention on IT skills for future public servants. The present regulation of public administration education does not demand training IT skills for working in digital economy. Changes in the list of competences for bachelor and master students and elaboration of postgraduate programs in digital technologies could improve the situation.

The main goal of the article is to identify whether the existing regulation of civil service and the regulation of education in public administration meets the needs of the development of digital economy in Russia. We study the congruence of education of public servants for the development of digital economy. Our research questions are:

- Is it possible to prepare public servants for the development of digital economy with the actual regulation of public administration education?
- How to influence the development of digital economy by the improvement of education of public servants?

Methodically our research includes the following steps.

1 Step. The analysis of the basic strategic documents that identifies the main directions of the development of digital economy, the main competences that the public servants should have and the main risks and difficulties in the implementation of the digital technologies in public administration.

2 Step. We analyze to see if the actual regulation of civil service corresponds to the directions of the development of digital economy and if the public servants are ready for such changes. We think that readiness for changes can be measured by the analysis of their preparation for work with digital technologies. To understand the situation with education of public servants in digital technologies we analyze the Federal State Statistics Service's data on the civil servants' basic higher education and on postgraduate education in information technologies. We use the data on basic higher

education for 2009, 2011, 2013 and 2016 and the data on postgraduate education in information technologies for the period from 2009 to 2017 (except 2015, because the data for this year is not published). Such time intervals permit us to identify the trends and give more complete picture of the situation in the studied spheres.

3 Step. We analyze bachelor and master federal educational standards in public administration to understand if the actual official requirements in the education programs correspond to the main directions of the development of digital economy. We ask if they give students skills of working with digital technologies.

The main research technique is the analysis of the correspondence of regulation of public service and of regulation in public administration education with the goals of the development of digital economy. We juxtapose strategic regulation of the development of digital economy with the actual Federal Law "About public service", the Qualification requirements handbook compiled by the Ministry of Labor and Social Protection of the Russian Federation and bachelor and master federal educational standards in public administration.

2 The Main Directions of the Development of the Digital Economy in Russia

Three strategic documents regulate the development of digital economy in Russia.

The first is the Decree of the President of the Russian Federation "About the strategy of the development of the information society in the Russian Federation in 2017–2030" [19]. The strategy declares the main priorities of the development of digital economy:

- development of information space;
- information and communication infrastructure;
- creation of domestic software;
- creation of new technological basis for the development of the economy and social sphere;
- information security.

The program "Digital Economy of the Russian Federation" emerged to facilitate this strategy. [16] The program declares the main areas of the development of digital economy: regulation, education and human resources, research, infrastructure and security. Each direction is at the same time the special branch of public regulation. The program in fact intends projects in each area of regulation. The program will have the three-level system of management – strategic, tactical, and operative levels with the division of functions. The functions of the system of management are determined by the projects including adjustment of the system of management, resources provision, project portfolio management, the main directions and the organization of research and development, and project management. The representatives of governmental institutions, business, civil society and research and education community are expected to be involved in the management of the program. The program also requires the support of small and medium-sized enterprises working in the sphere of digital technologies (support includes business training, investment acceleration, and financial support).

The development of the digital economy is named among the main goals in the Decree of the President of the Russian Federation "About the national goals and objectives of strategic development of the Russian Federation until 2024" [18]. It aims for the creation of information and communication infrastructure, the rise of costs of the projects of the development of digital economy, and using mainly domestic software for governmental, municipal and other organizations. It demands civil servants to know how to work with digital technologies, but more often it requires combination of competencies in digital technologies with the project management. Regulation of digital economy and transformation of the economy and social sphere with digital technologies requires knowledge of actual regulation, including basic technologies and their influence on social and economic processes. Some objectives need mainly technical competences – for example:

- creation of the infrastructure for data transmission;
- processing and storage of information;
- information security on the base of the domestic software;
- implementation of information technology in public services.

Objectives connected with the financial management and development of projects of implementation of digital technologies and coordination among the members of the Eurasian economic Union demand organizational and managerial skills and knowledge of the main trends of the development of digital technologies.

Public administration has already changed and continues to change in the direction of increasing of use of information technologies. According to the strategic documents changes in everyday activities of civil servants will also continue: they will need to solve problems in the regulation of use of digital technologies and they will need to explore technologies to use them in everyday professional activities.

The implementation of digital technologies in public administration is connected with some risks and difficulties. Risks and problems could be classified into technical, regulative and personnel.

Technical risks are often connected with problems of security. For public administration the most important technical risks are connected with data security. Some risks are connected with the lack of regulation of the use and development of digital technologies or their regulation needs some improvement. These risks demand special research. Considering the main goal of our article we have to pay more attention to personnel risks. They are the following:

- absence of competences of working with information technologies of civil servants;
- lack of specialists in information technologies in public administration;
- administrative culture.

Overall, all this suggests that governmental institutions need specialists qualified in digital technologies. Though the need for IT-specialists is always discussed, the strategic documents indicate that the public administration schools should prepare specialists who will be able to combine competences in digital technologies with the competences of project work, such as communications and industrial management. Now this direction seems to be new for public administration and there are no special recommendations. We think that competences could be determined by the technologies that will be used. For example the program "Digital economy" names the following basic technologies that need to be used and developed: big data, neurotechnology and artificial intelligence, distributed registry systems, quantum technologies, new production technologies, industrial Internet, robotics and sensor technology, wireless communication, virtual and augmented reality [16].

Administrative culture means the change in communications with the citizens and business to use all the advantages of e-government and other digital technologies. For example digital technologies help to involve local community in the solution of local problems [1].

3   Digital Economy and Public Service

Civil servants are the main executors of the goals declared in the strategic documents that regulate the development of the digital economy. The quality of personnel and the skills of civil service determine the degree of the realization of the strategic goals. The overall statistics of the education of civil servants give some ideas about main trends regarding the connection between human resources policy and the development of digital economy (see Table 1).

Table 1. Civil servants' basic higher education (state bodies of the Russian Federation, federal level, total) [10]

Period	Social sciences and humanities, %	Economics and management, %	Physical, mathematical and natural sciences, %	Education and pedagogy, %	Health care, %	Culture and arts, %	Information security, %	Service, %	Agriculture & fisheries, %	Computer science and engineering, %	Others, %
2009	32.8	36.5	3.5	5.1	2.1	0.3	0.3	0.2	3.4	0	15.8
2011	35.1	35.9	3.2	4.8	2	0.3	0.4	0.4	2.9	0	15.3
2013	38	34.3	2.9	4.5	1.9	0.3	0.4	0.3	2.6	0	14.7
2016	40.1	35.6	2.4	3.7	1.7	0.3	0	0	2.1	1.5	12.5

The same is true regarding public service in specific fields. Specialists in the Humanities and Social sciences, Economics and Management dominate. There are very few specialists in information technologies: in 2009–2013 there were few specialists with the education in the field of information security and specialists in computer sciences and engineering even could not be identified as a special group. At the same time we cannot say that there were no such specialists in the civil service in that time. The appearance of this group (even if specialists in Informational security were counted in this group) can indicate the changes in the human resources policy – some kind of "turn" of the policy to the technical specialists, caused by the development and distribution of digital technologies. We can mention another detail - growth of the number of specialists in the field Social Sciences and Humanities in 2016. Among the 40.1% of humanitarians in the civil service 35.8% are lawyers. These statistic suggest not only the popularity of legal education among the humanitarians in Russia but also that the increase of the number of lawyers could be caused by the need of improvement of the actual regulation. From 2013 we can see some changes of the educational priority of civil service: from economics and management to law.

At the same time the majority of civil servants have postgraduate education. According to the statistical data not many civil servants had postgraduate education in information technologies from 2009 to 2017. The general trend of the change of the percentage of public servants with education in information technologies is presented on the Fig. 1.

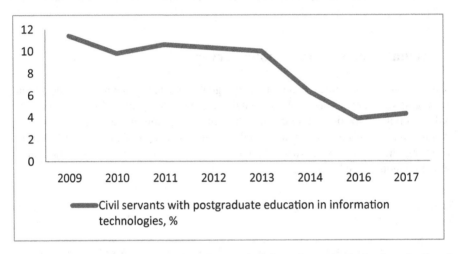

Fig. 1. Civil servants with postgraduate education in information technologies (state bodies of the Russian Federation, federal level, total) [11]

It is easy to notice that during the last two years there are fewer public servants prepared in postgraduate programs on information technologies then it was in 2011–2013. This situation does not correspond to the trends of development of digital economy – according to the strategic documents the percentage of civil servants with education in the sphere of informational technologies should increase. The first strategic document about the development of digital economy appeared in 2017, so we suppose that when the number of government projects in digital sphere increase digital skills for civil servants will become more important, and then the situation will change – we will see more civil servants with digital skills.

At present Federal Law "About public service" [21] does not mention the changes connected with digital economy and e-government though it has strong influence on the civil service that should change qualification requirements. These requirements on the education and professional skills are different in each state body. At the same time there is the Qualification requirements handbook compiled by the Ministry of Labor and Social Protection of Russia [17]. The handbook specifies requirements for positions connected with information security – including technical aspects. Requirements for some positions contain work with databases.

Regulation in the area of digital technologies as the special type of activity in public administration and civil service contain the following requirements: knowledge of the regulation and methodological base; of the basic directions of development of information security; of basic information resources; of the exchange and transmission of information. Civil servants in this sphere should know how to use information and communication networks, electronic workflow, as well as use search engines, legal databases, participate in the preparation of documents for procurement. Related area of activity is the information and network security and the development of information and communication infrastructure. Regulation of the Internet demands knowledge of the main principles of addressing in a data network. This type of activity demands the same skills and knowledge as the described kinds of activity. Implementation of the digital technologies for the public service demand knowledge of regulation and the procedure for registration of technical requirements for the development of automated information systems, the structure of the information and communication technology (ICT) market, actual trends of the development of ICT, processes of creation, implementation and development of software and technical information and communication environment, the main principles of the financial management and project work in ICT.

There are requirements for the subspecies of regulation in the field of information technology: regulation of the development of the digital technologies (innovative development, import substitution) and creation and development of technoparks. The listed knowledge and skills are relevant for these subspecies of professional activity and some kinds of activity can be added: project management, organization of interaction with public authorities on providing support for the creation of technoparks.

Another change touches the digitalization of public service – in 2018 public service should introduce electronic workflow on the federal level and automatic check of the information about the candidates for the position of public servant. By 2019 they should start to use a unified information system for the human resources management of the public service. As a result, it is planned to create information and communication environment in the public service [20].

4 Digital Economy and Public Administration Education

According to the Decree of the President one of the objectives of the development of digital economy is preparation of cadres for digitalization. It is very important for public administration education because the work of public servants becomes closely connected with digital technologies and they are the main executors of the goals of the digitalization. That's why it is important to find out whether the federal educational standards in public administration contain competences for working with digital technologies.

Information and methodological activities are mentioned in bachelor and master federal education standards. Bachelor federal education standards contain the competence of working with databases and the competences of participation in the implementation of the information technologies in the organization as well as the collection and processing the information. Graduates of a bachelor's degree should not only apply information and communication technologies in their work, but also know the main trends of their development [12].

Master's federal education standard is less oriented on digital economy. Consulting and information and analytical work means that master graduate should know how to work with databases: form, evaluate their completeness and quality, use data for the expertise and analytical work and also know how to use information technologies for solution of the research and administrative questions [13]. Work with databases is one of the most important requirements in public administration. Federal education standard gives rather uncertain formulation for master competences in information technologies: "to use information technologies to solve research problems" [13]. This formulation can mean different technologies. This requirement does not mean that the masters graduates will be able to orient themselves in digital technologies and main trends of its development, as it is required in the requirements of the Ministry of Labor and Social Protection. To fulfill this requirement it is enough to work in the basic Microsoft Office programs.

The existing federal education standards mention digital technologies very little and indefinably. Some universities have their own education standards in public administration that give them the opportunity to introduce new competences (for example, Russian Academy of National Economy and Public Administration, Higher School of Economics). In this case graduates of the programs of public administration from different universities and future public servants will have different competences. Subsequently they could be required to have competences that they have not obtained at the university. In our opinion such differences and little attention to the digital technologies in public administration federal education standards hampers the development of digital economy. This problem demands a system-wide national solution because the development of digital economy is one of the strategic goals of the state.

We think that federal education standards in public administration need to be improved in the strategic documents. Competences of working with digital technologies should appear in the standards. In particular, it should apply to practice-oriented master programs. Programs should teach how to use technologies and work in the projects of their implementation. Some competences could replicate the competences of specialists in information technologies. For example the digital competences for introduction in federal education standards in public administration could be the following.

At the bachelor level [14]:

- to identify information needs of users in the organization;
- to formulate requirements for the information system;
- to take part in management of the creation of information systems at stages of the life cycle.

At the master level [15]:

- to manage projects of informatization of applied tasks and creation of information systems of organizations;
- to organize negotiations and negotiate with customer representatives of IT-solutions in organizations;
- apply modern methods and tools of applied informatics for informatization of solution of applied problems.

These competences could help public servants better understand modern technologies and more professionally perform the goals of their projects, connect with digital technologies, and find common language with IT-specialists.

Also in bachelor and master studies it could be useful to give students more courses on different aspects of working with information technologies: work in Microsoft office, databases, visualization, big data analysis, and Internet searches, for example. Courses on digital technologies should be taught in all public administration programs. Master programs for preparing specialists in digital technologies in public administration need to be elaborated. These programs should combine several blocks of disciplines: disciplines connected with digital technologies, regulation of the use of digital technologies, and project management.

5 Conclusion

The analysis shows that the existing regulation of civil service and federal education standards needs to adapt to the changes in the digital economy. The current training of civil service does not fully meet the requirements of the digital economy. Federal law does not mention work with digital technologies though all strategic documents declare there needs to be an active role of the governmental institutions in the implementation of the digital technologies in different areas of economic and social activities and the usage of the technologies in everyday life of the public servants. The actual situation with IT knowledge of public servants gives reasons for the following changes.

- Introduce digital competences in the bachelor and master federal education standards.
- Elaborate methodical support for IT disciplines in public administration education programs with the help of professionals in digital technologies. This methodical support should become obligatory for all institutions teaching public administration.
- Elaborate postgraduate programs in digital technologies for the public servants, containing two or three levels of IT knowledge.
- Add digital competences as obligatory competences in the article of the Federal Law "About public service" about the qualification of public servants (art. 12). It could make IT certificates and the development of IT knowledge obligatory for public servants.

The need of coordination with strategic documents in the development of digital economy concerns also the Qualification requirements. Requirements for public servants who work with digital technologies now contain knowledge of trends of development of information and communication technologies and other special requirements. We think that the existing requirements should correspond with the actual strategic documents.

Summarizing the analysis we would like to mention that the adaptation of public administration education programs of all levels with the strategic regulation of the development of digital economy could be very beneficial. But it demands the improvement of the federal education standards with the competences of working with digital technologies, simplification of the creation of the master programs, and teaching more courses on the digital technologies on these programs. For courses on the digital technologies it is necessary to have modern equipment, software and access to the Internet in educational organizations, and to train information technology teachers to organize and teach such courses. Of course such programs will be more expensive at the start and throughout, but in the context of the actual goals of the strategic development of digital economy they seem to be necessary.

References

1. Allen, B.A., Luc, J., Paquet, G., Roy, J.: E-governance & government on-line in Canada: partnerships, people & prospects. Gov. Inf. Quart. **18**(2), 93–104 (2001). https://doi.org/10.1016/S0740-624X(01)00063-6
2. Brown, D.: Electronic government and public administration. Int. Rev. Adm. Sci. **71**(2), 241–254 (2005). https://doi.org/10.1177/0020852305053883
3. Bughin, J., Chui, M., Hazan, E., Manyika, J., Pelissie du Rausas, M., Said, R.: The macroeconomic impact of the Internet. In: Internet Matters. Essays in Digital Transformation. McKinsey & Company (2012)
4. Danziger, J.N., Viborg, A.K.: The impacts of information technology on public administration: an analysis of empirical research from the "Golden Age" of transformation. Int. J. Public Adm. **25**(5), 591–627 (2006). https://doi.org/10.1081/PAD-120003292
5. Digitalization of the entire country/The Free Economy Journal, p. 23 (2017)
6. Khan, M., Shah, K.S.: Data and information visualization methods, and interactive mechanisms: a survey. Int. J. Comput. Appl. **34**(1), 1–14 (2011). https://doi.org/10.5120/4061-5722
7. Stamoulis, D., Gouscos, D., Georgiadis, P., Martakos, D.: Revisiting public information management for effective e-government services. Inf. Manag. Comput. Secur. **9**(4), 146–153 (2001). https://doi.org/10.1108/09685220110400327
8. Wang, L., Wang, G., Cheryl, A.A.: Big data and vizualization: methods, challenges and technology progress. Digit. Technol. **1**(1), 33–38 (2015). https://doi.org/10.12691/dt-1-1-7
9. Williams, S.: More than data: working with big data for civics. I/S: J. Law Policy Inf. Soc. **11**(1), 1–21 (2015)
10. Byulleten' Federal'noy sluzhby gosudarstvennoy statistiki "Sostav rabotnikov, zameschayuschikh gosudarstvennye (munitsipal'nye) dolzhnosti i dolzhnosti gosudarstvennoy grazhdanskoy (munitsipal'noy) sluzhby, po polu, vozrastu, stazhu raboty, obrazovaniyu" [The Bulletin of Federal State Statistics Service "The composition of employees who replace state (municipal) posts and posts of the state civil (municipal) service, by sex, age, work experience, education"]. Electronic resource. http://www.gks.ru/wps/wcm/connect/rosstat_main/rosstat/ru/statistics/publications/catalog/doc_1237818141625. Accessed 24 July 2018
11. Byulleten' Federal'noy sluzhby gosudarstvennoy statistiki "Dopolnitel'noe professional'noe obrazovanie kadrov gosudarstvennoy grazhdanskoy i munitsipal'noy sluzhby" [The Bulletin of Federal State Statistics Service "Postgraduate education of cadres of the state civil and municipal service"]. Electronic resource. http://www.gks.ru/wps/wcm/connect/rosstat_main/rosstat/ru/statistics/publications/catalog/doc_1242887320828. Accessed 24 July 2018
12. Prikaz Ministerstva obrazovaniya i nauki Rossii ot 10.12.2014 № 1567 "Ob utverzhdenii federal'nogo gosudarstvennogo obrazovatel'nogo standarta vysshego obrazovaniya po napravleniyu podgotovki 38.03.04 Gosudarstvennoe i munitsipal'noe upravlenie (uroven' bakalavriata)" [The Decree of the Ministry of education and science of the Russian Federation of 10 December 2014 N 1567 "About the approval of federal education standard of higher education in the direction of training 38.03.04 Public administration (bachelor level)"]. Electronic resource. http://publication.pravo.gov.ru/Document/View/0001201502090042. Accessed 24 July 2018

13. Prikaz Ministerstva obrazovaniya i nauki Rossii ot 26.11.2014 № 1518 "Ob utverzhdenii federal'nogo gosudarstvennogo obrazovatel'nogo standarta vysshego obrazovaniya po napravleniyu podgotovki 38.03.04 Gosudarstvennoe i munitsipal'noe upravlenie (uroven' magistratury)" [The Decree of the Ministry of education and science of the Russian Federation of 26 November 2014 N 1518 "About the approval of federal education standard of higher education in the direction of training 38.04.04 Public administration (master level)"]. Electronic resources. http://www.consultant.ru/document/cons_doc_LAW_173666/. Accessed 24 July 2018

14. Prikaz Ministerstva obrazovaniya i nauki Rossii ot 27.03.2015 № 207 "Ob utverzhdenii federal'nogo gosudarstvennogo obrazovatel'nogo standarta vysshego obrazovaniya po napravleniyu podgotovki 09.03.03 Prikladnaya informatika (uroven' bakalavriata)" [The Decree of the Ministry of education and science of the Russian Federation of 27 March 2015 N 207 "About the approval of federal education standard of higher education in the direction of training 09.03.03 Applied computer science (bachelor level)"]. Electronic resource. http://publication.pravo.gov.ru/Document/View/0001201503310039?index=3&rangeSize=1. Accessed 24 July 2018

15. Prikaz Ministerstva obrazovaniya i nauki Rossii ot 28.10.2014 № 1404 "Ob utverzhdenii federal'nogo gosudarstvennogo obrazovatel'nogo standarta vysshego obrazovaniya po napravleniyu podgotovki 09.04.03 Prikladnaya informatika (uroven' magistratury)" [The Decree of the Ministry of education and science of the Russian Federation of 28 November 2014 N 1404 "About the approval of federal education standard of higher education in the direction of training 09.04.03 Applied computer science (master level)"]. Electronic resource. https://www.garant.ru/products/ipo/prime/doc/70632836/(accessed. Accessed 24 July 2018

16. Rasporyazhenie Pravitel'stva Rossiyskoy Federatsii ot 28 iyulya 2017 g. № 1632-r "Programma "Tsifrovaya ekonomika Rossiyskoy Federatsii" [The order of the Government of the Russian Federation of 28 July 2017 N 1632-p" About the approval of the program "Digital economy of the Russian Federation"]. Electronic resource. http://www.consultant.ru/document/cons_doc_LAW_221756/. Accessed 24 July 2018

17. Spravochnik kvalifikatsionnykh trebovaniy k spetsial'nostyam, napravleniyam podgotovki, znaniyam i umeniyam, kotorye neobkhodimy dlya zamescheniya dolzhnostey gosudarstvennoy grazhdanskoy sluzhby s uchetom oblasti i vida professional'noy sluzhebnoy deyatel'nosti gosudarstvennykh grazhdanskikh sluzhaschikh (utv. Mintrudom Rossii) [Qualification requirements handbook for the specialties, education, skills and knowledge that are necessary to replace the posts of the state civil service considering the scope and type of professional performance of state civil servants compiled by the Ministry of Labor and Social Protection of Russia]. Electronic resource. http://www.consultant.ru/document/cons_doc_LAW_219036/#dst0. Accessed 24 July 2018

18. Ukaz Prezidenta Rossiyskoy Federatsii ot 07 maya 2018 g. № 204 "O natsional'nykh tselyakh i strategicheskikh zadachakh razvitiya Rossiyskoy Federatsii na period do 2024 goda" [The Decree of the President of the Russian Federation of 17 May 2018 N 204 "About the national goals and objectives of strategic development of the Russian Federation until 2024"]. Electronic resource. http://publication.pravo.gov.ru/Document/View/00012018050 70038. Accessed 24 July 2018

19. Ukaz Prezidenta Rossiyskoy Federatsii ot 09 maya 2017 g. № 203 "O strategii razvitiya informatsionnogo obschestva v Rossiyskoy Federatsii na 2017–2030 gody" [The Decree of the President of the Russian Federation of 09 May 2017 N 203 "About the strategy of the development of the information society in the Russian Federation in 2017–2030"]/Electronic resource. http://www.consultant.ru/document/cons_doc_LAW_216363/. Accessed 24 July 2018

20. Ukaz Prezidenta Rossiyskoy Federatsii ot 11 avgusta 2016 g. № 403 "Ob osnovnykh napravleniyakh razvitiya gosudarstvennoy grazhdanskoy sluzhby Rossiyskoy Federatsii na 2016–2018 gg." [The Decree of the President of the Russian Federation of 11 August 2016 N 403 "About the main directions of the development of public service of the Russian Federation in 2016–2018"]. Electronic resource. http://pravo.gov.ru/proxy/ips/?docbody= &nd=102406096. Accessed 24 July 2018

21. Federal'nyy zakon "O gosudarstvennoy grazhdanskoy sluzhbe" ot 27 iyulya 2004 g. № 79-FZ [Federal Law "About public service" of 27 July 2004 N 79]. Electronic resource. http://www.consultant.ru/document/cons_doc_LAW_48601/. Accessed 24 July 2018

Mending Government-to-Business Communication Disruptions in Russia: Language Perspective

Ekaterina Baeva$^{(\boxtimes)}$ and Vladimir Bondar

Saint Petersburg State University, 199034 Saint Petersburg, Russia
{e.baeva, v.bondar}@spbu.ru

Abstract. Relations between government and various social entities often present serious challenges in many respects, among which communication is one of the most widespread and frequently neglected, especially when it comes to the sphere of government-to-business (G2B) communication. This paper addresses the issues in G2B interaction that pertain to the sphere of language and appear to be most vulnerable and fraught with possible communication failures. Though business and government discourse domains are regarded as separate, often unparalleled manifestations of language registers with their own established and long-standing traditions of specific usage of syntax, vocabulary, style etc, we argue that it is governmental communicators who are responsible for alleviating communication problems and taking additional language effort to adjust their messages to the rules of clear, concise and coherent business communication. Building on responses of surveyed employees from several firms, we devise a technique which shows in which cases governmental agents should abandon rigidity of communication behavior and succumb to changes in various language aspects. In particular, we propose to identify the so-called perception consistency which works as a benchmark in detecting which genre or/and which language aspect (style, grammar, vocabulary etc.) of governmental messages needs reformulation and readjustment. The paper contributes to a better understanding of multifaceted governmental transformations, an integral part of which is represented by a necessity of change in communication styles in the process of adaptation to constantly changing needs of society.

Keywords: G2B communication · Government transformations ·
Language perspective · Communication disruptions · Perception consistency

1 Introduction

It is a common knowledge that efficiency of any subject of social interactions (e.g., government, businesses, or individuals) can be measured by various indicators, among which communication is in the forefront. Polls conducted among business executives have confirmed that notion; take for instance the result of survey conducted in [1] which ranked communication skills as "very important" for business leadership by top managers.

© Springer Nature Switzerland AG 2019
A. Chugunov et al. (Eds.): EGOSE 2018, CCIS 947, pp. 481–491, 2019.
https://doi.org/10.1007/978-3-030-13283-5_36

However, one should bear in mind that government and corporate sector are essentially different with respect to their primary functions and goals they pursue to achieve. Therefore, this determines their choice of communication mode, channels, and strategies. For example, one of the crucial differences in communication between governments and businesses is that due to a lack of formalized communication structure, the former practice a decentralized approach to communication, whereas the latter practice more formal and centralized communication. Language, being an integral part of both discourse domains, exacerbates this divide even further. Government-to-business (G2B) interaction, while striving to benefit both entities, can often be inadvertently disrupted by the default communication settings of the party which initiates the communication but neglects or forgets to adjust its preferred interaction mode to that one of the counterpart.

Consequently, it is vital here for us to have a clear understanding of who and how initiates the communication process. Given that, in this paper we distinguish between two kinds of interaction: government-to-business (G2B) and business-to-government (B2G), each with their particularities and their own vector of communication directionality. In the current research we exclusively address the language perspective of G2B communication looking to the problem from the vantage point of the driving force of social development in contemporary society that is corporate sector. We claim that governmental discourse domain is traditionally more rigid as compared to the one of business which is profit-driven and thus more likely to change according to up-to-date trends. That is why in this paper we are going to demonstrate that it is the government that should alter, revise and adjust its communication policy and communication patterns in their willingness to transform.

It is often presumed that government bodies have to establish positive relationships and build rapport with various entities in society including businesses to function efficiently [2]. However, in reality it turns out that due to a number of factors companies in Russia are often faced with unexpected barriers which hinder their communication with government, leading to resentment and frustration [3, 4]. On the other hand, government communicators worldwide are bound by the inflexibility of their language register, while also encountering certain constraints from various spheres [5], law and politics among many others.

Our research aims to spot G2B communication problems and suggest relevant hands-on techniques and recommendations leading to bring the two discourse domains to a more or less common denominator which would allow government and business to better their communication processes. The current situation in Russian G2B communication is viewed from the perspective of business people for whom interaction with government appears to be most valuable and challenging at the same time.

In order to perceive and define potential communication pitfalls we specify the elements which constitute the act of communication. We talk about communication context, i.e. frequency, manner, forms, and channels of communication. Furthermore, provided that there is a limited set of tools for describing G2B communication in scholarly studies, we introduce and explore the following domains of G2B communication with regard to message transmission: the entities involved (sender vs receiver), perception consistency (sphere, genre, and the subjective vs objective nature of the message), discursive value of the message (complex vs simple). We come up with factors which in future studies should underscore the comprehensive algorithm of mending communication disruptions. Finally, based on our theoretical assumptions, we discuss an example of how perception consistency can be employed in real communication.

2   G2B Communication Context

2.1   Frequency

To avoid and fix any possible problems in G2B communication, governments should systematically assess the communication needs of various businesses.

It has been argued by Gelders and Ihlen [6] that governments need to stipulate the relevant criteria for good communication specifically and discuss them with all relevant businesses; however, we believe that the opposite is more urgent at the moment. Government seems to be in great need to revive its communication policies through business feedback because old communication strategies no longer appear to be effective in the fast-moving and digital world [7].

Once these communication methods have been designed and implemented, they need to be used on a daily basis. Evidence from Russian firms [8] suggests that there is a clear correlation between frequency and communication success. Nevertheless, high frequency of G2B interaction does not safeguard businesses from experiencing communication failures which seem to be evoked by purely linguistic issues and appear to be part of a more elaborate picture.

2.2   Types of Communication

There are two types of communication in every organization: internal and external. Internal communication is between members of the same organization. It can be both informal and formal, with smaller ventures tending to have more informal interactions than bigger ones [9, 10].

Effective internal communication for business means you can keep good employees longer and increase productivity, with communication being the ultimate tool of resolving conflicts and managing fruitful atmosphere in a company. Moreover, it ensures cooperation, efficiency and decision-making. Top executive managers are known to believe that it was communication skills that effected their career advancement [11].

External communication involves members of different organization and in our context government entities and other mediators. Ideally, both corporate sector and government will start their communication process based on the same premises and patterns. It has been established that in the spirit of mutual benefit, governmental organizations should be transparent, accessible and responsive [12]. This requires that government communicators should have the following core competencies: consistently confronting government organizations with the perspective of the outside world; and rendering significant information because information often needs to be adapted in order to be useful to the outside world [13].

2.3 Agents of Communication

However, it turns out that in companies various agents can be in charge of external communication, to a certain degree. It is more likely that a small team or a single person is responsible for the majority of contacts with government agencies and the search for public information. Addressing obligatory public matters is often a secondary task outside of the core business of organizations [14].

In Russian businesses communication with government traditionally can be delegated to economic departments, PR specialists, legal department, accounting department or even be supervised by representatives of the executive level. Given that, one may assume that it is thus possible to build a seamless communication flow. But in reality, despite their professional training and expertise, these communication agents tend to experience communication problems because the message they receive is often poorly tailored, from both language and communication perspective [15]. Even a simple, in terms of genre or register, message can be inadequately decoded by the receiver [8].

2.4 Channels of Communication

Communication channel is "the means by which a message is sent by a source or obtained by a receiver" [16, p. 13]. There are various channels employed by business in their operations. In Russia, the following channels seem to dominate: personal contact, telephone, Internet, e-mail, and mail [7]. The choice of channel usually depends on the communication style and pattern of an agent in charge. For example, in [17] it was found that there is a clear preference to face-to-face communication with personal sources, compared to the more formal ones.

The problem here is that since businesses have abundant potential channels to choose from, this increases the chance that they will choose inappropriate channels to fulfill their tasks. On the other hand, governments are not error-free in their choices of communication channels, preferring to use written types of interaction where other channels would fit in and yield better results [7]. Thus the wrong choice of communication channels on both sides potentially can do huge damage to communication. Overall, it is in the written form of communication that governments resort to the elaborate, complex, clichéd language which eventually impedes successful business procedure.

Analyzing G2B communication in this paper we focus exceptionally on the written communication because it has been widely accepted that written speech does not allow immediate restructuring, concomitant clarifications and is overall secondary to spoken speech. Therefore, it is in the written speech we can observe conspicuous obscurity which leads to communication breakdown. We distinguish between the so-called online (via the Internet) and offline communication. The former includes primarily emails and specific documents posted on certain websites of governmental and municipal agencies. The latter can be reduced to official letters.

2.5   Message Transmission

Sender-Receiver. There are two communicative roles in every interaction – a sender (encoder/speaker) and a receiver (decoder/listener). Some business studies have claimed that top managers regard sending messages as more important than receiving them [18], however, decoding skills are considered one of the six major dimensions of corporate effectiveness [19].

It has already been suggested that in order to provide efficient external communication and avoid raising unnecessary criticism or hostility, corporations should tailor their messages to different recipients [20]. We claim that the same is relevant for governments.

The B2G context is far more complex and networked than that faced by citizens, and there is a lack of substantial insights into this group [17]. Aspects indicating a complex and networked context include the following: (1) businesses have more contact moments with governments than citizens do because the former are subject to a greater number of rules and regulations; (2) some contact moments between governments and businesses are indirect – via intermediaries – whereas others are direct, which facilitates a network character [21].

One of the most crucial aspects indicating a complex context is characterized by the notion that businesses can take many forms, from self-employed to businesses with numerous employees. A business is a network of individuals, a network that can be partially influenced by and depend on the environment [22]. This argument suggests that different employees use government communication channels in a variety of ways. This characteristic makes it rather difficult to determine the unique contact point of a business and, therefore, hinders a government's ability to realize a straightforward service delivery strategy. This lack of clarity hinders the development of valuable insight into businesses' needs, expectations and search behaviors based on easy-to-obtain characteristics (e.g., an organization's size and form). Furthermore, e.g., Davis [23] argues that (1) individuals within a business differ in background, perceptions, and experiences, and (2) individuals react differently to situations.

As a result, we can distinguish some characteristics of government as a sender of communicative message. It is depersonalized. It operates with default messages. The social and ideological domain it represents demands constant reproduction of language messages vested in similar linguistic garments. In other words, a huge significance for government communication agents is ascribed to genre and register. Every individual sender is overshadowed by the specifics of domain itself. Although business as a domain also has specific features to abide with, it is, first and foremost, less generic and more independent. As receivers, business communicators can be discouraged by cumbersome clichéd language of official governmental style.

Perception Consistency. With regard to sender-receiver domain, it becomes clear that the relationship between government and business is fraught with subjective reactions in the course of communication. What we mean is that in modern Russian there is a definite stylistic and pragmatic gap between the administrative and business functional styles. Each language style represents a system of selected language means which can be chosen depending on a social situation. Since business and official language styles serve different social communicative acts, they should be operating different language means. Therefore, when a business communicator accustomed to their communicative style and patterns encounters a message built on a more convoluted government communication model, they can often be baffled and, as a result, fail to understand the message.

A question is bound to arise – how to reduce this level of subjectivity and avoid possible communication disruptions?

We claim that one of the most crucial components which contributes much to the efficiency of communication is what we call *perception consistency*. Under perception consistency we understand a psychological attitude, aptness and eagerness to decode a communicative message. In case of certain genres, no matter how strict and clichéd the language might be, it is the perception of the genre that triggers a subjective evaluation of the text as highly difficult and barely readable. This subjective perception can be exacerbated further by language flaws of the text, making it practically incomprehensible.

Certainly, this stressed feeling of confusion and communication bewilderment is exceptionally true when non-trained business agents get involved in communication with government bodies. Naturally enough, this problem could be overcome by hiring highly trained communication agents or investing in personnel communicative training, but one can find it a costly procedure which not every business can afford.

It is in perception consistency theory that we see a less cost-consuming and more ubiquitous method to mend G2B communicative problems. As we are going to show in the paper there virtually exist various situations when the culprit of the communication breakdown can be found on either side of communication. Thus one needs to find an effective way to identify who and how causes communication disruptions, i.e. the party who makes a major contribution to failures in a certain G2B interaction and the way how they do it. The main focus of the paper is elaboration of our theory and how it works, if applied to G2B communication needs.

Based on this, we formulate the following research questions:

(1) What key factors constitute perception consistency?
(2) How can we use perception consistency in mending G2B communication disruptions?

3   Research Method

This study is a part of an ongoing research into G2B communication in Russia. It is at the initial level and so far bears speculative nature. While analyzing the data presented in [8], we came up with a series of theoretical assumptions which are to be tested at consecutive stages of investigation. The abovementioned data was collected in St Petersburg in the period of 2016–2017. In total, 90 firms and SMEs took part in a survey. The questionnaire comprised 12 questions which aimed to obtain data about frequency, channels, and purposes of communication as well as issues related to language use in various interactions with governmental bodies.

The main aim of the survey was to identify certain communication barriers in B2G interaction with respondents' companies. The expressed concerns helped us to spot apprehension of business agents, in a variety in business communication perspectives, including the language one. To devise the foundation of perception consistency, we used the 2-step correlation analysis method: firstly, we assessed the statistical data for each rubric presented in [8] and afterwards we juxtaposed rubrics with the relevant statistical data.

4   Results and Discussion

4.1   Key Factors Constituting Perception Consistency

We presume that perception consistency is a combination of several subjective and objective factors.

Personal Assessment. By the subjective factor we mean *personal assessment* of the difficulty of the message by the receiver. If the level of difficulty is only defined by personal experience, frequency of interaction of the similar kind, familiarity with the genre or sphere the message belongs to, it certainly is subjective. Therefore, should the government want to improve its communication via solely training the recipients, it will be time-, effort- and cost-consuming because they would have to train each recipient individually in every separate component of communication.

As for the *sphere* and/or *genre* of the message, we believe that they can be ambivalent and regarded as either subjective or objective depending on the situation. For example, if a text belongs to the sphere of legal documents, it is, in a way, designed to be difficult for interpretation [24], while memos aspire to be concise and understood by a variety of people without any particular expertise [25]. This holds true until we take the receiver as the point of departure: any external communication agent, unless highly qualified, will be likely to abstain from dealing with intricate texts on account of anticipating language barriers. A vivid example of this kind can be drawn from a very common experience of signing certain legal documents of minor importance (such as terms and conditions of certain public services like entertainment ones and loyalty cards) without even reading them. Therefore text and genre become a subjective category.

To troublesome spheres one may refer such issues as taxation, licensing, health control, fire and explosion safety, etc. [8]. When potentially complex sphere occurs with inherently sophisticated theme, it amplifies the challenge of decoding in the subjective perception of the decoder.

Talking about the evaluation of the message complexity, we have to underscore another key issue affecting the success of the decoding process. We would call it *the extralinguistic factor* which includes emotional state of the individual, the circumstances and ambience of communication. It goes without saying that it is next to impossible to identify and measure all components of the extralinguistic factor. This is another argument to support the sender-driven model of evolution of communication process between the government and society. It is simply more productive to try to fix the template so that it would be more transparent to a receiver in any state of mind, any pressing circumstances etc.

Moreover, building the model of perception consistency we disregard such factor as the receiver's expertise, education and experience in decoding government's messages. This omission is justified by the fact that, although we consider these factors clearly important for successful communication, the target audience of our model is the so-called inexperienced users who in our case constitute the majority of communication agents. Thus, this model can be of use to those who strive to improve communication but lack specially trained personnel.

The objective criteria often lie within the linguistic domain and are shared by two categories, i.e. by personal assessment and text value. There is no doubt that employing linguistic factors helps the receiver spot troublesome communication areas which are identified as either too complicated vocabulary, extremely complex syntax or convoluted style. It is the objective nature of linguistic factors which underlie the category of text value that allows us to draw parallels between indicators of personal assessment and text value and further proceed with the overall perception consistency in the receiver's judgment of government's message.

Text Value. The Russian language is characterized by standardization which develops primarily in two directions: first, a wide use of ready-made formulas, language templates and clichés; second, frequent repetition of the same words and syntactic constructions, as well as avoidance of expressive language means and figures of speech. All of the above to a large extent simplifies and makes it easier for the officials to draw up typical documentation. Yet again, it is here that we encounter the same pitfall of lurking communication failure when the addressee of the message, who is at the receiving end, goes through a wrenching process of decoding the message without having enough expertise of doing it professionally.

In general, we can distinguish the following aspects of text value which play a significant role in the overall text perception: vocabulary, syntax, style, coherence and cohesion. As it has been shown in [8] the most distressing area of linguistic concern appears to be vocabulary issues which include abundance of irrelevant vocabulary, verbosity and words with vague and/or ambiguous meaning. Coupled with the complexity of the sphere or genre it decreases the readability level of the text and reduces the chances of clear perception of the message. No less annoying for the respondents was profuse usage of terms, words belonging to the formal register and foreignisms or loanwords. The sphere of syntax boils down to prevalence of complex sentence and obscure phrase structures that also obstruct understanding of the whole text. Another level where miscomprehension occurs is pragmatics, style and vague meaning alongside with poor text organization and lack of usage of signposting and relevant linking devices.

4.2   Using Perception Consistency in Mending G2B Communication Disruptions

Generally, we can think of various scenarios in which the perception consistency criteria can come into play and lead to different communication outcomes. Thus, if we assume that such text value indicators as genre, style and syntax in the government communicator's message are simple, easy to understand and, overall, are flawless but the business agent seems to feel difficulties in decoding the message, then we have to state that the problem lies within the scope of the business communicator. The reasons for this communication failure can be manifold and are not subject to analysis in this paper. On the contrary, if the personal assessment and text value criteria show a high level of complication, there is no doubt that it is the task of the government communicator to revise and adjust the message to the needs of the business communicator.

Figure 1 summarizes the criteria described above and gives an example of their application. There are two white boxes signaling for criteria beyond the score of our suggested algorithm of communication mending. This figure is rather sketchy, however, it reflects the basic theory we are proposing in our paper.

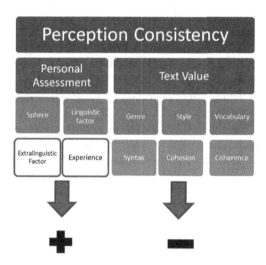

Fig. 1. Correlation of perception consistency with personal assessment and text value

The figure demonstrates the most salient example of application of our theoretical assumptions. The inexperienced receiver, in his overall personal assessment, views the message as simple (marked as "+"), while the text value of the same message is estimated as too obscure (marked as "−") . As a result, there is a clear distortion in the receiver's perception consistency which is an indicator that the sender is culpable of tailoring a poor message. Hence it is the task of the sender to reshape the language dimension of the message so as to make it more comprehensible.

The above mechanism of the perception consistency method can find a wider application, particularly, in the eGovernment sphere in Russia. In the process when all communication shifts to written offline form and excludes all possible ways of immediate repair of communication flaws, one should feel a drastic need to be armed with the method which will help to identify weaknesses in messages and convert them into communicative strengths. Perception consistency, thus, allows both parties, especially government communicators, to be flexible and tailor more reader-friendly and easy-to-decode messages.

5 Conclusion

Nowadays every government is striving for positive transformations. In the age of constant information flow it is important to ensure unimpeded communication, to mend barriers between different communication agents. In Russia, however reluctant it may traditionally seem in embracing changes, the government is currently undergoing transformations. Its communication patterns have shifted from strictly imposing to welcoming potential solutions of improving its modus operandi.

In our paper we suggested a tentative theory that, if applied to practice, eventually can substantially enhance communication between government and business, for both parties. Having analyzed some specific features of G2B communication, based on evidence from Russian firms, we got a clear vision of undeniable communication failures which are to be addressed urgently. In the course of our investigation we singled out key elements of G2B communication which led us to narrowing down a variety of objective and subjective criteria to two major categories that is personal assessment and text value. These categories and their correlation allowed us to come up with an indicator of communication efficiency which we called perception consistency. With the help of a simple but informative case we showed how this technique could be used in real life communicative situations.

However, more research on this matter is needed before a well-balanced and effective scheme can be designed and implemented. Our current study is likely to elucidate the importance of the altering communicative behavior on the part of government in the G2B context. We believe that the language perspective, and namely our concept of perception consistency, would ultimately benefit both parties of communication in question.

Acknowledgements. The authors would like to thank the anonymous reviewers for their valuable comments and suggestions to improve this paper.

References

1. Hildebrandt, H.W., Bond, F.A., Miller, E.L., Swinyard, A.W.: An executive appraisal of courses which best prepare one for general management. J. Bus. Commun. **19**, 5–15 (1982). https://doi.org/10.1177/002194368201900102
2. Kjellgren, H.: Staten som informatör eller propagandist? Om statssyners betydelse i svensk informationspolitik. Statsvetenskapliga Institutionen, Göteborgs Universitet, Göteborg (2002)
3. Yakovlev, A.: The evolution of business-state interaction in Russia: from state capture to business capture? Eur.-Asia Stud. **58**(7), 1033–1056 (2006). https://doi.org/10.1080/09668130600926256
4. Aidis, R., Estrin, S., Mickiewicz, T.: Institutions and entrepreneurship development in Russia: a comparative perspective. J. Bus. Ventur. **23**(6), 656–672 (2008). https://doi.org/10.1016/j.jbusvent.2008.01.005
5. Liu, B.F., Horsley, J.S., Levenshus, A.B.: Government and corporate communication practices: do the differences matter? J. Appl. Commun. Res. **38**(2), 189–213 (2010)

6. Gelders, D., Ihlen, Ø.: Government communication about potential policies: public relations, propaganda or both? Publ. Relat. Rev. **36**(1), 59–62 (2010). https://doi.org/10.1080/00909881003639528

7. Sanina, A., Balashov, A., Rubtcova, M., Satinsky, D.M.: The effectiveness of communication channels in government and business communication. Inf. Polity 1–17 (2017, preprint). https://doi.org/10.3233/IP-170415

8. Belov, S., Kropachev, N., Latukha, M., Orlova, E., Baeva, E., Bondar, V.: The role of language in the communication process between business and government: evidence from Russian firms. J. East-West Bus. 1–20 (2018). https://doi.org/10.1080/10669868.2018.1463341

9. Jenkins, H.: Small business champions for corporate social responsibility. J. Bus. Ethics **67** (3), 241–256 (2006). https://doi.org/10.1007/s10551-006-9182-6

10. Russo, A., Tencati, A.: Formal vs. informal CSR strategies: evidence from Italian micro, small, medium-sized, and large firms. J. Bus. Ethics **85**, 339–353 (2009). https://doi.org/10.1007/s10551-008-9736-x

11. Bennett, J.C., Olney, R.J.: Executive priorities for effective communication in an information society. J. Bus. Commun. **23**, 13–22 (1986). https://doi.org/10.1177/002194368602300202

12. Vos, M.: Communication quality measurement of councils. In: Proceedings of BledCom July 2003 in Conjunction with Euprera Annual Congress, Bled, Slovenia (2004)

13. Middel, R.: Daar hebben we toch communicatie voor; een beschouwing over de toegevoegde waarde van een discipline, L.S., Faculteit Communicatie en Journalistiek HU, Utrecht (2002)

14. Bergers, A.M.: Communication with SME Entrepreneurs: Assistance for Communication Advisors of the Federal Government (2003). http://communicatieplein.nl/dsc?c=getobject&s=obj&objectid. Accessed 12 June 2018

15. Sidorenko, E.V.: Trening kommunikativnoj kompetentnosti v delovom vzaimodejstvjj [Training communicative competencies in business communication]. Rech, St Petersburg (2003)

16. Pieterson, W.: Channel Choice: Citizens' Channel Behavior and Public Service Channel Strategy. Gildeprint B.V, Enschede (2009)

17. van den Boer, Y., Pieterson, W., Arendsen, R., van Dijk, J.: Towards a model of source and channel choices in business-to-government service interactions: a structural equation modeling approach. Gov. Inf. Q. **34**(3), 434–456 (2017). https://doi.org/10.1016/j.giq.2017.07.002

18. Carstens, J.: Perceptions of CEO's Personnel Managers, and Training Directors of Communication Practices and Listening Behavior in Large-Scale Organizations (1982)

19. Kaul, A.: Effective Business Communication. PHI Learning Pvt. Ltd., Delhi (2014)

20. Dawkins, J.: Corporate responsibility: the communication challenge. J. Commun. Manag. **9** (2), 108–119 (2005). https://doi.org/10.1108/13632540510621362

21. van den Boer, Y., van de Wijngaert, L., Pieterson, W., Arendsen, R.: On the interaction of source and channel choice in the government-to-business context. In: Scholl, H.J., Janssen, M., Wimmer, M.A., Moe, C.E., Flak, L.S. (eds.) EGOV 2012. LNCS, vol. 7443, pp. 27–39. Springer, Heidelberg (2012). https://doi.org/10.1007/978-3-642-33489-4_3

22. Jaffee, D.: Organization Theory: Tension and Change. McGraw-Hill, New York (2001)

23. Davis, K.: Human Behavior At Work: Organizational Behavior. McGraw-Hill, New York (1981)

24. Scalia, A.: A matter of Interpretation: Federal Courts and the Law: Federal Courts and the Law. Princeton University Press, Princeton (2018)

25. Guillory, J.: The memo and modernity. Crit. Inq. **31**(1), 108–132 (2004). https://doi.org/10.1086/427304

Author Index

Printed in the United States
By Bookmasters